World Trade Evolution

The book provides theoretical and empirical evidence on how world trade evolves, how trade affects resource allocation, how trade competition affects productivity, how China shock affects world trade and how trade affects large and small countries. It is a useful reference which focuses on new approaches to international trade by looking into country-specific as well as firm-product level-specific cases.

Lili Yan Ing is Lead Advisor, the Ministry of Trade of the Republic of Indonesia. She was Senior Economist at the Economic Research Institute of ASEAN and East Asia (ERIA) and Senior Lecturer at the University of Indonesia.

Miaojie Yu is Boya Chair Professor at Peking University, China, National Chang-jiang Scholar and National Distinguished Young Fellow.

T0371715

Routledge-ERIA Studies in Development Economics

World Trade Evolution

Growth, Productivity and Employment

Edited by
Lili Yan Ing and Miaojie Yu

Taylor & Francis Group

LONDON AND NEW YORK

First published 2019
by Routledge
2 Park Square, Milton Park, Abingdon, Oxon OX14 4RN

and by Routledge
605 Third Avenue, New York, NY 10017

First issued in paperback 2020

Routledge is an imprint of the Taylor & Francis Group, an informa business

British Library Cataloguing-in-Publication Data
A catalogue record for this book is available from the British Library

Library of Congress Cataloging-in-Publication Data
A catalog record for this book has been requested

ISBN 13: 978-0-367-50438-0 (pbk)
ISBN 13: 978-1-138-48003-2 (hbk)

Typeset in Times New Roman
by Apex CoVantage, LLC

Dedicated to our children with love

Michelle Lee and Han Na Lee
L.Y.I.

Yushen Yu
M.Y.

Contents

Figures

Tables

Contributors

Treb Allen is Distinguished Associate Professor of Economics and Globalization at Dartmouth College, USA.

Marco Del Angel is a PhD candidate at the University of California-Irvine, USA.

Pol Antràs is Robert G. Ory Professor of Economics at Harvard University, USA. He was Director of the International Trade and Organization Working Group at the National Bureau of Economic Research.

Costas Arkolakis is Henry Kohn Associate Professor of Economics at Yale University, USA.

David Autor is Ford Professor of Economics and Associate Head at the Department of Economics, Massachusetts Institute of Technology, USA.

Kyle Bagwell is Donald L. Lucas Professor in Economics at Stanford University, USA.

Andrew Bernard is Kadas Distinguished Professor at the Tuck School of Business, Dartmouth College, USA.

Esther Bøler is Assistant Professor at the Imperial College Business School, UK.

Lorenzo Caliendo is Professor of Economics at the School of Management, Yale University, USA.

Davin Chor is Associate Professor and Globalization Chair at the Tuck School of Business, Dartmouth College, USA, and Associate Professor at the Department of Economics, National University of Singapore.

Swati Dhingra is Associate Professor of Economics at the London School of Economics, UK.

David Dorn is Professor of International Trade and Labor Markets at the Department of Economics, University of Zurich, Switzerland.

Jonathan Eaton is Distinguished Professor of Economics at Pennsylvania State University, USA.

Robert Feenstra is Distinguished Professor at the Department of Economics, University of California-Davis, USA, and holds the C. Bryan Cameron Distinguished Chair in International Economics. He was Director of the International Trade and Investment Program at the National Bureau of Economic Research.

Sanjana Goswami is a PhD candidate at the University of California-Irvine, USA.

Gordon Hanson is Professor of Economics at the University of California San Diego (UCSD), USA, and holds the Pacific Economic Cooperation Chair in International Relations at UCSD's School of Global Policy and Strategy.

Lili Yan Ing is Lead Advisor, the Ministry of Trade of the Republic of Indonesia. She was Senior Economist at the Economic Research Institute of ASEAN and East Asia (ERIA) and Senior Lecturer at the University of Indonesia.

Samuel Kortum is James Burrows Moffatt Professor of Economics at Yale University, USA.

Lei Li is a Postdoctoral Researcher at the University of Zurich, Switzerland.

Marc Melitz is David A. Wells Professor of Political Economy at Harvard University, USA.

Ferdinando Monte is Assistant Professor of Strategy and Economics at the McDonough School of Business, Georgetown University, USA.

Scott Orr is a PhD candidate at the Department of Economics at the University of Toronto, Canada.

Antonio Rodriguez-Lopez is Associate Professor at the Department of Economics, University of California-Irvine, USA.

Esteban Rossi-Hansberg is Theodore A. Wells '29 Professor of Economics at the Department of Economics and WWS, Princeton University, USA.

Akira Sasahara is Assistant Professor of Economics at the University of Idaho, USA.

Robert W. Staiger is Roth Family Distinguished Professor in the Arts and Sciences and Professor of Economics at Dartmouth College, USA.

Daniel Trefler is Professor of Economics at the University of Toronto, Canada, and holds the J. Douglas and Ruth Grant Canada Research Chair in Competitiveness and Prosperity at the Rotman School of Management, University of Toronto.

Miaojie Yu is Boya Chair Professor at Peking University, China, National Chang-jiang Scholar and National Distinguished Young Fellow.

Rui Zhang is Research Fellow at CCER Peking University, China, and Visiting Scholar at Yale University, USA.

Acknowledgements

Trade economists were the least likely persons to be listened to by governments during the time when we were working on this book. After 70 years of trade liberalization, it has been challenged widely, even in the U.S. There has been rising anti-globalization sentiment. We voice what we believe true: trade liberalization increases economic growth through improved productivity. What is needed is improved management of trade liberalization through the improvement of domestic welfare systems, leaving both skilled and unskilled labour at least as well off as before liberalization, rather than the cessation of liberalization itself.

The book comprises new work from a stellar cast of authors, all experts in their fields, and benefits from constructive comments from Hidetoshi Nishimura, Gene Grossman, Martin Richardson, Olivier Cadot, Justin Yifu Lin, John Romalis, James Tybout, Taji Furusawa, Bradford Jensen, Daniel Yi Xu, Dominick Bartelme, Lee Sung Joon, Fukunari Kimura, Shujiro Urata and Chatib Basri. We thank Abigail Ho for her excellent research assistance. We specially thank Jennifer Bonnar and Fadriani Trianingsih, our book production managers. Elisa Ayu provided generous administrative support.

Finally, we thank the most inspiring people in our lives: our parents, spouses, friends, colleagues and students, for their love and endless support throughout our writing journey.

1   Introduction

Lili Yan Ing and Miaojie Yu

Trade shapes and directs the world. In the modern economy, we witness how trade liberalization has hugely contributed to world economic growth over the last 70 years. In one of the main economic ideas contained in the Ricardian model, dating back to 1817, is the observation that "a country's comparative advantage is essentially labour productivity that determines the pattern of world trade" (Ricardo 1817). Paul Krugman (1994) reiterates that "productivity is not everything, but in the long run, it is almost everything". Modern trade literature stresses how trade liberalization affects growth and productivity by improving firm productivity, either through competition or access to better quality or lower-priced inputs. Trade also affects real wages and the wages of skilled labour relative to those of unskilled labour and this will affect employment creation and movement of labour.

The next 12 chapters of this book explain how trade affects growth, productivity and employment. Chapters 2, 3 and 4 look theoretically at national sovereignty in an interdependent world, how trade competition affects a small open economy and how trade in services – dividing tangible and intangible services – affects trade in goods and real wages. The rest of the chapters present empirical exercises. Starting with Chapter 5, which explains "upstreamness" and "downstreamness" in global value chains, Chapters 6 to 10 detail how trade affects growth through improved firm productivity and through regional trade growth via industrial agglomeration, improved export quality, organizational change and firm-to-firm connections. They use very rich disaggregated data from China, France, Colombia and Indonesia. Chapters 11 to 13 examine how trade affects employment. The expansion of China has, of course, had a great deal of attention from trade economists. Chapter 11 examines how the growing of China's trade affects US occupational employment. Chapter 12 explores the "China shock" to employment in East and Southeast Asia. The last chapter develops a spatial economic model and tests it on trade in goods and migration.

The book starts by discussing trade in the multilateral context. Chapter 2 by Bagwell and Staiger reexamines the role of multilateral cooperation from the perspective of sovereign rights. What are the sovereign rights of nations in an interdependent world and to what extent do these rights stand in the way of achieving internationally efficient outcomes? The chapter proposes answers to these two questions. Their approach is to formalize the Westphalian norm of "non-intervention in the internal affairs of other states" in a way that captures several key features of Westphalian sovereignty emphasized in the international political economy literature. An important advantage of their approach is that it is analytically tractable. Using this formalization, Bagwell and Staiger show how Nash choice problems can be partitioned in a way that allows a characterization of the degree and nature of sovereignty that governments possess in the Nash equilibrium. This characterization, in turn, provides a benchmark from which to formally assess the implications for national sovereignty of international agreements of various designs.

In the context of the benchmark model of international interdependence, Bagwell and Staiger find that in principle there is no inherent conflict between the attainment of international efficiency through international agreements and preserving national sovereignty. As the benchmark model is general enough to cover channels of international interdependence that can take a variety of forms, this finding can be viewed as pointing to important possibilities for eliminating conflicts between international efficiency and national sovereignty through appropriate design of international agreements. Their findings highlight an important distinction between such agreements that mitigate international externalities and those that erode national sovereignty and point out that it can be possible to have the former without the latter.

Bagwell and Staiger find that the harmony in the benchmark model between international efficiency and national sovereignty is not always present in the universe of international relations among national governments. Rather, this harmony depends on the structure of the international externalities that define the nature of international interdependence and that give rise to the policy inefficiencies under non-cooperative policy setting. Together with other findings, this last point reinforces the importance of understanding the nature of the international externalities that are the source of the problem for an international agreement to solve, so that those tensions between sovereignty and efficiency that are unnecessary can be avoided, while those tensions that are inescapable can be anticipated and minimized through careful institutional design.

Where tensions between national sovereignty and international efficiency are inescapable, it may be that further refinements to the notion of national sovereignty could help to ease these tensions. A key message of the Bagwell and Staiger chapter, however, is that such refinements, to the extent they are possible, can be guided by the formal approach and instructive findings of this analysis. In this way, the chapter provides a framework for further systematic exploration into notions of sovereignty and their implications for efficiency.

Chapter 3 by Melitz provides exercises on trade competition and reallocations in a small open economy based on his highly referenced paper on measuring productivity in the heterogenous firm framework. The seminal Melitz (2003) paper offers elegant predictions on regarding changes in the extensive margin of trade in response to trade liberalization, yet it is largely silent on implications for the intensive margin from such trade liberalizations. To relax the constant markup feature associated with the constant elasticity of substitution, this chapter develops a setup of variable elasticities of substitution.

This model with endogenous markups is able to illustrate how trade liberalization induces intensive margin reallocations towards more productive firms that reinforce the extensive margin reallocations of Melitz (2003). When general equilibrium effects are incorporated, the theory also provides a decomposition of the impact of trade liberalization into a short-run component and a long-run component. In particular, the long-run component that incorporates the effects of firm entry and relative wage changes further contributes to the intensive margin reallocation. This extension is a significant milestone in research on firm heterogeneity and trade liberalization.

In Chapter 4, Eaton and Kortum examine some important and fundamental features of services trade and investigate how well current modelling strategies capture these features. They propose and quantify extensions to a baseline structural gravity model that incorporate these features. Their extended model allows us to handle goods trade and services trade in an encompassing framework.

Using OECD data and World Input-Output Database (WIOD), Eaton and Kortum explore basic features of services trade, documenting its growing differential and importance across countries. In particular, services exports now account for a third or more of the total exports of goods and services of the United Kingdom and United States but less than 20 per cent for Germany and Japan. In line with previous studies, they find that a standard gravity formulation with exporter–importer fixed effects captures bilateral trade both in services overall and in eight categories of services, nearly as well as trade in goods, with similar distance elasticities.

Eaton and Kortum then develop a model in which they divide services into tangible and intangible components. How to treat tangible services seems standard in the literature, but researchers have taken alternative approaches to intangibles. As Corrado, Hulten and Sichel (2009) point out, to constitute a source of growth using accumulation of intangibles, it requires information of a share in the production function just like physical capital, implying rivalry. Hence Eaton and Kortum include the accumulation of intangible capital as a source of growth that substantially reduces the "Solow residual" in growth accounting. The new approach introduced by Eaton and Kortum here, in treating intangibles as non-rival, considers the accumulation of intangibles as the source of this residual.

In this Eaton and Kortum service model, they treat tangible services and merchandise trade similarly. Absorption is related to current production and output is rivalrous. They model the output of the intangible services sector as non-rival intangible assets that provide technologies for the future production of goods and tangible services. For producers of tangibles to be able to compensate the original creators of their technology requires that they charge a mark-up over the cost of tangible inputs. Their market structure is consequently imperfectly competitive. Mark-ups on tangibles thus serve as the source of revenue for the creators of intangible assets. Finally, Eaton and Kortum implement the model numerically to explore its implications for trade in manufactures, tangible services and intangible assets. The numerical model illustrates how greater diffusion can benefit all countries, even though it can have negative implications for real wages in some countries.

Turning to the empirical chapters, in Chapter 5, Antràs and Chor examine variations in countries' and sectors' global value chain (GVC) positioning by developing a GVC theory amenable to quantitative general equilibrium trade modelling. With a quantifiable model that completely matches global bilateral trade flows in final goods/services and intermediate goods/services, this chapter analyzes the underlying forces that drive GVC positioning. The authors focus on the roles of trade costs and service sectors. Antràs and Chor first review several key measures of GVC positioning, namely indices to measure 'upstreamness' and 'downstreamness' of a country-sector pair. From the output side, a country/sector is considered upstream if it sells a small share of its output to final consumers and mainly sells its output to other sectors that sell little to final consumers. An upstream country/sector is thus remote from final consumers. From the input side, a country/sector is considered downstream if it uses a large share of intermediate inputs in its production and mainly uses inputs produced by sectors that intensively use intermediate inputs. A downstream country/sector thus uses little value-added overall.

Antràs and Chor then adopt the World Input-Output Database (WIOD) over the period 1995–2011 to construct measures of upstreamness and downstreamness and document two salient stylized facts: First, across years, an average country/sector has become more upstream (remote to final consumers) and more downstream (intensively use intermediate inputs) simultaneously. Second, across years, the positive correlation between upstreamness and downstreamness has increased. To interpret these two empirical findings, Antràs and Chor offer two explanations: trade costs and the rise of service sector. On the one hand, overall declining trade costs seem to suggest that the positive correlation between upstreamness and downstreamness should weaken over time. On the other hand, because the service sector is closer to final consumers (less upstream) and intensively uses primary factors and value-added in its production (less downstream), the rise of the service sector can generate the rising positive correlation between upstreamness and downstreamness via a composition effect.

To formally assess the effects of trade costs and the service sector in driving the observed variations in GVC positioning, Antràs and Chor develop a Ricardian model of the global economy with input-output linkages à la Caliendo and Parro (2015). Essentially, they extend the model by allowing trade costs for final goods/services to differ from those for intermediate goods/services. This richer structure of trade costs enables the model to completely match trade flows in both final goods/services and intermediate goods/services. The authors then show that counterfactual analysis can be readily performed conditional on the observed equilibrium using the "exact hat algebra" approach. In particular, declines in trade costs for services and the rising importance of the service sector both contribute to increases in the positive correlation between upstreamness and downstreamness.

In Chapter 6, Autor, Dorn, Hanson and Li argue that regional comparative advantage or industry agglomeration is another important reason to explain a region's export-growth potential. The impacts of the multilateral rules-based system (WTO) can be viewed in the following perspectives: First, reductions in import tariffs on both final goods and imported intermediate inputs can raise productivity. The gains from output trade liberalization are realized through competition (Brandt, Van Biesebroeck, Wang and Zhang, 2017), whereas the gains from input trade liberalization are mainly through cost saving effects (Yu, 2015). Second, the phase-out of multi-fiber agreements facing China in the US, EU, Japan and other OECD high-income countries also boosted China's exports (Khandelwal, Schott and Wei, 2013). Third, with WTO accession in 2001, China no longer faced the annual US reauthorization investigation of its "most favored nation" status. The phased-out US reauthorization investigation can significantly reduce trade uncertainty confronting Chinese exporters (Pierce and Schott, 2016; Handley and Limao, 2017; Feng, Li and Swenson, 2017).

However, these are not the only important factors in explaining China's dramatic fast trade growth in the first decade in the new century. The authors argue that regional comparative advantage or industry agglomeration is another important reason to explain a region's export-growth potential. They conduct their analysis by using disaggregated regional data on Chinese trade to access the channels through which the country's exports have surged. Inspired by the influential work of Autor, Dorn and Hanson (2013), they found that a simple Bartik measure is the strongest and most robust predictor of China's regional export growth. In particular, the spatial pattern of export growth can be explained by sectoral dynamic changes at the national level, even after controlling for reductions in tariff uncertainty, the phase-out of MFA quota eliminations and actual input and output tariff reductions.

Chapter 7, by Orr, Trefler and Yu, contributes to the literature on how to measure productivity using firm level data. They first review a number of prominent state-of-the-art methods of estimating firm productivity. The rise of China as the "world's manufacturer" has generated a growing interest for trade economists. Previous studies like Brandt, Van Biesesbroeck and Zhang (2012), Yu (2015), and Brandt, Van Biesesbroeck, Wang and Zhang (2017) consider the impact of trade liberalization on firm productivity. Yet, how to precisely estimate Chinese firm productivity still remains important.

The authors develop an augmented method to estimate Chinese firm productivity by incorporating China-specific economic characteristics such as the existence of state-owned enterprises (SOE) and foreign-invested enterprises (FIE). In particular, they estimate dozens of different specifications for around 30 Chinese industries for a total of 672 production function estimates using OLS and another five proxy-variable methods, by considering both gross output and value-added approaches with either Cobb-Douglas or translog specific functional forms.

The findings of the chapter of Orr, Trefler and Yu are rich. When comparing gross-output to value-added production functions, the former exhibits much less variation in returns to scale. When comparing translog gross-output to the Cobb-Douglas gross-output approach, estimates of output elasticities and returns to scale are stable across proxy-variable estimation approaches. Regarding the log TFP dispersion which is of interest for the macro misallocation and trade reallocation literature, the Orr, Trefler and Yu chapter finds that TFP dispersion is much larger for value-added production functions than for gross-output production functions. From reviewing many empirical exercises, they conclude that Chinese firms' TFP measures using gross-output production functions can yield the most reliable and sensible results.

In Chapter 8, Ing, Yu and Zhang illustrate the evolution of export quality. They employ very disaggregated micro-level firm-product-destination-year data to measure export quality for Indonesia (2008–2012) and China (2000–2013), employing a new approach based on an endogenous quality choice framework à la Feenstra and Romalis (2014). The theoretical framework explicitly encompasses the roles of production efficiency, consumer preferences, input costs and per-unit shipping costs in shaping individual firms' optimal quality choices, these all being widely recognized in the international trade literature as key driving forces of quality decisions.

By formalizing these intuitions, Ing, Yu and Zhang develop a procedure to estimate micro-level firm-product-destination-year export quality. Compared with the existing demand-side approaches like Khandelwal (2010), extensively used to infer product quality variations within a destination and a year, this estimation procedure ensures that the measured qualities are comparable both across destinations and over time. This important feature of the estimated quality allows for empirical analysis that focuses on quality variations across destinations and across years.

On empirical exercises, their exercises combine firm-level production data with transaction-level export data in both Indonesia and China to estimate micro-level export quality. The estimated export quality is positively associated with sales across firms within a destination, per capita income and geographic barriers across destinations. The estimation results show that there is substantial heterogeneity in export quality distributions across industries, ownership types and years. Moreover, goods with better quality are more likely to be sold to high-income destinations. Finally, when the aggregate weighted-average export quality of each country is decomposed into the intensive and extensive margins, it is found that the intensive margin plays a major role in Indonesia's exports, while the extensive margin plays a major role in China's exports. Future research can aim at understanding the underlying economic mechanisms and forces that drive these sorts of export quality variations along different dimensions.

Chapter 9 by Caliendo, Monte and Rossi-Hansberg empirically examines the effects of exporting on organizational change. Their findings contribute to a new perspective on the overall effects of trade liberalizations. Following the theoretical framework of Caliendo and Rossi-Hansberg (2012), their current chapter first derives the result that exporters are larger and have more organizational layers than non-exporters.

Using French employer–employee matched data from 2002 to 2007, together with data on a firm's exporting activity, Caliendo, Monte and Rossi-Hansberg find that exporters are larger, employ more hours of labour, pay higher wages and have more organizational layers than non-exporters. New exporters are more likely to add these layers than non-exporters. New exporters that add layers decrease average wages in existing layers while exporters that do not add layers increase them. Furthermore, firms that expand significantly as a result of exporting reduce average wages. In contrast, new exporters that do not change layers barely expand but do increase wages. The average effect on wages is positive albeit small. Furthermore, Caliendo, Monte and Rossi-Hansberg also find that firms that enter the export market and expand substantially reorganize by adding layers of management and hiring more workers in all pre-existing layers. In contrast, firms that enter the export market and expand little do not reorganize.

Caliendo, Monte and Rossi-Hansberg then present some evidence that these effects have causal explanations using pre-sample variation in the destination composition of exports, in conjunction with real exchange rate variation across countries. They find that for firms with one, two, or three layers, exporting does significantly increase the probability of adding layers. The causal effect of increases in the number of layers due to better access to foreign markets is to reduce wages in preexisting layers and to increase the number of employees in all of them. Overall, their results are consistent with a growing literature using occupations to study the internal structure of firms and how their organization responds to opportunities in export markets.

Chapter 10 by Bernard, Bøler and Dhingra examines very interesting and substantial firm-to-firm connections and the firm-level costs of trade using Colombian import data. The vast majority of world trade flows is between firms. The rise of a large literature on heterogeneous firms has recognized the importance of variation across exporters and to a lesser extent across importers, in determining aggregate trade flows. However, even in that firm-focused research, detailed trade transaction data are usually aggregated to the level of individual firms, summed across all buyers for exporters or, conversely, summed across all sellers for importers, before being used by researchers. Only very recently have some studies in international trade started to emphasize the importance of the connections between exporters and importers both in aggregate trade flows and in the negative relationship between trade and geographic distance. This chapter documents the role of firm-to-firm connections in trade flows and the formation and duration of these importer–exporter relationships by exploring the individual matches between exporters and importers and examining their evolution.

Bernard, Bøler and Dhingra explore a new comprehensive dataset of detailed firm-to-firm Colombian import transactions covering the period 1995–2014. The dataset is rich enough to identify both the exporter and the importer. Moreover, each import transaction can be linked to a specific seller in a source country and each Colombian firm's annual export transactions can be linked to specific buyers in every destination country. This allows the authors to develop a set of basic facts about sellers and buyers across markets at a point in time, as well as the evolution of those buyer–seller relationships over time. They find strong evidence that the extensive margin of importer–exporter connections is strongly correlated with aggregate country-level trade flows. In addition, there is substantial heterogeneity across both importers and exporters in terms of the numbers of partners and the levels of trade flows. Again, the extensive margin is crucial in explaining the variation in import levels across firms. Large importers do not import more from each partner but, rather, have many more partners than smaller importers.

Their study examining firms on both sides of trade transactions has important implications for policy and academic work on the origins of international trade. While substantial progress has been made on reducing tariffs on manufactured goods, especially for flows between higher income nations, empirical evidence suggests that substantial costs remain. Estimates of fixed and variable costs of trade are large, even as technology and policy have reduced costs of transport, communication and tariffs. To engender another round of global integration with its attendant increases in income, consumption and welfare, research must put more attention on the nature of the trade costs between the firms that engage in trade.

Chapter 11 by Del Angel, Goswami and Rodriguez-Lopez contributes to the literature by estimating the impact of the 'China shock' on U.S. occupational employment from 2002 to 2014. Their work is inspired by the influential papers of Autor, Dorn and Hanson (2013), Acemoglu, Autor, Dorn, Hanson and Price (2016) and Pierce and Schott (2016). The methodology of their chapter is similar to Acemoglu, Autor, Dorn, Hanson and Price (2016), but the main difference between it and its influential forerunners is that this chapter further distinguishes occupations according to wage, non-routineness and education characteristics by using occupational employment data, which are combined from the Occupational Employment Statistics (OES) database, the O*NET database, the United Nations Comtrade database and the Bureau of Economic Analysis (BEA).

Del Angel, Goswami and Rodriguez-Lopez implement three empirical specifications. First, the authors estimate the overall employment effects of direct import exposure and of two combined measures of import exposure – the first combined measure adds just the direct and upstream exposures, while the second adds the direct, upstream and downstream exposures. Second, this chapter considers occupational sorting under three criteria, which are real wage, non-routineness and education. Third, they investigate the effects of Chinese import exposure on occupational employment across three sectors, namely, directly Chinese-trade exposed sectors, non-exposed tradable sectors and non-exposed non-tradable sectors.

After sorting occupations, Del Angel, Goswami and Rodriguez-Lopez generate some new findings. First, they find that employment losses from occupational-level Chinese import exposure are concentrated in low-wage, routine, low-education occupations within both Chinese-trade exposed and non-exposed sectors. This finding of employment reductions in lower-indexed occupations in the non-exposed sectors is quite novel and they argue it to be the consequence of local labour market effects. What's more, the authors also find mild evidence that direct Chinese exposure drives an employment expansion in high-education occupations. For this effect they provide two possible explanations. The first is the existence of productivity effects within firms by the replacement of low-wage employment with imports from China. The second relates to the standard reallocation effects à la Melitz (2003): Low-productivity firms are washed out from the market in response to tougher Chinese import competition.

Chapter 12 by Feenstra and Sasahara, by using the Global Input-Output Table from the EORA database, adopts the demand-side technique proposed by Los, Timmer and de Vries (2015, 2016) to quantify China's employment change in response to China's growing exports to its neighbors in East Asia, including Southeast Asian countries and the other most important economic entities – Japan, South Korea and Taiwan (JKT). They find that China's exports to Southeast Asia, namely ASEAN and the other three economics, contributed 11 per cent annual employment growth during the period of 1990–2013. Such employment creation and its associated employment compensation is equivalent to 1.7 per cent of total GDP in the ASEAN + JKT area. They are able to unpack the job creation in China further to that due directly to trade liberalization and due to changes in China's final demand *per se*. Overall, the contribution of China's growing final demand is at least three times larger than that of gains due to trade liberalization.

As the world's largest "factory", China experienced a significant export boom in the first decade of the new century. In particular, China's share of global export grew more than threefold, rising from 4 per cent in 2000 to around 14 per cent in 2016. It is clearly important to understand how this came about. Previous studies have identified several key factors in explaining China's export boom. In addition to the continued phasing out of restrictions on foreign-invested enterprises (Bai, Krishna and Ma, 2017), easing credit constraints on firms' exports (Feenstra, Li and Yu, 2014) and the reform of state-owned enterprises (Hsieh and Song, 2015), trade economists have also found a significant impact of China's WTO accession.

The last chapter, Chapter 13 by Allen and Arkolakis, presents a gravity model of the movement of goods and labour. Previous literature including Baldwin and Taglioni (2006), Costinot and Rodríguez-Clare (2013), Head and Mayer (2013) and Redding and Rossi-Hansberg (2017) provide excellent reviews of the development of the gravity model. Allen and Arkolakis's foremost contribution is that they extend the gravity trade model to a gravity immigration model. They first document a number of stylized facts on spatial economics. The evidence shows clearly both the flows of commodities (trade) and labour (migration) exhibit gravity. In particular, bilateral trade is negatively correlated with distance, regardless of the specific functional form with which bilateral distance is modelled. As expected, both origin-specific "push" factors and destination-specific "pull" factors are strongly correlated with GDP and trade flows within and across countries. Allen and Arkolakis show that such positive correlations can be predicted by a spatial gravity model with symmetric trade costs and balanced trade.

More importantly, by constructing labour flow data across U.S. state of birth and current residing location (from Ruggles, Fitch, Kelly-Hall and Sobek, 2000), Allen and Arkolakis highlight a new finding that gravity relationships with "push" and "pull" factors in migration are substantially different for migration and trade. To shed light on this, inspired by Allen and Arkolakis (2014), they develop an indirect utility function relying both on the utility realized in the destination and on bilateral migration disutility to derive the labour demand for the gravity on migration. Accordingly, places with higher migration costs, places with higher trade costs, less productive places and lower amenity places will have lower populations.

The authors then take their model to the data by estimating bilateral frictions and recovering location fundamentals and estimating the model's related elasticities. After evaluating the related exact hat algebra, Allen and Arkolakis conduct a counterfactuals exercises and use Interstate Highway System data to serve as an illustration of their elegant spatial economics to examine trade flows as well as migration flows under different scenarios.

References

Acemoglu, D., Autor, D., Dorn, D., Hanson, G. H., & Price, B. (2016). Import Competition and the Great US Employment Sag of the 2000s. *Journal of Labor Economics*, 34 (S1), S141–S198.

Allen, T., & Arkolakis, C. (2014). Trade and the Topography of the Spatial Economy. *Quarterly Journal of Economics*, 129(3), 1085–1140.

Autor, D. H., Dorn, D., & Hanson, G. H. (2013). The China Syndrome: Local Labor Market Effects of Import Competition in the United States. *American Economic Review*, 103(6), 2121–2168.

Bai, X., Krishna, K., & Ma, H. (2017). How You Export Matters: Export Mode, Learning and Productivity in China. *Journal of International Economics*, 104, 122–137.

Baldwin, R., & Taglioni, D. (2006). Gravity for Dummies and Dummies for Gravity Equations. *National Bureau of Economic Research Working Paper No. w12516*, Cambridge, MA: NBER.

Brandt, L., Van Biesebroeck, J., Wang, L., & Zhang, Y. (2017). WTO Accession and Performance of Chinese Manufacturing Firms. *American Economic Review*, 107(9), 2784–2820.

Brandt, L., Van Biesebroeck, J., & Zhang, Y. (2012). Creative Accounting or Creative Destruction? Firm-level Productivity Growth in Chinese Manufacturing. *Journal of Development Economics*, 97(2), 339–351.

Caliendo, L., & Parro, F. (2015). Estimates of the Trade and Welfare Effects of NAFTA. *Review of Economic Studies*, 82(1), 1–44.

Caliendo, L., & Rossi-Hansberg, E. (2012). The Impact of Trade on Organization and Productivity. *Quarterly Journal of Economics*, 127(3), 1393–1467.

Corrado, C., Hulten, C., & Sichel, D. (2009). Intangible Capital and US Economic Growth. *Review of Income and Wealth*, 55(3), 661–685.

Costinot, A., & Rodríguez-Clare, A. (2013). Trade Theory With Numbers: Quantifying the Consequences of Globalization. National Bureau of Economic Research Working Papers *No. w18896*, Cambridge, MA: NBER.

Feenstra, R. C., Li, Z., & Yu, M. (2014). Exports and Credit Constraints Under Incomplete Information: Theory and Evidence From China. *Review of Economics and Statistics*, 96 (4), 729–744.

Feenstra, R. C., & Romalis, J. (2014). International Prices and Endogenous Quality. *Quarterly Journal of Economics*, 129(2), 477–527.

Feng, L., Li, Z., & Swenson, D. L. (2017). Trade Policy Uncertainty and Exports: Evidence From China's WTO Accession. *Journal of International Economics*, 106, 20–36.

Handley, K., & Limao, N. (2017). Policy Uncertainty, Trade and Welfare: Theory and Evidence for China and the United States. *American Economic Review*, 107(9), 2731–2783.

Head, K., & Mayer, T. (2013). Gravity Equations: Workhorse, Toolkit and Cookbook *(No. 9322)*. CEPR Discussion Papers.

Hsieh, C. T., & Song, Z. M. (2015). Grasp the Large, Let Go of the Small: The Transformation of the State Sector in China. National Bureau of Economic Research Working Paper *No. w21006*, Cambridge, MA: NBER.

Khandelwal, A. K. (2010). The Long and Short (of) Quality Ladders. *Review of Economic Studies*, 77(4), 1450–1476.

Khandelwal, A. K., Schott, P. K., & Wei, S. J. (2013). Trade Liberalization and Embedded Institutional Reform: Evidence From Chinese Exporters. *American Economic Review*, 103(6), 2169–2195.

Krugman, P. (1994). *The Age of Diminishing Expectations*. London: MIT Press.

Los, B., Timmer, M. P., & de Vries, G. J. (2015). How Important Are Exports for Job Growth in China? A Demand-side Analysis. *Journal of Comparative Economics*, 43 (1), 19–32.

Los, B., Timmer, M. P., & de Vries, G. J. (2016). Tracing Value-Added and Double Counting in Gross Exports: Comment. *American Economic Review*, 106(7), 1958–1966.

Melitz, M. J. (2003). The Impact of Trade on Intra-industry Reallocations and Aggregate Industry Productivity. *Econometrica*, 71(6), 1695–1725.

Pierce, J. R., & Schott, P. K. (2016). The Surprisingly Swift Decline of US Manufacturing Employment. *American Economic Review*, 106(7), 1632–1662.

Redding, S. J., & Rossi-Hansberg, E. (2017). Quantitative Spatial Economics. *Annual Review of Economics*, 9(1), 21–58.

Ricardo, D. (1817). *On the Principles of Political Economy and Taxation*. London: John Murray.

Ruggles, S., Fitch, C. A., Kelly-Hall, P., & Sobek, K. H. (2000). Integrated Public Use Microdata for the United States. In Hall, P.K., R. McCaa, & G. Thorvaldsen (eds.), *Handbook of International Historical Microdata for Population Research*. Minneapolis: University of Minnesota, pp. 259–286.

Yu, M. (2015). Processing Trade, Tariff Reductions and Firm Productivity: Evidence From Chinese Firms. *Economic Journal*, 125(585), 943–988.

2 National sovereignty in an interdependent world

Kyle Bagwell and Robert W. Staiger

Of all the rights possessed by a nation, that of sovereignty is doubtless the most important.

Emmerich de Vattel in *The Law of Nations*, as quoted in
Jeremy Rabkin, *Why Sovereignty Matters*, p. 27

1. Introduction

What are the sovereign rights of nations in an interdependent world, and to what extent do these rights stand in the way of achieving internationally efficient outcomes? These questions rest at the heart of contemporary debate over the role and design of international institutions as well as growing tension between globalization and the preservation of national sovereignty. But answers are elusive. This is attributable in part to the fact that national sovereignty is a complex notion, reflecting a number of different features. And it is attributable as well to the fact that nations interact in increasingly complex and interdependent ways, making it difficult to draw clear distinctions between international and domestic affairs.

In this chapter, we propose answers to these questions. We do so by first developing formal definitions of national sovereignty that build on features of sovereignty emphasized in the international political economy literature. We then utilize these definitions to describe the degree and nature of national sovereignty possessed by countries in a benchmark (Nash) world in which there exist no international agreements of any kind. And with national sovereignty characterized in this benchmark world, we evaluate the extent to which national sovereignty is violated by international agreements with specific design features. In this way, we delineate the degree of tension between national sovereignty and international efficiency and describe how that tension can be minimized – and sometimes in principle even eliminated – through careful institutional design.

We begin by describing a benchmark two-country model of international interdependence. In this benchmark model, an international "externality" variable defines the interdependence between the two countries, and this variable is modeled in a way that is general enough to allow the nature of this interdependence to take a variety of possible forms, ranging from international trade to the depletion of a common-pool resource to global climate change. Within this benchmark model, we develop a working definition of sovereignty.

Our starting point for defining sovereignty is the Westphalian norm of "non-intervention in the internal affairs of other states" (Krasner, 1999, p. 20). To make this norm operational, we must define "non-intervention" and "internal affairs." Building on the notions of sovereignty commonly discussed in the international political economy literature, we combine elements of several of these notions and say that a governmental decision problem concerns the country's internal affairs whenever its payoff in that decision problem does not depend on the actions of any extraterritorial agents; otherwise, we say that this decision problem concerns the country's "external affairs." In the context of voluntary international agreements, we then say that one state has intervened in the internal affairs of another state, and therefore that a violation of sovereignty has occurred, whenever an international agreement leads a country to make commitments over matters that concern its internal affairs or to make commitments that alter the normal operations of its domestic institutions within the domain of its internal affairs. We argue that our formal definition of sovereignty captures three key features of Westphalian sovereignty emphasized in the international political economy literature that seem especially relevant in the context of voluntary international agreements: first, commitments that result from voluntary international agreements do not necessarily violate Westphalian sovereignty (as when these commitments pertain only to a country's external affairs); second, international commitments over policies that concern "sufficiently domestic" affairs (i.e., internal affairs) *do* violate Westphalian sovereignty; and third, international commitments that distort the normal operation of domestic institutions also violate Westphalian sovereignty.

With our formal definition of sovereignty in hand, we then turn to a characterization of the nature and degree of sovereignty that countries possess according to this definition in various economic environments and institutional settings. We begin this characterization within our two-country benchmark model. To identify the degree of sovereignty that countries possess in this environment in the absence of an international agreement, we show that a government's policy choices in the Nash equilibrium can be partitioned into two choice problems: a choice of the externality variable and the contribution that this country makes to the determination of the externality variable, given the other government's policies; and a choice of how best to use its policy instruments to achieve its objectives while delivering the given contribution level. With this partition, we are able to associate a country's external affairs with the first choice problem, and its internal affairs with the second. Intuitively, when countries are mutually interdependent, the external affairs of each country consist of that country's choices over its contribution to the determination of the externality variable and the equilibrium level of the externality variable, since its payoff in this choice problem depends on the actions of external actors. By contrast, the matters that concern the internal affairs of each country are that country's choices among all its policy combinations that are consistent with a given contribution to and level of the externality variable, since its payoff in this choice problem is independent of the actions of external actors.

We put our definition of sovereignty to work by evaluating according to this definition the consequences of various forms of international agreements for national sovereignty. Specifically, we consider first whether it is possible to eliminate the inefficiencies that arise in the Nash equilibrium with international agreements that are limited only to the external affairs of each country, and thereby to navigate all the way to the international efficiency frontier without violating national sovereignty by means of such agreements. Our first main result is that this is indeed possible within the benchmark model. That is, we show that it is always possible within the benchmark model to pick any point on the international efficiency frontier that could be achieved by international negotiations over all policy instruments, and to achieve that point with international negotiations that are limited only to the external affairs of each country, i.e., to the level of the externality variable and each country's contribution to it.

We next consider the way in which a country's sovereignty is violated within our benchmark model when the country negotiates international commitments that concern its internal affairs. Such commitments directly violate a country's sovereignty, but we show that direct violations of sovereignty can also imply further indirect violations of sovereignty as well, under which government decisions that are not the subject of international negotiation are nevertheless distorted away from the decisions that would normally have been made under the domestic institutional arrangements of the country. We argue that this "contamination effect" generally prevents countries from containing violations of sovereignty caused by international agreements to narrow subsets of policy instruments. In fact, we establish as our second main result that within our benchmark model any international agreement that involves direct commitments over matters that are the internal affairs of a country must in general violate that country's sovereignty over at least as many policy instruments as it preserves.

Our first two results highlight an important distinction between international agreements that mitigate international externalities and international agreements that erode national sovereignty, and indicate that it can be possible to have the former without the latter and so allow national sovereignty and international efficiency to coexist in harmony. But questions remain as to (i) whether this harmony is likely to extend to environments beyond those captured by our benchmark model, and (ii) the degree to which prominent channels of interdependence between countries can be identified that find representation in the environment described by our benchmark model. These questions are taken up in the second half of the chapter.

We consider a variety of settings that go beyond our benchmark model, and find that the harmony between national sovereignty and international efficiency does not always survive in these extended settings. For example, we identify a conflict between national sovereignty and international efficiency that arises whenever an externality variable is completely determined by the policy choices of a single country. This is because in this case the externality variable becomes this country's internal affairs according to our definition, and subjecting the externality variable to the constraints of an international agreement (which would be necessary to achieve international efficiency in this case) would therefore violate the country's sovereignty.

Another particularly salient extension of the benchmark model that we consider is to a world of "small" countries. When all countries are small in relation to the externality variable, we show that each county's contribution to the externality variable again becomes its internal affairs. This in turn implies that, when all countries are small, any international agreement that constrains countries from pursuing their Nash policy choices must violate their sovereignty. Accordingly, as we demonstrate, whether the harmony between national sovereignty and international efficiency described above survives in a world of small countries hinges on whether governments agree or disagree in the Nash equilibrium over the direction that they would like the externality variable to move. If all governments agree, then the Nash equilibrium in the small-country case is inefficient and an international agreement will be required to reach the efficiency frontier, implying necessarily that national sovereignty and international efficiency will stand in conflict in this case. However, if there is disagreement, then the Nash equilibrium in the small-country case is efficient, and in this case the harmony between national sovereignty and international efficiency identified above survives in a world of small countries. Of course, which of these two cases is applicable will depend on the nature of the externality variable under consideration, but as we later demonstrate, the latter case has special significance in the context of international trade agreements.

Besides being of interest in their own right, these extensions of our benchmark model highlight an important feature of our approach: rather than tailoring our definition of sovereignty on a case-by-case basis so that national sovereignty is necessarily in harmony with international efficiency in all circumstances, we propose a formal definition of sovereignty and then evaluate the circumstances where a tradeoff between sovereignty and international efficiency is unavoidable.[1] As our benchmark model and its extensions reveal, the range of settings in which national sovereignty and international efficiency can coexist in harmony is non-trivial but also not exhaustive.

To explore whether prominent channels of interdependence between countries can be identified that find representation in the environment described by our benchmark model, we then consider the issue of national sovereignty within the particular context of international trade agreements, and we show that the trade setting fits well within the environment described by our benchmark model. To this end, we begin by briefly reviewing the two-country two-good competitive general equilibrium trade model adapted to allow for the possibility of both tariff and domestic regulatory policy choices as developed in Bagwell and Staiger (2001). We establish that this model is a special case of our benchmark model, in which the international externality variable is the terms of trade, and in which each country's contribution to the determination of the externality is the quantity of imports it demands at a given terms of trade, and so all of the results described above apply.

This leads to our third main result: when the results of our benchmark model are interpreted within the context of our trade model, they indicate that the fundamental principles underlying GATT/WTO market access agreements offer a way to achieve internationally efficient policies without sacrificing national sovereignty, and that attaining international efficiency is consistent with maintaining national sovereignty in this setting regardless of whether (all) countries are big or small. We also extend our analysis of trade agreements to a multilateral setting, and establish that agreement to abide by a non-discrimination principle such as the GATT/ WTO MFN rule does not violate a country's sovereignty. And finally, we identify a critical role for MFN if countries are to achieve internationally efficient policies without sacrificing national sovereignty when some (but not all) countries are small. In particular, we find that a non-discrimination rule can allow countries to sidestep the efficiency/sovereignty tradeoff that would otherwise exist in this extended setting, and we suggest that the MFN requirement is therefore "complementary" to preserving small-country sovereignty in the following sense: the sovereignty of small countries can be preserved under an internationally efficient agreement only if that agreement abides by the MFN requirement. More broadly, our results therefore suggest that a non-discrimination rule coupled with a market access agreement can facilitate the attainment of internationally efficient outcomes that do not compromise national sovereignty. In light of our findings, we discuss the basic harmony between the underlying GATT/WTO principles and the maintenance of national sovereignty, and we suggest that this harmony may be at risk as a result of changes that are occurring within the WTO.

The chapter proceeds as follows. Section 2 describes the two-country benchmark model. Section 3 develops our formal definition of sovereignty, characterizes the nature and degree of sovereignty in the Nash equilibrium, and relates this characterization to notions of sovereignty in the international political economy literature. Section 4 considers how national sovereignty is affected under international agreements that adopt alternative designs within the benchmark model, while Section 5 considers the issue of sovereignty within a number of extensions of the benchmark model. Section 6 establishes that the benchmark model and all its results can be given a trade interpretation, and extends the modeling environment to a multilateral setting to consider the implications of a non-discrimination rule for our sovereignty results. Section 7 concludes. An appendix contains proofs not included in the body of the chapter.

2.   A benchmark model

In this section we describe a benchmark model of international interdependence that is general enough to allow interdependence to take a wide variety of forms. Our benchmark model has two countries (territories), referred to respectively as the home and foreign country, in which private agents (home and foreign citizens) reside. Each country has a government, and each government is endowed with a set of (tax and/or regulatory) policy instruments, represented by the $1 \times I$ vector **i** for the home government and the $1 \times I^*$ vector $\mathbf{i}^*$ for the foreign government, that are applied by each government to activities within its territory. The objectives of the home and foreign governments are represented by the respective functions $G(\mathbf{i}, \tilde{x}(\mathbf{i}, \mathbf{i}^*))$ and $G^*(\mathbf{i}^*, \tilde{x}(\mathbf{i}, \mathbf{i}^*))$, with the equilibrium level of the "externality" variable $\tilde{x}(\mathbf{i}, \mathbf{i}^*)$ entering into each government objective function and embodying the nature of the policy spillovers between the two countries. The ability to represent government objectives in this way reflects an essential assumption of our benchmark model, namely, that there exists a well-defined channel (e.g., the level of a price or the quantity of a pollutant) through which the effect of each government's policy choices on the other government's objectives (the externality) travels.

Aside from global concavity assumptions on the G and G^* functions to ensure that second-order conditions are globally satisfied, the only additional structure we impose in the benchmark model is that $\tilde{x}(\mathbf{i}, \mathbf{i}^*)$ is a well-behaved function defined implicitly according to

$$
\begin{aligned}
f(g(\mathbf{i}, x), g^*(\mathbf{i}^*, x), x) &= 0, \\
\text{with } f_g g_{i_k} &\neq 0 \text{ for some } k \text{ and} \\
f_{g^*} g^*_{i_m} &\neq 0 \text{ for some } m,
\end{aligned}
\tag{2.1}
$$

where here and throughout we use subscripts on a function to denote the partial derivative of that function with respect to the subscripted argument. In effect, g represents the home country's "contribution" to the determination of the equilibrium level of the externality variable $\tilde{x}$, a contribution that is assumed to be impacted by at least one policy instrument of the home government (i.e., $g_{i_k} \neq 0$ for some k); and this contribution is defined for a given level of the externality once the home-country policy instruments are determined. An analogous interpretation holds for g^*. The function f then aggregates the contributions of the home and foreign country to determine the equilibrium level of the externality $\tilde{x}$ according to $f(\cdot) = 0$, under the assumption that f is impacted by changes in either country's contribution (i.e., $f_g \neq 0 \neq f_{g^*}$).

As we confirm in Section 6, this structure is consistent with a setting in which the interdependence across countries is purely pecuniary and takes the form of international trade, with (2.1) then amounting to a market-clearing condition. But this structure is general enough as well to include many other forms of interdependence.

For example, x might represent the density of the fish population in a common fishery, with g representing the home catch when the home fleet operates in the policy environment **i** and faces a fish population density x, and with g^* representing the foreign catch when the foreign fleet operates in the policy environment $\mathbf{i}^*$ and faces a fish population density x. In this setting, it would be natural that $g_x > 0$ and $g_x^* > 0$. The equilibrium density of the fish population, given the policy environment faced by home and foreign fleets, $\tilde{x}(\mathbf{i}, \mathbf{i}^*)$, is then determined according to (2.1). Alternatively, x might represent the temperature of the globe, with g representing the home country's carbon output when the home industry operates in the policy environment $\mathbf{i}$ and faces a global temperature x, and with g^* representing the carbon output of the foreign country when the foreign industry operates in the policy environment $\mathbf{i}^*$ and faces a global temperature x. Here it could be that $g_x \gtreqless 0$ and $g_x^* \gtreqless 0$ depending on circumstances. The equilibrium temperature of the globe, given the policy environment faced by home and foreign industries, $\tilde{x}(\mathbf{i}, \mathbf{i}^*)$, is then determined according to (2.1). Or, under the assumption that each government cares about infant mortality within its own borders but the home government also cares directly about infant mortality in the foreign country, x could represent the rate of infant mortality in the foreign country, with g representing the home country's crib exports to the foreign country when the home industry operates in the policy environment $\mathbf{i}$ and the foreign infant mortality rate is x, and with g^* representing the foreign country's crib sales in the foreign market when the foreign industry operates in the policy environment $\mathbf{i}^*$ and the foreign infant mortality rate is x. Here again it could be that $g_x \gtreqless 0$ and $g_x^* \gtreqless 0$ depending on circumstances. The equilibrium infant mortality rate in the foreign country, given the policy environment faced by home and foreign industries, $\tilde{x}(\mathbf{i}, \mathbf{i}^*)$, is then determined according to (2.1).

Importantly, the structure in (2.1) rules out the possibility that $f_g g_{i_k} = 0$ for all k and/or that $f_{g^*} g_{i_m}^* = 0$ for all m, and thereby excludes cases where the externality variable x cannot be impacted by the policy instruments of some government. We will extend the benchmark model to consider such cases in a later section.

In the absence of any international agreements, we assume that each government makes choices over its own set of policy instruments, taking as given the policy levels of the other government. This problem defines, for each government, its best-response policy choice problem, and the solution to this problem defines its best-response policy choices. Specifically, the home government chooses its best-response policies by solving $\max_{\mathbf{i}} G(\mathbf{i}, \tilde{x}(\mathbf{i}, \mathbf{i}^*))$ taking $\mathbf{i}^*$ as given, which using (2.1) we write in the equivalent form

Program 1: For a given $\mathbf{i}^*$, $\max_{\mathbf{i},x} G(\mathbf{i}, x)$ s.t. $f(g(\mathbf{i}, x), g^*(\mathbf{i}^*, x), x) = 0$,

at the same time that the foreign government chooses its best-response policies by solving $\max_{\mathbf{i}^*} G^*(\mathbf{i}^*, \tilde{x}(\mathbf{i}, \mathbf{i}^*))$ taking $\mathbf{i}$ as given, which using (2.1) we write in the equivalent form

Program 1*: For a given $\mathbf{i}$, $\max_{\mathbf{i}^*,x} G^*(\mathbf{i}^*, x)$ s.t. $f(g(\mathbf{i}, x), g^*(\mathbf{i}^*, x), x) = 0$.

Substituting the constraint into the objective function for each program, the I first-order conditions associated with Program 1 that define the home government's best-response policy choices are given by

$$G_{i_k} + G_x \tilde{x}_{i_k} = 0 \text{ for } k = 1, ..., I, \tag{2.2}$$

while the I^* first-order conditions associated with Program 1^* that define the foreign government's best-response policy choices are given by

$$G^*_{i_k^*} + G^*_x \tilde{x}_{i_k^*} = 0 \text{ for } k = 1, ..., I^*. \tag{2.3}$$

The joint solutions to (2.2) and (2.3) define the Nash equilibrium of the benchmark model, which throughout we assume exists and is unique.

We next characterize the international efficiency frontier and evaluate the efficiency properties of the Nash equilibrium. We define the international efficiency frontier with respect to the objectives of each government. Accordingly, the international efficiency frontier solves the following program:

Program 2: $\max\limits_{i, i^*, x} G(\mathbf{i}, x)$

s.t. (i) $G^*(\mathbf{i}^*, x) \geq \bar{G}^*$, and

(ii) $f(g(\mathbf{i}, x), g^*(\mathbf{i}^*, x), x) = 0$.

Using Program 2, and letting $k = 1$ denote a domestic and foreign policy instrument for which $g_{i_k} \neq 0$ and $g^*_{i_k^*} \neq 0$, it is direct to derive the first-order conditions that characterize the international efficiency frontier:

$$G_{i_k} = \frac{g_{i_k} G_{i_1}}{g_{i_1}} \text{ for } k = 2, ..., I, \tag{2.4}$$

$$G^*_{i_k^*} = \frac{g^*_{i_k^*} G^*_{i_1^*}}{g^*_{i_1^*}} \text{ for } k = 2, ..., I^*, \text{ and} \tag{2.5}$$

$$G_{i_1} G^*_{i_1^*} + G_{i_1} G^*_x \tilde{x}_{i_1^*} + G^*_{i_1^*} G_x \tilde{x}_{i_1} = 0, \tag{2.6}$$

along with the complementary slackness conditions ensuring that the Kuhn-Tucker multiplier on constraint (i) of Program 2 is non-negative:

$$-\frac{G_x}{G^*_x} + \frac{G_{i_1}[f_g g_x + f_{g^*} g^*_x + f_x]}{G^*_x f_g g_{i_1}} \geq 0 \text{ if } G^*_x \neq 0 \text{ and}$$

$$\frac{G_{i_1} f_{g^*} g^*_{i_k^*}}{G^*_{i_k^*} f_g g_{i_1}} \geq 0 \text{ for each } k \text{ for which } G^*_{i_k^*} \neq 0. \tag{2.7}$$

The efficiency properties of the Nash equilibrium may now be assessed. Using (2.2) and (2.3), whose joint solutions define the Nash equilibrium in our benchmark model, we may state:

Proposition 1. The Nash equilibrium of the benchmark model is inefficient if and only if $G_x \neq 0$ and $G^*_x \neq 0$ at the Nash policy choices.

Proof: See appendix.[2]

According to Proposition 1, the Nash equilibrium is inefficient – and hence a potential role for international agreements arises in our benchmark model – if and only if $G_x \neq 0$ and $G_x^* \neq 0$ at the Nash policy choices. We will refer to the case where $G_x \neq 0$ and $G_x^* \neq 0$ at the Nash policy choices as the case where the home and foreign countries are *mutually interdependent*. As our central purpose is to consider the implications of voluntary (i.e., mutually beneficial) international agreements for national sovereignty, and as the case of mutually interdependent countries is the only case in which voluntary international agreements can arise, this case will be a primary focus of the analysis to follow.

3. What is sovereignty?

With the essential elements of our benchmark model described, we now turn to develop a definition of sovereignty within the context of this model. Defining sovereignty is not a simple task. On the one hand, to be operational, our definition of sovereignty must be amenable to formal analysis. On the other hand, to be relevant, our definition of sovereignty must capture elements that feature prominently in the common usage of this term. This latter requirement is particularly difficult, because the international political economy literature within which sovereignty has been most discussed is not always clear about the precise meaning of the term and, when clear, does not always adopt a uniform meaning. In fact, Krasner (1999) identifies four distinct ways in which the term "sovereignty" has been commonly used in this literature. Krasner refers to these as *domestic sovereignty, international legal sovereignty, interdependence sovereignty* and *Westphalian sovereignty*. Domestic sovereignty refers to the organization and effectiveness of political authority within the state. International legal sovereignty refers to the mutual recognition of states. Interdependence sovereignty refers to the scope of activities over which states can effectively exercise control. And Westphalian sovereignty reflects as its central premise the rule of non-intervention in the internal affairs of other states.

Our starting point for defining sovereignty is the Westphalian norm of "non-intervention in the internal affairs of other states" (Krasner, 1999, p. 20). To formalize this definition, we must define "non-intervention" and "internal affairs."

What are the internal affairs of a state? One answer might be to equate internal affairs directly with those matters that no one outside the state cares about. But as a basis for defining national sovereignty, this approach has limitations, because it leads to a notion of sovereignty that is defined directly by the preferences of external actors: if an external actor decides that it cares about an issue over which a state is making a choice, then that issue is by this definition no longer an internal affair of the state.[3] We therefore look to the international political economy literature for guidance. In this literature, the internal affairs of a state are synonymous with its "domestic authority structures," a phrase that in turn has been interpreted to mean the state's authority to determine the institutions and policies that apply within its territorial boundaries. For example, according to Krasner (1999, p. 20), the concept of Westphalian sovereignty can be characterized as

> an institutional arrangement for organizing political life that is based on two principles: territoriality and the exclusion of external actors from domestic authority structures. Rulers may be constrained, sometimes severely, by the external environment, but they are still free to choose the institutions and policies they regard as optimal. Westphalian sovereignty is violated when external actors influence or determine domestic authority structures.

Here Krasner is drawing a distinction between the effectiveness with which control over outcomes can be exerted on the one hand, and the authority to choose institutions and policies on the other. The former is a concern of domestic sovereignty and interdependence sovereignty, but it is the latter that defines the internal affairs with which Westphalian sovereignty is concerned. In the international political economy literature, then, a nation's internal affairs – over which, according to Westphalian sovereignty, it must enjoy freedom from intervention by external actors – are considered to be its choice of domestic institutions and the operation of these institutions to translate the preferences of its citizens into policy choices.

To draw a connection between this notion of internal affairs and our benchmark model, we observe that our home and foreign government objectives G and G^* respectively can be said to reflect the particular set of "domestic authority structures" relevant for determining the levels of policy instruments within the territory of that government. For example, domestic authority may be concentrated in the hands of one individual, whose preferences are then the government objective function for that country. If that individual is subjected to lobbying by interest groups, then these interest groups also comprise a part of the domestic authority structure, and the government objective function for that country will reflect as well the influence wielded by these interest groups. Alternatively, domestic authority may be dispersed in the hands of the electorate and take the form of a direct democracy, in which case under appropriate assumptions the preferences of the median voter are then the government objective function for that country. Or domestic authority over different policies may be allocated across different domestic institutions: as long as coordination across domestic institutions (e.g., bargaining among them) is possible, our representation of government objectives allows a valid description of the domestic policy environment in this setting as well. The point is, each government's objective function as we have defined it reflects both the underlying preferences of the citizens of that country and the domestic authority structures under which those preferences are translated into choices over policy instruments in that country. According to the meaning of Westphalian sovereignty in the international political economy literature, then, within the context of our model the internal affairs of the home (foreign) country are embodied in its choice of G (G^*).

As for what constitutes intervention by external actors, Krasner (1999, Chapters 6 and 7) observes that coercion (as in international armed conflict) has frequently resulted in constitutional changes that explicitly alter the domestic institutions of a country and thereby violate its Westphalian sovereignty. Such explicit changes in domestic institutions could be interpreted within our benchmark model as alterations in the G and/or G^* functions, reflecting for example the forced removal of a dictator and the introduction of democratic institutions. However, our focus here is not on armed conflict, but rather on voluntary international agreements. Hence, violations of Westphalian sovereignty that would result in changes in the G and/or G^* functions are not our central concern.

But Krasner (1999, p. 22) observes that invitation (as in international contracts and conventions) can also violate Westphalian sovereignty, not necessarily by explicitly altering domestic institutions, but by "subjecting internal authority structures to external constraints." Rabkin (1998, p. 34) puts the point slightly differently: (Westphalian) sovereignty is violated by international commitments that "distort or derange the normal workings of our own system." In effect, international commitments need not alter the domestic institutions of a country in order to violate its Westphalian sovereignty: international commitments that distort the operation of domestic institutions will also violate Westphalian sovereignty.

Implicit in the above discussion is the notion that specific commitments arising out of voluntary international agreements would not ordinarily be viewed as violations of Westphalian sovereignty. For Westphalian sovereignty to be violated by invitation, a "deeper" intervention into the internal affairs of the state is required. Even here though, both Krasner (1999) and Rabkin (1998) suggest that there are limits to the appropriate matters for international agreement, and that a nation's Westphalian sovereignty would be violated by negotiated commitments over policies that cross these limits and stray into "sufficiently domestic" affairs. For instance, Krasner (1999, pp. 146–148) observes that the IMF routinely violates the norm of Westphalian sovereignty, in part because "a country entering into negotiations with the IMF could basically consider any aspect of its domestic economic policy open to discussion." Similarly, in the Preface to his book, Rabkin (1998, p. x) states that efforts to delineate the appropriate limits of international commitments are "particularly urgent now because, in the absence of any clear understandings on the matter, we seem to be letting international agreements and international authorities determine more and more of our policies." Neither Krasner nor Rabkin offer a precise method for defining the limits of proper subjects of international negotiation, though Rabkin (pp. 69–70) proposes several criteria.

In summation, three key features of Westphalian sovereignty that seem especially relevant in the context of voluntary international agreements can be identified from our discussion of the international political economy literature to this point: first, commitments that result from voluntary international agreements do not necessarily violate Westphalian sovereignty; second, international commitments over policies that concern "sufficiently domestic" affairs (i.e., internal affairs) *do* violate Westphalian sovereignty; and third, international commitments that distort the normal operation of domestic institutions also violate Westphalian sovereignty. We wish to construct a definition of sovereignty that reflects these three features.

To accomplish this, we maintain as our essential focus the Westphalian norm of non-intervention in the internal affairs of other states. And below we adopt a definition of non-intervention that is well-reflected in the discussion above. But in proposing a formal definition of internal affairs, we augment the Westphalian emphasis on authority over the determination of institutions and policies, and add to this an emphasis on authority and control over the determination of outcomes and therefore payoffs as well, all evaluated from the perspective of the Nash policy equilibrium of our model. In effect, our definition of sovereignty combines elements of authority with elements of control/effectiveness, and in so doing delivers a notion of sovereignty that exhibits traditional features (Krasner, 1999, p. 10) of Westphalian sovereignty (authority over institutions and policies), interdependence sovereignty (effective control over cross-border activities), and domestic sovereignty (authority and effective control over activities within the territory). As a result, the characterization of a country's internal affairs according to our definition will depend on the nature of interdependence across countries. With internal affairs so defined, our broad approach is then to characterize the normal operation of a country's domestic institutions in the domain of its internal affairs, and to say that a violation of sovereignty occurs whenever an international agreement leads the government of a country to make external commitments over matters that (i) concern the country's internal affairs or (ii) alter (and therefore influence/distort/derange) the normal operations of the country's domestic institutions within the domain of its internal affairs.

Our approach to defining national sovereignty has both advantages and disadvantages. On the minus side, our approach does not conform precisely to any one of the four notions of sovereignty commonly discussed in the international political economy literature: as we noted above, it combines elements of a number of these notions. On the plus side, however, our approach admits several advantages. First and foremost, as we demonstrate below this approach provides an analytically tractable way to capture the three key features of Westphalian sovereignty identified above. Second, because a country's internal affairs according to our definition will depend on the nature of interdependence across countries, as the nature of interdependence changes so too will the scope of a country's internal affairs and hence the domain of its sovereign rights.[4] And finally, by augmenting the Westphalian focus on authority over institutions/policies with a focus as well on authority over outcomes/payoffs, our approach may facilitate a more direct link to issues of *accountability* in an interdependent world than do any of the existing notions of sovereignty taken separately, and may thus be of some interest in its own right. For example, a government might maintain authority over its institutions and policies (and therefore maintain Westphalian sovereignty) and yet claim that it cannot be held accountable for its choices, as a consequence of a "race to the bottom" that external constraints have forced upon it. But in matters where the government maintains control over outcomes/payoffs as well (and hence in matters that are also the country's internal affairs according to our definition), this possibility of avoiding accountability by appealing to external constraints does not arise. As a consequence, our approach to defining national sovereignty can be used to forge a tighter link between international agreements that can be said to avoid an erosion of sovereignty and those that can be said to avoid an erosion of accountability.

3.1.   Sovereignty defined

We now proceed to develop our formal definitions in detail. To this end, we return to the benchmark model presented in Section 2, and consider the Nash policy choices made by each government. It is with respect to Nash choices, unconstrained by any international commitments, that a nation's internal affairs can be defined. As noted above, we adopt a definition of internal affairs that equates the internal affairs of a country with (i) the choice of domestic authority structures under which the preferences of its citizens are translated into choices over policy instruments in that country, as embodied in the home and foreign government objective functions G and G^* respectively, and (ii) the matters in which its government has control or "sole authority" over outcomes/payoffs (in the Nash equilibrium).

To develop this definition, we consider alternative representations of each government's best-response policy choice problem (that is, alternative representations of Program 1 and Program 1^* in Section 2) that *partition* this problem into a sequence of sub-problems, each of which can be considered a choice problem of its own, and where the solution to any such representation yields the original best-response policy choices of the government characterized by (2.2) and (2.3). Our approach is to use these partitions to identify the maximal set of choice problems over which a government can be said to exercise sole authority in the Nash equilibrium, and thereby (together with its choice of government objective function) identify the country's internal affairs according to our definition.

We begin by defining a partition of a government's best-response policy choice problem:

Definition 1. A *partition* $\mathcal{P}$ *of a government's best-response policy choice problem* is any sequence of choice problems whose solution yields the best-response policy choices of the government.

According to its definition, each element of $\mathcal{P}$ is a choice problem for the government, and when the government has solved each of these choice problems it arrives at the original best-response policies.[5] We also need a definition of authority:

Definition 2. A government has *sole authority* in a choice problem if and only if its payoff in that choice problem is independent of the actions of "external actors."

By the actions of external actors, we mean the setting of all policy instruments by the government of the other country and all decisions by private agents in the other country. Accordingly, a government has authority in a choice problem provided that its policy choices, together with the decisions of private agents operating within its borders, fully determine its payoffs in that choice problem.

We next define internal affairs and external affairs, conditional on the partition $\mathcal{P}$ under consideration:

Definition 3. For any partition $\mathcal{P}$ of its government's best-response policy choice problem, a country's $\mathcal{P}$-*internal affairs* consist of (i) the choice of domestic authority structures under which the preferences of its citizens are translated into choices over policy instruments in that country, as embodied in its government objective function, and (ii) the collection of choice problems in $\mathcal{P}$ over which the government has sole authority. The country's $\mathcal{P}$-*external affairs* are the remaining choice problems in $\mathcal{P}$.

In other words, conditional on a partition $\mathcal{P}$ of its government's best-response policy choice problem, a country's $\mathcal{P}$-internal affairs are its choice of government objective function and the choice problems over which its policy choices fully determine its payoffs, and its $\mathcal{P}$-external affairs are the remaining choice problems in the partition $\mathcal{P}$.

Definition 3 permits any choice problem to be assigned either to a country's internal affairs or to its external affairs. But these choice problems are defined relative to a specific partition of the government's best-response policy choice problem, and there are many such partitions. Hence, as a general matter, the internal affairs of a country as we have defined them in Definition 3 will depend on the partition under consideration, a dependence we have indicated with the terms $\mathcal{P}$-internal affairs and $\mathcal{P}$-external affairs.

However, if there exists a way to partition the government's best-response policy choice problem so that a *minimal* set of external affairs can be identified (in the sense that, as we formalize below, there is no partition under which a country's external affairs would be a proper subset of this set), then we prefer to select this partition among all possible partitions for purposes of defining a county's internal and external affairs. The minimal partition, when it exists, seems the reasonable partition on which to focus, because it would identify the smallest collection of choice problems over which the government does not enjoy sole authority in the Nash equilibrium, and by implication as well the largest collection of choice problems over which the government does enjoy sole authority in the Nash equilibrium. So in this case, the reference to dependence on the particular partition under consideration can be suppressed, and we can refer simply to internal and external affairs.

We next develop this preferred definition of internal and external affairs. To state this definition, we say that a collection of choice problems $\hat{s}$ contained in the partition $\hat{\mathcal{P}}$ is a *subset* of the collection of choice problems $\tilde{s}$ contained in the partition $\tilde{\mathcal{P}}$ provided that there exists a collection of choice problems $\tilde{s}'$ such that $\{\{\tilde{\mathcal{P}} \backslash \tilde{s}\} \cup \tilde{s}'\}$ is also a partition of the government's best-response policy choice problem and every choice problem in $\hat{s}$ is also in $\tilde{s}'$. Intuitively, $\hat{s}$ is a subset of $\tilde{s}$ if there is a way to write $\tilde{s}$ – which we denote $\tilde{s}'$, and with $\{\{\tilde{\mathcal{P}} \backslash \tilde{s}\} \cup \tilde{s}'\}$ also a partition of the government's best-response policy choice problem – so that $\hat{s}$ and $\tilde{s}'$ can be compared on a choice-problem by choice-problem basis, and when this comparison is made every element of $\hat{s}$ (every choice problem in $\hat{s}$) is also in $\tilde{s}'$; this would mean that $\tilde{s}$ can be thought of as $\hat{s}$ plus "stuff".[6] And we say that a collection of choice problems $\hat{s}$ contained in the partition $\hat{\mathcal{P}}$ is *equivalent* to the collection of choice problems $\tilde{s}$ contained in the partition $\tilde{\mathcal{P}}$ provided that there exists a collection of choice problems $\tilde{s}'$ such that $\{\{\tilde{\mathcal{P}} \backslash \tilde{s}\} \cup \tilde{s}'\}$ is also a partition of the government's best-response policy choice problem and a choice problem is in $\hat{s}$ if and only if it is also in $\tilde{s}'$.

We may now define a minimal partition:

Definition 4. A *minimal partition* $\hat{\mathcal{P}}$ of a government's best-response policy choice problem is a partition for which the government's $\hat{\mathcal{P}}$-external affairs are a subset of its $\mathcal{P}$-external affairs for all $\mathcal{P}$.

And with this we arrive at our preferred definition of internal and external affairs:

Definition 5. If there exists a minimal partition $\hat{\mathcal{P}}$ of its government's best-response policy choice problem, then a country's *internal affairs* consist of (i) the choice of domestic authority structures under which the preferences of its citizens are translated into choices over policy instruments in that country, as embodied in its government objective function, and (ii) its $\hat{\mathcal{P}}$-internal affairs; and the country's *external affairs* are its $\hat{\mathcal{P}}$-external affairs.

Notice that it is possible that a set of partitions may qualify as minimal partitions, but each partition in this set must (i) be payoff equivalent, because all partitions must lead to the same best-response policy choices, and (ii) deliver the same characterization of internal and external affairs according to Definitions 4 and 5. Hence, this possible non-uniqueness is immaterial for our purposes.[7]

To make use of Definition 5, we must establish the existence of minimal partitions of the home and foreign government best-response choice problems in our benchmark model. To this end, consider the alternative 2-step representation of Program 1:

Program 1':   *Step* 1. For a given (g,x): $\max_{\mathbf{i}} G(\mathbf{i},x)$

$$\text{s.t. } [g(\mathbf{i},x) - g] = 0.$$

Step 2. For a given $\mathbf{i}^*$: $\max_{g,x} L(\hat{\imath}(g,x), g, x)$

$$\text{s.t. } f(g, g^*(\mathbf{i}^*_x, x), x) = 0,$$

where $\hat{\imath}(g,x)$ is the solution from Step 1 and L is the Step-1 Lagrangean.[8] The Step-1 choice problem in Program 1' is solved conditional on a given level of the "externality" variable x and the home-country's "contribution" g to the externality variable, and has the home government making its preferred choices over domestic policy instruments $\mathbf{i}$ so as to deliver this contribution. The Step-2 choice problem has the home government then making its preferred choices over g and x subject to the constraint placed on its choices which is implied by a vector of foreign policy instruments $\mathbf{i}^*$.

Our first result is that Program 1' is indeed an equivalent way of characterizing the home-government's best-response policies in Program 1. We record this in:

Lemma 1. Program 1' is a partition of Program 1.

Proof: See appendix.

We prove Lemma 1 by establishing that the first-order conditions associated with Program 1$'$ are given by (2.2), the first-order conditions associated with Program 1, hence the solution of Program 1$'$ yields the best-response policy choices of the home government. While we have developed this partition from the perspective of the home government's problem Program 1, an exactly analogous partition (which we denote henceforth by Program 1$^{*\prime}$) can be developed for the foreign government's problem Program 1*. For future reference, we denote by P_0 the partition of the home-government's best-response policy choice problem defined by Program 1$'$, and by P_0^* the partition of the foreign-government's best-response policy choice problem defined by Program 1$^{*\prime}$.

We next use Program 1$'$ (and the analogous Program 1$^{*\prime}$ of the foreign government) to assess the internal affairs of each country according to the partitions P_0 and P_0^*. It is immediate from Program 1$'$ that the home government has sole authority over its payoff in the choice problem defined by Step 1, and hence the Step-1 choice problem concerns the home-country's P_0-internal affairs for this alternative partition. We refer henceforth to the home-government's Step-1 choice problem in the partition P_0 as its *choices over* $\mathbf{i}(g,x)$, and as noted above we denote its Step-1 choices by $\hat{i}(g, x)$. On the other hand, the home government would have sole authority over its payoff in the choice problem defined by Step 2 – and hence the Step-2 choice problem would concern the home-country's P_0-internal affairs for this alternative partition – if and only if the home government faced a non-binding constraint it its Step-2 choice problem, which cannot occur as long as G_x is non-zero.[9] We refer henceforth to the home-government's Step-2 choice problem in the partition P_0 as its *choices over g and x*. Completely analogous statements hold for the foreign government. Hence we have:

Lemma 2. The home country's P_0-internal affairs consist of its choice of G and its government's choices over $\mathbf{i}(g,x)$, and also its government's choices over g and x if and only if $G_x = 0$ when evaluated at the Nash policy choices. The foreign country's P_0^*-internal affairs consist of its choice of G^* and its government's choices over $\mathbf{i}^*(g^*,x)$, and also its government's choices over g^* and x if and only if $G_x^* = 0$ when evaluated at the Nash policy choices.

Finally, we now establish that the partitions P_0 and P_0^* are minimal partitions of the home and foreign government best-response choice problems, respectively. This is stated in:

Lemma 3. The partition P_0 is a minimal partition of the home-government's best-response choice problem, and the partition P_0^* is a minimal partition of the foreign-government's best-response choice problem.

Proof: If $G_x = 0$ and $G_x^* = 0$ when evaluated at the Nash policy choices, then according to P_0 and P_0^* there are no choices for either the home- or the foreign-government that concern its external affairs, and so P_0 and P_0^* must be minimal partitions in this case. Consider, then, the case in which $G_x \neq 0$ when evaluated at the Nash policy choices. According to $\mathcal{P}_0$, the home government's choices over g and x are its external affairs in this case. Suppose that $\mathcal{P}_0$ is not a minimal partition. Then there must exist a partition $\mathcal{P}'$ of the home government's best-response choice problem in which the home government's choices over g and x are not both included in its external affairs. In the partition $\mathcal{P}'$, it must then be possible for the home government to alter either g or x or both g and x in at least one choice problem contained in its internal affairs. Consider, then, any choice problem contained in the home government's $\mathcal{P}'$-internal affairs for which either g or x or both g and x can be altered. With $\mathbf{i}^*$ fixed and with $f_g \neq 0$ by assumption, g and x cannot be determined independently. Therefore, in this choice problem, the home government must face a constraint of the form $f(g,g^*(\mathbf{i}_x^*,x),x) = 0$ if it chooses g directly, or a constraint of the form $f(g(\mathbf{i},x), g^*(\mathbf{i}_x^*,x),x) = 0$ if it instead chooses g indirectly through its choice of elements of $\mathbf{i}$. But either way, the constraint ensures that the home government does not have sole authority in this choice problem – and this is inconsistent with the claim that this choice problem concerns a matter of internal affairs for the home government – as long as $G_x \neq 0$ when evaluated at the Nash policy choices, which is the case under consideration. Hence, we have derived a contradiction, and so $\mathcal{P}_0$ must be a minimal partition. An analogous argument holds for the foreign government. **QED**

As a result of Lemmas 1–3, we may then state:

Proposition 2. If countries are mutually interdependent so that $G_x \neq 0$ and $G_x^* \neq 0$ at the Nash policy choices, then in the benchmark model the home country's internal affairs are its choice of G and its government's choices over $\mathbf{i}(g,x)$, and the foreign country's internal affairs are its choice of G^* and its government's choices over $\mathbf{i}^*(g^*,x)$; and choices over g and x (g^* and x) represent the external affairs of the home- (foreign-) country. If countries are not mutually interdependent, then in the benchmark model: (a) if $G_x = 0$ at the Nash policy choices, the home country's internal affairs include as well its government's choices over g and x; and (b) if $G_x^* = 0$ at the Nash policy choices, the foreign country's internal affairs include as well its government's choices over g^* and x.

According to Proposition 2, when countries are mutually interdependent, the matters that concern the internal affairs of each country are the domestic authority structures under which the preferences of its citizens are translated into choices over policy instruments in that country, as embodied in its government objective function, and its government's choices among the set of policy combinations that are consistent with a given contribution to and level of the externality variable, since its payoff in this choice problem is independent of the actions of external actors. Notice that the policy choices made by each government in matters that concern its country's internal affairs, namely $\hat{\imath}(g,x)$ for the home government and $\hat{\imath}^*(g^*,x)$ for the foreign government, reflect both the underlying preferences of the citizens of that country and the normal operation of that country's domestic institutions under which those preferences are translated into choices over policy instruments. The external affairs of each country then consist of its government's choices over the country's contribution to the determination of the externality variable and the equilibrium level of the externality variable, since its payoff in this choice problem depends on the actions of external actors. And when countries are not mutually interdependent, *all* of their choices may become their internal affairs (and will be, when both $G_x = 0$ and $G_x^* = 0$) according to Proposition 2. In light of Proposition 1, an implication of Proposition 2 is that countries operating in an environment of mutual interdependency where a potential role for international agreements exists can claim national sovereignty only over a diminished range of choices (their internal affairs) even when they are not part of any international agreement.

In light of Proposition 2, we are now ready to define external intervention as it relates to voluntary international agreements:

Definition 6. An international agreement *subjects the internal affairs of a country to external constraints* if and only if: (i) the government of that country makes commitments in the agreement over matters that concern its internal affairs; and/or (ii) the agreement has the effect of altering the choices in any choice problem that concerns the country's internal affairs.

With this definition, we then say that a country's *sovereignty is violated by an international agreement* when its internal affairs are subjected to external constraints by that agreement.[10]

Returning now to the three key features that we described in Section 3 regarding Westphalian sovereignty as it relates to voluntary international agreements, we observe that our formalization of national sovereignty reflects each of these features. First, commitments that result from voluntary international agreements do not necessarily violate sovereignty since, according to Proposition 1, international agreements over g, x and g^* do not violate sovereignty as long as governments are mutually interdependent. Second, international commitments over policies that concern "sufficiently domestic" affairs (i.e., internal affairs) *do* violate Westphalian sovereignty since, according to Proposition 2, negotiated commitments over the elements of $\hat{\imath}(g,x)$ and/or $\hat{\imath}^*(g^*,x)$ always violate sovereignty. And third, international commitments that distort the normal operation of domestic institutions also violate sovereignty, if these distortions result in unilateral policy choices that do not conform to the corresponding elements of $\hat{\imath}(g,x)$ and/or $\hat{\imath}^*(g^*,x)$.

4.   Sovereignty, international agreements and efficiency

We now make use of our definition of sovereignty. In this section we consider international agreements of various kinds to explore within our benchmark model the nature of the tradeoff between the preservation of sovereignty and the attainment of international efficiency. Throughout we assume that, subsequent to the conclusion of negotiations of an international agreement, each government chooses its best-response policies unilaterally given the policies of the other government and subject to the constraints placed on it by the international agreement.

We first consider the possibility that international efficiency might be attained without violating national sovereignty. When countries are not mutually interdependent, it is direct from Propositions 1 and 2 that this is possible, as long as countries avoid being constrained by any international commitments. This follows because when countries are not mutually interdependent the Nash equilibrium is efficient by Proposition 1, and by Proposition 2 all of at least one country's choices are its internal affairs. When countries are mutually interdependent, however, an international agreement is required to achieve efficiency, as Proposition 1 implies. The question is whether an international agreement can in this case be designed to achieve international efficiency while not violating national sovereignty. The answer to this question within our benchmark model is affirmative, as we record in the next proposition:

Proposition 3. In the benchmark model, there is no inherent conflict between international efficiency and national sovereignty. When countries are not mutually interdependent, they can maintain their national sovereignty and attain international efficiency by avoiding international commitments. When countries are mutually interdependent, they can maintain their national sovereignty and attain international efficiency by negotiating commitments over g, x and g^*.

Proof: We focus on the case of mutually interdependent countries. If the home and foreign government negotiate commitments over g, x and g^*, then subsequent to the conclusion of negotiations the home government will, for the negotiated level of (g,x), choose its vector of policies $\mathbf{i}$ subject to the implied constraint $[g(\mathbf{i},x) - g] = 0$, and therefore solve Step 1 of Program 1′, and similarly the foreign government will, for the negotiated level of (g^*, x), choose its vector of policies $\mathbf{i}^*$ subject to the implied constraint $[g^*(\mathbf{i}^*,x) - g^*] = 0$, and therefore solve Step 1 of Program 1*′. With L and L^* the Step-1 Lagrangeans for the home and foreign government, respectively, negotiations over g, x, and g^* then solve the following program for some $\bar{L}^*$:

Program 3: $\max\limits_{g,x,g^*} L(\mathbf{i}(g,x),g,x)$

  s.t. (i) $L^*(\mathbf{i}^*(g^*,x),g^*,x) \geq \bar{L}^*$, and

  (ii) $f(g,g^*,x) = 0$.

It is now direct to derive that the first-order and complementary slackness conditions associated with Program 3 are identical to those associated with Program 2, and given by (2.4)–(2.6) and (2.7) respectively. Hence, negotiations over g, x and g^* achieve the international efficiency frontier without violating national sovereignty. **QED**

Proposition 3 implies that, in principle, countries need not confront a choice between preserving their sovereignty and attaining international efficiency when they negotiate international agreements, as long as they (*a*) negotiate agreements that impose commitments only on countries with which they are mutually interdependent, and (*b*) limit negotiations to direct commitments over the level of the externality (*x*) and each country's contribution to the externality (g and g^*).

Intuitively, the international externality is the source of both the mutual interdependence across countries and the inefficiency associated with their unilateral policy choices, and it also defines the domain of external affairs in the Nash equilibrium. Hence, international agreements that are targeted directly to addressing the international externality can solve the policy inefficiencies associated with the externality while avoiding intrusion on the internal affairs of either country. In this sense, Proposition 3 highlights an important distinction between international agreements that mitigate international externalities and international agreements that erode national sovereignty, and points out that it can be possible to have the former without the latter.

We next characterize the violation of national sovereignty that occurs in the benchmark model when international agreements involve direct commitments over elements of $i(g,x)$ and $i^*(g^*,x)$. In particular, we will show that the indirect encroachment on sovereignty associated with such commitments can be more extensive than the direct violations themselves.

When international agreements involve direct commitments over elements of $i(g,x)$ and/or $i^*(g^*,x)$, a country's sovereignty may be violated in two ways according to our definition. First, sovereignty is violated whenever a government makes such commitments in an international agreement, since the elements of $i(g,x)$ and $i^*(g^*,x)$ are matters that concern its internal affairs. In what follows, we say that the home (foreign) country's sovereignty over a policy instrument in $i(g,x)$ ($i^*(g^*,x)$) is *violated directly* by an international agreement whenever limits on this policy instrument are determined directly as a result of international negotiations. But a more subtle violation of sovereignty may also occur, if direct international commitments over elements of $i(g,x)$ and/or $i^*(g^*,x)$ result in unilateral choices over the remaining (non-negotiated) policy instruments that do not conform to the corresponding elements of $\hat{i}(g,x)$ and/or $\hat{i}^*(g^*,x)$, and therefore do not reflect the normal operation of a country's domestic institutions in the domain of its internal affairs. We will say that the home (foreign) country's sovereignty over a policy instrument is *violated indirectly* by an international agreement whenever the country's sovereignty over this instrument is not violated directly by the international agreement but the government's unilateral choice for this policy instrument differs from the corresponding element of $\hat{i}(g,x)$ ($\hat{i}^*(g^*,x)$) evaluated at the level of (g,x) ((g^*,x)) delivered under the agreement. Finally, we say that a country's sovereignty over a policy instrument is *violated* (*preserved*) whenever its sovereignty is violated directly or indirectly (neither directly nor indirectly).

As we next establish, direct violations of sovereignty typically imply further indirect violations as well, a feature that generally prevents governments from containing violations of sovereignty caused by international agreements to narrow subsets of policy instruments. In fact, as we now establish, this "contamination effect" implies that when an international agreement involves direct commitments over even a single element of $i(g,x)$ or $i^*(g^*,x)$, the number of policy instruments for which the agreement violates the associated country's sovereignty must be at least as great as the number of policy instruments for which the country's sovereignty is preserved under the agreement.

To establish this, we first introduce a notion of "interrelatedness" between policies. Taking the perspective of the domestic government, and recalling that L denotes the Step-1 Lagrangean for Program $1'$, we say that two policies u and v are *interrelated* if $L_{uv} \neq 0$ when L is evaluated at the maximized Step-1 choices $\hat{\imath}(g,x)$. In words, when u and v are interrelated, a change in v alters the level of u preferred by the domestic government for delivering a given level of contribution g to the (given level of the) externality variable x. An exactly analogous interpretation applies for the foreign government.

We may now state:

Proposition 4. An international agreement that specifies levels for a subset of the elements of $i(g,x)$ and $i^*(g^*,x)$ must (generically), for each country, violate that country's sovereignty over at least as many policy instruments as it preserves, provided that: (i) the agreement specifies at least one policy instrument for each government at a level different from its best-response level; and (ii) all policies are interrelated.

Proof: Consider an international agreement that specifies the levels for a subset of the elements of $i(g,x)$ and $i^*(g^*,x)$. We adopt the perspective of the domestic government. Let the elements of $i(g,x)$ that are not determined directly by the international agreement be contained in the set $\mathcal{H}$. If $\mathcal{H}$ is empty, then it is immediate that the statement of the proposition is satisfied, since in this case the sovereignty over all home-country instruments is violated (directly). If instead $\mathcal{H}$ is non-empty, then the proposition is proved if it can be established that, to preserve the sovereignty of m home-country policy instruments, at least m home-country policy instruments must be directly negotiated (and therefore the home country's sovereignty over these instruments is violated directly). Let $\mathbf{h}$ be the vector of non-negotiated home-country policies, and let $\bar{\mathbf{n}}$ be the vector of negotiated home-country policies whose levels are specified by the international agreement. Given any foreign policies $\mathbf{i}^*$, the home government's unilateral best-response choice of $\mathbf{h}$ must solve the program:

Program 4: For a given $\mathbf{i}^*$, $\max_{\mathbf{h}} G(\mathbf{h},\bar{\mathbf{n}},\tilde{x}(\mathbf{h},\bar{\mathbf{n}},\mathbf{i}^*))$.

The first-order conditions for Program 4 are given by the analogue of (2.2) for the home government's instrument choices contained in $\mathcal{H}$. Now consider the partition of this program into the alternative 2-step program:

Program $4'$: *Step* 1. For a given (g,x): $\max_{\mathbf{h}} G(\mathbf{h},\bar{\mathbf{n}},x)$

$$\text{s.t. } [g(\mathbf{h},\bar{\mathbf{n}},x) - g] = 0.$$

Step 2. For a given $\mathbf{i}^*$: $\max_{g,x} Q(\hat{\mathbf{h}}(g,x,\bar{\mathbf{n}}),\bar{\mathbf{n}},g,x)$

$$\text{s.t. } f(g,g^*(\mathbf{i}^*,x),x) = 0,$$

where $\hat{\mathbf{h}}(g,x,\bar{\mathbf{n}})$ is the solution from Step 1 and Q is the Step-1 Lagrangean. Arguments identical to those in the proof of Lemma 1 establish that Program $4'$

is a partition of Program 4. Hence, to complete the proof we need only observe that: (i) preserving the sovereignty of m home-country policy instruments requires that, with (g,x) set at the level delivered under the agreement, it must be possible to satisfy the Step-1 first-order conditions when evaluated at the corresponding m elements of $\hat{i}(g,x)$, with $\hat{i}(g,x)$ itself evaluated at the level of (g,x) delivered under the agreement; and (ii) with all policies interrelated, this in turn requires (generically) that there exist at least m policy instruments that are directly negotiated and can be used to "target" m of these Step-1 first-order conditions.[11] The only exception to this requirement occurs if the agreement fails to specify at least one policy instrument for each government at a level different from its best-response level, an exception that is ruled out by the condition (i) of the proposition. An analogous argument applies to the foreign government. **QED**

Hence, according to Proposition 4, if governments negotiate international agreements that encroach on the domain of their internal affairs with direct commitments over policy instruments in $\mathbf{i}(g,x)$ and $\mathbf{i}^*(g^*,x)$, national sovereignty will be violated, and the indirect erosion of sovereignty induced by these direct commitments may be greater and more far-reaching than the loss of sovereignty caused by the direct commitments themselves.

Moreover, Proposition 4 implies that, if national sovereignty has been violated in an international agreement by a direct commitment, the loss of sovereignty is not necessarily monotonic in the "depth" of the agreement, when depth is measured by the number of policy instruments in the domain of each country's internal affairs that the agreement subjects to direct commitments. This is because, once the first commitment that falls within the domain of a country's internal affairs has been added to an international agreement and hence violates directly the country's sovereignty, the indirect violations of the country's sovereignty induced by this direct commitment can be wide-spread (possibly covering *all* of the country's policy instruments), and the introduction of further commitments in the agreement on policies that fall within the domain of the country's internal affairs can then *reduce* the overall (direct plus indirect) violations of national sovereignty if those commitments reduce the number of policy instruments over which the country's sovereignty is violated *indirectly* by the agreement. We record this in:

Corollary 1. If national sovereignty has been violated in an international agreement by a direct commitment, the loss of sovereignty is not necessarily increasing in the depth of the agreement.

5.   Sovereignty and international agreements in an extended model

In the previous section we established that, in principle, countries need not confront a choice between preserving their sovereignty and attaining international efficiency when they negotiate international agreements (Proposition 3). This is a striking result, derived within our benchmark model of Section 2, and important questions remain as to (i) whether the result is likely to extend to environments beyond those captured by our benchmark model, and (ii) the degree to which prominent channels of interdependence between countries can be identified that find representation in the environment described by our benchmark model. We devote this and the next section to providing answers to these two questions.

As we noted in Section 2, the structure in (2.1) rules out the possibility that $f_g g_{i_k} = 0$ for all k and/or that $f_{g^*} g^*_{i_m} = 0$ for all m, and thereby excludes cases where the externality variable x cannot be impacted by the policy instruments of some government. The question we consider in this section is how our results are impacted when the possibility ruled out by (2.1) arises. To this end, we now consider several extensions of the benchmark model that do not conform to the structure imposed by (2.1).

5.1.   Small countries

An important possibility that is excluded from our benchmark model is that a country might be "small" in relation to its contribution to the externality variable x: if the home country is small in this sense, it would imply that $g_{i_k} = 0$ for all k (and hence $f_g g_{i_k} = 0$ for all k), while if the foreign country is small this would imply $g^*_{i_m} = 0$ for all m (and hence $f_{g^*} g^*_{i_m} = 0$ for all m).

We now consider an extension of the benchmark model in which there are many home and many foreign countries, each of which individually is small in the sense described just above. Formally, we subdivide the territory of the home country into N home countries and now assume that the overall contribution of the home countries to the externality is given by

$$g(\mathbf{i}^1, ..., \mathbf{i}^N, x) \equiv \frac{1}{N} \sum_{j=1}^{N} g^j(\mathbf{i}^j, x).$$

Similarly, we subdivide the territory of the foreign country into N foreign countries and now assume that the overall contribution of the foreign countries to the externality is given by

$$g^*(\mathbf{i}^{*1}, ..., \mathbf{i}^{*N}, x) \equiv \frac{1}{N} \sum_{j=1}^{N} g^{*j}(\mathbf{i}^{*j}, x).$$

In this setting, with $\frac{\partial g^j}{\partial i^j_k}$ and $\frac{\partial g^{*j}}{\partial i^{*j}_k}$ assumed finite and bounded, we then have

$$\frac{\partial g}{\partial i^j_k} = \frac{1}{N} \frac{\partial g^j}{\partial i^j_k} \longrightarrow 0 \text{ as } N \longrightarrow \infty \text{ for all } k \text{ and for } j \in \{1, ..., N\}, \text{ and}$$

$$\frac{\partial g^*}{\partial i^{*j}_m} = \frac{1}{N} \frac{\partial g^{*j}}{\partial i^{*j}_m} \longrightarrow 0 \text{ as } N \longrightarrow \infty \text{ for all } m \text{ and for } j \in \{1, ..., N\},$$

and so for all $j \in \{1, ..., N\}$ and for $N \to \infty$ we have $f_g g^j_{i^j_k} = 0$ for all k and $f_{g^*} g^{*j}_{i^{*j}_m} = 0$ for all m. An immediate implication is then that, as N goes to infinity, no single government acting alone can alter x with its policy choices: that is,

$\tilde{x}_{i_k^j} = 0$ and $\tilde{x}_{i_k^{*j}} = 0$ for all j and all k. For simplicity, we assume that each home country is identical, and that each foreign country is identical, so that we may refer to "representative" home and foreign governments, but this is not essential for our results. All other features of the benchmark model remain the same.

It is direct to confirm two important implications of this extension of the benchmark model. First, suppressing the j superscript, the Nash policy choices of a representative home and foreign government solve $G_{i_k} = 0$ for $k = 1, ..., I$ and $G^*_{i_k^*} = 0$ for $k = 1, ..., I^*$. And second, letting ι denote the vector of policies of all home governments $[\mathbf{i}^1\,\mathbf{i}^2...\mathbf{i}^N]$ and ι^* denote the vector of policies of all foreign governments $[\mathbf{i}^{*1}\,\mathbf{i}^{*2}...\mathbf{i}^{*N}]$, and with $\mathbf{i}^j$ the vector of policies of the jth home government and with ι^{-j} the vector of policies of all home governments other than j, $[\mathbf{i}^1...\mathbf{i}^{j-1}\,\mathbf{i}^{j+1}...\mathbf{i}^N]$, and finally with $g^{-j}(\iota^{-j},x) \equiv g(\iota,x) - g^j(\mathbf{i}^j,x)$, the minimal partition of the representative home government's best-response policy choice problem is:

Program S: *Step* 1. For a given x: $\max\limits_{\mathbf{i}^j} G(\mathbf{i}^j, x)$

$\qquad$ *Step* 2. For a given ι^{-j} and ι^*: $\max\limits_{x} Z(\hat{\imath}^j(x), x)$

$\qquad\qquad$ s.t. $f\left(g^j(\mathbf{i}^j, x) + g^{-j}(\iota^{-j}, x), g^*(\iota^*, x), x\right) = 0,$

where $\hat{\imath}^j(x)$ is the solution from Step 1 and Z is the Step-1 Lagrangean. The Step-2 determination of x is a trivial choice problem in Program S, because x is fully determined by the constraint once ι^{-j} and ι^* are given owing to the small size of country j. An analogous Program S* defines the minimal partition of the representative foreign government's best-response policy choice problem.

According to Programs S and S*, each country's contribution to the externality variable x is a matter of its internal affairs when this contribution is vanishingly small. To see why, consider home government j. As compared to the minimal partition $\mathcal{P}_0$ described by Program 1′ in the benchmark (large-country case) model, the key difference in the case of small countries is that g and hence f is unaffected by the choice of g^j, and so the home-government j's choice of g^j can be moved from Step 2 to Step 1 without affecting the validity of the partition. This results in a minimal partition for the small-country case – described by Program S – that treats the choice of g^j as the internal affairs of home country j. An analogous interpretation applies for foreign country j. In essence the externality variable x is completely out of government j's control owing to the vanishingly small impact of its contribution g^j, and government j has sole authority over everything else that matters for its objective function. As a consequence, when all countries are small, any international agreement that moves governments from their Nash policy choices must violate their sovereignty.

Together, these two implications lead to the following:

Proposition 5. When all countries are small in relation to their contribution to the externality variable x, attaining international efficiency is consistent with maintaining national sovereignty if and only if (i) governments are not mutually interdependent, or (ii) governments are mutually interdependent and $sign[G_x] \neq sign[G_x^*]$ when evaluated at the Nash policy choices. Under either condition (i) or condition (ii), the harmony between international efficiency and national sovereignty is preserved when small countries avoid making international commitments.

Proof: As implied by Programs S and S*, when all countries are small in relation their contribution to the externality variable x, sovereignty demands that each government be left to select its Nash policy choices. Hence, attaining international efficiency is consistent with maintaining sovereignty in the small-country case if and only if the associated Nash policy choices are efficient. If governments are not mutually interdependent, then arguments analogous to the proof of Proposition 1 establish that the Nash policy choices are efficient in the small-country case. Suppose, then, that governments are mutually interdependent. Evaluating the conditions for efficiency at the Nash policy choices of a representative home- and foreign- government, defined by $G_{i_k} = 0$ for $k = 1, ..., I$ and $G_{i_k^*}^* = 0$ for $k = 1, ..., I^*$, it is direct to confirm that (2.4)–(2.6) and the bottom line of (2.7) are satisfied, while the top line of (2.7) is satisfied if and only if $sign[G_x] \neq sign[G_x^*]$. **QED**

The interesting feature of Proposition 5 relates to the condition in part (ii). According to this condition, whether the apparent harmony between national sovereignty and international efficiency identified in Proposition 3 survives in a world of small countries hinges on whether governments agree or disagree in the Nash equilibrium over the direction that they would like the externality variable x to move. If all governments agree, then the Nash equilibrium in the small-country case is inefficient and an international agreement will be required to reach the efficiency frontier, implying necessarily that national sovereignty and international efficiency will stand in conflict in this case. However, if there is disagreement, then the Nash equilibrium in the small-country case is efficient, and in this case the harmony between national sovereignty and international efficiency identified in Proposition 3 survives in a world of small countries, though in this case as with condition (i) small countries must avoid international commitments to preserve this harmony. Of course, which of these two cases is applicable will depend on the nature of the externality variable x under consideration, but as we demonstrate in the next section, the latter case has special significance in the context of international trade agreements.[12]

5.2. *Authority over an externality variable*

At the opposite extreme of the small-country case considered above is the possibility that one country's policy choices completely determine the externality variable, so that either $f_g = 0$ or $f_{g^*} = 0$, a possibility that is ruled out in our benchmark model by (2.1). This possibility might arise, for example, if the foreign government determines the degree of religious freedom within its borders and the home-country government welfare is negatively impacted by religious persecution wherever it occurs.[13]

To capture this possibility, let us suppose that the objectives of the home and foreign governments are now represented by the respective functions $G(\mathbf{i}, \tilde{x}(\mathbf{i}, \mathbf{i}^*), \tilde{y}(\mathbf{i}^*))$ and $G^*(\mathbf{i}^*, \tilde{x}(\mathbf{i}, \mathbf{i}^*), \tilde{y}(\mathbf{i}^*))$, with the equilibrium level of the externality variable $\tilde{x}(\mathbf{i}, \mathbf{i}^*)$ determined as before according to (2.1) whereas the equilibrium level of the externality variable $\tilde{y}(\mathbf{i}^*)$ is completely determined by $\mathbf{i}^*$, the policy vector of the foreign government. And let us suppose further that the home and foreign countries are mutually interdependent with respect to both x and y, so that $G_x \neq 0$ and $G_x^* \neq 0$ and also $G_y \neq 0$ and $G_y^* \neq 0$ at the Nash policy choices. It is easy to show that the Nash policy choices of the two governments are internationally inefficient, and in this case *each* of the externality variables is a source of inefficiency in the Nash equilibrium.

The minimal partition of the home government's best-response choice problem is now

> **Program A :** *Step* 1. For a given (g, x, y): $\max_{\mathbf{i}} G(\mathbf{i}, x, y)$
>
> s.t. $[g(\mathbf{i}, x) - g] = 0.$
>
> *Step* 2. For a given $\mathbf{i}^*$: $\max_{g, x} L(\hat{i}(g, x, y), g, x, \tilde{y}(\mathbf{i}^*))$
>
> s.t. $f(g, g^*(\mathbf{i}^*, x), x) = 0,$

where $\hat{i}(g, x, y)$ is the solution from Step 1 and L is the Step-1 Lagrangean. Program A implies that g, x and y comprise the home country's external affairs and hence could be subjected to constraints in an international agreement without violating the home country's sovereignty.

By contrast, the minimal partition of the foreign government's best-response choice problem is given by the following program:

> **Program A*:** *Step* 1. For a given (g^*, x): $\max_{\mathbf{i}^*} G^*(\mathbf{i}^*, x, \tilde{y}(\mathbf{i}^*))$
>
> s.t. $[g^*(\mathbf{i}^*, x) - g^*] = 0.$
>
> *Step* 2. For a given $\mathbf{i}$: $\max_{g^*, x} L^*(\hat{i}^*(g^*, x), g, x, \tilde{y}(\mathbf{i}^*))$
>
> s.t. $f(g(\mathbf{i}, x), g^*, x) = 0,$

where $\hat{i}^*(g^*, x)$ is the solution from Step 1 and L^* is the Step-1 Lagrangean. Program A* implies that g^* and x – but not y – comprise the foreign country's external affairs. From this we may conclude that any commitment made by the foreign country in an international agreement beyond commitments to levels of g^* and/or x would violate its sovereignty. In particular, if national sovereignty is to be preserved, then the foreign government can make no commitments over $\mathbf{i}^*$ and hence $\tilde{y}(\mathbf{i}^*)$, indicating that this source of international inefficiency in the Nash equilibrium must then go unaddressed. This points to an unavoidable tension between national sovereignty and international efficiency in this case.

We summarize with:

Proposition 6. The harmony between national sovereignty and international efficiency breaks down whenever one country's policies completely determine the level of an international externality variable.

5.3.   *A pure externality*

A final case that we consider where the harmony between national sovereignty and international efficiency indicated by Proposition 3 can break down is when there exists an international externality variable that represents a "pure externality," in the sense that the country generating the externality with its policy choices is not impacted by the externality variable. In our benchmark model with one externality variable, we allowed for this possibility (e.g., $G_x \neq 0 = G_x^*$) and showed that it implied an efficient Nash equilibrium under the conditions of our benchmark model (Proposition 1; see also note 2). But with multiple externalities, the required conditions for inefficiency of the Nash equilibrium are weakened, and the harmony between national sovereignty and international efficiency can be disrupted in the presence of pure externalities as a result. Here we consider a simple extension of our benchmark model to illustrate the point.

In particular, we introduce a second externality variable, y, whose determination can be characterized in an analogous fashion to the determination of x, but we assume that y is a concern only to the foreign government. And we now assume that the externality variable x is a concern only to the home government. That is, in this extension of the benchmark model, the objectives of the home and foreign governments are represented by the respective functions $G(\mathbf{i}, \tilde{x}(\mathbf{i}, \mathbf{i}^*))$ and $G^*(\mathbf{i}^*, \tilde{y}(\mathbf{i}, \mathbf{i}^*))$, with the two externality variables $\tilde{x}(\mathbf{i}, \mathbf{i}^*)$ and $\tilde{y}(\mathbf{i}, \mathbf{i}^*)$ defining the nature of the interdependence between the two countries. The new externality variable $\tilde{y}(\mathbf{i}, \mathbf{i}^*)$ is a pure externality imposed by the home government's policy choices on the foreign country, and it could, for example, represent the level of water pollution which flows in one direction from the "upstream" home country (who is therefore not affected by the polluted water) to the "downstream" foreign country (who is affected by the polluted water). And similarly, we are assuming that the externality variables $\tilde{x}(\mathbf{i}, \mathbf{i}^*)$ is now also a pure externality imposed by the foreign government's policy choices on the home country, and it could for example represent the level of air pollution which flows in one direction from the "upwind" foreign country (who is therefore not affected by the polluted air) to the "downwind" home country (who is affected by the polluted air). In analogy with the benchmark model and (2.1), the externality variables $\tilde{x}(\mathbf{i}, \mathbf{i}^*)$ and $\tilde{y}(\mathbf{i}, \mathbf{i}^*)$ are defined implicitly according to

$$f(g(\mathbf{i}, x), g^*(\mathbf{i}^*, x), x) = 0, \text{ and}$$

$$c(q(\mathbf{i}, y), q^*(\mathbf{i}^*, y), y) = 0,$$

where in analogy with the benchmark model we impose $f_g g_{i_k} \neq 0$ and now also $c_q q_{i_k} \neq 0$ for some k and $f_{g^*} g_{i_m^*}^* \neq 0$ and now also $c_{q^*} q_{i_m}^* \neq 0$ for some m. We also impose $G_x \neq 0$ and $G_y^* \neq 0$, but note that the home and foreign countries are not mutually interdependent with regard to either x or y (because $G_y = 0 = G_x^*$).

By construction, in this extension of the benchmark model the home government's best-response policy choice problem can be represented by Program 1' as in the benchmark model, and so it is direct to confirm that the home country's external affairs continue to be its choices over g and x, and do not include its choices over q and y. In an analogous fashion, it is direct to confirm that the foreign government's external affairs in this extended benchmark model are its choices over q^* and y, and do not include its choices over g^* and x.

In this setting, it is easy to see that a requirement for international efficiency is that the home government's policy instruments must be set so that the home government is indifferent to small changes in its policies that leave the externality variable y unaltered (since the foreign government would be indifferent to such changes). Formally, and letting $k = 1$ denote a domestic policy instrument for which $g_{i_k} \neq 0$ and $q_{i_k} \neq 0$, this condition may be written as:

$$\left[\frac{G_x f_g}{[f_g g_x + f_g^* g_x^* + f_x]} \right] \times [g_{i_1} g_{i_k}] \times \left[\frac{g_{i_k}}{g_{i_1}} - \frac{q_{i_k}}{q_{i_1}} \right] = q_{i_k} \times \left[G_{i_k} - \frac{g_{i_k} G_{i_1}}{g_{i_1}} \right] \quad (5.1)$$

$$\text{for } k = 2, 3, ...I.$$

But as we have just observed, the external affairs of the home government are limited to its choices over g and x. Consequently, the international commitments that the home government can take on without violating its sovereignty are limited to commitments over g and x, and result in unilateral choices over its instruments **i** in light of any such commitments that solve Step 1 of Program 1' for a given (g,x):

$$\max_{\mathbf{i}} \ G(\mathbf{i}, x)$$

$$\text{s.t. } [g(\mathbf{i}, x) - g] = 0.$$

The first order conditions associated with this problem are:

$$\left[G_{i_k} - \frac{g_{i_k} G_{i_1}}{g_{i_1}} \right] = 0 \text{ for } k = 2, 3, ...I. \quad (5.2)$$

Consider now the home government's Nash policy choices. These choices solve Step 1 of Program 1' for the Nash levels of (g,x), and they must therefore satisfy (5.2). But these choices then violate (5.1), and must therefore be inefficient from an international perspective, unless

$$g_{i_k} \times \left[\frac{g_{i_k}}{g_{i_1}} - \frac{q_{i_k}}{q_{i_1}} \right] = 0 \text{ for } k = 2, 3, \ldots I, \tag{5.3}$$

which is to say unless all adjustments of the home-government policies that leave $\tilde{x}$ unchanged also leave $\tilde{y}$ unchanged. Intuitively, the home government will only be indifferent in the Nash equilibrium over small changes in its policies that leave $\tilde{y}$ unchanged if these same policy changes leave $\tilde{x}$ unchanged, because the home government cares about changes in $\tilde{x}$, but does not care about changes in $\tilde{y}$. But in fact, since (5.2) must hold for the domestic choices of **i** given any level of (g,x), it follows that any international agreement that commits the home government to a level of (g,x) must fail to attain the international efficiency frontier unless (5.3) holds. With the sovereignty of the home government violated by any international agreement that goes further than commitments over g and x, and with (5.3) violated except by chance, a conflict between national sovereignty and international efficiency is effectively unavoidable.

We summarize with:

Proposition 7. The harmony between national sovereignty and international efficiency can break down in the presence of international externalities that take the form of pure externalities.

6. Sovereignty, international trade agreements and the GATT/WTO

We now return to our benchmark model and ask: Can prominent channels of interdependence between countries be identified that find representation in the environment described by our benchmark model? To some extent we have already answered this question in the affirmative, by offering in Section 2 a number of specific illustrations of interdependencies that can be captured within the structure implied by (2.1). In this section we develop in detail the implications of our results in the particular context of international trade as a source of interdependence between countries. We begin in the next subsection by briefly reviewing the two-country two-good competitive general equilibrium trade model adapted to allow for the possibility of both tariff and domestic regulatory policy choices as developed in Bagwell and Staiger (2001). We establish that this model is a special case of the benchmark model developed in Section 2, and so all the results of Sections 2–4 apply. We then show that when these results are interpreted within the context of our trade model, they indicate that the fundamental principles underlying GATT/WTO market access agreements offer a way to achieve internationally efficient policies without sacrificing national sovereignty, and that attaining international efficiency is consistent with maintaining national sovereignty in this setting regardless of whether (all) countries are big or small. We also extend our analysis of trade agreements to a multilateral setting, establish that agreement to abide by a non-discrimination principle such as the GATT/WTO MFN rule does not violate a government's sovereignty, and identify a critical role for MFN if governments are to achieve internationally efficient policies without sacrificing national sovereignty when some (but not all) countries are small.[14]

6.1. *Sovereignty in the basic two-country trade model*

We first describe the essential features of the two-country trade model of Bagwell and Staiger (2001). The home country exports good y to the foreign country in exchange for imports of good x. The local price of good x relative to good y in the home (foreign) country is denoted by p (p^*). The "world price" (i.e., relative exporter price or terms of trade) is denoted by p^w, and international arbitrage links each country's local price to the world price in light of its (non-prohibitive) tariff according to $p = \tau p^w \equiv p(\tau, p^w)$ and $p^* = p^w/\tau^* \equiv p^*(\tau^*, p^w)$, where τ (τ^*) is one plus the ad valorem import tariff of the home (foreign) country. In addition to its tariff, each country also imposes a vector of local regulations, $\mathbf{r}$ (with length R) for the home country and $\mathbf{r}^*$ (with length R^*) for the foreign country, that may impact local production and/or consumption decisions at given prices. Each country's vector of local regulations therefore acts as a vector of "shift" parameters in its import demand and export supply functions, and we assume that these functions are differentiable in their respective regulation levels.

Incorporating each country's vector of regulations into its import demand and export supply functions, we denote these functions for the home country by $M(\mathbf{r}, p, p^w)$ and $E(\mathbf{r}, p, p^w)$ and for the foreign country by $M^*(\mathbf{r}^*, p^*, p^w)$ and $E^*(\mathbf{r}^*, p^*, p^w)$, respectively. The home and foreign budget constraints, which must hold for any p^w, may then be written as

$$p^w M(\mathbf{r}, p, p^w) = E(\mathbf{r}, p, p^w) \tag{6.1}$$

$$M^*(\mathbf{r}^*, p^*, p^w) = p^w E^*(\mathbf{r}^*, p^*, p^w). \tag{6.2}$$

The equilibrium world price, $\tilde{p}^w(\mathbf{r}, \tau, \mathbf{r}^*, \tau^*)$, is determined by the x-market-clearing requirement

$$M(\mathbf{r}, p(\tau, p^w), p^w) = E^*(\mathbf{r}^*, p^*(\tau^*, p^w), p^w), \tag{6.3}$$

where we have made explicit the dependence of the local prices on the tariffs and the world prices, and market clearing for good y is then implied by (6.1), (6.2) and (6.3).

Finally, we represent the objectives of the home and foreign governments with the general functions $W(\mathbf{r}, p, \tilde{p}^w)$ and $W^*(\mathbf{r}^*, p^*, \tilde{p}^w)$, respectively. These objective functions reflect an important assumption: governments care about the regulatory (and tariff) choices of their trading partners only because of the trade impacts of these choices (and therefore only because of the impacts of these choices on the equilibrium world price $\tilde{p}^w$). We assume that, holding its regulations and its local price fixed at levels that do not imply autarky, each government would prefer an improvement in its terms of trade,

$$
\begin{aligned}
W_{\tilde{p}^w}(\mathbf{r},p,\tilde{p}^w) &< 0 \text{ for } M(\mathbf{r},p,p^w) > 0, \text{ and} \\
W^*_{\tilde{p}^w}(\mathbf{r}^*,p^*,\tilde{p}^w) &> 0 \text{ for } M^*(\mathbf{r}^*,p^*,p^w) > 0.
\end{aligned}
\tag{6.4}
$$

According to (6.4), governments like transfers of revenue from their trading partners. In the case of autarky, a change in the terms of trade holding its regulations and local price fixed should be irrelevant to a government, since there is no trade volume and continues to be no trade volume after the change, and so we assume as well that

$$
\begin{aligned}
W_{\tilde{p}^w}(\mathbf{r},p,\tilde{p}^w) &= 0 \text{ for } M(\mathbf{r},p,p^w) = 0, \text{ and} \\
W^*_{\tilde{p}^w}(\mathbf{r}^*,p^*,\tilde{p}^w) &= 0 \text{ for } M^*(\mathbf{r}^*,p^*,p^w) = 0.
\end{aligned}
\tag{6.5}
$$

We leave government objectives otherwise unrestricted, and observe that these objectives are consistent with a wide variety of models of government behavior (see Bagwell and Staiger, 1999, 2002).

To establish that the trading environment we have just described is a special case of the benchmark model described in Section 2, we define $\mathbf{i} \equiv [\mathbf{r} \ \tau]$ and $\mathbf{i}^* \equiv [\mathbf{r}^* \ \tau^*]$, and then define

$$
\begin{aligned}
G(\mathbf{i},\tilde{p}^w) &\equiv W(\mathbf{r},p(\tau,\tilde{p}^w),\tilde{p}^w) \\
G^*(\mathbf{i}^*,\tilde{p}^w) &\equiv W^*(\mathbf{r}^*,p^*(\tau^*,\tilde{p}^w),\tilde{p}^w)
\end{aligned}
$$

and define

$$
\begin{aligned}
m(\mathbf{i},p^w) &\equiv M(\mathbf{r},p(\tau,p^w),p^w) \\
m^*(\mathbf{i}^*,p^w) &\equiv M^*(\mathbf{r}^*,p^*(\tau^*,p^w),p^w).
\end{aligned}
$$

We then substitute (6.2) into (6.3) to rewrite the x-market-clearing requirement as

$$
p^w m(\mathbf{i},p^w) - m^*(\mathbf{i}^*,p^w) = 0.
\tag{6.6}
$$

It is now direct to confirm that (6.6) is a special case of (2.1) in which $x \equiv p^w$, $g(\mathbf{i},x) \equiv m(\mathbf{i},p^w)$, $g^*(\mathbf{i}^*,x) \equiv m^*(\mathbf{i}^*,p^w)$, and where

$$
f(g(\mathbf{i},x),g^*(\mathbf{i}^*,x),x) \equiv [xg(\mathbf{i},x) - g^*(\mathbf{i}^*,x)],
$$

with $p^w > 0$ and with the natural restrictions on the import demand functions $m(\mathbf{i},p^w)$ and $m^*(\mathbf{i}^*,p^w)$ that $m_{i_k} \neq 0$ for some k and $m^*_{i^*_h} \neq 0$ for some h then ensuring that $f_g g_{i_k} \neq 0$ for some k and $f_{g^*} g^*_{i_h} \neq 0$ for some h, as required for the benchmark model under (2.1). In words, our two-country trade model is a special case of our benchmark model in which the international externality variable is the terms of trade, in which each country's contribution to the determination of the externality is the quantity of imports it demands at a given terms of trade, and in which these contributions are aggregated according to a market-clearing condition to determine the equilibrium level of the externality.

The minimal partition of the home government's best-response policy choice problem in the international trade setting, corresponding to Program 1′ in the benchmark model, is then:

Program 1′ (Trade): *Step* 1. For a given (m, p^w): $\max_{\mathbf{i}} G(\mathbf{i}, p^w)$

$$\text{s.t. } [m(\mathbf{i}, p^w) - m] = 0.$$

Step 2. For a given $\mathbf{i}^*$: $\max_{m, p^w} L(\hat{i}(m, p^w), m, p^w)$

$$\text{s.t. } [p^w m - m^*(\mathbf{i}^*, p^w)] = 0,$$

where $\hat{i}(m, p^w)$ is the solution from Step 1 and L is the Step-1 Lagrangean. The analogous minimal partition for the foreign government's best-response policy choice problem in the international trade setting is:

Program 1*′ (Trade): *Step* 1. For a given (m^*, p^w): $\max_{i^*} G^*(\mathbf{i}^*, p^w)$

$$\text{s.t. } [m^*(\mathbf{i}^*, p^w) - m^*] = 0.$$

Step 2. For a given $\mathbf{i}$: $\max_{m^*, p^w} L^*(\hat{i}^*(m^*, p^w), m^*, p^w)$

$$\text{s.t. } [p^w m(\mathbf{i}, p^w) - m^*] = 0,$$

where $\hat{i}^*(m^*, p^w)$ is the solution from Step 1 and L^* is the Step-1 Lagrangean.

Provided governments are mutually interdependent, which according to (6.4) and (6.5) will be the case in this setting if and only if they trade positive amounts in the Nash equilibrium, we may then conclude from Propositions 1–4 that, when the nature of interdependence across countries takes the form of international trade: (i) if governments negotiate commitments over policy instruments in $\mathbf{i}$ and $\mathbf{i}^*$, their sovereignty will be violated, and the extent of the violation will in general not be limited only to those policy instruments that are directly negotiated; and (ii) governments may negotiate commitments over m, p^w and m^* which then hold the home (foreign) government to policy choices satisfying $[m(\mathbf{i}, p^w) - m] = 0$ ($[m^*(\mathbf{i}^*, p^w) - m^*] = 0$) and attain a position on the international efficiency frontier without violating their sovereignty.

Consider now what these findings suggest regarding the implication for national sovereignty of commitments negotiated in the GATT/WTO. In Bagwell and Staiger (2001), we observed that, when a government agrees to "bind" a tariff in a GATT/WTO negotiation, this government is not making a commitment that (i) holds it rigidly to its bound tariff level in the future and (ii) implies no obligations regarding future choices over its remaining policy instruments. Rather, the government is making a *market access commitment*, which is interpreted in the GATT/WTO as a commitment by the home (foreign) government to establish and maintain certain "conditions of competition for exporters into the domestic market." Two important observations follow. First, a government can in principle fulfill a market access commitment with any combination of policy instruments that implies the agreed-upon conditions of competition for exporters into the domestic market.[15] And second, a commitment to certain conditions of competition for exporters into the domestic market implies in turn a commitment to an import level m (m^*) in the home (foreign) market when exporters price at p^w, and hence subjects the home (foreign) government to an implied constraint of the form $[m(\mathbf{i}, p^w) - m] = 0$ $([m^*(\mathbf{i}^*, p^w) - m^*] = 0)$ when making its policy choices. From these two observations, we may conclude that the fundamental commitments negotiated in the GATT/WTO are best interpreted as commitments over m, p^w and m^* rather than as commitments over policy instruments in $\mathbf{i}$ and $\mathbf{i}^*$ (see Bagwell and Staiger, 2002, for further elaboration on the interpretation of GATT/WTO market access commitments along these lines).[16]

Under this interpretation, then, Propositions 1–4 lend some formal support to the fundamental approach that rests at the heart of the GATT/WTO, in the sense that the negotiation of market access commitments can in principle allow governments to attain the international efficiency frontier without sacrificing national sovereignty.[17] We summarize this finding in:

Proposition 8. A market access agreement between the home and the foreign government can achieve the international efficiency frontier without violating the sovereignty of either country.

Proposition 8 is related to Propositions 3 and 4 of Bagwell and Staiger (2001), but recasts these results from the perspective of the formal definitions of national sovereignty that we develop here.

Finally, we observe that the harmony between national sovereignty and international efficiency survives in a world of (all) small countries when the nature of interdependence across countries takes the form of international trade. To see this, note that by our definitions we have $G_{\tilde{p}^w} = \tau W_p + W_{\tilde{p}^w}$ and $G^*_{\tilde{p}^w} = (1/\tau^*)W^*_{p^*} + W^*_{\tilde{p}^w}$. When the two-country trade model is extended to allow for many small home and foreign countries as in the analogous Section 5.1 extension of our benchmark model, it is direct to show that the Nash equilibrium policy choices satisfy $W_p = 0$ $(W^*_{p^*} = 0)$ for a representative home (foreign) government. Hence, when all countries are small we have $G_{\tilde{p}^w} = W_{\tilde{p}^w}$ and $G^*_{\tilde{p}^w} = W^*_{\tilde{p}^w}$ when evaluated at the Nash equilibrium. But using (6.4) and (6.5), Proposition 5 then implies that, when the nature of interdependence across countries takes the form of international trade, the harmony between national sovereignty and international efficiency survives in a world of (all) small countries: focusing on case (ii) of Proposition 5 where countries are mutually interdependent, the key point is that, in the international trade setting, governments generally disagree in the Nash equilibrium over the direction they would like the terms of trade (the externality variable) to move, as (6.4) indicates, and so in a world of small countries the Nash equilibrium is efficient and national sovereignty can be preserved at no cost with the avoidance of international commitments.

Together with Proposition 8, this last result is suggestive of a broad compatibility between maintaining national sovereignty and achieving international efficiency in trade matters. However, these findings fall short of establishing this claim in the multilateral setting in which real trade agreements (e.g., the GATT/WTO) operate, where some countries may be large, others small, and the non-discrimination (MFN) rule plays a prominent role. In the next section, we extend our two-country trade model to a three-country model in order to consider these issues.

6.2. MFN and sovereignty in a three-country trade model

We now consider a three-country trade model analogous to Bagwell and Staiger (1999), extended to include standards. The home country exports good y to foreign countries 1 and 2 and imports good x from each of them. For simplicity, we do not allow trade between the two foreign countries, and so only the home country has the opportunity to set discriminatory tariffs across its trading partners. The local price of good x relative to good y in the home country (foreign country j) is denoted by p (p^{*j}, $j = 1, 2$). The "world price" (i.e., relative exporter price) for trade between the home country and foreign country j is denoted by p^{wj}, and international arbitrage links each country's local price to the relevant world price in light of its (non-prohibitive) tariff according to $p = \tau^j p^{wj} \equiv p(\tau^j, p^{wj})$, and $p^{*j} = p^{wj}/\tau^{*j} \equiv p^{*j}(p^{wj}, \tau^{*j})$ for $j = 1, 2$, where τ^j (τ^{*j}) is one plus the ad valorem import tariff that the home country (foreign country j) applies to the imports from foreign country j (the home country). This implies in turn that world prices are *linked* across bilateral relationships:

$$p^{w1} = \left[\frac{\tau^2}{\tau^1}\right] \times p^{w2}. \tag{6.7}$$

We note in particular that an MFN rule requires $\tau^1 = \tau^2 \equiv \tau$ and therefore implies $p^{w1} = p^{w2} \equiv p^w$ by (6.7). As in the two-country trade model above, in addition to its tariff, each country also imposes a vector of local regulations, $\mathbf{r}$ (with length R) for the home country and $\mathbf{r}^{*j}$ (with length R^{*j}) for foreign country j, that may impact local production and/or consumption decisions at given prices. Each country's vector of local regulations will therefore act as a vector of "shift" parameters in its import demand and export supply functions, and as before we assume that these functions are differentiable in their respective regulation levels. For future reference, we denote the home government's vector of policy instruments by $\mathbf{i} \equiv [\mathbf{r} \ \tau^1 \ \tau^2]$, and we denote the vector of policy instruments for foreign government j by $\mathbf{i}^{*j} \equiv [\mathbf{r}^{*j} \ \tau^{*j}]$.

Incorporating each country's vector of regulations into its import demand and export supply functions, we denote functions for the home country by $M(\mathbf{r},p,T)$ and $E(\mathbf{r},p,T)$ and for foreign country j by $M^{*j}(\mathbf{r}^{*j},p^{*j},p^{wj})$ and $E^{*j}(\mathbf{r}^{*j},p^{*j},p^{wj})$, respectively, where T is the home-country's multilateral terms of trade, and is defined by

$$T(\mathbf{r}^{*1},p^{*1},\mathbf{r}^{*2},p^{*2},p^{w1},p^{w2}) \equiv \sum_{k=1}^{2} s^{*k}(\mathbf{r}^{*1},p^{*1},\mathbf{r}^{*2},p^{*2},p^{w1},p^{w2}) \times p^{wk}$$

with

$$s^{*j}(\mathbf{r}^{*1},p^{*1},\mathbf{r}^{*2},p^{*2},p^{w1},p^{w2}) \equiv \frac{E^{*j}(\mathbf{r}^{*j},p^{*j},p^{wj})}{\sum_{k=1}^{2} E^{*k}(\mathbf{r}^{*k},p^{*k},p^{wk})} \quad \text{for } j = 1,2.$$

Observe that an MFN rule requiring $\tau^1 = \tau^2$ implies $p^{w1} = p^{w2} = T \equiv p^w$ by (6.7). In any event, with T defined, the home and foreign budget constraints may then be written as

$$T \times M(\mathbf{r},p,T) = E(\mathbf{r},p,T), \text{ and} \tag{6.8}$$

$$M^{*j}(\mathbf{r}^{*j},p^{*j},p^{wj}) = p^{wj}E^{*j}(\mathbf{r}^{*j},p^{*j},p^{wj}) \text{ for } j = 1,2. \tag{6.9}$$

The pair of equilibrium world prices, $\tilde{p}^{wj}(\mathbf{i},\mathbf{i}^{*1},\mathbf{i}^{*2})$ for $j = 1, 2$, are then determined by the linkage condition (6.7) together with the requirement of market clearing for good x,

$$M(\mathbf{r},p,T) = \sum_{k=1}^{2} E^{*k}(\mathbf{r}^{*k},p^{*k},p^{wk}), \tag{6.10}$$

with market clearing for good y then implied by (6.8) and (6.9).

Finally, in analogy with the two-country trade model, we represent the objectives of the home and foreign government $j = 1, 2$ with the general functions $W(\mathbf{r},p,T)$ and $W^{*j}(\mathbf{r}^{*j}, p^{*j}, \tilde{p}^{wj})$, respectively. As before, we assume that, holding its regulations and its local price fixed, and provided that its regulations and local price do not imply autarky, each government would prefer an improvement in its terms of trade:

$$W_T(\mathbf{r},p,T) < 0 \text{ for } M(\mathbf{r},p,T) > 0, \text{ and}$$

$$W_{\tilde{p}^{wj}}^{*j}(\mathbf{r}^{*j},p^{*j},\tilde{p}^{wj}) > 0 \text{ for } M^{*j}(\mathbf{r}^{*j},p^{*j},p^{wj}) > 0.$$

For simplicity in this section we consider only the case where Nash policy choices do not imply autarky. We leave government objectives otherwise unrestricted.

In the Nash equilibrium of the three-country trade model, the home government chooses its best-response policies by solving

Program 5: For a given $\mathbf{i}^{*1}$ and $\mathbf{i}^{*2}$, $\max\limits_{\mathbf{i}} W(\mathbf{r}, p(\tau^j; \tilde{p}^{wj}), T)$,

at the same time that foreign government j, for $j = 1, 2$, chooses its best response policies by solving

Program 5^{*j}: For a given $\mathbf{i}$ and $\mathbf{i}^{*-j}$, $\max\limits_{\mathbf{i}^{*j}} W^{*j}(\mathbf{r}^{*j}, p^{*j}(\tau^{*j}, \tilde{p}^{wj}), \tilde{p}^{wj})$.

We next show that the Nash policy choices defined by the simultaneous solutions to Program 5 and Program 5^{*j} may be written in an equivalent form in which each government's best-response program is partitioned into a two-step choice problem.

Because foreign countries 1 and 2 each trade with only one partner (the home country), they each face a single international externality variable ($\tilde{p}^{wj}$), and so the minimal partition of Program 5^{*j} into a two-step choice problem is completely analogous to Program $1^{*\prime}$, the minimal partition of the foreign country in the two-country trade model of the previous section. However, the international externality faced by the home country is more complicated, owing to the possibility that it trades with two trading partners at two different bilateral world prices.

Nevertheless, as we now demonstrate, an analogous 2-step partition can be developed for the home government's best-response problem. In particular, consider the following 2-step program for the home government:

Program $5'$: *Step* 1. For a given (M, T): $\max\limits_{r, p} W(\mathbf{r}, p, T)$

$$\text{s.t. } [M(\mathbf{r}, p, T) - M] = 0.$$

Step 2. For a given $\mathbf{i}^{*1}$ and $\mathbf{i}^{*2}$: $\max\limits_{M, p^{w1}, p^{w2}} Y(\hat{\mathbf{r}}(M, T(\cdot)), \hat{p}(M, T(\cdot)), M, T(\cdot))$

$$\text{s.t. } [M - \sum_{k=1}^{2} E^{*k}(\mathbf{r}^{*k}, p^{*k}(\tau^{*k}, p^{wk}), p^{wk})] = 0,$$

where $\hat{\mathbf{r}}(M, T(\cdot))$ and $\hat{p}(M, T(\cdot))$ are the solutions from Step 1 and Y is the Step-1 Lagrangean, and where $T(\cdot)$ denotes $T(\mathbf{r}^{*1}, p^{*1}(p^{w1}, \tau^{*1}), \mathbf{r}^{*2}, p^{*2}(p^{w1}, \tau^{*1}), p^{w1}, p^{w2})$. Observe that a value for T is determined for given $\mathbf{i}^{*1}$ and $\mathbf{i}^{*2}$ once p^{w1} and p^{w2} are determined, and so the Step-2 choice problem over M, p^{w1} and p^{w2} determines a value for M and T, which are each taken as given in the Step-1 choice problem. We first state:

Lemma 4. Program $5'$ is a minimal partition of the home-government's best-response choice problem defined by Program 5.

Proof: See appendix.

According to Lemma 4, we may conclude that the external affairs of the home country are its government's choices over M, p^{w1} and p^{w2} (and by implication M and T). In analogy with the two-country trade model, these choices can be interpreted as determining the level of market access that the home country affords to each of its trading partners (as defined by the volume of imports it would accept at a particular multilateral terms of trade). The matters that concern the home country's internal affairs are then its choice of G and its government's choices over $\mathbf{r}(M,T(\cdot))$ and $p(M,T(\cdot))$. However, observing that $p = \tau^1 p^{w1} = \tau^2 p^{w2}$, we may restate the home government's choice over $p(M,T(\cdot))$ equivalently as a choice over $\tau^1(M,T,p^{w1})$ and $\tau^2(M,T,p^{w2})$ where $\tau^1(M,T,p^{w1}) \equiv p(M,T)/p^{w1}$ and $\tau^2(M,T,p^{w2}) \equiv p(M,T)/p^{w2}$. Recalling now that the MFN rule requires $\tau^1 = \tau^2 \equiv \tau$ and hence $p^{w1} = p^{w2} = T \equiv p^w$ by (6.7), but that the MFN rule leaves the level of τ and therefore p unrestricted, it follows that the MFN rule places restrictions on the home country's external affairs (its Step-2 choices) but places no restrictions nor introduces any distortions in the home country's internal affairs (its Step-1 choices). We may therefore state:

Proposition 9. Abiding by the non-discrimination rule does not violate national sovereignty.

Proposition 9 reflects the following intuition. Discriminatory tariffs make possible certain market access choices that would be impossible under MFN. But market access (Step-2) choices are the external affairs of a country, and so restrictions can be placed on these choices through voluntary international agreement without violating national sovereignty. And given any market access choices that would be feasible under MFN, discriminatory tariffs do not create any additional possibilities for delivering these market access levels. This feature is reflected in the fact that the Step-1 choices of Program 5′ may be expressed as choices over domestic regulations $\mathbf{r}$ and the domestic price level p, and for these choices the MFN restriction has no bearing. Hence, a country's sovereignty is violated neither directly nor indirectly when it agrees to abide by the MFN rule.[18]

According to Proposition 9, an agreement to abide by the MFN rule in the three-country trade model does not violate the sovereignty of any country. But once the MFN rule is imposed, it is direct to show that the three-country trade model is a straightforward extension of the two-country trade model, and exhibits all the same properties. In particular, it then follows by Propositions 8 and 9 that a market access agreement between the home and foreign governments in the three-country trade model that also imposes an MFN requirement can achieve the international efficiency frontier without violating the sovereignty of any country. This falls short of the stronger claim that the MFN rule is *required* to make the attainment of internationally efficient outcomes compatible with the maintenance of national sovereignty. But as we next show, this stronger claim can be made when the three-country trade model is extended to allow that some (but not all) countries are small.

To see this, let us suppose that foreign country 2 in the three-country trade model is now decomposed into a region of small foreign countries as with our small-country extension in Section 5.1, so that no single government k in foreign region 2 can, acting alone, alter $\tilde{p}^{w2}$ with its policy choices. As we established in Section 5.1, small countries must avoid international commitments in order to maintain their sovereignty, and so any international agreement that moves the governments in foreign region 2 from their best-response policy choices must violate their sovereignty. It is easy to see from Program 5^{*j} that the best-response policy choices of a representative government in foreign region 2 (suppressing the individual country superscript k) solve

$$W_{p^{*2}}^{*2} = 0 \text{ and } W_{r_i^{*2}}^{*2} = 0 \text{ for } i = 1, 2, ... R^{*2.} \tag{6.11}$$

The question, then, is whether the home government and foreign government 1 can undertake commitments that (i) do not violate their sovereignty and (ii) attain a position on the international efficiency frontier when the governments in foreign region 2 choose policies that satisfy (6.11).

We first establish:

Proposition 10. An international agreement can attain a point on the international efficiency frontier and satisfy (6.11) if and only if it satisfies the MFN rule.

Proof: See appendix.

As we establish in the appendix, to achieve international efficiency and satisfy (6.11), the home government and foreign government 1 must adopt policies that abide by the MFN rule and satisfy

$$W_p = 0 = W_{p^{*1}}^{*1} , \ W_{r_i} = 0 \text{ and } W_{r_i^{*1}}^{*1} = 0 \text{ for } i = 1, 2, ... R^{*1.} \tag{6.12}$$

Referring to market access agreements that achieve the market access levels implied by (6.11), (6.12) and the MFN restriction as *non-discriminatory politically optimal market access agreements*, and utilizing Propositions 8–10, we may now state:

Proposition 11. If some (but not all) countries are "small," then achieving international efficiency and preserving national sovereignty are mutually consistent goals of an international agreement if and only if the agreement satisfies the MFN requirement. In particular, non-discriminatory politically optimal market access agreements provide the unique path to achieving international efficiency while preserving national sovereignty in this setting.

In effect, if small countries are asked to make market access commitments, their sovereignty will be violated. If this is to be avoided, then small countries must be left unconstrained to choose their best-response policies in any international agreement. This requirement, though, is consistent with international efficiency only when tariffs also conform to the MFN requirement, as indicated by

Proposition 10. As a consequence, in an international trade setting Proposition 11 suggests that a non-discrimination rule is "complementary" to preserving the national sovereignty of small countries in the following sense: the sovereignty of small countries can be preserved under an internationally efficient agreement only if that agreement abides by the MFN requirement. More broadly, and in light of our finding in Proposition 9 that the MFN requirement itself involves no compromise of national sovereignty, our three-country results suggest that a non-discrimination rule coupled with a market access agreement can facilitate the attainment of internationally efficient outcomes that do not compromise national sovereignty.

6.3.   *Sovereignty, GATT and the WTO*

When viewed together, the results from the previous two subsections have potentially important implications for the design of the WTO and its predecessor, the GATT. The GATT/WTO has from its inception been concerned most fundamentally with non-discriminatory market access commitments, and it has traditionally sought to anchor these commitments with negotiations over border measures (e.g., tariffs) that are "multilateralized" through the MFN requirement. But this tradition is being eroded on two fronts. First, the extent and importance of discriminatory trade agreements (permitted by GATT/WTO exceptions to its MFN requirement) has increased dramatically in recent decades. And second, increasingly the WTO is thought of as a potential forum for the negotiation of international commitments on a host of non-border policies that are deemed to have important market access consequences, ranging from labor standards to environmental regulations to domestic subsidies to competition policy. Our results highlight the fundamental implications of these developments for the potential conflicts between international efficiency and national sovereignty within the WTO. Specifically, when international externalities flow only through world prices, the further the WTO departs from facilitating agreements that take the form of non-discriminatory market access commitments, the more it is likely to pose a (direct and indirect – and in principle, unnecessary) threat to the sovereignty of its member countries.

7.   Conclusion

What are the sovereign rights of nations in an interdependent world, and to what extent do these rights stand in the way of achieving internationally efficient outcomes? In this chapter, we have proposed answers to these two questions. Our answers, of course, depend on the definition of national sovereignty. Sovereignty is a complex concept with many features, and any definition has advantages and disadvantages. Our approach is to formalize the Westphalian norm of "non-intervention in the internal affairs of other states" in a way that we believe captures several key features of Westphalian sovereignty emphasized in the international political economy literature, features that seem especially relevant in the context of voluntary international agreements. An important advantage of this approach is that it is analytically tractable. Using this formalization, we show how Nash choice problems can be partitioned in a way that allows a characterization of the degree and nature of sovereignty that governments possess in the Nash equilibrium. This characterization, in turn, provides a benchmark from which to formally assess the implications for national sovereignty of international agreements of various designs.

In the context of our benchmark model of international interdependence, we find that in principle there is no inherent conflict between the attainment of international efficiency through international agreements and preserving national sovereignty. As our benchmark model is general enough to cover channels of international interdependence that can take a variety of forms, we view this finding as pointing to important possibilities for eliminating conflicts between international efficiency and national sovereignty through appropriate design of international agreements. Our findings here highlight an important distinction between international agreements that mitigate international externalities and international agreements that erode national sovereignty, and point out that it can be possible to have the former without the latter.

In the particular case of international trade relations, which we argue is captured well by our benchmark model, we find that a number of the foundational aspects of the GATT/WTO, such as its emphasis on market access commitments and the MFN rule, offer a possible means of achieving international efficiency without eroding national sovereignty. In this regard, we give formal support to the observation of Rabkin (1998, pp. 85–86):

> Probably the single most effective and consequential international program of the postwar era has been the mutual reduction of trade barriers under the General Agreement on Tariffs and Trade, initiated in 1947. Reasonable questions may be raised about certain aspects of the World Trade Organization, established in 1995 to help administer GATT norms. But, fundamentally, the trading system is quite compatible with traditional notions of sovereignty. It was developed on the foundations of much older sorts of international agreement, which would have been quite recognizable to the Framers of the Constitution.

However, our results suggest that the maintenance of this compatibility depends crucially on being true to these fundamental principles: the further away the WTO moves from a market-access focus and adherence to MFN, the more likely will conflicts arise within the WTO between international efficiency and national sovereignty.

Importantly, we also find that the harmony in our benchmark model between international efficiency and national sovereignty is not always present in the universe of international relations among national governments. Rather, as the various extensions to our benchmark model illustrate, this harmony depends on the structure of the international externalities that define the nature of international interdependence and that give rise to the policy inefficiencies under non-cooperative policy setting. Together with our other findings, this last point reinforces the importance of understanding the nature of the international externalities that are the source of the problem for an international agreement to solve, so that those tensions between sovereignty and efficiency that are unnecessary can be avoided, while those tensions that are inescapable can be anticipated and minimized through careful institutional design.

Where tensions between national sovereignty and international efficiency are inescapable according to our formal analysis, it may be that further refinements to the notion of national sovereignty, perhaps tailored to the case at hand, could help to ease these tensions. A key message of our chapter, however, is that such refinements, to the extent they are possible, can be guided by our formal approach and instructive findings. In this way, our analysis provides a framework for further systematic exploration into notions of sovereignty and their implications for efficiency.

At the same time, in circumstances where a tension between national sovereignty and international efficiency is inescapable, our formal analysis leaves unanswered an important question: in such circumstances, is the preservation of national sovereignty worth the sacrifice of international efficiency? At a general level, there are two ways that this question might be approached.

First, if as we assume the general government objectives in our formal analysis capture all relevant considerations for the associated countries, then there is a clear case for governments to pursue international efficient agreements, even if national sovereignty as we define that term is violated. From this perspective, the contribution of our analysis is to identify settings in which international efficiency can be achieved without violating national sovereignty.

Second, if there are explicit costs associated with the erosion of national sovereignty that are not captured in our formal analysis, then a formal answer to this question would require introducing those costs into the model. For example, such costs might arise if the quality of information depreciates with the distance between the decision-maker and those most directly impacted by the decision. Alternatively, the erosion of national sovereignty might have direct utility costs, if governments and their constituents have a preference for maintaining sovereignty aside from any economic benefits they may enjoy. In either case, once these costs were introduced into the model, there would again be a clear case for governments to pursue internationally efficient agreements even if national sovereignty as we define that term is violated, though in the latter case efficiency would be defined relative to government objective functions that include national sovereignty as an argument and hence sovereignty would become an explicit goal to be weighed against the other goals that governments also value. Introducing such micro-foundations for concerns about violations of sovereignty is an important area for further research.

Notes

Acknowledgement: This is a revised and updated version of our working paper Bagwell and Staiger (2004). For many helpful comments on the previous version, we thank Robert Keohane, Stephen Krasner, Alberto Martin, Jon Pevehouse, Jeremy Rabkin, Donald Regan, Guido Tabellini and seminar participants at Berkeley, Notre Dame, the Stockholm School and the NOITS Workshop in Copenhagen, and we thank the National

Science Foundation (award number SES-0214021) for support. We are also grateful to Lili Yan Ing and Miaojie Yu for providing very helpful comments on this version.

1 As we discuss later (see notes 4 and 13), in his reconsideration of the concept of sovereignty Jackson (2003) takes the first approach, and proposes a notion of "sovereignty modern" that according to Jackson is capable of maintaining harmony between sovereignty and international efficiency in the context of modern sensibilities.

2 The required conditions for inefficiency of the Nash equilibrium in the benchmark model would be weakened if the ability to make explicit international transfers were introduced. This can be done without changing the nature of any of our results, but we prefer to keep explicit international transfer instruments out of our model for simplicity. We also consider several extensions of the benchmark model in a later section where the Nash inefficiencies take more complicated forms.

3 For a related discussion of the practical difficulties associated with the implementation of Mill's "harm principle," see, for example, Gray (1991).

4 In arguing for the need to update the traditional Westphalian concept of sovereignty, Jackson (2003) states:

> Much has been said and written about "globalization"; despite being an ambiguous term of controversial connotation, it is reasonably well understood to apply to the exogenous world circumstances of economic and other forces that have developed in recent decades owing, in major part, to the sharply reduced costs and time required for the transport of goods (and services), and similar reductions in costs and time requirements for communication. These circumstances have led to new structures of production; they, in turn, have resulted in greatly enhanced (and sometimes dangerous) interdependence, which we can do little to remedy and which often renders the older concepts of "sovereignty" or "independence" fictional. ... these circumstances often demand action that no single nation-state can satisfactorily carry out, and thus require some type of institutional "coordination" mechanism. In some of these circumstances, therefore, a powerful tension is generated between traditional core "sovereignty," on the one hand, and the international institution, on the other hand.
>
> (Jackson, 2003, p. 784, footnotes omitted)

Jackson's approach is to propose an updated concept of Westphalian sovereignty that he terms "sovereignty-modern," and which is meant to be more consistent with international efficiency and the need for international policy coordination in the modern world. Our approach provides a formal definition of sovereignty which achieves some of what Jackson has in mind, in that according to our definition the domain of sovereignty will evolve as the nature of international interdependence evolves; but we do not tailor our definition of sovereignty on a case-by-case basis to necessarily be in harmony with international efficiency, and instead evaluate formally the circumstances when a tradeoff between maintaining national sovereignty and achieving international efficiency can be avoided versus when this tradeoff will necessarily arise.

5 Notice that, as the home government's best-response policy choices are defined by the vector of domestic policies $\mathbf{i}$ that solve 2.2, the choice problems in any partition $\mathcal{P}$ of the home government's best-response policy choice problem cannot include (trivial or otherwise) choices over foreign policies in $\mathbf{i}^*$, and similarly the choice problems in any partition $\mathcal{P}$ of the foreign government's best-response policy choice problem cannot include (trivial or otherwise) choices over home policies in $\mathbf{i}$.

6 Note that according to our definition, it is possible that $\hat{s}$ is a subset of $\tilde{s}$ and yet the cardinality of $\hat{s}$ is greater than the cardinality of $\tilde{s}$. This possibility would simply reflect that $\hat{s}$ had not been written in a form that had allowed direct comparison with $\tilde{s}$ on a choice-problem by choice-problem basis (and that by such rewriting it became possible to show that in fact $\hat{s}$ was a subset of $\tilde{s}$ according to our definition).

7   As a general matter, we do not have an existence proof for a minimal partition, which is why we state the definition of internal and external affairs conditional on the existence of a minimal partition. But as we next show, we are able to establish existence in the formal setting of our benchmark model.

8   It should be understood that the set of g and x for which Step-1 is solved are those for which there exists a vector of instruments $\mathbf{i}$ such that $[g(\mathbf{i}, x) - g] = 0$ is satisfied.

9   Forming the Lagrangean associated with the home government's Step-2 problem, it is direct to confirm that the expression for the Lagrange multiplier is $\lambda = G_x/[f_g g_x + f_{g^*} g_x^* + f_x]$, from which the statement above can be confirmed.

10   A distinction may be made between explicit and tacit agreements. We focus here on how sovereignty might be violated by an explicit agreement. A related possibility is that governments may achieve a tacit agreement that emerges from repeated interaction, for example. We do not explore that possibility here.

11   The qualifier to generic cases in Proposition 4 refers to the possibility that optimal unilateral choices for some instruments might by chance happen to correspond to the policy levels needed for "targeting" other first-order conditions as described in the proof of the proposition.

12   To state Proposition 5 we have adopted a binary distinction between the limiting case of small countries that individually make a zero contribution to the externality variable and "non-small" countries that individually make a non-zero contribution to the externality variable. If countries were defined to be non-small only when their individual contributions to the externality variable exceeded some de-minimis level, then countries falling below this de-minimis level could not accept international commitments without violating their national sovereignty, and the potential conflicts between achieving international efficiency and maintaining national sovereignty described in Proposition 5 would be amplified.

13   This possibility could also include, for example, the sorts of actions described by Jackson (2003, p. 790) that might have been included in the original definition of Westphalian sovereignty ("the nation-state's power to violate virgins, chop off heads, arbitrarily confiscate property, torture citizens and engage in all sorts of other excessive and inappropriate actions"). As we discussed above in note 4, Jackson's approach is to update the definition of sovereignty so that there is no tradeoff between sovereignty and international intervention to address these kinds of actions. Our approach is to not tailor our definition of sovereignty on a case-by-case basis so that tradeoffs between sovereignty and international efficiency never exist, but rather to point out where such tradeoffs will be unavoidable, a result that is reported for this case in our Proposition 6.

14   The other important non-discrimination rule in the GATT/WTO is that of "national treatment," which applies to non-border measures. In our formal model, the MFN rule would apply to tariffs, while the national treatment rule would apply to regulations. We focus here on the implications of the MFN rule for national sovereignty, but we conjecture that analogous findings could be formalized with regard to national treatment.

15   We say "in principal" because, as pointed out in Bagwell and Staiger (2001), under current GATT/WTO practice the flexibility to fulfill market access commitments with any combination of policy instruments is not unlimited, and in particular would not be sufficient in certain circumstances to achieve internationally efficient outcomes in the way that we describe here. See also Bagwell, Mavroidis and Staiger (2002) for a more detailed discussion on this point and proposals that would introduce the required additional flexibility.

16   In interpreting GATT/WTO commitments as commitments over m, p^w, and m^*, we are implicitly conditioning on economic fundamentals (preferences, technologies, endowments); but the same statement applies to our efficiency characterizations, so this seems the appropriate reference point.

17 This is not to say that the GATT and now the WTO poses no threat to the national sovereignty of its member countries. Rather, our claim here is simply that market access commitments are consistent with the preservation of national sovereignty, and that the GATT/WTO can in principle steer clear of violations of the sovereignty of its members by adhering closely to the market access approach. Even then, in practice the process by which market access commitments are interpreted and enforced may place the sovereignty of members at risk in ways that are not captured by our formal modeling. For example, Keohane (2002, p. 8) points out that "the classic conception of [Westphalian] sovereignty prohibits a government from agreeing to rules defining a process, over which it does not have a veto, that can confer obligations not specifically provided for in the original agreement," and Barfield (2001, pp. 42–69) argues that in practice the WTO Dispute Settlement Body may pose just such a threat to the Westphalian sovereignty of its members (though see also Keohane, 2002, p. 17, for a more qualified view). While such threats to sovereignty may indeed be real in practice, it is clear that in principle the WTO is designed not to pose such a threat: as Article 3.2 of the WTO Dispute Settlement Understanding states, "Recommendations and rulings of the [WTO Dispute Settlement Body] cannot add to or diminish the rights and obligations provided in the covered agreements."

18 We also note that Proposition 9 is in line with Rabkin (2004, pp. 131–134) who, arguing from an historical and legal perspective, concludes that MFN obligations are consistent with the preservation of national sovereignty.

References

Bagwell, Kyle, Petros C. Mavroidis and Robert W. Staiger, "It's a Question of Market Access," *The American Journal of International Law*, January 2002, pp. 56–76.

Bagwell, Kyle, and Robert W. Staiger, "An Economic Theory of GATT," *American Economic Review*, March 1999, pp. 215–248.

Bagwell, Kyle, and Robert W. Staiger, "Domestic Policies, National Sovereignty and International Economic Institutions," *Quarterly Journal of Economics*, May 2001, pp. 519–562.

Bagwell, Kyle, and Robert W. Staiger, *The Economics of the World Trading System*, MIT Press, Cambridge, MA. 2002.

Bagwell, Kyle, and Robert W. Staiger, "National Sovereignty in an Interdependent World," NBER Working Paper No 10249, January 2004.

Barfield, Claude E., *Free Trade, Sovereignty, Democracy: The Future of the World Trade Organization*, The AEI Press, Washington, DC. 2001.

de Vattel, Emmerich, *The Law of Nations*, Translated by Joseph Chitty, T. and J. W. Johnson & Co., Law Booksellers, Philadelphia, PA. 1872.

Gray, John, "Introduction," in *John Stuart Mill: On Liberty and Other Essays*, Oxford World's Classics, Oxford University Press, Oxford. 1991.

Jackson, John H., "Sovereignty-Modern: A New Approach to an Outdated Concept," *American Journal of International Law*, vol 97, 2003, pp. 782–802.

Keohane, Robert O., "Ironies of Sovereignty: The European Union and the United States," *JCMS: Journal of Common Market Studies*, vol 40, 2002, pp. 743–765.

Krasner, Stephen D., *Sovereignty: Organized Hypocrisy*, Princeton University Press, Princeton, NJ. 1999.

Rabkin, Jeremy, *Why Sovereignty Matters*, The AEI Press, Washington, DC. 1998.

Rabkin, Jeremy, *The Case for Sovereignty*, The AEI Press, Washington, DC. 2004.

Appendix

In this appendix, we provide proofs of all lemmas and propositions that are not proved in the body of the chapter.

Proposition 1. The Nash equilibrium of the benchmark model is inefficient if and only if $G_x \neq 0$ and $G_x^* \neq 0$ at the Nash policy choices.

Proof: Using (2.1), we may derive that

$$\tilde{x}_{i_k} = \frac{-f_g g_{i_k}}{f_g g_x + f_{g^*} g_x^* + f_x} \quad \text{for } k = 1, 2, \ldots I, \tag{A1}$$

$$\tilde{x}_{i_k^*} = \frac{-f_{g^*} g_{i_k^*}^*}{f_g g_x + f_{g^*} g_x^* + f_x} \quad \text{for } k = 1, 2, \ldots I^*. \tag{A2}$$

With (A1) and (A2), it is direct to show that the Nash conditions (2.2) and (2.3) imply efficiency conditions (2.4) and (2.5). Further, substituting the Nash conditions (2.2) and (2.3) into efficiency condition (2.6) yields

$$G_x^* \tilde{x}_{i_1^*} G_x \tilde{x}_{i_1} = 0,$$

which is violated at the Nash policy choices if and only if $G_x \neq 0$ and $G_x^* \neq 0$ at these policy choices. Finally, it may be confirmed that (2.7) will be satisfied at the Nash policy choices if either $G_x = 0$ or $G_x^* = 0$ at these policy choices. **QED**

Lemma 1. Program 1$'$ is a partition of Program 1.

Proof: We prove this by establishing that the first-order conditions associated with Program 1$'$ are equivalent to the first-order conditions associated with Program 1, given by (2.2). Letting λ_1 denote the Lagrange multiplier associated with the constraint in Step 1 of Program 1$'$, and letting λ_2 denote the Lagrange multiplier associated with the constraint in Step 2 of Program 1$'$, the first-order conditions associated with Step 1 are given by

$$G_{i_k} - \lambda_1 g_{i_k} = 0 \quad \text{for } k = 1, 2, \ldots, I, \tag{A3}$$

while the first order conditions associated with Step 2 are given by

$$\lambda_1 - \lambda_2 f_g = 0, \text{ and}$$

$$G_x - \lambda_1 g_x - \lambda_2 [f_{g^*} g_x^* + f_x] = 0.$$

(A4)

Eliminating λ_1 and λ_2 from (A3)–(A4) yields (2.2). **QED**

Lemma 4. Program $5'$ is a minimal partition of the home-government's best-response choice problem defined by Program 5.

Proof: We first establish that Program $5'$ is a partition of Program 5 (Part I). We then argue that it is a minimal partition (Part II).

Part I: The first-order conditions associated with Program 5 are

$$W_{r_i} + \tau^j W_p \times \frac{\partial \tilde{p}^{wj}}{\partial r_i} + W_T \times \frac{dT}{dr_i} = 0 \text{ for } i = 1, 2, ..., R, \text{ and}$$

(A5)

$$W_p + \theta^j W_T = 0 \text{ for } j = 1, 2,$$

(A6)

where $\theta^j \equiv \frac{dT/d\tau^j}{dp/d\tau^j}$. Observe that by (6.7), $\tau^1 [\partial \tilde{p}^{w1}/\partial r_i] = \tau^2 [\partial \tilde{p}^{w2}/\partial r_i]$, and so (A5) may be equivalently evaluated for either $j = 1, 2$. The first-order conditions associated with Step 1 and Step 2 of Program $5'$, with γ_1 and γ_2 denoting the Lagrange multiplier on the constraints in Step 1 and Step 2, respectively, are

$$W_{r_i} + \gamma_1 M_{r_i} = 0 \text{ for } i = 1, 2, ..., R,$$

(A7)

$$W_p + \gamma_1 M_p = 0,$$

(A8)

$$-\gamma_1 + \gamma_2 = 0,$$

(A9)

$$\tau^1 W_p + \gamma_1 \tau^1 M_p + [W_T + \gamma_1 M_T] \times \left[\frac{1}{\tau^{*1}} \frac{\partial T}{\partial p^{*1}} + \frac{\partial T}{\partial p^{w1}} \right]$$

(A10)

$$- \gamma_2 \left[\frac{1}{\tau^{*1}} E_{p^{*1}}^{*1} + E_{p^{w1}}^{*1} \right] = 0, \text{ and}$$

$$[W_T + \gamma_1 M_T] \times \left[\frac{1}{\tau^{*2}} \frac{\partial T}{\partial p^{*2}} + \frac{\partial T}{\partial p^{w2}} \right] - \gamma_2 \left[\frac{1}{\tau^{*2}} E_{p^{*2}}^{*2} + E_{p^{w2}}^{*2} \right] = 0.$$

(A11)

By using (A9) and (A11) to derive an expression for γ_1 and noting that $\frac{dT}{dp^{w2}} = \left[\frac{1}{\tau^{*2}} \frac{\partial T}{\partial p^{*2}} + \frac{\partial T}{\partial p^{w2}} \right]$, (A8) may be written as

$$W_p + \left[\frac{M_p \frac{dT}{dp^{w2}}}{E_{p^{w2}}^{*2} - M_T \frac{dT}{dp^{w2}}} \right] \times W_T = 0.$$

(A12)

Next, we observe that (A6) implies $\theta^1 = \theta^2$, which can be manipulated to yield

$$\frac{\partial \tilde{p}^{w1}}{\partial \tau^2} = \left[\frac{\tilde{p}^{w2}}{\tilde{p}^{w1}}\right] \times \left[\frac{dT/dp^{w2}}{dT/dp^{w1}}\right] \times \left[\frac{\partial \tilde{p}^{w2}}{\partial \tau^1}\right],$$

which in turn allows θ^2 to be written as

$$\theta^2 = \left[\frac{dT}{dp^{w2}}\right] \times \frac{\left[\frac{\partial \tilde{p}^{w2}}{\partial \tau^2}\right] + \left[\frac{\tilde{p}^{w2}}{\tilde{p}^{w1}}\right]\left[\frac{\partial \tilde{p}^{w2}}{\partial \tau^1}\right]}{\tilde{p}^{w2} + \tau^2\left[\frac{\partial \tilde{p}^{w2}}{\partial \tau^2}\right]}. \tag{A13}$$

Using the linkage condition (6.7) and the market-clearing condition (6.10), expressions for $\frac{\partial \tilde{p}^{w2}}{\partial \tau^1}$ and $\frac{\partial \tilde{p}^{w2}}{\partial \tau^2}$ may be derived which, when substituted into (A13), yield

$$\theta^2 = \frac{M_p \times \left[\frac{dT}{dp^{w2}}\right]}{E_{p^{w2}}^{*2} - M_T \frac{dT}{dp^{w2}}}. \tag{A14}$$

Therefore, by substituting (A14) into (A6) and observing that the resulting expression is identical to (A12), we may conclude that (A9), (A11), and (A8) imply (A6). Similarly, we use (A9) and (A10) to derive an alternative expression for γ_1, which allows (A7) to be written as

$$W_{r_i} + \tau^1 W_p \times \left[\frac{M_{r_i}}{E_{p^{w1}}^{*1} - M_{p^{w1}}}\right] + W_T \times \left[\frac{dT}{dp^{w1}}\right] \times \left[\frac{M_{r_i}}{E_{p^{w1}}^{*1} - M_{p^{w1}}}\right] = 0. \tag{A15}$$

Now using (6.7) and (6.10), we may derive that

$$\frac{\partial \tilde{p}^{w1}}{\partial r_i} = \left[\frac{M_{r_i}}{E_{p^{w1}}^{*1} - M_{p^{w1}}}\right]. \tag{A16}$$

Substituting (A16) into (A15) yields an expression identical to (A5). Hence, we may conclude that (A9), (A10), and (A7) imply (A5).

Part II: The proof that Program 5′ is a minimal partition of Program 5 proceeds in the same way as the proof of Lemma 3. **QED**

Proposition 10. An international agreement can attain a point on the international efficiency frontier and satisfy (6.11) if and only if it satisfies the MFN rule.

Proof: To prove this proposition, we first characterize the efficiency frontier of the three-country model (that is, for notational simplicity, we treat the foreign governments in region *2 as if they were all identical, but this is not essential for the result). To this end, fix foreign welfare levels $\bar{W}^{*j}$ for $j = \{1, 2\}$ and define $\tilde{p}^{wj}(\mathbf{r}^{*j}, \tau^{*j}, \bar{W}^{*j})$ implicitly by $W^{*j}(\mathbf{r}^{*j}, p^{*j}(\tau^{*j}, \tilde{p}^{wj}), \tilde{p}^{wj}) = \bar{W}^{*j}$ for $j = \{1, 2\}$. Observe that

$$\frac{\partial \tilde{p}^{wj}}{\partial \tau^{*j}} = \frac{p^{*j} W_{p^{*j}}^{*j}}{W_{p^{*j}}^{*j} + \tau^{*j} W_{\tilde{p}^{wj}}^{*j}}; \text{ and } \frac{\partial \tilde{p}^{wj}}{\partial r_i^{*j}} = \frac{-\tau^{*j} W_{r_i^{*j}}^{*j}}{W_{p^{*j}}^{*j} + \tau^{*j} W_{\tilde{p}^{wj}}^{*j}}, \tag{A17}$$

for $i = 1, 2, ..., R^{*j}$ and $j = \{1, 2\}$. We may now define

$$\bar{T}(\{\mathbf{r}^{*j}\}, \{\tau^{*j}\}, \{\bar{W}^{*j}\}) \equiv T(\{\mathbf{r}^{*j}\}, \{p^{*j}(\tau^{*j}, \tilde{p}^{wj}(\mathbf{r}^{*j}, \tau^{*j}, \bar{W}^{*j}))\}, \{\tilde{p}^{wj}(\mathbf{r}^{*j}, \tau^{*j}, \bar{W}^{*j})\}),$$

and observe that, by the market-clearing condition (6.10), a value of p is implied, which we denote by $\bar{p}(\mathbf{r}, \mathbf{r}^{*j}, \tau^{*j}, \bar{W}^{*j})$. We may thus write domestic government welfare as a function of the domestic regulatory choices, the foreign regulatory choices and foreign tariffs, and the foreign welfare levels, or

$$W(\mathbf{r}, \bar{p}(\mathbf{r}, \mathbf{r}^{*j}, \tau^{*j}, \bar{W}^{*j}), \bar{T}(\{\mathbf{r}^{*j}\}, \{\tau^{*j}\}, \{\bar{W}^{*j}\})). \tag{A18}$$

Fixing foreign welfare levels and choosing domestic and foreign regulations and foreign tariffs to maximize domestic welfare given by (A18) then defines a point on the efficiency frontier. The first order conditions that define the efficiency frontier are

$$W_{r_i} + W_p \frac{\partial \bar{p}}{\partial r_i} = 0 \text{ for } i = 1, 2, ..., R, \tag{A19}$$

$$W_p \frac{\partial \bar{p}}{\partial r_i^{*j}} + W_{\bar{T}} \frac{\partial \bar{T}}{\partial r_i^{*j}} = 0 \text{ for } i = 1, 2, ..., R^{*j} \text{ and } j = 1, 2, \text{ and} \tag{A20}$$

$$W_p \frac{\partial \bar{p}}{\partial \tau^{*j}} + W_{\bar{T}} \frac{\partial \bar{T}}{\partial \tau^{*j}} = 0 \text{ for } i = 1, 2. \tag{A21}$$

Now consider the efficiency properties of policy choices that satisfy (6.11) and also (6.12). By (A19)–(A21), these policies are efficient if and only if

$$\frac{\partial \bar{T}}{\partial r_i^{*j}} = 0 = \frac{\partial \bar{T}}{\partial \tau^{*j}} \text{ for } i = 1, 2, ..., R^{*j} \text{ and } j = 1, 2. \tag{A22}$$

But by (A17), (A22) is satisfied at policies that satisfy (6.11) and (6.12) if and only if

$$\frac{E_{r_i^{*j}}^{*j}}{M} [\tilde{p}^{wj} - \bar{T}] = 0 = \frac{E_{p^{*j}}^{*j}}{M} [\tilde{p}^{wj} - \bar{T}] \text{ for } i = 1, 2, ..., R^{*j} \text{ and } j = 1, 2. \tag{A23}$$

Hence, by (A23), policy choices that satisfy (6.11) and (6.12) are efficient if and only if the tariffs conform to MFN (so that $\tilde{p}^{wj} - \bar{T}$ for $j = 1, 2$). Further, at policies satisfying (6.11), (A17)–(A23) can be used to show that efficiency requires that these policies satisfy (6.12) as well and abide by MFN. Hence, an international agreement can attain a point on the international efficiency frontier and satisfy (6.11) if and only if it satisfies the MFN rule. **QED**

3 Trade competition and reallocations in a small open economy

Marc Melitz

1. Introduction

In this chapter, I develop a simple model of firm heterogeneity with endogenous markups. The endogenous markups stem from preferences that feature variable elasticities of substitution (VES) in a monopolistically competitive environment. Although the model is kept general along some key dimensions (both preferences and technology heterogeneity are left un-parametrized), I show how it is still amenable to simple, mostly graphical, comparative statics analyses of asymmetric trade liberalization (for either imports or exports) by applying these to the case of a "small" open economy.[1] The comparative statics analyses for trade liberalization are applied to describe both short-run and long-run effects of liberalization – where the latter allows for a response of firm entry to liberalization. These effects are described both in a partial equilibrium setting where wages in a given sector are fixed and trade need not be balanced; as well as in a general equilibrium setting where wages across countries adjust to balance trade. Although the preferences are left un-parametrized, they are restricted to a broad class of additively separable preferences that generates predictions for markups under monopolistic competition that are consistent with a large set of established empirical patterns. These patterns include evidence for markup differences across firms (larger firms set larger markups), as well as for changes in markups associated with incomplete pass-through of cost changes into prices.[2]

A substantial portion of the theoretical trade literature analyzing the response of heterogeneous exporters assumes constant markups – based on the assumptions of constant elasticity of substitution (CES) preferences along with monopolistic competition.[3] These models do a good job of capturing the extensive margin of trade: the selection effects that determine which products are sold where. However, those models cannot capture the intensive margin reallocations – between producers selling in the same market – stemming from trade, even though there is growing empirical evidence for this phenomenon.[4] The current model with endogenous markups highlights how trade liberalization induces such intensive margin reallocations towards more productive producers that reenforce the extensive margin reallocations that are stressed by models with exogenous markups – because they do not feature intensive margin reallocations. This generates another channel for the productivity enhancing effects of trade liberalization.[5]

2. Closed economy

I start with a description of a closed economy with monopolistic competition, heterogeneous producers and endogenous markups.[6] This introduces the key equilibrium concept of competition in a market, which in turn shapes the whole distribution of producer markups. I develop both a general equilibrium version with a single differentiated good sector for the whole economy, and a partial equilibrium version focusing on a single sector among many in the economy. In the latter, I also introduce a short-run version where entry is restricted (general equilibrium is inherently a long-run scenario). This closed economy setup is also used to examine an initial globalization scenario for an integrated world economy with no trade costs – captured by an overall increase in market size.

Consider a sector with a single productive factor, labor. I will distinguish between two scenarios. The first is the standard general equilibrium (GE) setup with a single sector. The exogenous labor endowment L indexes both the number of workers L^w with inelastic supply and consumers L^c. I choose the endogenous wage as the *numeraire*. Thus, all revenue and expenditure flows are measured in units of the wage.[7] Aggregate expenditures are then given by the exogenous labor endowment. In the partial equilibrium (PE) scenario, I focus on the sector as a small part of the economy. I take the number of consumers L^c as well as their individual expenditures on the sector's output as exogenously given. The supply of labor L^w to the sector is perfectly elastic at an exogenous economy-wide wage. This involves a normalization for the measure of consumers L^c in that sector: Aggregate accounting then implies that this normalized number of consumers L^c represents a fraction of the labor endowment L.[8]

2.1. Consumer optimization

There is a continuum of differentiated varieties indexed by $i \in [0, I]$, where I is the measure of products available. The demand for differentiated varieties q_i is generated by the L^c consumers who solve:[9]

$$\max_{q_i \geq 0} \int_0^I u(q_i)di \text{ s.t. } \int_0^I p_i q_i di = 1.$$

So long as

(A1) $u(0) = 0$; $u'(q_i) > 0$; and $u''(q_i) < 0$ for $q_i \geq 0$

this leads to a downward sloping inverse demand function (per consumer)

$$p(q_i; \lambda) = \frac{u'(q_i)}{\lambda}, \text{ where } \lambda = \int_0^I u'(q_i)q_i di > 0 \qquad (1)$$

is the marginal utility of income (spent on differentiated varieties). Given the assumption of separable preferences, this marginal utility of income λ is the unique endogenous aggregate demand shifter. Higher λ shifts all residual demand curves *inward*, which represents an increase in competition for a given level of market demand L^c.

Strict concavity of $u(q_i)$ ensures that the chosen consumption level from (1) also satisfies the second order condition for the consumer's problem. This residual demand curve (1) is associated with a marginal revenue curve

$$\phi(q_i; \lambda) = \frac{u'(q_i) + u''(q_i)q_i}{\lambda}. \tag{2}$$

Let $\varepsilon_p(q_i) \equiv -p'(q_i)q_i/p(q_i)$ and $\varepsilon_\phi(q_i) \equiv -\phi'(q_i)q_i/\phi(q_i)$ denote the elasticities of inverse demand and marginal revenue.[10] Thus $\varepsilon_p(q_i) \geq 0$ is the inverse price elasticity of demand (less than 1 for elastic demand), capturing the sensitivity of price to changes in quantities. $\varepsilon_\phi(q_i)$ captures the sensitivity of marginal revenue to changes in quantities, which combines both the response of the price of the marginal unit as well as the impact on revenue from the change in price on infra-marginal units. Additional demand restrictions imposed later will ensure that this sensitivity measure is non-negative for profit maximizing firms.

Although the demand and marginal revenue curves are residual (they depend on λ), their elasticities are nonetheless independent of λ. These preferences nest the case of CES preferences where the elasticities $\varepsilon_p(q_i)$ and $\varepsilon_\phi(q_i)$ are constant.[11]

2.2.   *Firm optimization*

The market structure is monopolistically competitive. There is an unbounded set of entrants who can pay a sunk entry cost f_E (in units of labor) for a variety blueprint with uncertain productivity. After this cost is incurred, the productivity φ of the blue print is revealed as a draw from a common continuous differentiable distribution $G(\varphi)$ with support over $[0, \infty)$.[12] This productivity is the inverse unit labor requirement for producing this variety, which can also be thought of as product quality.[13] Producing and selling this variety in the domestic market also entails a fixed cost f – assumed to be common across firms. Technology therefore exhibits increasing returns to scale at the product level. This production structure can also be extended to incorporate multi-product firms, as developed in Mayer et al. (2016).

A firm with productivity φ that produces positive output and faces market competition λ chooses an output level that maximizes operating profit per-consumer:

$$\pi(\varphi, \lambda) = \max_{q_i} [p(q_i, \lambda)q_i - q_i/\varphi], \tag{3}$$

$$q(\varphi, \lambda) = \arg\max_{q_i} [p(q_i, \lambda)q_i - q_i/\varphi]. \tag{4}$$

The first order condition for this optimization problem is the well known equalization of marginal revenue with marginal cost:

$$\phi(q(\varphi, \lambda); \lambda) = 1/\varphi. \tag{5}$$

In order to ensure that the solution to this problem exists (for at least some $\varphi > 0$) and is unique, I further restrict the specification of preferences to satisfy:

(**A2**) $2u''(q_i) + u'''(q_i)q_i < 0$ for $q_i \geq 0$.

This assumption ensures that marginal revenue $\varphi(q_i; \lambda)$ is decreasing for all output levels and positive for at least some output levels (as $q \to 0$). It also guarantees that demand is elastic along a top portion of the demand curve. One can also measure a firm's output using its generated revenues per consumer:

$$r(\varphi, \lambda) = q(\varphi, \lambda)p(q(\varphi, \lambda), \lambda). \tag{6}$$

Note that all these performance measures (operating profit, output, sales) are increasing in firm productivity φ and decreasing in the endogenous competition level λ: More productive firms are larger and earn higher profits than their less productive counterparts; and an increase in competition λ lowers production levels and profits for all firms.

A firm with productivity φ earns total – across consumers – net profit

$$\Pi(\varphi, \lambda) = L^c \pi(\varphi, \lambda) - f.$$

This is also increasing in firm productivity, leading to a unique cutoff productivity φ^* satisfying

$$\Pi(\varphi^*, \lambda) = 0. \tag{7}$$

Firms with productivity below this cutoff do not produce: they shut down in the short run, and exit in the long run. Tougher competition thus leads to tougher selection: only a proper subset of higher productivity firms survive.

2.3. Free entry in the long run

In the long run when entry is unrestricted, the expected profit of a prospective entrant adjusts to match the sunk cost:

$$\int_{\varphi^*}^{\infty} \Pi(\varphi, \lambda)dG(\varphi) = f_E. \tag{8}$$

This free entry condition, along with the zero cutoff profit condition (7), jointly determine the equilibrium cutoff φ^* along with the competition level λ. The number of entrants N^E, which includes some firms with productivity below the cutoff φ^* that do not produce, is then determined by the consumer's budget constraint:

$$N^E \int_{\varphi^*}^{\infty} r(\varphi, \lambda) dG(\varphi) = 1. \tag{9}$$

These conditions hold in both the GE and PE scenarios.

Aggregating employment over all firms yields the aggregate labor demanded:

$$L^w = N^E \left\{ f_E + \int_{\varphi^*}^{\infty} [f + L^c q(\varphi, \lambda)/\varphi] dG(\varphi) \right\}.$$

As the free entry condition (8) entails no ex-ante aggregate profits (aggregate revenue is equal to the payments to all workers, including those employed to cover the entry costs), this aggregate labor demand L^w will be equal to the number of consumers L^c. This ensures labor market clearing in the GE scenario. In the PE scenario, this implies that the endogenous labor supply adjusts so that it equals the normalized number of consumers (recall that this is an exogenous fraction of the economy-wide labor endowment).[14] Thus, in this closed economy setup, the determination of the endogenous cutoff φ^* and competition λ will be identical in both long-run scenarios (GE and PE). This equivalence will be broken in the open economy where the two scenarios feature different wage responses.

2.3.1.   *Graphical representation of equilibrium*

The determination of the long run equilibrium cutoff is represented in Figure 3.1 below. Consider a plot of total firm profit $\Pi(\varphi, \lambda)$ as a function of productivity φ for any given level of competition λ. In Figure 3.1, the productivity levels are rescaled to an index between 0 and 1 using the distribution $G(\varphi)$. The cutoff

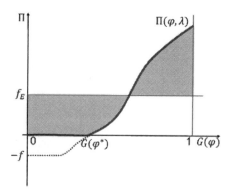

Figure 3.1 Graphical representation of equilibrium

productivity φ^* from (7) is given by the intersection of the curve with the horizontal axis. This curve is strictly increasing for all firms with productivity above this cutoff. (The dashed line represents the hypothetical total profit from the maximization of operating profit from (3); unlike the case of CES preferences operating profits may be zero for firms with low productivity and marginal cost above a choke price.) Firms with productivity below the cutoff φ^* do not produce and earn zero total profit. Given our rescaling of productivity, the area below the profit curve (up to the maximum productivity index $G(\varphi) = 1$) represents the average profit (and hence the expected profit) from the left-hand side of the free entry condition (8). At the equilibrium level of competition λ, this area must be equal to the sunk entry cost – represented in the graph by the rectangle above the axis up to the f_E line. Or, rearranging, the two shaded areas in the graph must be equalized. The area above the f_E line to the right represents the post-entry gains by firms with high productivity while the area below the line to the left captures the post-entry losses by the low productivity firms. This includes firms that exit as well as some that produce. In the latter case, the firms' total profit $\Pi(\varphi, \lambda)$ is positive, but below the sunk entry cost.

2.4. Short-run equilibrium

I now consider an alternative short-run situation in which the number of incumbents is fixed at $\bar{N}$ in the PE scenario (with the same exogenous distribution of ex-ante productivity $G(\varphi)$). In this case, free entry (8) no longer holds: firms with productivity above the cutoff φ^* in (7) produce while the remaining firms shutdown. However, the budget constraint (9) still holds with the exogenous number of incumbents $\bar{N}$ now replacing the endogenous number of entrants N^E. Together with the zero cutoff profit (7), those two conditions jointly determine the endogenous cutoff φ^* and competition level λ.

2.5. Aggregate productivity

As previously mentioned, the symmetric representation for quantities in the preferences assumes that those quantities have been adjusted for quality (in order to equate utility in the consumer's eye). A theoretical aggregation of productivity can therefore sum the quantity produced per worker:

$$\Phi = \frac{\int_{\varphi^*}^{\infty} q(\varphi, \lambda) d\mu(\varphi)}{L^w},$$

where $\mu(\varphi) = N^E G(\varphi)$ represents the cumulative mass of producing firms. This is a theoretical measure however, as the correspondence between physical and quality-adjusted units is not observed (even physical quantities are often poorly measured). Typically, labor productivity is measured as deflated aggregate sales (or value-added, when intermediates are used in production) per worker; where percentage changes in the price deflator capture expenditure weighted percentage changes in individual prices. The best representation of such a productivity measure within the structure of the model is:

$$\hat{\Phi} = \frac{\int_{\varphi^*}^{\infty} r(\varphi, \lambda) d\mu(\varphi)/P}{L^w},$$

where the price deflator

$$P = \frac{\int_{\varphi^*}^{\infty} r(\varphi, \lambda) p(q(\varphi, \lambda); \lambda) d\mu(\varphi)}{\int_{\varphi^*}^{\infty} r(\varphi, \lambda) d\mu(\varphi)}$$

is defined as the revenue-weighted average of firm-level prices.

3.   Curvature of demand

Up to now, I have placed very few restrictions on the shape of (residual) demand that the firms face, other than the conditions (A1)–(A2) needed to ensure a unique monopolistic competition equilibrium. The shape of demand determines how tougher competition λ (an inward shift of residual demand) impacts firm prices and markups. At their chosen production level $q(\varphi, \lambda)$, a firm sets a markup $\mu(q_i)$ (the ratio of price to marginal cost) that is tied down (inversely) by the price elasticity of demand: $\mu(q_i) = 1/(1 - \varepsilon_p(q_i))$. Thus, the response of markups is tied to changes in the price elasticity of demand (along the residual demand curve). If, moving up residual demand, demand becomes more elastic, $\varepsilon_p'(q_i) > 0$, then tougher competition λ leads to a lower markup (and hence price) for any given firm with productivity φ.[15] And conversely, if demand becomes more inelastic (again, moving up the demand curve), then tougher competition leads to higher markups and prices. Although theoretically possible, this latter case seems counter-intuitive. Indeed, this case was excluded by Marshall (1890) in his original exposition defining demand curves; it is often referred to as "Marshall's Second Law of Demand" (MSLD)[16] – that elasticity of demand increases with price along a demand curve, or alternatively that the demand curve is log-concave in log-price.[17] This is also the main demand assumption made "without apology" by Krugman (1979) (in order to yield "reasonable results") in his seminal paper on trade with economies of scale.

   Violations of MSLD would also directly contradict the evidence on markups and pass-through that were mentioned in the introduction. Within a monopolistic competition framework (required for a well-defined residual demand curve), MSLD is equivalent to the property that more productive firms set higher markups. It is also equivalent to the property of incomplete pass-through: that a change to marginal cost is passed-on less than one-for-one into prices – with the remaining variation absorbed into the markup. Under CES preferences, markups are constant, both across firms and with respect to changes in competition λ. Changes to marginal costs are passed on one-for-one into prices, and pass-through is therefore complete. Lastly, the endogenous markups generated by MSLD demand also induce a pattern of endogenous trade elasticities that are broadly consistent with the empirical evidence.[18]

Under MSLD, the elasticity of inverse demand $\varepsilon_p(q_i)$ increases with output q_i. Since marginal revenue is everywhere below the inverse demand, its elasticity – on average – must also increase with output. A slightly stronger assumption than MSLD is that the elasticity of marginal revenue $\varepsilon_\varphi(q_i)$ smoothly increases with output: $\varepsilon'_\phi(q_i) > 0$. I refer to this assumption as MSLD', which implies MSLD. Figure 3.2 depicts a log-log graph of the inverse demand and marginal revenue curves satisfying these restrictions. On its own, MSLD is equivalent to the concavity of the demand curve in log-log space. MSLD' is equivalent to the concavity of the marginal revenue curve in that space (relative to MSLD, it eliminates the possibility of inflection points in the marginal revenue curve).[19] From here on out, I assume that MSLD' holds ($\varepsilon'_\phi(q_i) > 0$), which implies that MSLD ($\varepsilon'_p(q_i) > 0$) also holds. I am tempted to add "without apology," but instead will lean on the accumulated empirical research in the intervening 30 years since Krugman (1979) and point out that violations of this demand-side restriction would generate counterfactual predictions against overwhelming empirical support on firm markup differences and how they respond to various shocks.[20]

Given MSLD', an increase in competition induces a downward shift in markups (lower markup at any given productivity level φ) as firms are pushed up their demand curves. This increase in price elasticities also results in a reallocation of output (and hence labor), revenue and operating profit towards more productive firms. Put another way, for any two firms with productivity φ_1 and $\varphi_2 < \varphi_1$, the ratios $q(\varphi_1, \lambda)/q(\varphi_2, \lambda)$, $r(\varphi_1, \lambda)/r(\varphi_2, \lambda)$, $\pi(\varphi_1, \lambda)/\pi(\varphi_2, \lambda)$ increase with competition λ (so long as both firms produce after the increase in competition). This intensive margin reallocation of resources towards more productive firms generates an increase in aggregate productivity for a given set of producing firms. There is also an extensive margin effect that contributes to aggregate productivity changes. If selection toughens (higher cutoff φ^*), then this margin also contributes to an aggregate productivity increase; and conversely weaker selection (lower cutoff φ^*) contributes to lower aggregate productivity.[21]

This MSLD' restriction on preferences excludes the very common case of CES preferences where the elasticities $\varepsilon_p(q_i)$ and $\varepsilon_\phi(q_i)$ are constant – and hence all

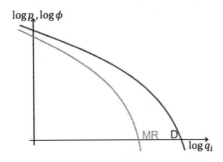

Figure 3.2 Graphical representation of demand assumptions

firms share the same constant markup. In this case, no intensive margin reallocations are possible: the output, revenue and operating profit ratios $q(\varphi_1, \lambda)/q(\varphi_2, \lambda)$, $r(\varphi_1, \lambda)/r(\varphi_2, \lambda)$, $\pi(\varphi_1, \lambda)/\pi(\varphi_2, \lambda)$ no longer vary with competition λ: they only depend on the productivity differential φ_1/φ_2 and exogenous parameters. In an open economy setting, such a model emphasizes the impact of trade (and trade liberalization) at the extensive margin (firm selection). The model developed in this chapter with MSLD' preferences will feature similar extensive margin predictions, but adds another important channel operating through intensive margin reallocations. In the following globalization scenarios, I will emphasize how these intensive margin reallocations generate a more robust prediction linking globalization to increased aggregate productivity.

4.　Market size

Before developing the open economy version of the model and analyzing various trade liberalization scenarios, I examine the impact of increased market size. This corresponds to a globalization scenario for an integrated world economy (with no additional frictions to international trade). I consider first the short-run response to an increase in the number of consumers L^c with a fixed number of producers (no entry). On impact (keeping the competition level λ fixed), an increase in market size increases firm net profit $\Pi(\varphi, \lambda) = L^c\pi(\varphi, \lambda) - f$ even though the operating profit per consumer $\pi(\varphi, \lambda)$ does not change. This is represented by the change from the solid line to the dotted line in Figure 3.3. This implies that some firms that previously entered and found production to be unprofitable (with productivity below the cutoff φ^*) now find it profitable to produce. This, in turn, increases competition λ leading to a short-run equilibrium with both higher competition λ and a lower cutoff φ^* as depicted by the dashed line in the figure. More formally, it is straightforward to show that this is the comparative static implied by the cutoff (7) and budget constraint (9) conditions for the short run.[22]

The short-run equilibrium depicted in Figure 3.3 clearly violates the free entry condition: Average firm profit – the area below the net profit curve – increases from its long-run equilibrium level matching the sunk entry cost (this is represented by the area below the solid line). This increase in average net profit in

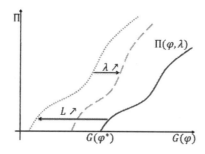

Figure 3.3 Increased market size: short run

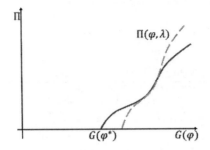

Figure 3.4 Increased market size: long run

the short run induces entry in the long run. This entry further raises the competition level λ. Figure 3.4 shows the new long-run equilibrium profit curve (dashed curve) along with the same old long-run equilibrium profit curve (solid curve). The new net profit curve now satisfies the free-entry condition: so long as the area between the two profit curves – above and below their intersection – are equal, the total area below the new profit curve will be equal to the entry cost f_E (as is also the case for the old equilibrium profit curve). As depicted in the figure, the new profit curve must be steeper than the old one, and must intersect it only once, given that the ratio of operating profit $\pi(\varphi_1, \lambda)/\pi(\varphi_2, \lambda)$ increases (with competition λ) for any two producing firms with $\varphi_1 > \varphi_2$.[23] This further implies that the cutoff φ^* rises indicating tougher selection. As I previously discussed, this new long run equilibrium applies to both the GE and PE versions of the model in a closed world economy (the same cutoff and free entry condition applies in both cases). Lastly, I note that the demand assumptions play a critical role in generating this prediction for selection. Under CES preferences, changes in competition λ would not affect the steepness of the profit curves, and the new long-run equilibrium curve would coincide with the old equilibrium curve: only the number of firms would change.[24]

Thus, we see how more realistic demand assumptions strengthen the link between this initial globalization scenario and aggregate productivity. In both the short- and long-run, an increased market size for the world economy induces an increase in competition that generates intensive margin reallocations towards more productive firms. As production resources (labor in this one-factor model) are reallocated towards more productive firms, aggregate productivity increases. In the long run, the impact on aggregate productivity is compounded by the extensive margin reallocations triggered by tougher selection. In the short run, the extensive margin reallocations go in the opposite direction as selection weakens (the productivity cutoff φ^* decreases). Aggregate productivity increases so long as the impact of the intensive margin reallocations dominate. These predictions for aggregate productivity contrast with the case of CES preferences and exogenous markups where productivity remains constant in the long-run and decreases in the short run (only the extensive margin effect is operative).

5.   Small open economy

In order to analyze globalization scenarios in a world that is not completely integrated, I now develop an open economy with trade frictions. For simplicity, I consider the same domestic economy that was previously developed along with a unique foreign trading partner (F). This "rest of the world" economy is structured in the same way as the domestic economy. It features a market size indexed by L_F^c consumers and an equilibrium level of competition λ_F. Thus, a foreign firm with productivity φ will earn an operating profit per-consumer in F, $\pi(\varphi, \lambda_F)$, given by the same optimization problem (3) as was solved by firms in the domestic economy – though these profits are denominated in units of the foreign wage (just like the domestic profits are denominated in units of the domestic wage). Note that this per-consumer operating profit function – and the associated output and revenue per-consumer given by (4) and (6) – depends only on preferences, which we assume to be identical across countries.[25]

Domestic firms can export to F but then incur both a per-unit "iceberg" trade cost $\tau \geq 1$ as well a fixed export market access cost f_X (denominated in units of domestic labor). Thus, if a domestic firm with productivity φ exports to F, it would earn an operating profit per-consumer in F (in units of the foreign wage) given by $\pi(w_F \tau^{-1} \varphi, \lambda_F)$, where w_F indexes the relative wage difference in F (the foreign wage divided by the domestic wage).[26] Converting this export profit to the domestic wage numeraire then yields total (across consumers) net export profits

$$\Pi_X(\varphi, \lambda_F) = w_F L_F^c \pi(w_F \tau^{-1} \varphi, \lambda_F) - f_X.$$

This is increasing in firm productivity, leading to a unique export cutoff productivity φ_X^* satisfying

$$\Pi_X(\varphi_X^*, \lambda_F) = 0. \tag{10}$$

Firms with productivity below this cutoff do not export.

As in the closed economy, a domestic firm with productivity φ would also earn a total net profit from domestic sales given by

$$\Pi_D(\varphi, \lambda) = L^c \pi(\varphi, \lambda) - f,$$

where λ still indexes the level of competition in the domestic market. The same cutoff condition also holds:

$$\Pi_D(\varphi^*, \lambda) = 0. \tag{11}$$

Firms with productivity below this cutoff cannot profitably operate in their domestic market and do not produce. Here, we have assumed that market conditions in the export market are not so favorable relative to the trade costs that firms would find it profitable to export and not produce for their domestic market.

Hence, we assume that selection into the export market is tougher, $\varphi_X^* > \varphi^*$, so that some firms with productivity in between those two cutoffs produce for the domestic market but do not export.[27] Total net profit for a firm with productivity φ then reflects both selection decisions and can be written:

$$\Pi(\varphi, \lambda, \lambda_F) = \mathbf{1}_{[\varphi \geq \varphi^*]} \Pi_D(\varphi, \lambda) + \mathbf{1}_{[\varphi \geq \varphi_X^*]} \Pi_X(\varphi, \lambda_F). \tag{12}$$

As previously mentioned, the foreign economy is structured in the same way as the domestic economy, though with its own set of parameters. There are N_F^E entrants with a productivity distribution $G_F(\varphi)$. These foreign firms can then export into the domestic economy, subject to per-unit trade costs $\tau_F \geq 1$ and an overhead fixed costs $f_{F,X}$ (in units of foreign labor). As with the domestic economy, the foreign firms sort into production and exports given cutoffs φ_F^* and $\varphi_{F,X}^*$.

5.1. *Small open economy restriction*

In order to analyze asymmetric trade liberalization scenarios with the simple graphical tools developed for the closed economy, I additionally assume that the domestic economy is small relative to its rest-of-the-world trading partner. I follow Demidova and Rodríguez-Clare (2013) in defining a small open economy with product differentiation and monopolistic competition. This amounts to assuming that changes in the domestic economy do not have repercussions for market aggregates in the foreign economy (other than its trade with the domestic economy). Thus, from the perspective of the domestic economy, the number of entrants N_F^E, the production cutoff φ_F^*, and the level of competition λ_F in foreign are all fixed and do not respond to domestic changes (including all trade costs to/from the domestic economy). The only foreign variables that remain endogenous are the relative wage w_F and the export cutoff into the domestic economy $\varphi_{F,X}^*$.[28]

5.2. *Long-run equilibrium*

In the long run with free-entry, average post-entry profits for all firms must still match the sunk entry cost, yielding the same free-entry condition (8) as for the closed economy – except that profits in the open economy now involve the potential for export profits as shown in (12).

In the PE version of the model, the relative wage w_F is fixed as the wage in the sector is fixed relative to the economy-wide wage in both countries. Since the competition level λ_F in F is exogenous, the export cutoff condition (10) then independently determines the export cutoff φ_X^*. Given this cutoff, one can solve for the domestic economy cutoff φ^* and competition λ using the free-entry condition (8) and domestic cutoff condition (11). Given a domestic competition level λ, one can then sequentially solve for the foreign export cutoff using a cutoff condition that is analogous to the one for the domestic exporters (10):

$$w_F^{-1} L^c \pi(w_F^{-1} \tau_F^{-1} \varphi_{F,X}^*, \lambda) - f_{F,X} = 0. \tag{13}$$

Lastly, the number of domestic entrants is then determined by the budget constraint:

$$N^E \int_{\varphi^*}^{\infty} r(\varphi, \lambda) dG(\varphi) + N_F^E \int_{\varphi_{F,X}^*}^{\infty} r(w_F^{-1} \tau_F^{-1} \varphi, \lambda) dG_F(\varphi) = 1. \tag{14}$$

In the GE version of the model, the relative wage w_F is endogenous and adjusts to balance trade:

$$w_F N^E \int_{\varphi_X^*}^{\infty} r(w_F \tau^{-1} \varphi, \lambda_F) dG(\varphi) = N_F^E \int_{\varphi_{F,X}^*}^{\infty} r(w_F^{-1} \tau_F^{-1} \varphi, \lambda) dG_F(\varphi), \tag{15}$$

with the aggregate domestic exports on the left-hand side and the aggregate foreign exports on the right-hand side. Together with the five equilibrium conditions from the PE version – budget constraint (14), free-entry (8) and three cutoff conditions (10,11,13) – this yields a system of six equations in the six endogenous variables $(\varphi^*, \varphi_X^*, \varphi_{F,X}^*, \lambda, N^E, w_F)$. Since the relative wage appears in all but one of the 6 conditions, these variables can no longer be solved sequentially as in the PE equilibrium.

5.3.   Short-run equilibrium

As was the case in the closed economy, the short-run equilibrium features a fixed number of firms $\bar{N}$ with the same exogenous distribution of ex-ante productivity $G(\varphi)$ and the free-entry condition no longer applies. This exogenous number of firms then replaces the endogenous number of entrants in the budget constraint (14). Again, I only consider the PE version in the short run (the GE relative wage adjustments are inherently a long-run phenomenon). Given an exogenous relative wage w_F, the export cutoff φ_X^* is again independently determined by its cutoff condition (10). The remaining three endogenous variables (domestic cutoff φ^*, foreign export cutoff $\varphi_{F,X}^*$, competition λ) are solved using the remaining two cutoff conditions (11,13) and the budget constraint (14) with the exogenous number of firms.

6.   Globalization scenarios

One of the main advantages of the small open economy that I have just described is that it is easily amenable to the analysis of asymmetric trade liberalization. In order to build the intuition for those comparative statics, I begin with a simpler setup where trade runs in a single direction: only imports into or exports out of the small open economy. I will then discuss how the asymmetric trade liberalization scenarios with two-way trade feature very similar predictions. By construction, a scenario with one-way trade applies only to the PE case of an individual sector – and not the GE version that is economy wide. (Clearly, balanced trade cannot be imposed with one-way trade.)

6.1. One-way trade

6.1.1. Imports only

I start by describing the impact of opening the PE version of the closed economy to imports. Firms in the small open economy cannot export (again, this relates to a specific sector), so there are no export profits and no associated export cutoff.[29] The free-entry condition for average profits thus only includes profits from domestic sales; and hence depends only on the domestic cutoff φ^*. Along with its associated cutoff condition (11), those conditions solve for that cutoff φ^* and the domestic competition level λ. Given this competition level, the foreign export cutoff condition (13) then solves for that cutoff $\varphi^*_{F,X}$. In the short run, those two cutoff conditions (11, 13) along with the budget constraint (14) jointly solve for those cutoffs φ^*, $\varphi^*_{F,X}$ and the competition level λ.

Now consider the short-run impact of opening up the closed economy to import competition. The new imports reduce the market share of domestic firms below one (in the domestic consumers' total expenditure). This, in turn, must lead to an increase in competition λ for the domestic economy.[30] The impact of the increase in competition λ on the domestic firms' profit curve is shown in figure 3.5 (the change from the solid curve to the dotted one). As depicted in the figure, this increase in competition is then associated with an increase in the domestic cutoff φ^*: the least productive firms are forced to shut-down in the short run.

The solid profit curve in Figure 3.5 represents the domestic firms' profits before opening to imports in the closed economy long run equilibrium. The free-entry condition then holds so that the area below this solid curve (average

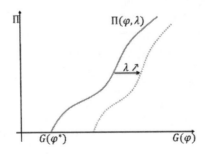

Figure 3.5 Opening the economy to imports

profits) is equal to the sunk entry cost. The short-run response to the import competition (dotted curve) clearly violates free-entry as the average profits are driven down. In the long run, this leads to reduced entry, which then results in lower competition λ. This process unfolds until the free-entry condition is re-established: the average profits are driven back up to equal the sunk entry cost. As the figure makes clear, this occurs when the increase in competition λ from the short run is fully reversed to its previous long-run competition level: this is the competition level that satisfies free-entry. Another way of seeing this is to note that the same free-entry and cutoff profit condition for domestic production φ^* hold in both the closed economy and the open economy with imports. They must then both exhibit the same competition level λ and cutoff φ^*.

Note that the impact of opening the economy to imports is very different than the impact of reducing the size of the domestic economy in terms of the number of consumers L^c. The latter would be associated with lower competition in both the short- and long-run. In both cases, the domestic sales are reduced. But in the case of import competition, a higher level of competition is sustained because the lost domestic sales and associated product variety is compensated from the consumer's perspective with increased imports and the associated imported product variety.

Starting in this economy open to imports, the impact of further import liberalization – a reduction in either the per-unit or fixed import costs τ_F and $f_{F,X}$ – will be similar to the impact of opening up from the closed economy that was just described. In other words, there are no discontinuities for the impact of lower import costs, starting with a limiting case when they are arbitrarily large and imports are non-existent: Decreases in those trade costs lead to increased competition λ and tougher selection in the short run; in the long run, decreases in entry reverse this increase in competition and it returns to its initial level. These effects also apply to a decrease in the relative wage w_F, which also induces an increase in imports – just like reductions in import trade costs.

Thus, we see how asymmetric import trade liberalization generates a force towards increased productivity. In the short run, increased competition from imports generates both extensive margin reallocations (shut-down of least productive firms) as well as intensive margin reallocations towards more productive firms. This second channel is not operative in a model with CES preferences and exogenous markups. The model predicts that these productivity gains are erased in the long run. I will show later that this reversal no longer holds in the GE version featuring an adjustment in the relative wage. Furthermore, even in the PE version, the long-run transition can unfold very slowly implying a substantial net present value effect for the productivity gain.

6.1.2.   *Exports only*

I now describe the impact of opening the small open economy to exports – with no foreign imports. As was previously noted, the exogenous relative wage w_F in this PE version implies that the export cutoff φ_X^* is independently determined by its cutoff condition (10). Given this cutoff, one can then solve for the domestic economy cutoff φ^* and competition level λ using the free-entry condition (8) and domestic cutoff condition (11). In the short run, the budget constraint (14) – which now only includes domestic sales and depends only on the domestic cutoff φ^* and competition λ – replaces the free entry condition; and determines the equilibrium levels of those variables (along with the domestic cutoff condition).

Now consider the impact of opening up the closed economy to exports. The new export opportunities increase the total profits $\Pi(\varphi, \lambda, \lambda_F)$ for high productivity firms with $\varphi \geq \varphi_x^*$ who start exporting. This is shown in Figure 3.6 along with the domestic profits $\Pi_D(\varphi, \lambda)$ (dotted curve) for all producing firms. The export profits $\Pi_X(\varphi, \lambda_F)$ are represented by the difference between the other two profit curves. In the short run, these increased profits do not affect the domestic cutoff φ^* and competition λ, which are still determined by the same budget constraint and domestic cutoff condition.

The dotted profit curve in Figure 3.6 also represents total firm profits before opening to exports in the closed economy long run equilibrium. The free-entry condition then holds so that the area below this dotted curve (average profits) is equal to the sunk entry cost. The short-run response in total profits (solid curve), which includes the new export profits, clearly violates free-entry as the average profits are driven up. In the long run, this leads to increased entry, which then results in increased competition λ. This process unfolds until the free-entry condition is re-established: The average profits are driven back down to equal the sunk entry cost. This is depicted in Figure 3.7, where the areas between the new total profit curve (including export profits) in the solid line and the old domestic profit curve in the dotted line are equal.

Predictions for the impact of further export liberalization – a reduction in either the per-unit or fixed export costs τ and f_X – will be similar to the impact of opening up from the closed economy that was just described. In other words, there are no discontinuities for the impact of lower export costs, starting with a limiting case when they are arbitrarily large and exports are non-existent: Decreases in those trade costs do not affect competition in the domestic market in the short run. Aggregate productivity increases nonetheless as market shares

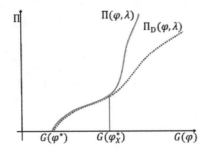

Figure 3.6 Opening the economy to exports

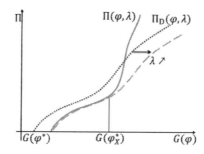

Figure 3.7 Opening the economy to exports in the long run

are reallocated towards more productive firms who export.[31] This is an extensive margin effect driven by changes in the set of markets served by a given firm.

In the long run, decreases in the export costs induce entry into the domestic market, along with increased competition λ and tougher selection. This generates additional extensive margin reallocations (shut-down of least productive firms) as well as new intensive margin reallocations: increased competition shifts domestic sales towards more productive firms. Again, this intensive margin channel is not operative in a model with CES preferences and exogenous markups. All of these effects also apply to an increase in the relative wage w_F, which also induces an increase in export and the associated profit (just like reductions in export trade costs).

6.2. Two-way trade

I now return to the model with two-way trade that was developed in the previous section and describe the impact of asymmetric trade liberalization (for both imports and exports).

6.2.1. Exogenous relative wage (PE)

When the relative wage w_F is fixed, both import and export liberalization will have the same effects in an economy open to two-way trade as in the special case of one-way trade that we just analyzed. The consequences for aggregate productivity – including both extensive and intensive margin reallocations – will therefore also be identical.

Consider first the case of import trade liberalization. Unlike the case of one-way import trade, the export profits will play a role in determining the equilibrium levels of competition λ and production cutoff φ^* in the domestic economy. However, changes in import costs τ_F or $f_{F,X}$ then do not have any impact on those export profits. Thus, the effects of this liberalization will unfold just like the case of one-way trade: Increased imports from Foreign raises competition λ and induces tougher selection in the short run; these effects are then reversed in the long run with decreased entry.

Now consider the case of export trade liberalization. Unlike the case of one-way export trade, the imports from Foreign will play a role in determining the equilibrium levels of competition λ and production cutoff φ^* in the domestic economy. In the short run, however, changes in export costs τ or f_X will have no impact on those imports from Foreign – because those trade costs do not affect the competition level λ in the domestic economy. The lower export costs induce higher export profits for domestic firms and the entry of new exporters (lower export cutoff φ_X^*), but this only feeds back into the determination of the equilibrium competition level λ in the domestic economy in the long run. The increased export profits then induce increased entry into the domestic economy, raising competition λ and generating tougher selection (higher cutoff φ^*). This increase in competition λ then induces a decrease in foreign imports and fewer foreign exporters (higher cutoff $\varphi_{F,X}^*$). However, there is no feedback from those reduced imports to the determination of the competition level λ in the long run: that level is determined by the free-entry (8) and cutoff profit (11) conditions.[32]

6.2.2. Endogenous relative wage (GE)

As discussed in the previous section, the relative wage w_F connects all but one of the equilibrium conditions, and these can no longer be solved sequentially as was done for the PE version in the long run. Although this makes a formal solving of the full equilibrium cumbersome, the direction of the comparative statics in response to asymmetric trade liberalization are nonetheless straightforward – because the direction of change for the relative wage is known in these cases. This relative wage must adjust to rebalance trade following an asymmetric liberalization. If imports are liberalized (which induces an increase in imports and no change in exports for the domestic economy at a constant relative wage), then the relative wage w_F must increase in order to rebalance trade. When exports are liberalized (which induces an increase in exports and a decrease in imports for the domestic economy at a constant relative wage), then the relative wage w_F must decrease in order to rebalance trade.

Consider first the case of import liberalization. At a constant relative wage w_F, the small open economy returns to a long-run equilibrium with the same competition level λ and domestic cutoff φ^* (see previous subsection). However, this leads to a (negative) trade imbalance and an ensuing increase in the relative wage w_F. This relative wage adjustment increases export profits for the domestic firms, and induces similar effects to a decrease in export costs (as was previously discussed). Relative to the long-run equilibrium with a constant relative wage, this implies higher domestic entry associated with increased competition λ and tougher selection (higher production cutoff φ^*). Since import liberalization does not affect the equilibrium in the long run at a given relative wage, the additional relative wage adjustment in GE must therefore induce increases in competition and tougher selection in response to import liberalization in the long run.

Consider now the case of export liberalization. At a constant relative wage w_F, the increased export profits generate additional entry in the domestic economy and tougher competition and selection. This leads to a (positive) trade imbalance and an ensuing decrease in the relative wage w_F. This decrease in the relative wage partially offsets the increase in export profits (for any given firm); it also induces an increase in imports from foreign (and new foreign exporters). These effects dampen – but cannot overturn – the entry response into the domestic economy. Therefore, the same qualitative predictions hold as with the case of an exogenous relative wage in PE: Increased export liberalization leads to tougher competition and selection in the domestic market (as well as increased exports and new exporters).

Thus, we have just seen how both import and export trade liberalization lead to tougher competition and selection in the small open economy; and higher export profits and new domestic exporters. This involves some extensive margin reallocations towards more productive producers: the exit of the least productive firms and reallocations towards more productive exporters. These effects would all be present in a model with CES preferences and exogenous markups.[33] However, the current model with endogenous markups also features additional intensive margin reallocations towards more productive producers – driven by the increase in competition in the domestic market. Those intensive margin reallocations further contribute to an aggregate productivity increase in response to asymmetric trade liberalization in either direction.

7.   Conclusion

I have just developed a simple model of firm heterogeneity with endogenous markups. Those endogenous markups stem from preferences that feature variable elasticities of substitution. These preferences are left un-parametrized within a broad class that generates empirical predictions for markups that are consistent with a large set of established empirical patterns. On the production side, the shape of the productivity distribution for firms is also left un-parametrized. By appealing to the concept of a small open economy, I have shown how comparative statics for the impact of asymmetric trade liberalization can be easily obtained without imposing any further parametric assumptions. Relative to a model with constant elasticities (CES) and exogenous markups, the current model highlights how trade liberalization – in either direction – induces intensive margin reallocations towards more productive producers that reenforce the extensive margin reallocations that are stressed by models with exogenous markups (because they do not feature intensive margin reallocations). Both of these reallocation margins generate aggregate productivity gains in response to asymmetric trade liberalization – especially when relative wage responses are incorporated. The predictions for the impact of trade liberalization are decomposed into a short-run response and then a long-run version that further incorporates the response of entry and potentially changes in relative wages induces by trade imbalances.

Notes

Acknowledgement: I thank Xiang Ding for superb research assistance, and Gene Grossman and Lili Yan Ing for their comments and feedback.

1 Demidova and Rodríguez-Clare (2013) show how to extend the standard competitive version of a small open economy to the case of product differentiation and imperfect competition with heterogeneous producers. This is the same version that is applied here.

2 See the evidence reviewed in De Loecker and Goldberg (2014), Burstein and Gopinath (2014).

3 See Melitz and Redding (2014) for a survey.

4 In those models with constant markups and CES preferences, the relative market share of two firms in any market is determined by the productivity ratio between those two firms. Mayer et al. (2016) reviews this evidence and also provides some additional empirical support for intensive margin product reallocation by French firms.

5 Dhingra and Morrow (2018) analyze the efficiency properties of a monopolistic competition equilibrium with similar additively separable preferences. They show how the new intensive margin reallocations induced by the endogenous markups generate an additional channel for the gains from trade (increased market size).

6 The closed economy is a simplified version of the model developed in Mayer et al. (2016) without multi-product firms; it is also very similar to the model developed by Zhelobodko et al. (2012).

7 In the closed economy, this is equivalent to normalizing the wage and per-consumer expenditure to 1. In the open economy, I will introduce a relative wage across countries.

8 I will be using additively separable preferences that are non-homothetic. Thus, changes in consumer income will have different effects than changes in the number of consumers L^c. I focus on this functional form for tractability and do not wish to emphasize its properties for income elasticities. As summarized in Deaton and Muellbauer (1980, chapter 5, section 3, pp. 138–140), additively separable preference imply a specific relationship between price and income elasticities that does not fit empirical consumption patterns well. I emphasize the properties of demand for those price elasticities. Thus, I analyze changes in the number of consumers L^c holding their income fixed. This is akin to indexing the preferences to a given reference income level.

9 Note that the symmetric representation for these preferences assumes that these quantity units have been implicitly normalized to equate utility (and hence adjusted for quality); these quantity units should therefore not be interpreted as physical units for heterogeneous goods.

10 Note that $\phi(q_i;\lambda) = p(q_i;\lambda)[1 - \varepsilon_p(q_i)]$.

11 In the case of CES preferences, the marginal utility of income λ is an inverse monotone function of the CES price index.

12 This assumption of infinite support is made for simplicity only to rule out the possibility of an equilibrium without any firm selection.

13 I leave the concept of a physical unit of the product undefined. The units for the product are the ones that equate utility in the consumer's eye based on the symmetric preferences. Thus, higher productivity can also represent the production of a good with more utility units per worker.

14 This sector-level adjustment for labor supply is very similar to the case of CES product differentiation within sectors and Cobb-Douglas preferences across sectors. In the latter case, the sector's labor supply adjusts so that it is equal (as a fraction of the aggregate labor endowment) to the exogenous Cobb-Douglas expenditure share for the sector. See Melitz and Redding (2014) for an example of those preferences with firm heterogeneity.

15 Recall that firm output per consumer $q(\varphi, \lambda)$ is decreasing in competition λ.

16 Marshall's First Law of Demand is that it is downward sloping; this too can be violated with rational utility maximizing consumers.

17 Several other terms have been used to describe MSLD demand in the literature on monopolistic competition with endogenous markups. Zhelobodko et al. (2012) describe those preferences as exhibiting increasing "relative love of variety" (RLV); Mrázová and Neary describe this as the case of "sub-convex" demand; and Bertoletti and Epifani (2014) use the term "decreasing elasticity of substitution."

18 It is the key characteristic of the demand systems analyzed by Spearot (2013), Novy (2013), and Arkolakis et al. (2018) in order to explain the empirical variations in the trade elasticity (at the intensive product margin).

19 $u(q_i)$ quadratic, leading to linear demand $p(q_i)$ is a simple functional form satisfying MSLD' (and hence MSLD).

20 Mayer et al. (2016) reviews this evidence and also provides some additional empirical support for MSLD' based on the pattern of intensive margin product reallocation for French firms.

21 Dhingra and Morrow (2018) show how these productivity gains induced by both intensive and extensive margin reallocations under endogenous markups generate additional welfare gains – over and above the standard channels for welfare gains under exogenous markups.

22 Assume that competition λ were to *decrease* following an increase in market size L^c. Then, from (7), the export cutoff φ^* must decrease. This would then violate the budget constraint (9) as spending must then rise. So competition λ must increase; and given this, the cutoff φ^* must decrease to satisfy the budget constraint (9).

23 One can choose the firm at the intersection of the two curves as the reference firm to show this directly.

24 See Melitz (2003) and Melitz and Redding (2014) for a more detailed discussion of the equilibrium with CES preferences.

25 In other words, the same per-consumer performance functions $\pi(\varphi, \lambda)$, $q(\varphi, \lambda)$ and $r(\varphi, \lambda)$ apply to both the domestic and foreign economy.

26 Note that the productivity shifter $w_F \tau^{-1}$ in the operating profit function represents the unit-cost differential between a Foreign and domestic firm with productivity φ.

27 If this were not the case, we would then need to account for the overhead production cost – a portion of the fixed cost f – into the fixed export cost f_X and remove that portion from the fixed cost of serving the domestic market f.

28 This is identical to assuming an exogenous foreign wage level and an endogenous domestic wage. If we pick the foreign wage as numeraire, then the domestic wage would be $1/w_F$.

29 Alternatively, one can think of this as a case where the export costs and foreign competition level λ_F are such that no domestic firms find it profitable to export.

30 This can be shown by contradiction. A (weak) decrease in competition λ, given the cutoff conditions for domestic sales and foreign export sales would necessarily violate the budget constraint (14).

31 If only the fixed export costs f_X are reduced, then the market share of existing exporters does not change. Only the new exporters expand their market share. The impact on aggregate productivity will nonetheless be positive so long as those new exporters are more productive than the industry average: $\varphi_X^* > \Phi$.

32 Only equilibrium entry into the domestic market is affected by those reduced imports in the long run (given the budget constraint).

33 Demidova and Rodríguez-Clare (2013) develop such a model with CES preferences for a small open economy (in GE with a relative wage adjustment to balance trade). The predictions for the relative wage change and all the cutoffs are identical to the model developed here.

References

Arkolakis, C., Costinot, A., Donaldson, D., and Rodríguez-Clare, A. (2018). *The Elusive Pro-Competitive Effects of Trade: The Review of Economic Studies*, forthcoming.

Bertoletti, P. and Epifani, P. (2014). Monopolistic Competition: CES Redux? *Journal of International Economics*, 93(2): 227–238.

Burstein, A. and Gopinath, G. (2014). International Prices and Exchange Rates. In Gita Gopinath, Elhanan Helpman and Kenneth Rogoff, editors, *Handbook of International Economics*, Volume 4, pages 391–451. Amsterdam: Elsevier.

Deaton, A. and Muellbauer, J. (1980). *Economics and Consumer Behavior*. New York: Cambridge University Press.

De Loecker, J. and Goldberg, P. K. (2014). Firm Performance in a Global Market. *Annual Review of Economics*, 6(1): 201–227.

Demidova, S. and Rodríguez-Clare, A. (2013). The Simple Analytics of the Melitz Model in a Small Economy. *Journal of International Economics*, 90(2): 266–272.

Dhingra, S. and Morrow, J. (2018). Monopolistic Competition and Optimum Product Diversity Under Firm Heterogeneity. *Journal of Political Economy*, forthcoming.

Krugman, P. R. (1979). Increasing Returns, Monopolistic Competition and International Trade. *Journal of International Economics*, 9(4): 469–479.

Marshall, A. (1890). *The Principles of Economics*. London: Macmillan.

Mayer, T., Melitz, M. J., and Ottaviano, G. I. P. (2016). Product Mix and Firm Productivity Responses to Trade Competition. Working Paper 22433, National Bureau of Economic Research.

Melitz, M. J. (2003). The Impact of Trade on Intra-Industry Reallocations and Aggregate Industry Productivity. *Econometrica*, 71(6): 1695–1725.

Melitz, M. J. and Redding, S. J. (2014). Heterogeneous Firms and Trade. In Gita Gopinath, Elhanan Helpman and Kenneth Rogoff, editors, *Handbook of International Economics*, Volume 4, pages 1–54. Amsterdam: Elsevier.

Mrazova, M. and Neary, J. P. (2017). Not So Demanding: Demand Structure and Firm Behavior. *American Economic Review*, 107(12): 3835–3874.

Novy, D. (2013). International Trade Without CES: Estimating Translog Gravity. *Journal of International Economics*, 89(2): 271–282.

Spearot, A. C. (2013). Variable Demand Elasticities and Tariff Liberalization. *Journal of International Economics*, 89(1): 26–41.

Zhelobodko, E., Kokovin, S., Parenti, M., and Thisse, J.-F. (2012). Monopolistic Competition: Beyond the Constant Elasticity of Substitution. *Econometrica*, 80(6): 2765–2784.

4　Trade in goods and trade in services

Jonathan Eaton and Samuel Kortum

1.　Introduction

Structural gravity modeling has advanced substantially in the last two decades. Trade in merchandise, particularly in manufactures, has either explicitly or implicitly inspired most modeling approaches. In fact, manufactures constitute the largest component of trade, but, according to data reported to the Organization for Economic Cooperation and Development (OECD), trade in services has grown enormously in the last several decades, to the point where it now constitutes about a quarter of total trade involving OECD countries. Our goal in this chapter is to examine basic features of services trade and to ask how well current modeling strategies capture these features. We then propose and quantify extensions to a basic structural gravity model that we think incorporate these features. Our extended model allows us to handle goods trade and services trade in an encompassing framework.

Modeling such trade is daunting because traded services include such diverse activities as tourism, financial services, wholesale and retail trade, innovation and artistic creation. In an attempt to systematize thinking, the General Agreement on Trade in Services (GATS) of the World Trade Organization (WTO) classifies services exports into four modes of supply:

> Mode 1 constitutes a cross-border export. The service is provided by resources located in the exporting country and delivered to a consumer in the importing country. An example would be technical help provided by a customer service representative in India to a U.S. household whose computer has been infected by a virus.
> Under mode 2 a person from the importing country travels to the exporting country to consume the service. An example is U.S. college students on spring break traveling to Cancun to buy margaritas at a Mexican bar.
> Under mode 3 the exporter provides a commercial presence in the importer. An example is German technology brought to the BMW plant in Spartanburg, South Carolina.
> Under mode 4 (the opposite of mode 2), a natural person from the exporter travels to the location of the consumer to provide the service. An example is the Rolling Stones visiting the United States on a concert tour.[1]

These different modes have different implications for introducing services trade into a general equilibrium economic model. Much services trade under modes 1, 2 and 4 would appear to resemble trade in merchandise in two respects. For one thing, the consumption of the service by the importer involves the recent or contemporaneous employment of factors in the exporter (e.g., the Mexican bartender serving a drink to the inebriated U.S. student). For another, the exports are rival (only one student can sip the margarita at a time). Under mode 3, however, the consumption of the service could occur much later than its production. The research and development (R&D) investment behind BMW's engineering technology may have occurred years ago. Moreover, BMW could use the same technology in its plant in Germany or in South Africa.

To capture these distinctions we follow Hill (1999) in classifying services exports into two categories, tangible and intangible. Tangible services exports are produced in the exporting country in the same period in which they are consumed in the importing country and they are rival. Intangible services exports could have been produced in the origin long before their use in the destination and are nonrival.

An example illustrating both of these distinctions is that viewers in nearly 200 destinations can simultaneously watch *The Big Sleep* on Netflix, enjoying the efforts of Humphrey Bogart, Lauren Bacall, Howard Hawks and William Faulkner from seven decades ago, but generating export revenues for Netflix and Warner Brothers even now. We treat the streaming from the Netflix library as a tangible service export. We treat the rights to the *The Big Sleep* as an intangible asset created by Warner Brothers in 1946. It constitutes an intangible asset that Netflix uses for its tangible services export.

Reinsdorf and Slaughter (2009) and Robbins (2009) discuss the thorny accounting issues that trade in intangibles raises. Until recently, producing intangibles has been treated as an intermediate expense for investors, but in 2013 the U.S. Bureau of Economic Analysis (BEA) began treating research and development spending by firms as equivalent to their investment spending on tangible capital assets.[2] As with physical capital, the effort involved in creating intangible assets represents current economic activity (e.g., composing a rock song is like building a house), whether it's counted as investment or intermediate production, but earning income from the asset may involve little or no current resources (earning royalties when the rock song is played on the radio or renting out the house). One distinction between capital and intangible assets, however, is that physical capital is typically rival while intangible assets are not. In contrast to our *Big Sleep* example, if Lufthansa rents a Boeing 777 from Ireland's GE Capital Aviation Services, that airplane is not available for Air Canada. Another distinction in the national accounts is that, while returns to a country's physical and intangible capital used abroad contribute to its GNP, they are part of its GDP only for intangible assets or physical capital that is "moveable," e.g., a French-owned aircraft in Ireland but not a U.K. family's vacation apartment in Torremolinos.

Of course, how we model trade in services relates to how we model the production and consumption of services generally. How to treat tangible services doesn't seem to generate controversy. They're like merchandise. But researchers have taken alternative approaches to intangibles. Corrado et al. (2009), in particular, propose a (closed economy) accounting framework in which intangibles receive the same treatment as physical capital in three respects: (1) investment (whether construction of capital or creation of intangibles) constitutes a contemporaneous contribution to GDP on the production side; (2) earnings on the assets (whether tangible or intangible) constitute a contemporaneous contribution to GDP on the income side; and (3) the accumulation of assets (whether tangible or intangible) constitute a "source of growth" based on the change in the stock of the asset and its share in production.

While the approach we take to intangible assets here is consistent with the first two characteristics, with the third it is not. As Corrado et al. (2009) point out, for the accumulation of intangibles to constitute a source of growth requires that they have a share in the production function just like physical capital, implying rivalry. Hence their respecification of the accounts to include the accumulation of intangible capital as a source of growth substantially reduces the "Solow residual" in growth accounting. In contrast, our approach, in treating intangibles as nonrival, considers the accumulation of intangibles as the source of this residual.[3] In turning to trade in intangibles, McGrattan and Prescott (2010) and Ramondo (2014) follow Corrado et al. (2009) in treating intangibles as rival, in contrast to our approach here.

We begin with an exploration of data on services trade, documenting its growing and differential, importance across countries. In particular, services exports now constitute a third or more of the total exports of goods and services of the United Kingdom and United States, but less than 20 per cent for Germany and Japan. In line with previous studies, we find that a standard gravity formulation with exporter–importer fixed effects captures bilateral trade both in services overall and in eight categories of services, nearly as well as trade in goods, with similar distance elasticities.

We then develop a model of trade in goods and services, where we divide services into a tangible and intangible component. We treat tangible services and merchandise similarly. Absorption is related to current production, and output is rival. We model the output of the intangible services sector as nonrival intangible assets that provide technologies for the future production of goods and tangible services. For producers of tangibles to be able to compensate the original creators of their technology requires that they charge a markup over the cost of tangible inputs. Our market structure is consequently imperfectly competitive. Markups on tangibles thus serve as the source of revenue for the creators of intangible assets.

We implement the model numerically to explore its implications for trade in manufactures, tangible services and intangible assets. The numerical model illustrates, for example, how greater diffusion can benefit all countries, even though it can have negative implications for real wages in some countries.

The next section reviews some basic facts about services trade. In Section 3 we present our model of trade in goods and in services. Section 4 presents some quantitative implications of the model. Section 5 concludes the chapter.

2. Basic facts

According to OECD data, goods continue to dominate services in international trade, but trade in services is growing and for some countries now constitutes a major source of export revenue. Table 4.1 reports services exports (as a share of total exports) and services imports (as a share of total imports) for 20 OECD countries for 1985, 2000 and 2015.[4] Only for Luxembourg in 2000 and in 2015 does services constitute the majority of trade, but the share of services in trade grew in all but a handful of cases. For some large economies, such as the United Kingdom and United States, services exports represent more than a third of the total.[5] But for others, such as Japan and Germany, the services share is less than 20 per cent.

Services trade comprises a wide ranging set of activities. To get a more detailed breakdown of services trade we turn to the World Input-Output Database (WIOD).[6] The WIOD reports annual amounts of production, absorption, and bilateral trade among 43 countries, partitioning economic activity into around 50 sectors. Table 4.2 provides a list of the different subcategories of services in

Table 4.1 Services trade

Country	Services exports (% of total exports)			Services imports (% of total imports)		
	1985	*2000*	*2015*	*1985*	*2000*	*2015*
Australia	16.5	23.0	21.9	23.7	22.0	22.2
Austria	30.8	26.9	29.2	17.0	20.7	24.6
Canada	10.8	12.2	16.3	15.4	15.0	18.8
Denmark	24.6	33.0	38.4	20.3	33.5	39.9
Finland	12.9	14.9	30.3	17.2	23.3	33.5
France	24.4	22.2	28.4	20.7	19.1	28.0
Germany	10.9	13.8	17.3	20.0	23.0	22.4
Greece	26.8	55.9	48.4	11.3	23.1	19.5
Iceland	31.3	37.0	48.3	29.7	31.4	36.4
Israel	33.6	34.4	39.4	24.7	26.4	29.0
Italy	20.4	20.2	17.9	15.5	20.6	20.5
Japan	11.6	12.5	19.6	20.3	25.1	20.3
Korea	15.4	15.2	12.3	11.8	16.8	19.9
Luxembourg	37.2	73.2	85.1	25.4	58.9	82.0
Netherlands	16.2	20.4	22.8	17.5	24.3	27.3
Norway	27.5	23.2	29.3	28.8	31.8	36.7
Sweden	17.5	19.3	32.1	20.0	26.6	31.4
Switzerland	27.9	33.1	28.1	17.9	24.8	27.4
United Kingdom	24.7	30.5	44.2	17.6	23.7	25.9
United States	25.0	27.3	33.9	17.7	15.0	17.9

Notes:
German data before 1991 are estimated based on today's boundaries.
Total trade (exports or imports) designates goods and services.
Source: OECD National Accounts Data (all OECD countries with complete data as of 1985).

Table 4.2 Industry correspondence

Category	Industry description
Omitted	Electricity, gas, steam and air conditioning supply
Omitted	Water collection, treatment and supply
Omitted	Sewerage; waste collection, treatment and disposal activities; materials recovery; remediation activities and other waste management services
Construction	Construction
Wholesale Retail	Wholesale and retail trade and repair of motor vehicles and motorcycles
Wholesale Retail	Wholesale trade, except of motor vehicles and motorcycles
Wholesale Retail	Retail trade, except of motor vehicles and motorcycles
Transportation	Land transport and transport via pipelines
Transportation	Water transport
Transportation	Air transport
Transportation	Warehousing and support activities for transportation
Transportation	Postal and courier activities
Accommodation	Accommodation and food service activities
Communication	Publishing activities
Communication	Motion picture, video and television program production, sound recording and music publishing activities; programming and broadcasting activities
Communication	Telecommunications
Communication	Computer programming, consultancy and related activities; information service activities
Professional	Financial service activities, except insurance and pension funding
Professional	Insurance, reinsurance and pension funding, except compulsory social security
Professional	Activities auxiliary to financial services and insurance activities
Professional	Real estate activities
Professional	Legal and accounting activities; activities of head offices; management consultancy activities
Professional	Architectural and engineering activities; technical testing and analysis
Professional	Scientific research and development
Professional	Advertising and market research
Professional	Other professional, scientific and technical activities; veterinary activities
Administration	Administrative and support service activities
Other	Public administration and defence; compulsory social security
Other	Education
Other	Human health and social work activities
Other	Other service activities
Omitted	Activities of households as employers; undifferentiated goods- and services-producing activities of households for own use
Omitted	Activities of extraterritorial organizations and bodies

the WIOD. For the purposes of our analysis here we aggregate them into eight categories indicated on the first column of the table (with some codes omitted from our categorization).

Table 4.3 provides a breakdown of total services exports into the eight categories for 43 countries in 2010 based on the WIOD. They demonstrate some striking patterns of specialization. For France, 37.6 per cent of services exports are in wholesale and retail trade, while communications constitute 39.6 per cent of India's services exports. While call centers may explain India's revealed comparative advantage in communications, other patterns may reflect differences in how different countries classify different activities.[7]

To what extent does services trade resemble trade in merchandise, for which data have been available much more comprehensively? Let's first gauge the extent to which services are traded across countries compared with merchandise and manufactures. Based on the WIOD for 2010, we calculate, for each sector, the sum of what's traded between countries relative to total world production, which equals total world absorption. Specifically, denoting sales in sector j to destination n from source i as X_{ni}^j, we calculate:

$$O_{ni}^j = \frac{\sum_{i,n,i \neq n} X_{ni}^j}{\sum_{i,n} X_{ni}^j}.$$

The bottom row of Table 4.4a, labeled "off diagonal ratio," reports the results (repeated in Tables 4.4b and 4.4c for convenience) . For goods, what's internationally traded is 21 per cent of total production and the traded share for manufactures is slightly higher. In contrast, the share for total services is only 3 per cent. Only for transportation is the traded share even one third of what it is for all goods or for manufactures.

To the extent that services are traded internationally, do geographic barriers such as distance play the same role in services trade as in merchandise trade? For decades the standard gravity model has been the workhorse tool for describing bilateral trade patterns. We use WIOD data from 2010 to look at patterns of bilateral trade in all goods, manufactures, services and our eight categories of services.[8] We relate destination n's imports from source i in sector j, X_{ni}^j, $n \neq i$, to a fixed effect S_i^j for sector j in source i, to a fixed effect D_n^j for sector j in destination n, and to characteristics connecting origin i and destination n, Our bilateral indicators indexed by k, t_{ni}^k, are the log of the distance between n and i and fixed effects for countries n and i sharing a common language, common border and former colonial connection, all taken from the CEPII website. We estimate three versions of a gravity specification found in the literature.

Table 4.4a reports the results of estimating the equation:

$$\ln(X_{ni}^j) = S_i^j + D_n^j + \sum_k \gamma_k^j t_{ni}^k + \varepsilon_{ni}^j \tag{1}$$

Table 4.3 Services export shares

Country	Code	Construction	Wholesale retail	Transportation	Accomodation	Communication	Professional	Administration	Other
Australia	AUS	1.6	35.6	26.6	6.2	2.3	16.0	4.9	5.6
Austria	AUT	2.2	31.9	21.2	6.4	6.4	16.9	3.4	2.6
Belgium	BEL	4.2	27.3	18.8	1.1	5.7	28.1	4.8	1.6
Bulgaria	BGR	5.6	9.1	29.7	0.6	9.1	20.7	3.8	1.3
Brazil	BRA	2.0	7.2	15.7	2.8	2.6	43.3	14.9	7.0
Canada	CAN	1.5	14.9	15.8	12.1	7.1	18.8	15.2	7.8
Switzerland	CHE	0.2	16.5	10.6	3.8	4.4	50.1	4.1	3.0
China	CHN	0.4	3.0	29.6	2.9	1.4	50.0	–	10.9
Cyprus	CYP	0.8	2.6	56.8	0.2	2.7	26.3	6.6	1.2
Czech Republic	CZE	5.0	9.2	27.5	1.0	14.4	20.7	3.1	2.0
Germany	DEU	1.2	33.1	10.7	2.3	9.2	29.1	4.9	1.7
Denmark	DNK	3.9	27.9	34.8	0.2	5.0	12.5	5.4	3.1
Spain	ESP	2.2	29.6	19.6	9.0	8.6	13.8	8.9	3.0
Estonia	EST	3.5	4.1	44.1	0.3	8.0	15.5	8.4	0.8
Finland	FIN	0.3	7.2	25.7	0.6	7.7	31.2	14.2	5.4
France	FRA	–	37.6	15.6	–	4.8	19.2	15.7	2.8
United Kingdom	GBR	0.2	30.7	4.9	1.4	8.7	32.9	13.2	4.5
Greece	GRC	2.8	3.8	69.6	0.0	5.1	12.5	1.5	1.5
Croatia	HRV	3.3	0.3	28.7	0.2	12.9	31.3	1.8	7.4
Hungary	HUN	1.7	32.4	23.0	1.1	11.8	14.7	8.4	1.2
Indonesia	IDN	1.8	0.0	15.2	18.2	13.0	30.5	10.1	8.9
India	IND	0.2	1.2	4.5		39.6	20.4	–	34.2
Ireland	IRL	0.1	4.7	5.3	1.5	32.1	37.0	16.8	2.5

Italy	ITA	1.4	26.7	17.3	0.1	12.7	21.5	13.5	3.2
Japan	JPN	0.0	5.1	44.1	10.1	2.9	25.0	6.7	4.6
Korea	KOR	0.2	29.0	21.4	1.8	1.9	35.9	5.6	2.7
Lithuania	LTU	1.8	14.3	58.9	1.0	4.5	8.8	1.2	0.9
Luxembourg	LUX	1.8	5.6	3.5	0.1	9.9	70.8	5.7	1.2
Latvia	LVA	3.0	12.7	48.6	0.2	3.8	16.4	5.3	0.7
Mexico	MEX	–	70.5	24.9	–	0.7	3.1	0.0	–
Malta	MLT	0.5	1.9	5.4	0.3	1.6	63.8	4.6	21.4
Netherlands	NLD	1.8	34.7	17.7	0.1	4.0	20.0	14.2	1.4
Norway	NOR	1.6	1.3	27.1	0.1	7.4	38.8	15.0	3.6
Poland	POL	8.5	53.7	14.4	0.1	4.0	12.7	1.1	1.6
Portugal	PRT	3.3	13.8	45.0	4.5	5.8	13.2	6.4	1.3
Romania	ROM	7.1	8.7	46.0	3.7	9.1	12.3	0.9	6.7
Russia	RUS	0.1	45.3	51.3	0.0	0.6	0.0	1.2	0.1
Slovakia	SVK	5.6	35.2	25.5	0.2	6.7	12.7	4.5	3.1
Slovenia	SVN	4.1	7.9	38.7	0.1	8.2	19.9	1.5	1.2
Sweden	SWE	0.8	28.9	26.0	0.1	8.5	22.7	9.0	0.8
Turkey	TUR	9.5	34.3	41.1	0.2	0.8	5.6	4.5	1.5
Taiwan	TWN	0.0	46.8	29.8	3.3	1.3	11.0	3.6	4.0
United States	USA	0.0	7.6	19.5	0.3	15.7	32.0	14.6	1.8

Export share is taken as a share of total export of services.
Source: World Input-Output Tables, 2010.

Table 4.4a Gravity model estimates (ordinary least squares)

Industry	Merchandise	Manufactures	Services	Construction	Wholesale retail	Transportation	Accomodation	Communication	Professional	Administration	Other
	(1)	(2)	(3)	(4)	(5)	(6)	(7)	(8)	(9)	(10)	(11)
Distance (logarithm)	-1.376***	-1.334***	-1.363***	-1.010***	-1.370***	-1.500***	-1.691***	-1.472***	-1.362***	-1.372***	-1.197***
	(-39.69)	(-38.91)	(-26.86)	(-12.83)	(-21.52)	(-22.25)	(-21.88)	(-22.11)	(-19.29)	(-16.30)	(-16.33)
Contiguity	0.336***	0.331***	0.135	0.588**	0.0482	0.130	0.205	0.184	-0.0808	-0.00583	0.315
	(3.84)	(3.83)	(1.06)	(3.00)	(0.30)	(0.76)	(1.06)	(1.09)	(-0.45)	(-0.03)	(1.74)
Common language	0.203*	0.223**	-0.101	-0.0646	0.0614	-0.224	-0.231	-0.222	-0.0533	-0.130	0.0783
	(2.24)	(2.48)	(-0.76)	(-0.31)	(0.37)	(-1.27)	(-1.13)	(-1.28)	(-0.29)	(-0.60)	(0.41)
Common colonizer	1.137***	1.254***	0.867**	0.865	0.620	1.440***	1.637***	-0.155	0.987*	2.411***	0.732
	(5.47)	(6.09)	(2.85)	(1.91)	(1.65)	(3.56)	(3.43)	(-0.39)	(2.33)	(4.55)	(1.70)
Constant	20.64***	19.63***	19.54***	12.27***	18.21***	19.76***	19.58***	17.14***	16.88***	15.49***	14.80***
	(49.30)	(47.43)	(31.90)	(12.94)	(23.76)	(24.28)	(20.99)	(21.33)	(19.81)	(15.30)	(16.73)
Origin fixed effect	Yes	Yes	Yes	Yes	Yes	Yes	Yes	Yes	Yes	Yes	Yes
Destination fixed effect	Yes	Yes	Yes	Yes	Yes	Yes	Yes	Yes	Yes	Yes	Yes
N	1806	1806	1806	1676	1783	1806	1654	1805	1806	1704	1756
Zero trade observation	0	0	0	130	23	0	152	1	0	102	50
R-sq	0.914	0.917	0.875	0.791	0.933	0.740	0.770	0.748	0.741	0.794	0.730
Off diagonal ratio	0.210	0.221	0.03	0.004	0.051	0.086	0.016	0.042	0.032	0.070	0.007

The dependent variable is the logarithm of a destination country's imports from an origin country.

t statistics in parentheses.

* $p < 0.05$

** $p < 0.01$

*** $p < 0.001$

Table 4.4b Gravity model estimates (Poisson pseudo-maximum likelihood)

Industry	Merchandise	Manufactures	Services	Construction	Wholesale retail	Transportation	Accomodation	Communication	Professional	Administration	Other
	(1)	(2)	(3)	(4)	(5)	(6)	(7)	(8)	(9)	(10)	(11)
Distance (logarithm)	-0.885***	-0.872***	-0.639***	-1.153***	-0.817***	-0.747***	-1.130***	-0.762***	-0.452***	-0.495***	-0.450***
	(-25.13)	(-24.44)	(-14.59)	(-6.01)	(-12.60)	(-14.19)	(-11.75)	(-9.45)	(-5.92)	(-2.83)	(-5.26)
Contiguity	0.461***	0.410***	0.0719	-0.0579	0.167	0.167	0.781***	-0.118	0.00228	-0.521	0.817***
	(6.33)	(5.97)	(0.66)	(-0.21)	(1.55)	(1.36)	(3.45)	(-0.69)	(0.01)	(-1.08)	(4.07)
Common Language	0.146	0.222**	0.390**	0.0730	0.501**	0.136	0.0959	0.365*	0.404*	0.475	0.321
	(1.46)	(2.63)	(2.72)	(0.33)	(2.63)	(1.06)	(0.42)	(2.11)	(2.42)	(1.14)	(1.37)
Common colonizer	0.0466	0.149	0.582	1.980***	-0.230	1.056	1.460***	0.531	0.301	1.809	-1.236
	(0.18)	(0.56)	(1.50)	(4.37)	(-0.67)	(1.62)	(3.32)	(0.93)	(0.61)	(1.75)	(-1.31)
Constant	17.08***	15.81***	12.68***	14.66***	13.45***	12.71***	15.70***	10.83***	8.681***	7.526***	8.138***
	(33.40)	(32.79)	(20.66)	(7.55)	(14.86)	(20.63)	(16.12)	(12.25)	(9.02)	(3.82)	(7.40)
Origin fixed effect	Yes	Yes	Yes	Yes	Yes	Yes	Yes	Yes	Yes	Yes	Yes
Destination fixed effect	Yes	Yes	Yes	Yes	Yes	Yes	Yes	Yes	Yes	Yes	Yes
N	1806	1806	1806	1722	1806	1806	1680	1806	1806	1722	1764
Zero trade observation	0	0	0	84	0	0	126	0	0	84	42
R-sq	0.912	0.932	0.806	0.549	0.827	0.746	0.898	0.800	0.731	0.558	0.690
Off diagonal ratio	0.210	0.221	0.03	0.004	0.051	0.086	0.016	0.042	0.032	0.070	0.007

The dependent variable is the level of a destination country's imports from an origin country.

t statistics in parentheses.

* $p < 0.05$

** $p < 0.01$

*** $p < 0.001$

Table 4.4c Gravity model estimates (multinomial pseudo maximum likelihood)

Industry	Merchandise	Manufactures	Services	Construction	Wholesale retail	Transportation	Accomodation	Communication	Professional	Administration	Other
	(1)	(2)	(3)	(4)	(5)	(6)	(7)	(8)	(9)	(10)	(11)
Distance (logarithm)	-1.070***	-1.066***	-0.838***	-0.857***	-1.0006***	-0.922***	-1.273***	-0.788***	-0.788***	-0.591***	-0.193
	(-23.05)	(-23.33)	(-9.28)	(-5.16)	(-9.73)	(-12.10)	(-12.89)	(-8.40)	(-7.85)	(-4.15)	(-1.13)
Contiguity	0.455***	0.430***	0.235	0.530	0.0828	0.466**	0.377*	-0.437	0.00752	-0.457	1.376***
	-5.32	-5.36	-0.89	-2.06	(0.36)	-1.67	-2.33	-2.58	(-0.03)	(-0.80)	-4.51
Common language	0.263*	0.261*	0.0405	0.283	0.537	0.142	0.0648	0.39	-0.232	0.281	0.354
	-2.34	-2.34	(-0.12)	-1.19	-1.41	(-0.90)	(-0.36)	-1.85	(-0.73)	-0.52	-1.16
Common colonizer	0.879**	0.946***	1.644***	1.982***	0.582	2.991***	2.172***	0.543	1.014*	2.292***	0.799
	-3.06	-3.43	-5.57	-4.67	-1.49	-8.24	-3.48	-1	(-0.79)	-4.24	-1.25
Constant	5.086***	4.501***	0.129	-1.64	2.641	2.650**	6.006***	-0.996	-0.927	-2.839	-7.112***
	-9.02	-8.63	-0.12	(-0.87)	-1.84	-2.58	-6.07	(-0.95)	(-0.79)	(-1.61)	(-3.44)
Origin fixed effect	Yes	Yes	Yes	Yes	Yes	Yes	Yes	Yes	Yes	Yes	Yes
Destination fixed effect	Yes	Yes	Yes	Yes	Yes	Yes	Yes	Yes	Yes	Yes	Yes
N	1806	1806	1806	1722	1806	1806	1680	1806	1806	1722	1764
Zero trade observation	0	0	0	130	0	0	152	1	0	102	50
R-sq	0.831	0.852	0.496	0.815	0.526	0.75	0.836	0.639	0.597	0.479	0.881
Off diagonal ratio	0.210	0.221	0.03	0.004	0.051	0.086	0.016	0.042	0.032	0.070	0.007

The dependent variable is the logarithm of a destination country's imports from an origin country.
t statistics in parentheses.
* $p < 0.05$
** $p < 0.01$
***$p < 0.001$

by ordinary least squares (OLS). Here γ_k^j is the coefficient on the relevant bilateral indicator ι_{ni}^k and ε_{ni}^j is an error term reflecting idiosyncratic components of exports from source i to destination n in sector j. With 43 countries there are a total of 1806 ($= 43^2 - 43$) observations of bilateral trade. For several of the services categories we have had to drop observations for which $X_{ni}^j = 0$, reducing the number of observations accordingly (as reported in the row labeled "N").

Note first that the coefficients on distance are very similar for all goods, manufactures and services. Trade decays with distance with an elasticity around 1.33 to 1.38. Somewhat surprisingly, services appear slightly less sensitive to the trading partners' sharing a common border or language.

Note also that, with the exception of wholesale and retail trade, gravity is less robust for services. The R^2's for goods and manufactures are solidly above 0.9 but with services dip as low as 0.73. But for services as a whole the R^2 is 0.875. The overall picture is that gravity plays nearly as strong a role in services trade as it does in goods trade.

To avoid the loss of information in removing observations of zero trade in OLS estimation, Santos Silva and Tenreyro (2006) propose estimating the gravity equation:

$$X_{ni}^j = \exp\left(S_i^j + D_n^j + \sum_k \gamma_k^j \iota_{ni}^k \right) + \varepsilon_{ni}^j \tag{2}$$

by Poisson pseudo-maximum likelihood (PPML). Table 4.4b reports the results of applying this estimation strategy to our data. Some observations still have to be dropped (in increments of 42) if a country doesn't report any exports or any imports in some category (which prevents estimation of the corresponding exporter or importer fixed effect).

Eaton et al. (2013), henceforth EKS, derive a theory of zeros in the trade data due to a finite number of firms. They propose estimating the gravity equation:

$$\frac{X_{ni}^j}{X_n^j} = \exp\left(S_i^j + D_n^j + \sum_k \gamma_k^j \iota_{ni}^k \right) + \varepsilon_{ni}^j \tag{3}$$

by multinomial pseudo maximum likelihood (MPML). Table 4.4c presents the results of applying this estimation strategy to our data.

In almost all sectors the distance elasticities are lower using PPML and somewhere in between using MPML. Otherwise the results are very similar.

Despite the lower overall tradability of services, as we saw in Table 4.1, services account for a large share of exports from certain countries (related to the large share of services in their GDP). To explore relative specialization in services versus manufactures Figures 4.1 to 4.3 report the exporter fixed effects from our gravity regressions for the 43 countries in our sample (with the relevant

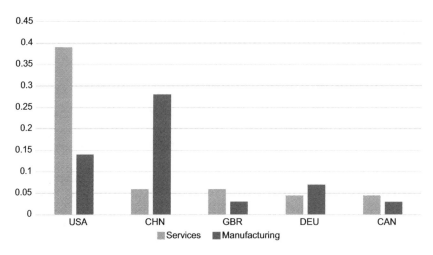

Figure 4.1 Gravity exporter effects (top 5 for services)

three-letter country code indicated in Table 4.3). Specifically, for each country i we calculate:

$$\Psi_i^j = \frac{\exp(S_i^j)}{\sum_{i'=1}^{N} \exp(S_{i'}^j)},$$

for j corresponding to services (S) and to manufactures (M), using the results from OLS estimation (Table 4.4a). To accommodate the vast size differences across countries we organize the countries in descending order of their gravity exporter effects Ψ_i^S into three different charts. Note the different scales across the three figures.

Figure 4.1 reveals a striking degree of specialization across the largest exporters. The United States, United Kingdom and Canada contribute much more to services exports while China and Germany are heavily skewed toward manufactures. The remaining figures reveal similarly strong patterns of specialization for smaller countries.

To summarize, while services are much less traded than goods or manufactures, gravity provides a good statistical description. Exporter fixed effects reflect surprising degrees of specialization. We now turn to a model designed to capture these patterns.

3.   A model of trade in goods and services

We build on Eaton and Kortum (1999), henceforth EK (1999); Eaton and Kortum (2001), henceforth EK (2001); Eaton and Kortum (2002), henceforth EK (2002); Bernard et al. (2003), henceforth BEJK (2003); Eaton and Kortum (2007),

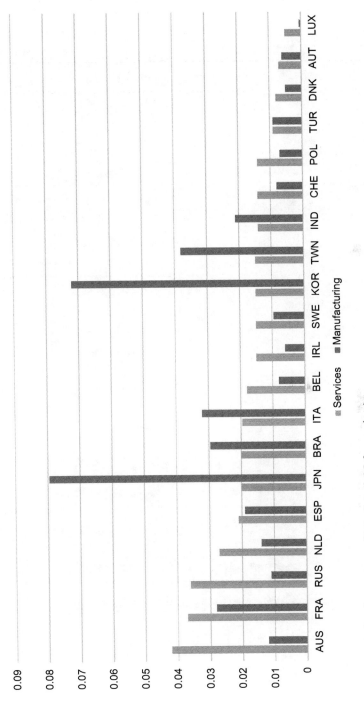

Figure 4.2 Gravity exporter effects (top 6–25 for services)

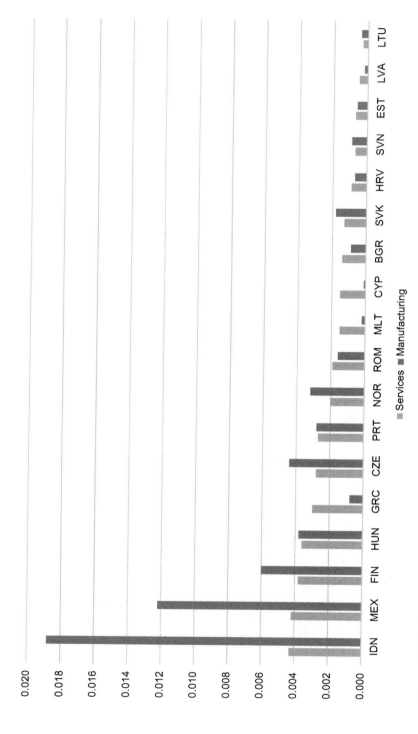

Figure 4.3 Gravity exporter effects (bottom 18 for services)

henceforth EK (2007); Ramondo and Rodríguez-Clare (2013), henceforth RR-C (2013); and Arkolakis et al. (2014), henceforth ARR-CY (2014). As in EK (1999) and EK (2007) intangible ideas emerge from a process of invention. These ideas, each associated with a potential production technology, diffuse over time across countries, with the original inventors earning royalties from the use of their ideas around the world. These royalties constitute earnings on intangibles, a component of services exports. EK (1999) ignored international trade, so that the correlation of productivities around the world implied by the use of the same technology in different countries was irrelevant. EK (2007) assumed that diffusion led to perfect correlation of efficiency across borders, which made their model difficult to apply to multicountry data. RR-C (2013) and ARR-CY (2014) assumed instantaneous diffusion, but allow for positive but imperfect correlation.

Our model of production and trade reflects the fact that services can sometimes take the form of a rival service currently provided by inputs in the selling country to consumers in the buying country. It may also reflect the return on nonrival intangible assets produced in the past by what we will call the "intangibles sector."

We consider an arbitrary integer number N of countries, indexed by i (as innovators), by l (as producers) and by n (as destinations). Each country has three sectors, (tangible) manufactures M, (tangible) services S and intangibles I. In each tangible sector there are a unit continuum of varieties. The output of each tangible sector is a constant elasticity of substitution (CES) aggregate over its varieties, with elasticity of substitution $\sigma^j, j \in \{M, S\}$. Final absorption consists entirely of tangibles, with manufactures having a Cobb-Douglas share α^M and services a share $\alpha^S = 1 - \alpha^M$ in preferences.[9] The intangibles sector is the source of new production technologies, which we turn to next.

3.1. Technologies

Each sector produces output by combining, in a Cobb-Douglas production function, three rival inputs: labor and intermediates from each of the two tangible sectors. For sector $j' \in \{M, S, I\}$, we denote the output elasticity of the sector j intermediate by $\beta^{j'j}, j \in \{M, S\}$. Due to constant returns to scale, the output elasticity of labor is:

$$\beta^{j'L} = 1 - \beta^{j'M} - \beta^{j'S}.$$

Production of each variety in each tangible sector also requires a non-rival input, which we call the production technology. While we treat the output elasticities of rival inputs as common across the continuum of varieties within a tangible sector, the production technology varies across varieties and countries.

A production technology is the output, at some date in the past, of the intangible sector in some country i, which we assume maintains property rights over it. We distinguish a technology by this origin country, by the sector and variety to which it applies, and by whether it's exclusively available in country i or has diffused everywhere.[10] We can ignore the age of a technology, since its value is based on its productive efficiency relative to other available technologies. As this description makes clear, a technology is an intangible asset and, as we describe later, producers will pay for the right to use one.[11]

Consider first technologies for producing varieties in tangible sector j that were developed in country i and remain exclusive to it, so that i is the only possible producer (i.e., $l = i$). These intangibles do not generate services exports for country i since the technology can only be used domestically.

As we show in appendix equation (27), our assumptions about the stochastic arrival of ideas imply that the number of such technologies to produce a variety with efficiency above z is distributed Poisson with parameter:

$$\lambda_i^{j,E}(z) = T_i^{j,E} z^{-\theta^j}. \tag{4}$$

Here the parameter $T_i^{j,E}$ reflects the size of country i's pool of exclusive technology in sector j. The probability distribution of country i's most efficient exclusive technology for a variety in sector j, delivering output per bundle of inputs $Z_i^{j,E}$, is thus:

$$\Pr[Z_i^{j,E} \leq z] = \exp(-T_i^{j,E} z^{-\theta^j}), \tag{5}$$

which is the Poisson probability that no technology better than z is available. Realizations are independent across source countries i for these exclusive technologies.

We now turn to technologies from country i that have diffused everywhere. Since these technologies may be used by producers in other countries, these intangibles can generate services exports for country i.

A diffused technology delivers a different efficiency in each potential production location l, but we allow for that efficiency to be correlated across countries. Furthermore, following RR-C (2013) and Ramondo (2014), we assume that diffusion of a technology from an origin country i to a producer in location l diminishes its productivity there by a factor $h_{li}^j \geq 1$, where we normalize $h_{ii}^j = 1$. These parameters, which we call iceberg transfer costs (for technology), moderate the level of intangible services exports much like iceberg transport costs (introduced in the next section) moderate the level of goods and tangible services exports.

As we show in appendix equation (28), our assumptions about the diffusion of ideas imply that the number of technologies diffused from i for producing a variety with efficiency above z_l in at least one location l is distributed Poisson with parameter:

$$\lambda_i^{j,D}(z_1, z_2, ..., z_N) = T_i^{j,D} \left(\sum_{l=1}^{N} (z_l h_{li})^{-\theta^j/(1-\rho^j)} \right)^{1-\rho^j}. \tag{6}$$

Here $T_i^{j,D}$ reflects the size of country i's pool of diffused ideas in sector j and $\rho^j \in [0, 1)$ reflects the correlation across locations of the efficiency delivered by a diffused technology.

Consider the most efficient such technology from the perspective of a producer of a variety in a given location l, delivering output per bundle of inputs $Z_{li}^{j,D}$. The joint distribution of the $Z_{li}^{j,D}$ across all potential production locations is:

$$\Pr[Z_{1i}^{j,D} \le z_1, Z_{2i}^{j,D} \le z_2, ..., Z_{Ni}^{j,D} \le z_N] \tag{7}$$

$$= \exp\left(-T_i^{j,D}\left(\sum_{l=1}^{N}\left(z_l h_{li}^j\right)^{-\theta^j/(1-\rho^j)}\right)^{1-\rho^j}\right),$$

which is the Poisson probability that no technology better than z_l, for any location l, is available. Realizations are still independent across source countries i, but are correlated across production locations l, with the correlation increasing in ρ^j. For a given set of $\{z_l\}_{l=1}^N$, the probability (7) is increasing in the technology transfer costs, since a larger h_{li}^j reduces the likelihood that a technology from i will yield high efficiency when used in any location $l \ne i$.

3.2. Costs

We denote the price index of tangible sector j output in country l as p_l^j, $j \in \{M, S\}$. With a wage w_l, the cost of a bundle of inputs to produce sector $j' \in \{M, S, I\}$ output in production location l is thus:

$$b_l^{j'} = \left(p_l^M\right)^{\beta^{j'M}}\left(p_l^S\right)^{\beta^{j'S}}\left(w_l\right)^{\beta^{j'L}}.$$

Later, we will connect the price indices p_l^j to these input bundle costs, technologies and market structure. For now, we simply take them as given to focus on unit production costs in locations l, and costs of delivery to a destination n, which inherit a distribution from the technologies underlying these costs.

The unit cost of producing a variety of tangible sector j in country l is b_l^j/Z_l^j, where Z_l^j is the random level of efficiency of the best available technology. We posit an iceberg transport cost $d_{nl}^j \ge 1$ to deliver a unit to n from l. The unit cost of producing a variety of tangible sector j in country l after delivery to destination n is then:

$$C_{nl}^j = \frac{b_l^j d_{nl}^j}{Z_l^j}.$$

For location l to be able to provide the variety at a cost $C_{nl}^j \le c$ thus requires that its efficiency satisfies:

$$Z_l^j \ge \frac{b_l^j d_{nl}^j}{c}. \tag{8}$$

Applying equation (4), the number of exclusive technologies from l that exceed this threshold is distributed Poisson with parameter

$$\lambda_l^{j,E}\left(\frac{b_l^j d_{nl}^j}{c}\right) = T_l^{j,E}\left(b_l^j d_{nl}^j\right)^{-\theta^j} c^{\theta^j}. \tag{9}$$

For a diffused technology that originated in country i to serve destination n at a cost below c its efficiency in at least one production location l must also satisfy (8). From (6), the number of such technologies is distributed Poisson with parameter:

$$\lambda_i^{j,D}\left(\frac{b_1^j d_{n1}^j}{c}, \frac{b_2^j d_{n2}^j}{c}, ..., \frac{b_N^j d_{nN}^j}{c}\right) = T_i^{j,D}\left(\sum_{l=1}^{N} \left(b_l^j d_{nl}^j h_{li}^j\right)^{-\theta^j/(1-\rho^j)}\right)^{1-\rho^j} c^{\theta^j}. \tag{10}$$

Since technologies from different countries, and those that are exclusive and diffused, are all independent of each other, the number of technologies that can provide a sector j variety to destination n at unit cost below c, regardless of source or diffusion status, is distributed Poisson with parameter:

$$\lambda_n^j(c) = \sum_{l=1}^{N} \lambda_l^{j,E}\left(\frac{b_l^j d_{nl}^j}{c}\right) + \sum_{i=1}^{N} \lambda_i^{j,D}\left(\frac{b_1^j d_{n1}^j}{c}, \frac{b_2^j d_{n2}^j}{c}, ..., \frac{b_N^j d_{nN}^j}{c}\right) = \Phi_n^j c^{\theta^j} \tag{11}$$

where:

$$\Phi_n^j = \sum_{l=1}^{N} T_l^{j,E}\left(b_l^j d_{nl}^j\right)^{-\theta^j} + \sum_{i=1}^{N} T_i^{j,D}\left(\sum_{l=1}^{N} \left(b_l^j d_{nl}^j h_{li}^j\right)^{-\theta^j/(1-\rho^j)}\right)^{1-\rho^j}. \tag{12}$$

We can now derive the distribution of the lowest cost of a tangible sector j variety available in country n (produced in any location l using technologies from any source i). The probability that all costs are above c (hence the lowest as well) is the probability that no cost is below c. The distribution of this lowest cost C_n^j is:

$$G_n^j(c) = \Pr[C_n^j \leq c] = 1 - \exp\left(-\Phi_n^j c^{\theta^j}\right), \tag{13}$$

which is 1 minus the Poisson probability that no cost is below c. The distribution of costs in n depends, through Φ_n^j, on all iceberg transport costs into n and on all iceberg transfer costs between every pair of countries.

3.3. Sources of production and technology

We now turn to which location l can serve market n at the lowest cost with a technology originating from i. We start with the probability that a technology originating from i supplies n at the lowest cost.

First consider technology that's exclusive to i, so that $l = i$. The probability that such a technology is lowest cost in supplying n is the ratio of the Poisson parameter (9) to the Poisson parameter (11):

$$\pi_{ni}^{j,E} = \frac{T_i^{j,E}\left(b_i^j d_{ni}^j\right)^{-\theta^j}}{\Phi_n^j}. \tag{14}$$

Note how c cancels. This share is like that in EK (2002), as country i's share depends on its pool of exclusive technology downweighted by its cost of inputs and the iceberg transport cost of delivering tangible goods to country n. The response of the share to these costs is governed by θ^j. The new piece is in the denominator (12), which includes terms capturing the possibility that n is supplied using a technology that is not exclusive to any country.

For technology that's diffused from i, the probability that such a technology is lowest cost in supplying n (from any location l') is the ratio of the Poisson parameter (10) to the Poisson parameter (11):

$$\pi_{n\cdot i}^{j,D} = \frac{T_i^{j,D}\left(\sum_{l'=1}^{N}\left(b_{l'}^j d_{nl'}^j h_{l'i}^j\right)^{-\theta^j/(1-\rho^j)}\right)^{1-\rho^j}}{\Phi_n^j},$$

where the dot in the subscript indicates that the production location l could be anywhere. Here, country i's share (in supplying the technology) depends on its pool of diffused technology downweighted by the iceberg transfer cost of getting the technology from i to any of the potential producing countries l' together with the cost of inputs in l' and the iceberg transport cost of shipping goods from l' to n.

As we show in appendix equation (30), the probability that country l is the supplier, when a technology that diffused from i is used to supply n, is:

$$\pi_{nl|i}^{j,D} = \frac{\left(b_l^j d_{nl}^j h_{li}^j\right)^{-\theta^j/(1-\rho^j)}}{\sum_{l'=1}^{N}\left(b_{l'}^j d_{nl'}^j h_{l'i}^j\right)^{-\theta^j/(1-\rho^j)}},$$

where the vertical bar in the subscript indicates conditioning on a diffused technology from i being used to supply n. In this expression, since each producing country has access to the same technologies that diffuse from i, the shares do not depend on pools of technology. Instead l's share depends on its access to i's diffused technology (as governed by the iceberg transfer cost), its cost of inputs and its access to country n (as governed by the iceberg transport cost). The response of this share to these costs is governed by $\theta^j/(1-\rho^j)$, which is increasing in the correlation parameter ρ^j. If the efficiency in different production locations of the same diffused technology is quite similar (ρ^j near 1), slight differences in input or transport costs across locations will have a large effect on which location ends up producing with such technologies.

The probability that country l supplies n using a technology that diffused from i is the product of the probability that such a technology provides the lowest cost in n and the probability that country l is the lowest cost location for using it, when serving destination n:

$$\pi_{nli}^{j,D} = \pi_{n\cdot i}^{j,D} \cdot \pi_{nl|i}^{j,D} \tag{15}$$

$$= \frac{T_i^{j,D}\left(\sum_{l'=1}^{N}\left(b_{l'}^j d_{nl'}^j h_{l'i}^j\right)^{-\theta^j/(1-\rho^j)}\right)^{1-\rho^j}}{\Phi_n^j} \cdot \frac{\left(b_l^j d_{nl}^j h_{li}^j\right)^{-\theta^j/(1-\rho^j)}}{\sum_{l'=1}^{N}\left(b_{l'}^j d_{nl'}^j h_{l'i}^j\right)^{-\theta^j/(1-\rho^j)}}.$$

Combining (15) and (14), the probability that a variety purchased in n is produced in l using an idea from i is:

$$\pi_{nli}^{j} = \delta_{li}\pi_{ni}^{j,E} + \pi_{nli}^{j,D} \tag{16}$$

where $\delta_{li} = 0$ if $l \neq i$ and $\delta_{li} = 1$ if $l = i$. We now have a full description of how technology from different sources is used in different production locations to serve different markets. Since country n is necessarily supplied (with a variety of tangible sector j) by some country l using a technology from some country i, the probabilities satisfy:

$$\sum_{i=1}^{N} \sum_{l=1}^{N} \pi_{nli}^{j} = 1.$$

3.4.   Market structure and markups

We treat the difference between revenues and costs in using a technology as a return to the creator of the technology, which we refer to as a royalty. Deriving the royalty share of revenues requires our characterizing the distribution of the markups, which we turn to now.

We assume that potential producers of a tangible variety engage in Bertrand competition in each market n where they sell, regardless of whether the buyer is another producer or a household. A result of this competition is that the low-cost producer of a variety serves the market and its price equals either the cost of the second lowest-cost potential supplier of that variety to market n or the monopoly price, whichever is lower.

This market structure leads to random markups $\bar{M}_{n}^{j}$ for a variety of tangible sector j supplied to country n. As we show in appendix equation (31), the distribution of these markups takes the very convenient form of a truncated Pareto distribution:

$$\Pr\left[\bar{M}_{n}^{j} \leq m\right] = \begin{cases} 1 - m^{-\theta^{j}} & 1 \leq m < \bar{m}^{j} \\ 1 & m = \bar{m}^{j} \end{cases},$$

where the truncation point is the monopoly markup:

$$\bar{m}^{j} = \frac{\sigma^{j}}{\sigma^{j} - 1}.$$

This distribution of markups, together with the distribution of costs (13), determines the distribution of tangible sector j prices in country n.

3.5.   The price index

Until this point, our derivations applied to a particular variety (such as the probability π_{nli}^{j} that a variety of tangible sector j is supplied to n by l using a technology from i). In deriving the price index, however, we need to integrate across varieties, so it's convenient to give them an index. Let $P_n^j(\omega)$ denote the price in country n of variety ω in tangible sector j. The price index is thus:

$$p_n^j = \left(\int_0^1 \left[P_n^j(\omega) \right]^{1-\sigma^j} d\omega \right)^{1/(1-\sigma^j)}.$$

By treating the individual prices as random variables, as we show in appendix equation (34), we obtain an expression connecting this price index to the parameter of the cost distribution (12):

$$p_n^j = \gamma^j \left(\Phi_n^j \right)^{-1/\theta^j}, \tag{17}$$

where:

$$\gamma^j = \Gamma \left(\frac{2\theta^j - (\sigma^j - 1)}{\theta^j} \right)^{1/(1-\sigma^j)} \left(1 + \frac{\sigma^j - 1}{\theta^j - (\sigma^j - 1)} \left(\bar{m}^j \right)^{-\theta^j} \right)^{1/(1-\sigma^j)}.$$

The CES parameter σ^j matters (in this model) only through the constant γ^j.

3.6. Royalties

Tangible goods are sold in country n at a markup over the cost of the inputs used to produce them (including any transport cost to deliver them). We interpret the resulting wedge between revenue and tangible cost as the value of the intangible services embodied in country n's absorption. Ultimately, this value of intangible services will flow in the form of royalties to the country whose intangible sector generated the intangible assets.

As we show in appendix equation (35), the value of intangible services $X_n^{j,I}$ embodied in country n's absorption of tangible sector j goods is:

$$X_n^{j,I} = \frac{1}{1 + \theta^j} X_n^j.$$

We return to the trade shares to track how the payments for these intangible services flow as royalties earned by the owners of the intangible assets that generate them.

Since there are a continuum of varieties in each tangible sector, the probability π_{nli}^j that a variety consumed in n was produced in l using a technology from i is also the share of spending on such varieties in n. An implication is that the share of l's production in n's sector j absorption (without regard to the source of the technology i) is:

$$\pi_{nl}^{j,T} = \sum_{i=1}^{N} \pi_{nli}^j, \tag{18}$$

where the T superscript indicates that this term is the share of n's spending on tangible sector j goods imported from country l.

The share of origin i's technologies used in n's sector j absorption (without regard to the production location l) is:

$$\pi_{n \cdot i}^{j,I} = \sum_{l=1}^{N} \pi_{nli}^{j},$$

(19)

where the I superscript indicates that this term is the share of n's absorption of intangible services (embodied in n's spending on tangible sector j) ultimately paid as royalties to country i.

The royalties earned by country i's sector j technologies used for production in l and absorbed in destination n is:

$$X_{nli}^{j,I} = \pi_{nli}^{j} X_{n}^{j,I} = \frac{1}{1+\theta^{j}} \pi_{nli}^{j} X_{n}^{j}.$$

We treat royalty income as collected at the point of production rather than at the point of absorption, so that if a producer in l uses a technology from i to supply a consumer in n, we count i as exporting the intangible to country l not to n. In this case sector j intangible services exports from origin i to location l are:

$$X_{\cdot li}^{j,I} = \sum_{n=1}^{N} X_{nli}^{j,I}.$$

Summing over production locations (including country i itself), royalty income of country i from sector j technologies is:

$$R_{i}^{j} = \sum_{l=1}^{N} X_{\cdot li}^{j,I}.$$

Summing over sectors, country i's total royalty income is:

$$R_{i} = \sum_{j \in \{M,S\}} R_{i}^{j}.$$

(20)

3.7.   *Production and absorption*

We denote the gross output of sector j' in country l as $Y_{l}^{j'}$, $j' \in \{M,S,I\}$. For the two tangible sectors, $j \in \{M, S\}$:

$$Y_{l}^{j} = \sum_{n=1}^{N} \pi_{nl}^{j,T} X_{n}^{j}.$$

Sector j tangible absorption in country n consists of final demand $X_n^{j,F}$ plus intermediate demand, so that total absorption of tangible sector j by country n is:

$$X_n^j = X_n^{j,F} + \beta^{lj} Y_n^I + \sum_{j' \in \{M,S\}} \beta^{j'j} \frac{\theta^{j'}}{1 + \theta^{j'}} Y_n^{j'}.$$

Final demand for sector j output in country n is a share α^j of total final absorption, which itself consists of labor income $w_n L_n$, royalty income R_n from intangibles, less what's invested in intangibles Y_n^I together with any net exports N_n:

$$X_n^{j,F} = \alpha^j \left(w_n L_n + R_n - Y_n^I - N_n \right). \tag{21}$$

Labor income is simply labor's share of total production costs in each sector:

$$w_n L_n = \sum_{j \in \{M,S\}} \beta^{jL} \frac{\theta^j}{1 + \theta^j} Y_n^j + \beta^{IL} Y_n^I.$$

3.8.   Equilibrium

We can combine these various pieces to form three systems of equations. The first system gives absorption of each country's tangibles in each sector given final sectoral demand and trade shares:

$$X_l^j = X_l^{j,F} + \beta^{lj} Y_l^I + \sum_{j' \in \{M,S\}} \beta^{j'j} \frac{\theta^{j'}}{1 + \theta^{j'}} \sum_{n=1}^{N} \pi_{nl}^{j',T} X_n^{j'}. \tag{22}$$

The second system gives labor income in terms of sectoral absorption:

$$w_l L_l = \beta^{IL} Y_l^I + \sum_{j \in \{M,S\}} \beta^{jL} \frac{\theta^j}{1 + \theta^j} \sum_{n=1}^{N} \pi_{nl}^{j,T} X_n^j. \tag{23}$$

Incorporating (21) and (20) into (22) gives:

$$\begin{aligned} X_l^j &= \alpha^j \left(w_l L_l + R_l - Y_l^I - N_l \right) + \beta^{lj} Y_l^I + \sum_{j' \in \{M,S\}} \sum_{n=1}^{N} \beta^{j'j} \frac{\theta^{j'}}{1 + \theta^{j'}} \pi_{nl}^{j',T} X_n^j \\ &= \alpha^j \left(w_l L_l - Y_l^I - N_l \right) + \beta^{lj} Y_l^I \\ &\quad + \sum_{j' \in \{M,S\}} \sum_{n=1}^{N} \left(\alpha^j \frac{1}{1 + \theta^{j'}} \pi_{n,l}^{j',J} + \beta^{j'j} \frac{\theta^{j'}}{1 + \theta^{j'}} \pi_{nl}^{j',T} \right) X_n^{j'}. \end{aligned} \tag{24}$$

Given wages, prices are determined by the third system of equations, for $j \in \{M, S\}$ and $j' \neq j$:

$$
\left(p_n^j\right)^{-\theta^j} = \gamma^j \sum_{l=1}^{N} T_l^{j,E} \left(w_l^{1-\beta^{lj}-\beta^{lj'}} \left(p_l^j\right)^{-\beta^{lj}} \left(p_l^{j'}\right)^{-\beta^{lj'}} d_{nl}^j \right)^{-\theta^j}
$$
$$
+ \gamma^j \sum_{i=1}^{N} T_i^{j,D} \left(\sum_{l=1}^{N} \left(w_l^{1-\beta^{lj}-\beta^{lj'}} \left(p_l^j\right)^{-\beta^{lj}} \left(p_l^{j'}\right)^{-\beta^{lj'}} d_{nl}^j h_{li}^j \right)^{-\theta^j/(1-\rho^j)} \right)^{1-\rho^j}. \quad (25)
$$

Together, the system of equations (23), (24) and (25) determine wages w_l, price indices p_l^j, and final absorption $X_n^{j,T}, j \in \{M, S\}$, given each country's production of intangibles Y_l^I, which we take as exogenous in this static analysis.

3.9.   *International income accounts*

Having laid out the model, we can now discuss how it maps into an international system of accounts with trade in services and intangibles. Doing so will help to connect the model to the data. Two additional definitions will make this task easier.

First, we define the concept of sectoral value added. For the intangible sector, value added is standard:

$$
y_i^I = Y_i^I - \beta^{IM} Y_i^I - \beta^{IS} Y_i^I = \beta^{IL} Y_i^I = w_i L_i^I.
$$

where L_i^j denotes labor employed in sector $j \in \{M, S, I\}$. Since there is no physical capital in the model, and since we have assumed that the intangible sector does not itself use specific technologies to invent new ones, value added reduces to labor income earned in the sector. For the two tangible sectors, $j \in \{M, S\}$, we include intangible inputs in value added since they represent a return on intangible assets:

$$
y_i^j = Y_i^j - \beta^{jM} \frac{\theta^j}{1+\theta^j} Y_i^j - \beta^{jS} \frac{\theta^j}{1+\theta^j} Y_i^j
$$
$$
= \frac{\theta^j}{1+\theta^j} \beta^{jL} Y_i^j + \frac{1}{1+\theta^j} Y_i^j = w_i L_i^j + \frac{1}{1+\theta^j} Y_i^j.
$$

Our treatment of the services of intangibles in value added (for the tangible goods sectors) is parallel to how we would treat physical capital (if it were included in the model) where the value of capital services is part of value added even if the sector rents the capital from elsewhere.

Second, since there is no final demand for intangibles, we define demand for intangibles used in tangible good production in country l as:

$$
X_l^I = \sum_{j \in \{M,S\}} \frac{1}{1+\theta^j} Y_l^j.
$$

To complete the accounts for intangibles, we can define bilateral trade in intangibles by:

$$X_{\cdot li}^{I} = \sum_{j \in \{M,S\}} X_{\cdot li}^{j,I}.$$

Using this expression for bilateral trade, demand for intangibles by country l satisfies:

$$X_{l}^{I} = \sum_{i=1}^{N} X_{\cdot li}^{I},$$

and royalty income of country i satisfies:

$$R_{i} = \sum_{l=1}^{N} X_{\cdot li}^{I}.$$

3.9.1. Income side

We let y_{i} denote GDP of a country i. From the income side, GDP is measured as payments to the two factors, wage income to rival labor and royalty income to non-rival technology assets:

$$y_{i} = w_{i}L_{i}^{I} + w_{i}L_{i}^{M} + w_{i}L_{i}^{S} + R_{i}^{M} + R_{i}^{S}$$

$$= w_{i}L_{i} + R_{i}.$$

3.9.2. Production side

From the production side, we can sum sectoral value added of a country l to get:

$$y_{l}^{I} + y_{l}^{M} + y_{l}^{S} = w_{l}L_{l}^{I} + w_{l}L_{l}^{M} + \frac{1}{1+\theta^{M}}Y_{l}^{M} + w_{l}L_{l}^{S} + \frac{1}{1+\theta^{S}}Y_{l}^{S}$$

$$= w_{l}L_{l} + \frac{1}{1+\theta^{M}}Y_{l}^{M} + \frac{1}{1+\theta^{S}}Y_{l}^{S}$$

$$= w_{l}L_{l} + X_{l}^{I}.$$

We can therefore express GDP in country l as:

$$y_{l} = y_{l}^{I} + y_{l}^{M} + y_{l}^{S} + N_{l}^{I},$$

where the last term is country l's net exports of intangibles:

$$N_l^I = R_l - X_l^I = \sum_{l' \neq l}^{N} X_{\cdot l' l}^I - \sum_{i \neq l}^{N} X_{\cdot li}^I.$$

3.9.3.   Expenditure side

Since we do not model physical investment, spending on investment I_n in country n is equal to its intangible sector output $I_n = Y_n^I$. Spending on consumption (broadly interpreted) is final demand for tangible goods:

$$C_n = \sum_{j \in \{M,S\}} X_n^{j,F}$$

$$= \sum_{j \in \{M,S\}} \left(X_n^j - \beta^{lj} Y_n^I - \beta^{Mj} \frac{\theta^M}{1+\theta^M} Y_n^M - \beta^{Sj} \frac{\theta^S}{1+\theta^S} Y_n^S \right).$$

Thus, from the spending side:

$$C_n + I_n = \sum_{j \in \{M,S\}} \left(X_n^j - \beta^{Mj} \frac{\theta^M}{1+\theta^M} Y_n^M - \beta^{Sj} \frac{\theta^S}{1+\theta^S} Y_n^S \right) + \left(Y_n^I - \beta^{IM} Y_n^I - \beta^{IS} Y_n^I \right)$$

$$= \sum_{j \in \{M,S\}} \left(X_n^j - \beta^{Mj} \frac{\theta^M}{1+\theta^M} Y_n^M - \beta^{Sj} \frac{\theta^S}{1+\theta^S} Y_n^S \right) + y_n^I$$

$$= \sum_{j \in \{M,S\}} \left(X_n^j - Y_n^j + y_n^j \right) + y_n^I$$

$$= y_n^I + y_n^M + y_n^S + \sum_{j \in \{M,S\}} \left(X_n^j - Y_n^j \right).$$

We can therefore express GDP in country n as:

$$y_n = C_n + I_n + R_n - X_n^I + \sum_{j \in \{M,S\}} \left(Y_n^j - X_n^j \right)$$

$$= C_n + I_n + N_n,$$

where, recall, N_n is country n's total net exports across all three sectors.

4.   Quantitative experiments

As a first step in exploring the quantitative implications of this model, we have developed a numerical version of it using Matlab for a world of three hypothetical countries. We label the countries the United States, Germany and China since our parameterization is meant to capture some key features of these economies. The numerical implementation allows us to examine the model's general equilibrium implications for trade in manufactures, tangible services and intangible services

Table 4.5 Parameters common to all countries

	Manufacturing	Services
Theta	4.00	4.00
Rho	0.80	0.40
Alpha	0.30	0.70
Sigma	4.00	4.00
Beta (using sector):		
manufacturing	0.50	0.16
services	0.08	0.30
intangibles	0.08	0.30

Labor is residual share

as well as for sectoral employment, aggregate income and welfare. Of particular interest is understanding how these outcomes vary as we change deep parameters in the model.

Table 4.5 reports our baseline values for parameters that are common across countries (such as θ^j and ρ^j). Table 4.6 reports baseline values for parameters that are country specific (such as L_i and $T_i^{j,E}$). Table 4.7 displays key outcomes generated by our baseline parameters. The first row of the table shows labor income. World income (normalized to 100) serves as our numéraire.

Where possible we have chosen parameter values that are common in the literature (such as $\theta^M = 4$) or that can be calibrated directly to data (such as $\beta^{MS} = 0.16$ based on Input-Output Tables). The relative size of the three economies is largely determined by L_i, with China's labor force twelve times Germany's and four times that of the United States. We have chosen the iceberg costs ($d_{nl}^M = 1.7$ and $d_{nl}^S = 3.0$, for $n \neq l$) so that the model yields plausible outcomes for the fraction of manufacturing output (22 per cent) and services output (3 per cent) that is traded. In some cases the parameters are new to this model (such as $\rho^M = 0.8, h_{li}^M = 1.7, h_{li}^S = 2.0$ for $l \neq i$), and we get little direct guidance from data without a more formal calibration strategy, which is beyond the scope of this chapter.

The technology parameters ($T_i^{j,E}$ and $T_i^{j,D}$) play a central role in our analysis, and the model helps us understand the mapping between them and basic observable outcomes. These parameters vary along three dimensions, which we consider in turn. Along the country dimension, we have chosen the technology parameters to deliver the large real income advantage of the United States over China, while keeping Germany slightly below the level of the United States. We report these outcomes in the second to fourth rows of Table 4.7. Real income adds royalty income to wage income, while real consumption, in turn, subtracts investments in intangibles. Along the industry dimension, we have chosen the technology parameters to deliver Germany and China's specialization in manufacturing relative to the United States. These outcomes appear in the sectoral employment shares in Table 4.7. The final dimension is between exclusive and diffused

Table 4.6 Country-specific parameters

	United States	Germany	China
Labor endowment	3.00	1.00	12.00
Investment in intangibles	1.50	0.20	0.50
Aggregate trade deficit	0.00	0.00	0.00
Exclusive technology:			
manufacturing	10.00	10.00	0.50
services	8.00	5.00	0.25
Diffused technology:			
manufacturing	4.00	1.00	0.25
services	2.00	0.50	0.02
Iceberg costs:			
manufacturing (importer):			
United States	1.00	1.50	1.50
Germany	1.50	1.00	1.50
China	1.50	1.50	1.00
services (importer):			
United States	1.00	4.00	4.00
Germany	4.00	1.00	4.00
China	4.00	4.00	1.00
Diffusion costs:			
manufacturing (receiving):			
United States	1.00	1.70	1.70
Germany	1.70	1.00	1.70
China	1.70	1.70	1.00
services (receiving):			
United States	1.00	2.00	2.00
Germany	2.00	1.00	2.00
China	2.00	2.00	1.00

technology. Here we gave the United States an advantage in diffused technology to capture the large magnitude of U.S. intangible services exports. The outcomes for international trade in Table 4.7 show the United States running a large trade deficit in manufacturing and a large surplus in intangible services.

Having described our baseline, we now consider some numerical experiments. The first moves exclusive U.S. manufacturing technologies to U.S. diffused technologies. Specifically, we hold all other parameters at their baseline values while, for the United States, we lower $T^{M,E}$ from 10 to 0 while raising $T^{M,D}$ from 4 to 14. China is the big beneficiary of this shift, as China's low wage allows it to exploit manufacturing technology originating in the United States. China's real wage increases nearly 20 per cent. The U.S. real wage doesn't fall, and real income actually rises by 3 per cent as royalties rise. While income effects are positive, the US manufacturing sector shrinks dramatically. The manufacturing share of employment falls by 3 percentage points and U.S. exports of manufactures shrivel.

Table 4.7 Baseline outcomes

	United States	*Germany*	*China*
Aggregate labor income	48.9	16.0	35.1
Real income per worker	7.6	6.6	1.6
Real consumption per worker	6.0	6.0	1.4
Real wage	5.1	4.3	1.2
Sectoral employment shares (%):			
manufacturing	17.0	22.0	25.0
services	64.0	70.0	66.0
intangibles	19.0	7.7	8.8
International trade:			
manufacturing:			
imports	8.1	5.3	4.2
exports	4.2	5.0	8.5
tangible services:			
imports	1.0	0.9	0.0
exports	0.2	0.1	1.6
intangible services:			
imports	0.0	0.1	5.9
exports	4.8	1.3	0.0

The correlation of diffused technology ρ is a prominent (yet elusive) parameter in our model. To explore its role, we repeat the first experiment, but now with $\rho^M = 0$ (rather than $\rho^M = 0.8$). In this scenario, diffused technology will have very different realizations depending on where it is put to use in production. With $\rho^M = 0$ we find that U.S. income is even higher and the U.S. manufacturing sector remains more competitive in world markets. China experiences roughly the same increase in its real wage, and Germany's also rises a bit. The lower value of ρ^M raises the benefit of diffusion since ideas experience a greater transformation as they spread. A diffused idea is thus less substitutable across locations.

5.   Conclusion

While we have applied our framework to a hypothetical three-country, three-sector world, the apparatus is flexible enough to deal with an arbitrary number of countries and alternative sectoral breakdowns. We've kept the analysis here static, but activity in the intangibles sector could be tied to the expectation of future royalty earnings as in EK (1999), EK (2001) and EK (2007).

These extensions are conceptually fairly straightforward. A barrier to future quantitative work in these directions is the remaining gap between key concepts in the theory and the data that are reported. The availability of data on services trade has improved dramatically in the last few years, but separating its tangible and intangible components remains a daunting challenge. Overcoming that challenge is essential to understanding the role of creativity in driving growth in the world economy.

Notes

Acknowledgement: We thank Yuta Watabe for excellent research assistance. We thank Costas Arkolakis, Lili Yan Ing and an anonymous reviewer for very helpful comments.

1 According to Reinsdorf and Slaughter (2009), whether a transaction under this fourth mode constitutes a service export depends on the length of stay of the natural person. If she stays over a year she becomes a resident of the destination so her service is considered part of the gross domestic product of the destination.
2 See Santacreu (2016).
3 Corrado et al. (2009) include in their definition of intangible investment both worker training and advertising, which are quantitatively important in the U.S. economy. The assets created by such investments, human capital in the first case and firm goodwill in the second, would seem rival. While we don't model either training or advertising here, we would exclude such investments and subsequent assets from our concept of intangibles. We think of worker training, like education in general, as contributing to the supply of skills to be treated in the accounts accordingly. The goodwill a company creates through advertising, while an asset to the investing firm, is also a liability for its competitors. We treat the net contribution as zero. We have trouble envisioning an economy that could grow simply through the proliferation of ads, unless we take the view that an ad can make a consumer happier with a given physical allocation.
4 We extracted these figures from the OECD National Accounts. The sample are the 20 countries with data going back to 1985. Lipsey (2009) provides a depressing account of myriad conceptional and practical problems associated with the measurement of service trade. In particular he documents how services trade in earlier periods may have been more severely underreported, rendering the apparent rise in services trade illusional. Borga (2009) reports how the United States Bureau of Economic Analysis (BEA) has changed how it measures U.S. trade in three service sectors.
5 Reported figures may significantly understate U.S. service exports. See in particular Mutti and Grubert (2009), Robbins (2009), Moris (2009), McGrattan and Prescott (2010) and Guvenen et al. (2017) . A reason is that U.S. tax policy makes it advantageous for U.S. corporations to shift profits overseas, creating an incentive to underreport exports of intangible services. The U.S. Bureau of Economic Analysis reports U.S. foreign investment receipts of a similar magnitude to U.S. service exports, suggesting a large upper bound on the degree of underreporting.
6 See Timmer et al. (2015) for a description of the data.
7 To quote van der Marel and Shepherd (2013a), "It is well known that services data become increasingly inaccurate as they are disaggregated."
8 We are, of course, not the first to apply gravity analysis to trade in services. Without needing data on bilateral trade flows in services, Jensen and Kletzer (2005) assess the tradability of different service sectors by looking at the concentration of occupations employed extensively in these sectors across U.S. Metropolitan Statistical Areas (inferring that greater concentration is made possible by greater tradability). Lejour and Verheijden (2007) make use of bilateral data on services trade from the Canadian provinces and the European Union to estimate a gravity model for services. Egger et al. (2012) use data from the Organization for Economic Cooperation and Development to estimate a structural gravity model of trade in goods and services. Anderson et al. (2014) compare the role of distance and national borders in trade in goods and services among Canadian provinces and between individual provinces and the United States. Anderson et al. (2016) use OECD data to estimate a

structural gravity equation for 12 individual service sectors. Van der Marel and Shepherd (2013a, 2013b) examine how regulation affects the tradability of services using a dataset developed by Francois and Pindyuk (2013), combining data from Eurostat, the International Monetary Fund (IMF), the OECD and United Nations. Gervais and Jensen (2013) estimate a model of services trade among U.S. states based on differences between demand and supply at different U.S. BEA labor market areas. Miroudot et al. (2016) examine the effect of services trade on measured productivity in services.

9 Pursuing the example above, we treat a current Netflix viewer of the *Big Sleep* as consuming the tangible services of Netflix and Netflix as purchasing the intangible services of Warner Brothers as an input into its streaming services.

10 One can conceive of much more complex patterns of diffusion. For simplicity we stick here with this simple dichotomy.

11 Consider the iPhone. While various rival inputs are used to produce it and deliver it to consumers (production labor, glass, aluminum and employees at the Apple store), much of its value is due to the non-rival intangible assets embodied in it (engineering, software and sleek design). The abstraction of our model is to lump these multiple dimensions of the non-rival inputs into a single intangible that we call the "technology."

12 As discussed in Arkolakis et al. (2014), for $\rho = 0$, an idea provides an efficiency $Q_l > \underline{q}_l$ in only one location l. Everywhere else the efficiency is $\underline{q}_{l'}$.

References

Anderson, James E., Ingo Borcher, Aaditya Mattoo, and Yoto V. Yotov (2016) "Dark Costs, Missing Data: Shedding Some Light on Services Trade," *NBER Working Paper No. 21546*.

Anderson, James E., Catherine A. Milot, and Yoto V. Yotov (2014) "How Much Does Geography Deflect Services Trade," *International Economic Review*, 55: 791–818.

Arkolakis, Costas, Natalia Ramondo, Andrés Rodríguez-Clare, and Stephen Yeaple (2014) "Innovation and Production in the Global Economy," unpublished.

Bernard, Andrew B., Jonathan Eaton, J. Bradford Jensen, and Samuel Kortum (2003) "Plants and Productivity in International Trade," *American Economic Review*, 93: 1268–1290.

Borga, Maria (2009) "Improved Measures of U.S. International Services: The Cases of Insurance, Wholesale and Retail Trade, and Financial Services," in *International Trade in Services and Intangibles in the Era of Globalization, Studies in Income and Wealth Volume 29*, edited by Marshall Reinsdorf and Matthew J. Slaughter. Chicago: The University of Chicago Press.

CEPII (2017) Geography Database (website).

Corrado, Carol, Charles Hulten, and Daniel Sichel (2009) "Intangible Capital and U.S. Economic Growth," *Review of Income and Wealth*, 55(3): 661–685.

Eaton, Jonathan and Samuel Kortum (1999) "International Technology Diffusion: Theory and Measurement," *International Economic Review*, 40: 537–570.

Eaton, Jonathan and Samuel Kortum (2001) "Technology, Trade and Growth: A Unified Framework," *European Economic Review: Papers and Proceedings*, 45: 742–755.

Eaton, Jonathan and Samuel Kortum (2002) "Technology, Geography, and Trade," *Econometrica*, 70: 1741–1779.

Eaton, Jonathan and Samuel Kortum (2007) "Innovation, Diffusion, and Trade," in *Entrepreneurship, Innovation and the Growth Mechanism of the Free-Enterprise Economies*, edited by Eytan Sheshinski, Robert J. Strom and William J. Baumol. Princeton: Princeton University Press.

Eaton, Jonathan, Samuel Kortum, and Sebastian Sotelo (2013) "International Trade: Linking Micro and Macro," in *Advances in Economics and Econometrics, Volume II*, edited by Daron Acemoglu, Manuel Arellano and Eddie Dekel. Cambridge: Cambridge University Press, 329–372.

Egger, Peter, Mario Larch, and Kevin E. Staub (2012) "Trade Preferences and Bilateral Trade in Goods and Services: A Structural Approach," *CEPR Discussion Paper No. 9051*.

Francois, Joseph and Olga Pindyuk (2013) "Consolidated Data on International Trade in Services v8.7," *IIDE Discussion Paper 20130101*.

Gervais, Antoine and J. Bradford Jensen (2013) "The Tradability of Services: Geographic Concentration and Trade Costs," *NBER Working Paper 19759*.

Guvenen, Fatih, Raymond Mataloni, Dylan Rassier, and Kim Ruhl (2017) "Offshore Profit Shifting and Domestic Productivity Measurement," *NBER Working Paper 23324*.

Hill, Peter (1999) "Tangibles, Intangibles and Services: A New Taxonomy for the Classification of Output," *Canadian Journal of Economics*, 32: 426–446.

Jensen, J. Bradford and Lori G. Kletzer (2005) "Tradable Services: Understanding the Scope and Impact of Services Offshoring," *Brookings Trade Forum*, 75–133.

Lejour, Arjan and Jan-Willem de Paiva Verheijden (2007) "The Tradability of Services Within Canada and the European Union," *The Services Industry Journal*, 27: 389–409.

Lipsey, Robert E. (2009) "Measuring International Trade in Services," in *International Trade in Services and Intangibles in the Era of Globalization, Studies in Income and Wealth Volume 29*, edited by Marshall Reinsdorf and Matthew J. Slaughter. Chicago: The University of Chicago Press.

McGrattan, Ellen and Edward Prescott (2010) "Technology Capital and the U.S. Current Account," *American Economic Review*, 100(4): 1493–1522.

Miroudot, Sebastien, Jehan Sauvage, and Ben Shepherd (2016) "Trade Costs and Productivity in Services," *Economic Letters*, 114: 36–38.

Moris, Francisco (2009) "R&D Exports and Imports: New Data and Methodological Issues," in *International Trade in Services and Intangibles in the Era of Globalization, Studies in Income and Wealth Volume 29*, edited by Marshall Reinsdorf and Matthew J. Slaughter. Chicago: The University of Chicago Press.

Mutti, John and Harry Grubert (2009) "The Effect of Taxes on Royalties and the Migration of Intangible Assets Abroad," in *International Trade in Services and Intangibles in the Era of Globalization, Studies in Income and Wealth Volume 29*, edited by Marshall Reinsdorf and Matthew J. Slaughter. Chicago: The University of Chicago Press.

Ramondo, Natalia (2014) "A Quantitative Approach to Multinational Production," *Journal of International Economics*, 93: 108–122.

Ramondo, Natalia and Andrés Rodríguez-Clare (2013) "Trade, Multinational Production and the Gains From Openness," *Journal of Political Economy*, 121: 273–322.

Reinsdorf, Marshall and Matthew Slaughter (2009) "Introduction," in *International Trade in Services and Intangibles in the Era of Globalization, Studies in Income and Wealth Volume 29*, edited by Marshall Reinsdorf and Matthew J. Slaughter. Chicago: The University of Chicago Press.

Robbins, Carol A. (2009) "Measuring Payments for the Supply and Use of Intellectual Property," in *International Trade in Services and Intangibles in the Era of Globalization, Studies in Income and Wealth Volume 29*, edited by Marshall Reinsdorf and Matthew J. Slaughter. Chicago: The University of Chicago Press.

Santacreu, Ana Maria (2016) "Impact of Including R&D in GDP," *On the Economy Blog*, Federal Reserve Bank of St. Louis.

Santos Silva, J.M.C. and Silvana Tenreyro (2006) "The Log of Gravity," *The Review of Economics and Statistics*, 88: 641–658.

Timmer, Marcel, Hendrikus Dietzenbacher, Bart Los, Robert Stehrer, and Gaaitzen de Vries (2015), "An Illustrated User Guide to the World Input-Output Database: The Case of Global Automotive Production," *Review of International Economics*, 23: 575–605.

van der Marel, Erik and Ben Shepherd (2013a) "International Tradability Indices for Services," *Policy Research Working Paper No. 6712*, International Trade Unit, The World Bank.

van der Marel, Erik and Ben Shepherd (2013b) "Services Trade, Regulation and Regional Integration: Evidence From Sectoral Data," *The World Economy*, 36: 1393–1405.

Appendix A

Deriving the efficiency distributions

Here we derive the distributions of efficiency posited in the text from more primitive assumptions about the discovery and diffusion of ideas, extending the model in EK (2001) to incorporate technology diffusion.

Creators in country i generate ideas about how to produce some variety in some sector $j \in \{M, S\}$ at different locations l in the world. By date t the number of ideas originating in country i for a variety in sector j is distributed Poisson with parameter $\bar{a}T^j_{i,t}$. In what follows we consider a particular variety within a particular sector j at a particular date t and, for parsimony, drop the j superscript and t subscript.

Once diffused, an idea from origin i enables the variety to be produced in different countries l with efficiencies Q_{li}, for $l = 1, \ldots, N$. As in Arkolakis et al. (2014), we assume that these efficiencies are realizations from the joint distribution:

$$\Pr[Q_{1i} \le q_1, Q_{2i} \le q_2, \ldots, Q_{Ni} \le q_N] = F^D_i(q_1, q_2, \ldots, q_N)$$

$$= 1 - \bar{a}^{-1} \left(\sum_{l=1}^{N} (q_l h_{li})^{-\theta/(1-\rho)} \right)^{1-\rho}, \tag{26}$$

where $\rho \in [0, 1)$ and $h_{li} \ge 1$ with $h_{ii} = 1$. To insure that this distribution is nonnegative we assume that it is defined only for

$$q_l \ge \underline{q}_{li} = \underline{q}/h_{li}$$

where:

$$\underline{q} = \bar{a}^{-1/\theta} N^{(1-\rho)/\theta}.$$

Note that:

$$F^D_i(\underline{q}_{1i}, \underline{q}_{2i}, \ldots, \underline{q}_{Ni}) = 0.$$

Sending $q_{l'} \to \infty$, $l' \ne l$, the marginal distribution is:

$$F^D_{li}(q_l) = 1 - \bar{a}^{-1}(q_l h_{li})^{-\theta}.$$

Evaluating the marginal distribution at the lower bound:

$$F_{li}^{D}(\underline{q}_{li}) = 1 - N^{-(1-\rho)},$$

implying a mass at the lower bound of the marginal distribution.[12]

Upon its creation, an idea may not be immediately available for production. The technology diffuses over time to ever greater sets of countries. While the dynamics of diffusion could be quite general, for our purposes here we've limited diffusion to a one-step process. An idea is initially "exclusive" and available only in the country where it originated. Then, at some random date, it "diffuses," becoming available to all countries. The date at which it diffuses is independent of the values of the Q_l's the idea delivers. Hence the distribution of the Q_l's is the same regardless of whether the idea has diffused or not.

Say that the probability that an idea from i has diffused is p_i. Defining $T_i^{D} = p_i T_i$ and $T_i^{E} = (1 - p_i)T_i$, it follows that the number of ideas that have diffused is distributed Poisson with parameter $\bar{a}T_i^{D}$ while the number that remain exclusive is distributed Poisson with parameter $\bar{a}T_i^{E}$. The efficiencies of these two sets of ideas are independent of one another.

An idea from i that's diffused has an efficiency distribution $F_i^{D}(q_1, q_2, \ldots, q_N)$ given by (26). An idea from country i that has not diffused, since it is only available for use in country i, has an efficiency distribution derived from (26) by letting $q_l \to \infty$ for all $l \neq i$; that is:

$$F_i^{E}(q) = 1 - \bar{a}^{-1}q^{-\theta},$$

for $q \geq \bar{a}^{-1/\theta}$.

The number of exclusive ideas from i with efficiency above z is distributed Poisson with parameter:

$$\bar{a}T_i^{E}\left[1 - F_i^{E}(z)\right] = T_i^{E}z^{-\theta}, \tag{27}$$

so that $\bar{a}$ cancels out. By letting $\bar{a} \to \infty$ we get full support $z \geq 0$.

We can follow a similar strategy to derive the joint distribution of the best ideas that have diffused from country i. With probability $1 - F_i^{D}(z_1, z_2, \ldots, z_N)$ an idea from i has efficiency exceeding $z_1, z_2, \ldots, z_N$ in at least one location l. Hence the number of ideas from i that provide efficiencies above $z_1, z_2, \ldots, z_N$ in at least one location is distributed Poisson with parameter:

$$\bar{a}T_i^{D}\left[1 - F_i^{D}(z_1, z_2, \ldots, z_N)\right] = T_i^{D}\left(\sum_{l=1}^{N}\left(z_l h_{li}\right)^{-\theta/(1-\rho)}\right)^{1-\rho}. \tag{28}$$

Once again $\bar{a}$ drops out. Again, by letting $\bar{a} \to \infty$ this distribution applies to the positive orthant.

Appendix B

Deriving conditional probabilities

If country n obtains a variety of tangible sector j produced using technology that diffused from country i, what is the probability that country l is the producer of this variety for country n? Since different countries l' may find the very same technique to be the lowest cost, our approach in the text, which relied on independent Poisson distributions, won't work in this context. Instead, this derivation starts from the joint complementary distribution of costs across producing countries l when using technology that's diffused from i.

Denote the lowest cost, using a technology diffused from i to serve n from location l, by $C_{nli}^{j,D}$. From (7), their joint complementary distribution across production locations l is:

$$
\begin{aligned}
\bar{G}_{n \cdot i}^{j,D}(c_1, c_2, \ldots c_N) &= \Pr[C_{n1i}^{j,D} > c_1, C_{n2i}^{j,D} > c_2, \ldots, C_{nNi}^{j,D} > c_N] \\
&= \Pr\left[Z_{1i}^{j,D} \leq \frac{b_1^j d_{n1}^j}{c_1}, Z_{2i}^{j,D} \leq \frac{b_2^j d_{n2}^j}{c_2}, \ldots, Z_{Ni}^{j,D} \leq \frac{b_N^j d_{N1}^j}{c_N}\right] \\
&= \exp\left(-T_i^{j,D}\left(\sum_{l'=1}^{N} \left(b_{l'}^j d_{nl'}^j h_{l'i}^j\right)^{-\theta^j/(1-\rho^j)} c_{l'}^{\theta^j/(1-\rho^j)}\right)^{1-\rho^j}\right).
\end{aligned}
\tag{29}
$$

Differentiating (29) with respect to its l'th argument and evaluating at $c_{l'} = c$ for $l' = 1, \ldots, N$, we get:

$$
\begin{aligned}
\frac{\partial \bar{G}_{n \cdot i}^{j,D}(c, c, \ldots, c)}{\partial c_l} &= -\exp\left(-T_i^{j,D}\left(\sum_{l'=1}^{N} \left(b_{l'}^j d_{nl'}^j h_{l'i}^j\right)^{-\theta^j/(1-\rho^j)} c^{\theta^j}\right)^{1-\rho^j}\right) \\
&\quad \times (1-\rho^j) T_i^{j,D}\left(\sum_{l'=1}^{N} \left(b_{l'}^j d_{nl'}^j h_{l'i}^j\right)^{-\theta^j/(1-\rho^j)}\right)^{-\rho^j} c^{-\theta^j \rho^j/(1-\rho^j)} \\
&\quad \times \left(b_{l'}^j d_{nl'}^j h_{l'i}^j\right)^{-\theta^j/(1-\rho^j)} \frac{\theta^j}{1-\rho^j} c^{\theta^j/(1-\rho^j)-1},
\end{aligned}
$$

which simplifies to:

$$
\frac{\partial \bar{G}_{n\cdot i}^{j,D}(c, c, ..., c)}{\partial c_l} = -\exp\left(-T_i^{j,D}\left(\sum_{l'=1}^{N} \left(b_{l'}^{j} d_{nl'}^{j} h_{l'i}^{j}\right)^{-\theta^j/(1-\rho^j)}\right)^{1-\rho^j} c^{\theta^j}\right)
$$

$$
\times T_i^{j,D}\left(\sum_{l'=1}^{N} \left(b_{l'}^{j} d_{nl'}^{j} h_{l'i}^{j}\right)^{-\theta^j/(1-\rho^j)}\right)^{-\rho^j} \left(b_{l'}^{j} d_{nl'}^{j} h_{l'i}^{j}\right)^{-\theta^j/(1-\rho^j)} \theta^j c^{\theta^j - 1}
$$

$$
= \frac{\left(b_{l'}^{j} d_{nl'}^{j} h_{l'i}^{j}\right)^{-\theta^j/(1-\rho^j)}}{\sum_{l'=1}^{N} \left(b_{l'}^{j} d_{nl'}^{j} h_{l'i}^{j}\right)^{-\theta^j/(1-\rho^j)}} \frac{d\bar{G}_{n\cdot i}^{j,D}(c)}{dc},
$$

where, we define:

$$
\bar{G}_{n\cdot i}^{j,D}(c) = \exp\left(-T_i^{j,D}\left(\sum_{l'=1}^{N} \left(b_{l'}^{j} d_{nl'}^{j} h_{l'i}^{j}\right)^{-\theta^j/(1-\rho^j)}\right)^{1-\rho^j} c^{\theta^j}\right).
$$

Since $\bar{G}_{n\cdot i}^{j,D}(c)$ is itself a complementary distribution (the probability that all the $C_{nl'i}^{j,D}$, for $l' = 1, ..., N$, exceed c), we can see that $\bar{G}_{n\cdot i}^{j,D}(0) = 1$ and $\bar{G}_{n\cdot i}^{j,D}(\infty) = 0$.

Setting all but the l'th argument in (29) to 0, we obtain the marginal complementary distribution of $C_{nli}^{j,D}$:

$$
\bar{G}_{nli}^{j,D}(c) = \exp\left(-T_i^{j,D}\left(b_{l'}^{j} d_{nl'}^{j} h_{l'i}^{j}\right)^{-\theta^j} c^{\theta^j}\right).
$$

Hence:

$$
g_{nli}^{j,D}(c) = -\frac{d\bar{G}_{nli}^{j,D}(c)}{dc}
$$

is the corresponding density.

The probability that l is the lowest cost supplier, conditional on delivering to n at unit cost c, is:

$$
\pi_{nli}^{j,D}(c) = -\frac{\partial \bar{G}_{n\cdot i}^{j,D}(c, c, ..., c)/\partial c_l}{g_{nli}^{j,D}(c)}.
$$

Unconditionally, the probability that l is the lowest cost supplier is therefore:

$$
\pi_{nl|i}^{j,D} = \int_0^\infty \pi_{nli}^{j,D}(c) g_{nli}^{j,D}(c) dc
$$

$$
= -\int_0^\infty \frac{\partial \bar{G}_{n\cdot i}^{j,D}(c, c, ..., c)}{\partial c_l} dc
$$

$$
= -\frac{\left(b_{l'}^{j} d_{nl'}^{j} h_{l'i}^{j}\right)^{-\theta^j/(1-\rho^j)}}{\sum_{l'=1}^{N} \left(b_{l'}^{j} d_{nl'}^{j} h_{l'i}^{j}\right)^{-\theta^j/(1-\rho^j)}} \int_0^\infty \frac{d\bar{G}_{n\cdot i}^{j,D}(c)}{dc} \qquad (30)
$$

$$
= \frac{\left(b_{l}^{j} d_{nl}^{j} h_{li}^{j}\right)^{-\theta^j/(1-\rho^j)}}{\sum_{l'=1}^{N} \left(b_{l'}^{j} d_{nl'}^{j} h_{l'i}^{j}\right)^{-\theta^j/(1-\rho^j)}}.
$$

Appendix C

Deriving the distribution of markups

Denote the unit cost of the lowest cost supplier of a variety to market n as $C_n^{(1)j}$ and the unit cost of the second-lowest cost (potential) supplier as $C_n^{(2)j}$. If $\sigma^j < 1$ there is no finite monopoly price so that the markup is simply:

$$M_n^j = \frac{C_n^{(2)j}}{C_n^{(1)j}}.$$

If $\sigma^j > 1$ the monopoly price is a markup:

$$\bar{m}^j = \frac{\sigma^j}{\sigma^j - 1},$$

over $C_n^{(1)j}$. The markup the seller will charge is thus:

$$\bar{M}_n^j = \min\{M_n^j, \bar{m}^j\}.$$

To derive the distribution of this markup, it's useful to condition on a cost c_2 such that $C_n^{(1)} < c_2 < C_n^{(2)}$. Defining:

$$\tilde{M}_n = \frac{c_2}{C_n^{(1)j}},$$

the distribution of $\tilde{M}$ under this condition is:

$$\Pr[\tilde{M}_n \le m]$$

$$= \frac{\Phi_n^j(1 - m^{-\theta^j}) c_2^{\theta^j} \exp[-\Phi_n^j(1 - m^{-\theta^j}) c_2^{\theta^j}] \cdot \exp[-\Phi_n^j(c_2/m)^{\theta^j}]}{\exp[-\Phi_n^j c_2^{\theta^j}] \cdot \Phi_n^j c_2^{\theta^j}}.$$

Looking at the right-hand side, the first term in the numerator is the probability of exactly one cost in the interval between $m^{-1}c_2$ and c_2. The second term in the numerator is the probability that $C_n^{(1)j} \ge c_2/m$. The term in the denominator is the probability that $C_n^{(1)j} < c_2 < C_n^{(2)j}$. Simplifying, this expression becomes:

$$\Pr[\tilde{M}_n \le m] = 1 - m^{-\theta^j}.$$

Key for what follows is that this distribution does not depend on c_2. It follows that the distribution of M_n^j is:

$$H(m) = \Pr\left[M_n^j \leq m\right] = 1 - m^{-\theta^j}, \tag{31}$$

which is independent of $C_n^{(2)j}$. Taking account of the upper bound $\bar{m}^j$, we get the distribution of $\bar{M}_n^j$.

Appendix D

Deriving the price index

To derive the price index consider the price of a variety of tangible sector j, with second lowest cost $C_n^{(2)j}$ (we return to our convention of dropping the variety index, ω). We can write its price P_n^j as:

$$P_n^j = \begin{cases} C_n^{(2)j} & M_n^j \leq \bar{m}^j \\ \bar{m}^j \left(C_n^{(2)j} / M_n^j \right) & M_n^j > \bar{m}^j \end{cases}.$$

The independence of M_n^j and $C_n^{(2)j}$ allows us to write:

$$\left(p_n^j \right)^{1-\sigma^j} = \left[\int_0^\infty c^{1-\sigma^j} dG_n^{(2)j}(c) \right] \cdot \left[\theta^j \int_1^{\bar{m}^j} m^{-\theta^j - 1} dm + \theta^j \bar{m}^{j(1-\sigma^j)} \int_{\bar{m}^j}^\infty m^{\sigma^j - \theta^j - 2} dm \right] \quad (32)$$

where $G_n^{(2)j}$ is the distribution of $C_n^{(2)j}$. Since $C_n^{(2)j}$ lies below a cost c only if there are two or more below c, this distribution is:

$$G_n^{(2)j}(c) = \Pr[C_n^{(2)j} \leq c] = 1 - \exp(-\Phi_n^j c^{\theta^j}) - \Phi_n^j c^{\theta^j} \exp(-\Phi_n^j c^{\theta^j}),$$

that is, 1 minus the probability that there are zero or one. The corresponding density is:

$$dG_n^{(2)j}(c) = \theta^j \left(\Phi_n^j \right)^2 c^{2\theta^j - 1} \exp(-\Phi_n^j c^{\theta^j}) dc.$$

Attacking the first expression in (32):

$$\int_0^\infty c^{1-\sigma^j} dG_n^{(2)j}(c) = \theta^j \left(\Phi_n^j \right)^2 \int_0^\infty c^{2\theta^j - \sigma^j} \exp(-\Phi_n^j c^{\theta^j}) dc$$

$$= \Gamma\left(\frac{2\theta^j - (\sigma^j - 1)}{\theta^j} \right) \Phi_n^{-(1-\sigma^j)/\theta^j}, \quad (33)$$

where $\Gamma(\alpha) = \int_0^\infty x^{\alpha-1} e^{-x} dx$ is the gamma function. Attacking the second term in (32):

$$\theta^j \int_1^{\bar{m}^j} m^{-\theta^j-1} dm + \theta^j \bar{m}^{j(1-\sigma)} \int_{\bar{m}^j}^\infty m^{\sigma^j-\theta^j-2} dm = (1 - (\bar{m}^j)^{-\theta^j}) + \frac{\theta^j}{\theta^j - (\sigma^j - 1)} (\bar{m}^j)^{-\theta^j}$$

$$= 1 + \frac{\sigma^j - 1}{\theta^j - (\sigma^j - 1)} (\bar{m}^j)^{-\theta^j}$$

giving us the price index:

$$p_n^j = \gamma^j (\Phi_n^j)^{-1/\theta^j}, \tag{34}$$

where:

$$\gamma^j = \Gamma \left(\frac{2\theta^j - (\sigma^j - 1)}{\theta^j} \right)^{1/(1-\sigma^j)} \left(1 + \frac{\sigma^j - 1}{\theta^j - (\sigma^j - 1)} (\bar{m}^j)^{-\theta^j} \right)^{1/(1-\sigma^j)}.$$

Appendix E

Deriving the royalty share

Having derived the price index for sector j in destination n, we now turn to the royalties generated there. Consider a variety ω in sector j in country n with a price $P(\omega)$. Our CES demand system implies that its sales there are:

$$X(\omega) = A_n^j P(\omega)^{1-\sigma^j}$$

where:

$$A_n^j = \frac{X_n^j}{P_n^{j\,1-\sigma^j}}.$$

Here X_n^j is total absorption of sector j. The cost of tangible inputs to produce this variety are:

$$I(\omega) = \frac{X(\omega)}{M(\omega)}.$$

Input costs can be expressed as:

$$I(\omega) = \begin{cases} A_n^j \dfrac{[C^{(2)}(\omega)]^{1-\sigma^j}}{M(\omega)} & M(\omega) \leq \bar{m}^j \\[3mm] A_n^j \left(\dfrac{C^{(2)}(\omega)}{M(\omega)}\right)^{1-\sigma^j} (\bar{m}^j)^{-\sigma^j} & M(\omega) > \bar{m}^j. \end{cases}$$

Integrating across varieties ω, using (33), input costs in sector j in country n are:

$$I_n^j = A_n^j \int_0^\infty c^{1-\sigma^j} dG_n^{(2)}(c) \left[\int_1^{\bar{m}^j} m^{-1} dH(m) + (\bar{m}^j)^{-\sigma^j} \int_{\bar{m}^j}^\infty m^{\sigma^j-1} dH(m) \right]$$

$$= A_n^j \Gamma\left(\frac{2\theta^j - (\sigma^j - 1)}{\theta^j}\right) \Phi_n^{-(1-\sigma^j)/\theta^j} \frac{\theta^j}{\theta^j + 1}\left(1 + \frac{\sigma^j - 1}{\theta^j - (\sigma^j - 1)}(\bar{m}^j)^{-\theta^j}\right).$$

Combined with the price index (17), this complicated expression reduces to:

$$\frac{I_n^j}{X_n^j} = \frac{\theta^j}{1 + \theta^j}.$$

It follows that intangible services (embodied in n's absorption of tangible sector j goods) are:

$$X_n^{j,I} = X_n^j - I_n^j = X_n^j - \frac{\theta^j}{1 + \theta^j} X_n^j$$

$$= \frac{1}{1 + \theta^j} X_n^j.$$

(35)

5 On the measurement of upstreamness and downstreamness in global value chains

Pol Antràs and Davin Chor

1. Introduction

In 2017, international trade economists celebrated the 200th anniversary of the birth of their field, as marked by the publication of David Ricardo's *On the Principles of Political Economy and Taxation*. This treatise is widely recognized to contain the first lucid exposition of the concept of comparative advantage. Although the notion of comparative advantage is as relevant today as it was 200 years ago, the nature of international trade flows has dramatically changed in recent decades. Technological, institutional, and political developments in the last 30 years have led to a sharp disintegration of production processes across borders, as firms found it more and more profitable to organize production on a global scale. Countries are no longer exchanging "cloth for wine", to quote Ricardo's famous example. Instead, world production is now structured into global value chains (GVCs, hereafter) in which firms source parts, components, or services from producers in several countries, and in turn sell their output to firms and consumers worldwide.

By dramatically altering the international organization of production, the rise of GVCs has placed the specialization of countries *within* GVCs at center stage. Where in GVCs are different countries specializing? What are the determinants of a country's positioning in GVCs? What are the real income implications of moving up or down GVCs? Although we still lack definitive answers to these questions, a recent body of work in international trade has contributed to our understanding by developing measures of the positioning of countries and industries in GVCs (see Fally, 2012, Antràs et al., 2012, Antràs and Chor, 2013, Alfaro et al., 2017, Miller and Temurshoev, 2017, Wang et al., 2017, Fally and Hillberry, 2018).[1] The intellectual foundation and computation of these measures is based on Input-Output (I-O) analysis. The application of Input-Output techniques by trade economists has in turn been reciprocated by an increased interest by Input-Output practitioners on the global dimension of inter-industry linkages. Indeed, a big contributing factor to the popularization of the literature on GVC positioning has been the construction and widespread availability of Global Input-Output Tables, which provide a detailed picture of inter-industry commodity flows both within and across countries.

A key limitation of existing approaches to measuring the positioning of countries in GVCs is that they lack a theoretical foundation within the realm of modern general equilibrium models of international trade. With information on the various entries of a Global Input-Output Table, a researcher can compute the implied upstreamness or downstreamness of specific industries and countries. But without knowledge of what shapes these I-O entries, a researcher cannot tease out the primitive determinants of GVC positioning or elucidate how changes in the economic environment (e.g., changes in trade costs) are likely to affect the specialization of countries within GVCs. To be clear, we do not mean to imply that the literature on GVCs has been atheoretical in nature. On the contrary, in recent years, various theoretical frameworks have been developed highlighting the implications of the rise of GVCs for the workings of general equilibrium models of international trade.[2] Nevertheless, the vast majority of theoretical models developed to date are too stylized to easily map to Global Input-Output Tables.[3]

This chapter makes four contributions to the literature on GVCs. First, we provide a succinct overview of various measures developed in the literature to capture the upstreamness or downstreamness of industries and countries in GVCs. Second, we employ data from the World Input-Output Database (WIOD) to document the empirical evolution of these measures over the period 1995–2011. Third, we develop a theoretical framework – which builds on Caliendo and Parro (2015) – that provides a structural interpretation of *all* the entries of the WIOD in a given year. Fourth, we then resort to a calibrated version of the model to perform counterfactual exercises that: (i) sharpen our understanding of the independent effect of several factors in explaining the observed empirical patterns between 1995 and 2011; and (ii) provide guidance for how future changes in the world economy are likely to shape the positioning of countries in GVCs.

The key measures of upstreamness explored in this chapter are introduced in Section 2. These measures envision a world in which production in GVCs features some element of sequentiality.[4] We first consider a measure of distance or *upstreamness* of a production sector from final demand which was developed independently by Fally (2012) and Antràs and Chor (2013), and consolidated in Antràs *et al.* (2012). This measure (which we label *U*) aggregates information on the extent to which an industry in a given country produces goods that are sold directly to final consumers or that are sold to other sectors that themselves sell disproportionately to final consumers. A relatively upstream sector is thus one that sells a small share of its output to final consumers, and instead sells disproportionately to other sectors that themselves sell relatively little to final consumers. A second related measure, originally proposed by Fally (2012), captures the distance or *downstreamness* of a given sector from the economy's primary factors of production (or sources of value-added). According to this measure (which we denote by *D*), an industry in a given country will appear to be downstream if its production process uses little value-added relative to intermediate inputs, and particularly so when it purchases intermediate inputs from industries that themselves use intermediate inputs intensively. In addition, we also discuss simpler versions of these two measures of GVC positioning: the first reduces the measure in Antràs *et al.* (2012) to simply the share of a country-industry's output that is sold directly to final consumers (denoted by F/GO), while the second reduces the Fally (2012) measure of distance from value-added to simply the share of a country-industry's payments accounted for by payments to primary factors (denoted by VA/GO).

Although these measures were initially developed at the industry-level with National Input-Output Tables in mind, we show that it is straightforward to define them and compute them at the country-industry level with data from Global Input-Output Tables, as in the recent work of Miller and Temurshoev (2017) and Fally and Hillberry (2018). Similarly, taking weighted averages of these indices across sectors, one can easily compute the average upstreamness or downstreamness of specific countries in GVCs, which we will adopt as summary measures of countries' GVC positioning.

With these definitions in hand, in Section 3 we use data from the WIOD to compute these measures for the period 1995–2011. We unveil two systematic and somewhat surprising facts. First, countries that appear to be upstream according to their production-staging distance from final demand (U) are at the same time recorded to be downstream according to their production-staging distance from primary factors (D). This puzzling finding is also observed when working with the simpler F/GO and VA/GO measures. More specifically, countries that sell a disproportionate share of their output directly to final consumers (thus appearing to be downstream in GVCs according to U) tend to also feature high value-added over gross output ratios, reflecting a limited amount of intermediate inputs embodied in their production (thus appearing to be upstream in GVCs according to D). Our second main empirical finding relates to the evolution of these measures. Not only is the puzzling positive correlation between U and D (and between F/GO and VA/GO) present in all the years in our sample, but it actually appears to have intensified between 1995 and 2011. While we first illustrate these results using the GVC measures aggregated at the country level, we further show that these positive correlations (as well as their increase over time) are also observed in the GVC measures as originally computed at the country-industry level.

In Section 4, we provide a tentative investigation of the possible causes behind these salient and puzzling facts from the data. We first explore the role of trade costs. Note that in a closed economy, value-added coincides with final consumption as a national accounting identity; thus, in a cross-section of closed economies that differ in their value-added intensity in production, one would expect to record a perfect positive correlation between F/GO and VA/GO. This suggests that the observed positive correlation between these measures (and between U and D) might reflect the persistence of large trade barriers across countries. When applying the Head and Ries (2001) approach to back out implied trade costs, we indeed find these costs to be substantially high, even towards the end of our sample. Nevertheless, we also find that average trade barriers fell significantly in the period 1995–2011 (especially prior to the Global Financial Crisis), while the positive correlation between the various pairs of country-level GVC measures actually intensified. This suggests that other mechanisms must have been in play to explain the puzzling facts unveiled in Section 3. As a second candidate explanation, we provide evidence for the importance of compositional effects related to the differential (and growing) importance of services. Intuitively, service sectors feature short production chain lengths, with both a high ratio of sales to final consumers and little use of intermediate inputs in production. The cross-country variation in our measures of upstreamness (as well as the positive correlation among U and D) thus partly reflects variation in the importance of service sectors in the production structure of different countries.[5]

In order to better elucidate the quantitative importance of these alternative explanations, and also to be able to interpret the data in a structural manner, we turn in Section 5 to develop a theoretical model. We begin by reviewing Caliendo and Parro's (2015) extension of the Eaton and Kortum (2002) Ricardian model of trade. In its closed economy version, the Cobb-Douglas structure of the demand and production sides of this model are closely related to the framework in Acemoglu *et al.* (2012). As is well known, the demand and technological Cobb-Douglas parameters of that model can easily be recovered from expenditure shares reported in National Input-Output Tables. In the type of open-economy equilibrium corresponding to a Global Input-Output Table, cross-country and cross-industry expenditure shares are less straightforward to map structurally to a model because they are the outcome of competition across potential sources, and are thus shaped by differences in productivity and trade costs across countries. Caliendo and Parro (2015) showed, however, that a variant of the Eaton and Kortum (2002) framework could be used to interpret structurally the share of purchases of a given type of industry good originating from different source countries.

We develop in Section 5 an extension of the Caliendo and Parro (2015) model that features a more flexible formulation of trade costs, in order to be able to fully match *all* entries of a World Input-Output Table (WIOT) that relate to trade in intermediate inputs and trade in goods/services designated for final consumption. In its original form, the Caliendo and Parro (2015) model does not allow these "trade shares" to vary depending on the identity of the purchasing entity, that is, depending on whether they are sold to final consumers or to different industries as inputs. Instead, the model (implicitly) imposes certain restrictions on these entries that need not (and typically do not) hold in the actual data. Given our objective of providing a structural interpretation of the GVC measures described in Section 2, it is instead desirable to correctly match both the intermediate-use and final-use trade shares, since the implied values of upstreamness and downstreamness will clearly depend on the extent to which a sector's output is sold to final consumers or to other industries.[6] For the extension we develop, we further show – in line with Dekle *et al.* (2008) and Caliendo and Parro (2015) – that in order to perform various counterfactuals, all that is required are: (i) initial trade shares available from a WIOT; (ii) demand and technological Cobb-Douglas parameters easily recoverable from the same WIOT; and (iii) a vector of sectoral parameters shaping the elasticity of trade flows (across source countries) to trade barriers.

In Section 6, we leverage this result to undertake several counterfactual exercises. We first attempt to trace the relative contribution of trade cost reductions and the growing share of final consumption of services for explaining the puzzling increase in the key correlations between F/GO and VA/GO (and between U and D) over the 1995–2011 period. Our quantitative results confirm that declining trade costs tend only to aggravate the high-correlation puzzle. On the other hand, we find that changes in final consumption shares did contribute – but only modestly – to the observed increase in the correlation between these GVC measures. We next use our model to shed light on the potential future evolution of the positioning of industries and countries in GVCs. We do so by experimenting with possible scenarios involving different trade cost reductions, as well as further increases in the share of countries' spending on services. Interestingly, we find that a trade cost reduction that is disproportionately larger for services than for goods industries can induce a further increase in the correlation between F/GO and VA/GO (and between U and D); this is because a change in trade costs of this nature would tend to reinforce initial patterns of specialization for countries with comparative advantage in services.

The rest of the chapter is structured as follows. In Section 2, we review the empirical measures of GVC positioning. In Section 3, we compute these measures using data from the WIOD for the period 1995–2011 and discuss several patterns that emerge. In Section 4, we explore two possible explanations for these patterns. In Section 5, we turn to a theoretical model to interpret the data structurally, and, in Section 6, we use the framework to perform counterfactual exercises. Last, in Section 7, we offer some concluding comments (the appendix contains some technical details of our model).

2. An overview of four measures of GVC positioning

In this section, we develop the main measures of GVC positioning we will work with throughout the chapter.[7] Our unit of analysis is a country-industry pair such as Electrical and Optical Equipment in Australia. The goal is to devise measures of the extent to which a country-industry is relatively upstream or downstream in global value chains. These measures are built with the type of data available from Global Input-Output Tables. We shall refer to a World Input-Output Table as a WIOT, and Figure 5.1 provides a schematic version of one such WIOT.

The WIOT in Figure 5.1 considers a world economy with J countries (indexed by i or j) and S sectors (indexed by r or s). In its top left $J \times S$ by $J \times S$ block, the WIOT contains information on intermediate purchases by industry s in country j from sector r in country i. We denote these intermediate input flows by Z_{ij}^{rs}. To the right of this block, the WIOT contains an additional $J \times S$ by J block with information on the final-use expenditure in each country j on goods originating from sector r in country i. We denote these final consumption flows by F_{ij}^{r}. The sum of

Figure 5.1 The structure of a World Input-Output Table

		Input use & value added							Final use			Total use
Output supplied		**Country 1**			⋯	**Country J**			**Country 1**	⋯	**Country J**	
		Industry 1	⋯	Industry S	⋯	Industry 1	⋯	Industry S				
Country 1 — Industry 1		Z_{11}^{11}	⋯	Z_{11}^{1S}	⋯	Z_{1J}^{11}	⋯	Z_{1J}^{1S}	F_{11}^1	⋯	F_{1J}^1	Y_1^1
Country 1 — ⋯		⋯	Z_{11}^{rs}	⋯	⋯	⋯	Z_{1J}^{rs}	⋯	⋯	⋯	⋯	⋯
Country 1 — Industry S		Z_{11}^{S1}	⋯	Z_{11}^{SS}	⋯	Z_{1J}^{S1}	⋯	Z_{1J}^{SS}	F_{11}^S	⋯	F_{1J}^S	Y_1^S
⋯		⋯	⋯	⋯	Z_{ij}^{rs}	⋯	⋯	⋯	⋯	F_{ij}^r	⋯	Y_i^r
Country J — Industry 1		Z_{J1}^{11}	⋯	Z_{J1}^{1S}	⋯	Z_{JJ}^{11}	⋯	Z_{JJ}^{1S}	F_{J1}^1	⋯	F_{JJ}^1	Y_J^1
Country J — ⋯		⋯	Z_{J1}^{rs}	⋯	⋯	⋯	Z_{JJ}^{rs}	⋯	⋯	⋯	⋯	⋯
Country J — Industry S		Z_{J1}^{S1}	⋯	Z_{J1}^{SS}	⋯	Z_{JJ}^{S1}	⋯	Z_{JJ}^{SS}	F_{J1}^S	⋯	F_{JJ}^S	Y_J^S
Value added		VA_1^1	⋯	VA_1^S	VA_j^s	VA_J^1	⋯	VA_J^S				
Gross output		Y_1^1	⋯	Y_1^S	Y_j^s	Y_J^1	⋯	Y_J^S				

the $(J \times S) + J$ terms in each row of a WIOT represents the total use of output of sector r from country i, and naturally coincides with gross output in that sector and country (denoted by Y_i^r). More formally, we have

$$Y_i^r = \sum_{s=1}^{S} \sum_{j=1}^{J} Z_{ij}^{rs} + \sum_{j=1}^{J} F_{ij}^{r} = \sum_{s=1}^{S} \sum_{j=1}^{J} Z_{ij}^{rs} + F_i^r, \tag{1}$$

where we will hereafter denote the *total* final use of output originating from sector r in country i by $F_i^r = \sum_{j=1}^{J} F_{ij}^r$.

As illustrated by the two bottom rows of the WIOT, gross output in industry s in country j is also equal to the sum of: (i) all intermediate purchases made from source sectors r in countries i; and (ii) country j's value-added employed in the production of industry s itself (the latter denoted by VA_j^s). More formally:

$$Y_j^s = \sum_{r=1}^{S} \sum_{i=1}^{J} Z_{ij}^{rs} + VA_j^s. \tag{2}$$

As described, the WIOT contains information on linkages in a full production network, where each country-industry could potentially be traversed in a large number of production chains. In this complex setting, the measures of GVC positioning described below will seek to capture the average position of each country-industry in the production chains in which it is involved. The first two measures introduced below will take as a point of reference the sources of final demand at the end of each production chain, and compute the upstreamness of the country-industry relative to final use. The second set of measures will instead capture the downstreamness of each country-industry from where production processes commence, namely from sources of value-added by primary factors.

2.1.   Upstreamness from final use

How upstream or downstream in GVCs is a given sector r from a given country i? A first possible approach to tackling this question is to consider the extent to which a country-industry pair sells its output for final use to consumers world-wide or instead sells intermediate inputs to other producing sectors in the world economy. The idea is that a sector that sells disproportionately to final consumers would appear to be downstream in value chains, while a sector that sells little to final consumers is more likely to be upstream in value chains. Invoking equation (1), a simple measure of this notion of GVC positioning is the ratio F_i^r / Y_i^r, which equals the share of gross output in sector r in country i that is sold to final consumers. We will refer to this measure as *F/GO*. Note that a lower value of this ratio is associated with a higher upstreamness from final use.

An unappealing feature of the simple measure *F/GO* is that it does not capture variation in the upstreamness of country-industry pairs that goes beyond the extent to which their output is directly sold to final consumers or to other industries. In order to transition to a more satisfactory measure, let us first define $a_{ij}^{rs} = Z_{ij}^{rs}/Y_j^s$ as the dollar amount of sector r's output from country i needed to produce one dollar worth of industry s's output in country j. With this notation, equation (1) becomes:

$$Y_i^r = \sum_{s=1}^{S} \sum_{j=1}^{J} a_{ij}^{rs} Y_j^s + F_i^r. \tag{3}$$

Iterating this identity, we can express industry r's output in country i as an infinite sequence of terms which reflect the use of this country-industry's output at different positions in global value chains, starting with its use as a final good/service, as a direct input in the production of final goods/services in all countries and industries, as a direct input of a direct input in the production of final goods/services in all countries and industries, and so on:

$$Y_i^r = F_i^r + \sum_{s=1}^{S} \sum_{j=1}^{J} a_{ij}^{rs} F_j^s + \sum_{s=1}^{S} \sum_{j=1}^{J} \sum_{t=1}^{S} \sum_{k=1}^{J} a_{ij}^{rs} a_{jk}^{st} F_k^t + \dots \tag{4}$$

Building on this identity, Antràs and Chor (2013) suggested computing the (weighted) average position of a country-industry's output in global value chains by multiplying each of the terms in (4) by its respective production-staging distance from final use plus one, and dividing by Y_i^r, or:

$$U_i^r = 1 \times \frac{F_i^r}{Y_i^r} + 2 \times \frac{\sum_{s=1}^{S} \sum_{j=1}^{J} a_{ij}^{rs} F_j^s}{Y_i^r} + 3 \times \frac{\sum_{s=1}^{S} \sum_{j=1}^{J} \sum_{t=1}^{S} \sum_{k=1}^{J} a_{ij}^{rs} a_{jk}^{st} F_k^t}{Y_i^r} + \dots \tag{5}$$

It is clear that $U_i^r \geq 1$, and that larger values are associated with relatively higher levels of *upstreamness* of the output originating from sector r in country i.

Although computing (5) might appear to require computing an infinite power series, provided that $\sum_{r=1}^{S} \sum_{i=1}^{J} a_{ij}^{rs} < 1$ for all j-s pairs (a natural assumption), the numerator of the above measure is actually equal to the $((i-1) \times S + r)$-th element of the $J \times S$ by 1 column matrix $[I - A]^{-2} \mathbf{F}$; here, $\mathbf{A}$ is a $J \times S$ by $J \times S$ matrix whose $((i-1) \times S + r, (j-1) \times S + s)$-th element is a_{ij}^{rs}, while $\mathbf{F}$ is a column matrix with F_i^r in its $((i-1) \times S + r)$-th row. Using the fact that the stacked column matrix of gross output also satisfies $\mathbf{Y} = [I - A]^{-1} \mathbf{F}$ – which is easily verified from (3) – the numerator is thus also equal to the $((i-1) \times S + r)$-th element of the $J \times S$ by 1 matrix $[I - A]^{-1} Y$, where Y is a $J \times S$ by 1 column matrix with Y_i^r in its $((i-1) \times S + r)$-th row. Because a WIOT provides direct information on A and Y, computing the upstreamness of output of each sector r in each country i thus amounts to a straightforward matrix inversion.[8]

Fally (2012) instead proposed a measure of upstreamness (or distance from final use) based on the notion that industries selling a disproportionate share of their output to relatively upstream industries should be relatively upstream themselves.[9] In particular, he posited the following linear system of equations that implicitly defines upstreamness for each sector r in country i:

$$\tilde{U}_i^r = 1 + \sum_{s=1}^{S} \sum_{j=1}^{J} b_{ij}^{rs} \tilde{U}_j^s, \tag{6}$$

where note that $b_{ij}^{rs} = Z_{ij}^{rs}/Y_i^r = a_{ij}^{rs} Y_j^s/Y_i^r$ is the share of total output of sector r in country i that is purchased by industry s in country j. Again, it is clear that $\tilde{U}_i^r \geq 1$. Less obviously, one can demonstrate using matrix algebra that $\tilde{U}_i^r$ and U_i^r are in fact equivalent; this is the key theoretical result in Antràs *et al.* (2012).

2.2.   Downstreamness from primary factors

We next turn to alternative measures of GVC positioning based on a country-industry pair's use of intermediate inputs and primary factors of production. These measures are based on the identity in (2), which describes the technology for producing output in industry s in country j. Other things equal, it seems plausible that production processes that embody a larger amount of intermediate inputs relative to their use of primary factors of production will be relatively downstream in value chains. Conversely, if an industry relies disproportionately on value-added from primary factors of production, then it would appear that this industry is relatively upstream. In light of equation (2), a simple measure to capture such GVC positioning is the ratio VA_j^s/Y_j^s, with large values of this measure being associated with higher upstreamness or lower downstreamness. We will refer to this measure as *VA/GO*.

As in the case of the sales-based measure of *F/GO*, a limitation of *VA/GO* is that it does not take into account potential heterogeneity in the upstreamness of the inputs used in the production process of a country-industry pair. With that in mind, we next develop a more informative measure of downstreamness from primary factors of production. Recall that $b_{ij}^{rs} = Z_{ij}^{rs}/Y_i^r$ denotes the share of sector r's output in country i that is used in industry s in country j. Then equation (2) can be written as:

$$Y_j^s = \sum_{r=1}^{S} \sum_{i=1}^{J} b_{ij}^{rs} Y_i^r + VA_j^s.$$

Iterating this identity, we can express:

$$Y_j^s = VA_j^s + \sum_{r=1}^{S} \sum_{i=1}^{J} b_{ij}^{rs} VA_i^r + \sum_{r=1}^{S} \sum_{i=1}^{J} \sum_{t=1}^{S} \sum_{k=1}^{J} b_{ki}^{tr} b_{ij}^{rs} VA_k^t + \cdots$$

Notice that the first term captures the direct use of primary factors in the production of industry s in country j. The second term reflects the use of intermediate inputs that are themselves produced directly with primary factors. The third term captures intermediate input purchases produced with inputs produced with primary factors, and so on. The larger are the terms associated with further iterations, the more intensive is that country-industry's use of inputs far removed from primary factors, and thus the more downstream is production relative to these primary factors.

Building on Antràs and Chor (2013), Miller and Temurshoev (2017) propose the following measure of downstreamness of a given country-industry pair from primary factors of production:

$$D_j^s = 1 \times \frac{VA_j^s}{Y_j^s} + 2 \times \frac{\sum_{r=1}^{S} \sum_{i=1}^{J} b_{ij}^{rs} VA_i^r}{Y_j^s} + 3 \times \frac{\sum_{r=1}^{S} \sum_{i=1}^{J} \sum_{t=1}^{S} \sum_{k=1}^{J} b_{ki}^{tr} b_{ij}^{rs} VA_k^t}{Y_j^s} + \cdots \tag{7}$$

As in the case of U_i^r, it is clear that $D_j^s \geq 1$, with larger values being associated with relatively higher levels of *downstreamness* of industry s in country j. Given the similar structure of U_i^r in (5) and D_j^s in (7), it should come as no surprise that one need *not* approximate the infinite sum in (7) to compute D_j^s. By defining a matrix **B** analogous to the matrix **A** invoked in the construction of U_i^r and computing $[I - B]^{-1} Y$, the various elements of the numerator of D_j^s are easily retrieved. Furthermore, there is an analogous foundation for the measure D_j^s building on the following recursive definition:

$$\tilde{D}_j^s = 1 + \sum_{i=1}^{J} \sum_{r=1}^{S} a_{ij}^{rs} \tilde{D}_i^r. \tag{8}$$

This system of equations defining downstreamness $\tilde{D}_j^s$ was first suggested by Fally (2012), who associated it with the average number of production stages embodied in a sector's output. As pointed out by Miller and Temurshoev (2017), $\tilde{D}_j^s$ in (8) and D_j^s in (7) are in fact mathematically equivalent.[10]

2.3. *Aggregation*

So far we have developed measures of GVC positioning at the country-industry level, but for some applications a researcher might be interested in the *average* position of countries in GVCs. An example of such a focus on the country dimension rather than the country-industry dimension is provided by Antràs and de Gortari (2017).

In principle, there are two alternative ways to compute country-level measures of upstreamness/downstreamness. First, one can take a WIOT and simply collapse its entries at the country-by-country level. More specifically, one can compute the total purchases of intermediate inputs by country j from country i as $Z_{ij} = \sum_{r=1}^{S} \sum_{s=1}^{S} Z_{ij}^{rs}$, and then generate a $J \times J$ block matrix with elements Z_{ij}. Similarly, a $J \times J$ block matrix of aggregate final-use sales can be computed with entries $F_{ij} = \sum_{r=1}^{S} F_{ij}^{r}$. With this collapsed country-level WIOT, it is then straightforward to compute country-level variants of the measures of upstreamness and downstreamness developed above. A second potential approach maintains the country-industry level dimension of the data and the GVC positioning measures, but instead computes a weighted-average measure of upstreamness/downstreamness at the country level by averaging the industry-level values of those measures within a country.

For the two basic measures F/GO and VA/GO, it turns out that these two approaches deliver the exact same country-level positioning numbers when using the shares of a country's gross output accounted for by different industries as weights in the second approach. To see this equivalence result for the F/GO measure, note that:

$$\sum_{r=1}^{S} \frac{F_i^r}{Y_i^r} \times \frac{Y_i^r}{\sum_{s=1}^{S} Y_i^s} = \frac{\sum_{r=1}^{S} F_i^r}{\sum_{r=1}^{S} Y_i^s} = \frac{F_i}{Y_i}, \tag{9}$$

where the left-hand side is the gross-output weighted-average of final-use shares, while F_i/Y_i (in the right-hand side) is the aggregate ratio of final use to gross output in country i; the latter is naturally the ratio F/GO that would be computed with a WIOT collapsed at the country level. Similarly, for the measure VA/GO, we have:

$$\sum_{s=1}^{S} \frac{VA_j^s}{Y_j^s} \times \frac{Y_j^s}{\sum_{r=1}^{S} Y_j^r} = \frac{\sum_{s=1}^{S} VA_j^s}{\sum_{s=1}^{S} Y_j^s} = \frac{VA_j}{Y_j}, \tag{10}$$

where the right-hand side term, VA_j/Y_j, would naturally be the value for the country-level value-added over gross output ratio resulting from a WIOT collapsed at the country level.

When considering the more involved measures U and D, such an equivalence result between the two aggregation approaches no longer holds. In the empirical analysis to be performed in the next section, we have nevertheless found the two approaches to deliver extremely highly correlated country-level indices of GVC positioning (see, in particular, footnote 16).[11]

Finally, one might also be interested in computing a *worldwide* average measure of GVC positioning. A natural way to do so would be to compute a weighted sum of the respective measures, F/GO, VA/GO, U, and D, with weights given by gross output in each country-industry. From simple inspection of (9) and (10), it is straightforward to see that the worldwide averages for F/GO and VA/GO will coincide with the ratio of aggregate world final consumption to aggregate world gross output and the ratio of aggregate world value-added to aggregate world gross output, respectively. Furthermore, because the world as a whole is a closed economy, the aggregate world value of final-use expenditures is necessarily equal as an accounting identity to the aggregate payments made to primary factors. Denoting these aggregates with upper bars, we thus have $\bar{F}/\overline{GO} = \overline{VA}/\overline{GO}$ at the level of the world economy. There is a similar though far less obvious relationship connecting the world measures of U and D. More specifically, Proposition 1 in Miller and Temurshoev (2017) establishes that the gross-output weighted-average $\bar{U}$ value across country-industries is in fact exactly equal to the corresponding gross-output weighted-average $\bar{D}$.[12]

This suggests that one should *not* interpret these world averages as measures of GVC positioning. Instead, these world averages should be viewed as measures of the complexity of world production patterns, as captured by the extent to which production processes are sliced across industries and countries. When $\bar{U} = \bar{D}$ is large (or $\bar{F}/\overline{GO} = \overline{VA}/\overline{GO}$ is low), GVCs are more complex in the sense that world production uses inputs far removed from final use, but also highly processed inputs far removed from the primary factors that initiated production. Conversely, a world with a low value of $\bar{U} = \bar{D}$ and a high value of $\bar{F}/\overline{GO} = \overline{VA}/\overline{GO}$ is a world with little intermediate input use and short production chains.

3. The empirical evolution of GVC positioning

We turn now to the annual World Input-Output Database (WIOD) to compute the four measures of GVC positioning defined in the previous section, and document how these have evolved in recent decades. The WIOD is well-suited for this exercise: It contains detailed information on country-industry production linkages and final-use expenditures for a large panel of $J = 41$ countries (including a rest-of-the-world aggregate), a common set of $S = 35$ consistently-defined industries in each country, at an annual frequency, as described in Timmer *et al.* (2015). We work with the 2013 edition of the WIOD, which covers the years 1995–2011. This is in practice a very large dataset. Looking at the entries that correspond to input purchases across country-industry pairs (i.e., the Z_{ij}^{rs}'s in the schematic in Figure 5.1), there are already a total of $(35 \times 41)^2 = 2{,}059{,}225$ such data points in any single year. Looking at the entries that report the value of each country's purchases for final-use from each country-industry source (i.e., the

F_{ij}^r's in Figure 5.1), this yields an additional $35 \times 41^2 = 58{,}835$ observations per year.[13]

In terms of practical implementation, we calculate the four GVC measures for each industry r in each country i in each year, after first performing a "net inventory" correction. For expositional purposes, equation (1) presented earlier had simplified the components of gross output, Y_i^r: Apart from the value of that output that is purchased for intermediate and final uses (the Z_{ij}^{rs}'s and F_{ij}^r's), gross output in the Input-Output accounts includes an additional third component equal to the net value that is inventorized (which we denote by N_i^r).[14] To fully account for how these net inventories affect the measurement of production staging, one would need to observe the identities of the industries s that undertake this inventorization. However, a breakdown of N_i^r by the identity of purchasing industries is not available in the WIOD. We therefore follow Antràs *et al.* (2012) in applying a "net inventory" correction that apportions N_i^r across purchasing countries and industries, in proportion to the corresponding breakdown seen in the intermediate use entries (i.e., the Z_{ij}^{rs}'s). This correction boils down to rescaling each Z_{ij}^{rs} and F_{ij}^r term by a multiplicative factor equal to $Y_i^r / (Y_i^r - N_i^r)$ before we compute the GVC measures at the country-industry level.[15]

To more succinctly illustrate the broad trends in countries' GVC positioning over time, we will find it useful to begin by working with a collapsed version of the World Input-Output Tables (WIOT), in which we aggregate out the industry dimension – by summing over all industry entries for each source-by-destination country pair – to obtain a panel of country-by-country Input-Output Tables, as described in Section 2.3. From this collapsed WIOT, one can compute a set of country-level measures of F/GO, VA/GO, U, and D (with a corresponding net inventory correction based on country-level aggregate inventories) to summarize the GVC positioning of each country, and more easily illustrate how this has evolved over time.[16]

3.1. The GVC positioning of countries over time

Figure 5.2 provides an overview of how GVCs have evolved for the world economy as a whole. Here, we have taken two of the country-level measures of GVC positioning, namely F/GO and U, computed the gross-output weighted-average of each measure (across the 41 countries in the 2013 WIOD), and plotted these over time.

The upper panel reveals that the final-use share in gross output in the world economy ($\overline{F/GO}$) has been on the decline over this period. While the magnitude of this change was fairly small (from 0.526 in 1995 to 0.486 in 2011), the drop was nevertheless perceptible and steady, particularly after 2002. Put otherwise, production and trade in intermediate inputs has risen relative to that in final goods, which would be consistent with a rise in GVC activity around the world. The lower panel corroborates this interpretation. There, we see that the

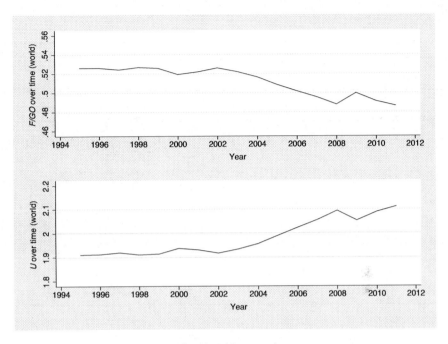

Figure 5.2 GVC positioning over time (world average)

world average upstreamness $\bar{U}$ has been on the uptick, suggesting that production processes have become fragmented into more stages.

What about the other two measures of GVC positioning? Remember from Section 2.3 that the aggregate world value of final-use expenditures is equal to the aggregate world payments made to primary factors. A plot of $\overline{VA/GO}$ over time would thus be identical to the upper panel in Figure 5.2. As previously discussed, the gross-output weighted-average U value is in fact also equal to the gross-output weighted-average of D, and thus a separate figure for the evolution of $\bar{D}$ over time would also be redundant.

In Figure 5.3, we take a more detailed look at these aggregate patterns, by plotting the respective GVC measures for the countries at the 25th, 50th, and 75th percentiles of the cross-country distribution in each year. Note that the worldwide equivalence between F/GO and VA/GO, as well as that between U and D, no longer holds for individual countries, so we can now meaningfully examine the evolution of the four separate GVC measures. The plots in the left column of Figure 5.3 verify that the downward trend in F/GO, and the converse upward trend in U, both hold across these different percentiles of the cross-country distribution. Viewed from the perspective of these two GVC measures, it appears that countries have been broadly moving *more upstream relative to final demand* in the nature of the production activities that are conducted. On the

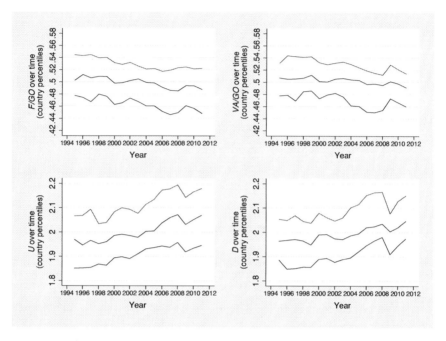

Figure 5.3 GVC positioning over time (25th, 50th, 75th country percentiles)

other hand, the plots in the right column indicate that the value-added to gross-output ratio (*VA/GO*) has been falling over this period, while the measure of production staging relative to sources of value-added (*D*) has been rising. The distribution of countries' GVC positioning has thus simultaneously become *more downstream in relation to primary factors*. Taken together, these observations suggest that GVCs have become more complex, as the average global production chain "length" from primary factors to a particular country, and onward from that country to final demand, have both increased.

It is useful to discuss how the above stylized facts relate to the broader empirical literature on GVC positioning. We are admittedly not the first to document the gradual rise in *U* and *D* over time: Miller and Temurshoev (2017) have also reported this pattern both across countries and across industries in the 2013 WIOD. In the regression analysis that we present below, we will extend this finding by showing that these trends are present too when examining the within country-industry variation in these GVC measures (see Table 5.2). In contrast, Fally (2012) has documented a fall over time in the number of production stages from primary factors to industries, i.e., in the *D* measure, using U.S. Input-Output Tables that span 1947 to 2002. Nevertheless, the bulk of the decline documented by Fally (2012) occurred in the 1980s and early 1990s, prior to the period considered in this chapter, and thus prior to the explosion in GVC activity. Furthermore, in the ongoing revision of his work, Fally documents an uptick in *D* over the period 1997–2007, which is consistent with our findings.

While Figures 5.2 and 5.3 point to broad trends that apply across the country sample, these may mask significant movements in individual countries' GVC positioning. A simple rank correlation test nevertheless indicates that each country's position in GVCs vis-à-vis other countries has remained remarkably stable. In particular, we obtain Spearman coefficients in excess of 0.75 for each of the country-level GVC measures when comparing their cross-country rank order in 1995 against that in 2011. Table 5.1 confirms that there is a striking persistence in countries' GVC position over time, even in the tail ends of the rank order. For example, focusing on the left half of the table, China, Luxembourg, and the Czech Republic were among the five most upstream countries relative to final demand in both 1995 and 2011, based on either the country rank by *F/GO* or *U*. On the other hand, Brazil, Greece, and Cyprus have remained in the five most downstream countries over this period in their proximity to final-use. A similar persistence can also be seen in the right half of Table 5.1, which reports the rank order of countries in terms of their GVC position relative to primary factors (based on either *VA/GO* or *D*).

The above discussion has described patterns in the evolution of GVC positioning across countries, in terms of the broad decline in *F/GO* and *VA/GO*, as well as the accompanying rise in *U* and *D* over time. We next establish that these patterns are also borne out when focusing instead on variation within countries – and more specifically, within country-industry – over time. For this, we turn to the more disaggregate GVC measures computed at the country-industry level. To tease out the desired "within"-variation, we run a series of regressions of the following form:

$$GVC_{j,t}^s = \beta_1 Year_t + FE_j^s + \epsilon_{j,t}^s. \tag{11}$$

On the left-hand side, $GVC_{j,t}^s$ denotes the GVC measure for industry s in country j during year t. We will use each of the four measures (*F/GO*, *VA/GO*, *U*, and *D*) as this dependent variable; summary statistics for these country-industry GVC measures are presented in appendix Table 5.A1. On the right-hand side, the FE_j^s's denote country-industry fixed effects. The variable $Year_t$ then seeks to pick up whether there is a simple linear time trend in the evolution of $GVC_{j,t}^s$ within country-industry. In more detailed specifications, we will replace $Year_t$ with a full set of year dummies to trace the year-by-year evolution in the respective GVC measures. We report conservative standard errors that are multi-way clustered by country, industry, and year, to accommodate possible correlation in the $\epsilon_{j,t}^s$'s along each of these dimensions (Cameron *et al.* 2011).

Table 5.2 reports the results from this regression exercise. These confirm that the broad patterns documented earlier are present too in the evolution of GVC positioning within country-industry: Both the final-use share in gross output $((F/GO)_{j,t}^s$, Columns 1–2) and the value-added share in gross output $((VA/GO)_{j,t}^s$, Columns 3–4) have declined steadily over time. Conversely, upstreamness relative to final demand has been rising ($U_{j,t}^s$, Columns 5–6), as

Table 5.1 Country-level GVC position by rank (top and bottom five)

Rank:	F/GO (1995)		F/GO (2011)		Rank:	VA/GO (1995)		VA/GO (2011)	
1.	China	0.384	Luxembourg	0.296	1.	China	0.373	China	0.325
2.	Luxembourg	0.388	China	0.340	2.	Czech Rep.	0.403	Luxembourg	0.362
3.	Slovakia	0.394	Korea	0.377	3.	Slovakia	0.416	Korea	0.372
4.	Czech Rep.	0.408	Taiwan	0.396	4.	Estonia	0.430	Czech Rep.	0.383
5.	Russia	0.444	Czech Rep.	0.401	5.	Romania	0.454	Bulgaria	0.401
37.	Denmark	0.558	Brazil	0.557	37.	Austria	0.563	Brazil	0.561
38.	Brazil	0.572	USA	0.569	38.	Turkey	0.575	USA	0.562
39.	Turkey	0.605	Mexico	0.586	39.	Brazil	0.575	Mexico	0.581
40.	Greece	0.625	Cyprus	0.637	40.	Greece	0.576	Cyprus	0.586
41.	Cyprus	0.709	Greece	0.668	41.	Cyprus	0.625	Greece	0.628

Rank:	U (1995)		U (2011)		Rank:	D (1995)		D (2011)	
1.	Cyprus	1.451	Greece	1.546	1.	Cyprus	1.662	Greece	1.657
2.	Greece	1.611	Cyprus	1.617	2.	Brazil	1.748	Cyprus	1.763
3.	Turkey	1.666	Mexico	1.737	3.	Turkey	1.758	Mexico	1.779
4.	Brazil	1.755	USA	1.786	4.	Greece	1.759	Brazil	1.806
5.	Denmark	1.810	Brazil	1.824	5.	Austria	1.800	USA	1.808
37.	Russia	2.185	Czech Rep.	2.358	37.	Romania	2.155	Luxembourg	2.348
38.	Luxembourg	2.242	Taiwan	2.463	38.	Estonia	2.209	Bulgaria	2.370
39.	Czech Rep.	2.331	Korea	2.544	39.	Slovakia	2.306	Czech Rep.	2.444
40.	Slovakia	2.389	Luxembourg	2.581	40.	Czech Rep.	2.344	Korea	2.534
41.	China	2.535	China	2.819	41.	China	2.591	China	2.900

Notes: Rank order based on the respective GVC measures computed at the country level, i.e., based on the WIOD aggregated to a country-by-country panel of Input–Output Tables. The top and bottom five countries in the rank order are reported, for both 1995 and 2011.

Table 5.2 Evolution of GVC measures within country-industries over time

Dependent variable:	$(F/GO)^s_{jt}$ (1)	$(F/GO)^s_{jt}$ (2)	$(VA/GO)^s_{jt}$ (3)	$(VA/GO)^s_{jt}$ (4)	$(U)^s_{jt}$ (5)	$(U)^s_{jt}$ (6)	$(D)^s_{jt}$ (7)	$(D)^s_{jt}$ (8)
Year	-0.0009* [0.0004]		-0.0017*** [0.0005]		0.0064*** [0.0015]		0.0084*** [0.0017]	
Dum: Year=1996		-0.0002 [0.0025]		-0.0012 [0.0026]		-0.0060 [0.0083]		0.0019 [0.0079]
Dum: Year=1997		-0.0015 [0.0020]		-0.0024 [0.0020]		0.0026 [0.0068]		0.0061 [0.0062]
Dum: Year=1998		0.0026** [0.0010]		0.0002 [0.0015]		-0.0129*** [0.0032]		-0.0085* [0.0043]
Dum: Year=1999		0.0029*** [0.0004]		-0.0005 [0.0005]		-0.0086*** [0.0010]		-0.0073*** [0.0025]
Dum: Year=2000		-0.0015 [0.0014]		-0.0094*** [0.0016]		0.0140*** [0.0045]		0.0311*** [0.0045]
Dum: Year=2001		-0.0022 [0.0020]		-0.0122*** [0.0021]		0.0182*** [0.0065]		0.0394*** [0.0053]
Dum: Year=2002		-0.0010 [0.0024]		-0.0091*** [0.0022]		0.0069 [0.0069]		0.0218*** [0.0054]
Dum: Year=2003		-0.0033 [0.0027]		-0.0102*** [0.0022]		0.0204** [0.0082]		0.0334* [0.0059]
Dum: Year=2004		-0.0052 [0.0030]		-0.0135*** [0.0025]		0.0346*** [0.0100]		0.0490*** [0.0079]
Dum: Year=2005		-0.0061* [0.0031]		-0.0153*** [0.0032]		0.0421*** [0.0099]		0.0657*** [0.0101]

(Continued)

Table 5.2 (Continued)

Dependent variable:	$(F'/GO)^s_{j,t}$ (1)	$(F/GO)^s_{j,t}$ (2)	$(VA/GO)^s_{j,t}$ (3)	$(VA/GO)^s_{j,t}$ (4)	$(U)^s_{j,t}$ (5)	$(U)^s_{j,t}$ (6)	$(D)^s_{j,t}$ (7)	$(D)^s_{j,t}$ (8)
Dum: Year=2006		-0.0084**		-0.0208***		0.0598***		0.0919***
		[0.0033]		[0.0036]		[0.0117]		[0.0115]
Dum: Year=2007		-0.0119***		-0.0237***		0.0797***		0.1103***
		[0.0038]		[0.0039]		[0.0137]		[0.0133]
Dum: Year=2008		-0.0130***		-0.0287***		0.0894***		0.1333***
		[0.0044]		[0.0048]		[0.0159]		[0.0154]
Dum: Year=2009		-0.0075		-0.0164***		0.0562***		0.0746***
		[0.0052]		[0.0052]		[0.0171]		[0.0150]
Dum: Year=2010		-0.0102*		-0.0211***		0.0738***		0.1027***
		[0.0055]		[0.0053]		[0.0180]		[0.0167]
Dum: Year=2011		-0.0111*		-0.0226***		0.0822***		0.1110***
		[0.0055]		[0.0054]		[0.0179]		[0.0168]
Country-Industry FE?	Y	Y	Y	Y	Y	Y	Y	Y
Observations	24,076	24,076	24,395	24,395	24,395	24,395	24,395	24,395
R^2	0.9709	0.9709	0.9491	0.9495	0.9632	0.9636	0.9444	0.9460

Notes: The sample comprises all countries (41), industries (35), and years (17) in the WIOD. Standard errors are multi-way clustered by country, industry, and year; ***, **, and * denote significance at the 1%, 5%, and 10% levels respectively. The dependent variables are respectively the GVC measures computed at the country-industry level for each year. All columns control for country-industry (i.e., j-s) pair fixed effects; columns (2), (4), (6), and (8) further include year fixed effects, with the omitted category being the dummy for 1995.

has been its production-staging distance from primary factors ($D^s_{j,t}$, Columns 7–8). The estimates in the odd-numbered columns point to a significant linear time trend, this being negative in the case of *F/GO* and *VA/GO*, while positive in the case of *U* and *D*. Inspecting more closely the coefficients of the year dummies in the even-numbered columns, most of the movement over time in these GVC measures appears to have kicked in starting in 2000.[17,18]

In sum, the decline in *F/GO* and *VA/GO*, and the rise in *U* and *D*, appear to be pervasive phenomena. These patterns are clearly visible in how the country-level measures of GVC positioning have moved over time. They also emerge robustly from more formal regressions that exploit within country-industry movements in the GVC measures.

3.2. Puzzling correlations

The findings in the previous subsection hint at interesting patterns of co-movement among the GVC positioning measures. We explore this dimension of the data more carefully now, specifically the correlation between *F/GO* and *VA/GO* (respectively, *U* and *D*) across countries, and how this correlation has behaved over the period 1995–2011.

As GVCs have grown in importance as a mode of production, one might have imagined that individual countries would have gradually positioned themselves (on average) in particular segments of these GVCs in which they have comparative advantage. For example, one might have expected that countries with comparative advantage in natural resources or basic parts and components would have increasingly specialized in early stages of production processes, and would have consequently experienced a downward shift in *F/GO* and an increase in *VA/GO*. Conversely, countries with comparative advantage in production stages that are closer to final assembly would have been expected to experience a rise in *F/GO* and a decline in *VA/GO*.[19] If such a scenario had indeed played out, this should have led any positive correlation between *F/GO* and *VA/GO* to weaken over time, and perhaps even turn negative.

Figure 5.4 reveals, however, that the actual patterns in the data are surprisingly at odds with this prior intuition. The upper row in this figure plots the country-level measures of *F/GO* against *VA/GO* in 1995 and 2011 respectively. A positive relationship between these two measures stands out in both years, and this relationship actually appears to have tightened around the line of best fit by the end of the period. The plots in the bottom row demonstrate that a similarly strong positive relationship has persisted between the country-level measures of *U* and *D*. These observations are moreover consistent with what was seen earlier in the country rank lists in Table 5.1. We saw there that countries such as China and Luxembourg were among the bottom-five according to *both F/GO* and *VA/GO* across the sample period. Similarly, countries such as Brazil, Greece, and Cyprus were consistently ranked in the top-five of both of these GVC measures. This persistent correlation between *F/GO* and *VA/GO* is surprising, as it is a

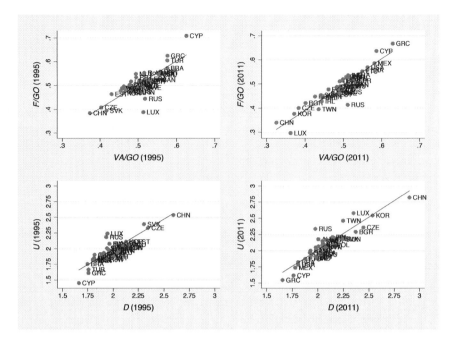

Figure 5.4 GVC positioning measures and their correlation over time

feature that would be more consistent with a world in which trade costs have remained relatively high. Recall in particular from the discussion in the Introduction that in the extreme case of autarky, the cross-country correlation between *F/GO* and *VA/GO* would a perfect one. Taken at face value, this suggests that trade costs have perhaps not fallen enough to cause any significant dampening in this positive correlation.

Taking a more detailed look at the annual data, Figure 5.5 shows that these correlations are not anomalous or specific to 1995 or 2011. The upper panel here plots the pairwise correlation between *F/GO* and *VA/GO* at the country level for each year in the sample. The correlation was already strong at the beginning of the period (equal to 0.825 in 1995), and contrary to what we might expect in an age of rising GVC activity, it in fact strengthened gradually over time (0.925 by 2011). The bottom panel provides a closely related illustration. There, we have run a simple bivariate regression of the country-level measures of *F/GO* against *VA/GO*, separately for each year between 1995 and 2011. The estimates of the coefficient of *VA/GO* have been plotted, together with their associated 95 per cent confidence interval bands. The positive partial correlation between the final-use and the value-added shares of gross output is always precisely estimated, with the slope coefficient itself hovering around 1 in each year. In sum, the positive correlation between *F/GO* and *VA/GO* has shown no sign of waning over time.

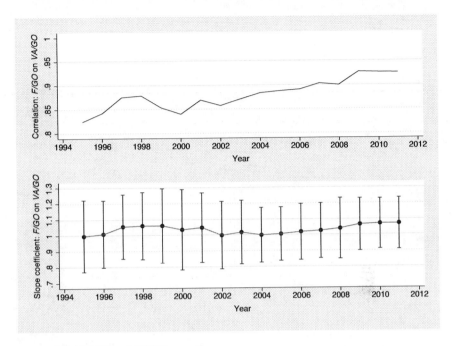

Figure 5.5 FU/GO and VA/GO over time

An analogous set of correlations can be documented between the country-level measures of U and D. As seen in Section 2, the definition of U would lead us to expect that it would be inversely correlated with F/GO, as the more upstream a country is from sources of final demand, the lower would be the share of country output that goes directly to final-use. Similarly, D exhibits a negative correlation with VA/GO, so that the more downstream a country is from primary factors, the lower would be the share of gross output that goes towards direct payments to those factors.[20] We therefore obtain a positive correlation in Figure 5.6 between U and D in each year, in line with what was seen earlier for F/GO and VA/GO. We find once again that there are no clear signs of a weakening in the positive U-D correlation in more recent years (upper panel), while the bivariate slope coefficient is positive and relatively stable over time (lower panel).

The positive association between F/GO and VA/GO, as well as that between U and D, are robust features even when we turn to the more detailed country-industry measures of GVC positioning. Toward this end, we have run a series of regressions of the form:

$$(F/GO)_{j,t}^s = \beta_1 (VA/GO)_{j,t}^s + FE_j + FE^s + \epsilon_{j,t}^s, \tag{12}$$

to uncover how the country-industry measures of F/GO and VA/GO are correlated in any given year t. In the interest of space, we have reported the findings for $t =$

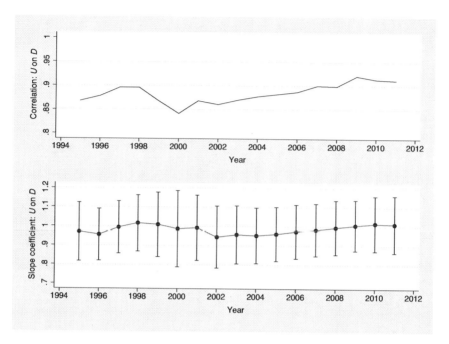

Figure 5.6 *U* and *D* over time

1995 and $t = 2011$ in Table 5.3, but the results for other years are very similar. For each year, the table reports the estimates from three different specifications, namely: (i) a simple bivariate regression with no fixed effects, to assess the unconditional cross-sectional correlation between *F/GO* and *VA/GO*; (ii) a second regression that then controls for country fixed effects (FE_j); and (iii) a last regression that further includes industry fixed effects (FE^s) as in (12) above. These results are presented in the upper row of Table 5.3, while the bottom row performs the analogous exercise from regressing *U* against *D*. (The standard errors in the table are two-way clustered, by country and industry.)

Even in the simple bivariate regressions, we already find a positive association between *F/GO* and *VA/GO* (respectively, between *U* and *D*) in the raw cross-section (Columns 1, 4, 7, 10). The R^2's for these regressions range from 0.1–0.2, pointing to a fair bit of unexplained variation in the data, but the highly significant slope coefficient estimates clearly point at a positive correlation. Controlling for country fixed effects (Columns 2, 5, 8, 11), and further for industry fixed effects (Columns 3, 6, 9, 12), successively reduces the magnitude of this slope coefficient, but it always remains statistically significant except in Column 3 for the relationship between *F/GO* and *VA/GO* at the start of the sample period. In short, the positive associations between *F/GO* and *VA/GO*, as well as between *U* and *D*, are present even when we focus on these different

Table 5.3 Correlation between country-industry GVC measures

Dependent variable:	$(F/GO)^s_{j,t}$ 1995	$(F/GO)^s_{j,t}$ 1995	$(F/GO)^s_{j,t}$ 1995	$(F/GO)^s_{j,t}$ 2011	$(F/GO)^s_{j,t}$ 2011	$(F/GO)^s_{j,t}$ 2011
	(1)	(2)	(3)	(4)	(5)	(6)
$(VA/GO)^s_{j,t}$	0.5438***	0.5196**	0.0775	0.6543***	0.6373***	0.2647***
	[0.1815]	[0.1924]	[0.0543]	[0.1647]	[0.1740]	[0.0527]
Country FE?	N	Y	Y	N	Y	Y
Industry FE?	N	N	Y	N	N	Y
Observations	1,417	1,417	1,417	1,414	1,414	1,414
R^2	0.1285	0.1488	0.8392	0.1927	0.2033	0.8479

Dependent variable:	$(U)^s_{j,t}$ 1995	$(U)^s_{j,t}$ 1995	$(U)^s_{j,t}$ 1995	$(U)^s_{j,t}$ 2011	$(U)^s_{j,t}$ 2011	$(U)^s_{j,t}$ 2011
	(7)	(8)	(9)	(10)	(11)	(12)
$(D)^s_{j,t}$	0.5308***	0.4820**	0.2413***	0.6213***	0.5707***	0.3772***
	[0.1640]	[0.1902]	[0.0604]	[0.1454]	[0.1698]	[0.0617]
Country FE?	N	Y	Y	N	Y	Y
Industry FE?	N	N	Y	N	N	Y
Observations	1,435	1,435	1,435	1,435	1,435	1,435
R^2	0.1350	0.1742	0.8264	0.1946	0.2232	0.8325

Notes: The sample comprises all countries (41), industries (35), and years (17) in the WIOD. Standard errors are multi-way clustered by country and industry; ***, **, and * denote significance at the 1%, 5%, and 10% levels respectively. The dependent variables are GVC measures computed at the country-industry level for each year. The upper row reports regressions of F/GO against VA/GO, while the lower row reports regressions of U against D. Regressions are run for both 1995 and 2011; for each year, three specifications are reported: (i) with no fixed effects; (ii) with country fixed effects; and (iii) with country and industry fixed effects.

sources of variation in the measures of GVC positioning at the country-industry level.[21]

4. Proximate explanations

The correlations that we have just documented warrant closer investigation, as their persistence runs counter to what one might expect in an era of global production fragmentation. We take a first look in this section at two proximate explanations that could account (at least qualitatively) for these puzzling correlations, before turning to a model-based investigation in Sections 5 and 6.

4.1.   Trade costs

A first possibility is that trade costs might not in actuality have fallen as much as commonly perceived. If cross-border trade frictions have remained relatively high, this would provide an immediate explanation for the significant and persistent correlation between F/GO and VA/GO (and by extension, between U and D). One could naturally argue that high cross-border trade costs would in principle discourage rather than facilitate the formation of GVCs. But for the sake of argument, let us for now suspend that concern and instead examine what the data tell us about trade costs over this sample period.

We make use of the Head and Ries (2001) index as a measure of these cross-border trade costs, since this can readily be computed from information that is already contained in the WIOD. The Head-Ries index is usually constructed at the country level to yield a measure of bilateral trade costs. We extend this concept to the country-industry level, to capture trade costs from country i to j in industry r, and moreover distinguish between trade costs that are incurred when the good/service from industry r is being used as an intermediate input and when it is destined instead for final-use. Specifically, for each $i \neq j$, we compute:

$$\tau_{ij}^{rs} = \left(\frac{Z_{ij}^{rs} Z_{ji}^{rs}}{Z_{ii}^{rs} Z_{jj}^{rs}} \right)^{-\frac{1}{2\theta}} \text{, and} \tag{13}$$

$$\tau_{ij}^{rF} = \left(\frac{F_{ij}^{r} F_{ji}^{r}}{F_{ii}^{r} F_{jj}^{r}} \right)^{-\frac{1}{2\theta}}. \tag{14}$$

Note that τ_{ij}^{rs} denotes the trade costs associated with exporting sector-r intermediates from country i to country j when these are purchased as inputs by industry s. On the other hand, τ_{ij}^{rF} captures the corresponding trade costs incurred when the exports in question are purchased for final-use. From the above formulae, one can see that the Head-Ries index infers the magnitude of cross-border trade costs from the observed values of bilateral trade flows relative to domestic absorption.

The θ that appears in the exponent in (13) and (14) is the familiar trade elasticity with respect to iceberg trade costs, which we assume satisfies $\theta > 1$. Intuitively, the greater is the level of cross-border trade relative to domestic absorption, the lower would be the inferred iceberg trade costs; moreover, the greater is the trade elasticity, the lower will be the trade costs required to rationalize a given ratio of cross-border to domestic sales.

As is well-known, the Head-Ries index is an exact way to back out the iceberg trade cost when bilateral flows are characterized by a gravity equation with a constant trade elasticity θ, subject to two further assumptions. First, within-country trade costs are uniformly equal to 1; in our context, this amounts to normalizing $\tau_{ii}^{rs} = 1$ and $\tau_{ii}^{rF} = 1$ for all countries i and industry pairs r and s. Second, cross-border trade costs are directionally symmetric; in other words, we have $\tau_{ij}^{rs} = \tau_{ji}^{rs}$ and $\tau_{ij}^{rF} = \tau_{ji}^{rF}$ for all industries r and s, so that the cost of exporting for intermediate-use (respectively, for final-use) is equal regardless of whether one is exporting from country i to j or from j to i. The latter assumption in particular is more restrictive. As we shall see in Section 5, it potentially limits the flexibility of the model there to fully match all entries of a WIOT. That said, absent more direct measures of trade costs, the Head-Ries index provides a convenient empirical handle to assess how trade costs have been moving on average.

To get a sense of aggregate trends, we first use the country-by-country version of the WIOT (i.e., with the industry dimension collapsed out) to calculate the standard Head-Ries index of bilateral trade costs between country pairs.[22] We adopt a baseline value of $\theta = 5$ for the trade elasticity. We take for each year a simple average of the Head-Ries index over all country pairs with $i < j$ (bearing in mind the symmetric nature of the index), and then plot the trends over time in Figure 5.7. This is done separately for intermediate-use and final-use trade costs.[23]

Several observations emerge from Figure 5.7. Trade costs remain high in absolute levels, with the average iceberg friction still roughly 300 per cent in *ad valorem* equivalent terms even at the end of the sample period. That said, the overall trend between 1995 and 2011 has been one of declining trade costs, this being especially marked in the first half of the sample period.[24] Absent other forces, this fall in trade costs is difficult to reconcile with the persistence over time in the positive correlation between F/GO and VA/GO (as well as between U and D). Interestingly, while trade costs have fallen for both intermediate- and final-use, the average level of trade frictions faced by intermediate inputs has been lower than that for final-use throughout this period. This is consistent with a "tariff escalation" intuition: there is less incentive to impose barriers on trade in intermediates, since a country may end up bearing a portion of these trade costs if the inputs are embodied in final goods/services that the country eventually consumes.

This message of a broad decline in trade costs is reinforced when we examine the Head-Ries indices constructed at the country-industry level, as given by (13)

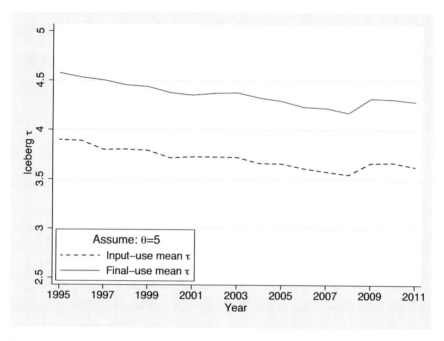

Figure 5.7 Head-Ries τ's (country-level) over time

and (14). With these measures, we find that even within narrowly defined country-industry pairs, there is strong evidence of a downward trend over time in trade costs. More specifically, we regress the log of each Head-Ries index against a linear time trend (*Year$_t$*) and an extensive set of fixed effects, as follows:

$$\ln \tau_{ij,t}^{rs} = \beta_0 Year_t + FE_{ij}^{rs} + \epsilon_{ij,t}^{rs}, \text{ and} \tag{15}$$

$$\ln \tau_{ij,t}^{rF} = \beta_0 Year_t + FE_{ij}^{r} + \epsilon_{ij,t}^{r}. \tag{16}$$

In the first regression involving trade costs for intermediate inputs, we include a full set of source country-industry by destination country-industry dummies (FE_{ij}^{rs}), this being the most comprehensive set of fixed effects that can be used while allowing us to identify the coefficient of the time trend. Similarly, in the second regression explaining trade costs for final-use, we include a full set of source country-industry by destination country dummies (FE_{ij}^{r}). The above regressions thus seek to isolate what could be called the pure "within" component of the time variation in these trade costs. The findings from estimating (15) and (16) are reported in Tables 5.4 and 5.5 respectively, based on Head-Ries indices calculated once again using a common value of $\theta = 5$. Given the directional symmetry described earlier, we include in Table 5.4 only those trade cost observations

Table 5.4 Head-Ries trade costs for intermediate inputs over time

Dependent variable:			log trade costs for intermediate inputs			
Industries:	(1) All	(2) All	(3) Goods	(4) Goods	(5) Services	(6) Services
Year	-0.0164***		-0.0181***		-0.0150***	
	[0.0022]		[0.0024]		[0.0026]	
Dum: Year=1996		-0.0052		-0.0211*		0.0085
		[0.0093]		[0.0108]		[0.0142]
Dum: Year=1997		-0.0782***		-0.0982***		-0.0609***
		[0.0048]		[0.0075]		[0.0061]
Dum: Year=1998		-0.1108***		-0.1503***		-0.0768***
		[0.0039]		[0.0077]		[0.0055]
Dum: Year=1999		-0.1129***		-0.1598***		-0.0725***
		[0.0048]		[0.0074]		[0.0063]
Dum: Year=2000		-0.1562***		-0.1850***		-0.1313***
		[0.0056]		[0.0079]		[0.0086]
Dum: Year=2001		-0.1653***		-0.2021***		-0.1336***
		[0.0067]		[0.0093]		[0.0099]
Dum: Year=2002		-0.1594***		-0.1936***		-0.1299***
		[0.0064]		[0.0079]		[0.0107]
Dum: Year=2003		-0.1778***		-0.2141***		-0.1465***
		[0.0100]		[0.0123]		[0.0154]
Dum: Year=2004		-0.2019***		-0.2219***		-0.1846***
		[0.0097]		[0.0115]		[0.0155]
Dum: Year=2005		-0.2239***		-0.2558***		-0.1965***
		[0.0109]		[0.0147]		[0.0159]

(Continued)

Table 5.4 (Continued)

Dependent variable:			log trade costs for intermediate inputs			
Industries:	(1) All	(2) All	(3) Goods	(4) Goods	(5) Services	(6) Services
Dum: Year=2006		-0.2491*** [0.0107]		-0.2781*** [0.0154]		-0.2241*** [0.0152]
Dum: Year=2007		-0.2629*** [0.0108]		-0.2895*** [0.0153]		-0.2400*** [0.0157]
Dum: Year=2008		-0.2697*** [0.0122]		-0.3055*** [0.0158]		-0.2387*** [0.0182]
Dum: Year=2009		-0.2727*** [0.0123]		-0.2991*** [0.0146]		-0.2499*** [0.0188]
Dum: Year=2010		-0.2425*** [0.0124]		-0.2989*** [0.0146]		-0.1939*** [0.0188]
Dum: Year=2011		-0.2544*** [0.0125]		-0.3157*** [0.0148]		-0.2016*** [0.0190]
Input Country-Industry by Destination Country-Industry FE?	Y	Y	Y	Y	Y	Y
Observations	17,491,215	17,491,215	8,101,928	8,101,928	9,389,287	9,389,287
R^2	0.8602	0.8604	0.7408	0.7414	0.8806	0.8808

Notes: The left-hand side variable is the Head-Ries index (computed with $\theta = 5$) associated with trade costs for intermediate inputs, from industry r in country i purchased by industry j in country j; for trade costs that correspond to input purchases that lie above the main diagonal of the WIOT in each year. Standard errors are multi-way clustered by source country-industry (i,r), destination country-industry (j,s), and year; ***, **, and * denote significance at the 1%, 5%, and 10% levels respectively. All columns control for source country-industry by destination country-industry fixed effects. Columns (3)–(4) restrict to the subsample of trade costs where the industry r is from the goods sectors, while Columns (5)–(6) restrict to the subsample where the industry r is from the services sectors.

Table 5.5 Head-Ries trade costs for final-use over time

		log trade costs for final goods/services				
Dependent variable:						
Industries:	(1) All	(2) All	(3) Goods	(4) Goods	(5) Services	(6) Services
Year	−0.0212*** [0.0039]		−0.0231*** [0.0041]		−0.0196*** [0.0051]	
Dum: Year=1996		−0.0217 [0.0332]		−0.0510* [0.0278]		0.0029 [0.0550]
Dum: Year=1997		−0.1123*** [0.0104]		−0.1306*** [0.0146]		−0.0968*** [0.0115]
Dum: Year=1998		−0.1588*** [0.0099]		−0.2095*** [0.0116]		−0.1161*** [0.0168]
Dum: Year=1999		−0.1479*** [0.0193]		−0.1910*** [0.0090]		−0.1115** [0.0441]
Dum: Year=2000		−0.2001*** [0.0257]		−0.2445*** [0.0162]		−0.1628*** [0.0456]
Dum: Year=2001		−0.2370*** [0.0233]		−0.2708*** [0.0245]		−0.2084*** [0.0360]
Dum: Year=2002		−0.2295*** [0.0179]		−0.2589*** [0.0238]		−0.2047*** [0.0359]
Dum: Year=2003		−0.2500*** [0.0251]		−0.2825*** [0.0251]		−0.2225*** [0.0423]
Dum: Year=2004		−0.2814*** [0.0304]		−0.2951*** [0.0303]		−0.2699*** [0.0435]
Dum: Year=2005		−0.3024*** [0.0323]		−0.3417*** [0.0372]		−0.2693*** [0.0435]

(Continued)

Table 5.5 (Continued)

Dependent variable:		log trade costs for final goods/services				
Industries:	(1) All	(2) All	(3) Goods	(4) Goods	(5) Services	(6) Services
Dum: Year=2006		-0.3260***		-0.3652***		-0.2930***
		[0.0307]		[0.0372]		[0.0425]
Dum: Year=2007		-0.3470***		-0.3764***		-0.3223***
		[0.0317]		[0.0399]		[0.0429]
Dum: Year=2008		-0.3524***		-0.3858***		-0.3244***
		[0.0391]		[0.0386]		[0.0555]
Dum: Year=2009		-0.3588***		-0.3964***		-0.3272***
		[0.0392]		[0.0397]		[0.0547]
Dum: Year=2010		-0.3250***		-0.3899***		-0.2704***
		[0.0413]		[0.0380]		[0.0576]
Dum: Year=2011		-0.3421***		-0.4137***		-0.2818***
		[0.0421]		[0.0437]		[0.0585]
Source Country-Industry by Destination Country FE?	Y	Y	Y	Y	Y	Y
Observations	487,900	487,900	223,040	223,040	264,860	264,860
R^2	0.9002	0.9005	0.7109	0.7119	0.9140	0.9143

Notes: The left-hand side variable is the Head-Ries index (computed with $\theta = 5$) associated with trade costs for final-use sales, from industry r in country i purchased by country j, for all $i < j$. Standard errors are multi-way clustered by source country-industry (i,r), destination country (j), and year; ***, **, and * denote significance at the 1%, 5%, and 10% levels respectively. All columns control for source country-industry by destination country fixed effects. Columns (3)–(4) restrict to the subsample where the industry r is from the goods sectors, while Columns (5)–(6) restrict to the subsample where the industry r is from the services sectors.

corresponding to input-use purchases that lie above the main diagonal of the matrix of Z_{ij}^{rs}'s in the WIOT in any given year, while we include in Table 5.5 only observations for which the country index satisfies $i < j$. Even so, the regression sample is very large, especially in Table 5.4: For trade costs related to intermediate inputs, we will report results for specifications with close to 17.5 million observations, with more than 1 million fixed effects used!

Turning now to these results, we obtain coefficients on $Year_t$ that are negative and highly significant in Column 1 in both Tables 5.4 and 5.5. (The standard errors are multi-way clustered by source country-industry, destination country-industry, and year in Table 5.4, while clustered by source country-industry, destination country, and year in Table 5.5.) For trade in intermediates, the point estimate indicates an average fall in trade costs of about 1.6 per cent per year. The corresponding fall has been slightly faster for final-use trade costs, namely a 2.1 per cent decrease per year. A very similar pattern emerges in Column 2, when replacing the linear time trend with a full set of year dummies. Over the course of 1995–2011, the average within-category fall in intermediate input trade costs was a cumulative 25.4 per cent, while the corresponding decline for final-use trade costs was 34.2 per cent.

We have also explored whether there are differences in the manner of these trade cost movements across goods versus service industries, given that this sectoral distinction will play an important part in the next subsection. This is done in the remaining columns of Tables 5.4 and 5.5, which look at trade in goods (Columns 3–4) versus trade in services (Columns 5–6). From these columns, it is clear that the decrease in trade costs is a feature shared by both goods and service industries. Separately, we have found similar patterns when allowing for differences across industries in the trade elasticity used to compute the Head-Ries indices, specifically when using the industry-level estimates of θ from Caliendo and Parro (2015) matched to the WIOD industry categories.[25] The conclusion of a broad decline in trade costs is also robust to dropping the largest 1 per cent, 5 per cent, 10 per cent, 25 per cent, and even 50 per cent of the trade cost observations in each table (results available on request), so that the patterns are unlikely to be driven by observations that correspond to small trade flows.[26]

Ceteris paribus, the widespread decrease in cross-border trade costs would in principle have spurred GVC activity, which in turn might lead us to expect that the link between F/GO and VA/GO would have weakened. It is thus difficult to rationalize the persistence in the correlation between F/GO and VA/GO (as well as that between U and D) on the basis of the observed movements in trade costs alone. We are left to conclude that other forces must have been at play that account for these puzzling correlations between the GVC measures.

4.2.   Composition of industries: goods versus services

As a second proximate explanation, we explore the possibility of shifts in the underlying composition of industrial activity. This is motivated by the observation from appendix Table 5.A1, that there are distinct differences between goods and service industries in the nature of their GVC positioning. Goods-producing industries feature on average a lower share of their output going directly to final-use and are more upstream relative to final demand when compared against service industries, likely reflecting that the manufacturing process for goods can be more easily fragmented into stages involving separate parts and components. At the same time, goods industries also exhibit a lower share of payments to primary value-added and are more downstream relative to primary factors than service industries, presumably because payments to labor comprise a larger share of the production costs in service industries. Goods industries thus appear to be positioned in "longer" production chains – with more stages both upstream and downstream – than service industries.

This raises a potential explanation for the positive correlation between *F/GO* and *VA/GO* at the country level: Suppose that countries differ in their comparative advantage across goods versus services. Countries with comparative advantage in services would then feature low final-use and value-added shares in gross output ("short" GVCs), with the converse being true for countries that have comparative advantage in goods-producing industries ("long" GVCs). In the cross-section of countries, this would manifest itself as a positive correlation between *F/GO* and *VA/GO* (as well as between *U* and *D*). Pursuing this logic further, a decline in cross-border trade costs of the type documented in Figure 5.7, applying broadly to both goods and services, would reinforce this pre-existing pattern of comparative advantage, and could even strengthen these positive correlations.

To explore whether such a mechanism may have been at play, we examine how patterns of specialization across countries in goods versus services have evolved over time. We do so by looking at the service sector's share of gross output within each country. (Recall from footnote 17 that industries 17–35 in the WIOD are classified as services, while industries 1–16 are goods-producing.) This services share has been on the rise, from an average across countries of 59.5 per cent in 1995 to 65.6 per cent in 2011. At the same time, this secular rise in recorded service activity was accompanied by a mild increase in dispersion in the services share across economies. This is illustrated in Figure 5.8, where we have plotted these services shares after demeaning by the cross-country average in each respective year. The figure points to an increase between 1995 and 2011 in the observed spread in the services share: Countries such as Luxembourg, Cyprus, and Great Britain that initially were relatively specialized in services have become even more so, while economies such as China, Korea, and Taiwan have become more skewed towards producing goods.[27] These compositional shifts in output between goods and services thus appear to be moving in the right direction to help account for the cross-country correlation puzzle among the GVC measures. Admittedly, however, our empirical results so far cannot help us elucidate the extent to which the shifts observed in Figure 5.8 are directly related to the trade cost reductions documented in Figure 5.7. We will return to this point in Section 6, after having developed our quantitative model.

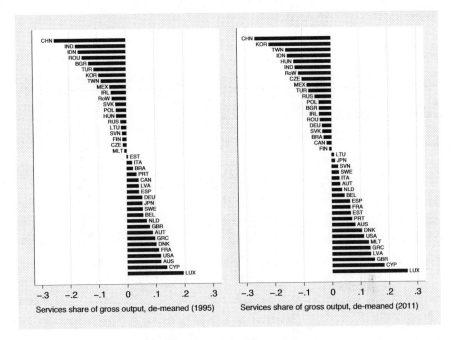

Figure 5.8 Services share of gross output over time

Can the rise of services help to account too for the correlation puzzle at the *country-industry* level? Figure 5.9 plots the relationship between *F/GO* and *VA/GO*, constructed at the country-industry level, for the goods and services sectors separately; a third subplot illustrates the relationship when pooling across all industries. While the figures are drawn for 2011, the message is similar if one were to look at 1995 instead. A quick comparison of the first two subplots confirms that goods industries tend to feature lower final-use and value-added to gross-output ratios than service industries. The respective lines of best fit (drawn with 95 per cent confidence interval bands) moreover demonstrate that it is the service industries that are driving the overall positive correlation between *F/GO* and *VA/GO*; the corresponding correlation when looking at goods industries is in fact weakly negative. Figure 5.10 performs the analogous exercise for the country-industry measures of *U* and *D*. In line with appendix Table 5.A1, the service industries are on average more proximate to final-use, as well as to primary factors, when compared to the goods industries. The raw correlation between *U* and *D* is now slightly positive when examining just the industries in the goods sector. But this relationship is particularly marked for the service sector, which ultimately contributes to the strong positive slope seen between *U* and *D* when pooling across all industries. Put otherwise, absent the service industries, the correlations between *F/GO* and *VA/GO* (as well as between *U* and *D*) would clearly be much weaker.

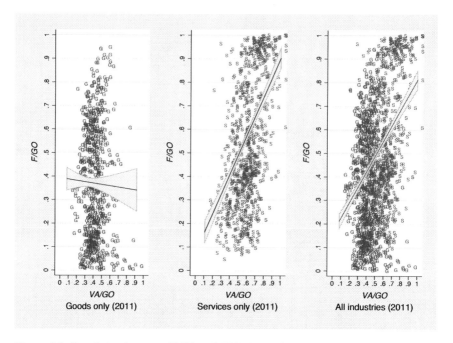

Figure 5.9 Correlation between *F/GO* and *VA/GO*: goods versus services

We round off this subsection by further documenting that there has been a compositional shift away from goods and towards services over the sample period. This is important for translating the positive correlations described above at the country-industry level into a corresponding set of correlations at more aggregate levels (say when aggregating over all industries within a country). More specifically, we show that over time: (i) services have risen as a share of final-use expenditures; and (ii) service inputs have risen as a share of gross-output value.

Focusing first on (i), we calculate the share of industry s in the final-use expenditures of country j as: $\alpha_j^s = (\sum_{i=1}^J F_{ij}^s)/(\sum_{i=1}^J \sum_{s=1}^S F_{ij}^s)$. Pooling these α_j^s's over all years t in the WIOD, we then explore how these shares have evolved over time with the following regression:

$$\ln \alpha_{j,t}^s = \beta_0 Year_t + FE_j^s + \epsilon_{j,t}^s. \tag{17}$$

As before, the use of the FE_j^s fixed effects means that we are estimating the $Year_t$ coefficient off time variation within the industry-by-country bins. Table 5.6 presents these regression results; multi-way clustered standard errors (by country, industry, and year) are reported. Since the $\alpha_{j,t}^s$'s sum up to 1 in any given country and year, any increases over time in the expenditure shares on particular goods or services would need to be offset by decreases in the shares spent on

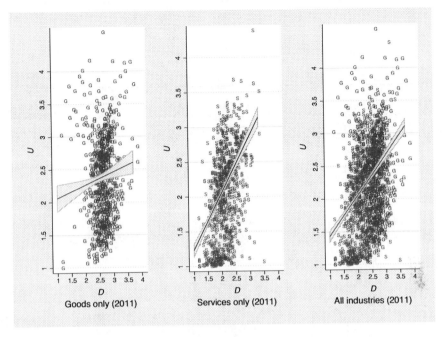

Figure 5.10 Correlation between *U* and *D*: goods versus services

other industries; in line with this, we find no significant time trend on average when pooling across all industries (Columns 1–2). However, a distinct pattern emerges when we separate goods from services and re-run (17): There has been a significant decline in the goods industries' shares in final demand over time (Columns 3–4), and this has been accompanied correspondingly by an increase in the expenditure shares on services (Column 5–6). While the coefficient on the linear time trend in Column 5 is marginally insignificant, the more flexible specification with year dummies in Column 6 uncovers a positive effect over time (albeit one that has tapered off slightly in the last few years).

Turning to (ii), we take a similar look at how the importance of goods versus service inputs has shifted. This is done by computing (once again from the WIOD) the following measures of the share of sector-*r* inputs in the value of gross output of industry *s* in country *j*, namely: $\gamma_j^{rs} = (\sum_{i=1}^{J} Z_{ij}^{rs})/(Y_j^s)$. We focus on the variation over time within each *r*-by-*s*-by-*j* bin using:

$$\ln \gamma_{j,t}^{rs} = \beta_0 Year_t + FE_j^{rs} + \epsilon_{j,t}^{rs}, \tag{18}$$

where FE_j^{rs} denotes a full set of industry-pair by destination country fixed effects. The results in Table 5.7 highlight the rising importance of services versus goods, this time as an input in production processes. There is no distinct pattern seen in these input purchase shares over time when looking over all inputs (Columns 1

Table 5.6 Final-use expenditure shares over time

Dependent variable:		log expenditure shares, a_j^s				
Industries:	(1) All	(2) All	(3) Goods	(4) Goods	(5) Services	(6) Services
Year	-0.0038 [0.0025]		-0.0127*** [0.0037]		0.0037 [0.0025]	
Dum: Year=1996		0.0016 [0.0148]		-0.0087 [0.0183]		0.0104 [0.0200]
Dum: Year=1997		-0.0078 [0.0117]		-0.0230* [0.0127]		0.0050 [0.0137]
Dum: Year=1998		-0.0139 [0.0081]		-0.0493*** [0.0158]		0.0160** [0.0059]
Dum: Year=1999		-0.0070*** [0.0022]		-0.0633*** [0.0077]		0.0405*** [0.0036]
Dum: Year=2000		0.0028 [0.0060]		-0.0497*** [0.0130]		0.0470*** [0.0086]
Dum: Year=2001		-0.0013 [0.0099]		-0.0718*** [0.0119]		0.0582*** [0.0155]
Dum: Year=2002		-0.0123 [0.0144]		-0.0991*** [0.0104]		0.0609** [0.0231]
Dum: Year=2003		-0.0192 [0.0159]		-0.1171*** [0.0134]		0.0633** [0.0222]
Dum: Year=2004		-0.0165 [0.0185]		-0.1130*** [0.0250]		0.0648*** [0.0212]

	(1)	(2)	(3)	(4)	(5)	(6)
Dum: Year=2005		-0.0136		-0.1123***		0.0697***
		[0.0216]		[0.0344]		[0.0232]
Dum: Year=2006		-0.0207		-0.1164**		0.0601**
		[0.0234]		[0.0396]		[0.0245]
Dum: Year=2007		-0.0226		-0.1188**		0.0584**
		[0.0235]		[0.0405]		[0.0247]
Dum: Year=2008		-0.0315		-0.1409***		0.0607**
		[0.0256]		[0.0440]		[0.0225]
Dum: Year=2009		-0.0687**		-0.2297***		0.0670**
		[0.0303]		[0.0345]		[0.0311]
Dum: Year=2010		-0.0645**		-0.2103***		0.0583*
		[0.0294]		[0.0373]		[0.0373]
Dum: Year=2011		-0.0579*		-0.1938***		0.0567*
		[0.0292]		[0.0403]		[0.0403]
Input Industry by Purchasing Country FE?	Y	Y	Y	Y	Y	Y
Observations	24,392	24,392	11,152	11,152	13,240	13,240
R^2	0.9833	0.9834	0.9713	0.9715	0.9872	0.9872

Notes: The sample comprises all countries (41), industries (35), and years (17) in the WIOD. Standard errors are multi-way clustered by country, industry, and year; ***, **, and * denote significance at the 1%, 5%, and 10% levels respectively. The dependent variable is the log expenditure share in country j on final-use purchases from industry s. All columns control for country-industry (i.e., j-s) pair fixed effects; columns (2), (4), and (6) further include year fixed effects, with the omitted category being the year dummy for 1995. Columns (1)–(2) run the regression on all observations; columns (3)–(4) restrict to expenditure shares for purchases from goods industries; while columns (5)–(6) restrict to expenditure shares for purchases from services industries.

Table 5.7 Input-use shares over time

| Dependent variable: | | | log input-use shares, γ_{ij}^{rs} | | | |
Industries:	(1) All	(2) All	(3) Goods	(4) Goods	(5) Services	(6) Services
Year	0.0000 [0.00031]		-0.0113** [0.0043]		0.0097*** [0.0031]	
Dum: Year=1996		0.0098 [0.0160]		-0.0050 [0.0186]		0.0227 [0.0142]
Dum: Year=1997		0.0093 [0.0134]		-0.0209 [0.0167]		0.0351** [0.0167]
Dum: Year=1998		-0.0031 [0.0110]		-0.0580*** [0.0186]		0.0437*** [0.0130]
Dum: Year=1999		0.0013 [0.0043]		-0.0728*** [0.0087]		0.0643*** [0.0087]
Dum: Year=2000		0.0204*** [0.0032]		-0.0544*** [0.0091]		0.0840*** [0.0062]
Dum: Year=2001		0.0450*** [0.0119]		-0.0660*** [0.0103]		0.1391*** [0.0157]
Dum: Year=2002		0.0335** [0.0154]		-0.0894*** [0.0116]		0.1377*** [0.0193]
Dum: Year=2003		0.0234 [0.0183]		-0.1068*** [0.0166]		0.1337*** [0.0209]
Dum: Year=2004		0.0353 [0.0230]		-0.1028*** [0.0276]		0.1524*** [0.0242]

	(1)	(2)	(3)	(4)	(5)	(6)
Dum: Year=2005		0.0353		-0.1032**		0.1526***
		[0.0260]		[0.0372]		[0.0250]
Dum: Year=2006		0.0300		-0.1072**		0.1462***
		[0.0269]		[0.0415]		[0.0235]
Dum: Year=2007		0.0309		-0.1154**		0.1549***
		[0.0292]		[0.0437]		[0.0254]
Dum: Year=2008		0.0226		-0.1298**		0.1518***
		[0.0318]		[0.0494]		[0.0264]
Dum: Year=2009		-0.0112		-0.2111***		0.1581***
		[0.0363]		[0.0440]		[0.0298]
Dum: Year=2010		-0.0044		-0.1891***		0.1520***
		[0.0352]		[0.0460]		[0.0297]
Dum: Year=2011		-0.0021		-0.1773***		0.1463***
		[0.0350]		[0.0486]		[0.0300]
Input industry by Purchasing Country-Industry FE?	Y	Y	Y	Y	Y	Y
Observations	826,130	826,130	378,258	378,258	447,872	447,872
R²	0.9622	0.9623	0.9543	0.9543	0.9662	0.9662

Notes: The sample comprises all input industries (35), purchasing country-industry pairs (41x35), and years (17) in the WIOD. Standard errors are multi-way clustered by input industry, purchasing country-industry, and year; ***, **, and * denote significance at the 1%, 5%, and 10% levels respectively. The dependent variable is the log share of purchases on inputs from industry r by industry s in country j. All columns control for country by industry by country fixed effects; columns (2), (4), and (6) further include year fixed effects, with the omitted category being the year dummy for 1995. Columns (1)–(2) run the regression on all observations; columns (3)–(4) restrict to input shares for purchases from goods industries; while columns (5)–(6) restrict to input shares for purchases from services industries.

and 2). When separately examining goods and services purchases though, we immediately detect a downward time trend in the purchases of inputs from goods industries (Columns 3 and 4), and a corresponding rise over time in that associated with services (Columns 5 and 6). Comparing the point estimates in Column 5 across Tables 5.6 and 5.7, each successive year is associated with an increase in the services input-use share of about 0.97 per cent per annum, versus an increase in the final-use share of about 0.37 per cent per annum; the rise in purchases of services has thus been larger in proportional terms for intermediate input-use than for final-use.

This observed increase in the use of services as an intermediate input warrants some discussion. One interpretation is that production technologies have indeed shifted toward substituting the use of more service for goods inputs. This view would be in line with the "servification" hypothesis, as articulated for example by Baldwin and Ito (2014). An alternative interpretation is that the use of services is now recorded more comprehensively as a result of a rise in outsourcing. Services that previously were performed in-house – ranging from basic janitorial services to more complex accounting work – are now increasingly performed by sub-contractors that are independent entities located outside of firm headquarters. Such activity might in the past have been recorded as payments to labor within the firm, but are now picked up instead as payments across establishments and firms with the rise of such outsourcing practices. The observed increase in services purchases may thus be a reflection of such organizational rather than technological change *per se*.[28]

Distinguishing between these two hypotheses is an interesting research question, but one that lies beyond the scope of this chapter. What should be clear is that the shifting composition of goods versus services industries – with the latter rising in importance in both final expenditures and input purchases – has potential to explain why F/GO and VA/GO (respectively, U and D) have remained positively correlated at both the country and country-industry levels.

5.   A structural interpretation of the data

We turn next to develop a theoretical framework that provides a structural interpretation of all the cells in a WIOT, and that hence allows for a basic quantitative assessment of the extent to which trade cost declines and the rising importance of services can help to account for the correlations seen over time between the various GVC measures.

5.1.   A useful starting point

The Caliendo and Parro (2015) model provides a useful starting point. Consider a world with $J \geq 1$ countries and $S \geq 1$ sectors or industries. This gives rise to a $J \times S$ by $J \times S$ matrix of bilateral country-industry trade shares for trade in intermediate inputs, and a $J \times S$ by J matrix of trade shares for trade designated for final-use.

For the purposes of clarity, let us establish upfront the notation to index the economic variables in the exposition, which deviates from Caliendo and Parro (2015). As in our empirical sections, we use the *subscripts i* and *j* to refer throughout to countries; whenever a pair of subscripts is used (e.g., to describe a trade flow variable), the left subscript will denote the source country, while the right subscript will denote the destination country (so *ij* corresponds to a flow from *i* to *j*). On the other hand, we use the *superscripts r* and *s* to refer to industries; once again, whenever a pair of superscripts is used on a variable, the left superscript will be the identity of the source (i.e., selling) industry, while the right superscript will be the identity of the destination (i.e., buying) industry (so *rs* is a purchase from industry *r* by industry *s*).

5.1.1. Model set-up and equilibrium

Preferences are country-specific and take the form:

$$u(C_j) = \prod_{s=1}^{S} \left(C_j^s \right)^{\alpha_j^s}, \tag{19}$$

where C_j^s denotes consumption of a sector-*s* aggregate, C_j denotes the vector of the C_j^s's consumed in country *j*, α_j^s is the share of industry *s* in the expenditure of the country-*j* representative consumer, and $\sum_{s=1}^{S} \alpha_j^s = 1$.

Within each industry *s*, there is a continuum of varieties indexed by $\omega^s \in [0, 1]$. Production of each variety is a Cobb-Douglas function of equipped labor, as well as intermediate inputs. More specifically, in country *j*, the production function for each industry-*s* variety is given by:

$$y_j^s(\omega^s) = z_j^s(\omega^s) \left(l_j^s(\omega^s) \right)^{1-\sum_{r=1}^{S} \gamma_j^{rs}} \prod_{r=1}^{S} \left(\mathcal{M}_j^{rs}(\omega^s) \right)^{\gamma_j^{rs}}. \tag{20}$$

Note that $\mathcal{M}_j^{rs}(\omega^s)$ is the amount of composite intermediates from industry *r* used in the production of variety ω^s in country *j*. The exponent γ_j^{rs} is the (constant) share of production costs spent on intermediate inputs from sector *r* by each industry-*s* producer in country *j*. We assume that $0 < \gamma_j^{rs} < 1$, and moreover that $0 < \sum_{r=1}^{S} \gamma_j^{rs} < 1$, so that the equipped labor share (or simply, value-added share) of production costs is strictly positive in all sectors and countries. The productivity shifter $z_j^s(\omega^s)$ is an i.i.d. draw from a Fréchet distribution with cumulative density function: $\exp\{-T_j^s z^{-\theta^s}\}$. The scale parameter T_j^s governs the state of technology of country *j* in industry *s*, while $\theta^s > 1$ governs (inversely) the dispersion of productivity in industry *s* across producers worldwide, thereby shaping comparative advantage.

The country-j composite in industry s, which is used both for final consumption (C_j^s), as well as to provide inputs to other sectors r ($\mathcal{M}_j^{sr}$), is a CES aggregate over the set of varieties on the unit interval:

$$Q_j^s = \left(\int q_j^s(\omega^s)^{1-1/\sigma^s} \, d\omega^s \right)^{\sigma^s/(\sigma^s-1)}, \tag{21}$$

where $q_j^s(\omega^s)$ denotes the quantity of variety ω^s that is ultimately purchased, naturally from the lowest-cost source country. Note that the same CES aggregator over varieties applies to the industry-s composite, whether it is being consumed in final demand or being used as an intermediate input; this is a key feature of the model that will be relaxed below.

Consider the decision problem of either the representative consumer or a firm in country j, regarding which country to purchase variety ω^s from. As in Eaton and Kortum (2002), this corresponds to choosing the lowest-cost source country across $i \in \{1, \ldots, J\}$, after factoring in the unit production costs c_i^s and iceberg trade costs τ_{ij}^s across all potential source countries i.[29] The solution to this discrete choice problem and the law of large numbers yields an expression for the expenditure share of country j spent on industry-s varieties that come from country i:

$$\pi_{ij}^s = \frac{T_i^s \left(c_i^s \tau_{ij}^s \right)^{-\theta^s}}{\sum_{k=1}^J T_k^s \left(c_k^s \tau_{kj}^s \right)^{-\theta^s}}. \tag{22}$$

In turn, the unit production cost c_j^s is obtained as the solution to the cost-minimization problem faced by each industry-s firm in country j, based on the production function (20). This is given by:

$$c_j^s = \Upsilon_j^s w_j^{1-\sum_{r=1}^S \gamma_j^{rs}} \prod_{r=1}^S \left(P_j^r \right)^{\gamma_j^{rs}}, \tag{23}$$

where Υ_j^s is a constant that depends only on the parameters γ_j^{rs}, and P_j^r is the ideal price index of the industry-r composite being used as an intermediate input in country j. Following Eaton and Kortum (2002), the expression for P_j^r is given explicitly by:

$$P_j^r = A^r \left[\sum_{i=1}^J T_i^r \left(c_i^r \tau_{ij}^r \right)^{-\theta^r} \right]^{-1/\theta^r}, \tag{24}$$

where A^r is a constant that depends only on σ^r and θ^r.[30]

Let X_{ij}^s denote the expenditure of country j on industry-s varieties from country i. This is the sum of country-j expenditures on the industry-s composite from country i, over both its use as an intermediate input and for final consumption. In turn, define: (i) $X_j^s = \sum_{i=1}^J X_{ij}^s$ as the total expenditure of country j on industry-s varieties; and (ii) Y_j^s as the value of gross output in industry s produced in country j. Having defined these objects, we can close the model by clearing the market for each industry in each country:

$$X_j^s = \sum_{r=1}^S \gamma_j^{sr} \underbrace{\sum_{i=1}^J X_i^r \pi_{ji}^r}_{Y_j^r} + \alpha_j^s \left(w_j L_j + D_j \right). \tag{25}$$

Note that the first term on the right-hand side of (25) is equal to the total purchases of intermediate inputs from industry s, where the sum is taken over all industries r that purchase intermediate inputs from s.[31] D_j is the national deficit of country j, computed as the sum of all sectoral and final-use imports of a country minus the sectoral and final-use outputs. Then, the second term on the right-hand side is the total purchases by country j on industry s for final consumption.

We finally impose trade balance, equating a country j's imports to its exports plus its observed deficit D_j:

$$\sum_{s=1}^S X_j^s = \sum_{s=1}^S \sum_{i=1}^J X_j^s \pi_{ij}^s = \sum_{s=1}^S \sum_{i=1}^J X_i^s \pi_{ji}^s + D_j \tag{26}$$

One can show that this last equilibrium condition can alternatively be derived from the equality of (equipped) labor income and total value-added.[32]

The equilibrium of the model is then pinned down by the system of equations: (22), (23), (24), (25), and (26).[33]

5.1.2. *Mapping the model to empirical counterparts*

How does the model map to the available data from Global Input-Output Tables? Remember that a WIOT contains information on intermediate purchases by industry s in country j from sector r in country i, which we denote by Z_{ij}^{rs}. It also contains information on the final-use expenditure in each country j on goods/services originating from sector r in country i, which we denote by F_{ij}^r. Finally, the values of country-industry gross output Y_j^s and value-added V_j^s, as well as country-specific trade deficits D_j, can all be computed from the WIOT. For clarity, we denote the observed values for these variables that come from the WIOT data with tildes (e.g., $\tilde{Z}_{ij}^{rs}$).

The main limitation of this framework as it stands is that it imposes the same market share of a given country i in the sales of output of a given sector r to a destination country j regardless of whether that output is designated for final-use or for use as an intermediate by other industries. In particular, note that the model imposes:

$$\pi_{ij}^r = \frac{\tilde{F}_{ij}^r}{\sum_{k=1}^{J} \tilde{F}_{kj}^r} = \frac{\tilde{Z}_{ij}^{rs}}{\sum_{k=1}^{J} \tilde{Z}_{kj}^{rs}} \quad \text{for } j = 1, \ldots, J. \tag{27}$$

Prior to the WIOD, the standard proportionality assumptions used to infer these import shares from available data would have generated identical shares across both final-use and input purchases. One of the contributions of the WIOD was to bring additional information to bear to distinguish imports across different end-use categories (see Dietzenbacher *et al.*, 2013, for details). In the WIOD data, the J input shares on the right-end of equation (27) and the final-use shares in the middle term would thus differ from each other, except by extreme coincidence. Hence, the Caliendo and Parro (2015) model cannot *exactly* match all the entries of a generic WIOT. For certain applications, this mismatch may of course not be too important. But in using the WIOT to make sense of the positioning of a country in GVCs, it stands to reason that it would be important for the model to be able to fully account for all final-use and intermediate-use trade shares.

5.2.   A more flexible model

We now present a more flexible version of the Caliendo and Parro (2015) model. In particular, we relax their assumption that iceberg trade costs τ_{ij}^s are only country-pair and (selling) industry specific.

5.2.1.   New assumptions and equilibrium

Instead of the previous formulation of trade costs, consider the case in which trade costs are denoted by τ_{ij}^{rs} when goods/services in sector r from country i are shipped to industry s in country j. Similarly, denoted by τ_{ij}^{rF}, the trade costs incurred when goods/services in sector r from country i are shipped to final consumers in country j. This variation could reflect, for instance, underlying heterogeneity in the characteristics (weight, value, etc.) of the various inputs and final goods that are lumped together into a sector in the WIOD. Naturally, it might also be driven by heterogeneity in the man-made trade barriers applied to these various industry subcategories. To the extent that different sectors buy different types of inputs in a given sector in different proportions, they will effectively face different trade costs, with the same being true of purchasers of final varieties.

As noted in the Introduction (see footnote 6 in particular), the proportionality assumptions used to construct WIOTs would generate identical trade shares, π_{ij}^r, across all input-purchasing industries s.[34] This suggests that an extension of the Caliendo and Parro (2015) framework that simply allowed for distinct trade costs for shipments of inputs and final-goods for a given country pair i-j and selling sector r would be sufficient to match all the entries of a WIOT. In practice, the WIOD used in our empirical analysis features minor deviations from these proportionality assumptions, so we develop here a model with more flexible input trade shares that vary depending on the identity of the purchasing industry.[35] Although this added flexibility is likely to be of little quantitative importance for our exercise centered on the WIOD, there are good reasons to believe (see de Gortari, 2017) that trade shares do vary significantly in the real world depending on what the input is used for, and we expect future WIOTs to more effectively exploit firm-level import and export data to document larger departures from the commonly-used proportionality assumptions.

How does this more general formulation of trade costs affect the equilibrium conditions of the model developed above? Following the same exact steps as in our derivations in the Caliendo-Parro model, it is easy to verify that producers in industry s in country j now spend on inputs from different sectors r and countries i according to the input trade shares:

$$\pi_{ij}^{rs} = \frac{T_i^r (c_i^r \tau_{ij}^{rs})^{-\theta^r}}{\sum_{k=1}^{J} T_k^r (c_k^r \tau_{kj}^{rs})^{-\theta^r}}.$$ (28)

Meanwhile, consumers in j spend a share π_{ij}^{rF} of their sector-r final consumption on varieties from country i, where π_{ij}^{rF} is given by:

$$\pi_{ij}^{rF} = \frac{T_i^r (c_i^r \tau_{ij}^{rF})^{-\theta^r}}{\sum_{k=1}^{J} T_k^r (c_k^r \tau_{kj}^{rF})^{-\theta^r}}.$$ (29)

These expressions are analogous to equation (22), but they now define $(S+1) \times J$ distinct trade shares, rather than only J.

On the cost side, we now have the following counterpart to equation (23):

$$c_j^s = \Upsilon_j^s w_j^{1-\sum_{r=1}^{S} \gamma_j^{rs}} \prod_{r=1}^{S} \left(P_j^{rs}\right)^{\gamma_j^{rs}},$$ (30)

where Υ_j^s is again a constant that depends only on the parameters γ_j^{rs}, but P_j^{rs} is now the ideal price index of the sector-r composite good in country j when purchased by industry-s producers. This price index is given by:

$$P_j^{rs} = A^r \left[\sum_{i=1}^{J} T_i^r \left(c_i^r \tau_{ij}^{rs}\right)^{-\theta^r} \right]^{-1/\theta^r},$$ (31)

where A^r is again a constant that depends only on σ^r and θ^r. The main difference relative to equation (24) is that this price index is now rs-specific, rather than just *r*-specific. For similar reasons, we now have to separately define the price index for final consumption for each sector in each country *j*:

$$P_j^{rF} = A^r \left[\sum_{i=1}^{J} T_i^r \left(c_i^r \tau_{ij}^{rF} \right)^{-\theta^r} \right]^{-1/\theta^r}. \tag{32}$$

Note that the price index for overall consumption is now given by:

$$P_j^F = \prod_{s=1}^{S} \left(P_j^{sF}/\alpha_j^s \right)^{\alpha_j^s}. \tag{33}$$

Consider next the goods-market clearing conditions. As in the previous less flexible model, the equality of total expenditure of country *j* on industry-*s* varieties can still be expressed as the sum of total expenditure on inputs and on final consumption in that sector:

$$X_j^s = \sum_{r=1}^{S} \gamma_j^{sr} Y_j^r + \alpha_j^s \left(w_j L_j + D_j \right). \tag{34}$$

However, it is now not so straightforward to express Y_j^r as a function of X_i^r in other sectors and countries, as we did in equation (25). Instead, we need to consider final sales and intermediate input sales separately, which leads us to develop a linear system of equations in the gross output levels:

$$Y_j^s = \underbrace{\sum_{k=1}^{J} \pi_{jk}^{sF} \alpha_k^s (w_k L_k + D_k)}_{\text{final-use sales}} + \underbrace{\sum_{r=1}^{S} \sum_{k=1}^{J} \pi_{jk}^{sr} \gamma_k^{sr} Y_k^r}_{\text{intermediate-input sales}}. \tag{35}$$

In words, the gross output of sector *s* in country *j* is either used for final consumption in all countries around the world (the first term in (35)) or as an input by all industries in all countries (the second term in (35)).

We finally impose trade balance, equating a country *j*'s imports to the sum of its exports and its trade deficit D_j. After some simplifications, this can be written as:

$$\sum_{i=1}^{J} \sum_{r=1}^{S} \sum_{s=1}^{S} \pi_{ij}^{sr} \gamma_j^{sr} Y_j^r + w_j L_j = \sum_{i=1}^{J} \sum_{r=1}^{S} \sum_{s=1}^{S} \pi_{ji}^{sr} \gamma_i^{sr} Y_i^r + \sum_{s=1}^{S} \sum_{i=1}^{J} \pi_{ji}^{sF} \alpha_i^s (w_i L_i + D_i). \tag{36}$$

One can show that this last equilibrium condition can again be written as (equipped) labor income being equal to value-added.[36]

The equilibrium is now defined by equations (28), (29), (30), (31), (32), (35), and (36). Note that (28) comprises $J \times (J-1) \times S \times S$ independent equations, since the shares π_{ij}^{rs} need to sum to 1 for each *j-rs* pair; for a similar reason, (29) comprises $J \times (J-1) \times S$ independent equations. In turn, (30) and (32) comprise $J \times S$

equations each, while (31) comprises $J \times S \times S$ equations. Finally, the market-clearing conditions in (35) comprise $J \times S{-}1$ independent equations, since one of these is redundant by Walras' Law, and we also have J trade balance conditions from (36). On the other hand, the equilibrium seeks to solve for the following objects: the π_{ij}^{rs}'s (of which there are $J \times (J-1) \times S \times S$ independent shares); the π_{ij}^{rF}'s (of which there are $J \times (J-1) \times S$ independent shares); the unit production costs c_j^s, and price indices P_j^{rs} and P_j^{rF} (of which there are $J \times S$, $J \times S \times S$, and $J \times S$ terms respectively); the $J-1$ wage levels w_j's (with one country's wage picked as the numéraire); as well as the $J \times S$ gross output levels Y_j^s's. Thus, we have as many equilibrium conditions as variables to be solved for. With wages and the gross output levels, we can also easily solve for the expenditure levels X_j^s using equation (34).

We shall not concern ourselves with proving the sufficient conditions for the existence and uniqueness of an equilibrium. Such a proof could be carried out following the approach in Alvarez and Lucas (2007). In discussing how our extended Caliendo-Parro model maps to a WIOT, we will however discuss issues that relate to the existence of an equilibrium.

5.2.2. *Mapping to empirical counterparts*

We now turn to evaluate the ability of our model to match the type of data available in World Input-Output Tables. Our main result will be that, via a suitable choice of parameter values for trade costs, our extended model will be able to match all entries of a WIOT that relate to intermediate-use and final-use expenditures. This will in turn allow us to provide a structural interpretation of a WIOT and of the measures of GVC positioning computed from its entries. We will also show in the next section, that one can perform interesting counterfactuals with information on only a small subset of the primitive parameters of the model, a subset that crucially does not include the complex matrix of trade costs that ensure a perfect fit of our model.

Before discussing the mapping between model and data, remember that a WIOT contains information on country-industry pair input flows (Z_{ij}^{rs}), country-pair final-use trade flows by sector (F_{ij}^r), country-sector-specific gross output Y_j^s and value-added V_j^s, and country-specific trade deficits D_j. As before, we denote the observed values of these variables in the WIOT with tildes.

It is useful to begin by considering the mapping between the data and both the input share parameters γ_j^{rs} and final expenditure share parameters α_j^s. As in the benchmark Caliendo-Parro framework developed above, the Cobb-Douglas structure of the model allows us to easily recover all these parameters from observed trade flows. In particular, we have:

$$\gamma_j^{rs} = \frac{\sum_{i=1}^{J} \tilde{Z}_{ij}^{rs}}{\tilde{Y}_j^s}, \tag{37}$$

and:

$$\alpha_j^s = \frac{\sum_{i=1}^{J} \tilde{F}_{ij}^s}{\sum_{r=1}^{S} \widetilde{VA}_j^r + \tilde{D}_j}. \tag{38}$$

Furthermore, the value-added share in sector s can be recovered as $1 - \sum_{r=1}^{S} \gamma_j^{rs}$.

Let us now turn to the ability of the model to replicate observed inter-industry and final-use flows, this being a limitation of the benchmark Caliendo-Parro model. With our more flexible trade cost formulation, we now have:

$$Z_{ij}^{rs} = \pi_{ij}^{rs} \gamma_j^{rs} Y_j^s, \tag{39}$$

and:

$$F_{ij}^r = \pi_{ij}^{rF} \alpha_j^r \left(\sum_{r=1}^{S} VA_j^r + D_j \right). \tag{40}$$

The key novelty is that the trade shares π_{ij}^{rs} now vary both across buying and selling industries, and are also distinct from the trade shares for final consumption (π_{ij}^{rF}). This feature in turn implies that, conditional on the observed values of gross output $\tilde{Y}_j^s$, value-added in all sectors $\widetilde{VA}_j^r$, and the trade deficits $\tilde{D}_j$, together with the recovered values of γ_j^{rs} and α_j^s in (37) and (38), there exist values for the trade cost parameters τ_{ij}^{rs} and τ_{ij}^{rF} that lead the model to *exactly* match all the empirically observed values of $\tilde{Z}_{ij}^{rs}$ and $\tilde{F}_{ij}^r$.

To illustrate this result, focus first on the π_{ij}^{rs} trade shares. Let us define: $b_i^r = T_i^r \left(c_i^r \right)^{-\theta^r}$ and $\rho_{ij}^{rs} = \left(\tau_{ij}^{rs} \right)^{-\theta^r}$. Combining equation (39) with the definition of the input trade shares π_{ij}^{rs} in (28), we then obtain:

$$\rho_{ij}^{rs} = \frac{\tilde{Z}_{ij}^{rs}}{\sum_{l=1}^{J} \tilde{Z}_{lj}^{rs}} \sum_{k=1}^{J} \frac{b_k^r}{b_i^r} \rho_{kj}^{rs}. \tag{41}$$

For each destination country j and each sector pair rs, equation (41) defines a system of J linear equations in the power transformation of trade costs $\left(\rho_{1j}^{rs}, \ldots, \rho_{ij}^{rs}, \ldots, \rho_{Jj}^{rs} \right)$. Clearly, the system is linearly dependent: given a solution, if all the ρ_{ij}^{rs} are multiplied by a common constant κ_j^{rs}, these alternative trade costs also solve the system. One can thus normalize one of the J trade cost parameters to 1, and it is natural to set the domestic trade cost to $\rho_{jj}^{rs} = 1$ (i.e., $\tau_{jj}^{rs} = 1$). Under weak invertibility conditions, the system in (41) with $\rho_{jj}^{rs} = 1$ delivers a unique solution for the matrix of ρ_{ij}^{rs}'s, given a vector of observed input flows $\tilde{Z}_{ij}^{rs}$ as well as values for the terms b_i^r.

Similarly, from equations (40) and (29), we obtain the following system of linear equations:

$$\rho_{ij}^{rF} = \frac{\tilde{F}_{ij}^{r}}{\sum_{l=1}^{J} \tilde{F}_{lj}^{r}} \sum_{k=1}^{J} \frac{b_k^r}{b_i^r} \rho_{kj}^{rF}, \tag{42}$$

which also delivers, under weak invertibility conditions, a unique solution for the matrix of τ_{ij}^{rF}'s conditional on values for observed final-use flows $\tilde{F}_{ij}^{r}$ and the values of the terms b_i^r, after setting $\rho_{jj}^{rF} = 1$ (i.e., $\tau_{jj}^{rF} = 1$).

It is worth stressing that our results above are not sufficient to provide a method to recover a unique set of values of the trade cost parameters, τ_{ij}^{rs} and τ_{ij}^{rF}, that ensure a perfect match between the trade shares in the model and in the data. More specifically, the trade cost parameters implicitly defined by (41) and (42) are a function of the terms b_i^r, which are in turn shaped by the unobserved technology parameters T_i^r and by the (endogenous) unit cost variables c_i^r. Furthermore, transitioning from ρ_{ij}^{rs} to τ_{ij}^{rs} requires knowledge of the trade elasticity parameters θ^r.

For these reasons, backing out the values of τ_{ij}^{rs} and τ_{ij}^{rF} that ensure that the model perfectly matches the data is not straightforward. Fortunately, we will demonstrate in the next section that this does not preclude a structural interpretation of the data and the implementation of interesting counterfactuals. For our purposes, it will suffice to show that there *exists* at least one set of values for the trade cost parameters τ_{ij}^{rs} and τ_{ij}^{rF} such that the model exactly replicates the data. Our derivations above indicate that this is certainly the case (under weak invertibility conditions) conditional on the values of b_i^r. In the appendix, we demonstrate that when allowing the values of b_i^r to be determined by the technology parameters T_i^r and by the general equilibrium of the model, this existence result persists. As long as the general equilibrium of the model exists (regardless of whether that equilibrium is unique or not), the equilibrium will deliver a well-defined vector of values for b_i^r, which also ensures that the model can exactly match the input and final-use trade shares, π_{ij}^{rs} and π_{ij}^{rF}; it follows immediately that the model will also match the country-sector-specific gross output Y_j^s and value-added V_j^s, and country-specific trade deficits D_j.

There is one additional issue with regard to mapping the model exactly to the data. The underlying Eaton-Kortum structure of the model implies that all of the trade shares, π_{ij}^{rs} and π_{ij}^{rF}, are strictly positive. In particular, this means that the production of each good s in country j would source a positive amount of inputs from all sectors r in all countries i. In the WIOD data, however, zero entries are relatively common. To address this, we have taken the pragmatic approach of replacing each zero input-purchase or final-use entry in the WIOD with a positive constant ($1e^{-18}$) that is less than the smallest positive entry seen in the WIOD. This naturally precludes us from evaluating interesting counterfactuals that pertain to how the extensive margin of sourcing would adjust. In what follows, we have therefore focused on counterfactual outcomes that pertain to the aggregate economy (rather than on the effects on specific entries in the WIOT).

6.   Counterfactuals

We conclude the chapter by illustrating how the theoretical results derived in the last section can be used to deliver quantitative insights related to where countries are positioned in GVCs. First, we will extend the "hat algebra" results in Dekle *et al.* (2008) and Caliendo and Parro (2015), to show that in order to perform various counterfactuals with the model, all that is required are: (i) the initial trade shares, π_{ij}^{rs} and π_{ij}^{rF}, available from a WIOT; (ii) the demand and technological Cobb-Douglas parameters γ_j^{rs} and α_j^s, which we have also shown are easily recoverable from the same WIOT; and (iii) a vector of sectoral parameters θ^r shaping the elasticity of trade flows (across source countries) to trade barriers. In particular, although the existence of flexible trade costs τ_{ij}^{rs} and τ_{ij}^{rF} is crucial to ensure that the model is able to fit the WIOT data exactly, knowledge of the precise values of these trade cost parameters is *not* necessary to conduct counterfactuals. Similarly, although the technological parameters T_i^r certainly shape the values of the trade costs, τ_{ij}^{rs} and τ_{ij}^{rF}, that would enable the model to fit the data, the specific values of T_i^r are not essential for these counterfactuals. Having derived these sufficient statistics results, we then perform a series of counterfactual exercises, in order to shed light on the possible determinants of the evolution of our various GVC positioning measures over time.

6.1.   The hat algebra approach

We are interested in obtaining the values of the counterfactual entries of a WIOT following a shock to some of the parameters of the model. In practice, we will focus in our applications on changes in trade costs, τ_{ij}^{rs} and τ_{ij}^{rF}, and in the final demand Cobb-Douglas parameters α_j^r; our exposition below will therefore consider the case where only these parameters change in the model.[37] For simplicity, we will also assume that deficits D_j are held constant in the counterfactuals we will study. We denote the counterfactual value of a parameter or variable X with a prime (e.g., X') and use hats to denote the relative change in these variables, i.e., $\hat{X} = X'/X$.

With this notation, and invoking equations (39) and (40), we can express the counterfactual input and final-use flows as:

$$\left(Z_{ij}^{rs}\right)' = \left(\pi_{ij}^{rs}\right)' \gamma_j^{rs} \left(Y_j^s\right)',$$

(43)

and:

$$\left(F_{ij}^r\right)' = \left(\pi_{ij}^{rF}\right)' \left(\alpha_j^r\right)' \left(\sum_{r=1}^{S} \left(VA_j^r\right)' + D_j\right).$$

(44)

Clearly, to obtain the specific counterfactual values of these entries, one needs to figure out how the trade shares π_{ij}^{rs} and π_{ij}^{rF}, as well as gross output Y_j^s and value-added levels VA_j^r, are affected by changes in trade costs or final-consumption shares.

Consider first trade shares. Using the hat algebra notation, it is easy to verify that (28) and (29) result in:

$$
\hat{\pi}_{ij}^{rs} = \left(\frac{\hat{c}_i^r \hat{\tau}_{ij}^{rs}}{\hat{P}_j^{rs}} \right)^{-\theta^r} \tag{45}
$$

and:

$$
\hat{\pi}_{ij}^{rF} = \left(\frac{\hat{c}_i^r \hat{\tau}_{ij}^{rF}}{\hat{P}_j^{rF}} \right)^{-\theta^r} . \tag{46}
$$

In words, the percentage response of trade shares is purely shaped by the trade elasticity parameters θ^r and by the percentage shifts of the various trade cost parameters, as well as the percentage responses of the unit costs c_i^r, and the price indices P_j^{rs} and P_j^{rF}. It is worth stressing that (45) and (46) are not approximations: They hold exactly for any shock to trade costs (or to final consumption shares), regardless of the size of the shock. Notice also, that the level of trade costs or the unobserved technological parameters T_i^r do not appear directly in these equations.

The responses of the unit costs c_i^r and the price indices P_j^{rs} and P_j^{rF} to changes in the environment can be obtained from simple manipulations of equations (30), (31), and (32). More specifically, plugging in the expressions for the trade shares from (28) and (29), we obtain:

$$
\hat{c}_j^s = \left(\hat{w}_j \right)^{1-\sum_{r=1}^S \gamma_j^{rs}} \prod_{r=1}^S \left(\hat{P}_j^{rs} \right)^{\gamma_j^{rs}}, \tag{47}
$$

$$
\hat{P}_j^{rs} = \left[\sum_{i=1}^J \pi_{ij}^{rs} \left(\hat{c}_i^r \hat{\tau}_{ij}^{rs} \right)^{-\theta^r} \right]^{-1/\theta^r} , \tag{48}
$$

and:

$$
\hat{P}_j^{rF} = \left[\sum_{i=1}^J \pi_{ij}^{rF} \left(\hat{c}_i^r \hat{\tau}_{ij}^{rF} \right)^{-\theta^r} \right]^{-1/\theta^r} . \tag{49}
$$

There are two key features of these three sets of equations. First, the only variables in levels that appear in these equations are the trade shares prior to the shocks (which are obviously observable), the Cobb-Douglas technological parameters γ_j^{rs} (which are retrievable from the data in a WIOT), and the trade elasticity parameters θ^r. Second, it is clear from inspection that combining (47) and (48), one should be able to solve – albeit computationally – for $\hat{c}_j^s$ and $\hat{P}_j^{rs}$ as a function of these initial trade shares, as well as the percentage changes in wages ($\hat{w}_j$) and input trade costs ($\hat{\tau}_{ij}^{rs}$). Similarly, combining (47) and (49), we can obtain $\hat{P}_j^{rF}$ as a function of these same initial trade shares, as well as the percentage changes in wages ($\hat{w}_j$) and final-use trade costs ($\hat{\tau}_{ij}^{rF}$).

Plugging these resulting values of $\hat{c}_j^s$, $\hat{P}_j^{rs}$, and $\hat{P}_j^{rF}$ into (45) and (46), this then allows us to express the changes in trade shares as a function of observables (π_{ij}^{rs}, π_{ij}^{rF}, and γ_j^{rs}), the trade elasticity parameters θ^r, and the percentage changes in wages and trade costs.

We finally discuss how to trace the response of wages, as well as gross output and value-added, to the shocks. For that, we invoke the goods-market clearing conditions (35) and the trade balance conditions (36). In the counterfactual equilibrium, these can be re-written as:

$$\left(Y_j^s\right)' = \sum_{k=1}^{J}\left(\pi_{jk}^{sF}\right)'\left(\alpha_k^s\right)'(\hat{w}_k w_k L_k + D_k) + \sum_{r=1}^{S}\sum_{k=1}^{J}\left(\pi_{jk}^{sr}\right)'\gamma_k^{sr}\left(Y_k^r\right)', \qquad (50)$$

and:

$$\sum_{i=1}^{J}\sum_{r=1}^{S}\sum_{s=1}^{S}\left(\pi_{ij}^{sr}\right)'\gamma_j^{sr}\left(Y_j^r\right)' + \hat{w}_j w_j L_j = \sum_{i=1}^{J}\sum_{r=1}^{S}\sum_{s=1}^{S}\left(\pi_{ji}^{sr}\right)'\gamma_i^{sr}\left(Y_i^r\right)'$$

$$+ \sum_{s=1}^{S}\sum_{i=1}^{J}\left(\pi_{ji}^{sF}\right)'\left(\alpha_i^s\right)'(\hat{w}_i w_i L_i + D_i). \qquad (51)$$

Noting that $\left(\pi_{ij}^{sr}\right)' = \hat{\pi}_{ij}^{sr} \cdot \pi_{ij}^{sr}$, this system of equations delivers solutions for $\left(Y_j^s\right)' = \hat{Y}_{ij}^s \cdot Y_{ij}^s$ and $\hat{w}_j$ as a function of the changes in trade costs and Cobb-Douglas demand parameters ($\hat{\tau}_{ij}^{rs}$, $\hat{\tau}_{ij}^{rF}$, and $\hat{\alpha}_j^s$). Plugging these values into (39) and (40), and noting that $\left(VA_j^r\right)' = \widehat{VA_j^r} \cdot VA_j^r = \hat{Y}_j^r \cdot VA_j^r$ (due to the Cobb-Douglas assumption in technology), this then allows us to obtain the counterfactual values of all the entries in a WIOT.

In sum, we have demonstrated that in order to perform counterfactual exercises that shock trade costs or the demand parameters α_j^s while holding all other parameters constant, all that is required is the initial values of a set of variables that are easily retrieved from a WIOT, as well as values for the trade elasticities θ^r.[38] We next turn to an application of this result to various counterfactual scenarios of interest.

6.2. Applications

We will perform two types of counterfactuals, using the system of equations in "hat algebra" form just laid out in (43)–(51). First, we will study how much changes in trade costs and changes in the α_j^s preference parameters can help explain the evolution of the GVC positioning of industries and countries over the period 1995–2011. More specifically, we will hold all other parameters of the model (including trade deficits) to their 1995 levels, and allow first trade costs and then the parameters α_j^s to jump to their 2011 levels. This will shed light on the extent to which these factors might help in resolving the empirical puzzles identified in Section 3. We will later consider further counterfactual trade cost reductions and changes in demand parameters starting from their 2011 levels, to offer projections for the future positioning of countries in GVCs.

We should stress that the exercise here is not meant to be an exhaustive exploration of the forces that could account for the persistent correlations in the country-level GVC measures. The counterfactuals that we run here speak to the two candidate explanations posited earlier in Section 4, namely movements in trade costs and shifts in sectoral composition. Even so, we are unable to explore the effect of changes in the input purchase share parameters (the γ_j^{rs}'s), though these have likely contributed too to the realignments in sectoral composition, as such shifts cannot be analyzed using the "hat algebra" techniques within the current model with Cobb-Douglas production functions.[39] Likewise, we do not explore the possible role of changes in the fundamental technology levels (the T_i^r's), since these are harder to discipline empirically with available data. (Note that in the exercises below, we adopt $\theta^r = 5$ throughout for simplicity.)

In Table 5.8 below, we explore the model's implications for shifts in country GVC positioning over the 1995–2011 period. Panel A reports several key moments and correlations related to the country-level GVC measures, including the values computed directly from the 1995 and 2011 WIOTs. Consider first the effect of a change in trade costs from 1995 to 2011 levels. Since we encounter a non-trivial number of zero entries in the WIOT in each year (which would inconveniently imply that the Head-Ries trade cost index is infinite for these entries), we opt to aggregate the industries in the WIOT into two broad sectors, namely goods versus services. We thus compute Head-Ries indices associated with trade in intermediates between any country-sector pair (based on the goods and services sectoral aggregates), as well as the Head-Ries indices associated with final-use trade between any country pair in goods and in services.[40]

What are the quantitative implications of the empirically observed reductions in trade costs? We argued in Section 4.1 that falling trade costs would tend to weaken the correlation between the final-use and value-added shares in gross output across countries, as production along GVCs becomes more fragmented across borders. Yet, in Section 4.2 we also put forth the view that the increased

Table 5.8 Evaluating the role of changes in trade costs and expenditure shares

A: Country-level GVC measures

	Mean F/GO	Mean VA/GO	Correlation F/GO, VA/GO	Mean U	Mean D	Correlation U, D	Real wage change (Min, Mean, Max)
1995 baseline (from data)	0.507	0.503	0.825	1.976	1.987	0.868	—
2011 baseline (from data)	0.484	0.487	0.925	2.085	2.070	0.912	—
1995 to 2011 shifts							
Change trade costs	0.518	0.502	0.612	1.940	1.984	0.666	(1.003, 1.104, 1.512)
Change expenditure shares	0.516	0.513	0.857	1.945	1.953	0.889	(0.993, 1.001, 1.017)
Both changes	0.525	0.511	0.660	1.917	1.952	0.705	(1.002, 1.093, 1.434)

B: Country-industry GVC measures

	Regress $(F/GO)^s_{j,t}$ on $(VA/GO)^s_{j,t}$ (Coefficient on $(VA/GO)^s_{j,t}$)		Correlation F/GO, VA/GO	Regress $(U)^s_{j,t}$ on $(D)^s_{j,t}$ (Coefficient on $(D)^s_{j,t}$)		Correlation U, D
1995 baseline (from data)	0.5434***	0.5184**	0.0851	0.5337***	0.4839**	0.2564***
2011 baseline (from data)	0.6543***	0.6373***	0.2647***	0.6286***	0.5785***	0.4156***
1995 to 2011 shifts						
Change trade costs	0.5534***	0.5321***	0.1101*	0.5270***	0.4844***	0.2474***
Change expenditure shares	0.5942***	0.5760***	0.1029*	0.5930***	0.5540***	0.2753***
Both changes	0.6009***	0.5854***	0.1193**	0.5856***	0.5512***	0.2609***
Country FE?	N	Y	Y	N	Y	Y
Industry FE?	N	Y	Y	N	Y	Y

Notes: Quantitative evaluations based on the multi-country, multi-industry general equilibrium model described in Section 5. Panel A reports moments and correlations for the country-level GVC measures, as well as real wage changes. Panel B reports the partial correlation between the country-industry level GVC measures based on the regression specifications in Table 5.3; standard errors are multi-way clustered by country and industry; ***, **, *, and ° denote significance at the 1%, 5%, and 10% levels respectively. For the "1995 baseline" and "2011 baseline" rows, the moments and correlations are calculated directly from the WIOT data. Under "Change trade costs", this simulates the effect of the observed change between 1995 and 2011 in the Head-Ries trade costs indices computed at the country-sector level after aggregating the industries up to broad sectoral aggregates (i.e., Goods versus Services). The trade costs indices are computed separately for intermediate-use and final-use shipments; for each of these categories, changes in trade costs that fall below the 1st percentile (respectively, above the 99th percentile) are bottom-coded (respectively, top-coded). Under "Change expenditure shares", this simulates the effect of the observed change between 1995 and 2011 in the final-use expenditure shares. The "Both changes" row simulates the combined effect of both the above changes in trade costs and final-use expenditure shares.

specialization in services and in goods production illustrated in Figure 5.8 – which tended to increase the correlation between F/GO and VA/GO – could also well be driven by trade cost reductions. Which of these forces dominated over the period 1995–2011? Our results in Table 5.8 indicate that, in isolation, trade costs would have led to a *reduction* in the correlation between F/GO and VA/GO from a value of 0.825 in the initial year to 0.612 by the end of the period. This contrasts against the fact that this correlation actually moved in the opposite direction in the data, and stood at 0.925 in 2011. Along a similar vein, the changes in trade costs alone would have generated a drop in the correlation between the country-level production staging measures (U vs D), from 0.868 to 0.666, whereas the WIOT data point to an increase in this correlation to 0.912.

We next consider the effects of holding trade costs constant while feeding into the model the observed change in the α_j^s preference parameters seen between 1995 and 2011. As reported under "Change expenditure shares" in Panel A, this generates a moderate increase in the correlation between F/GO and VA/GO to 0.857, as well as in the correlation between U and D to 0.889. As services have become more important in consumption relative to goods, the model implies that service industries would have expanded across most countries, which in turn would reinforce the aforementioned positive correlations among these country-level measures of GVC positioning. Note that, quantitatively, the change in the α_j^s's on their own brings us about a third to a half of the way towards bridging the gap between the correlations recorded in 1995 and in 2011.

However, when the changes in trade costs and the final-use expenditure shares are considered simultaneously, the effect of the trade cost declines dominates: The correlations of interest all weaken relative to 1995, although the extent of this decline is not as large compared to the first counterfactual where only trade cost movements were considered. This leaves us to conclude that other forces which we are not able to accommodate with the current framework – such as shifts in the use of inputs (the γ_j^{rs}'s) towards services – would have had to be at play, in order to rationalize the rising correlation between the country-level GVC measures from 1995 to 2011.

A similar conclusion is reached if we look at Panel B of Table 5.8. There, we have re-run the same series of regressions as in Table 5.3, to estimate the partial correlation between the counterfactual GVC measures at the country-industry level (i.e., between $(F/GO)_j^s$ and $(VA/GO)_j^s$, as well as between $(U)_j^s$ and $(D)_j^s$). These regressions have been run in the pure cross-section with no fixed effects, with country fixed effects, and further including industry fixed effects. The simulations point to an increase in the slope coefficients across all columns, which is consistent with what we see in the actual evolution of the country-industry GVC measures between 1995 and 2011. That said, the combined effect of the trade costs and expenditure share shifts ("Both changes") is only able to partially account for the increase seen in the slope coefficients; in particular, these forces alone do not do particularly well in explaining the magnitude of the increase in the slope coefficient when both country and industry dummies are controlled for.

We turn to some forward projections in Table 5.9. For this exercise, we now calibrate the model to the 2011 WIOT as a starting point, and then ask what would happen to the country-level GVC measures if shifts in trade costs (and/ or the final-use expenditure shares) were to persist for a further 16 years. We take guidance from the average rates of decline in trade costs estimated earlier in Tables 5.4 and 5.5 for intermediate and final-use trade, for goods and services separately. For example, we assume in these simulations that trade costs for goods shipped for intermediate use continue to decline at the rate of 1.81 per cent per annum (based on the coefficient estimate in Column 3, Table 5.4); the assumed rates of decline for trade in final-goods, as well as for trade in services are drawn from these tables in an analogous manner.[41] For the projected changes in the expenditure shares, we likewise simulate the effects of a decrease in the α_j^s's associated with goods industries of 1.27 per cent per year (taking guidance from Column 3, Table 5.6), coupled with a rise in the α_j^s's associated with services of 0.37 per cent per year (Column 5, Table 5.6); the counterfactual α_j^s shares are re-scaled proportionally to ensure that they sum to 1 for each country.

We once again find in Table 5.9 that a decline in trade costs alone would tend to reduce the country-level correlations between the final-use and value-added shares in gross output (from 0.925 to 0.840), as well as that between U and D (from 0.912 to 0.815). A more nuanced view emerges when we consider changes in the trade costs associated with shipping goods and shipping services separately. A hypothetical decline in trade costs for goods ("Goods only") would tend to reduce the cross-country correlations, as expected. However, a decline in trade costs for services ("Services only") instead sees the correlation between U and D rise to 0.908, and that between F/GO and VA/GO rise to 0.914. It thus appears that if trade costs for services were to fall relatively more than trade costs for goods, this would reinforce comparative advantage in services for those countries that were already initially specializing in those industries; this in turn would be sufficient to raise the cross-country correlation between the GVC measures. Thus, depending on whether trade costs declines are larger for goods versus services, there appears to be scope for trade cost movements to generate a between-industry shift in specialization patterns.

As in our counterfactuals in Table 5.8, the effects of an isolated shift in the final expenditure shares (continuing their 1995–2011 trajectory) would tend to increase the country-level correlations between the final-use and value-added shares in gross output. Even though the initial correlations are already very high, they increase even further to 0.934 (between F/GO and VA/GO) and to 0.923 (between U and D), respectively. When considered in conjunction with the trade cost movements, the shifts in the α_j^s's act to moderate the decline in these key correlations induced when trade cost decreases are applied to both goods and services; the shift in consumption towards services is however not

Table 5.9 Counterfactual projections

Country-level measures	Mean F/GO	Mean VA/GO	Correlation F/GO, VA/GO	Mean U	Mean D	Correlation U, D	Real wage change (Min, Mean, Max)
2011 baseline (from data)	0.484	0.487	0.925	2.085	2.070	0.912	—
1995 to 2011 shifts							
Change trade costs	0.482	0.476	0.840	2.095	2.101	0.815	(1.070, 1.207, 1.485)
Change trade costs (goods only)	0.483	0.480	0.836	2.089	2.091	0.811	(1.058, 1.151, 1.269)
Change trade costs (services only)	0.486	0.485	0.914	2.081	2.073	0.908	(1.010, 1.048, 1.286)
Change expenditure shares	0.492	0.494	0.934	2.054	2.042	0.923	(0.997, 1.000, 1.006)
Change trade costs (goods & services) and expenditure shares	0.489	0.483	0.867	2.066	2.072	0.849	(1.064, 1.189, 1.456)

Notes: Quantitative evaluations based on the multi-country, multi-industry general equilibrium model described in Section 5. Moments and correlations for the country-level GVC measures, as well as real wage changes, are reported. The "2011 baseline" row reports summary statistics calculated directly from the 2011 WIOT data. Under "Change trade costs", this simulates the effects of a decrease commencing in 2011 for 16 more years, in which trade costs for intermediate goods decline at a rate of 1.81% per year, trade costs for intermediate service inputs decline at a rate of 1.50% per year, trade costs for final goods decline at a rate of 2.31% per year, and trade costs for final-use services decline at a rate of 1.96% per year, these being the rates of change estimated from Tables 5.4 and 5.5. The subsequent two rows simulate the effects of this trade cost decrease, but applying the decrease to Goods (respectively, Services) industries only. Under "Change expenditure shares", this simulates the effects of a decrease commencing in 2011 for 16 more years, in which the expenditure share for goods industries falls at a rate of 1.27% per year, and that for services industries rises at a rate of 0.37% per year; the expenditure shares are re-scaled proportionally to ensure that they sum to 1 for each country. The "Both changes" row simulates the combined effect of both the changes in trade costs and final-use expenditure shares.

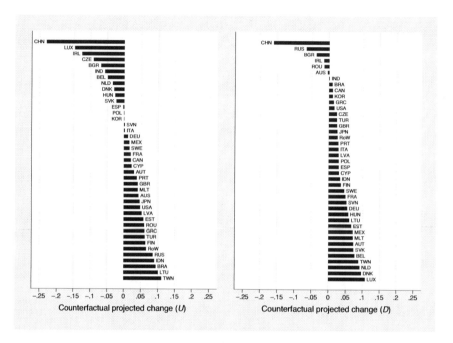

Figure 5.11 Further declines in trade costs and country GVC position

sufficiently large to fully undo or reverse the overall weakening in these correlations between the country GVC measures.

We round off this discussion of counterfactuals by taking a more detailed look at the projected shift in countries' GVC positioning should trade costs continue to decline. Figure 5.11 plots the changes in country-level upstreamness (*U*) and downstreamness (*D*) based on the "Change trade costs" simulation from Table 5.9. The figure points to interesting variation across countries in response to a continued fall in trade costs applied to both goods and services. China stands out as a country that records a large decrease in its production staging distance according to both *U* and *D*. A closer look at the underlying sectoral shifts reveals that this is driven by a further decline in output in Mining and Quarrying (an industry with a particularly high value of *U*), as the fall in trade costs reinforces China's production patterns towards other goods and service industries in which it has stronger comparative advantage. On the other hand, economies like Taiwan, Finland, and Japan exhibit an increase in both *U* and *D*, and thus appear to become more embedded in longer value chains that place them at a greater production staging distance from both end-consumers and primary factors.

7.   Conclusion

This chapter aims to contribute to our understanding of the positioning of countries and industries in GVCs. We have relied on data from the World Input-Output

Database (WIOD) to document the evolution of the upstreamness and down-streamness of various countries and industries in GVCs during the period 1995–2011. We have emphasized, in particular, the presence of a puzzling positive correlation between several pairs of GVC measures at both the country and country-industry levels. More specifically, countries and country-industries far removed from final demand also tend to be far removed from the use of primary factors in production. We have explored potential explanations for this phenomenon and have assessed the quantitative role of two factors: a reduction in trade costs and an increase in the share of world spending on services. This quantitative evaluation is based on a theoretical model of GVCs that we have built, by extending the framework of Caliendo and Parro (2015) in a way that allows the model to match *all* the entries of a World Input-Output Table. We have finally used the model to conjecture on the future evolution of the positioning of industries and countries in GVCs. By introducing considerations related to the positioning of countries and industries in GVCs into a general equilibrium model of trade with cross-sectoral linkages, we hope to contribute a useful bridge between two literatures: On the one hand, the body of empirical work on GVCs employing Input-Output analysis techniques, and on the other hand, the theoretical literature on quantitative trade models that facilitate a structural interpretation of input flows across countries (c.f., Costinot and Rodríguez-Clare 2014). We also hope that the modeling framework will in turn provide scope for future research, to arrive at a more complete decomposition of the forces that account for the evolution of GVC activity. In this regard, a potentially fruitful line of work would be to generalize the production setup to a constant elasticity of substitution (CES) specification, in order to assess the role of shifts in input-use shares (the γ's) in accounting for the observed trends in the measures of GVC positioning.

Notes

Acknowledgement: We are grateful to Lorenzo Caliendo, Thibault Fally, Gene Grossman, Lili Yan Ing, and John Romalis for helpful comments, as well as to Jiacheng (Jack) Feng for extremely valuable research assistance. Antràs acknowledges support from the NSF (proposal #1628852). Chor acknowledges support from the Global Production Networks Center at the National University of Singapore (GPN@NUS).

1   These contributions relate to a parallel body of work, starting with the seminal piece of Johnson and Noguera (2012), that has been concerned with tracing the value-added content of trade flows and the participation of various countries in GVCs (see Koopman *et al.*, 2014, Johnson, 2014, Timmer *et al.*, 2014, de Gortari, 2017).

2   See, among others, Harms *et al.* (2012), Baldwin and Venables (2013), Costinot *et al.* (2013), Antràs and Chor (2013), Tyazhelnikov (2017), Fally and Hillberry (2018), and Kikuchi et al. (2018). This literature is in turn inspired by earlier contributions to modeling multi-stage production, such as Dixit and Grossman (1982), Sanyal and Jones (1982), Kremer (1993), Yi (2003, 2010), and Kohler (2004).

3   Two recent exceptions are the work of Antràs and de Gortari (2017) and de Gortari (2017), who develop multi-country models that emphasize the sequential nature of trade flows in GVCs. Their frameworks provide a structural interpretation of Global Input-Output Tables, but the calibration of those models requires a much more

cumbersome estimation procedure than is required for the model developed in this chapter.

4 Baldwin and Venables (2013) famously introduced the term "snakes" to refer to purely sequential value chains, in which each production stage obtains its inputs from a unique upstream stage. They distinguished "snakes" from "spiders", which are flatter GVCs in which each production stage sources from several upstream suppliers simultaneously. The measures of GVC positioning that we review in Section 2 are defined in a general way, so that they can be computed for production processes that have both "snake"-like as well as "spider"-like features.

5 In a revision of his 2012 working paper, Fally studies the role of the growth of the service sector in explaining the downward trend in D observed in U.S. Input-Output Tables in the period 1947 to 2002.

6 A recent paper by Alexander (2017) extends the Caliendo and Parro (2015) framework by allowing trade shares to vary depending on whether goods are sold to final consumers or to other industries, but imposes a common trade share for all intermediate input purchasing industries. Readers familiar with the construction of WIOTs will be aware that proportionality assumptions are commonly adopted that would imply identical trade shares for all input purchasing industries. In practice though, the World Input-Output Database (WIOD) used in this chapter introduces minor adjustments that generate some variation in input trade shares in the data. Following the lead of de Gortari (2017), we hypothesize that future WIOTs will make better use of firm-level import and export data to generate even larger departures from such proportionality assumptions.

7 See Johnson (2017) for a recent complementary overview of these and other measures of GVC activity.

8 It may be tempting heuristically to view the exercise here as one of projecting the information on production linkages within the WIOT into a stylized linear production chain. We should however caution against this interpretation, since the intention of the GVC measures is not to literally arrange the country-industries in a WIOT into a unique production sequence. To give an example, if the Mining and Quarrying industry in Australia has the next largest U value compared to the Rubber and Plastics industry in China, it does not mean that the former is necessarily being purchased as an input by the latter industry; instead, what this means is that the former industry tends on average to enter production chains at a larger number of stages relative to final demand.

9 We should stress that although they were developed independently, Fally's (2012) measure chronologically preceded that in Antràs and Chor (2013).

10 Miller and Temurshoev (2017) refer to U_j^s as the "output upstreamness" of sector s in country j, and D_j^s as the "input downstreamness" of the same sector.

11 Our numerical results also suggest that the gross-output weighted-average of the country-industry U's (respectively, D's) is slightly larger than the country-level U's (respectively, D's) computed from a collapsed WIOT. This would be consistent with the matrix inverse used in the computation of these indices being a convex transformation.

12 The proof relies on the fact that: (i) U can be computed from the Leontief inverse matrix, $\mathbf{L} = [\mathbf{I} - \mathbf{A}]^{-1}$; (ii) D can be computed from the Ghosh inverse matrix, $\mathbf{G} = [\mathbf{I} - \mathbf{B}]^{-1}$; and (iii) the Leontief and Ghosh inverse matrices are closely related to each other. Facts (i) and (ii) were discussed earlier in Section 2, while (iii) is made explicit in Miller and Temurshoev (2017). In particular, define Y to be a square matrix whose diagonal entries are equal to gross output in each country-industry, and whose non-diagonal entries are all equal to zero. Then, we have: $Y\mathbf{G} = \mathbf{L}Y$.

13 We have separately verified that similar patterns hold in the recent 2016 release of the WIOD. Relative to the 2013 edition, the 2016 WIOD includes 44 countries and 56 industries from 2000–2014. The increase in the number of industries covered arises

mainly from a more detailed breakdown of service industries. We have nevertheless based the analysis in this chapter on the 2013 WIOD, in order to trace the evolution of GVCs starting from an earlier year.

14 The full output identity should thus be:

$$Y_i^r = \sum_{s=1}^{S}\sum_{j=1}^{J} Z_{ij}^{rs} + \sum_{j=1}^{J} F_{ij}^r + N_i^r.$$

15 See Antràs *et al.* (2012) for a derivation of this correction term and how it arises from proportionality assumptions.

16 As mentioned in Section 2.3, an alternative approach would be to work directly with the country-industry measures of GVC positioning in a given year, and take weighted-averages of these to obtain their analogues at the country level. As explained in Section 2, the two approaches clearly yield exactly the same country-level values for *F/GO* and *VA/GO* if weights equal to gross output in each country-industry are used. While the two approaches are not equivalent for *U* and *D*, they nevertheless result in highly correlated GVC measures at the country level (with a correlation higher than 0.98, for both *U* and *D*). The trends that we document are thus not sensitive to the approach taken to compute the country-level GVC measures. In practice, the net inventory correction introduces small discrepancies between the country-level GVC measures computed under either approach, but the correlation remains very high.

17 We have found no major differences in the within country-industry time trends when re-running the Table 5.2 regressions restricting to either goods-producing or service industries. The time trends for each of the GVC measures retain the same sign as in Table 5.2; statistical significance on the *Year_t* variable is lost in only one case, for the regression involving *F/GO* for goods industries (results available on request). The goods-producing industries are defined as industries 1–16 in the WIOD, these being industries in agriculture, mining, and manufacturing activities; the service industries are defined as industries 17–35.

18 In separate unreported results, we have found similar time trends when weighting each observation by the gross output of the country-industry in question. Likewise, the results are robust when adopting a less stringent set of fixed effects, namely when the FE_j^s's are replaced with a set of country fixed effects instead.

19 Costinot *et al.* (2013) and Antràs and de Gortari (2017) develop models in which countries specialize in equilibrium in particular segments of the global value chain: some countries have comparative advantage in more upstream stages, while others specialize in more downstream stages.

20 The correlation between the country-level measures of *F/GO* and *U*, as well as between the country-level measures of *VA/GO* and *D*, is indeed negative and lower than −0.96 in any given year.

21 We have verified that the patterns documented in this section are not unduly driven by the small economies in the WIOD sample. In particular, similar time trends are obtained when: (i) dropping Malta, Cyprus, Estonia, Latvia, and Lithuania, these being the five smallest countries by GDP; (ii) using aggregate gross output as regression weights in the cross-country regressions underlying the lower panels in Figures 5.5 and 5.6; or (iii) weighting the Table 5.3 regressions by the gross output of the country-industry in question.

22 Using the notation in Section 2.3, this is calculated for any country pair (i, j) as: $((Z_{ij}Z_{ji})/(Z_{ii}Z_{jj}))^{-1/2\theta}$ for trade in intermediates and as: $((F_{ij}F_{ji})/(F_{ii}F_{jj}))^{-1/2\theta}$ for final-use trade. Note that the formulae for the Head-Ries indices imply that trade costs are infinite when either the value of trade from i to j or that from j to i is zero. For

practical purposes, we therefore add a small constant to all Z_{ij}^{rs} and F_{ij}^r entries that are equal to zero, before collapsing the WIOT to a country-by-country set of tables, in order to bound the implied trade costs away from infinity. The constant added ($1e^{-18}$) is less than the smallest positive entry seen in the WIOT in any year.

23 When plotting Figure 5.7, we have dropped the largest 1 per cent of values for both intermediate-use and final-use trade costs. In practice, this helps to smooth out the time trend in the figure, ensuring that the patterns are not being driven by outliers that correspond to very small trade flows that are most prone to being measured with error.

24 There appears to be a small rise in trade costs around the onset of the Global Financial Crisis, consistent with the collapse in trade flows experienced during that episode.

25 These industry-level elasticities are for goods-producing sectors, and so we continue to set $\theta = 5$ for trade flows involving services in this robustness exercise.

26 Similar results are obtained when dropping the industries related to transport services, namely Inland Transport (23), Water Transport (24), Air Transport (25), and Other Transport Activities and Travel Agencies (26).

27 The coefficient of variation of the service share in gross output rose slightly from 0.159 in 1995 to 0.167 in 2011.

28 See Berlingieri (2014) for a related discussion based on the U.S. Domestic Input-Output Tables.

29 We ignore tariffs and their implied tariff revenue for simplicity.

30 We assume that $\sigma^r < 1 + \theta^r$ for each r, in order for the ideal price index over this industry-r CES aggregate to be well-defined.

31 The manipulation uses the fact that gross output of industry r in country j is equal to the world's total purchases from this country-industry.

32 Aggregating (25) across sectors, and using (26), one obtains after some manipulations:

$$w_j L_j = \sum_{r=1}^{S} \left(1 - \sum_{s=1}^{S} \gamma_j^{sr}\right) \sum_{i=1}^{J} \pi_{ji}^r X_i^r = \sum_{r=1}^{S} \left(1 - \sum_{s=1}^{S} \gamma_j^{sr}\right) Y_j^r.$$

In words, the total wage payments to labor in country j are equal to total value-added across all sectors of j.

33 Note that (22) comprises $J \times (J - 1) \times S$ independent equations, since the shares π_{ij}^s need to sum to 1 for each j-s pair. Also, (23) and (24) each comprise $J \times S$ equations. The market-clearing condition (25) comprises $J \times S - 1$ independent equations, since one of these is redundant by Walras' Law. Finally, there are J trade balance conditions in (26). On the other hand, the equilibrium seeks to solve for the following objects: The shares π_{ij}^s (of which there are $J \times (J - 1) \times S$ independent shares), the unit production costs c_j^s and price indices P_j^s (of which there are $J \times S$ each), as well as the $J - 1$ wage levels w_j's (with one country's wage chosen as the numéraire) and the $J \times S$ expenditure levels X_j^s's. Thus, we have as many equilibrium conditions as variables to be solved for.

34 In other words, given the identities of i, j and r, $\tilde{Z}_{ij}^{rs} / \sum_{k=1}^{J} \tilde{Z}_{kj}^{rs}$ would be equal for all purchasing industries s.

35 These deviations arise from adjustments made by the WIOD to reconcile the information contained on bilateral trade flows; see in particular Section 5 of Dietzenbacher et al. (2013).

36 In particular, and just as in footnote 32, aggregating (25) across sectors, and using (26), one obtains after some manipulations:

$$w_j L_j = \sum_{r=1}^{S} \left(1 - \sum_{s=1}^{S} \gamma_j^{sr}\right) Y_j^r.$$

37 One could also easily use this approach to explore changes in the technology parameters T_i^r. It would also be interesting to explore shocks to the Cobb-Douglas technological parameters γ_j^{rs}, but the sufficient statistics results derived below do not easily generalize to this type of shocks.

38 As pointed out by a reviewer, for the approach to work, it is important that the sectoral trade elasticities do not vary across importing countries.

39 To accommodate changes in the γ_j^{rs}'s, one would require a more flexible production specification, such as CES production functions in each industry.

40 In other words, we calculate $(2J)^2$ instead of $(J \times S)^2$ trade costs for intermediate inputs, and $2J^2$ instead of $J^2 \times S$ trade costs for final-use trade. We adopt $\theta = 5$ when computing these Head-Ries indices. Even after aggregating to the broad sectoral level, there are still a number of zeros in the matrix. We therefore bottom-code $\hat{\tau}_{ij}^{rs}$ and $\hat{\tau}_{ij}^{rF}$ at their respective first percentile values if these proportional changes fall below this percentile threshold. Likewise, we top-code large values of $\hat{\tau}_{ij}^{rs}$ and $\hat{\tau}_{ij}^{rF}$ at their respective 99th percentile values.

41 Specifically, trade costs for goods shipped for final-use are assumed to decline at the rate of 2.31 per cent per annum (Column 3, Table 5.5); trade costs for services shipped for intermediate use decline at 1.50 per cent per annum (Column 5, Table 5.4); and trade costs for services shipped for final-use decline at 1.96 per cent per year (Column 5, Table 5.5).

42 Strictly speaking, one should also be concerned with the model satisfying the equilibrium condition (32), which solves for the matrix of final-use price indices P_j^{rF}. These price indices are however not directly observable in a WIOT, so this condition is not relevant for the purposes of the result we are proving.

References

Acemoglu, Daron, Vasco M. Carvalho, Asuman Ozdaglar, and Alireza Tahbaz-Salehi (2012), "The Network Origins of Aggregate Fluctuations," *Econometrica* 80(5): 1977–2016.

Alexander, Patrick D. (2017), "Vertical Specialization and Gains From Trade," Bank of Canada Staff Working Paper 2017–17.

Alfaro, Laura, Pol Antràs, Davin Chor, and Paola Conconi (2017), "Internalizing Global Value Chains: A Firm-Level Analysis," *Journal of Political Economy*, forthcoming.

Alvarez, Fernando, and Robert E. Lucas (2007), "General Equilibrium Analysis of the Eaton-Kortum Model of International Trade," *Journal of Monetary Economics* 54(6): 1726–1768.

Antràs, Pol, and Davin Chor (2013), "Organizing the Global Value Chain," *Econometrica* 81(6): 2127–2204.

Antràs, Pol, Davin Chor, Thibault Fally, and Russell Hillberry (2012), "Measuring the Upstreamness of Production and Trade Flows," *American Economic Review Papers & Proceedings* 102(3): 412–416.

Antràs, Pol, and Alonso de Gortari (2017), "On the Geography of Global Value Chains," mimeo Harvard University.

Baldwin, Richard, and Tadashi Ito (2014), "The Smile Curve: Evolving Sources of Value Added in Manufacturing," mimeo.

Baldwin, Richard, and Anthony Venables (2013), "Spiders and Snakes: Offshoring and Agglomeration in the Global Economy," *Journal of International Economics* 90(2): 245–254.

Berlingieri, Giuseppe (2014), "Outsourcing and the Rise in Services," CEP Discussion Paper No. 1199.

Caliendo, Lorenzo, and Fernando Parro (2015), "Estimates of the Trade and Welfare Effects of NAFTA," *Review of Economic Studies* 82(1): 1–44.

Cameron, Colin, Jonah Gelbach, and Douglas Miller (2011), "Robust Inference With Multi-way Clustering," *Journal of Business and Economic Statistics* 29(2): 238–249.

Costinot, Arnaud, and Andres Rodríguez-Clare (2014), "Trade Theory with Numbers: Quantifying the Consequences of Globalization," *Handbook of International Economics*, 4: 197–261.

Costinot, Arnaud, Jonathan Vogel, and Su Wang (2013), "An Elementary Theory of Global Supply Chains," *Review of Economic Studies* 80(1): 109–144.

de Gortari, Alonso (2017), "Disentangling Global Value Chains," mimeo Harvard University.

Dekle, Robert, Jonathan Eaton, and Samuel Kortum (2008), "Global Rebalancing With Gravity: Measuring the Burden of Adjustment," *IMF Economic Review* 55(3): 511–540.

Dietzenbacher, Erik, Bart Los, Robert Stehrer, Marcel Timmer, and Gaaitzen J. de Vries (2013), "The Construction of World Input-Output Tables in the WIOD Project," *Economic Systems Research* 25(1): 71–98.

Dixit, Avinash, and Gene Grossman (1982), "Trade and Protection With Multistage Production," *Review of Economic Studies* 49(4): 583–594.

Eaton, Jonathan, and Samuel Kortum (2002), "Technology, Geography, and Trade," *Econometrica* 70(5): 1741–1779.

Fally, Thibault (2012), "Production Staging: Measurement and Facts," mimeo UC Berkeley.

Fally, Thibault, and Russell Hillberry (2018), "A Coasian Model of International Production Chains," *Journal of International Economics* 114: 299–315.

Harms, Philipp, Oliver Lorz, and Dieter Urban (2012), "Offshoring Along the Production Chain," *Canadian Journal of Economics* 45(1): 93–106.

Head, Keith, and John Ries (2001), "Increasing Returns Versus National Product Differentiation as an Explanation for the Pattern of U.S.-Canada Trade," *American Economic Review* 91(4): 858–876.

Johnson, Robert C. (2014), "Five Facts About Value-Added Exports and Implications for Macroeconomics and Trade Research," *Journal of Economic Perspectives* 28(2): 119–142.

Johnson, Robert C. (2017), "Measuring Global Value Chains," NBER Working Paper 24027.

Johnson, Robert C., and Guillermo Noguera (2012), "Accounting for Intermediates: Production Sharing and Trade in Value Added," *Journal of International Economics* 86(2): 224–236.

Kikuchi, Tomoo, Kazuo Nishimura, and John Stachurski (2018), "Span of Control, Transaction Costs and the Structure of Production Chains," *Theoretical Economics* 13(2): 729–760.

Kohler, Wilhelm (2004), "International Outsourcing and Factor Prices With Multistage Production," *Economic Journal* 114(494): C166–C185.

Koopman, Robert, Zhi Wang, and Shang-Jin Wei (2014), "Tracing Value-Added and Double Counting in Gross Exports,"*American Economic Review* 104(2): 459–494.

Kremer, Michael (1993), "The O-Ring Theory of Economic Development," *Quarterly Journal of Economics* 108(3): 551–575.

Mas-Colell, Andreu, Michael Whinston, and Jerry Green (1995), *Microeconomic Theory*, Oxford: Oxford University Press.

Miller, Ronald E., and Umed Temurshoev (2017), "Output Upstreamness and Input Downstreamness of Industries/Countries in World Production," *International Regional Science Review* 40(5): 443–475.

Sanyal, Kalyan K., and Ronald W. Jones (1982), "The Theory of Trade in Middle Products," *American Economic Review* 72(1): 16–31.

Timmer, Marcel P., Eric Dietzenbacher, Bart Los, Robert Stehrer, and Gaaitzen J. de Vries (2015), "An Illustrated User Guide to the World Input-Output Database: The Case of Global Automotive Production," *Review of International Economics* 23(3): 575–605.

Timmer, Marcel P., Abdul Azeez Erumban, Bart Los, Robert Stehrer, and Gaaitzen J. de Vries (2014), "Slicing Up Global Value Chains," *Journal of Economic Perspectives* 28(2): 99–118.

Tyazhelnikov, Vladimir (2017), "Production Clustering and Offshoring," mimeo UC Davis.

Wang, Zhi, Shang-Jin Wei, Xinding Yu, and Kunfu Zhu (2017), "Measures of Participation in Global Value Chains and Global Business Cycles," NBER Working Paper 23222.

Yi, Kei-Mu (2003), "Can Vertical Specialization Explain the Growth of World Trade?" *Journal of Political Economy* 111(1): 52–102.

Yi, Kei-Mu (2010), "Can Multistage Production Explain the Home Bias in Trade?" *American Economic Review* 100(1): 364–393.

Appendix

In this appendix, we first outline the main steps involved in proving the existence of equilibrium in our extension of the Caliendo and Parro (2015) model. We also expand our discussion from the main text regarding the ability of the model to match all the entries of a WIOT.

Let us first tackle the issue of existence of equilibrium. The key equations characterizing such an equilibrium are (28), (29), (30), (31), (32), (35), and (36). We begin by noting that the system of equations in (31), after plugging in (30), can be written as

$$
\left(P_j^{rs}\right)^{-\theta^r} = \left(A^r\right)^{-\theta^r} \sum_{i=1}^{J} T_i^r \left(\tau_{ij}^{rs}\right)^{-\theta^r} \left(\Upsilon_i^r w_i^{1-\sum_{t=1}^{S} \gamma_i^{tr}} \prod_{t=1}^{S} \left(P_i^{tr}\right)^{\gamma_i^{tr}}\right)^{-\theta^r}.
$$

Following the same approach as in Alvarez and Lucas (2007) or Antràs and de Gortari (2017), one can verify that as long as trade costs are bounded and $\sum_{t=1}^{S} \gamma_i^{tr} < 1$ for all i and r, the system above delivers a unique mapping between the vector of wages $\mathbf{w} = \left\{w_j\right\}_{j=1}^{J}$ and the matrix of price indices P_j^{rs}. From equation (30), this in turn implies that, under the same conditions, there exists a unique matrix of unit costs c_i^r given a vector of wages $\mathbf{w}$.

The proof of the existence of a vector of wages is more involved, and we shall not develop it in full detail here, but such a proof would proceed as follows. First, notice that the system of equations defined in (35) can be inverted – under weak invertibility conditions – to express the matrix of gross output levels as a function of the equilibrium vector of wages $\mathbf{w}$. In doing so, one would invoke that trade shares are only a function of wages and parameters once plugging in the values of c_i^r as a function of the same vector of wages. With this result in hand, the last step is to simply plug trade shares – in (28) and (29) – and gross output levels – in (35) – into the trade balance condition (36) to obtain a system of J equations in the J equilibrium wages $\mathbf{w}$. Following Alvarez and Lucas (2007) or Antràs and de Gortari (2017), one would then define an excess demand function $Z(\mathbf{w})$ and show that it satisfies the conditions in Propositions 17.C.1 in Mas-Colell *et al.* (1995, p.585), namely continuity, homogeneity of degree 0 in wages, Walras' Law, the existence of a lower bound, and a limit condition.

The existence of an equilibrium does not of course guarantee that it is unique. In fact, even in the simpler one-sector Eaton and Kortum (2002) model, uniqueness has only been demonstrated under certain (sufficient) conditions on the matrix of trade costs (see Alvarez and Lucas, 2007). To derive the analogous sufficient conditions, one would need to verify the restrictions on trade costs that guarantee that the excess demand function $Z(\mathbf{w})$ has the gross substitutes property in $\mathbf{w}$ (see Proposition 17.F.3 in Mas-Colell *et al.*, 1995, p. 613).

Let us now return to the issue of whether our more flexible formulation of trade costs allows our model to match all the entries of a WIOT, no matter their values. A first obvious observation is that, if an equilibrium of the model exists, then given matrices of input and final-use trade costs, there exists equilibrium commodity flows Z_{ij}^{rs} and F_{ij}^r across sectors and industries, as well as country-sector-specific gross output Y_j^s and value-added VA_j^s levels. In other words, the model produces values for all the entries of a WIOT.

Now suppose that we begin with the empirical entries of an actual WIOT. Suppose you fix the vector of equipped labor $\mathbf{L} = \{L_j\}_{j=1}^J$ to some arbitrary values (e.g., the labor force in each country). Given $\mathbf{L}$ and the vector of aggregate value-added in each country, we obtain a vector of empirical wages $\tilde{\mathbf{w}}$, where we again use tildes to denote empirical values. It is clear that plugging the empirically observed trade shares $\tilde{\pi}_{ij}^{rs}$ and $\tilde{\pi}_{ji}^{rF}$, and gross output and deficit levels $\tilde{Y}_j^r$ and $\tilde{D}_j$, as well as the easily recoverable parameters γ_j^{sr} and α_i^s (see (37) and (38)), the goods-market and trade balance conditions (35) and (36) will hold as identities.

As demonstrated in the main text, defining $b_i^r = T_i^r (c_i^r)^{-\theta^r}$ and $\rho_{ij}^{rs} = \left(\tau_{ij}^{rs}\right)^{-\theta^r}$, we can write equations (28) and (29) as:

$$\rho_{ij}^{rs} = \tilde{\pi}_{ij}^{rs} \sum_{k=1}^J \frac{b_k^r}{b_i^r} \rho_{kj}^{rs}, \tag{A.1}$$

and:

$$\rho_{ij}^{rF} = \tilde{\pi}_{ij}^{rF} \sum_{k=1}^J \frac{b_k^r}{b_i^r} \rho_{kj}^{rF}. \tag{A.2}$$

We now further note that the values of (transformed) trade costs ρ_{ij}^{rs} and the term b_i^r need also satisfy the two remaining equilibrium conditions (30) and (31), which further imposes:

$$\left(b_j^s\right)^{-1/\theta^s} = \Psi_j^s (\tilde{w}_j)^{1-\sum_{r=1}^S \gamma_j^{rs}} \prod_{r=1}^S \left[\sum_{i=1}^J b_i^r \rho_{ij}^{rs}\right]^{-\gamma_j^{rs}/\theta^r}, \tag{A.3}$$

where the constant Ψ_j^s is given by $\Psi_j^s = T_j^s \Upsilon_j^s (A^r)^{\gamma_j^{rs}}$.[42] Fixing the parameters T_j^s, as well as σ^r and θ^r (shaping A^r), the system provides a second set of equilibrium conditions relating trade costs ρ_{ij}^{rs} and the term b_i^r (while involving other parameters and "observables"). Combining (A.1) and (A.3) one should, under the necessary invertibility conditions solve for the matrix of values for b_j^s consistent with the observables in the WIOT and the general equilibrium of the model. With those in hand, it just suffices to plug them back into (A.1) and (A.2) to obtain the matrices of trade costs ρ_{ij}^{rs} and ρ_{ij}^{rF} that make the model replicate all the entries of a WIOT exactly. Although it should be clear from our proof, obtaining those parameters requires however fixing the other unobserved (and not easily retrieved) parameters L_j, T_j^s, σ^r and θ^r.

Table 5.A1 Summary statistics: country-industry GVC measures

	10th	Median	90th	Mean	Std Dev	N
F/GO						
All industries	0.125	0.444	0.901	0.473	0.271	24,076
Goods industries only	0.076	0.373	0.700	0.379	0.240	11,105
Service industries only	0.216	0.496	0.956	0.553	0.270	12,971
VA/GO						
All industries	0.279	0.456	0.738	0.489	0.186	24,395
Goods industries only	0.247	0.360	0.499	0.371	0.118	11,152
Service industries only	0.378	0.575	0.812	0.589	0.175	13,243
U						
All industries	1.153	2.126	2.914	2.098	0.649	24,395
Goods industries only	1.523	2.298	3.048	2.291	0.605	11,152
Service industries only	1.055	1.982	2.771	1.936	0.640	13,243
D						
All industries	1.502	2.141	2.624	2.092	0.450	24,395
Goods industries only	2.033	2.381	2.728	2.376	0.316	11,152
Service industries only	1.356	1.846	2.363	1.852	0.404	13,243

Notes: Based on the country-industry GVC measures calculated from the WIOD for 1995–2011; the sample comprises all 41 countries, 35 industries, and 17 years. Goods industries are defined as primary and manufacturing industries, namely industries 1–16 in the WIOD classification. The service industries are industries 17–35 in the WIOD classification.

6 Understanding regional export growth in China

David Autor, David Dorn, Gordon Hanson and Lei Li

1. Introduction

Over the last quarter century, China has emerged as the world's most dynamic manufacturing nation. Based on data from the World Development Indicators, between 1991 and 2013 the country's share of global manufacturing value added grew more than six fold, rising from 4 per cent to 24 per cent. Having surpassed the United States in 2010, China is now the world's largest producer of manufactured goods. As China's manufacturing sector has grown, so too has its presence in global markets. Between 1991 and 2014, China's share of world manufacturing exports increased more than seven times, from 2 per cent to 17 per cent, with most of this growth having occurred by 2010, when the global financial crisis dented growth in world trade. Today, China is the world's factory.

Most discussions of China's manufacturing boom center on economic reforms that the country enacted in the 1980s and 1990s, which initiated a process of export-led development similar to that of the Asian Tigers – Hong Kong, Singapore, South Korea, and Taiwan – in earlier decades (Rodrik, 2006; Hsieh and Ossa, 2016). Initial reforms created special economic zones in which foreign enterprises set up export processing plants to import parts and components for the assembly of final exports (Wang, 2013; Alder, Shao, and Zilibotti, 2016). By the late 1990s, export-processing plants accounted for over half of China's manufacturing exports (Yu and Tian, 2012 and 2017), with most of this production occurring in establishments owned by multinational corporations. A second phase of reforms closed and consolidated state-owned enterprises, allowing higher productivity private manufacturers to expand (Hsieh and Song, 2015). At the same time, the de facto relaxation of barriers on internal migration permitted over 150 million workers to reallocate from rural farms to urban factories (Li, Li, Wu, and Xiong, 2012; Fan, 2015; Zi, 2016).

China's outward-oriented economic-policy changes culminated with its accession to the World Trade Organization in 2001, which reduced tariff barriers on imported intermediate inputs (Yu, 2015; Amiti, Dai, Feenstra, and Romalis, 2017; Brandt, Van Biesebroeck, Wang, and Zhang, 2017; Yu and Tian, 2017), phased out restrictions on which firms are allowed to export directly (Ding, Sun, and Jiang, 2015; Bai, Krishna, and Ma, 2017), and attenuated uncertainty over China's access to foreign markets, the United States in particular (Pierce and Schott, 2016; Handley and Limao, 2017; Erten and Leight, 2017). Together, these modifications helped China's manufacturing sector achieve annual rates of productivity growth of nearly 8 per cent, on a value-added basis, and of nearly 3 per cent, on a gross-output basis, in the 10 years preceding the onset of the global financial crisis (Brandt, Van Biesebroeck, and Zhang, 2012).

In this chapter, we use disaggregated regional data on Chinese trade to assess the channels through which the country's exports have surged. We begin the analysis by describing how the composition of exports in China changed during the period spanning the country's accession to the WTO. Since 2000, the share of export processing in China's exports has declined, as China has shifted into more vertically integrated forms of production for global markets. Due in large part to the liberalization of foreign trading rights, the share of exports by state-owned enterprises has plummeted. In their place, the share of exports by foreign-owned enterprises has grown steadily, while the share by private domestic enterprises has skyrocketed. Also over this time period, China's exports shifted from traditionally labor-intensive goods, such as apparel, footwear, furniture, and toys, to more sophisticated electronics products, including cellphone handsets and laptop computers (Xu and Lu, 2009). Two decades ago, China had few brands that were recognized globally. Today, Huawei (telecommunications equipment) and Lenovo (personal computers) are the largest global producers in their respective industries, while three of the top five producers of smartphones are Chinese companies (Huawei, Oppo and Vivo).

As a starting point for our analysis, we use a Bartik (1991) shift-share approach to evaluate the common component of industry-level export growth across regions in China. Applied in our context, this approach, which takes the method in Autor, Dorn and Hanson (2013) for modeling the growth in U.S. imports from China down to the level of Chinese regions, involves predicting a region's manufacturing export growth over the 2000s by combining the initial regional share of economic activity in each industry with national export growth in that industry and then summing across industries. Regions are "exposed" to better export-growth opportunities if they begin specialized in industries that subsequently experience rapid growth at the national level.

We thus imagine that a region's pattern of industrial specialization as of the late 1990s is predictive of its later export growth. Predictability may arise from stability in regional comparative advantage over time (or at least over the 10-year period that we examine) or from the geographic clustering of related industries, such that growth in one industry (textiles) tends to be related to growth in upstream industries (chemicals) or downstream industries (apparel). Our reduced-form empirical approach allows us to be agnostic about the origins of regional export growth. Variation in regional export growth may reflect regional stability in relative factor supplies (which would determine comparative advantage in a Heckscher-Ohlin setting), in relative industry technological capabilities (which would determine comparative advantage in a Ricardian setting), or in localization patterns arising from agglomeration economies. Our use of a Bartik measure to explain China's export growth is similar in spirit to Bombardini and Li (2016), who examine the consequences of China's export boom for pollution-related mortality in the country, and Cheng and Potlogea (2015), who study how trade-related economic linkages affect local economic development in China.

Of course, regional comparative advantage or industry agglomeration are not the only factors that indicate a region's export-growth potential. The substantial changes in China's economic policy over the time period that we study are also potentially important determinants of regional export growth, at least to the extent that regions differ in their exposure to these policy changes. Our analysis also considers the impact on exports of explicit measures of policy change that the literature has identified as important drivers of China's trade expansion, in particular, and post-trade liberalization episodes, in general. These include the reduction of barriers on imported intermediate inputs, the Pierce and Schott (2016) measure of policy uncertainty confronting China in the U.S. market (Feng, Li and Swenson, 2017), and reductions in quotas on apparel and textile products mandated by the end of the Multi-Fiber Arrangement (Khandelwal, Schott and Wei, 2013). To avoid the confounding effects of the surge in state lending that China undertook to combat the global financial crisis (Bai, Hsieh and Song, 2016), we focus our analysis on the years 2000 to 2010, which captures a period of accelerated export and productivity growth in China (Brandt, Wang and Zhang, 2017) and coincides with the most intense phase of China's export boom.

We find that a simple Bartik measure has substantial predictive power for China's regional export growth. Even though China's regional development has been highly uneven, the spatial pattern of regional export growth is to a large extent explained by industry trends at the national level. Our results indicate that a region at the 75th percentile of exposure to China's national export boom would have had growth in export intensity 0.1 standard deviations higher than a region at the 25th percentile of exposure. Once we add the Bartik measure to the regression, the estimated impact of reduced input tariffs on China's export growth falls substantially and loses statistical significance. A similar outcome is observed for the Pierce and Schott and Handley and Limao uncertainty measures, whose impacts on export growth falls to zero with the inclusion of the Bartik measure. The ability of these tariff-based measures to predict export growth also declines considerably when province dummies or controls for the initial specialization of cities in the textile/apparel and electronics/machinery sectors are added to the regression analysis. Whereas exposure to different tariff regimes appears to vary to a large extent across rather than within provinces and sectors, the Bartik measure provides a consistently strong prediction of export growth even when province-level and sector-level trends are absorbed into control variables. We see little evidence that regions more exposed to the elimination of MFA quotas enjoyed faster export growth.

Next, we examine the importance of export regimes (processing versus ordinary exports) and firm ownership type (state-owned, foreign-owned, domestic privately owned establishments) in China's export growth. If some regions – say, because of their proximity to ports – are better suited to export processing, they may have enjoyed relatively rapid growth (Brandt and Morrow, 2017; Dai, Maitra and Yu, 2016). Similarly, regions that were initially more dominated by state-owned enterprises may have seen slower growth as foreign and private domestic firms outpaced SOEs in their ability to attract resources and penetrate foreign markets (Hsieh and Song, 2015). We find that ordinary exports and processing exports operate as independent drivers of regional export growth, while among firm types it is national growth in industry exports by foreign-owned enterprises – rather than by state-owned or private domestic enterprises – that is the strongest predictor of regional expansion in exports. The initial attractiveness of regions to foreign-owned companies, driven in part perhaps by Deng Xiaoping's early experiments in opening locations to foreign investment and trade, appears to have laid the foundation for China's 2000s export boom.

The result of our analysis is a reduced-form model of regional export growth in China, which can be used to support analysis of the local-labor-market impacts of deeper global economic integration. The rapidly growing literature on how import competition from lower-income countries has affected labor markets in developed economics (e.g., Autor, Dorn and Hanson, 2013 and 2016; Autor, Dorn, Hanson and Song, 2014; Acemoglu, Autor, Dorn, Hanson and Price, 2016) has not been matched by an equivalent volume of work on how China's export growth has affected its own local labor markets. A newly emerging literature examines how export growth in China affects local pollution (Bombardini and Li, 2016), enhances incentives for skill and capital accumulation (Cheng and Potlogea, 2015; Li, 2015), and induces reallocation of labor out of agriculture and into manufacturing (Fan, 2015; Zi, 2016; Leight, 2016; Erten and Leight, 2017). If regional comparative advantage or industry agglomeration patterns are roughly stable over decadal time periods, then export growth across regions will vary according to their initial patterns of industrial specialization and which industries enjoyed rapid export growth at the national level. We also consider the impact of explicit measures of policy change that the literature has identified as drivers of China's trade expansion, including reductions of tariffs on final goods, tariffs on imported intermediate inputs, trade-policy uncertainty for China in the U.S. market, and MFA quotas on apparel and textile products.

We find that a simple Bartik measure has substantial predictive power for China's regional export growth. Once we add the Bartik measure to the analysis, the impacts of reduced input and output tariffs or trade-policy uncertainty on China's export growth fall substantially and become statistically insignificant. These tariff-based predictors of export growth are also very sensitive to the inclusion of time trends across provinces and broad sectors, whereas the Bartik measure has considerably more success in predicting variation in export growth within provinces and sectors. There is little evidence that regions more exposed to the elimination of MFA quotas enjoyed faster export growth. Our results provide a foundation for the analysis of how China's export boom affected China's regional economies.

2. Background on China's export growth

China's quarter century of export growth began in the early 1990s. Although Deng Xiaoping initiated economic reform in the late 1970s, the early emphasis was on improving incentives for agricultural production and relaxing centralized control over industry. In 1989, after more than a decade of reform, China still remained a small player in global manufacturing, accounting for only 1.8 per cent of global manufacturing exports. When hardliners re-established control over economic policy following the events at Tiananmen Square in 1989, reform stalled and there was doubt about the sustainability of China's transition toward a market economy (Naughton, 2007). It was not until the reformist camp reaffirmed its authority over economic policy in the early 1990s that China fully embraced export-led development. Deng's famous "southern tour" in 1992 focused national attention on the successes of earlier policy experiments in a handful of locations on China's east coast (Vogel, 2011). These efforts had included the creation of special economic zones (SEZs), which allowed foreign companies to set up export processing plants that imported inputs and exported final outputs, relatively free from government interference (Yu and Tian, 2017; Alder, Shao and Zilibotti, 2016). As the number of SEZs grew from 20 in 1991 to 150 in 2010, foreign-owned export plants proliferated. According to the World Development Indicators, inflows of foreign direct investment, which averaged only 0.7 per cent of GDP during the 1980s, rose to 4.2 per cent of GDP during the 1990s and 2000s.

China's economic isolation under Mao created abundant opportunities for later catch up (Zhu, 2012; Brandt, Ma and Rawski, 2016). Because the distortions of the Maoist era kept China far inside its production frontier, market opening ignited a phase of transitional growth that was governed in large part by the country's accumulated productivity gap with the developed world (Song, Storesletten and Zilibotti, 2011). A key feature of this transitional growth was China realizing its long dormant comparative advantage in manufacturing. Whereas many large emerging economies specialize in primary commodities – including Brazil in iron ore, Indonesia in rubber, Russia in oil and gas, and South Africa in minerals – China's advantage is overwhelmingly in industrial goods. Over the period 1990 to 2013, manufacturing averaged 88 per cent of China's total exports of goods and services. This fraction of manufacturing exports was higher than any other country with consistent data over this time period, and simply stunning for such a large economy. Relative to other major emerging economies, China's manufacturing export share over this time period compares to 77 per cent in South Korea, 69 per cent in Mexico, 60 per cent in Thailand, 59 per cent in the Philippines, 49 per cent in India, 48 per cent in Vietnam, 42 per cent in Indonesia, 41 per cent in Brazil, 40 per cent in South Africa, and 18 per cent in Russia. To the extent that China's regions varied either in their comparative advantage within manufacturing (e.g., coal supplies in China's northeast may account for the region's strength in steel production) or their access to foreign markets (e.g., the proximity of Guangdong province to Hong Kong may have helped its local firms make connections with multinational enterprises), the country's transitional growth may have favored particular industries in particular locations. It is the combination of China's dramatic market opening and its latent relative strength in manufacturing production that we exploit in specifying a Bartik-style, reduced-form model for export growth in China.

The culmination of China's entry onto the world economic stage was its accession to the WTO in 2001. The country's entry occurred over the course of nearly a decade. In 1996, China began to meet preconditions for its WTO accession by removing its most restrictive non-tariff barriers. Trade licenses, special import arrangements, and discriminatory policies against foreign goods were reduced or eliminated, thereby making import tariffs the primary instruments of protection. In 2001, China began to reduce tariffs themselves. The simple average tariff (across six-digit HS products) fell from 17 per cent in 2000 (with a standard deviation of 12 per cent) to 6 per cent by the end of 2005 (with a standard deviation that was nearly 50 per cent smaller). Since 2005, average tariffs have remained stable (Amiti, Dai, Feenstra and Romalis, 2017).

Changes in tariffs have meant increased competition from imports in China's domestic market and improved access to imported intermediate inputs. A now substantial literature documents the positive impact of lower barriers on imported inputs on the productivity of manufacturing plants, including work by Amiti and Konings (2007) on Indonesia; Topalova and Khandelwal (2011) and Goldberg, Khandelwal, Pavcnik and Topalova (2010) on India; and Yu (2015) and Brandt, Van Biesebroeck, Wang and Zhang (2017) on China itself. Thus, one indirect way in which the WTO accession may have enhanced China's export performance was by raising productivity through lower-cost access to foreign inputs and capital goods and the advanced technology that they embody.

The WTO accession also inspired other reforms. One was privatization (Berkowitz, Ma and Nishioka, 2017). In the late 1990s and early 2000s, China idled many state-owned manufacturing enterprises, helping the country move towards compliance with WTO provisions that restrict state subsidies to domestic industries. Capital and labor were consequently reallocated from smaller, less productive state-owned companies to privately owned manufacturing plants, helping raise productivity and output in the sector (Hsieh and Song, 2015). Joining the WTO also obligated China to phase out requirements that had mandated most private establishments to export through state-run intermediaries.

Such restrictions constitute barriers to exporting, which the WTO expressly forbids. Bai, Krishna and Ma (2017) estimate that had private firms not been granted direct foreign trading rights, China's manufacturing exports in the 2000s would have been one third smaller than they were. A further consequence of China's WTO entry regards the insecurity of its access to the U.S. market on a most-favored nation (MFN) basis. Prior to 2001, China's MFN status in the United States was subject to annual reauthorization by Congress. Although Congress never failed to reauthorize China's MFN status, the annual ritual possibly created risk in the minds of investors regarding the stability of China's economic relations with the United States. Pierce and Schott (2016) and Handley and Limao (2017) argue that the lurking prospect of a return to non-MFN tariffs, which averaged 37.0 per cent in 1999 and compared to average MFN tariffs of only 3.4 per cent in that year, dissuaded Chinese firms from investing in operations dedicated expressly to exporting to the United States. WTO accession removed this uncertainty, potentially encouraging increased trade between China and the United States through this channel.

Finally, China's entry into the WTO allowed the country to benefit from reduced quotas on its exports of apparel and textile products, which WTO members had long retained alongside tariff reductions in other manufacturing industries under the Multi-Fiber Arrangement (Khandelwal, Schott and Wei, 2013). The MFA quotas, after a staged phase out beginning in 1995, were fully eliminated in 2005. China would have begun to enjoy the impacts of relaxed MFA quotas in 2001, by which point two MFA quota reductions had occurred, in 1995 and 1998, and a third, in 2002, was about to occur. As MFA quotas in China prior to 2001 appeared to be allocated disproportionately to state-owned enterprises, their termination may have especially benefited foreign and domestic private enterprises in apparel and textile sectors.

Motivated by this context, we utilize four measures of the determinants of regional export growth in China: (i) the reduction in tariffs on output and on imported intermediate inputs, (ii) the reduction in uncertainty regarding China's access to the U.S. market, (iii) the elimination of MFA quotas, and (iv) underlying comparative advantage. Given the importance of multinational enterprises for China's exports, in a second stage of our analysis we evaluate export growth by firm ownership, in which we separate foreign-owned firms from domestically owned private firms and state-owned enterprises. The ownership distinction allows us to examine the differential performance of state-owned firms in reaching foreign markets, after the loss of their privileged control over foreign trading rights, MFA quotas, explicit government subsidies, and other benefits.

3. Patterns of export production in China

In this section, we summarize the data we use in our analysis and describe patterns of export production in China by regime, firm ownership type, sector, and region.

3.1. Data sources

Trade data are from China's Customs Bureau, which gives details on export activity by HS 8-digit product (of which there are roughly 7,000), customs-district (which are roughly at the prefectural level and of which there were 742 in 2010), trade regime (discussed below and of which there were 15 in 2010), and ownership type of firm (discussed below and of which there were 7 in 2010). The separation of exports by trade regime and ownership type, as well as by detailed product code and regional identifier, provides an enormous amount of detail on trade in China. We elect to use these data, rather than commonly used firm-level data on trade in China, as the matching of firms to the customs data results in a substantial loss in total trade activity. We have data for the years 1997, 2000 and 2010 and we focus the analysis on the key 2000 to 2010 period. The year 1997 is the first for which prefectural level trade data are available, and, as mentioned, 2000 to 2010 spans the most intense phase of China's post-trade liberalization export growth.

To analyze regional export growth, we need to define geographic markets in China. Administrative units in the county are defined at four levels: provinces, prefectures, counties, and townships. We select the prefecture to be the target of our analysis, which leads us to aggregate more than 700 customs districts into 337 quasi-prefectural-level entities, which are roughly the equivalent of large metropolitan zones. We refer to these entities as cities. There are three justifications for this choice. First, people in China usually live and work within the same prefecture. (An exception to this regularity is the four large municipalities – Beijing, Chongqing, Shanghai and Tianjin – which are provinces in themselves but are generally regarded as unified local labor markets.) The prefecture thus approximates a local labor market, which would be of interest in many applications of our results. Combining customs districts within a prefecture into a single entity implicitly allows shocks to one zone of a city (e.g., special economic zones in Xiamen) to affect exports in other zones of a city (e.g., locations outside SEZs in Xiamen). Second, many government policies – e.g., those related to migration restrictions, social policy, land-use policy, or infrastructure investments – are implemented at the provincial or prefecture level. Third, most data released by China's National Bureau of Statistics data are at the provincial or prefecture level, whereas county, township, or customs area level data are limited in availability. Analysis of local labor markets in the country would thus likely occur at the prefectural level.

3.2. Export regimes and ownership types

We next describe export patterns by trading regime and firm ownership type. By far and away the two dominant regimes are ordinary exports – which are exports by firms that enjoy no special benefits regarding imported inputs – and processing exports – which encompass exports under in-bond arrangements in which firms post a bond equal to the value of duties on imported inputs and have the bond

Table 6.1 Export share by trading regime

Year	Export share	
	Processing trade	*Ordinary trade*
1997	0.547	0.453
2000	0.553	0.447
2010	0.470	0.530

Note: Processing trade is defined as processing with imported materials and processing and assembling. Ordinary trade includes all other trade regimes, such as ordinary trade, warehousing trade, entrepot trade by bonded area and border trade.

returned once they export their output, giving them tariff-free access to foreign intermediate goods under the constraint that all output is shipped abroad.

It is common for a country in the early stages of export-led growth to have processing exports dominate its shipments to foreign markets. This was the case in Hong Kong, Singapore and Taiwan (Naughton, 1996), where firms entered export-oriented production by serving as assembly shops for foreign contractors. China has followed a similar pattern. Under export processing, a foreign firm typically provides the specifications for a product, orders or selects the inputs to be used in production, and handles distribution, while the firm in China simply provides the labor and other factors used to assemble or otherwise process the inputs into a final good (Feenstra and Hanson, 2005). Often, but not always, the foreign contractor owns the Chinese export-processing plant outright. In China's case, Hong Kong and Taiwan are the two primary economies involved in establishing and (or) contracting with export processing plants.

Table 6.1 shows that processing exports as a share of total exports stood at 55 per cent in both 1997 and 2000, and then declined over the 2000s, dropping to 47 per cent by 2010. Brandt and Morrow (2017) argue that the reduction in barriers on imported inputs induced many firms to reorient themselves from being export processors to becoming ordinary exporters, so as to relax the constraint of having to export the entirety of their output. The WTO accession thus may have encouraged China's move toward more vertically integrated production within manufacturing and in production by plants that ship to foreign markets in particular.

Given the importance of multinational enterprises in export processing, it is no surprise that foreign-owned enterprises (FOEs) account for the majority of exports under this regime. Table 6.2 shows that, in 1997, foreign-owned firms represented 64 per cent (0.350/(0.350+0.196)) of China's processing exports, compared to their accounting for just 13 per cent (0.061/(0.061+0.392)) of the country's ordinary exports. The foreign-firm share of processing exports rises over time, to 71 per cent in 2000 and to 84 per cent in 2010. The foreign-firm share of ordinary exports also rises over time, reaching 29 per cent by 2010.

In the 1990s, the foreign-owned firms that obtained permission to operate in China were freed from having to export their output through state-owned intermediaries. Privately owned domestic enterprises (POEs) could not avoid this requirement. Table 6.2 shows that in 1997 all processing and ordinary exports

Table 6.2 Export share by firm ownership and trading regime

Year		Export share		
	Firm type	Processing trade	Ordinary trade	Total
1997	SOE	0.196	0.392	0.588
1997	POE	0.000	0.000	0.000
1997	FOE	0.350	0.061	0.411
2000	SOE	0.162	0.349	0.511
2000	POE	0.001	0.009	0.010
2000	FOE	0.391	0.089	0.480
2010	SOE	0.047	0.133	0.180
2010	POE	0.029	0.244	0.273
2010	FOE	0.394	0.153	0.547

Note: See Table 6.1 for definitions of processing trade and ordinary trade. SOEs (state-owned enterprises) include collective enterprises and state-owned enterprises. POE is short for private-owned firms. FOEs (foreign firms) include Sino-foreign contractual joint ventures, Sino-foreign equity joint ventures and foreign-owned enterprises.

by non-foreign firms were by state-owned enterprises (SOEs), which reflects the mandate still in effect at this time. As the government relaxed and then eliminated the control of foreign trading rights by state-owned firms, private domestic firms began to play a larger role in exports. The domestic private enterprise (POE) share of ordinary exports reached 46 per cent in 2010 (from 0 per cent in 1997) and of processing exports reached 6 per cent in 2010 (also from 0 per cent in 1997). By 2010, foreign-owned enterprises accounted for 55 per cent of China's overall exports, followed by private domestic firms at 27 per cent of overall exports and state-owned firms at 18 per cent of the total. The relative decline of the state-owned sector in exporting is even more rapid than its decline in industrial production, which falls from one half in 1998 to just over one quarter in 2010 (Hsieh and Song, 2015).

3.3.   *Measuring export growth and shocks to export growth*

In specifying regional export growth, we need to account for the fact that some prefectures begin the sample period with relatively low levels of exports. These low export levels reflect the weak direct integration of many Chinese regions into the global economy, prior to China's accession to the World Trade Organization in 2001. Simply using the change in log exports to measure the expansion of exports would possibly create a distorted sense of growth in these locations. The obvious solution is to scale export growth by the size of the local economy. Because exports are a gross sales value, the value of gross output by prefecture would be a suitable scaling variable. In China, however, local- and industry-level output data are likely to be of low quality over our sample period. Because city boundaries changed dramatically in the 2000s, we would need to aggregate county-level data to construct city-level data. County-level data are likely subject to particularly severe measurement error, and have a large number of missing values which are unlikely to be random. Absent reliable local output data, we instead scale export growth by prefectural population at the beginning of the sample period. China's population census provides complete county-level data for the population based on the place of residence (rather than based on the location of one's official registration, or hukou status) in 1990, 2000, and 2010. Our resulting measure of regional export growth Δx_{it} is:

$$\Delta x_{it} = \left(\frac{X_{it} - X_{it-1}}{X_{it-1}}\right)\frac{X_{it-1}}{P_{it-1}} = \frac{X_{it} - X_{it-1}}{P_{it-1}}, \tag{1}$$

where X_{it} is exports by city i in final year t (2010 in our analysis) and P_{it-1} is the residence-based population in city i in the initial period, $t-1$ (2000 in our analysis). Table 6.3 presents summary statistics. The average growth in exports per capita across Chinese regions is 1.036 (measured in units of 1,000 U.S. dollars, and thus corresponding to \$1,036 per person), with an interquartile range of 0.034 to 0.463, implying substantial skewness in this measure. We address skewness by presenting results with and without four outlier cities that have exceptionally high levels of exposure to export growth, Dongguan, Shenzhen, Suzhou, and Zhuhai. The first two are cities in Guangdong Province, which lie immediately to the north of Hong Kong; the third is a city that borders Shanghai; and the fourth is a city that borders Macao. Hence, the outliers in terms of export growth are cities that have access to major international ports and that were among the earliest locations in which special economic zones were established (Yu and Tian, 2012).

Table 6.3 Summary statistics

Variable	mean	sd	min	p25	p75	max	N
Export Growth per Capita	1.036	2.855	−0.043	0.034	0.463	23.097	337
Predicted Export Growth (PEG)	0.999	3.727	0.000	0.018	0.432	41.282	337
$\triangle$log(Output Tariff+1)	−0.066	0.027	−0.186	−0.083	−0.053	0.094	337
$\triangle$log(Input Tariff+1)	−0.032	0.016	−0.072	−0.044	−0.022	0.005	337
NTR Gap	0.321	0.131	0.000	0.275	0.393	0.596	337
Trade Policy Uncertainty (TPU)	0.481	0.177	0.000	0.460	0.583	0.734	337
MFA Share	0.018	0.017	0.000	0.005	0.027	0.116	337
Export Share of Textile/Apparel in 2000	0.245	0.204	0.000	0.090	0.369	1.000	337
Export Share of Electronics/ Machinery in 2000	0.151	0.164	0.000	0.019	0.237	0.847	337

Note: Export growth per capita and predicted export growth are both measured in thousand U.S. dollars. The statistics are weighted by residence-based population in 2000.

3.3.1. Bartik predicted export growth

Our first shock to export growth is a Bartik (1991) type measure, a variant of shift-share growth decomposition which is commonly applied in labor economics (e.g., Diamond, 2016) to capture how national-level shocks are transmitted to local economies. We project national export growth onto Chinese regions by multiplying industry export growth in outside regions (i.e., excluding a given city i) by the initial share of an industry in city i's exports and then summing across industries in the city. The resulting Bartik measure is:

$$
\Delta b_{it} = \left[\sum_j \frac{X_{ijt-1}}{X_{it-1}} \left(\frac{X_{jt}^{-i} - X_{jt-1}^{-i}}{X_{jt-1}^{-i}} \right) \right] \frac{X_{i0}}{P_{i0}},
\tag{2}
$$

where X_{ijt-1}/X_{it-1} is the share of industry j in city i's exports in the initial period, which captures regional comparative advantage in the industry, and X_{jt}^{-i} is national exports in industry j and year t excluding the province in which city i is located.

The logic behind the expression in equation (2) as a determinant of export growth is that the initial pattern of export specialization in a city exposes the city to national-level shocks more in some industries than in others. There is a clear theoretical logic behind using initial city industry export shares to characterize the exposure of a city to national export growth opportunities. Taking a trade model with a gravity structure, one can easily show that regional or national exposure to global industry shocks (due, e.g., to trade reform or technological change at home or abroad) is summarized by the initial pattern of regional or national specialization by industry (Autor, Dorn, and Hanson, 2013 and 2016). Indeed, in the exact hat algebra of Dekle, Eaton, and Kortum (2008) for general-equilibrium trade models, these initial industry shares of activity in an economy fully summarize initial patterns of comparative advantage. As mentioned in Section 1, our approach to measuring regional exposure to export growth opportunities does not require us to take a stand as to whether specialization patterns reflect comparative advantage, agglomeration economies, or their interaction. All that is required is that initial patterns of regional specialization are useful for predicting regional export growth, which we show empirically to be the case.

To avoid introducing a common source of measurement error on both sides of the regression equation, we measure the scaling variable in (2), X_{i0}/P_{i0}, using values from a pre-sample year (1997 in our analysis, which is the first year for which we have regional trade data). We define the population level for the pre-sample period in a region as the geometric mean of population levels in 1990 and 2000, given that population measures are only available in census years (e.g., 1990, 2000, 2010). In (2), we define industries at the HS 2-digit product level, in order to limit the distorting effects of zero values on measuring initial regional comparative advantage. Whereas in 2000 zero values populate

89 per cent of city-HS-6-digit-product combinations and 81 per cent of city-HS-4-digit-product combinations, zero export values account for just 54 per cent of the city-HS-2-digit-product combinations.

To give an initial view of the data, Figures 6.1a and 6.1b plot the Bartik variable in equation (2) against export growth per capita in equation (1). In Figure 6.1a, we see both a strong positive correlation between the two variables (correlation coefficient of 0.61) and the presence of the four outlier cities in terms of export growth; in Figure 6.1b, we see that the correlation between Bartik-predicted and observed export growth remains strongly positive (correlation coefficient of 0.86) when the four outlier cities are dropped from the sample. We will report regression results with and without controls for the four outlier cities in the analysis.

3.3.2. Industry tariffs

We include in the analysis measures of regional exposure to changes in output tariffs and to changes in input tariffs. To utilize the tariff data, we need to account for the fact that tariff measures for a given year are defined in terms of the HS product codes which apply to that year. The tariff data for 2000 are based on the 1996 HS codes, whereas the tariff data for 2010 are based on 2007 HS codes. To create a common basis for measurement, we first take the simple average of tariffs across HS 8-digit products within an HS 6-digit product in each year and then use the WITS crosswalk to convert the 2000 tariffs to the 1996 HS codes. Using as weights the share of each HS 6-digit product within China's HS 2-digit exports in 2000, we calculate the average HS 2-digit tariffs in 2000 and 2010, respectively. With these tariffs in hand, we then calculate the average change in output tariffs that apply to city i as:

$$\Delta \tau_{it}^{O} = \sum_{j} \frac{X_{ijt-1}}{X_{it-1}} \left[\ln \left(1 + \tau_{jt} \right) - \ln \left(1 + \tau_{jt-1} \right) \right], \tag{3}$$

where X_{ijt-1}/X_{it-1} is the share of HS 2-digit product j in city i's exports in the initial period and τ_{jt} is the tariff that applies to HS 2-digit product j in year t.

To calculate changes in tariffs that apply to intermediate inputs, we use the 2002 Input/Output Table for China, which is defined for I/O 5-digit sectors (of which there are 122) at the national level.[1] The construction of the input tariff proceeds in three steps. First, we convert HS 6-digit-product tariffs to 5-digit I/O sectors. Second, we calculate the change in input tariffs for I/O sector j in city i as:

$$\Delta \tau_{ijt}^{I} = \sum_{j'} \gamma_{jj'} \left[\ln \left(1 + \tau_{ij't} \right) - \ln \left(1 + \tau_{ij't-1} \right) \right], \tag{4}$$

where $\gamma_{jj'}$ is the share of inputs from I/O sector j' in total input purchases by I/O sector j. Third, we calculate the average change in input tariffs for city i by

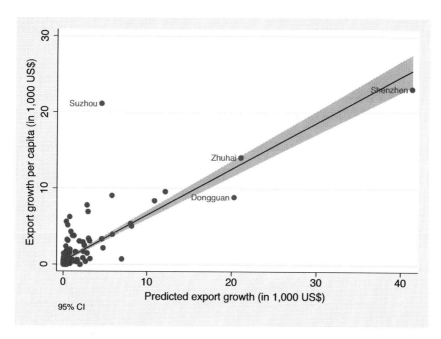

Figure 6.1a Predicted export growth and export growth per capita (2000–2010)

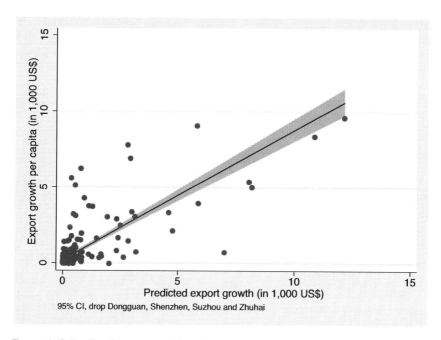

Figure 6.1b Predicted export growth and export growth per capita (2000–2010), dropping outlier cities

combining industry changes in input tariffs $\Delta\tau_{ijt}^I$ with initial city importing patterns. The resulting value is,

$$\Delta\tau_{it}^I = \sum_{j'} \frac{M_{ijt-1}}{M_{it-1}} \Delta\tau_{ijt}^I, \tag{5}$$

where M_{ijt-1}/M_{it-1} is the share of I/O industry j in total imports by city i in the initial period. Because we cannot separate a city's imports in an industry into those used for intermediate inputs versus those used in final consumption, we impose the assumption that input and consumption shares for imports are the same within each industry and within each city.

In Figures 6.2a and 6.2b, we plot regional exposure to changes in output and input tariffs in equations (3) and (5) against regional weighted average initial tariffs. The strong, linear, and negative relationships between initial tariffs and tariff changes indicate that the magnitude of tariff reductions were driven largely by the level of China's pre-WTO tariff protection. As part of China's WTO accession, the country reduced both the mean and variance of tariffs, such that initially more-protected industries saw larger increases in foreign competition and in access to foreign inputs. After 2001, the regions in which these industries were concentrated thus also saw larger increases in import competition and imported-input access. This pattern of tariff change derives largely from the fact that the WTO mandates maximum levels for tariffs at the industry level.

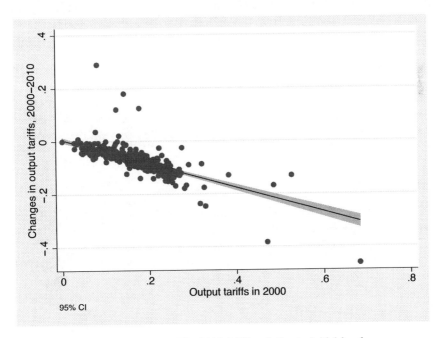

Figure 6.2a Changes in output tariffs, 2000–2010, relative to initial levels

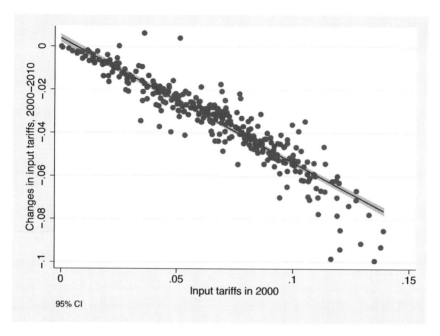

Figure 6.2b Changes in input tariffs, 2000–2010, relative to initial levels

Initially high-tariff industries were thus mechanically subject to larger reductions in tariffs, as China brought its trade barriers in line with WTO guidelines.

In Figures 6.3a and 6.3b, we plot regional export growth against regional exposure to changes in input tariffs, first including all observations (in Figure 6.3a) and then dropping the four outliers cities. There is an apparent negative correlation between regional export growth and exposure to input tariff changes, indicating that cities enjoying fast increases in exports per capita were those specialized in industries that saw larger reductions in tariffs on imported inputs. The slope of the regression line falls sharply in absolute value when outlier cities for export growth are dropped.

3.3.3.   NTR gap (Pierce and Schott tariff uncertainty measure)

Pierce and Schott (2016) measure uncertainty in trade policy confronting China before its accession to the WTO using the difference in U.S. non-MFN and MFN tariffs, which they refer to as the normal trade relations (NTR) tariff gap. This gap represents the increase in tariffs that would have occurred had U.S. Congress not reauthorized China's MFN status in the U.S. market. While China was granted MFN status in the United States in 1980, Congress instituted a requirement for annual reauthorization after the events at Tiananmen Square in 1989. Once China became a WTO member in 2001, it was no longer subject to this annual reauthorization risk. U.S. non-MFN tariffs have changed only modestly

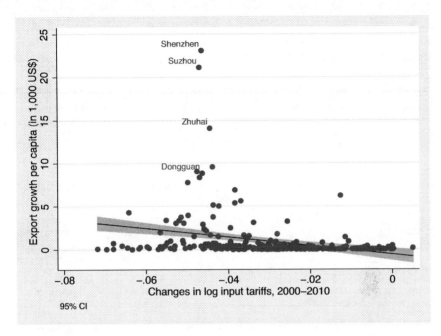

Figure 6.3a Changes in input tariffs and export growth per capita (2000–2010)

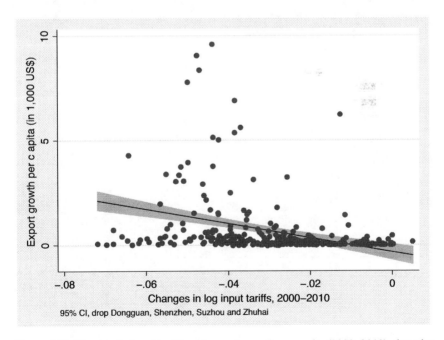

Figure 6.3b Changes in input tariffs and export growth per capita (2000–2010), dropping outlier cities

since the 1930s. We take the simple average of HS 8-digit NTR and non-NTR tariffs within HS 6-digit products for the year 1999. We then calculate the average NTR gap among the HS-6-digit products that are contained in a HS 2-digit code, using as weights the share of an HS 6-digit product in China's HS 2-digit exports to the United States. Finally, we calculate the regional NTR gap by combining NTR gaps at the HS 2-digit level with the initial composition of a region's exports across HS 2-digit products, yielding the following measure:

$$NTR_i = \sum_j \frac{X_{ijt-1}}{X_{it-1}} \left[\sum_{k \in j} \gamma_{jkt-1} \left(\tau_{k,1999}^{non-NTR} - \tau_{k,1999}^{NTR} \right) \right], \tag{6}$$

where X_{ijt-1}/X_{it-1} is the share of HS 2-digit product j in city i's exports in the initial period, γ_{jk} is the share of HS 6-digit product k in China's exports of HS 2-digit product j to the United States in the initial period, and $\tau_{k,1999}^{non-NTR}$ ($\tau_{k,1999}^{NTR}$) is the U.S. non-NTR (NTR) tariff for HS 6-digit product k in 1999. The average NTR gap has a mean value of 32 per cent (standard deviation of 13 per cent) across Chinese regions (see Table 6.3).

3.3.4. *MFA quotas*

To capture the exposure of regions to the removal of MFA quotas, we calculate the export share of products subject to MFA quotas within each HS 2-digit product in the year 2000, where we account for the fact that some HS 8-digit products may be subject to a quota in one market (e.g., the United States) but not in other markets (e.g., Canada). The resulting measure of exposure to the elimination of MFA quotas for city i is, in 2000:

$$MFA_i = \sum_j \frac{X_{ijt-1}}{X_{it-1}} MFA_{j2000}, \tag{7}$$

where MFA_{j2000} is the share of exports in HS 2-digit product j subject to MFA quotas in the year 2000. The average value for this share is 2 per cent, with a maximum value of 12 per cent (Table 6.3).

4.   Empirical results

The specification for regional export growth that we estimate is the following:

$$\Delta x_{it} = \alpha_s + \beta_1 \Delta b_{it} + \beta_2 \Delta \tau_{it}^O + \beta_3 \Delta \tau_{it}^I + \beta_4 NTR_i + \beta_5 MFA_i + \epsilon_{it}, \tag{8}$$

where Δx_{it} is growth in exports per capita for city i from (1), α_s is a dummy variable for the province in which city i is located, Δb_{it} is the Bartik predictor of regional export growth in (1), $\Delta \tau_{it}^O$ is the exposure of city i to changes in output tariffs in (3), $\Delta \tau_{it}^I$ is the exposure of city i to changes in input tariffs in (5), NTR_i is the average NTR gap confronting city i as of 1999 in (6), MFA_i is the average share of exports by city i subject to MFA quotas as of 2000 in (7), and ϵ_{it} is an error term. $\Delta \tau_{it}^{O}$ ($\Delta \tau_{it}^{I}$) is replaced as zero for cities with no export (import) in 2000. Accordingly, a dummy variable for the 18 cities with no import or export in 2000 is included. The time period for the analysis is 2000 to 2010, meaning that we estimate a single long difference for 337 cities, which are approximately at the prefectural level. The province-managing counties (accounting for 1 per cent of China's population in 2000) which the provincial government could by-pass the prefecture government to control directly are merged into prefectures which used to govern the counties. Standard errors are clustered at the province level (of which there are 31 and which include 5 autonomous regions and 4 municipalities).

4.1. Results for the Bartik predictor and industry tariffs

Table 6.4 presents our main estimation results. Panel (A) shows baseline regressions that do not include any covariates other than an indicator variable for the small number of cities that lack foreign trade in the base year. The column (1) estimate indicates that the shift-share instrument is a strong and precise predictor of local export growth (t-statistic of 7.3). The large R-squared value of 0.63 indicates that patterns of local export growth largely reflect national industry trends in exporting, rather than city-specific shocks.

In column (2), we replace the shift-share variable with regional exposure to the change in output tariffs. The negative coefficient indicates that regions whose industries have been subject to larger reductions in output tariffs had more rapid export growth, a finding that we will see is not robust. A negative coefficient also appears on regional exposure to changes in input tariffs, in column (3). When we include both input and output tariff exposure together in the regression, in column (4), a similar result obtains. Exposure to output-tariff changes enters negatively, indicating that cities exposed to larger increases in foreign competition have greater export growth. Exposure to input-tariff changes also enters negatively, indicating that cities enjoying greater improvements in access to imported inputs experience faster export growth. The coefficients are precisely estimated and quantitatively sizable.

The finding on input tariffs is consistent with substantial evidence that reductions in barriers to foreign inputs raise industry productivity and output (Yu, 2015; Brandt, Van Biesebroeck, Wang and Zhang, 2017). Comparing cities at the 25th and 75th percentiles of exposure to output-tariff reductions, the latter has greater export growth by 483 U.S. dollars per person ((.08 − .05) × 16.1 units of 1,000 dollars per capita), or 0.2 standard deviations; comparing cities at the 25th and 75th percentiles of exposure to input-tariff reductions, the latter has export growth that is greater by 904 dollars per person ((.04 − .02) × 45.2 × 1000), or 0.3 standard deviations. These impacts fall substantially, however, when further controls are added to the regression.

Table 6.4 Impact of predicted export growth and changes in tariffs
Dependent variable: △ export/residence-based population (in 1,000 US$)

	(1)	(2)	(3)	(4)	(5)	(6)	(7)
			Panel A: Baseline				
Predicted Export Growth	0.606*** (0.083)				0.595*** (0.078)	0.587*** (0.075)	0.582*** (0.073)
△log(Output Tariff+1)		−24.342** (9.289)		−16.135** (6.420)	−10.090** (4.900)		−6.920* (3.832)
△log(Input Tariff+1)			−53.242*** (17.586)	−45.216*** (14.874)		−22.346** (8.517)	−19.143*** (7.302)
R-squared	0.628	0.048	0.081	0.099	0.635	0.641	0.644
		Panel B: Controlling for Province Dummies					
Predicted Export Growth	0.600*** (0.067)				0.599*** (0.066)	0.597*** (0.066)	0.597*** (0.066)
△log(Output Tariff+1)		−6.219 (3.827)		−3.911 (3.349)	−3.519 (2.809)		−3.021 (2.679)
△log(Input Tariff+1)			−25.929* (13.198)	−24.746* (13.104)		−6.380** (3.080)	−5.473* (2.708)
R-squared	0.764	0.347	0.356	0.357	0.765	0.765	0.765
	Panel C: Controlling for Province Dummies and Dummies for Four Outlier Cities						
Predicted Export Growth	0.726*** (0.100)				0.725*** (0.099)	0.720*** (0.101)	0.719*** (0.100)
△log(Output Tariff+1)		−3.331* (1.741)		−1.994 (1.441)	−1.455 (1.057)		−1.258 (1.022)

	(1)	(2)	(3)	(4)	(5)	(6)	(7)
△log(Input Tariff+1)			−15.099** (5.695)	−14.500** (5.600)		−2.646 (2.368)	−2.279 (2.343)
R-squared	0.955	0.888	0.892	0.892	0.955	0.955	0.956
Panel D: Controlling for Each City's Initial Export Share of Textile/Apparel and Electronics/Machinery Sectors							
Predicted Export Growth	0.548*** (0.066)				0.548*** (0.066)	0.547*** (0.065)	0.547*** (0.065)
△log(Output Tariff+1)		−4.816 (3.177)		−4.554 (3.247)	−0.459 (2.688)		−0.340 (2.702)
△log(Input Tariff+1)			−14.231* (7.594)	−14.029* (7.587)		−6.912 (4.327)	−6.898 (4.288)
R-squared	0.663	0.233	0.236	0.237	0.663	0.664	0.664
Panel E: Controlling for Province Dummies, Outlier Cities and Export Shares of Two Sectors							
Predicted Export Growth	0.701*** (0.100)				0.701*** (0.100)	0.700*** (0.101)	0.700*** (0.101)
△log(Output Tariff+1)		0.138 (1.652)		0.124 (1.737)	−1.013 (1.284)		−1.013 (1.295)
△log(Input Tariff+1)			−7.409 (5.175)	−7.408 (5.186)		−0.914 (3.272)	−0.914 (3.291)
R-squared	0.956	0.899	0.900	0.900	0.956	0.956	0.956

Note: $N = 337$. Panel C and E include dummy variables for the four outlier cities, namely Dongguan, Shenzhen, Suzhou, and Zhuhai. A dummy variable for cities with no export or import in 2000 is included in all regressions. Textile/apparel and electronics/machinery include 2-digit I/O industries 17 to 19 and 35 to 41, respectively. All observations are weighted by city-level residence-based population in 2000. Robust standard errors in parentheses are clustered on province.

*** $p < 0.01$

** $p < 0.05$

* $p < 0.1$

In columns (5) to (7) of Table 6.4 (panel A), we add the Bartik predictor of city export growth to the specifications with tariff variables. The result is a substantial increase in the explanatory power of the regression, with the adjusted R-squared rising from 0.10 in column (4) – with just output and input tariffs as regressors – to 0.64 in column (7) – with the Bartik measure added to the specification. Using the column (7) results, moving a city from the 25th to the 75th percentile of exposure to national-industry export growth leads to higher export growth of 238 dollars per person ((.43 – .02) × 0.58 × 1000), or 0.08 standard deviations. Further, the inclusion of the Bartik predictor leads to a substantial reduction in the estimated impacts of output-tariff or input-tariff changes on regional export growth. Adding the Bartik variable causes the coefficients on both tariff variables to fall by nearly three fifths (when comparing column 7 to column 4), though both variables remain at least marginally statistically significant.

Panel (B) of Table 6.4 repeats the regressions in panel (A), now with province dummies added to the specification. Comparing column (1) in panels (A) and (B), we find no impact of these geographic controls on the coefficient estimate for predicted export growth, while the precision of the estimate improves. Columns (2)–(4) in panels (A) and (B) however show that the inclusion of province dummies leads the absolute magnitude of the coefficients on output-tariff changes to fall by about three-quarters and input-tariff changes to fall by half. The sensitivity of exposure to tariff changes to the inclusion of provincial dummies suggests that these measures could be correlated with unobserved regional shocks – e.g., regarding the establishment of SEZs, openness to internal migration, or the phaseout of state-owned enterprises. When we further add the Bartik predictor of regional export growth, the tariff coefficients fall further. In column (7), the panel (B) coefficient on output tariffs is only two-fifths as large and the coefficient on input tariffs is only one-quarter as large, when compared to the coefficients in panel (A); with province dummies included, the first variable is insignificant while the second is marginally significant. By contrast, the coefficient on the Bartik predictor remains strongly positive and precisely estimated, increasing slightly in absolute value when provincial controls are added to the regression. The stability of the coefficient on Bartik-predicted exports to the inclusion of provincial dummy variables indicates that this variable captures robust explanatory factors behind regional export growth, including the exposure of regions to comparative-advantage or industry-agglomeration driven export expansions associated with China's phase of post-reform transitional growth.

In panel (C) of Table 6.4 we further add dummies for the four outlier cities seen in Figure 6.1a. The absolute coefficient magnitudes on output tariffs and input tariffs decline further, while for the Bartik variable they increase modestly. Considering the results in column (7), output and input tariff coefficients fail to achieve statistical significance. Comparing cities at the 25th versus 75th percentiles of exposure to output-tariff reductions, the latter would have export growth that is 0.01 standard deviations higher, while comparing cities at the 25th versus 75th percentiles of exposure to input-tarriff reductions, the latter would also have export growth that is 0.02 standard deviations higher. The Bartik variable continues to be strongly positive and precisely estimated. Comparing cities at the 25th versus 75th percentiles of exposure to national-industry export growth, the latter would have export growth that is 0.10 standard deviations higher.

The shift-share variable and the tariff variables are all functions of a city's export composition across industries in the base year 2000. It is therefore possible that any of these variables could be correlated with unobserved sectoral shock such as different technology trends. Panel (D) of Table 6.4 augments the baseline model of panel (A) with two control variables for the share of textile and apparel, and the share of electronics and machinery in a city's exports in 2000. In 1997, both of these sectors accounted for over a quarter of all Chinese exports (29 per cent textile and apparel, 27 per cent electronics and machinery). By 2010, the fraction of textile and apparel had declined to 15 per cent, while exports of electronics and machinery had expanded to 50 per cent of all exports. The results in column (1) of panel (D) indicate that the inclusion of these controls modestly reduces the coefficient estimate for predicted export growth compared to the baseline model in panel (A) while precision improves. All coefficient estimates for the tariff variables in the subsequent columns of panel (D) are much smaller than the initial estimates in panel (A), and none reaches a high level of signficance.

The final panel (E) of Table (4) includes both the geographic controls from panel (C) and the two controls for sectorial composition from panel (D). The estimate for the Bartik variable retains a similar magnitude as in the previous specifications, and it remains highly significant. By contrast, estimates for the tariff variables are modest in magnitude and never significantly different from zero, irrespective of the exclusion or inclusion of the Bartik variable in the regression model (columns 2–4 vs columns 5–7).

There are three primary lessons from these results. First is that for explaining regional export growth in China, the variation in regional exposure to output- and input-tariff changes that is independent from regional exposure to national-industry export growth is modest. The Bartik predictor functionally operates as an omnibus measure of the sources of export growth in China, implicitly capturing a substantial portion of the trade-policy shocks associated with explicit output- and input-tariff changes. Second, and related, is that because the magnitude of tariff reductions in China was largely determined by the level of initial tariffs (Figures 6.2a, 6.2b), it appears to be the strong comparative-advantage industries – i.e., industries that following the phaseout of Maoist-era distortions were most primed for export growth – that were initially the most protected. Thus, when we add the Bartik predictor to the regression, the impact of output- and input-tariff changes is diminished, while the explanatory power of the regressions improves sharply. The increase in explanatory power suggests that there are non-tariff policy distortions that kept China's comparative-advantage industries artificially small in the pre-reform period, such that their removal helped unleash a surge in growth in the regions in which these industries were concentrated. Evidently, regional exposure to the removal of these other distortions is far from fully encapsulated by regional exposure to industry tariff changes. Third, the Bartik predictor yields stable results across regression models that do or do not control for province dummies, outlier cities and initial sectorial composition. This pattern indicates that the shift-share variable is able to predict variation in export growth across cities within the same province, and across cities that had a similar pattern of specialization across broad industrial sectors. The variation in export growth that is related to the tariff variables instead gets largely absorbed by a parsimonious set of geography and sector controls, which implies that it is difficult to separate the impact of tariffs from other shocks that operate at the level of provinces or broad sectors.

4.2.   *Results on the NTR gap and MFA quotas*

In Table 6.5, we expand the analysis to include the NTR gap, which is the Pierce and Schott (2016) measure of pre-WTO tariff uncertainty confronting China in the U.S. market. Accordingly, we use regional growth in exports to the United States instead of regional export growth to construct the dependent variable in equation (1) for Table 6.5. The Bartik predicted export growth is constructed in a similar way by using predicted export growth to the United States. The NTR gap enters positively and is precisely estimated in column (1) of panel (A), a specification with no other controls in the regression. This finding indicates that regions more specialized in industries subject to greater uncertainty over U.S. trade policy in the 1990s enjoyed faster export growth in the 2000s, once China had joined the WTO. However, the coefficient on the NTR gap falls substantially and loses significance in column (3), with the Bartik predictor and output and input tariffs added to the specification.

For completeness, we also examine results using an alternative measure of trade policy uncertainty. Columns (4) to (6) of panel (A) of Table 6.5 use the Handley and Limao (2017) measure of pre-WTO U.S. trade policy uncertainty for China. We see a similar pattern for coefficient estimates on this variable as for the NTR gap, with a large, positive and precisely estimated effect with no other controls in the regression (column 4), which falls to near zero when additional controls are included (column 6). With either measure of trade-policy uncertainty included in the regression, coefficient estimates on tariff variables have similar values and patterns of statistical significance as in Table 6.4.

We obtain considerably smaller coefficient estimates on the NTR gap and the Handley and Limao (2017) trade-policy uncertainty measure in panel (B) of Table 6.5, which reports specifications that incorporate dummy variables for provinces and four outlier cities. It is now the case that both trade-policy uncertainty measures are highly insignificant in all specifications, no matter whether or not the Bartik and tariff variables appear in the regression. In columns (3) and (6), the NTR gap and the Handley-Limao measure have t-statistics of 0.38 and 0.30, respectively. It thus appears that regional exposure to uncertainty over U.S. trade policy can only predict spatial variation in export growth to the United States across Chinese provinces, but not across cities within provinces.

Table 6.5 Impact of predicted export growth and trade policy uncertainty
Dependent variable: △ export to the U.S./residence-based population (in 1,000 US$)

	(1)	(2)	(3)	(4)	(5)	(6)
			Panel A: Baseline			
NTR Gap	0.447** (0.185)	0.331** (0.151)	0.057 (0.093)			
Trade Policy Uncertainty				0.442** (0.179)	0.332** (0.148)	0.104 (0.079)
Predicted Export Growth (U.S.)		0.233*** (0.064)	0.214*** (0.057)		0.232*** (0.063)	0.214*** (0.057)
△log(Output Tariff+1)			-1.756** (0.792)			-1.702** (0.754)
△log(Input Tariff+1)			-6.204*** (2.185)			-6.030*** (2.088)
R-squared	0.013	0.176	0.215	0.019	0.179	0.216
	Panel B: Controlling for Province Dummies and Dummies for Four Outlier Cities					
NTR Gap	0.043 (0.077)	0.033 (0.056)	0.021 (0.055)			
Trade Policy Uncertainty				0.047 (0.058)	0.024 (0.042)	0.012 (0.040)
Predicted Export Growth (U.S.)		0.753*** (0.222)	0.739*** (0.222)		0.752*** (0.222)	0.739*** (0.222)
△log(Output Tariff+1)			-0.209 (0.150)			-0.216 (0.146)
△log(Input Tariff+1)			-0.839 (0.776)			-0.835 (0.775)
R-squared	0.901	0.946	0.946	0.901	0.946	0.946

(Continued)

Table 6.5 (Continued)

	(1)	(2)	(3)	(4)	(5)	(6)
Panel C: Controlling for Each City's Initial Export Share of Textile/Apparel and Electronics/Machinery Sectors						
NTR Gap	0.204	0.141	0.105			
	(0.151)	(0.120)	(0.113)			
Trade Policy Uncertainty				0.181	0.137	0.101
				(0.124)	(0.098)	(0.094)
Predicted Export Growth (U.S.)		0.175***	0.175***		0.175***	0.174***
		(0.052)	(0.052)		(0.052)	(0.052)
$\triangle$log(Output Tariff+1)			0.062			0.050
			(0.452)			(0.455)
$\triangle$log(Input Tariff+1)			-2.317*			-2.233*
			(1.230)			(1.242)
R-squared	0.186	0.268	0.271	0.187	0.268	0.271

Note: $N = 337$. The NTR gap is the difference between non-NTR tariffs (column 2 tariffs) and NTR tariffs (column 1 tariffs) in 1999. Trade policy uncertainty (TPU) is a non-linear measure of the difference between non-NTR tariffs and NTR tariffs based on Handley and Limao (2017). Panel B includes the dummy variables for the four outlier cities, namely Dongguan, Shenzhen, Suzhou, and Zhuhai. A dummy variable for cities with no export or import in 2000 is included in all regressions. Textile/apparel and electronics/machinery include 2-digit I/O industries 17 to 19 and 35 to 41, respectively. All observations are weighted by city-level residence-based population in 2000. Robust standard errors in parentheses are clustered on province.

*** $p < 0.01$

** $p < 0.05$

* $p < 0.1$

The regression models in panel (C) of Table 6.5 omit the province and outlier city dummies, but control for initial export shares of the textile/apparel and electronics/machinery sectors. These controls for broad sectorial composition of export activity reduce the panel (A) estimates for NTR gap and trade policy uncertainty by more than half in most models, suggest that tariff uncertainty varies primarily across rather than within broad sectors. Taken together, the panel (B) and (C) results imply that it is difficult to separate effects of tariff uncertainty from province-level and sector-level shocks.

Table 6.6 expands the analysis to include regional exposure to the elimination of MFA quotas. We report results with and without provincial dummy variables, control for the four outlier cities (which accounted for a large fraction of China's apparel and tariff production in its pre-WTO era), and control for the initial export shares of the textile/apparel and electronics/machinery sectors. In no specification is the coefficient on MFA quotas precisely estimated. There is little change in the results when the Bartik predictor, tariff variables and the NTR gap are added to the specification (columns 4–6). We conclude that there is little evidence regional exposure to the elimination of MFA quotas affected regional export growth in China during the 2000s.

Table 6.6 Impact of predicted export growth and MFA quota share
Dependent variable: $\triangle$ export/residence-based population (in 1,000 US$)

	(1)	*(2)*	*(3)*	*(4)*	*(5)*	*(6)*
MFA Share	8.790	0.911	8.551	2.387	2.199	1.661
	(12.004)	(3.039)	(6.183)	(5.156)	(5.173)	(5.343)
Predicted Export Growth				0.700***	0.699***	0.699***
				(0.098)	(0.099)	(0.098)
$\triangle$log(Output Tariff+1)					−0.987	−0.751
					(1.268)	(1.376)
$\triangle$log(Input Tariff+1)					−0.762	−0.703
					(3.322)	(3.367)
NTR Gap						0.390
						(0.379)
Province Fixed Effects	N	Y	Y	Y	Y	Y
Dummies for Outliers	N	Y	Y	Y	Y	Y
Controlling for Export Shares of Two Sectors	N	N	Y	Y	Y	Y
R-squared	0.007	0.350	0.888	0.955	0.956	0.956

Note: $N = 337$. The four outlier cities are Dongguan, Shenzhen, Suzhou, and Zhuhai. A dummy variable for cities with no export or import in 2000 is included in all regressions. Models in Column (3)–(6) control for the initial export shares of the textile/apparel and electronics/machinery sectors which include 2-digit I/O industries 17 to 19 and 35 to 41, respectively. All observations are weighted by city-level residence-based population in 2000. Robust standard errors in parentheses are clustered on province.
*** $p < 0.01$
** $p < 0.05$
* $p < 0.1$

4.3.   Results on exports by trade regime and firm ownership type

In Table 6.7, we expand the analysis by disaggregating exports by customs trade regime. Column (1) replicates results from column (7) and panel C of Table 6.4. Column (2) uses processing exports alone (rather than total exports) to construct the dependent variable in equation (1), while column (3) uses ordinary exports in the equivalent variable construction. Bartik predicted export growth is based on all trade. We see qualitatively similar results to those in Table 6.4. Overall Bartik-predicted export growth is strongly positive correlated with regime-specific export growth, both under the ordinary trade regime and the export-processing regime. Columns (4) and (5) repeat the analysis, now using regime-specific trade to construct Bartik-predicted export growth, with broadly similarly results. Finally, in column (6) we return to total export growth as the dependent variable and include regime-specific Bartik-predicted exports. With both Bartik variables in the regression, we see that predicted growth in processing exports is the stronger variable of the two, with a coefficient of 1.11 for Bartik-predicted processing exports compared to 0.33 for Bartik-predicted ordinary exports, where the former is very precisely estimated while the latter fails to achieve statistical significance.

Table 6.7 Predicted export growth and export growth per capita by trading regime
Dependent variable: $\triangle$ export/residence-based population by trading regime (in 1,000 US$)

	(1)	(2)	(3)	(4)	(5)	(6)
			Export growth per capita			
	Total export	*Processing*	*Ordinary*	*Processing*	*Ordinary*	*Total export*
Predicted Export	0.719***	0.383***	0.336***			
Growth	(0.100)	(0.057)	(0.046)			
Predicted Processing				0.721***		1.108***
Export Growth				(0.113)		(0.088)
Predicted Ordinary					0.477***	0.332
Export Growth					(0.121)	(0.238)
$\triangle$log(Output Tariff+1)	−1.258	−0.787	−0.471	−0.554	−0.647	−0.917
	(1.022)	(0.531)	(0.549)	(0.471)	(0.589)	(0.961)
$\triangle$log(Input Tariff+1)	−2.279	0.918	−3.197	−0.851	−4.029	−3.822
	(2.343)	(1.040)	(2.098)	(0.795)	(2.968)	(2.801)
R-squared	0.956	0.963	0.89	0.969	0.863	0.957

Note: $N = 337$. Province dummies, dummies for outlier cities, namely Dongguan, Shenzhen, Suzhou, and Zhuhai, and a dummy variable for cities with no export or import in 2000 are controlled. Please refer to Table 6.1 for definitions of the trading regimes. All observations are weighted by city-level residence-based population in 2000. Robust standard errors in parentheses are clustered on province.
*** $p < 0.01$
** $p < 0.05$
* $p < 0.1$

Table 6.8 Predicted export growth and export growth per capita by firm ownership
Dependent variable: △ export/residence-based population by firm ownership (in 1,000 US$)

	(1)	(2)	(3)	(4)	(5)	(6)	(7)
	Export growth per capita						
	SOE	POE	FOE	SOE	POE	FOE	Total export
Predicted Export Growth	0.059** (0.025)	0.191*** (0.019)	0.469*** (0.068)				
Predicted Export Growth of SOE				0.350** (0.143)			0.674 (0.446)
Predicted Export Growth of POE					0.405*** (0.070)		−0.601 (0.490)
Predicted Export Growth of FOE						0.084*** (0.022)	1.088*** (0.216)
△log(Output Tariff+1)	−0.041 (0.172)	−0.504 (0.455)	−0.718 (0.483)	−0.312 (0.232)	−0.641 (0.529)	−0.008 (0.159)	−1.267 (1.070)
△log(Input Tariff+1)	−0.696 (0.574)	−1.734** (0.726)	0.164 (1.602)	−0.671 (0.550)	−4.733*** (1.554)	−1.012* (0.538)	−3.855 (2.325)
R-squared	0.874	0.833	0.966	0.870	0.776	0.871	0.960

Note: Province dummies, dummies for outliers and a dummy variable for cities with no export or import in 2000 are included. The four outliers are Dongguan, Shenzhen, Suzhou, and Zhuhai. Please refer to Table 6.2 for definitions of firm ownership types. All observations are weighted by city-level residence-based population. Robust standard errors in parentheses are clustered on province.
*** $p < 0.01$
** $p < 0.05$
* $p < 0.1$

Finally, we turn to exports by firm ownership type in Table 6.8. We perform an analysis similar to that in Table 6.7, in which we analyze export growth separately for state-owned enterprises (SOEs) in columns (1) and (4), private domestic enterprises (POEs) in columns (2) and (5), and foreign-owned enterprises (FOEs) in columns (3) and (6). In columns (1)–(3), we see that overall Bartik-predicted export growth is strongly positively correlated with export growth of each ownership type; in columns (4)–(6) we see that Bartik-predicted export growth for each ownership type is strongly positively correlated with export growth of that type (i.e., predicted SOE export growth has a strong positive impact on actual SOE export growth, etc.). In column (7), we combine the three Bartik-predicted export growth measures together to explain total city export growth. Strikingly, while Bartik-predicted export growth for foreign-owned enterprises has a positive and precisely estimated impact on overall export growth, predicted export growth for SOEs and POEs enter insignificantly, and the latter with a negative sign. Of the components of predicted city export growth that matter for overall export expansion, it is growth related to foreign-owned firms that appears to be the most important, both economically and statistically.

Why might the shift-share analysis show that the local presence of foreign-owned enterprises – and their associated national growth – is the strongest predictor of regional export booms among the three ownership types? One possibility is that foreign-owned firms may be a channel through which local firms learn about foreign market opportunities. That is, export production by foreign firms may generate positive spillovers to nearby firms by showing them the types of goods to produce (helping spread product innovations), how to manufacture them (helping spread process innovations), and where to sell them (helping spread marketing knowledge). Another possibility is that local governments successful in attracting foreign firms may offer a policy environment that is conducive to trade growth for all firm types. Such policies could include the more efficient operation of customs, relatively low regulatory burdens, and greater ease of resolving commercial disputes. A third possibility is that Deng's experiments in creating SEZs had long-lasting effects. Initially, foreign-owned firms were confined to operate in SEZs, which were concentrated in a few select locations in the country. Over time, SEZs proliferated and private firms, both foreign and domestic, were permitted to produce for export in many locations. The early establishment of SEZs may have shaped later local industrial development, and perhaps policy-makers attitudes toward foreign trade, in a manner that had persistent effects on regional export activity.

5. Discussion

Over the last quarter century, China has experienced one of the greatest manufacturing booms that the world has ever seen. The country's dramatic expansion in the supply of exports and in the demand for imported inputs have upended markets globally. The China export-supply shock has contributed to reductions in manufacturing employment in regions specialized in labor-intensive manufacturing in Germany, Mexico, Norway, Spain, and the United States, among other countries (Autor, Dorn, and Hanson, 2016). In turn, the China import-demand shock contributed to spikes in global commodity prices in the mid- to late 2000s, with concomitant sharp increases in export earnings in commodity exporting economies. Although the China shock appears to have peaked in the late 2000s, the two-decade-long period of growth in the country's manufacturing sector has enduringly transformed the global economy.

Driving China's export growth is the country's greater openness to foreign trade and investment. Although there is a long list of potential factors that are responsible for China's export surge, most literature to date has focused on one or another factor, without considering them in concert. Our goal in this chapter is to evaluate the contributions of exposure to changes in output tariffs, input tariffs, uncertainty over trade policy, and MFA apparel and textile quotas to regional export growth in China. We compare the role of these specific measures of policy change to a Bartik predictor, which captures differential regional exposure to export growth tied to China's underlying comparative advantage. That is, while industry-specific changes in trade policy surely matter for explaining China's recent trade expansion, what has also driven manufacturing export growth is the country's once-in-an-epoch transition from near economic isolation to a high degree of openness. During this process of transitional growth, regions more specialized in strong comparative-advantage industries (or strong agglomeration-economy industries) would have experienced larger increases in production, as China reoriented from production for its domestic market to production for the global economy and moved from a distorted equilibrium far inside its technology frontier to an equilibrium more closely aligned with world relative prices for goods and services.

Our findings indicate that a simple Bartik measure is the strongest and most robust predictor of China's regional export growth among those examined. It consistently explains a larger share of the spatial variation in export growth than any of the tariff-based variables, and remains a significant predictor of export growth also in regressions that allow for different time trends across provinces and broad sectors. With other controls in the regression, changes in output tariffs and input tariffs, trade-policy uncertainty, and MFA quota elimination instead appear to be only weakly related to China's regional export growth. These results imply that regional variation in Chinese export growth, and particular spatial variation within provinces, has important determinants beyond tariff policy which are captured by the Bartik measure.

Looking forward, one would expect that the contribution of China's initial comparative advantage for its regional export growth may attenuate. As China's period of post-transition growth comes to an end, the country appears to be engaging in more concerted industrial policy, as indicated by intensifying government efforts to move the country into the production of high-end electronics, renewable energy technologies, and sophisticated transportation equipment. Similarly, the effects of changes in specific trade policies may also recede in importance for China's regional export growth. Reductions in import barriers were most intense in the half-decade immediately after China's WTO accession. These impacts will likely lessen in importance as the country moves further away from its entry date. If, indeed, industrial policy increasingly supplants the role of China's market transition in guiding the expansion of its export activity, other factors may rise in importance in explaining the regional distribution of export production. These factors may include the ability of regional government officials to steer industrial policies in favor of their local industries and firms.

Note

Acknowledgement: We thank Lili Yan Ing, Miaojie Yu and an anonymous reviewer for helpful comments.

1 At the provincial level, I/O tables are calculated at the I/O 2-digit level (42 industries). Because these data use more aggregate industry categories (and may be subject to measurement error in smaller provinces), we elect to use national I/O tables.

References

Acemoglu, Daron, David Autor, David Dorn, Gordon H. Hanson, and Brendan Price. 2016. "Import Competition and the Great US Employment Sag of the 2000s". *Journal of Labor Economics*, 34(S1): S141–S198.

Alder, Simon, Lin Shao, and Fabrizio Zilibotti. 2016. "Economic Reforms and Industrial Policy in a Panel of Chinese Cities". *Journal of Economic Growth*, 21(4): 305–349.

Amiti, Mary, Mi Dai, Robert C. Feenstra, and John Romalis. 2017. "How Did China's WTO Entry Benefit US Consumers?". NBER Working Paper No. 23487.

Amiti, Mary, and Jozef Konings. 2007. "Trade Liberalization, Intermediate Inputs and Productivity: Evidence From Indonesia". *American Economic Review*, 97(5): 1611–1638.

Autor, David H., David Dorn, and Gordon H. Hanson. 2013. "The China Syndrome. Local Labor Market Effects of Import Competition in the United States". *American Economic Review*, 103(6): 2121–2168.

Autor, David H., David Dorn, and Gordon H. Hanson. 2016. "The China Shock: Learning From Labor-market Adjustment to Large Changes in Trade". *Annual Review of Economics*, 8: 205–240.

Autor, David H., David Dorn, Gordon H. Hanson, and Jae Song. 2014. "Trade Adjustment. Worker Level Evidence". *Quarterly Journal of Economics*, 129(4): 1799–1860.

Bai, Chong-En, Chang-Tai Hsieh, and Zheng Michael Song. 2016. "Crony Capitalism With Chinese Characteristics". University of Chicago, Working Paper.

Bai, Xue, Kala Krishna, and Hong Ma. 2017. "How You Export Matters: Export Mode, Learning and Productivity in China". *Journal of International Economics*, 104: 122–137.

Bartik, Timothy J. 1991. "Who Benefits From State and Local Economic Development Policies?" W.E. Upjohn Institute for Employment Research. Kalamazoo, MI.

Berkowitz, Daniel, Hong Ma, and Shuichiro Nishioka. 2017. "Recasting the Iron Rice Bowl: The Reform of China's State Owned Enterprises". *Review of Economics and Statistics*, forthcoming..

Bombardini, Matilde, and Bingjing Li. 2016. "Trade, Pollution and Mortality in China". NBER Working Paper No. 22804.

Brandt, Loren, Debin Ma, and Thomas Rawski. 2016. "Industrialization in China". IZA Discussion Papers 10096, Institute for the Study of Labor (IZA).

Brandt, Loren, and Peter Morrow. 2017. "Tariffs and the Organization of Trade in China". *Journal of International Economics*, 104: 85–103.

Brandt, Loren, Johannes Van Biesebroeck, Luhang Wang, and Yifan Zhang. 2017. "WTO Accession and Performance of Chinese Manufacturing Firms". *American Economic Review*, forthcoming.

Brandt, Loren, Johannes Van Biesebroeck, and Yifan Zhang. 2012. "Creative Accounting or Creative Destruction? Firm-Level Productivity Growth in Chinese Manufacturing". *Journal of Development Economics*, 97(2): 339–351.

Brandt, Loren, Luhang Wang, and Yifan Zhang. 2017. "Productivity in Chinese Industry: 1998–2013". Working Paper.

Cheng, Wenya, and Andrei Potlogea. 2015. "Trade Liberalization and Economic Development: Evidence From China's WTO Accession". Working Paper.

Dai, Mi, Madhura Maitra, and Miaojie Yu. 2016. "Unexceptional Exporter Performance in China? The Role of Processing Trade". *Journal of Development Economics*, 121: 177–189.

Dekle, Robert, Jonathan Eaton, and Samuel Kortum. 2008. "Global Rebalancing With Gravity: Measuring the Burden of Adjustment". *IMF Economic Review*, 55: 511–540.

Diamond, Rebecca. 2016. "The Determinants and Welfare Implications of US Workers' Diverging Location Choices by Skill: 1980–2000". *American Economic Review*, 106 (3): 479–524.

Ding, Sai, Puyang Sun, and Wei Jiang. 2015. "The Effect of Foreign Entry Regulation on Downstream Productivity: Microeconomic Evidence From China". Working Paper.

Erten, Bilge, and Jessica Leight. 2017. "Exporting Out of Agriculture: The Impact of WTO Accession on Structural Transformation in China". Working Paper.

Fan, Jingting. 2015. "Internal Geography, Labor Mobility and the Distributional Impacts of Trade". Working Paper.

Feenstra, Robert C., and Gordon H. Hanson. 2005. "Ownership and Control in Outsourcing to China: Estimating the Property-rights Theory of the Firm". *Quarterly Journal of Economics*, 120(2): 729–761.

Feng, Ling, Zhiyuan Li, and Deborah L. Swenson. 2017. "Trade Policy Uncertainty and Exports: Evidence From China's WTO Accession". *Journal of International Economics*, 106: 20–36.

Goldberg, Pinelopi, Amit Khandelwal, Nina Pavcnik, Petia Topalova. 2010. "Imported Intermediate Inputs and Domestic Product Growth: Evidence From India". *Quarterly Journal of Economics*, 125(4): 1727–1767.

Handley, Kyle, and Nuno Limao. 2017. "Policy Uncertainty, Trade and Welfare: Theory and Evidence for China and the U.S.". *American Economic Review*, forthcoming.

Hsieh, Chang-Tai, and Ralph Ossa. 2016. "A Global View of Productivity Growth in China". *Journal of International Economics*, 102: 209–224.

Hsieh, Chang-Tai, and Zheng Song. 2015. "Grasp the Large, Let Go of the Small: The Transformation of the State Sector in China". NBER Working Paper No. 21006.

Khandelwal, Amit K., Peter K. Schott, and Shang-Jin Wei. 2013. "Trade Liberalization and Embedded Institutional Reform: Evidence From Chinese Exporters". *American Economic Review*, 103(6): 2169–2195.

Leight, Jessica. 2016. "Complementarity Between Non-agricultural and Agricultural Shocks in Rural Industrialization: Evidence From China". Working Paper.

Li, Bingjing. 2015. "Export Expansion, Skill Acquisition and Industry Specialization: Evidence From China". Working Paper.

Li, Hongbin, Lei Li, Binzhen Wu, and Yanyan Xiong. 2012. "The End of Cheap Chinese Labor". *Journal of Economic Perspectives*, 26(4): 57–74.

Naughton, Barry. 1996. *Growing Out of the Plan: Chinese Economic Reform, 1978–1993*. Cambridge: Cambridge University Press.

Naughton, Barry. 2007. *The Chinese Economy: Transitions and Growth*. Cambridge, MA: MIT Press.

Pierce, Justin R., and Peter K. Schott. 2016. "The Surprisingly Swift Decline of U.S. Manufacturing Employment". *American Economic Review*, 106(7): 1632–1662.

Rodrik, Dani. 2006. "What's So Special About China's Exports?". *China and World Economy*, 14(5): 1–19.

Song, Zheng, Kjetil Storesletten, and Fabrizio Zilibotti. 2011. "Growing Like China". *American Economic Review*, 101(1): 196–233.

Topalova, Petia, and Amit Khandelwal. 2011. "Trade Liberalization and Firm Productivity: The Case of India". *Review of Economics and Statistics*, 93(3): 995–1009.

Vogel, Ezra F. 2011. *Deng Xiaoping and the Transformation of China*. Vol. 10. Cambridge, MA: Belknap Press of Harvard University Press.

Wang, Jin. 2013. "The Economic Impact of Special Economic Zones: Evidence From Chinese Municipalities". *Journal of Development Economics*, 101: 133–147.

Xu, Bin, and Jiangyong Lu. 2009. "Foreign Direct Investment, Processing Trade, and the Sophistication of China's Exports". *China Economic Review*, 20(3): 425–439.

Yu, Miaojie. 2015. "Processing Trade, Tariff Reductions, and Firm Productivity: Evidence From Chinese Firms". *Economic Journal*, 125(585): 943–988.

Yu, Miaojie, and Wei Tian. 2012. "China's Processing Trade: A Firm-Level Analysis," in Huw McMay and Ligang Song (eds.) *Rebalancing and Sustaining Growth in China*. Australian National University E-press: 111–148.

Yu, Miaojie, and Wei Tian. 2017. "Processing Trade, Export Intensity, and Input Trade Liberalization: Evidence From Chinese Firms". *Journal of Asia-Pacific Economy*, forthcoming.

Zhu, Xiaodong. 2012. "Understanding China's Growth: Past, Present, and Future". *Journal of Economic Perspectives*, 26(4): 103–124.

Zi, Yuan. 2016. "Trade Liberalization and the Great Labor Reallocation". Working Paper.

7 Estimating productivity using Chinese data: methods, challenges and results

Scott Orr, Daniel Trefler and Miaojie Yu

1. Introduction

The rise of China as the world's manufacturer has generated considerable interest in the evolution of Chinese productivity, e.g., Yu (2015) and Brandt et al. (2017). Yet how productivity is and should be estimated remains an area of active research. In this chapter we review some state-of-the-art methods for estimating productivity, always adopting a practitioner's perspective. We then apply these methods to Chinese manufacturing data over the 2000–2006 period. We estimate dozens of different specifications for 28 industries for a total of 672 production function estimates. We then compare results across specifications and draw conclusions about the strengths and pitfalls of each.

To obtain an estimate of firm-level productivity, the researcher typically estimates some variant of the following model:

$$y_{it} = f(x_{it}) + \omega_{it} \tag{1}$$

where y_{it} is log output of firm i, x_{it} is a vector of inputs used by firm i, $f(\cdot)$ is the production function, and ω_{it} is log total factor productivity (TFP).

Generally, the researcher observes y_{it} and x_{it}, while the production function and TFP are unknown. However, if the production function can be estimated, firm-level TFP can be obtained as the estimated *residual* from (1). For example, in the simplest case of Cobb-Douglas production, the researcher estimates the following linear model:

$$y_{it} = \beta_L l_{it} + \beta_K k_{it} + \omega_{it} \tag{2}$$

where l_{it} and k_{it} are the logs of the labour and capital inputs, and the parameters β_L and β_K govern the marginal products of labour and capital. TFP is then the portion of firm-level output that is unexplained by input use. To obtain this object, we need estimates of the production function parameters.

Since (2) is a simple linear model, one might be tempted to estimate the production function parameters using OLS. This would likely lead to biased coefficients of the production function parameters and, as a result, misleading estimates of productivity. Since each firm likely knows its own productivity, labour, and capital inputs are likely *correlated* with ω_{it}. For example, since high-productivity firms have lower costs of production, they have lower prices and sell more output, requiring that they buy more labour and capital than low-productivity firms. This leads to an *upward* bias in estimated production function coefficients and hence to an upward bias in the estimated returns to scale $\beta_L + \beta_K$. It may even lead to estimates of increasing returns to scale ($\beta_L + \beta_K > 1$) when in fact there are decreasing returns ($\beta_L + \beta_K < 1$). This would be a very misleading picture of the nature of production. Similarly, since by construction OLS chooses production function parameters to minimize the variance of the residual, this approach will tend to *underestimate* productivity dispersion within an industry. This is problematic because accurate measurements of productivity dispersion are central to the literature on macroeconomic misallocation (e.g., Hsieh and Klenow 2009) and the literature on international trade (e.g., Eaton and Kortum 2002 and Melitz 2003).

The problems with using OLS to estimate production functions have been recognized at least since Marschak and Andrews (1944). Fortunately, there has been enormous progress since then in developing alternative methods to estimate production functions that alleviate these concerns. See Griliches and Mairesse (1995) and Ackerberg et al. (2007) for a review of some of this literature.

Our chapter focuses on one popular approach that has been extensively used in the applied literature over the last 20 years, the so-called "proxy-variable" approach of Olley and Pakes (1996), Levinsohn and Petrin (2003), and Ackerberg et al. (2015). In this approach one uses first-order conditions for inputs (such as capital and labour) to proxy for the direct effect of TFP in (1).[1]

In this chapter, we estimate the production function using five different versions of the proxy-variable estimation procedure described in Ackerberg et al. (2015) as well as De Loecker and Warzynski (2012). We then compare the production function parameters and productivity estimates obtained across the different methods.

Our main conclusions are as follows. First, gross-output production functions tend to display returns to scale that are centred between 0.9 and 1.1. In contrast, value-added production functions display much greater variation in scale returns (between 0.5 and 1.5). Second, translog gross-output production functions are very stable across proxy-variable methods. The same is not true of the other three production functions (Cobb-Douglas gross-output, Cobb-Douglas value-added, and translog value-added). Third, we examine log TFP dispersion, a topic of great interest for thinking about the macro misallocation literature (Hsieh and Klenow 2009) and the literature on international trade (Eaton and Kortum 2002 and Melitz 2003). We find that the choice of proxy-variable method makes little difference to the estimated dispersion in TFP. However, dispersion is much lower for gross-output production functions than for value-added production functions. Fourth, when examining the TFP premia associated with either capital intensity or size, the premia are present for value-added production functions, but much less so for gross-output production functions. *We conclude from these four observations that gross-output production functions tend to produce more sensible estimates than value-added production functions.*

The outline of the chapter is as follows. In Section 2 we describe the basic model underlying the estimation routine, while in Section 3 we describe the estimation of productivity in more detail than is typically done. This makes this section more technical than the rest of the chapter. Our expectation is that the casual reader will race through it, ignoring the details. However, for those wishing to estimate state-of-the-art productivity, Section 3 provides a line-by-line guide to all of the details that practitioners need, including some common extensions such as correcting for attrition bias (Olley and Pakes 1996) and the impact of exporting on productivity (De Loecker 2013). Section 4 describes the data and implementation. Sections 5 and 6 present the estimated parameters. Section 7 describes the results for TFP dispersion. Section 8 describes results for the TFP premia associated with capital intensity, size, and exporting. Section 9 concludes.

2. Model

Before we outline the actual estimation procedure, it is useful to describe a simple model of firm-level production. This discussion will highlight the basic assumptions we need to obtain consistent estimates of the production function parameters.

Suppose each firm i produces output using the following technology:

$$y_{it} = f(l_{it}, k_{it}, m_{it}; \beta) + \omega_{it} + \epsilon_{it} \tag{3}$$

where t indexes years, y_{it}, l_{it}, k_{it}, and m_{it} are the natural logarithms of output, labour input, capital input, and materials input, respectively; β is a vector of production function parameters, ω_{it} is firm-level productivity, and ϵ_{it} is an *ex-post* productivity shock that is not realized until after a firm has made its production decisions.[2] While y_{it}, l_{it}, k_{it}, and m_{it} are observable, ω_{it} and ϵ_{it} are not.[3]

To obtain an estimate of ω_{it}, our primary object of interest, we estimate (3) using the two-step proxy-variable estimation procedure described in Ackerberg et al. (2015). For this approach to identify the production function, we need to make some further assumptions. First, we assume that ω_{it} evolves over time according to a fixed Markov process, i.e.,

$$\omega_{it} = g(\omega_{i,t-1}, X_{i,t-1}) + \xi_{it} \tag{4}$$

where $X_{i,t-1}$ is a vector of firm-level characteristics that potentially affect the law of motion for productivity and $g(\omega_{i,t-1}, X_{i,t-1}) = \mathbb{E}[\omega_{it}|\omega_{i,t-1}, X_{i,t-1}]$ is expected productivity conditional on past productivity and $X_{i,t-1}$. Note that by construction, $\mathbb{E}[\xi_{it}] = 0$, $Cov(\omega_{i,t-1}; \xi_{it}) = 0$ and $Cov(X_{i,t-1}; \xi_{it}) = 0$. As in Ackerberg et al. (2015) we assume that (4) is known by each firm.

Next we assume that capital requires time to build, with the firm-level capital stock at time t being determined by investment at time $t - 1$. Formally, we assume that capital follows a deterministic law of motion given by:

$$k_{it} = \kappa\left(k_{i,t-1}, i_{i,t-1}\right) \tag{5}$$

where $i_{i,t-1}$ is investment in capital at time $t - 1$.

While (5) implies that capital is predetermined at the beginning of each period t, we assume that labour, materials, and investment, are determined by the firm after observing ω_{it}. The particular timing assumptions we make are graphically described in Figure 7.1. At the beginning of period t, we assume that each firm i inherits a predetermined capital stock k_{it}, and then observes ω_{it}. The firm then chooses $\{l_{it}, m_{it}, i_{it}\}$ to maximize the present discounted value of profits. After making these input decisions, ϵ_{it} is realized. Finally, investment is realized, generating $k_{i,t+1}$, which takes us to the start of period $t + 1$. Following Ackerberg et al. (2015), we assume that labour may have dynamic implications (e.g., adjustment costs), while materials inputs are "static," in the sense that they have no dynamic implications. This means materials demand will only depend on current state variables of the firm (e.g., current productivity, capital, and labour), while labour demand may depend on past realizations of labour input.

Finally, we assume that the conditional demand function for m_{it} only depends on a single unobservable, ω_{it}, and the conditional demand function is strictly increasing in ω_{it}. Let W_{it} denote a vector of firm-level observable characteristics (aside from labour and capital) that may affect materials demand. The final set of assumptions can then be written compactly as:

$$m_{it} = h_t(l_{it}, k_{it}, W_{it}, \omega_{it}), \qquad \frac{\partial h_t}{\partial \omega_{it}} > 0 . \tag{6}$$

3. Estimation

The estimation procedure is primarily based on the two-step "proxy-variable" approach described in Ackerberg et al. (2015), while also incorporating some insights from De Loecker and Warzynski (2012). In this section, we describe the details of our empirical implementation of this procedure. Afterwards, we describe some extensions to the general estimation approach that we implement, including estimation with over-identification restrictions, and correcting for attrition bias using a selection-correction approach as in Olley and Pakes (1996).

3.1. First stage

To generate the first-stage estimating equation, note that equation (6) is invertible since we assume conditional materials demand is strictly increasing in ω_{it}. As a result, we can write:

$$\omega_{it} = h_t^{-1}(l_{it}, k_{it}, m_{it}, W_{it}) . \tag{7}$$

Figure 7.1 Timeline

Note that all the variables on the right-hand side of (7) are observable. As a result, we should be able to non-parametrically account for the effect of ω_{it} in the production function. In particular, substitute (7) into (3), yielding:

$$y_{it} = \phi_t(l_{it}, k_{it}, m_{it}, W_{it}) + \epsilon_{it} \qquad (8)$$

where

$$\phi_t(l_{it}, k_{it}, m_{it}, W_{it}) \equiv f(l_{it}, k_{it}, m_{it}; \beta) + h_t^{-1}(l_{it}, k_{it}, m_{it}, W_{it}) \,.$$

Equation (8) is the first-stage estimating equation. Although the production function parameters β cannot be identified from this equation,[4] estimating (8) allows us to obtain estimates of ϵ_{it}, the productivity shocks that the firm observes *after* it has made its input decisions. In practice, we treat ω_{it} as fundamental firm productivity and treat ϵ_{it} as noise that we net out when examining productivity empirically.

There are a variety of ways one could non-parametrically estimate (8). The standard approach in the literature, which we also follow, is to approximate ϕ_t by a cubic polynomial in l_{it}, k_{it}, m_{it}, and W_{it}. Since in our particular application, we take W_{it} to only consist of an indicator for whether a firm exports or not, we can write the first stage estimating equation as follows:[5]

$$y_{it} = \alpha_0 + V_{it}\alpha_1 + E_{it}V_{it}\alpha_2 + \alpha_t + \epsilon_{it} \qquad (9)$$

where

$$V_{it} = \left(l_{it}, l_{it}^2, l_{it}^3, k_{it}, k_{it}^2, k_{it}^3, m_{it}, m_{it}^2, m_{it}^3, l_{it}k_{it}, l_{it}^2k_{it}, l_{it}k_{it}^2, l_{it}m_{it}, l_{it}^2m_{it}, l_{it}m_{it}^2, m_{it}k_{it}, m_{it}^2k_{it}, m_{it}k_{it}^2, l_{it}k_{it}m_{it}\right)$$

is a vector of input interaction terms, E_{it} is equal to 1 if a firm exports (and is equal to zero otherwise), α_t is a vector of year fixed effects (to control for the variation in ϕ_t over time), and α_0, α_1, α_2 are parameters to be estimated. We then estimate (9) using OLS.

3.2. Second stage

To obtain the second-stage estimating equation we need to take a stance on the particular functional form $f(\cdot)$ takes in (3). We consider four different functional forms for the production function: Cobb-Douglas value added (CD VA), translog value added (TL VA), Cobb-Douglas gross output (CD GO), and translog gross output (TL GO). Letting y_{it}^{VA} be the log of value added (sales minus material costs), the two different value-added functional forms are described by:

$$y_{it}^{VA} = \beta_L l_{it} + \beta_K k_{it} + \omega_{it} + \epsilon_{it} \qquad \text{(CD VA)}$$

and

$$y_{it}^{VA} = \beta_L l_{it} + \beta_K k_{it} + \beta_{LL}(l_{it})^2 + \beta_{KK}(k_{it})^2 + \beta_{LK}l_{it}k_{it} + \omega_{it} + \epsilon_{it} \,. \qquad \text{(TL VA)}$$

The gross-output functional forms are described by:

$$y_{it} = \beta_L l_{it} + \beta_K k_{it} + \beta_M m_{it} + \omega_{it} + \epsilon_{it} \tag{CD GO}$$

and

$$y_{it} = \beta_L l_{it} + \beta_K k_{it} + \beta_M m_{it} + \beta_{LL} (l_{it})^2 + \beta_{KK} (k_{it})^2 + \beta_{MM} (m_{it})^2$$
$$+ \beta_{LK} l_{it} k_{it} + \beta_{LM} l_{it} m_{it} + \beta_{KM} k_{it} m_{it} + \omega_{it} + \epsilon_{it} \, . \tag{TL GO}$$

We begin by discussing the estimator for the simplest case of Cobb-Douglas value added, and then conclude by discussing modifications needed for the more complicated functional forms described by (TL VA), (CD GO), and (TL GO). When the production function is given by (CD VA), the second-stage estimator is based on the following two moment conditions:

$$\mathbb{E} \left[\xi_{it} \begin{pmatrix} l_{i,t-1} \\ k_{it} \end{pmatrix} \right] = \begin{pmatrix} 0 \\ 0 \end{pmatrix} . \tag{10}$$

We discuss these in turn. The second moment condition, $\mathbb{E}[\xi_{it} k_{it}] = 0$, follows from the fact that capital is predetermined (through equation (5)), and as such should not be correlated with the innovation to productivity, ξ_{it}.

Next consider the first moment condition $\mathbb{E}[\xi_{it} l_{i,t-1}] = 0$. Since ω_{it} (and therefore ξ_{it}) is observed before the firm chooses labour input, $\mathbb{E}[\xi_{it} l_{it}] \neq 0$. Following Ackerberg et al. (2015), we instrument for labour using its lagged value, since this choice is made before ξ_{it} is revealed, and hence we should have $\mathbb{E}[\xi_{it} l_{i,t-1}] = 0$. Relevancy of the instrument is justified by labour adjustment costs (as we assumed in Section 2) or serial correlation in firm-level wages.

To estimate the model by GMM using the moment conditions (10), one must first obtain ξ_{it} as a function of β_L, β_K, and observable parameters. This can be done as follows. First, note that since $\phi_t(l_{it}, k_{it}, m_{it}, W_{it}) = f(l_{it}, k_{it}, m_{it}; \beta) + h_t^{-1}(l_{it}, k_{it}, m_{it}, W_{it})$, we can write $\omega_{it} = \phi_t(l_{it}, k_{it}, m_{it}, W_{it}) - \beta_L l_{it} - \beta_K k_{it}$ using (7) and (CD VA). Since ϕ_t has been estimated in the first stage, we can obtain an estimate of ω_{it} as a function of β_L, β_K and observable parameters, as follows:

$$\hat{\omega}_{it}(\beta_l, \beta_k) = \hat{\phi}_{it} - \beta_L l_{it} - \beta_K k_{it} \tag{11}$$

where $\hat{\phi}_{it}$ is the predicted value of each observation from the first-stage regression, i.e., $\hat{\phi}_{it} \equiv \hat{\alpha}_0 + V_{it} \hat{\alpha}_1 + E_{it} V_{it} \hat{\alpha}_2 + \hat{\alpha}_t$.

Next, note that by (4), $\xi_{it} = \omega_{it} - g(\omega_{i,t-1}, X_{i,t-1})$. Hence, if $g(\omega_{i,t-1}, X_{i,t-1})$ were known, we could recover ξ_{it} using (11). In practice, we do this by estimating $g(\cdot)$ non-parametrically for every potential value of (β_L, β_K).[6] In particular, suppose, as in our application, that $X_{i,t-1}$ only consists of an indicator variable for whether a firm exports or not (denoted, as before, by $E_{i,t-1}$). Approximating $g(\cdot)$ using a cubic polynomial in $\hat{\omega}_{i,t-1}$ and $E_{i,t-1}$, we then estimate the following model by OLS for every candidate value of (β_L, β_K):

$$\hat{\omega}_{it}(\beta_L, \beta_K) = \gamma_0 + \tilde{V}_{it}(\beta_L, \beta_K)\gamma_1 + \left(E_{i,t-1}\tilde{V}_{it}(\beta_L, \beta_K)\right)\gamma_2 + \xi_{it} \tag{12}$$

where $\tilde{V}_{it}(\beta_L, \beta_K) = (\hat{\omega}_{i,t-1}(\beta_L, \beta_K), \hat{\omega}_{i,t-1}^2(\beta_L, \beta_K), \hat{\omega}_{i,t-1}^3(\beta_L, \beta_K))$.

Having estimated (12) for a given value of (β_L, β_K), we can now obtain an estimate for ξ_{it} for any trial value of (β_L, β_K), which we denote by:

$$\hat{\xi}_{it}(\beta_L, \beta_K) = \hat{\omega}_{it}(\beta_L, \beta_K) - \hat{\gamma}_0(\beta_L, \beta_K) - \tilde{V}_{it}(\beta_L, \beta_K)\hat{\gamma}_1(\beta_L, \beta_K) \tag{13}$$
$$- \left(E_{i,t-1}\tilde{V}_{it}(\beta_L, \beta_K)\right)\hat{\gamma}_2(\beta_L, \beta_K)$$

where $\hat{\gamma}_i(\beta_L, \beta_K)$ denotes the OLS estimate of γ_i in (12), given (β_L, β_K).

We then use (13) to estimate the remaining parameters using standard GMM techniques. In particular, a Nelder-Mead optimization routine is used to choose the value of β that minimizes a quadratic form of the sample equivalent of the moments conditions described by (10). Formally, we choose (β_L, β_K) to solve:[7]

$$\min_{\beta} Q(\beta) = \left(Z'\hat{\xi}(\beta)\right)'\left(Z'\hat{\xi}(\beta)\right) \tag{14}$$

where, for example, if we observe a balanced panel of n firms for T periods, $\hat{\xi}(\beta)$ is an $n(T-1) \times 1$ vector with typical element given by (13) and Z is an $n(T-1) \times 3$ matrix of instruments, with each column corresponding to $l_{i,t-1}$, k_{it}, and a constant, respectively. Note that $(Z'\hat{\xi}(\beta))'(Z'\hat{\xi}(\beta))$ is just the standard (unweighted) GMM criterion function for the moment conditions described by (10).

This completes the estimation algorithm for the Cobb-Douglas value-added case. As discussed by De Loecker and Warzynski (2012), estimation using more complicated functional forms follows the same general procedure. The only modification that needs to be made is the inclusion of extra moment conditions in the GMM criterion function to identify any extra parameters. For example, in the translog value-added case, where the production function is given by (TL VA) above, we define the following moments to estimate the production function:

$$\mathbb{E}\left[\xi_{it}\begin{pmatrix} l_{i,t-1} \\ k_{it} \\ l_{i,t-1}^2 \\ k_{it}^2 \\ l_{i,t-1}k_{it} \end{pmatrix}\right] = \begin{pmatrix} 0 \\ 0 \\ 0 \\ 0 \\ 0 \end{pmatrix}, \tag{15}$$

i.e., we obtain more moments by interacting the instruments in the same manner these variables are being interacted within the production function. In this case, the system is still exactly identified so the form of the criterion function does not change. Note, however, that the matrix of instruments Z will now include the "extra" instruments, $l_{i,t-1}^2$, k_{it}^2 and $l_{i,t-1}k_{it}$.

Estimation of gross-output production functions, as in (CD GO) and (TL GO), proceed analogously, with the extra moment condition for identifying the materials coefficient(s) being given by:

$$\mathbb{E}\left(\xi_{it}m_{i,t-1}\right) = 0, \tag{16}$$

i.e., we use lagged materials to identify the materials input elasticity, because we would expect current materials to be correlated with the innovation to firm i's current productivity, as in De Loecker and Warzynski (2012) and Brooks et al. (2016).[8]

Having discussed the basic estimation procedure, we now consider some of the extensions to the main approach that we will be using.

3.3. Extensions: over-identification and attrition

3.3.1. Over-identification

Note that we can also use $k_{i,t-1}$ as an "extra" instrument for k_{it}. In this case, we have more identifying moments than we have parameters to identify and, as a result, we minimize the standard weighted GMM criterion function to identify β. In particular, we solve:

$$\min_{\beta} Q(\beta) = \left(Z'\hat{\xi}(\beta)\right)'(Z'Z)^{-1}\left(Z'\hat{\xi}(\beta)\right) \tag{17}$$

where, in the Cobb-Douglas case, Z is now an $n(T-1) \times 4$ matrix with columns corresponding to a constant, $l_{i,t-1}$, k_{it} and $k_{i,t-1}$, respectively.[9]

3.3.2. Attrition

The methods described so far have implicitly been for balanced panels. However, our data involves an unbalanced panel of firms due to firms exiting the market. As a result, our estimates will suffer from attrition bias since firms with high values of ω will tend to stay in our dataset, i.e., high-productivity firms are less likely to exit while low-productivity firms (low ω) are more likely to exit as they are not productive enough to survive in the current market place.

Following Olley and Pakes (1996), we can include an extra selection term in the procedure to correct for attrition bias. In particular, suppose that firm exit is endogenous in the sense that a firm (rationally) decides to exit if it draws a value of ω_{it} that is sufficiently low. Olley and Pakes (1996) point out that if we model entry and exit using the tools developed in Ericson and Pakes (1995), then firm i will exit the market whenever $\omega_{it} < \overline{\omega}_{it} = \overline{\omega}_t(k_{it})$, where $\overline{\omega}_t(k_{it})$ is the cutoff value of ω_{it}, which will depend on k_{it} as well as any other state variables of the firm's dynamic programming problem.

Having put some structure on the firm's exit decision, we can now characterize the probability that a firm in period $t - 1$ continues into period t. Let P_{it} denote the probability that we observe firm i at time t, *conditional* on the firm's information set at the end of period $t - 1$. Given the optimal cutoff rule, this probability is given by:

$$P_{it} = \Pr\left(\omega_{it} \geq \overline{\omega}_{it} | \overline{\omega}_{it}, \omega_{i,t-1}\right) = \wp_t\left(\overline{\omega}_{it}, \omega_{i,t-1}\right) \tag{18}$$

where $\wp_t$ is some unknown function. Note that since we are conditioning on the firm's information set at the end of period $t - 1$, $\overline{\omega}_{it} = \overline{\omega}_t(k_{it})$ is *known*, because capital is predetermined.

Notice that we can estimate (18) via a probit regression using the information that we have. In particular, note that while a firm's capital stock at time t will not be observed if a firm has exited by time t, we can still infer the level of the capital stock from investment behaviour using (5). As a result, k_{it} is going to be some deterministic function of past investment and capital, $\kappa(k_{i,t-1}, i_{i,t-1})$. Substituting (5) and (7) into (18) then yields:

$$\begin{aligned} P_{it} &= \wp_t\left(\overline{\omega}_{it}\left(\kappa(k_{i,t-1}, i_{i,t-1})\right), h^{-1}\left(l_{i,t-1}, k_{i,t-1}, m_{i,t-1}, W_{i,t-1}\right)\right) \\ &= \wp_t\left(k_{i,t-1}, i_{i,t-1}, l_{i,t-1}, m_{i,t-1}, W_{i,t-1}\right) . \end{aligned} \tag{19}$$

Hence, we can obtain an estimate of the probability of remaining in the dataset at time t by running a non-parametric selection probit on a cubic polynomial in $k_{i,t-1}$, $i_{i,t-1}$, $l_{i,t-1}$, $m_{i,t-1}$, and $W_{i,t-1}$. Call the predicted values from this regression $\widehat{P}_{it}$.

The final step, following Olley and Pakes (1996), is to note that the bias term that shows up due to non-random exit in the second-stage regression is given by $\mathbb{E}[\omega_{it} | \omega_{i,t-1}, \omega_{it} \geq \overline{\omega}_{it}] = \bar{g}(\omega_{i,t-1}, \overline{\omega}_{it})$. Hence, to correct for this bias we need to include a non-parametric function of $\overline{\omega}_{it}$ and $\omega_{i,t-1}$ in the second-stage regression. While we have already discussed in Sections 3.1 and 3.2 how to recover estimates of lagged productivity, $\overline{\omega}_{it}$ still needs to be estimated.

To estimate $\overline{\omega}_{it}$, note that since (18) is a conditional survival probability, it *must* be monotonically decreasing in $\overline{\omega}_{it}$. As a result, we can invert (18), yielding:

$$\overline{\omega}_{it} = \wp_t^{-1}\left(P_{it}, \omega_{i,t-1}\right) . \tag{20}$$

Since we already have estimates for the probability of staying in the market, $\widehat{P}_{it}$, and we also have estimates of past productivity, $\widehat{\omega}_{i,t-1}$, we actually do not need to estimate $\overline{\omega}_{it}$. Rather, the "bias" term $\bar{g}(\cdot)$ can simply be written as $\bar{g}(\omega_{i,t-1}, \wp_t^{-1}(P_{it}, \omega_{i,t-1}))$, i.e., we can control for endogenous exit by including a cubic in the estimated survival probability $\widehat{P}_{it}$ and lagged productivity $\widehat{\omega}_{i,t-1}$

in the regression model (12) (i.e., the regression for the law of motion for productivity, where we now include the bias correction terms in this regression). In particular, define the following vector of cubic terms for $\hat{P}_{it}$ and $\hat{\omega}_{i,t-1}$:

$$\bar{V}_{it}(\beta) = (\hat{\omega}_{i,t-1}(\beta), \hat{\omega}^2_{i,t-1}(\beta), \hat{\omega}^3_{i,t-1}(\beta), \hat{P}_{it}, \hat{P}^2_{it}, \hat{P}^3_{it}, \hat{P}_{it} \times \hat{\omega}_{i,t-1}(\beta), \hat{P}^2_{it}$$
$$\times \hat{\omega}_{i,t-1}(\beta), \hat{P}_{it} \times \hat{\omega}^2_{i,t-1}(\beta)) \ .$$

Continuing to take lagged export status $E_{i,t-1}$ as the only other firm-level variable that affects the law of motion for productivity, we can then estimate the following model by OLS for each candidate value of β:

$$\hat{\omega}_{it}(\beta) = \theta_0 + \bar{V}_{it}(\beta)\theta_1 + \left(E_{i,t-1}\bar{V}_{it}\right)\theta_2 + \xi_{it} \ . \tag{21}$$

As before, we then construct an estimate of $\hat{\xi}_{it}$, for each potential value of β, as follows:

$$\widehat{\xi_{it}}(\beta) = \widehat{\omega_{it}}(\beta) - \hat{\theta}_0(\beta) - \tilde{V}_{it}(\beta)\hat{\theta}_1(\beta) - \left(E_{i,t-1}\tilde{V}_{it}(\beta)\right)\hat{\theta}_2(\beta) \tag{22}$$

which we then use to construct the criterion function (14).

4. Data and empirical implementation

We use firm-level data from the 2000–2006 Chinese Manufacturing Enterprises (CME) dataset. The dataset includes information on all state-owned enterprises (SOEs) as well as non-SOEs with annual sales of more than RMD 5 million. We first clean these data according to the method described in Feenstra et al. (2014) by eliminating observations with (i) incomplete or internally inconsistent financial variables, (ii) fewer than 8 employees, (iii) missing firm identification, or (iv) invalid entries for year. We then drop firms based on four extra criteria that are relevant for productivity analysis. First, the firms must have complete data on sales, employment, material costs, and capital. Second, they cannot have "holes" over time, i.e., if they appear in years t_0 and t_1 then they must appear in all years between t_0 and t_1. Third, they cannot switch industries or cities over time (city switching is very rare). Industries are defined at the 2-digit Census Industry Classification level (CIC-2). Fourth, we drop Tobacco (CIC-2 = 16) because it has too few firms. This leaves us with 772,788 firm-years and 298,259 firms in 28 industries. See Table 7.1.

To prepare the data for estimation, we deflate each firm's sales using an industry-level price deflator. We deflate materials input expenditures at the industry level using input price deflators that have been filtered through the Chinese Input-Output Tables.[10] We estimate the production function by CIC-2 industry

Table 7.1 Number of firm-years

CIC-2	Industry name	Observations
17	Textiles	74,088
31	Non-metallic minerals	70,632
26	Raw chemicals	65,328
35	General machinery	59,285
18	Apparel	49,456
30	Plastics	43,153
13	Food processing	39,270
37	Transport equipment	32,269
36	Special machinery	31,077
39	Electrical machinery	32,131
34	Metal	30,295
22	Paper	22,733
23	Printing	21,319
32	Smelting, ferrous metals	21,468
19	Leather	20,590
20	Timber	16,724
14	Food manufacturing	16,862
27	Medicines	15,633
40	Communication equipment	16,435
33	Smelting, non-ferrous metals	14,328
42	Art	13,775
24	Toys	11,830
21	Furniture	11,524
15	Beverages	11,103
29	Rubber	10,031
41	Measuring instruments	9,319
25	Petroleum	6,780
28	Chemical fibers	4,676
	Total	772,114

using six different methods: OLS and five different variants of the proxy-variable approach outlined in Section 3. The five proxy-variable estimators are:

1 Case 1 (Vanilla): This specification is exactly as described in Sections 3.1 and 3.2, except that we do not allow the law of motion for ω_{it} to depend on observables.[11]

2 Case 2 (Exporting): Same as vanilla except we allow the law of motion for firm level productivity to depend on lagged export status. This controls for learning-by-exporting effects as in De Loecker and Warzynski (2012) and De Loecker (2013).

3 Case 3 (Attrition): Same as vanilla, except we include the selection correction terms to correct for attrition bias. See Section 3.3.2.

4   Case 4 (Over-identification): Same as vanilla, except we include $k_{i,t-1}$ as an extra instrument. We also include $k_{i,t-1}^2$ as an extra instrument in the translog case. See Section 3.3.1.

5   Case 5 (Full Model): The case 2–4 modifications of case 1 are all introduced simultaneously.

We apply each of these estimation strategies to each of the four functional forms for the production function described in Section 3.2.

1   Cobb-Douglas, Value Added
2   Cobb-Douglas, Gross Output
3   Translog, Value Added
4   Translog, Gross Output

This yields $6 \times 4 = 24$ methods for calculating productivity for each of the 28 industries we observe. Since this results in 672 different production function estimates, to convey a representative picture of the production functions of firms in China we will often present histograms of coefficients *weighted* by the number of observations in Table 7.1. In particular, this approach is ideal for Cobb-Douglas specifications, since many important features of the production function are characterized by production function parameters that only vary across industries, not firms, e.g., the derivative of the log production function with respect to log labour is β_L. On the other hand, this is no longer the case for translog production functions, as even simple features of the production function, such as derivatives, depend on where the firm is located on the production function. Restated, simple features of the production function vary across firm-year observations, even within an industry. In this case, we will summarize our production function results by showing histograms of various firm-level characteristics, e.g., the derivative of log production function with respect to log labour inputs, at the firm level.

5. Results using Cobb-Douglas

There are a number of possible Cobb-Douglas specifications. We start with *value-added* production functions and consider three cases: OLS, Case 1 (vanilla) and Case 5 (full model). The top panel of Figure 7.2 reports the labour coefficients β_L. Each curve is a histogram (or, more accurately, smoothed kernel) of the 28 industry-level β_L, but weighted by the number of observations in Table 7.1.[12] The dotted line is OLS histogram, the dashed line is the case 1 (vanilla) histogram, and the solid line is the case 5 (full model) histogram.

Consider the top panel for labour (β_L). The OLS line is left-shifted compared to cases 1 and 5, indicating that the OLS coefficients tend to be smaller. This may be surprising, as we expect OLS to be upward biased. The middle panel is for capital (β_K) and, as expected, OLS tends to generate relatively larger values of β_K than proxy-variable methods. Assuming that our proxy-variable strategy is indeed

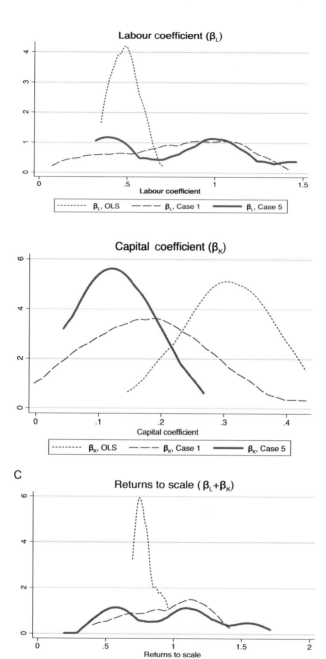

Figure 7.2 Cobb-Douglas, value-added production functions

Notes: The top panel reports the labour coefficients β_L. Each curve is a weighted histogram (or more accurately, a smoothed kernel) of the 28 industry-level β_L. The weights are the number of firm-year observations reported in Table 7.1 so that the histograms are representative of the underlying population of firms. We trim outliers when estimating the kernels; see the appendix for point estimates for all industries. The three lines correspond to three different specifications: OLS (dotted line), case 1 or vanilla (dashed line), and case 5 or full model (solid line). The middle panel repeats the exercise for the capital coefficient β_K. The bottom panel repeats the exercise for scale returns $\beta_L + \beta_K$.

solving the OLS bias, this may simply indicate that high productivity firms tend to accumulate more capital than labour.

The bottom panel reports the estimated returns to scale, $\beta_L + \beta_K$. OLS estimates almost always display decreasing returns to scale. In contrast, the proxy-variable approaches display much more heterogeneity: There are large masses of firms both above and below unity. While this is surprising, this could also be due to the fact that using a value-added production function does not directly account for the role of materials in production, and therefore we are simply missing the contribution of a very important factor of production.

We can account for this by instead turning to the gross-output production functions in Figure 7.3. Here we see *much* less variation in the degree of returns to scale. The proxy-variable methods provide estimates of returns to scale in the narrower range of 0.9 to 1.15. These seem much more reasonable than the value-added estimates.[13]

6. Results using translog

Since translog coefficients are hard to interpret on their own, we instead plot the distribution of the *output elasticities* for each input, $\partial f/\partial l$ where f is log output and l is log labour. In the Cobb-Douglas case this is just β_L. In the translog case this is:

$$\beta_L + 2\beta_{LL}l_{it} + \beta_{LK}k_{it} + \beta_{LM}m_{it}$$

that is, it depends on where the firm is on the production function.

The distribution of labour output elasticities for the translog value-added specifications appear in the top left panel of Figure 7.4. There are five histograms, one for each of our 5 cases. We find that the particular method used to estimate the production function can matter a great deal. While a particular pattern is hard to see in the labour elasticities, which vary widely across firms over the a priori unlikely range (0,2), note that the capital elasticities systematically decrease once we over-identify the capital coefficient using cases 4 and 5. This is a bit puzzling, as these values on the capital coefficient are smaller than we would expect. This may be worth examining more carefully in future research.

It is tedious but straightforward to prove that summing the labour and capital input elasticities gives us a *local* measure of returns to scale at the firm level. This measure of local returns to scale is plotted in the bottom panel of Figure 7.4. We find very wide variation in the degree of returns to scale across firms, with many operating in regions far from unity (constant returns to scale). Case 5 is of particular note, as it appears to generate a bimodal distribution, with a large set of firms operating subject to decreasing returns, and another set operating subject to constant or slightly increasing returns. However, once we allow for materials in the production function, we end up with less exotic histograms.

In Figure 7.5 we turn to the gross-output production functions and plot the distributions of the three output elasticities and local returns to scale. In particular,

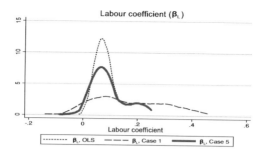

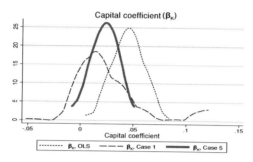

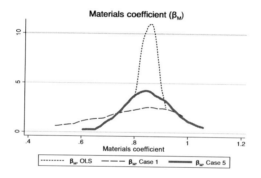

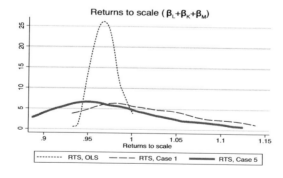

Figure 7.3 Cobb-Douglas, gross-output production functions

Notes: This figure is identical to that in Figure 7.2, but with three minor differences. First, it is for Cobb-Douglas gross-output production functions (rather than value added). Second, because it is for gross output, there is an additional panel for the materials coefficient β_M. Third, scale returns in the bottom panel is now defined as $\beta_L + \beta_K + \beta_M$. See Figure 7.2 for additional details.

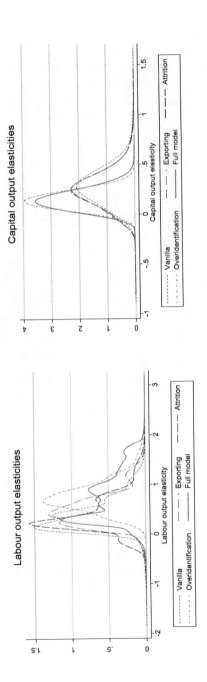

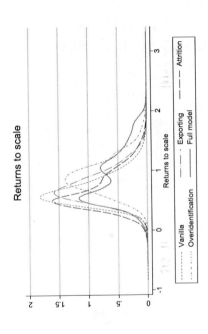

Figure 7.4 Translog value added: output elasticities and returns to scale

Notes: Each panel displays 5 histograms and each histogram corresponds to one of the 5 cases described at the start of Section 4. The panels report labour output elasticities ($\beta_L + 2\beta_{LL}l_{it} + \beta_{LK}k_{it}$), capital output elasticities ($\beta_K + 2\beta_{KK}k_{it} + \beta_{LK}l_{it}$), and returns to scale (the sum of the labour and capital elasticities). Since output elasticities vary across firm-year observations, the histograms are estimated from the 772,788 firm-year observations.

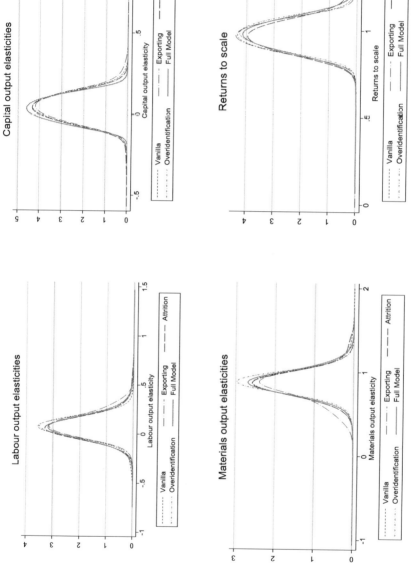

Figure 7.5 Translog gross output: output elasticities and returns to scale

Notes: This figure is identical to that in Figure 7.4, but with three minor differences. First, it is for translog gross-output production functions (rather than value added). Second, because it is for gross output, there is an additional panel for the materials output elasticity ($\beta_M + 2\beta_{MM}m_{it} + \beta_{LM}l_{it} + \beta_{KM}k_{it}$). Third, returns to scale in the bottom panel is now defined as the sum of the labour, capital, and materials output elasticities. See Figure 7.4 for additional details.

the returns to scale elasticities are fairly evenly centred around one for all estimation approaches. Moreover, as with the Cobb-Douglas case, allowing for a gross-output production function appears to generate much less dispersion in the returns to scale, with most firms operating in regions with local returns to scale between 0.75 and 1.3.

One of the most striking features of Figure 7.5 is how each method appears to provide essentially the same picture of the production technology.

It is often the case that estimates of the labour and capital output elasticities (β_L and β_K) are small and even negative for Cobb-Douglas gross-output production functions. Because there is no parameter counterpart to these output elasticities under translog, it is unclear whether this problem persists under translog. Figure 7.5 illustrates that it does. There is a sizeable number of firms operating in regions where increasing labour or capital *decreases output*. In particular, slightly more than 10 per cent of firms have negative labour and capital output elasticities.

This calls for an explanation. One possibility is that there is a problem with the underlying data. According to the Chinese Manufacturing Enterprises dataset, Chinese manufacturers have low labour shares. For the median firm it is 26 per cent in 2000–2006. This is low relative to the aggregate Chinese economy, whose labour share averaged above 40 per cent during 2000–2006 Karabarbounis and Neiman (2014).[14] To investigate the impact of reported labour shares, we re-estimated all of our specifications using the wage bill in place of the number of workers. This did not systematically raise the estimated coefficients associated with labour. Given that small labour and capital coefficients appear in many productivity studies, the explanation is deeper than an appeal to China-specific factors.

It would be useful for future research to determine why these methods generate such small output elasticities for labour and capital and how we are to understand why some firms produce in a region where the increased use of an input decreases output.

7. Measures of within-industry productivity dispersion

In this section, we ask whether the sizeable difference in the production function parameters that we found across many estimation methods in Sections 5 and 6 provide different estimates of productivity dispersion. The magnitude of productivity dispersion within an industry is a question of substantive economic interest since industries with greater productivity dispersion have a greater scope for *across-firm* allocative productivity gains. For example, the international trade literature has found that trade liberalization leads to aggregate productivity improvements by reallocating resources away from low productivity firms towards higher productivity firms. See Melitz and Trefler (2012) for a review of this literature. Similarly, a growing literature in macroeconomics and development has argued that various firm-level *wedges* or *distortions* such as taxes and subsidies can generate significant resource misallocation, which can explain a sizeable portion of the large differences in aggregate productivity observed across countries. See Restuccia and Rogerson (2017) for a review of this literature. To quantify the extent to which these mechanisms matter for aggregate productivity and welfare, estimates of industry dispersion in productivity are needed.[15] As a result, it is important to know whether different approaches to estimating productivity will significantly change the degree of dispersion we find in the data.

In Figure 7.6, we plot the estimated density of log TFP obtained using the five different proxy-variable approaches, for each of the four functional forms of the production function.[16] The most important takeaway from these pictures is how *little* the particular estimation method appears to matter for obtaining an estimate of productivity dispersion, as most of the densities closely align with one another. To see this, note from Figure 7.6 that in any single panel all 5 curves largely overlap. For the translog value-added production function, which has the largest dispersion, the standard deviations of the 5 estimates range tightly between 0.84 to 0.97. For the Cobb-Douglas gross-output production function, which has the smallest dispersion, the standard deviations of the 5 estimates range tightly between 0.24 to 0.29.

While we obtain similar pictures of TFP dispersion across estimation methods, the assumed functional form of the production function has much larger implications for measuring productivity dispersion. In Figure 7.7, we plot the dispersion of productivity for our 4 different functional forms using estimation method 5. From the figure, there is *much less* dispersion in productivity when we use a gross-output specification, compared to a value-added specification, with the ratio of standard deviations varying by more than a factor of 3. These are massive differences, likely due to the fact that value-added specifications load the effect of materials on production into the productivity residual. Since accurately estimating the degree of productivity dispersion matters a great deal for questions related to input reallocations and aggregate efficiency, Figure 7.7 tells us that thinking carefully about which model more accurately reflects production within the industry is likely of first order importance, as has also been recently argued by Gandhi et al. (2016).

8.   Assessing differences in estimated productivity – economic metrics

We have seen that very different conclusions emerge about productivity dispersion when we compare different methods of estimating TFP. However, with over 700,000 firm-years and 24 different methods of estimating TFP, it is challenging to decide whether these differences carry over to other economic questions of interest. In this section we examine three questions: (1) Are more capital-intensive firms more productive? (2) Are larger firms more productive? (3) Are exporters more productive?

8.1.   Capital intensity and productivity

Figure 7.8 reports four TFP histogram/kernels for translog specifications. In each panel are two kernels: The solid line is for firms with above-average

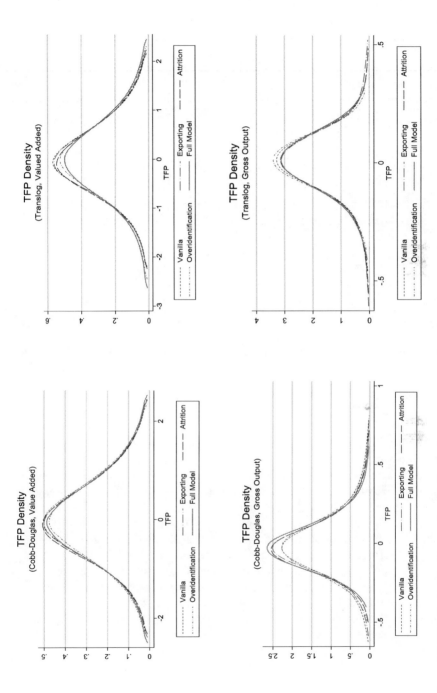

Figure 7.6 TFP dispersion across estimation methods

Notes: Each panel plots 5 TFP histograms (kernels), one for each of our 5 cases. TFP has been demeaned at the 2-digit industry level so that the histograms capture within-industry TFP dispersion.

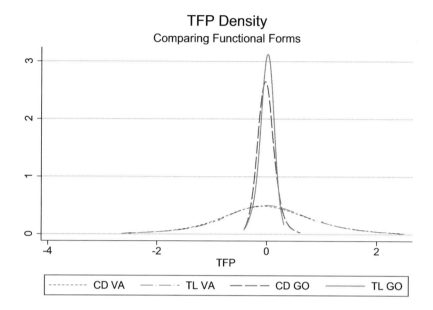

Figure 7.7 TFP dispersion across functional forms for full model

Notes: The figure plots 4 TFP histograms (kernels), one for each of our 4 functional forms. CD VA = Cobb-Douglas value added; TL VA = translog value added; CD GO = Cobb-Douglas gross output; TL GO = translog gross output. Only case 5 (Full Model) is used. TFP has been demeaned at the 2-digit industry level so that the histograms capture within-industry TFP dispersion.

capital-labour intensities and the dashed line is for firms with below-average capital-labour intensities. On the top left is the kernel associated with a vanilla (case 1) value-added translog production function. It shows that labour-intensive firms are slightly more prominent in the middle of the TFP distribution and capital-intensive firms are slightly more prominent at the top of the TFP distribution. When we move to case 5 (bottom left panel), there is a much clearer separation of the two lines, meaning that there is a much more pronounced 'capital-intensity premium', i.e., capital-intensive firms are more productive.

This is something of a puzzling result given our assumption that, once controlling for capital and labour, we can pool across firms within an industry. The puzzle is resolved by the right-hand panels of Figure 7.8 which report gross-output translog production functions. In these two pictures, there is very little evidence of a capital-intensity premium. This points to a satisfying feature of gross-output production functions relative to value-added production functions.

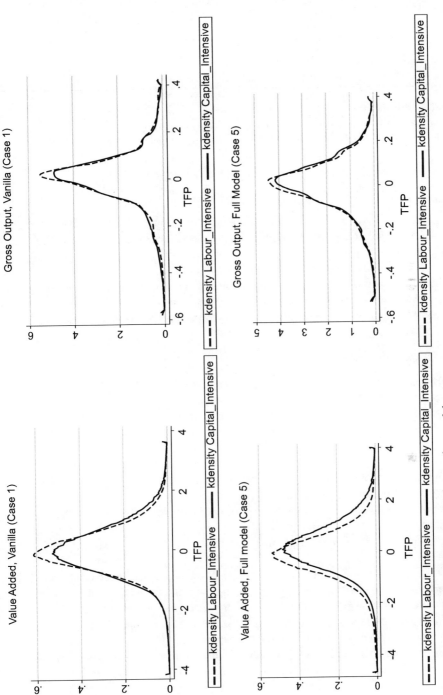

Figure 7.8 The capital-intensity premium in the translog model

Notes: This figure plots histograms (kernels) of TFP. TFP has been demeaned at the 2-digit industry level so that the histograms capture within-industry TFP dispersion. There are two histograms per panel. The solid histogram is for capital-intensive firms and the dashed histogram is for labour-intensive firms. A firm is capital-intensive (labour-intensive) if its capital-labour ratio is above (below) the industry's average capital-labour ratio.

8.2. *Sales and productivity*

It is natural to expect that more productive firms will capture a larger share of the market. Without suggesting that we are estimating a causal relationship running from productivity to sales, we can examine the correlation between sales and productivity. To this end, within each industry we divide firms into two groups based on whether the firm has above-average or below-average log sales. We emphasize that this split is done *within* industry.

Each of the four panels in Figure 7.9 reports two TFP kernels: The solid line is for big firms and the dashed line is for small firms. Consider first the two left panels, which are for value-added production functions. We see that there is a very clear "size premium", by which we mean that big firms have higher TFP. The two right panels are for gross-output production functions. They also display a size premium, but it is less pronounced. This is of interest because translog production functions display non-homotheticities in inputs, i.e., the ratio of inputs to output are allowed to vary with output. Stated more graphically, output expansion paths need not be linear. The difference in size premia between value-added and gross output production functions suggests that much of the non-homotheticities load on capital and labour rather than on materials. This is sensible: A car needs four wheels so the ratio of material inputs (four wheels) to output (cars) is four, independently of the number of cars produced.

8.3. *Exporting and productivity*

It has long been asserted that exporters are more productive than non-exporters (e.g., Bernard and Jensen 1995) and this relationship appears to be at least partially causal (e.g., Lileeva and Trefler 2010). To examine the export premium we divide firms into two groups based on whether they export. In each of the four panels in Figure 7.10, the solid line is the TFP kernel for exporters and the dashed line is the TFP kernel for non-exporters. We only report results for the translog production function and we demean TFP by subtracting off the mean TFP of the firm's 2-digit industry.

For the vanilla (case 1) value-added translog production function in the top left panel of Figure 7.10, the exporter premium is very clear. The solid line is shifted towards higher TFP levels, indicating that there is indeed an exporter TFP premium.

Recall that in the full model (case 5) we have included a lagged exporter dummy in the equation determining the evolution of productivity (equation (4)).[17] As pointed out by De Loecker (2013), if one theorizes that exporting affects productivity then this is the right thing to do. One then assesses the impact of exporting on productivity by examining the export dummy coefficient in the evolution-of-productivity equation. It is thus of interest that when looking at the value-added translog production function (left panels of Figure 7.10) and comparing cases 1 with 5, there is a much less pronounced exporter premium. In case 5,

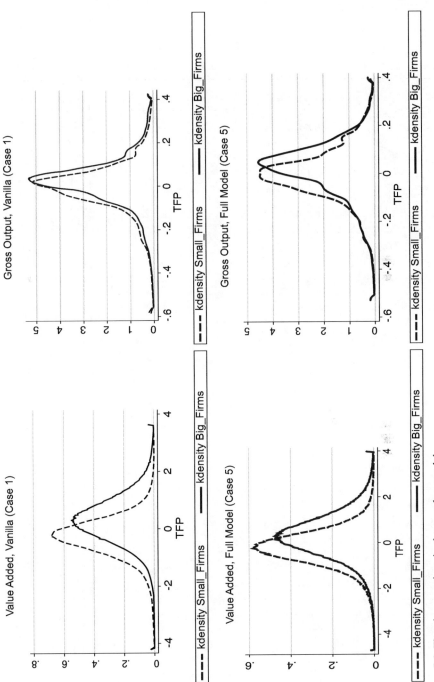

Figure 7.9 The size premium in the translog model

Notes: This figure plots histograms (kernels) of TFP. TFP has been demeaned at the 2-digit industry level so that the histograms capture within-industry TFP dispersion. There are two histograms per panel. The solid histogram is for big firms and the dashed histogram is for small firms. A firm is big (small) if its log sales are above (below) its 2-digit industry's average log sales.

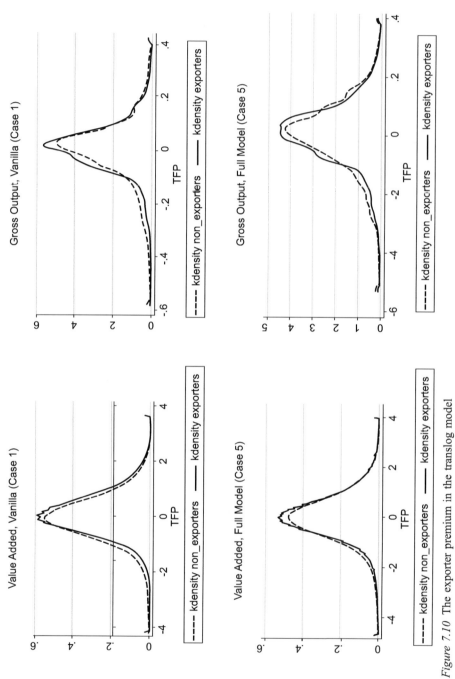

Figure 7.10 The exporter premium in the translog model

Notes: This figure plots histograms (kernels) of TFP. TFP has been demeaned at the 2-digit industry level so that the histograms capture within-industry TFP dispersion. There are two histograms per panel. The solid histogram is for firm-years where the firm exports and the dashed histogram is for firm-years where the firm does not export.

where exporting has already been controlled for, there is only a very small exporter premium.

A different conclusion emerges when looking at gross output. See the two right panels of Figure 7.10. First, the exporter premium in case 1 is confined to firms with productivity below approximately 0.03, which is about 40 per cent of all firms. Second, cases 1 and 5 do not appear to be all that different in terms of inferences about the exporter premium. This may point to the difficulty of including the exporter dummy directly into the evolution-of-productivity equation. Including it solves the problems identified by De Loecker (2013), but the resulting exporter premium may not capture a causal effect because at least some and maybe most of the sample variation in the exporter premium is across firms rather than within firms.[18] In contrast, studies such as Lileeva and Trefler (2010) do not allow for exporting directly in the evolution-of-productivity equation (a drawback), but are able to purely exploit within-firm switching into and out of exporting (an advantage). Tying the two approaches together would be an interesting area for future research.

9. Conclusions

We estimated production functions for:

1   28 industries,
2   OLS plus five proxy-variable methods,
3   gross output and value added, and
4   Cobb-Douglas and translog.

That is, we estimated 672 production functions. While generalizations are somewhat difficult, we find the following empirically.

1   When comparing value-added to gross-output production functions, the former yield very large variations in returns to scale. Looking across specifications, returns to scale ranging to the extremes of 0.5 and 1.5 are not uncommon. In contrast, gross-output production functions display much less variation in returns to scale, which tend to be strongly centred between 0.9 and 1.1. In short, gross-output production functions display more sensible returns to scale.
2   Using the translog gross-output function, estimates of output elasticities and returns to scale are extremely stable across proxy-variable estimation methods. This is not true of Cobb-Douglas or value-added production functions.
3   We examine log TFP dispersion, a topic of great interest for thinking about the macro misallocation literature and the international trade reallocation literature. Conditional on functional form (e.g., Cobb-Douglas value added), the choice of proxy-variable method makes little difference to the estimated

dispersion in TFP. However, dispersion is much lower for gross-output production functions than for value-added production functions.

4   When looking at the TFP-premium associated with both capital intensity and size, the premium was present for value-added production functions, but much less so for gross-output production functions.

In collecting these many results, it appears that greater efforts must be made in the literature to demonstrate robustness of results to alternative production function specifications and proxy-variable methods. One theme that appears repeatedly is that we often obtain empirically more sensible results using gross-output production functions rather than value-added production functions.

Notes

Acknowledgement: We are indebted to David Rivers and Frederic Warzynski for helpful discussions. Trefler thanks the Canadian Institute for Advance Studies (CIFAR) Program in Institutions, Organizations and Growth, the Social Sciences and Humanities Research Council of Canada (SSHRC) and the Bank of Canada for generous intellectual and financial support.

1   See also Gandhi et al. (2016) whose first-order-condition approach we do not consider, but only in the interest of space.
2   ϵ_{it} may also be interpreted as measurement error in output.
3   Ideally, all inputs should be measured in productivity adjusted units; otherwise, differences in input quality show up in ω_{it} or ϵ_{it}.
4   This is because we cannot separately identify $f(l_{it}, k_{it}, m_{it}; \beta)$ from $h_t^{-1}(l_{it}, k_{it}, m_{it}, W_{it})$.
5   Note that y_{it} in the first stage estimating equation should either be in gross-output or value-added units, depending on the exact specification of the production function one wishes to estimate.
6   This is equivalent to "concentrating out" the parameters governing $g(\cdot)$ in the overall GMM estimation procedure.
7   Note that β in the GMM criterion function always includes a constant term as well as (β_L, β_K).
8   Note that Gandhi et al. (2016) have recently pointed out that this sort of identification strategy, which has previously been used in the literature, may run into some identification problems. In particular, they show that proxy-variable approaches that use lagged materials as an instrument for a gross-output production function are non-parametrically non-identified. Put differently, functional form restrictions are not innocuous when one uses this type of estimation strategy, because the production function parameters will only be identified off of these restrictions. This may lead to misleading inference if the functional form restrictions do not hold in practice.
9   If we are considering the translog case, Z also contains $l_{i,t-1}^2$, k_{it}^2, $l_{i,t-1}$, k_{it}, $k_{i,t-1}$, $k_{i,t-1}^2$ and $l_{i,t-1}k_{i,t-1}$.
10 We measure labour input using employment and thus do not need a labour deflator. However, capital is simply measured in RMB.
11 Put differently, X_{it} in (4) is empty. Note, however, that W_{it} is not empty. (Recall that W_{it} is the vector of firm-level variables that affect demand for inputs.) Following De Loecker and Warzynski (2012), W_{it} always includes an export dummy. For the reader interested in the exporting-and-productivity literature, this means that we are *not* allowing exporting to affect the law of motion for productivity in the vanilla case. This is allowed only in cases 2 and 5.

12 Point estimates by industry can be found in the appendix.
13 Note that for labour and intermediates, all three cases have the same central tendency, but the proxy-variable methods have greater dispersion. In contrast, for capital, the proxy-variable methods yield smaller estimates of β_K.
14 The difference between 26 per cent and 40 per cent might be explained by the fact that services are more labour-intensive than manufacturing. We are skeptical that this is the only reason for the difference.
15 See Melitz and Redding (2015) for a recent discussion on when detailed estimates of micro-level productivity dispersion matter for quantifying the aggregate gains from trade. Similarly, see Hsieh and Klenow (2009) for a detailed discussion on how dispersion in *revenue TFP* can be used to measure the degree of resource misallocation within an industry.
16 We demean log TFP within an industry in these diagrams, so that we only capture within-industry dispersion in productivity.
17 This dummy is interacted with lagged productivity.
18 This is what we expect from work on the sunk costs of exporting by Roberts and Tybout (1997).

References

Ackerberg, Daniel A., Kevin Caves, and Garth Frazer, "Identification Properties of Recent Production Function Estimators," *Econometrica*, November 2015, *83* (6), 2411–2451.

Ackerberg, Daniel A., Benkard Lanier, Steven Berry, and Ariel Pakes, "Econometric Tools for Analyzing Market Outcomes," in J. J. Heckman and E.E. Leamer, eds., *Handbook of Econometrics*, Vol. 6, Elsevier, 2007.

Bernard, Andrew B. and J. Bradford Jensen, "Exporters, Jobs, and Wages in U.S. Manufacturing: 1976–1987," *Brookings Papers on Economic Activity, Microeconomics*, 1995, 67–112.

Brandt, Loren, Johannes Van Biesebroeck, Luhang Wang, and Yifan Zhang, "WTO Accession and Performance of Chinese Manufacturing Firms," *American Economic Review*, September 2017, *107* (9), 2784–2820.

Brooks, Wyatt J., Joseph P. Kaboski, and Yao Amber Li, "Growth Policy, Agglomeration, and (the Lack of) Competition," Working Paper, National Bureau of Economic Research, 2016.

De Loecker, Jan, "Detecting Learning by Exporting," *American Economic Journal: Microeconomics*, August 2013, *5* (3), 1–21.

———— and Frederic Warzynski, "Markups and Firm-Level Export Status," *American Economic Review*, October 2012, *102* (6), 2437–2471.

Eaton, Jonathan and Samuel Kortum, "Technology, Geography, and Trade," *Econometrica*, September 2002, *75* (5), 1741–1779.

Ericson, Richard and Ariel Pakes, "Markov-Perfect Industry Dynamic: A Framework for Empirical Work," *Review of Economic Studies*, January 1995, *62* (1), 53–82.

Feenstra, Robert C., Zhiyuan Li, and Miaojie Yu, "Exports and Credit Constraints Under Incomplete Information: Theory and Evidence From China," *Review of Economics and Statistics*, October 2014, *96* (4), 729–744.

Gandhi, Amit, Salvador Navarro, and David Rivers, "On the Identification of Production Functions: How Heterogeneous is Productivity?" Working Paper, 2016.

Griliches, Zvi and Jacques Mairesse, "Production Functions: The Search for Identification," 1995. NBER Working Paper No. 5067.

Hsieh, Chang-Tai and Peter J. Klenow, "Misallocation and Manufacturing TFP in China and India," *Quarterly Journal of Economics*, November 2009, *1403* (4), 1403–1448.

Karabarbounis, Loukas and Brent Neiman, "The Global Decline of the Labor Share," *Quarterly Journal of Economics*, February 2014, *129* (1), 61–103.

Levinsohn, James and Amil Petrin, "Estimating Production Functions Using Inputs to Control for Unobservables," *Review of Economic Studies*, April 2003, *70* (2), 317–341.

Lileeva, Alla and Daniel Trefler, "Improved Access to Foreign Markets Raises Plant-Level Productivity . . . for Some Plants," *Quarterly Journal of Economics*, August 2010, CXXV (3), 1051–1100.

Marschak, Jacob and William H. Andrews, "Random Simultaneous Equations and the Theory of Production," *Econometrica*, July–October 1944, *12* (3/4), 143–205.

Melitz, Marc J., "The Impact of Trade on Intra-Industry Reallocations and Aggregate Industry Productivity," *Econometrica*, November 2003, *71* (6), 1695–1725.

——— and Stephen J. Redding, "New Trade Models, New Welfare Implications," *American Economic Review*, March 2015, *105* (3), 1105–1146.

——— and Daniel Trefler, "Gains From Trade When Firms Matter," *Journal of Economic Perspectives*, Spring 2012, *26* (2), 91–118.

Olley, G. Steven and Ariel Pakes, "The Dynamics of Productivity in the Telecommunications Equipment Industry," *Econometrica*, November 1996, *64* (6), 1263–1297.

Restuccia, Diego and Richard Rogerson, "The Causes and Costs of Misallocation," *Journal of Economic Perspectives*, Summer 2017, *31* (3), 151–174.

Roberts, Mark J. and James R. Tybout, "The Decision to Export in Colombia: An Empirical Model of Entry With Sunk Costs," *American Economic Review*, September 1997, *87* (4), 545–564.

Yu, Miaojie, "Processing Trade, Tari Reductions and Firm Productivity: Evidence From Chinese Firms," *Economic Journal*, June 2015, *125* (585), 943–988.

Appendix

Cobb-Douglas point estimates

CIC-2	Industry name	Case 1: value-added		Case 5: value-added		Case 1: gross output			Case 5: gross output		
		β_L	β_K	β_L	β_K	β_L	β_K	β_M	β_L	β_K	β_M
13	Food processing	0.62	0.20	0.42	0.17	0.33	0.02	0.67	0.11	0.04	0.76
14	Food manufacturing	1.42	0.00	0.90	0.12	0.03	0.05	0.87	0.03	0.02	0.94
15	Beverages	1.21	0.08	1.07	0.12	0.22	0.04	0.78	0.25	0.04	0.72
17	Textiles	0.30	0.26	0.35	0.17	0.17	0.03	0.73	0.09	0.03	0.79
18	Apparel	1.20	0.00	0.79	0.12	0.06	0.01	0.94	0.08	0.00	0.99
19	Leather	0.57	0.21	1.02	0.08	0.04	0.00	0.99	0.24	0.02	0.77
20	Timber	0.19	0.21	0.63	0.10	0.06	0.06	0.91	0.05	0.02	0.92
21	Furniture	1.29	−0.07	0.76	0.09	0.07	0.00	0.90	0.07	0.02	0.86
22	Paper	0.78	0.10	1.12	0.05	0.09	0.03	0.82	0.07	0.01	0.89
23	Printing	0.08	0.43	0.32	0.17	0.08	0.03	0.85	0.06	0.05	0.83
24	Toys	0.70	0.11	0.69	0.10	0.23	0.02	0.70	0.15	0.03	0.76
25	Petroleum	0.79	0.23	1.66	0.06	0.34	−0.05	0.85	0.01	0.02	0.86
26	Raw chemicals	0.45	0.29	0.34	0.18	0.36	0.01	0.73	0.06	0.02	0.86
27	Medicines	0.17	0.38	1.35	0.10	0.12	0.05	0.79	0.09	0.04	0.85
28	Chemical fibers	0.07	0.39	−0.07	0.27	−0.01	0.01	0.97	−0.08	0.03	0.96
29	Rubber	0.93	0.10	0.87	0.10	0.15	0.00	0.89	0.15	0.03	0.79
30	Plastics	0.84	0.13	1.11	0.07	0.04	0.00	0.96	0.07	0.02	0.86
31	Non-metallic minerals	1.00	0.16	1.46	0.04	0.28	0.12	0.53	0.05	0.02	0.89
32	Smelting, ferrous metals	0.71	0.25	0.50	0.16	0.03	0.00	0.97	0.06	0.03	0.84
33	Smelting, non-ferrous metals	0.66	0.19	0.46	0.15	−0.14	−0.11	1.44	0.02	0.02	0.91
34	Metal	0.88	0.20	0.49	0.19	0.03	0.01	0.97	0.19	0.03	0.76
35	General machinery	1.03	0.12	1.02	0.12	0.24	0.01	0.84	0.20	0.02	0.83
36	Special machinery	1.11	0.07	0.93	0.13	0.13	0.03	0.85	0.07	−0.01	1.06
37	Transport equipment	1.19	0.10	1.11	0.12	0.02	0.02	0.95	0.04	0.02	0.93

(*Continued*)

(Continued)

CIC-2	Industry name	Case 1: value-added		Case 5: value-added		Case 1: gross output			Case 5: gross output		
		β_L	β_K	β_L	β_K	β_L	β_K	β_M	β_L	β_K	β_M
39	Electrical machinery	0.79	0.25	1.56	0.08	0.46	0.05	0.59	0.59	0.02	0.61
40	Communication equipment	1.17	0.07	0.99	0.11	0.16	0.02	0.82	0.20	0.03	0.77
41	Measuring instruments	0.79	0.16	0.34	0.17	0.37	0.09	0.50	−0.01	0.03	0.88
42	Art	0.56	0.18	0.91	0.09	0.10	0.00	0.93	0.06	0.01	0.94

8 The evolution of export quality: China and Indonesia

Lili Yan Ing, Miaojie Yu and Rui Zhang

1. Introduction

The competitiveness of a country's exported products relies heavily on their quality. Better-quality products are preferred by consumers but are generally more expensive and more difficult to invent, innovate, and produce. Better-quality products are associated with more advanced technology, higher input quality, skill intensity, greater innovation, and more efficient management (Schott, 2004; Verhoogen, 2008; Khandelwal, 2010; Kugler and Verhoogen, 2012; Fan et al., 2015). Quality upgrading is widely interpreted as an indicator of the success of a firm at the disaggregate level and of an economy at the aggregate level. Quality is not only determined by a country or firm's capability and technology but is also affected by other factors. As argued by Alchian and Allen (1977) and supported by a great deal of empirical evidence, the per-unit trade cost (or specific trade cost) also significantly alters the product quality of trade. Specifically, proxies for higher per-unit trade cost (longer distance) tend to be positively associated with better-quality or higher unit values or prices (Hummels and Skiba, 2004; Baldwin and Harrigan, 2011; Manova and Zhang, 2012; Martin, 2012).

A classic argument to account for this finding is that higher per-unit trade costs lower the relative price of high-quality goods, so higher per-unit trade costs skew the composition of exports towards higher-quality goods (firms) and therefore, increase the average export quality (price). Feenstra and Romalis (2014) suggest that in addition to the effects across firms, a firm will also endogenously produce products at a higher quality when the unit trade cost is high, a within-firm effect that has been overlooked by previous research but is supported in empirical studies (for within-firm evidence using Chinese micro-level data, see Manova and Zhang, 2012; for within-firm evidence using French micro-level data, see Martin, 2012).

Empirical studies also document evidence that countries with higher per capita income tend to import and consume higher-quality goods (Hallak, 2006; Hallak and Schott, 2011; Fajgelbaum et al., 2011). Such evidence suggests that higher-income countries have higher tastes for quality, and these differences in taste can shape the composition and quality of the goods they demand.

Measuring product quality is useful in understanding the consequences of these quality variations on trade and the economy. We can learn how trade and industrial policies affect individual firm quality choice via the channels of innovation or reductions in costs. Meanwhile, quality choice can be associated with the destination country's characteristics, such as per capita income and shipping costs. These associations suggest that quality does not only reflect a firm's capability but also an economy's constraints for business, such as transport and logistics costs. The quality upgrading process can have significant consequences that affect many parties in an economy. Increases in the quality of imported goods can trigger tougher competition and have an impact on domestic firms and workers. At the aggregate level, quality and price are crucial for measuring the welfare of a country. Measuring quality is, therefore, an important empirical issue.

Quality is an attribute of a product that increases a consumer's satisfaction but at the same time requires extra costs. Our framework relies on the endogenous choice of quality for individual firms and includes the impact of production efficiency, consumers' tastes for quality, input costs, and per-unit shipping costs on quality choice. The cost minimization motive stemming from the trade-off between the production cost and the unit shipping cost, together with consumers' taste for quality, will determine the choices for optimal quality. The optimal quality will increase if the unit shipping cost is relatively higher than the unit production cost and if consumers' preferences for quality are higher. A firm combines production inputs and shipping inputs to serve each market, and the relative amount of production inputs with respect to shipping inputs (quantity used to ship goods) suggests the relative cost of shipping adjusted by the taste for quality.

We estimate the firm-product-destination-year-level export quality for Indonesia from 2008 to 2012 and for China from 2000 to 2013. Figure 8.1 shows that both countries experienced rapid export growth after 2000. Understanding the variations in export quality offers some insights into explaining the variations in export value. We also document and explore the rich variations in export quality along several dimensions. We present the evolution of export quality distribution in aggregate, by firm type, and by industry, for which we document substantial heterogeneity in both Indonesia and China. We also document the cross-sectional quality variations associated with the destination's per capita income and decompose the evolution of export quality into different sources. Our results show that export quality in Indonesia and China is driven by different sources of variation.

Since quality is difficult to observe, we need to develop indicators to measure quality using observable data. Convenient and straightforward measures of product quality are the prices or unit values obtained from trade data.[1] However, variations in prices and unit values reflect not only variations in quality but also variations in other determinants of prices, such as production

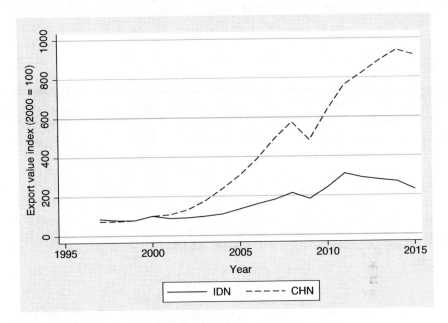

Figure 8.1 Export value index (2000 = 100), China and Indonesia

CHN = China, IDN = Indonesia

Source: Authors.

efficiencies, markups, and input costs. Hence, price is often considered to be a rough measure of quality.

The hedonic method, which links product quality directly to the specific attributes of a product, is also used in some cases. Examples include Goldberg and Verboven (2001), and Auer et al. (2014), who use horsepower, fuel consumption, and other attributes to measure the quality of an automobile; and Crozet et al. (2012) and Chen and Juvenal (2016), who, respectively, measure the quality of champagne using ratings from the Champagne Guide and ratings by wine experts. The hedonic method requires detailed information on a product's attributes, such as horsepower for a car or the number of processors for a laptop, and such information is generally not available in standard trade datasets.

In the last decade, substantial progress has been made in inferring quality via estimating the demand function. Quality is modelled as a demand shifter that measures the valuation consumers attach to a good. Therefore, if the demand function can be consistently estimated with observed quantity and price data, one can infer product quality as the residuals of the fitted demand function. Intuitively, higher product quality should be assigned to goods with larger market shares or sales conditional on price. This intuition is derived and applied by Khandelwal (2010) under a nested-logit preference and by Khandelwal et al. (2013) under a constant elasticity of substitution preference to estimate, respectively, the qualities of import varieties to the United States and the export qualities of Chinese textile exporters. Hallak and Schott (2011) also show that conditional on the export price, countries running trade surpluses are inferred to offer higher quality than countries running trade deficits. In these methods, since the determination of quality is not characterized, quality is expressed as a function of quantity and price together with some aggregate price index and expenditure measures. These aggregate variables are, in general, not observed. As a result, in empirical practice, these aggregate variables are often captured by destination- and time-specific fixed effects. Since the residuals of the estimated demand function are taken as measured qualities, the introduction of fixed effects makes the measured qualities difficult to compare across destinations or over time in absolute terms. This constrains the application of such demand-side methods when one wants to study the cross-destination variations or over-time evolution of quality.

Researchers then turn to the supply side to try to understand how quality is determined and pursue other methods of measuring quality. Schott (2004) finds that high-income countries tend to export better-quality goods. Kugler and Verhoogen (2012) introduce complementarity between input and firm capability in the production of quality and generate the implication that firms with higher capability produce better-quality goods. However, their focus is on the domestic market, and they do not consider the possibility that a firm may offer goods with different quality levels to different destinations. Feenstra and Romalis (2014) combine the per-unit trade cost with endogenous quality. The resulting optimal qualities, given a firm, vary across destinations. Using a zero-cut-off profit condition, they estimate the export and import qualities of different countries for different products. While Feenstra and Romalis (2014) provide measured qualities for each exporter and importer for each Standard International Trade Classification (SITC) product, there has so far been no attempt to measure the qualities at the micro level based on endogenous quality.

The method used in this study is built on the theoretical framework of Feenstra and Romalis (2014) but further exploits a firm's trade-off through which optimal quality choice is shaped by the per-unit shipping (trade) cost. A firm embeds more quality units into one physical unit to avoid incurring shipping costs when the per-unit shipping cost is high. The shipping cost therefore introduces economies of scale in quality production and shipping. This framework provides an explicit solution to optimal quality. Furthermore, it generates the endogenous reactions of quality to variations in the per-unit trade costs within a firm, which is consistent with previous empirical findings. For empirical analysis, Feenstra and Romalis (2014) rely on United Nations Comtrade data to estimate a country's import/export quality-adjusted price index and quality index for each SITC product. Our method is based on the same theoretical framework, but we use micro-level production and trade data to develop a procedure to measure the firm-product-destination-year-level product quality. As such, we are interested in estimating product quality at the micro level, compared with Feenstra and Romalis (2014) who focus on differences in quality at the macro level. In particular, we exploit the implication of the model that a firm combines production inputs and shipping inputs to serve its customers and we estimate the production function of the quality-adjusted outputs. Our method also ensures that the measured qualities are comparable both across destinations and over time.

The study is organized as follows. Section 2 presents the theoretical framework of endogenous quality choice and the implementation procedure for estimating the export quality. Section 3 discusses the data and estimation results. Section 4 shows the analyses of the export quality of Indonesia and China on quality evolution. Section 5 concludes.

2. Estimating micro-level export quality: approach and implementation

In this section, we describe how we measure export quality at the micro level. In our model, quality is the attribute of a product that increases consumer satisfaction but, meanwhile, is costly to produce, as in Hallak (2006), Verhoogen (2008), Khandelwal (2010), Hallak and Schott (2011), Johnson (2012), Khandelwal et al. (2013) and Feenstra and Romalis (2014). We first lay out the theoretical framework under which a firm's optimal quality choice is determined in a cost minimization problem. A firm incurs two types of costs in serving its customers: production costs and per-unit shipping costs. The cost of shipping relative to production determines the optimal quality level that minimizes the total cost. If the shipping cost is relatively high, then a firm tends to produce better-quality goods to avoid incurring the high shipping cost. Furthermore, because rich consumers value quality differently to poor consumers, a firm also sets different qualities according to the destination income levels.

We show that the total quality units being served to customers require both production inputs and shipping inputs, and the total physical units reveal information on the shipping inputs being used. Therefore, the ratio between the total physical units and production inputs implies the cost of shipping relative to production. We exploit these relationships to estimate export quality.

Our method differs from most of the existing literature, which mainly relies on the demand-side relationship between market share and price to identify quality. In particular, existing methods usually infer product qualities as the residuals of the market shares conditional on prices and the destination-year fixed effects. This implementation makes the estimated qualities incomparable across destinations and years. Our method, on the other hand, is able to identify quality variations across firms, across destinations and across years as we avoid using any destination-year fixed effects in the estimation procedure. Such variations are important in describing the over-time evolution of export quality both at the disaggregate level and the aggregate level.

2.1.   *Optimal quality and cost minimization*

We assume that the effective output of a firm is in terms of quality units. To be specific, the total quality unit Q is determined by the total physical unit q and quality level per physical unit z, namely

$$Q = q \cdot z$$

Quality z determines the satisfaction level a consumer obtains when consuming one unit of a particular variety and is related to the attractiveness of that variety. We assume that Q enters the consumer's utility U and U is increasing in Q. Therefore, quality increases a consumer's valuation of a particular variety and increases a consumer's utility.

We assume that in each destination market k there are multiple firms under monopolistic competition. Firms j differ in their exogenous production efficiency φ_j. Similar to Feenstra and Romalis (2014), the technology to produce quality z_{jk} is assumed as in equation (2.1):

$$z_{jk} = (\varphi_j \cdot l_{jk} + a_k)^{\theta} \tag{2.1}$$

l_{jk} is the quantity of effective composite inputs that a firm needs in order to produce quality z_{jk} for each unit of physical output.[2] $a_k > 0$ is the consumer's 'baseline' valuation when $l_{jk} = 0$ and varies by k. This parameter characterizes how consumers in different markets evaluate a firm's efforts in producing quality. To illustrate, suppose $a_k > a_l$ for two markets served by firm j. In order to ensure that consumers in the two markets obtain the same satisfaction level $z_{jk} = z_{jl}$, firm j should invest more in market l so that $l_{jl} > l_{jk}$. The inverse of a_k can therefore be interpreted as the taste for quality, and higher efforts in l_{jk} are required to "conquer" consumers with higher tastes for quality.[3] We therefore assume that a_k is decreasing in per capita income in market k to capture the association between per capita income and the taste for quality.

θ measures the diminishing returns to production inputs in producing quality z_{jk} and is assumed to lie between 0 and 1. Equation (2.1) implies the following unit cost function to produce one unit of physical output associated with quality level z_{jk}:

$$c_{jk} = wl_{jk} = \frac{w}{\varphi_j} \left(z_{jk}^{\frac{1}{\theta}} - a_k \right) \tag{2.2}$$

Equation (2.2) states that given a firm's quality choice z_{jk}, the unit cost to produce one unit of physical output, is increasing in input price w, increasing in product quality z_{jk}, decreasing in a_k, and decreasing in production efficiency φ_j. $0 < \theta < 1$ implies that quality upgrading is subject to diminishing marginal returns. When θ is higher, the marginal cost of upgrading quality is lower. A higher a_k suggests consumers' higher valuation when $l_{jk} = 0$, the lower taste for quality given the same level of production inputs used, and therefore, the lower unit cost of production to be incurred given z_{jk}.

When selling goods to a particular destination, k, firms are also subject to trade costs. There are two types of trade costs: the per-unit shipping cost T_{jk} (capturing additive trade costs, such as shipping, transportation and distribution costs) and the iceberg trade cost τ_{jk} (capturing multiplicative trade costs, such as tariffs). T_{jk} reflects the transportation and distribution costs associated with destination k, and we allow the costs to vary across firms. As a result, the total cost to produce and ship one unit of physical output becomes

$$UC_{jk} = \tau_{jk}(c_{jk} + T_{jk}) = \tau_{jk}\left(\frac{w}{\varphi_j}\left(z_{jk}^{\frac{1}{\theta}} - a_k\right) + T_{jk}\right)$$

Given the total quality unit firm j wants to produce to serve market k, Q_{jk}, the optimal quality that minimizes the total cost of production and shipping is

$$\min_{q_{jk}, z_{jk}} UC_{jk} \cdot q_{jk}, \ s.t. \ Q_{jk} = q_{jk} \cdot z_{jk}$$

$$\min_{z_{jk}} \frac{UC_{jk}}{z_{jk}} Q_{jk} = \frac{\tau_{jk}\left(\frac{w}{\varphi_j}\left(z_{jk}^{\frac{1}{\theta}} - a_k\right) + T_{jk}\right)}{z_{jk}} Q_{jk}$$

This motivation can be justified in a world where a consumer relies on the total quality units he/she consumes to derive utility. The optimal quality, z_{jk}, therefore minimizes the cost to produce and ship one quality unit:

$$\min_{z_{jk}} \frac{\tau_{jk}\left(\frac{w}{\varphi_j}\left(z_{jk}^{\frac{1}{\theta}} - a_k\right) + T_{jk}\right)}{z_{jk}}$$

The optimal quality is thus:

$$z_{jk} = \left[\frac{\theta}{1-\theta}\left(\frac{T_{jk}\varphi_j}{w} - a_k\right)\right]^{\theta} \tag{2.3}$$

Equation (2.3) suggests that quality is increasing in the term $\frac{T_{jk}\varphi_j}{w} - a_k$. When the per-unit shipping cost, T_{jk}, increases or when the firm-specific production cost, $\frac{w}{\varphi_j}$, decreases, the optimal quality choice of the firm increases.

When such a relative cost is high, firms tend to produce higher quality. The intuition is that when the cost of shipping is high compared with the cost of production, it is optimal to serve customers with fewer physical units and a higher quality per physical unit to avoid incurring too high shipping costs. A decrease in production input cost w or an increase in firm production efficiency φ_j causes a similar effect because the effective production cost decreases. Furthermore, when consumers have a higher taste for quality (lower a_k), firms also endogenously supply higher quality. A higher taste for quality lowers the baseline per-unit valuation of a particular product, equivalent to a higher per-unit cost for a firm to maintain its consumers at a given satisfaction level. Therefore, a higher taste for quality acts as a per-unit cost wedge and also introduces economies of scale in quality upgrading.

The trade-off between the average production cost and average shipping cost (and the wedge due to taste for quality) therefore determines the optimal quality. A higher shipping cost associated with a destination induces firms to ship better-quality goods to that destination. This is the within-firm "Washington apple effect". A lower input cost induces firms to upgrade quality, and more productive firms tend to produce higher-quality goods. Moreover, firms tend to serve high-income markets with higher quality. This property captures the idea that high-income countries demand high-quality goods.

The optimal quality in log form is, therefore:

$$\ln z_{jk} = \theta \ln \frac{\theta}{1-\theta} + \theta \ln \left(\frac{T_{jk}}{w} - \frac{a_k}{\varphi_j} \right) + \theta \ln \varphi_j \tag{2.4}$$

With the optimal quality solved, the production inputs used for each physical unit, l_{jk}, are

$$l_{jk} = \frac{z_{jk}^{\frac{1}{\theta}}}{\varphi_j} = \frac{\theta}{1-\theta} \left(\frac{T_{jk}}{w} - \frac{a_k}{\varphi_j} \right)$$

Therefore, we can define the total amount of production inputs used to produce q_{jk} units of physical output with quality level z_{jk} as X_{jk}, taking into account the iceberg trade cost, namely

$$X_{jk} = \tau_{jk} q_{jk} l_{jk} = \frac{\theta}{1-\theta} \left(\frac{T_{jk}}{w} - \frac{a_k}{\varphi_j} \right) \tau_{jk} q_{jk}$$

Defining free on board (FOB) physical unit as $q_{jk}{}^* = \tau_{jk} q_{jk}$ and rearranging, we get

$$\frac{X_{jk}}{q_{jk}{}^*} = \frac{\theta}{1-\theta} \left(\frac{T_{jk}}{w} - \frac{a_k}{\varphi_j} \right) \tag{2.5}$$

This expression suggests that the ratio between a firm's spending on production inputs, $w X_{jk}$, and a firm's spending on shipping inputs, $\left(T_{jk} - \frac{w a_k}{\varphi_j} \right) q_{jk}{}^*$, is constant. The per-unit shipping cost is adjusted by the taste for quality in market k as we highlight that a higher taste for quality (lower a_k) acts as a per-unit cost wedge that increases a firm's actual per-unit cost in serving consumers. Such a relationship stems from the firm's cost minimization behaviour.

The total FOB quality unit, $Q_{jk}^* \equiv q_{jk}^* \cdot z_{jk}$, is

$$Q_{jk}^* = q_{jk}^* \left[\frac{\theta}{1-\theta} \left(\frac{T_{jk}\varphi_j}{w} - a_k \right) \right]^{\theta} = (\varphi_j X_{jk})^{\theta} q_{jk}^{*\,1-\theta} \tag{2.6}$$

Therefore, the total quality units produced and shipped, Q_{jk}^*, is created by combining production inputs X_{jk} and shipping inputs q_{jk}^*. Productivity φ_j acts as a production input-augmented technology advancement. Using the ratio between the production inputs and shipping inputs and the total FOB quality units, we rearrange and arrive at the following equations:

$$\ln q_{jk}^* = \ln X_{jk} - \ln \left(\frac{T_{jk}}{w} - \frac{a_k}{\varphi_j} \right) - \ln \frac{\theta}{1-\theta} \tag{2.7}$$

$$\ln Q_{jk}^* = (1 - \theta) \ln q_{jk}^* + \theta \ln X_{jk} + \theta \ln \varphi_j \tag{2.8}$$

2.2. Implementation

With the subscripts indicating the different products, g (defined as the HS 6-digit product), and year, t, the expressions for the physical units, q_{jk}^*, and quality units, Q_{jk}^*, become

$$\ln q_{jkgt}^* = \ln X_{jkgt} - \ln \left(\frac{T_{jkgt}}{w_{gt}} - \frac{a_{kgt}}{\varphi_{jgt}} \right) - \ln \frac{\theta_g}{1-\theta_g} \tag{2.9}$$

$$\ln Q_{jkgt}^* = (1 - \theta_g) \ln q_{jkgt}^* + \theta_g \ln X_{jkgt} + \theta_g \ln \varphi_{jgt} + \varepsilon_{jkgt} \tag{2.10}$$

where ε_{jkgt} is a mean-zero error term due to either measurement error in the dependent variable or the idiosyncratic random output shocks that are realized after all the input decisions are made.

We now turn to additional parametric assumptions regarding the structure of composite input X_{jkgt}. Following Ackerberg et al. (2015), we assume X_{jkgt} to be Leontief in materials as in equation (2.11):

$$X_{jkgt} = \min\{K_{jkgt}^{\alpha_g} \cdot L_{jkgt}^{1-\alpha_g}, \beta_g M_{jkgt}\} \tag{2.11}$$

K_{jkgt}, L_{jkgt}, and M_{jkgt} are, respectively, the capital, labour, and materials used by firm j to produce product g shipped to k in year t. Capital and labour are assumed to be substitutable with each other with constant returns to scale, while materials are not substitutable for capital or labour. This production specification is defined as "structural value-added" and is motivated by Ackerberg et al. (2015) and Gandhi et al. (2017).[4]

The implied cost for a unit of composite input, w_{gt}, is therefore:

$$w_{gt} = \frac{r_{gt}^M}{\beta_g} + \left(\frac{r_{gt}^K}{\alpha_g}\right)^{\alpha_g} \cdot \left(\frac{r_{gt}^L}{1 - \alpha_g}\right)^{1-\alpha_g}$$

r_{gt}^M, r_{gt}^K, and r_{gt}^L are the prices of one unit of effective material, capital, and labour, respectively. Equation (2.11) simply states that

$$\ln X_{jkgt} = \alpha_g \ln K_{jkgt} + (1 - \alpha_g) \ln L_{jkgt} \tag{2.12}$$

The cost share of capital, α_g, is assumed to be dependent on g to reflect different production technologies across different products. Each α_g lies between 0 and 1. We combine equations (2.12), (2.9), and (2.10) to yield

$$\ln q_{jkgt}{}^* = \alpha_g \ln K_{jkgt} + (1 - \alpha_g) \ln L_{jkgt} - \ln \left(\frac{T_{jkgt}}{w_{gt}} - \frac{a_{kgt}}{\varphi_{jgt}}\right) - \ln \frac{\theta_g}{1 - \theta_g} \tag{2.13}$$

$$\ln Q_{jkgt}{}^* - (1 - \theta_g) \ln q_{jkgt}{}^*$$
$$= \theta_g \alpha_g \ln K_{jkgt} + \theta_g (1 - \alpha_g) \ln L_{jkgt} + \theta_g \ln \varphi_{jgt} + \varepsilon_{jkgt} \tag{2.14}$$

We use an iteration procedure to estimate $\ln z_{jkgt}$. The iteration procedure consists of three equations, namely equations (2.4), (2.13), and (2.14). With K_{jkgt}, L_{jkgt}, and $q_{jkgt}{}^*$ available, given θ_g, α_g, and $\ln \varphi_{jgt}$, one can calculate an estimate for $\ln \left(\frac{T_{jkgt}}{w_{gt}} - \frac{a_{kgt}}{\varphi_{jgt}}\right)$ according to equation (2.13). The estimated $\ln \left(\frac{T_{jkgt}}{w_{gt}} - \frac{a_{kgt}}{\varphi_{jgt}}\right)$, together with $\ln \varphi_{jgt}$ and θ_g, forms an estimate for $\ln z_{jkgt}$ according to equation (2.4). Combining $\ln z_{jkgt}$ and $\ln q_{jkgt}{}^*$, we again can estimate equation (2.14) to obtain estimates of θ_g, α_g, and $\ln \varphi_{jgt}$.

We develop a five-step iteration procedure to implement the estimation as follows.

Given the values of $\widehat{\theta}_g{}^n$ and $\widehat{\alpha}_g{}^n$ (superscript denotes the n-th iteration), first compute the estimated value of $\ln \left(\frac{\widehat{T_{jkgt}}}{w_{gt}} - \frac{a_{kgt}}{\varphi_{jgt}}\right)^n$ according to equation (2.13):

$$\ln \left(\frac{\widehat{T_{jkgt}}}{w_{gt}} - \frac{a_{kgt}}{\varphi_{jgt}}\right)^n = \widehat{\alpha}_g{}^n \ln K_{jkgt} + (1 - \widehat{\alpha}_g{}^n) \ln L_{jkgt} - \ln q_{jkgt}{}^* - \ln \frac{\widehat{\theta}_g{}^n}{1 - \widehat{\theta}_g{}^n}$$

Then, we construct the estimate of product quality $\ln \widehat{z}_{jkgt}{}^n$ according to equation (2.4), given the value of $\ln \widehat{\varphi}_{jgt}{}^n$ and $\ln \left(\frac{T_{jkgt}}{w_{gt}} - \frac{a_{kgt}}{\varphi_{jgt}}\right)^n$

$$\ln \widehat{z}_{jkgt}{}^n = \widehat{\theta}_g{}^n \ln \frac{\widehat{\theta}_g{}^n}{1 - \widehat{\theta}_g{}^n} + \widehat{\theta}_g{}^n \ln \left(\frac{T_{jkgt}}{w_{gt}} - \frac{a_{kgt}}{\varphi_{jgt}}\right)^n + \widehat{\theta}_g{}^n \ln \widehat{\varphi}_{jgt}{}^n$$

Generate the estimate of $\ln \widehat{Q_{jkgt}}^{*n}$, namely

$$\ln \widehat{Q_{jkgt}}^{*n} = \ln \widehat{z_{jkgt}}^n + \ln q_{jkgt}^*$$

Estimate equation (2.14) to generate updated estimates of $\ln \widehat{\varphi}_{jgt}^{n+1}$, $\widehat{\theta}_g^{n+1}$ and $\widehat{\alpha}_g^{n+1}$:

$$\ln \widehat{Q_{jkgt}}^{*n} - (1 - \widehat{\theta}_g^n) \ln q_{jkgt}^*$$
$$= \widehat{\theta}_g^{n+1}\widehat{\alpha}_g^{n+1} \ln K_{jkgt} + \widehat{\theta}_g^{n+1}(1 - \widehat{\alpha}_g^{n+1}) \ln L_{jkgt} + \widehat{\theta}_g^{n+1} \ln \widehat{\varphi}_{jgt}^{n+1} + \varepsilon_{jkgt}$$

Using ordinary least squares to estimate equation (2.14) incurs a potential simultaneity bias since inputs $\ln K_{jkgt}$ and $\ln L_{jkgt}$ are likely to be correlated with production efficiency $\ln \varphi_{jgt}$. To mitigate the potential simultaneity bias, we use the control function approach proposed by Ackerberg, Caves and Frazer (2015) (henceforth, ACF). We use intermediate input (materials) as a proxy variable to express production efficiency $\ln \varphi_{jgt}$ as a function of the materials, capital and labour being used, and identify $\theta_g \alpha_g$ and $\theta_g (1 - \alpha_g)$. Except for productivity, any other factors that move the quality unit output will operate through the input channel by increasing the input requirements. In the appendix, we describe in detail the algorithm for implementing the control function approach with the intermediate inputs (or materials) as the proxy variable. The estimation delivers the updated estimates of $\ln \widehat{\varphi}_{jgt}^{n+1}$, $\widehat{\theta}_g^{n+1}$, and $\widehat{\alpha}_g^{n+1}$.

If the following convergence condition is not met, we repeat Step 1 to Step 4.

$$\max\{|\widehat{\theta}_g^{n+1}\widehat{\alpha}_g^{n+1} - \widehat{\theta}_g^n\widehat{\alpha}_g^n|, |\widehat{\theta}_g^{n+1}(1 - \widehat{\alpha}_g^{n+1}) - \widehat{\theta}_g^n(1 - \widehat{\alpha}_g^n)|\} < tol$$

tol is set to be 0.0001. Once convergence is achieved, we repeat Step 1 and Step 2 to generate the final estimate of product quality $\ln z_{jkgt}$.

We implement the iteration procedure for each HS 4-digit product and obtain estimates of $\ln z_{jkgt}$ for each Chinese export j selling product g in each destination k in year t.[5] Distinct from the quality estimated using the demand-side approach, $\ln z_{jkgt}$ is comparable across destinations and years. This property allows us to construct a quality index that captures the quality shocks over time.

To ensure the qualities across different products are comparable, we normalize the estimated quality by subtracting $\ln z_{jkgt}$ from the "reference quality level" in its own product category, which we define as the 5 per cent quantile of the quality distribution of product g in the year when product g first appears in the sample:[6]

$$qual_{jkgt} = \ln z_{jkgt} - \ln z_{g0}^{5\%} \tag{2.15}$$

3.   Data and estimation

In this section, we first describe the micro-level data used to estimate export quality for Indonesia and China. We then present the estimation results, including the parameter estimates and several systematic variations in export quality across firms and destinations.

3.1.   *Data*

Our micro-level data involve both firm-level production data and product-level trade data. From the firm-level production data, we obtain information, among others, firm identity, total output, labour, capital stock and intermediate inputs. From the product-level trade data, we obtain information, among others, firm identity, product classification, destination country, export value and quantity.

3.1.1.   *Indonesian data*

The Indonesian firm-level production data are from the Manufacturing Survey of Large and Medium-sized Firms (Survey Industry, or SI), which we name the Indonesian Firm Dataset (IFD), issued by Statistics Indonesia (Badan Pusat Statistik, or BPS). The survey is conducted every year and covers all manufacturers in Indonesia with over 20 employees. The data period that we have access to is from 2008 to 2012. The IFD dataset contains necessary firm-level information on, among others, output, expenses on domestic materials and imported materials, capital, the number of employees, domestic sales, export and import status, the shares of exports and imports and other firm characteristics. All firms are classified according to ISIC revision 4, at the 4-digit industry level.

Indonesian product-level trade data are also available from 2008 to 2012. This dataset is also provided by Statistics Indonesia. The product-level trade data records information on domestic sales, export dollar value, export quantity, destination and product category up to HS 10-digits for each firm in each year. We aggregate each firm's export value (converted to Indonesian Rupiah) and quantity to each destination in each year to the HS 2007 6-digit level since the HS 6-digit level is the most disaggregated product level compatible across countries.

One important note is that the firm's identity numbers in the Indonesian product-level trade data are of the same coding system as those in the IFD dataset. Therefore, we can readily match the product-level information with the SI dataset using the firm identity number (Kode Identitas Pendirian Usaha, PSID), which is also cross-checked by a unique tax number, address and phone number.

3.1.2.   *Chinese data*

The Chinese firm-level production data are collected and maintained by China's National Bureau of Statistics (NBS). We refer to the dataset as the Chinese Firm Dataset (CFD). The dataset covers all state-owned industrial firms and all non-state-owned industrial firms with annual sales exceeding a certain threshold (RMB 5 million from 1998 to 2010 and RMB 20 million from 2011 to 2013). Therefore, the CFD dataset consists of large and medium-sized enterprises.[7] The dataset records comprehensive production information (gross output, material inputs, employment, export sales and other firm characteristics) and financial information (assets, fixed assets and other variables). The dataset spans from 1998 to 2013. All firms are classified according to the China Industrial Classification (CIC) at the 4-digit level, which is comparable to the ISIC 4-digit industries.

We acknowledge the shortcomings of the CFD according to Brandt et al. (2012) and Feenstra et al. (2014). A part of the sample in the CFD suffers from missing or misleading information. Hence, we conduct a data-filtering procedure before using the data. Following Yu (2015), we delete observations that have missing values for assets, the net value of fixed assets, sales, gross output or the firm's identity number; have greater values of current assets than total assets; have greater values of fixed assets than total assets; have greater values of the net value of fixed assets than total assets; or have an establishment month less than 1 or greater than 12.

The Chinese product-level trade dataset comes from the General Administration of Customs of China (Chinese Customs dataset, CC). The CC dataset records information on the export dollar value, export quantity, destination, product category up to the HS 8-digit level and export mode for each exporter. The time span we have access to is from 2000 to 2013. As noted by Yu (2015) and Dai et al. (2016), in China, processing exports possess entirely different production features than ordinary exports. To avoid unnecessary complications induced by the mixture of export modes, we keep only ordinary exports in our sample. We then combine each firm's export value and volume to the HS 2007 6-digit level for each destination in each year before constructing China's firm-product-year-level export quality.

One point worth noting is that the CC dataset and the CFD dataset have different coding systems for the firm identity numbers. We therefore follow Yu (2015) and Dai et al. (2016) to match the two datasets using each firm's Chinese name as well as the zip code and the last seven digits of the phone number.

3.2. Estimation results

The matched dataset for Indonesia and China contains all the variables needed for the calculation of export quality. The firm-level number of employees, L_{jt}, and materials inputs, M_{jt}, are available. The firm-level capital stock K_{jt} for Indonesia is directly available from the Indonesian dataset, and the firm-level capital stock for China can be constructed from the Chinese dataset via the perpetual inventory method proposed by Brandt et al. (2012).[8] Firm j's FOB export sales and quantity of product g to destination k in year t, $R_{jkgt}{}^{*}$ and $q_{jkgt}{}^{*}$, respectively, are also available.

We proxy K_{jkgt} and L_{jkgt} using the following formula:[9]

$$K_{jkgt} = \frac{R_{jkgt}^{*}}{R_{jt}^{*}} K_{jt}; \ L_{jkgt} = \frac{R_{jkgt}^{*}}{R_{jt}^{*}} L_{jt}$$

where $R_{jt}^{*} = \sum_{k,g} R_{jkgt}^{*}$.

We need an initial guess of $\ln \widehat{\varphi}_{jgt}^{\,0}$, $\widehat{\theta}_{g}^{\,0}$ and $\widehat{\alpha}_{g}^{\,0}$ to initialise the estimation. The initial guess of the production efficiency, $\ln \widehat{\varphi}_{jgt}^{\,0}$, is obtained by estimating equation (3.1) for each CIC 2-digit industry separately using the ACF algorithm:

$$\ln R_{jt}^{*} = \ln \varphi_{jt}^{Initial} + \rho_K \ln K_{jt} + \rho_L \ln L_{jt} \tag{3.1}$$

where we take $\ln \widehat{\varphi}_{jgt}^{\,0} = \ln \varphi_{jt}^{Initial}$. We can then obtain the estimated $\ln \widehat{\varphi}_{jgt}^{\,0}$, $\hat{\rho}_K$, and $\hat{\rho}_L$. The initial estimated $\widehat{\alpha}_{g}^{\,0}$ is computed as

$$\widehat{\alpha}_{g}^{\,0} = \frac{\hat{\rho}_K}{\hat{\rho}_K + \hat{\rho}_L}$$

For $\widehat{\theta}_{g}^{\,0}$, Feenstra and Romalis (2014) have estimates for each SITC 4-digit level product. We map their estimated values into the HS 6-digit level to generate θ_g^{FR} as initial values for θ_g.

With the initialization, the estimation is carried out for each HS 2007 4-digit level for Indonesia and China. Table 8.1a presents the distribution of the estimated θ for Indonesia and China separately. There are 307 HS 4-digit products for Indonesia and 750 HS 4-digit products for China in the sample. The mean and median values of the distribution concentrate around 0.55, while the first and third quartiles are around 0.48 and 0.62, respectively. The standard deviation reveals heterogeneity of θ, reflecting technology differences across products.

Although the estimation is conducted for the two countries separately, we still document considerable similarity in technology given a particular product across the two countries. Figure 8.2 presents the scatter plot of θ_{IDN} and θ_{CHN}. The cross-sectional correlation is 0.49. The high correlation between θ_{IDN} and θ_{CHN} suggests that the technology to produce quality for a particular product is highly correlated across the two countries.

Table 8.1a Summary of theta

Variable	Observations	Mean	Median	75% quantile	25% quantile	Std dev.
θ_{IDN}	307	0.566	0.558	0.640	0.480	0.127
θ_{CHN}	750	0.553	0.542	0.609	0.489	0.104

Note: θ_{IDN} stands for the estimated values obtained using the Indonesian data, while θ_{CHN} stands for the estimated values obtained using the Chinese data, both at the HS 4-digit level.
Source: Authors.

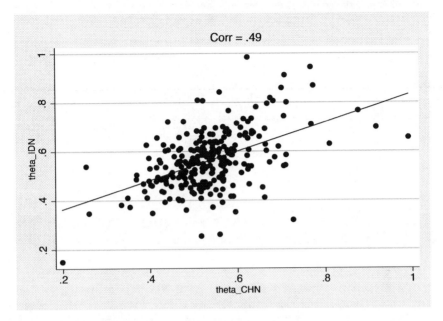

Figure 8.2 Theta comparison: Indonesia versus China
Source: Authors.

As unit value has been used to measure quality in a large number of previous studies, we first investigate how our measured quality varies with unit value. Specifically, we estimate the following specification:

$$\ln uv_{jkgt} = \beta_1 \cdot \ln z_{jkgt} + \beta_2 \cdot \ln z_{jkgt} \times Diff_g + \mu_{kgt} + \varepsilon_{jkgt} \qquad (3.2)$$

We introduce an interaction term of our measured quality and a dummy indicating whether product g is differentiated. The definition of $Diff_g$ follows Rauch (1999).[10] β_1 is expected to be positive, while β_2 is also expected to be positive. The intuition is that among differentiated products, the variation in price should be more informative for the variation in quality.

Table 8.1b reports the results that examine the correlation between unit value and the measured quality using Indonesian data. Both β_1 and β_2 are estimated to be positive at the 1 per cent significance level. This suggests that our measured quality is positively associated with unit value, and such a positive correlation is stronger for differentiated goods than for homogeneous goods. Table 8.1c reports similar results using Chinese data.

We next proceed to investigate the cross-sectional variations of $\ln z_{jkgt}$ along different dimensions. We first focus on the quality variations within a firm across different destinations. To illustrate, we estimate the following specification:

Table 8.1b Quality and unit value, Indonesia 2008–2012

Dependent variable: ln uv_{jkgt}	(1)	(2)	(3)	(4)
ln z_{jkgt}	0.159***	0.160***	0.325***	0.276***
	(0.005)	(0.005)	(0.013)	(0.024)
$Diff_g$	1.862***	1.867***		
	(0.024)	(0.024)		
ln $z_{jkgt} \times Diff_g$	0.365***	0.367***	0.180***	0.210***
	(0.007)	(0.007)	(0.014)	(0.026)
Year FEs	No	Yes	Yes	Yes
Product FEs	No	No	Yes	Yes
Product-destination-year FEs	No	No	No	Yes
Number of observations	99,451	99,451	99,451	99,451
R-squared	0.319	0.326	0.723	0.885

Note: Robust standard errors are in parentheses. *, ** and *** indicate significance at the 10%, 5% and 1% levels, respectively.

Source: Authors.

Table 8.1c Quality and unit value, China 2000–2013

Dependent variable: ln uv_{jkgt}	(1)	(2)	(3)	(4)
ln z_{jkgt}	1.066***	1.068***	1.203***	1.200***
	(0.001)	(0.001)	(0.001)	(0.001)
$Diff_g$	0.946***	0.921***		
	(0.004)	(0.004)		
ln $z_{jkgt} \times Diff_g$	0.199***	0.192***	0.030***	0.033***
	(0.001)	(0.001)	(0.001)	(0.001)
Year FEs	No	Yes	Yes	Yes
Product FEs	No	No	Yes	Yes
Product-destination-year FEs	No	No	No	Yes
Number of observations	7,639,763	7,639,763	7,639,763	7,639,763
R-squared	0.880	0.882	0.965	0.972

Note: Robust standard errors are in parentheses. *, ** and *** indicate significance at the 10%, 5% and 1% levels, respectively.

Source: Authors.

$$\ln z_{jkgt} = \beta' \cdot D_{kt} + \mu_{jgt} + \varepsilon_{jkgt} \tag{3.3}$$

We pay particular attention to the vector of destination attributes, D_{kt}, where we include the log per capita income, ln $GDPpc_{kt}$, and log population, ln pop_{kt}, of that destination in a year. We also include the geographic association between the destination and the source country, such as the log bilateral distance

Table 8.2a Quality across destinations, Indonesia 2008–2012

Dependent variable: ln z_{jkgt}	(1)	(2)	(3)	(4)
ln $GDPpc_{kt}$	0.014***		0.013***	0.013***
	(0.002)		(0.002)	(0.002)
ln pop_{kt}	−0.013***		−0.013***	−0.013***
	(0.002)		(0.002)	(0.002)
ln $dist_k$		0.018***	0.018***	0.016***
		(0.003)	(0.003)	(0.003)
$landlocked_k$		0.010	0.013	0.013
		(0.009)	(0.009)	(0.009)
$border_k$				−0.017
				(0.011)
Firm-product-year FEs	Yes	Yes	Yes	Yes
Number of observations	107,412	109,025	107,034	107,034
R-squared	0.973	0.973	0.973	0.973

Note: Robust standard errors are in parentheses. *, ** and *** indicate significance at the 10%, 5% and 1% levels, respectively.

Source: Authors.

ln $dist_k$, a dummy indicating whether the destination is a landlocked country, and a dummy indicating the contiguity between the destination and the source country. The inclusion of firm-product-year fixed effects, μ_{jgt}, ensures that our comparison is made across markets by holding firms, products, and years fixed.

Table 8.2a presents the estimation results of equation (3.3) for Indonesia, with the complete specification in the final column. ln $GDPpc_{kt}$ is positively associated with quality, consistent with our model prediction and the general hypothesis that higher-income countries demand high-quality goods because they have higher tastes for quality. Similar facts are also documented by Hallak (2006), Feenstra and Romalis (2014), and Manova and Zhang (2012). The population size, ln pop_{kt}, on the other hand, is negatively associated with quality. This is in contrast to any of the theories predicting the scale effect of market size on quality upgrading and might suggest that the fixed cost for quality upgrading, if any, is not paid for each market. An alternative interpretation could be that larger markets are associated with lower per-unit trade costs due to the possibility that the transportation and distribution margins are decreasing in market size.

Turning to the geographic variables, we find evidence supporting the existence of "Washington apple effects". Namely, better-quality goods are normally shipped to farther destinations associated with higher per-unit trade costs. A 1 per cent increase in bilateral distance increases quality by 0.018 per cent, which is aligned with the finding of Hummels and Skiba (2004), Baldwin and Harrigan (2011) and Manova and Zhang (2012), and also consistent with the prediction of the model presented in Section 2. Under a higher unit trade cost

Table 8.2b Quality across destinations, China 2000–2013

Dependent variable: ln z_{jkgt}	(1)	(2)	(3)	(4)
ln $GDPpc_{kt}$	0.016***		0.016***	0.016***
	(0.000)		(0.000)	(0.000)
ln pop_{kt}	−0.016***		−0.016***	−0.016***
	(0.000)		(0.000)	(0.000)
ln $dist_k$		−0.000	0.000	−0.000
		(0.001)	(0.001)	(0.001)
$landlocked_k$		0.013***	0.016***	0.016***
		(0.002)	(0.002)	(0.002)
$border_k$				−0.001
				(0.001)
Firm-product-year FEs	Yes	Yes	Yes	Yes
Number of observations	7,627,008	7,696,988	7,608,761	7,608,761
R-squared	0.963	0.963	0.963	0.963

Note: Robust standard errors are in parentheses. *, ** and *** indicate significance at the 10%, 5% and 1% levels, respectively.

Source: Authors.

(longer distance), a firm optimally chooses higher quality for each physical unit to avoid incurring shipping costs out of the cost-reduction motive. The landlocked and contiguity dummies have the right signs but are not significant.

Table 8.2b reports the estimation results of equation (3.3) for the Chinese sample. Again, Chinese firms tend to ship better-quality goods to destinations with higher per capita income. Meanwhile, population size is again negatively correlated with quality. It is also worth noting that the magnitudes of the quality elasticities with respect to income and population size in the Indonesian sample are close to those obtained in the Chinese sample. The geographical barriers to trade exhibit a different although broadly consistent picture. Despite that the log bilateral distance is not systematically associated with the quality level shipped (and the elasticity with respect to distance is virtually 0), a landlocked destination is significantly associated with higher quality, which is in general consistent with the rationale that quality should be increasing in per-unit trade cost.

We next turn to the quality variations across firms. We examine whether firm size and quality are positively correlated. We estimate the following specification:

$$\ln z_{jkgt} = \beta_1 \cdot \ln R_{jkgt} + \beta_2 \cdot FIE_{jt} + \beta_3 \cdot SOE_{jt} + \mu_{kgt} + \varepsilon_{jkgt} \tag{3.4}$$

We introduce destination-product-year fixed effects to restrict the comparison across firms. ln R_{jkgt} is the sales of product g in k by firm j in year t. FIE_{jt} and SOE_{jt} are dummies suggesting whether a firm is foreign owned or government owned.

Table 8.3a Quality and ownership, Indonesia 2008–2012

Dependent variable: ln z_{jkgt}	(1)	(2)	(3)	(4)
ln R_{jkgt}	0.044***	0.044***	0.036***	0.036***
	(0.001)	(0.001)	(0.003)	(0.003)
FIE_{jt}		0.046***		0.029**
		(0.008)		(0.013)
SOE_{jt}		−0.296***		−0.223***
		(0.048)		(0.083)
Year FEs	Yes	No	Yes	No
Product FEs	Yes	No	Yes	No
Product-destination-year FEs	No	Yes	No	Yes
Number of observations	109,795	109,795	109,795	109,795
R-square	0.629	0.629	0.842	0.842

Note: Robust standard errors are in parentheses. *, ** and *** indicate significance at the 10%, 5% and 1% levels, respectively.

FIE_{jt} equals 1 if the foreign share is larger than 50% and 0 otherwise. SOE_{jt} equals 1 if the central and local government share is larger than 50% and 0 otherwise.

Source: Authors.

Table 8.3a reports the estimation results of equation (3.4) for the Indonesian sample. Within a destination-product-year cell, higher quality is associated with larger sales, consistent with the conjecture that more productive firms are more likely to produce high-quality goods. Meanwhile, foreign-invested enterprises (FIEs) are associated with high-quality goods, while state-owned enterprises (SOEs) are associated with low-quality goods.

Table 8.3b reports the estimation results of equation (3.4) for the Chinese sample. Again, larger firms are systematically associated with high-quality goods, while foreign-owned firms and SOEs are both more likely to produce high-quality goods.

To summarize, the estimated qualities show cross-sectional variations that are consistent with previous theories and empirical findings. Within a firm, high-quality goods are more likely to be shipped to high-income and farther destinations, while within a destination, firms with larger sales are more likely to produce high-quality goods.

4. Evolution of export quality: Indonesia and China

In this section, we describe the evolution of export quality for Indonesia and China. Due to data limitations, the Indonesian sample spans from 2008 to 2012, while the Chinese sample spans from 2000 to 2013. We then continue to document the quality evolution by different ownership, industries and destinations. We finally conduct a dynamic decomposition to attribute the aggregate quality fluctuations into various margins.

Table 8.3b Quality and ownership, China 2000–2013

Dependent variable: $\ln z_{jkgt}$	(1)	(2)	(3)	(4)
$\ln R_{jkgt}$	0.056***	0.057***	0.059***	0.060***
	(0.000)	(0.000)	(0.000)	(0.000)
FIE_{jt}		0.141***		0.113***
		(0.001)		(0.001)
SOE_{jt}		0.194***		0.160***
		(0.002)		(0.003)
Year FEs	Yes	No	Yes	No
Product FEs	Yes	No	Yes	No
Product-destination-rear FEs	No	Yes	No	Yes
Number of observations	7,904,893	7,904,893	7,904,893	7,904,893
R-squared	0.583	0.585	0.689	0.690

Note: Robust standard errors are in parentheses. *, ** and *** indicate significance at the 10%, 5% and 1% levels, respectively.

FIE_{jt} equals 1 if a firm registered as a 'foreign-invested firm' or a 'Hong Kong/Macau/Taiwan-invested firm' and 0 otherwise. SOE_{jt} equals 1 if a firm registers as a 'state-owned firm' and 0 otherwise.
Source: Authors.

Prior to proceeding with our descriptive analysis, we conduct the following normalization for each HS 2007 6-digit product to ensure the comparability between different products. Specifically,

$$qual_{jkgt} = \ln z_{jkgt} - \ln z_{g0}^{5\%} \tag{4.1}$$

According to equation (4.1), we subtract the log quality by its "reference quality", which is the 5 per cent quantile of the quality distribution of HS 6-digit product g in the initial year when g first appears in the sample. The normalized log quality, $qual_{jkgt}$, is thus the percentage premium/discount with respect to the 'reference quality'. We use $qual_{jkgt}$ in the following analysis.

4.1.   The evolution of the overall distribution

We first present the evolution of the quality distribution over time for Indonesia and China. Table 8.4a reports the distribution of $qual_{jkgt}$ for the Indonesian sample by year. The whole distribution of the Indonesian export quality experiences an abrupt drop from 2008 to 2009. The mean and median values continue to drop from 2009 to 2010 and start to pick up from 2010 to 2012. The drop in the quality distribution is likely to have been induced by the global financial crisis in 2008, and its effect seems persistent. During the whole sample period, the mean and median quality drop by 21 per cent and 15 per cent, respectively.

The evolution of the standard deviation also reveals substantial heterogeneity in the quality evolution. It is worth noting that the standard deviation increases

Table 8.4a Quality distribution, Indonesia 2008–2012

Year	Obs.	Mean	Median	75% quantile	25% quantile	Std dev.
2008	15,623	1.029	0.754	1.382	0.272	1.130
2009	21,279	0.853	0.615	1.280	0.120	1.298
2010	22,331	0.803	0.548	1.333	0.046	1.359
2011	24,255	0.805	0.578	1.353	0.031	1.396
2012	26,260	0.810	0.602	1.360	0.052	1.390

Source: Authors.

Table 8.4b Quality distribution, China 2000–2013

Year	Obs.	Mean	Median	75% quantile	25% quantile	Std dev.
2000	131,098	1.217	1.072	1.677	0.550	1.018
2001	160,494	1.242	1.111	1.714	0.579	1.055
2002	232,899	1.242	1.105	1.704	0.588	1.057
2003	303,798	1.247	1.111	1.724	0.587	1.073
2004	478,296	1.293	1.151	1.772	0.621	1.092
2005	567,975	1.335	1.191	1.817	0.664	1.109
2006	672,284	1.383	1.232	1.882	0.684	1.156
2007	618,598	1.371	1.210	1.881	0.650	1.189
2008	716,510	1.444	1.267	1.968	0.689	1.249
2009	761,432	1.449	1.275	2.007	0.666	1.295
2010	739,582	1.470	1.297	2.038	0.689	1.302
2011	885,174	1.493	1.303	2.063	0.684	1.374
2012	823,269	1.558	1.351	2.184	0.687	1.448
2013	813,484	1.588	1.360	2.218	0.702	1.480

Source: Authors.

from 1.13 in 2008 to 1.39 in 2012. The evolutions of the 75 per cent and 25 per cent quantiles suggest that the upper tail of the quality distribution starts its recovery soon from 2009 to 2010, while the lower tail of the quality distribution keeps declining during 2008–2011. The distinct and divergent evolutions of the upper tail and lower tail give rise to the growing dispersion of Indonesian exports. Table 8.4b presents the quality distribution of China's exports from 2000 to 2013. Before 2007, the whole distribution keeps on improving, with the mean and median growing by around 16 per cent. The whole distribution decreases by 1.2 per cent to 2.2 per cent in 2007 and starts to grow again until 2013. From 2000 to 2013, the mean and median quality grow by 37 per cent and 29 per cent, respectively.

The dispersion within each year also increases as time goes by, from 1.02 in 2000 to 1.48 in 2013. Again, this is due to the fact that the upper tail of the distribution is growing faster than the lower tail. From 2000 to 2007, the 75 per cent quantile increases by 21 per cent, while the 25 per cent quantile only increases by

10 per cent. If we focus on the whole sample period, then the 75 per cent quantile grows by 54 per cent, while the 25 per cent quantile grows by 15 per cent. While these exercises simply display the evolution of the distribution of the normalized qualities, *qual*$_{jkgt}$, across years, we have not explored the driving forces behind these evolutions. In Section 4.5, we decompose these aggregate variations across years into the intensive and extensive margins and discuss which margin plays the main role.

4.2. Evolution of different ownerships

In this subsection, we divide the sample for each country into different ownerships and examine whether there are different trends for different types of firms. We divide the sample into three groups: private firms, SOE firms and FIE firms.

Table 8.5a shows the over-time variations for Indonesia. In 2008, the start of the period, the quality ranking is FIEs > private firms > SOEs. Since the number of observations for SOEs is fewer than 100 in the sample period, we focus on the comparison between private firms and FIE firms.

Both private firms and FIE firms exhibit a U-shaped trajectory during the sample period. However, although the gap between the median qualities widens during the period as FIE increases its relative quality premium to private firms, the quality gap between mean qualities decreases. This suggests that the upper tail for the private firms grows faster than that for FIE firms, while the rest of the quality distribution for private firms grows more slowly.

Table 8.5b reports the results for China. All of the three types keep growing during the sample period but experience a drop during the global financial crisis (2008–2010). From 2000 to 2013, the median export qualities for private firms, SOE firms and FIE firms grow by 25 per cent, 33 per cent, and 39 per cent, respectively. FIE remains the highest quality, and the quality premium of FIE relative to the other two types of firms widens during the sample period. SOE firms start with the lowest quality but end up with both higher mean and median qualities than private firms. The role of the extensive margin might account for the differences in the trends for private firms and SOE firms.

Table 8.5a Quality distribution by ownership, Indonesia 2008–2012

Year	Private			SOE			FIE		
	Obs.	*Mean*	*Median*	*Obs.*	*Mean*	*Median*	*Obs.*	*Mean*	*Median*
2008	8,953	0.938	0.752	62	0.571	0.532	6,608	1.157	0.759
2009	12,269	0.761	0.595	36	0.741	0.343	8,974	0.978	0.655
2010	13,085	0.709	0.532	48	0.482	0.200	9,198	0.937	0.589
2011	14,171	0.699	0.521	58	0.460	0.049	10,026	0.956	0.731
2012	15,874	0.740	0.586	98	0.342	0.256	10,288	0.922	0.657

Source: Authors.

Table 8.5b Quality distribution by ownership, China 2000–2013

Year	Private			SOE			FIE		
	Obs.	Mean	Median	Obs.	Mean	Median	Obs.	Mean	Median
2000	27,068	1.134	0.997	23,684	1.134	0.916	80,346	1.269	1.140
2001	45,314	1.113	0.991	20,114	1.143	0.949	95,066	1.323	1.196
2002	75,550	1.120	0.982	20,286	1.180	0.993	137,063	1.318	1.186
2003	108,411	1.120	0.977	18,681	1.162	0.989	176,706	1.333	1.205
2004	182,129	1.181	1.035	14,084	1.204	0.992	282,083	1.369	1.230
2005	225,292	1.239	1.084	12,356	1.196	1.016	330,327	1.406	1.266
2006	272,280	1.290	1.128	10,539	1.282	1.055	389,465	1.451	1.304
2007	275,726	1.298	1.115	5,940	1.303	1.035	336,932	1.431	1.288
2008	331,362	1.362	1.158	4,937	1.520	1.216	380,211	1.515	1.357
2009	359,081	1.343	1.154	5,614	1.542	1.320	396,737	1.544	1.379
2010	330,323	1.350	1.168	6,976	1.478	1.189	402,283	1.569	1.405
2011	468,642	1.404	1.196	5,610	1.516	1.206	410,922	1.595	1.425
2012	458,509	1.453	1.232	5,531	1.618	1.231	359,229	1.691	1.500
2013	474,434	1.478	1.243	3,494	1.569	1.247	335,556	1.742	1.530

Source: Authors.

Notice that during the sample period, the observations of private firms keep increasing, while those of SOE firms keep shrinking. This is consistent with the Chinese government's "grasp the large and let go of the small" strategy to keep SOEs with exceptional performance in control while privatizing SOEs that underperform. Because higher quality can reflect higher production efficiency, the selection channel might be responsible for the rapid growth in the mean and median export qualities of the SOE group.

4.3. Evolution of different industries

In this subsection, we restrict our attention to the quality evolution of different types of industries. We first divide the sample for each country into labour-intensive and capital-intensive industries. Specifically, we calculate the median capital-labour ratio in each two-digit industry and use the median capital-labour ratio to determine whether an industry is labour intensive or capital intensive.

Table 8.6a reports the comparison for the Indonesian sample. Notice that for Indonesia, most of the exports are concentrated in labour-intensive sectors. As for the over-time evolution, during 2008–2012, the mean and median export qualities of labour-intensive industries drop by 24 per cent and 17 per cent, respectively. The mean export quality of capital-intensive industries remains almost constant, while the median export quality of capital-intensive industries increases by 7 per cent.

Table 8.6b reports the same statistics for Chinese firms during 2000–2013. Clearly, most of China's exports shift from labour-intensive sectors to

Table 8.6a Quality distribution by factor intensity, Indonesia 2008–2012

Year	Labour intensive			Capital intensive		
	Obs.	Mean	Median	Obs.	Mean	Median
2008	11,318	0.912	0.706	4,305	1.337	0.947
2009	16,033	0.684	0.537	5,246	1.369	0.910
2010	17,928	0.648	0.480	4,403	1.432	1.244
2011	19,484	0.671	0.512	4,771	1.351	1.141
2012	20,678	0.670	0.531	5,582	1.330	1.016

Source: Authors.

Table 8.6b Quality distribution by factor intensity, China 2000–2013

Year	Labour intensive			Capital intensive		
	Obs.	Mean	Median	Obs.	Mean	Median
2000	83,635	1.203	1.086	47,463	1.241	1.045
2001	92,307	1.264	1.132	68,187	1.212	1.081
2002	96,361	1.362	1.208	136,538	1.156	1.040
2003	127,804	1.266	1.147	175,994	1.233	1.083
2004	224,188	1.407	1.243	254,108	1.191	1.065
2005	393,824	1.246	1.147	174,151	1.538	1.323
2006	321,339	1.335	1.171	350,945	1.427	1.284
2007	340,268	1.275	1.121	278,330	1.488	1.325
2008	335,304	1.400	1.235	381,206	1.483	1.294
2009	351,622	1.246	1.125	409,810	1.623	1.401
2010	403,964	1.330	1.209	335,618	1.639	1.435
2011	435,167	1.451	1.240	450,007	1.534	1.361
2012	439,920	1.466	1.298	383,349	1.663	1.413
2013	359,283	1.279	1.136	454,201	1.832	1.552

Source: Authors.

capital-intensive sectors. During the sample period, the mean and median export qualities of labour-intensive industries grow by 7 per cent and 5 per cent, while those of capital-intensive industries grow by 59 per cent and 51 per cent, respectively. The contrast suggests that China has experienced massive transformation, both in the composition of its export industries and in quality growth within labour-intensive and capital-intensive industries.

Table 8.7a presents the number of observations and the median Indonesian export quality for each ISIC rev. 4 two-digit industry in each year. In the final column, we also calculate the gap between the 2012 median and the 2008 median. It reveals substantial heterogeneity across different industries. Consistent with the aggregate pattern, most of the industries exhibit decreasing trends in export quality during 2008–2012. The machinery (28), computer (26), and electrical (27) industries experience the largest declines in median export quality at

Table 8.7a Quality by ISIC 2-digit industry, Indonesia 2008–2012

ISIC 2-digit industry	2008		2009		2010		2011		2012		2012–2008
	Obs.	Median	Obs.	Median	Obs.	Median	Obs.	Median	Obs.	Median	Median
Food 10	1,582	0.441	2,071	0.430	2,091	0.401	2,532	0.249	3,089	0.287	-0.154
Tobacco 12	13	1.350	25	2.062	26	1.182	109	0.932	116	1.196	-0.154
Textile 13	1,981	0.501	2,608	0.434	2,343	0.248	2,146	0.255	2,466	0.283	-0.218
Apparel 14	2,284	0.662	4,291	0.344	4,740	0.253	5,568	0.410	6,373	0.505	-0.157
Leather 15	323	0.772	528	0.707	507	0.644	545	0.691	633	0.567	-0.205
Wood 16	1,228	0.694	1,284	0.519	2,104	0.440	1,603	0.375	1,280	0.450	-0.244
Paper 17	142	0.692	232	0.343	239	0.438	238	0.577	227	1.354	0.662
Printing 18	52	1.792	71	1.031	103	2.004	114	1.421	120	2.114	0.322
Chemical 20	901	0.466	1,269	0.953	1,357	1.063	1,419	1.063	1,351	1.072	0.606
Medicine 21	27	2.775	50	2.544	88	2.340	100	2.328	118	2.377	-0.398
Rubber and plastic 22	1,279	0.908	1,405	0.808	1,439	0.708	1,436	0.743	1,419	0.771	-0.137
Non-metallic 23	197	0.669	290	0.828	313	0.875	352	0.771	396	0.968	0.299
Metals 24	136	0.550	248	0.479	232	0.210	214	0.269	234	0.212	-0.338
Metal products 25	352	1.071	553	1.059	684	0.907	696	0.645	722	0.929	-0.142
Computer 26	371	1.075	587	0.476	796	0.664	796	0.123	860	0.446	-0.629
Electrical 27	413	1.577	502	2.279	473	1.753	535	1.885	457	1.150	-0.426
Machinery 28	219	1.061	271	0.638	292	0.514	253	0.682	329	0.287	-0.774
Motor 29	803	1.159	697	1.065	711	2.213	844	1.299	800	1.219	0.059
Other transportation 30	87	1.738	102	2.311	67	2.124	194	2.650	219	2.243	0.505
Furniture 31	2,622	1.052	3,340	0.786	2,972	0.906	3,663	0.940	4,180	0.876	-0.176
Other 32	594	1.157	811	1.307	709	1.071	834	0.988	828	1.114	-0.042

Note: Industries with fewer than 100 observations in each year during the sample period are not reported.

Source: Authors.

77.4 per cent, 62.9 per cent and 42.6 per cent, respectively. The industries that experience the largest increases in median export quality are the paper (17), chemical (20) and other transportation (30) industries by 66.2 per cent, 60.6 per cent and 50.5 per cent, respectively.

Table 8.7b presents a similar exercise for the Chinese export quality at the CIC two-digit industry level in each year. The final three columns present the gap between medians: between 2007 and 2000, between 2013 and 2007, and between 2013 and 2000. The divisions allow us to separate the quality growth of each industry into the pre-and post-financial crisis periods. In the 2000–2007 subsample, the printing (23), furniture (21) and special machinery (36) industries have the largest increases in median quality, by 91.1 per cent, 79.7 per cent and 46.8 per cent, respectively. Meanwhile, the petroleum (25), chemical fibre (28) and beverage (15) industries have the largest declines in median quality, by 37.2 per cent, 27.1 per cent and 24.9 per cent, respectively. In the 2007–2013 subsample, the measuring and office (42), special machinery (36) and leather (19) industries have the largest increases in median quality by 57.4 per cent, 31.7 per cent and 30.4 per cent, respectively. Meanwhile, the petroleum (25), non-ferrous metals (33) and medicine (27) industries experience the largest declines in median quality by 59.8 per cent, 26.6 per cent and 24.0 per cent, respectively.

Summarizing the whole sample period from 2000 to 2013, the evolutions of export quality are still heterogeneous across industries. The printing (23), furniture (21) and measuring and office (42) industries improve their median qualities by 110.5 per cent, 83.6 per cent and 79.2 per cent, respectively, showing the largest increases in median quality. Meanwhile, the petroleum (25), beverage (15) and chemical fibre (28) industries experience the largest declines in median quality by 97.0 per cent, 21.7 per cent and 18.0 per cent, respectively.

4.4.   Quality leaders to each destination

We now turn to the cross-destination variation of export quality. Similar to Amiti and Khandelwal (2013), we first define the weighted-average quality, $qual_{kgt}$, as

$$qual_{kgt} = (value_{jkgt} \cdot qual_{jkgt}) / \sum_{s} value_{skgt}$$

We next define a product-destination-year dummy, $leader_{kgt}$, which defines whether Indonesia (or China) is offering its best quality product g to destination k in year t, namely:

$$leader_{kgt} = \begin{cases} 1, & if \ qual_{kgt} = \max_{s} qual_{sgt} \\ 0, & if \ qual_{kgt} \neq \max_{s} qual_{sgt} \end{cases}$$

Table 8.7b Quality by CIC 2-digit industry, China 2000–2013

CIC 2-digit industry	2000		2001		2002		2003		2004	
	Obs.	Median	Obs.	Median	Obs.	Median	Obs.	Median	Obs.	Median
Processing of food 13	3,813	0.802	2,138	0.816	2,761	0.810	3,880	0.709	6,242	0.695
Manufacturing of food 14	2,270	0.711	2,330	0.665	3,087	0.648	3,964	0.663	5,871	0.583
Beverage 15	466	0.920	662	0.958	966	0.740	1,338	0.797	1,023	0.738
Textile 17	13,448	0.833	18,838	0.883	29,613	0.817	42,832	0.842	76,056	0.877
Apparel 18	21,707	1.054	24,965	1.101	35,793	1.126	43,276	1.162	58,056	1.217
Leather 19	5,342	1.218	6,014	1.221	8,497	1.238	10,652	1.243	16,567	1.292
Wood 20	1,766	1.145	2,048	1.228	2,232	1.277	3,138	1.244	5,676	1.277
Furniture 21	2,435	1.175	2,650	1.303	3,394	1.519	4,834	1.620	10,186	1.637
Paper 22	645	1.067	632	1.106	1,043	0.897	1,564	0.871	3,164	1.184
Printing 23	811	0.919	813	1.099	860	1.270	1,476	1.397	2,453	1.512
Cultural and sports 24	6,990	1.015	9,412	1.034	13,176	1.022	16,264	1.102	23,329	1.187
Petroleum 25	208	0.449	128	0.331	209	0.269	222	0.241	428	0.330
Chemical 26	4,885	0.887	7,065	0.859	9,795	0.799	13,637	0.772	20,275	0.792
Medicine 27	1,404	1.302	1,918	1.398	2,581	1.282	3,297	1.301	4,128	1.360
Chemical fibre 28	894	0.980	1,160	1.127	1,427	0.981	970	0.572	1,004	0.877
Rubber 29	1,841	1.140	2,072	1.102	2,669	1.054	3,665	1.047	5,884	1.108
Plastic 30	5,402	1.137	6,543	1.185	9,620	1.231	12,458	1.207	20,646	1.269
Non-metallic 31	7,955	0.867	9,328	0.835	12,450	0.869	14,878	0.873	23,335	0.943
Ferrous metals 32	686	0.402	1,241	0.684	1,153	0.627	1,564	0.633	3,005	0.627
Non-ferrous metals 33	911	0.763	1,214	0.776	1,946	0.815	2,582	0.830	4,009	0.990
Metal products 34	8,870	1.113	11,751	1.156	17,263	1.160	19,802	1.151	31,053	1.161
General machinery 35	6,203	1.340	8,817	1.302	12,654	1.293	17,777	1.303	31,816	1.324
Special machinery 36	3,175	1.402	3,869	1.444	6,212	1.438	7,572	1.574	12,968	1.722
Transportation vehicle 37	3,051	1.325	4,030	1.323	5,371	1.295	8,205	1.184	13,769	1.317
Electrical 40	8,105	1.179	11,189	1.195	16,827	1.139	22,923	1.143	36,769	1.174
Communications and computer 41	5,248	1.549	6,259	1.597	9,666	1.590	13,413	1.666	21,996	1.717
Measuring and office 42	1,510	1.370	1,459	1.581	2,623	1.381	5,904	1.154	8,521	1.295
Artwork and other 43	11,047	1.224	11,939	1.308	19,011	1.311	21,700	1.317	30,067	1.297

(Continued)

Table 8.7b (Continued)

CIC 2-digit industry	2005		2006		2007		2008		2009	
	Obs.	Median	Obs.	Median	Obs.	Median	Obs.	Median	Obs.	Median
Processing of food 13	6,585	0.687	7,439	0.721	12,966	0.593	6,641	0.544	14,262	0.573
Manufacturing of food 14	6,513	0.608	7,499	0.621	6,870	0.625	7,202	0.600	8,251	0.515
Beverage 15	1,154	0.740	1,290	0.729	1,027	0.671	973	0.681	1,462	0.603
Textile 17	86,360	0.913	88,566	0.918	82,059	0.888	88,155	0.904	85,327	0.877
Apparel 18	76,319	1.248	85,979	1.283	81,399	1.290	95,233	1.289	88,843	1.278
Leather 19	20,197	1.332	22,840	1.358	20,965	1.358	22,261	1.426	22,187	1.663
Wood 20	5,686	1.270	6,008	1.239	8,659	0.935	9,727	0.935	9,869	0.957
Furniture 21	11,694	1.631	14,044	1.660	13,384	1.971	19,343	1.970	19,574	2.012
Paper 22	3,307	1.264	4,662	1.243	4,643	1.251	5,275	1.224	5,697	1.308
Printing 23	2,625	1.681	4,158	1.784	4,365	1.829	5,245	1.900	5,703	1.971
Cultural and sports 24	27,794	1.228	32,639	1.239	27,887	1.277	33,325	1.313	32,209	1.329
Petroleum 25	404	0.255	418	0.125	261	0.078	277	0.182	585	0.131
Chemical 26	23,021	0.815	28,008	0.798	20,972	0.786	23,350	0.840	29,560	0.835
Medicine 27	4,842	1.417	5,727	1.393	3,858	1.509	4,002	1.439	5,009	1.541
Chemical fibre 28	1,372	0.751	1,492	0.669	1,691	0.709	1,488	0.675	1,584	0.650
Rubber 29	6,809	1.134	8,306	1.180	7,669	1.081	8,950	1.191	10,043	1.102
Plastic 30	24,232	1.297	31,605	1.298	27,929	1.269	33,912	1.271	37,833	1.313
Non-metallic 31	25,873	0.981	31,931	1.019	27,057	0.958	30,544	0.971	33,637	0.931
Ferrous metals 32	3,130	0.549	4,992	0.472	5,100	0.445	5,484	0.504	4,562	0.405
Non-ferrous metals 33	4,275	1.054	5,485	1.032	4,595	1.028			22	1.873
Metal products 34	39,265	1.189	50,359	1.218	48,609	1.202	59,546	1.213	60,788	1.213
General machinery 35	38,448	1.390	47,206	1.498	41,922	1.494	55,000	1.574	64,656	1.575
Special machinery 36	15,444	1.821	21,157	1.876	19,168	1.870	25,654	2.008	29,398	2.017
Transportation vehicle 37	19,015	1.335	24,341	1.439	23,085	1.398	30,401	1.466	32,569	1.472
Electrical 40	42,647	1.181	52,476	1.212	46,514	1.171	61,576	1.255	71,188	1.279
Communications and computer 41	26,963	1.815	32,675	1.908	28,414	1.967	32,858	2.008	37,762	2.053
Measuring and office 42	9,848	1.402	12,291	1.566	8,912	1.633	10,647	1.707	10,959	1.841
Artwork and other 43	34,153	1.326	38,691	1.328	38,618	1.304	39,433	1.324	37,891	1.280

CIC 2-digit industry	2010		2011		2012		2013		2007–2000	2013–2007	2013–2000
	Obs.	Median	Obs.	Median	Obs.	Median	Obs.	Median	Median	Median	Median
Processing of food 13	9,422	0.673	15,712	0.719	13,009	0.637	13,536	0.683	-0.209	0.090	-0.119
Manufacturing of food 14	6,442	0.550	10,389	0.568	10,344	0.572	11,007	0.559	-0.086	-0.066	-0.152
Beverage 15	1,469	0.628	1,482	0.629	1,449	0.729	1,607	0.703	-0.249	0.032	-0.217
Textile 17	82,443	0.894	101,633	0.905	88,442	0.929	68,589	0.831	0.055	-0.057	-0.002
Apparel 18	81,346	1.312	78,433	1.369	57,971	1.368	82,244	1.317	0.236	0.027	0.263
Leather 19	21,835	1.601	24,199	1.703	20,655	1.732	30,464	1.662	0.140	0.304	0.444
Wood 20	7,630	1.009	9,155	0.990	10,007	1.084	8,420	1.092	-0.210	0.158	-0.052
Furniture 21	15,674	1.980	22,427	1.993	20,567	2.020	21,209	1.966	0.797	-0.005	0.792
Paper 22	5,214	1.220	6,305	1.288	6,348	1.359	6,228	1.325	0.184	0.074	0.258
Printing 23	5,130	1.892	7,019	1.890	6,636	1.980	7,662	2.023	0.911	0.194	1.105
Cultural and sports 24	31,434	1.276	32,813	1.389	28,421	1.400	57,271	1.326	0.262	0.050	0.311
Petroleum 25	621	0.231	287	0.076	498	-0.138	454	-0.521	-0.372	-0.598	-0.970
Chemical 26	28,692	0.867	34,090	0.829	34,285	0.810	37,102	0.833	-0.101	0.047	-0.054
Medicine 27	5,555	1.540	7,576	1.233	7,187	1.339	6,768	1.269	0.207	-0.240	-0.033
Chemical fibre 28	1,796	0.646	3,112	0.757	3,204	0.833	3,517	0.800	-0.271	0.090	-0.180
Rubber 29	10,315	1.183	12,499	1.098	12,267	1.119	11,756	0.981	-0.059	-0.100	-0.159
Plastic 30	35,776	1.341	44,493	1.346	43,528	1.373	39,326	1.436	0.132	0.167	0.299
Non-metallic 31	25,399	1.026	32,723	0.891	30,590	0.933	33,038	0.926	0.091	-0.032	0.060
Ferrous metals 32	5,619	0.365	6,166	0.371	6,102	0.384	9,697	0.665	0.043	0.221	0.264
Non-ferrous metals 33	6,020	0.956	7,881	0.867	7,554	0.907	4,885	0.761	0.264	-0.266	-0.002
Metal products 34	56,131	1.210	67,187	1.239	60,316	1.273	56,531	1.278	0.089	0.075	0.165

(Continued)

Table 8.7b (Continued)

CIC 2-digit industry	2010		2011		2012		2013		2007–2000	2013–2007	2013–2000
	Obs.	Median	Obs.	Median	Obs.	Median	Obs.	Median	Median	Median	Median
General machinery 35	67,333	1.619	77,141	1.610	75,357	1.706	79,993	1.777	0.154	0.283	0.437
Special machinery 36	32,043	2.005	38,750	1.995	41,628	2.129	46,068	2.187	0.468	0.317	0.784
Transportation vehicle 37	38,362	1.478	48,041	1.457	52,540	1.521	11,097	1.438	0.073	0.040	0.113
Electrical 40	64,628	1.236	86,232	1.264	84,580	1.305	88,437	1.381	−0.008	0.211	0.202
Communications and computer 41	40,240	2.068	51,938	2.118	51,361	2.231	55,593	2.260	0.417	0.293	0.710
Measuring and office 42	12,550	1.734	15,295	2.005	13,614	2.108	13,049	2.206	0.263	0.574	0.836
Artwork and other 43	40,457	1.313	42,184	1.334	34,803	1.318	7,933	1.481	0.080	0.178	0.257

Note: Industries with observations fewer than 100 in each year during the sample period are not reported.

Source: Authors.

Finally, we calculate the log of the number of quality leaders to each destination in each year:

$$\ln \#\_quaLleader_{kt} = \ln \left(1 + \Sigma_g leader_{kgt}\right) \tag{4.2}$$

We plot $\ln \#\_qual\_leader_{kt}$ against $\ln GDPpc_{kt}$ for each year. Figure 8.3a presents the scatter plots and the fitted lines for Indonesia in 2008 and 2012. The positive association between the two variables is obvious and straightforward, and the correlation is above 0.6. The positive correlation is a confirmation of the "preference for quality" hypothesis and is aligned with the empirical evidence of Hallak (2006) and Feenstra and Romalis (2014).

We also show that the cross-sectional correlation between quality and destination income is rather persistent. Table 8.8a reports the top five destinations with the largest number of quality leaders of Indonesia's export quality from 2008 to

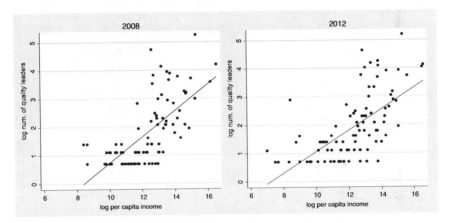

Figure 8.3a Quality leader versus income: Indonesia
Source: Authors.

Table 8.8a Destinations with the most quality leaders: Indonesia

Rank	2008	2009	2010	2011	2012
1	Japan	Japan	Japan	Japan	Japan
2	Singapore	Singapore	Singapore	Singapore	Singapore
3	United States	United States	Thailand	Malaysia	Thailand
4	Malaysia	Thailand	Australia	Australia	Malaysia
5	Thailand	Malaysia	Malaysia	Thailand	United States

Source: Authors.

2012. Japan and Singapore rank first and second, respectively, across all years, while the United States, Malaysia, Thailand and Australia rank third, fourth and fifth in all years. With the relative ranking of per capita income being persistent during the sample period, the top destinations with the highest quality from Indonesia also remain stable.

It may appear that the top destinations with the largest number of quality leaders are inconsistent with our model prediction. While our model predicts that a firm tends to offer higher quality for richer and more distant markets, many of the top destinations listed in Table 8.8a are actually countries near Indonesia. This is because the number of quality leaders reflects not only the average quality Indonesia offers to a market but also the probability of Indonesia's firms selling their products in that market. If a market is rich and far away from Indonesia, considering the relative cost of shipping costs to production, Indonesia will offer higher quality products in that market relative to the other markets, conditional on serving that market. As that market is distant and costly to enter, Indonesia may be able to sell only a few products there, decreasing the number of quality leaders. The number of quality leaders in a market reflects both Indonesia's capability of reaching that market and Indonesia's quality decision in that market, conditional on reaching that market.

Now, we turn to the case of China. Figure 8.3b presents the scatter plots and fitted line for $\ln \#\_qual\_leader_{kt}$ against $\ln GDPpc_{kt}$ for 2000, 2004, 2008 and

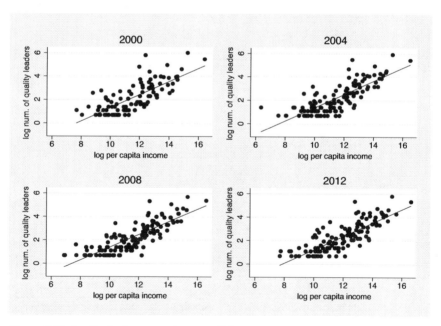

Figure 8.3b Quality leader versus income: China

Source: Authors.

Table 8.8b Destinations with the most quality leaders: China

Rank	2000	2003	2006	2009	2012
1	Japan	Japan	Japan	Japan	Japan
2	Hong Kong	Hong Kong	United States	United States	Hong Kong
3	United States	United States	Hong Kong	Hong Kong	United States
4	South Korea	South Korea	South Korea	South Korea	South Korea
5	Singapore	Taiwan	Taiwan	Taiwan	Germany

Source: Authors.

2012. There is a strong positive correlation between these variables shown by a correlation that is higher than 0.6 in each year.

Analogously, we present the top five destinations with the largest number of quality leaders in Table 8.8b. Japan ranks first across the whole sample period, while Hong Kong and the United States rank second and third. The Republic of Korea (henceforth, South Korea) constantly ranks fourth in the whole sample, while Singapore, Taiwan and Germany rank fifth. The ranking is also mostly persistent over time.

4.5. Margins of quality evolution: a dynamic decomposition

In this subsection, we focus on decomposing the aggregate weighted average export quality into various margins that contribute to its evolution. This calls for a dynamic decomposition framework that appropriately measures the contributions of survivors, entry, exit and the between-effect occurring among survivors.

After surveying the literature, we adopt the dynamic Olley-Pakes decomposition (henceforth, DOPD) proposed by Melitz and Polanec (2015). With the beginning period (defined by $t = 1$) and the ending period (defined by $t = 2$), we streamline the subscript by letting s be a firm-product-destination (jkg) combination, which we call "variety". Therefore, the aggregate weighted-average export quality in each period, Q_t, is

$$Q_t = \left(\sum_s value_{st} \cdot qual_{st} \right) \bigg/ \left(\sum_s value_{st} \right)$$

We define the sample as three subgroups. If s is present in both $t = 1$ and $t = 2$, then s is defined as "survivor" and $s \in S$. If s is present in $t = 1$ and absent in $t = 2$, then s is defined as "exit" and $s \in X$. If s is absent in $t = 1$ and present in $t = 2$, then s is defined as "entry" and $s \in E$. Finally, $G = \{S, X, E\}$.

Therefore, for different subgroups, G, we can define the group-specific market share, M_{Gt}, and the weighted-average export quality, Q_{Gt}:

$$M_{Gt} = \left(\sum_{s \in G} value_{st} \right) / \left(\sum_{s} value_{st} \right)$$

$$Q_{Gt} = \left(\sum_{s \in G} value_{st} \cdot qual_{st} \right) / \left(\sum_{s \in G} value_{st} \right)$$

Therefore, according to Melitz and Polanec (2015), Q_1 and Q_2 can be decomposed as the following:

$$Q_1 = M_{S1}Q_{S1} + M_{X1}Q_{X1} = Q_{S1} + M_{X1}(Q_{X1} - Q_{S1})$$

$$Q_2 = M_{S2}Q_{S2} + M_{E2}Q_{E2} = Q_{S2} + M_{E2}(Q_{E2} - Q_{S2})$$

The change of aggregate export quality is, therefore,

$$Q_2 - Q_1 = \underbrace{Q_{S2} - Q_{S1}}_{Survivor} + \underbrace{M_{E2}(Q_{E2} - Q_{S2})}_{Entry} + \underbrace{M_{X1}(Q_{S1} - Q_{X1})}_{Exit} \tag{4.3}$$

Equation (4.3) clearly shows that the aggregate quality upgrading comes from three margins. The survivor margin is positive if and only if the weighted-average quality of survivors increases. The entry margin is positive if and only if the weighted-average quality of entry is higher than the weighted-average quality of survivors in $t = 2$. Similarly, the exit margin is positive if and only if the weighted-average quality of exit is lower than the weighted-average quality of survivors in $t = 1$. The survivor margin is the intensive margin, while the sum of the entry and exit margins is the extensive margin.

We can further decompose the intensive margin into within-variety and between-variety margins:

$$Q_{S2} - Q_{S1} = \overline{Q_{S2}} - \overline{Q_{S1}} + \Delta cov \tag{4.4}$$

$\overline{Q_{S2}} - \overline{Q_{S1}}$ is the gap between the means of survivors in the two periods, and Δcov measures the contribution of market share reallocation among survivors. Δcov is positive if and only if the market share of high-quality variety increases across two periods.

According to equations (4.3) and (4.4), we conduct the DOPD approach for Indonesia and China separately. We first conduct the decomposition on a year-to-year basis, then we conduct the decomposition for the first and last years of the sample period. We also provide a sub-period decomposition for China's case.

Table 8.9a reports the decomposition results for Indonesia. Except for 2009–2010, other yearly intervals in the sample all feature a decrease in the overall

Table 8.9a Margins of quality evolution, Indonesia 2008–2012

Begin	End	(1)	(2)	(3)	(4)	(5)	(6)
		Overall	Survivor	Within	Between	Entry	Exit
2008	2009	−9.20%	−10.33%	−10.36%	0.03%	2.12%	−0.99%
2009	2010	7.14%	13.48%	−5.41%	18.88%	−7.67%	1.33%
2010	2011	−5.88%	−8.04%	1.28%	−9.32%	−0.03%	2.20%
2011	2012	−4.19%	−1.78%	4.31%	−6.09%	−0.27%	−2.14%
2008	2012	−12.14%	−15.24%	−10.05%	−5.18%	5.42%	−2.32%

Note: (1) = (2) + (5) + (6), (2) = (3) + (4).
Source: Authors.

weighted-average export quality. In most of the yearly intervals, the survivor margin plays the key role, while the entry and exit margins are less important. Turning to the whole period, the aggregate weighted-average export quality decreases by 12.14 per cent, with the survivor margin contributing to a decrease by 15.24 per cent. Entry contributes positively with a 5.42 per cent margin, suggesting that entering varieties are on average of higher quality than continuing varieties. The exit margin also contributes a −2.32 per cent margin, suggesting that exiting varieties are of higher quality compared with continuing varieties. Finally, within the survivor margin, both within-variety and between-variety contribute negatively, with the within-margin accounting for nearly two-thirds of the declining export quality in the survivor margin.

Table 8.9b reports the decomposition for China. In most of the yearly intervals, the weighted-average export quality increases, except for 2009–2010 where a massive drop in export quality happens due to the negative exit margin. Compared with Indonesia, the roles of entry and exit are more important in the case of China. The 2000–2007 and 2007–2013 sub-periods both feature aggregate quality upgrading of more than 20 per cent. In both periods, the extensive margin plays a major role in determining the aggregate quality upgrading pattern. In 2000–2007, both entry and exit margins contribute positively, totalling a 27.19 per cent margin. In 2007–2013, the exit margin contributes a 37.41 per cent margin, while the entry margin contributes a −13.25 per cent margin, totalling a 24.16 per cent margin. In these two sub-periods, the survivor margin provides slightly negative contributions, mainly due to the between-variety effects. Summing up the whole sample period, we find that the aggregate quality upgrading is 46.84 per cent, with entry and exit margins contributing 9.60 per cent and 24.71 per cent. Therefore, the extensive margin accounts for almost three-quarters of the total quality upgrading. Among the 12.53 per cent contribution of the survivor margin, within-variety contributes 31.37 per cent, while the market share reallocation mechanism deteriorates aggregate quality by 18.84 per cent.

Table 8.9b Margins of quality evolution, China 2000–2013

Begin	End	(1)	(2)	(3)	(4)	(5)	(6)
		Overall	*Survivor*	*Within*	*Between*	*Entry*	*Exit*
2000	2001	−2.07%	−2.12%	1.65%	−3.77%	−4.17%	4.22%
2001	2002	0.69%	−1.30%	−1.38%	0.08%	−3.50%	5.49%
2002	2003	1.12%	−0.08%	−0.63%	0.55%	−2.08%	3.28%
2003	2004	0.88%	0.79%	1.56%	−0.77%	−1.77%	1.86%
2004	2005	3.95%	2.06%	0.55%	1.51%	0.32%	1.57%
2005	2006	4.24%	0.73%	−0.16%	0.89%	0.88%	2.62%
2006	2007	16.59%	−1.97%	−0.42%	−1.56%	21.60%	−3.04%
2007	2008	15.64%	9.89%	0.12%	9.77%	−5.54%	11.29%
2008	2009	3.03%	0.28%	−0.19%	0.46%	−10.62%	13.38%
2009	2010	−29.06%	−8.85%	−3.33%	−5.52%	0.43%	−20.64%
2010	2011	20.75%	9.49%	6.42%	3.07%	14.49%	−3.23%
2011	2012	10.77%	13.59%	8.08%	5.51%	−0.85%	−1.98%
2012	2013	0.31%	−0.99%	2.64%	−3.62%	0.30%	1.00%
2000	2007	25.40%	−1.79%	8.29%	−10.08%	21.00%	6.19%
2007	2013	21.44%	−2.72%	16.34%	−19.06%	−13.25%	37.41%
2000	2013	46.84%	12.53%	31.37%	−18.84%	9.60%	24.71%

Note: (1) = (2) + (5) + (6), (2) = (3) + (4).
Source: Authors.

5.   Concluding remarks

In this study, we first employ an approach that allows for the estimation of firm-product-destination-year-level export quality for Indonesia and China. This approach is based on a theory where firms determine the optimal quality for each destination via a trade-off between the production cost and per-unit shipping cost, by taking into account different consumers' preferences for quality. An increase in the shipping cost relative to the production cost thus raises the optimal quality. Optimal quality is also higher when the consumer's preference for quality is stronger.

The estimated export quality is positively associated with sales across firms within a destination and positively associated with income and geographic barriers across destinations within a firm. We document the export quality evolutions of Indonesia and China in detail. Specifically, we present the aggregate export quality distribution over time for the two countries as well as the export quality distribution over time by firm type and industry. We observe substantial variation across types and industries.

We also show that better-quality goods are more likely to be sold to high-income destinations, and the ranking in terms of quality received remains rather stable over time. We finally decompose the aggregate weighted-average export quality into the intensive margin and extensive margin. We find that the intensive margin plays a major role for Indonesia, while extensive margin plays a major role for China.

Our estimations and descriptions generate variations in export quality along several dimensions, and we plan to explore these facts and evidence in further studies to identify and analyse the underlying economic mechanisms that determine the variation in export quality.

Notes

Acknowledgement: We thank Gene Grossman and Martin Richardson for their constructive comments on earlier drafts. Disclaimer: The study was conducted when Lili Yan Ing was with Economic Research Institute for ASEAN and East Asia (ERIA). The views expressed here do not represent views of the Ministry of Trade of Indonesia.

1 Hallak (2006), Bastos and Silva (2010), Auer and Chaney (2009) and Alessandria and Kaboski (2011).
2 We assume that l_{jk} is a combination of various inputs, for example, capital, labour and intermediate inputs. w is then defined as the composite input price associated with the combination of these inputs. In a later section, we describe how to construct the empirical counterpart of l_{jk} and the associated w, while presently, we simply regard l_{jk} as a composite input.
3 A lower a_k suggests that market k's consumers are more sensitive to variations in a firm's quality effort l_{jk} and forces a firm to put more effort into increasing quality. For example, compared with a poor country, a rich country may have stronger preferences for apparel products made from delicate materials with fashionable styles over basic-style apparel made of cotton.
4 The reason for specifying a "structural value-added" specification rather than a gross output specification (where the materials enter a Cobb-Douglas production function together with capital and labour) is that under the assumption of "scalar unobservable" (namely, a firm's investment or material use is a function of unobserved productivity), without further restrictions, the gross production function cannot be identified. This argument is shown by Bond and Soderbom (2005) for the case of a Cobb-Douglas production function and by Gandhi et al. (2017) for more general cases.
5 In principle, we can perform the estimation for each HS 6-digit product. However, since the average sample size for each product gets smaller when one moves from aggregate classification to disaggregate classification, we fail to generate sensible estimates for some HS 6-digit products due to insufficient observations. We therefore choose to perform our estimation at the HS 4-digit level in order to incorporate as much trade volume as possible while at the same time preserving the substantial technology variations across products.
6 For example, before normalization, we cannot compare a pencil's quality with a car's quality. After such a normalization, we can at least say a pencil's quality ranking in its own category is higher than a car's quality ranking in its own category.
7 We admit the limitation that some small manufacturers that also export may not be included in the CFD sample. However, since most of the trade volume comes from large manufacturers, we assume that neglecting those small exporters does not give rise to systematic measurement errors on aggregate export quality.
8 For the sample period where firm-level depreciation is available, we use the actual reported depreciation in the perpetual inventory method. For the sample period where firm-level depreciation is missing (2008–2010), we calculate the depreciation rate at the CIC 2-digit industry level (increase in accumulated depreciation of the whole industry in that year divided by the fixed asset at the original price of the whole industry in that year) and use this depreciation rate to calculate the firm-level depreciation in order to conduct the perpetual inventory method.

9 We admit that such an approximation can be subject to measurement errors because the input share of a product (to a market) is not necessarily proportional to the revenue share of that product (to that market). Therefore, when estimating the production function of quality units, we are exploiting the variations in input uses across firms to identify parameters.

10 If a product is defined as "differentiated" by Rauch (1999), we let $Diff_g = 1$. If a product is defined as "reference-priced" or "open exchange", we let $Diff_g = 0$. We use "conservative" classification in this practice.

References

Ackerberg, D.A., K. Caves, and G. Frazer (2015), 'Identification Properties of Recent Production Function Estimators', *Econometrica*, 83(6), 2411–2451.

Alchian, A.A. and W.R. Allen (1977), *Exchange and Production: Competition, Coordination and Control*. Belmont, CA: Wadsworth Publishing Company.

Alessandria, G. and J.P. Kaboski (2011), 'Pricing-to-Market and the Failure of Absolute PPP', *American Economic Journal: Macroeconomics*, 3(1), 91–127.

Amiti, M. and A.K. Khandelwal (2013), 'Import Competition and Quality Upgrading', *Review of Economics and Statistics*, 95(2), 476–490.

Auer, R. and T. Chaney (2009), 'Exchange Rate Pass-Through in a Competitive Model of Pricing-to-Market', *Journal of Money, Credit and Banking*, 41(s1), 151–175.

Auer, R., T. Chaney, and P. Saure (2014), 'Quality Pricing-to-Market', CEPR Discussion Papers.

Baldwin, R. and J. Harrigan (2011), 'Zeros, Quality, and Space: Trade Theory and Trade Evidence', *American Economic Journal: Microeconomics*, 3(2), 60–88.

Bastos, P. and J. Silva (2010), 'The Quality of a Firm's Exports: Where You Export to Matters', *Journal of International Economics*, 82(2), 99–111.

Bond, S. and M. Soderbom (2005), 'Adjustment Costs and the Identification of Cobb-Douglas Production Functions', Economics Department Working Paper, Oxford, W04.

Brandt, L., J. Van Biesebroeck, and Y. Zhang (2012), 'Creative Accounting or Creative Destruction? Firm-level Productivity Growth in Chinese Manufacturing', *Journal of Development Economics*, 97(2), 339–351.

Chen, N. and L. Juvenal (2016), 'Quality, Trade and Exchange Rate Pass-through', *Journal of International Economics*, 100(5), 61–80.

Crozet, M., K. Head, and T. Mayer (2012), 'Quality Sorting and Trade: Firm-level Evidence for French Wine', *Review of Economic Studies*, 79(2), 609–644.

Dai, M., M. Maitra, and M. Yu (2016), 'Unexceptional Exporter Performance in China? The Role of Processing Trade', *Journal of Development Economics*, 121, 177–189.

Fajgelbaum, P.D., G.M. Grossman, and E. Helpman (2011). 'Income Distribution, Product Quality and International Trade', *Journal of Political Economy*, 119(4), 721–765.

Fan, H., Y.A. Li, and S.R. Yeaple (2015), 'Trade Liberalization, Quality, and Export Prices', *Review of Economics and Statistics*, 97(5), 1033–1051.

Feenstra, R.C., Z. Li, and M. Yu (2014), 'Exports and Credit Constraints Under Incomplete Information: Theory and Evidence From China', *Review of Economics and Statistics*, 96(3), 729–744.

Feenstra, R.C. and J. Romalis (2014), 'International Prices and Endogenous Quality', *Quarterly Journal of Economics*, 129(2), 477–527.

Gandhi, A., S. Navarro, and D. Rivers (2017), 'On the Identification of Production Functions', *Working Paper*.

Goldberg, P.K. and F. Verboven (2001), 'The Evolution of Price Dispersion in the European Car Market', *Review of Economic Studies*, 68(4), 811–848.

Hallak, J.C. (2006), 'Product Quality and the Direction of Trade', *Journal of International Economics*, 68(1), 238–265.

Hallak, J.C. and P.K. Schott (2011), 'Estimating Cross-Country Differences in Product Quality', *Quarterly Journal of Economics*, 126(1), 417–474.

Hummels, D. and A. Skiba (2004), 'Shipping the Good Apples Out? An Empirical Confirmation of the Alchian-Allen Conjecture', *Journal of Political Economy*, 112(6), 1384–1402.

Johnson, R.C. (2012), 'Trade and Prices With Heterogeneous Firms', *Journal of International Economics*, 86(1), 43–56.

Khandelwal, A.K. (2010), 'The Long and Short (of) Quality Ladders', *Review of Economic Studies*, 77(4), 1450–1476.

Khandelwal, A.K., P.K. Schott, and S.J. Wei (2013), 'Trade Liberalization and Embedded Institutional Reform: Evidence From Chinese Exporters', *American Economic Review*, 103(6), 2169–2195.

Kugler, M. and E. Verhoogen (2012), 'Prices, Plant Size and Product Quality', *Review of Economic Studies*, 79(1), 307–339.

Manova, K. and Z. Zhang (2012), 'Export Prices Across Firms and Destinations', *Quarterly Journal of Economics*, 127(1), 379–436.

Martin, J. (2012). 'Markups, Quality and Transport Costs', *European Economic Review*, 56(4), 777–791.

Melitz, M.J., and S. Polanec (2015), 'Dynamic Olley-Pakes Productivity Decomposition With Entry and Exit', *RAND Journal of Economics*, 46(2), 362–375.

Rauch, J.E. (1999). 'Networks Versus Markets in International Trade', *Journal of International Economics*, 48(1), 7–35.

Schott, P.K. (2004). 'Across-Product Versus Within-Product Specialization in International Trade', *Quarterly Journal of Economics*, 119(2), 647–678.

Verhoogen, E.A. (2008), 'Trade, Quality Upgrading, and Wage Inequality in the Mexican Manufacturing Sector', *Quarterly Journal of Economics*, 123(2), 489–530.

Yu, M. (2015), 'Processing Trade, Tariff Reductions and Firm Productivity: Evidence From Chinese Firms', *Economic Journal*, 125(585), 943–988.

Appendix

Step 4 in estimating export quality

We propose a five-step iteration procedure to estimate quality. Among the five steps, step four includes an estimation of equation (2.14) using a two-stage control function approach proposed by ACF (2015) to mitigate the simultaneity problem.

$$\ln Q_{jkt}^{*} - (1 - \theta) \ln q_{jkt}^{*} = \theta\alpha \ln K_{jkt} + \theta(1 - \alpha) \ln L_{jkt} + \theta \ln \varphi_{jt} + \varepsilon_{jkt}$$

We describe this approach in detail in this appendix. Throughout this appendix, the two-stage estimation is done for each HS 4-digit product separately, so we abstract the subscript g for concision.

We first rewrite equation (2.14) as (A1):

$$y_{jkt} = \beta_k k_{jkt} + \beta_l l_{jkt} + \omega_{jt} + \varepsilon_{jkt} \qquad (A1)$$

y_{jkt} is $\ln Q_{jkgt}^{*} - (1 - \theta_g) \ln q_{jkgt}^{*}$. k_{jkt} and l_{jkt} are simply the log forms of K_{jkt} and L_{jkt}. ω_{jt} is $(\beta_k + \beta_l) \ln \varphi_{jt}$, and ε_{jkt} is the mean-zero error term due to measurement errors or idiosyncratic output shocks that are realized after a firm has made all its input decisions. Both ω_{jt} and ε_{jkt} are unobserved.

ω_{jt} is likely to be correlated with k_{jkt} and l_{jkt} and, therefore, induces endogeneity. We follow ACF (2015) to introduce an observable input demand proxy variable m_{jkt} which satisfies equation (A2):

$$m_{jkt} = g(\omega_{jt}, k_{jkt}, l_{jkt}) \qquad (A2)$$

Equation (A2) states that conditional on k_{jkt} and l_{jkt}, intermediate input m_{jkt} is the function of ω_{jt}. We impose the following assumption:

Assumption A1. *Conditional on k_{jkt} and l_{jkt}, $m_{jkt} = g(\omega_{jt}, k_{jkt}, l_{jkt})$ is invertible in ω_{jt}.*

Under the assumption that $g(\omega_{jt}, k_{jkt}, l_{jkt})$ is conditionally invertible, we can transform ω_{jt} into (A3):

$$\omega_{jt} = g_{\omega}^{-1}(m_{jkt}, k_{jkt}, l_{jkt}) \qquad (A3)$$

And we proxy m_{jkt} by

$$m_{jkgt} = \ln \left(\frac{R_{jkgt}^*}{R_{jt}^*} M_{jt} \right)$$

M_{jk} is the absolute value of real intermediate inputs, which is obtained from the Indonesian and Chinese firm-level data. R_{jkgt}^* is the total value of sales of firm j of product g to destination k in year t, while $R_{jt}^* = \sum_{k,g} R_{jkgt}^*$.

We plug (A2) into (A1) to obtain

$$\begin{aligned} y_{jkt} &= \beta_k k_{jkt} + \beta_l l_{jkt} + g_\omega^{-1}(m_{jkt}, k_{jkt}, l_{jkt}) + \varepsilon_{jkt} \\ &= \Phi(m_{jkt}, k_{jkt}, l_{jkt}) + \varepsilon_{jkt} \end{aligned} \qquad (A4)$$

We use third-order polynomials of $(m_{jkt}, k_{jkt}, l_{jkt})$ to non-parametrically approximate $\Phi(m_{jkt}, k_{jkt}, l_{jkt})$. Therefore, estimating equation (A4) generates an estimated $\widehat{\Phi}_{jkt} = \hat{\Phi}(m_{jkt}, k_{jkt}, l_{jkt})$ of Φ_{jkt}. This completes the first-stage estimation.

Before we proceed to the second-stage estimation, we specify that the production efficiency $\ln \varphi_{jt}$ follows an AR (1) process, which is equivalent to the claim that ω_{jt} follows an AR (1) process:

$$\omega_{jt} = \rho \omega_{jt-1} + \delta_{jt}$$

δ_{jt} is the innovation on production efficiency orthogonal to ω_{jt-1}. Therefore, the following moment condition holds:

$$E[\delta_{jt} + +\varepsilon_{jkt} \mid I_{jkt-1}] = 0$$

$$E[y_{jkt} - \beta_k k_{jkt} - \beta_l l_{jkt} - \rho(\Phi_{jkt-1} - \beta_k k_{jkt-1} - \beta_l l_{jkt-1}) \mid I_{jkt-1}] = 0 \qquad (A5)$$

We define y_{jt}, Φ_{jt-1}, $k_{jt(t-1)}$ and $l_{jt(t-1)}$:

$$y_{jt} = \sum_{k \in \Omega_{jt}} y_{jkt}; \quad \Phi_{jt-1} = \sum_{k \in \Omega_{jt}} \Phi_{jkt-1}$$

$$k_{jt(t-1)} = \sum_{k \in \Omega_{jt}} k_{jkt(t-1)}; \quad l_{jt(t-1)} = \sum_{k \in \Omega_{jt}} l_{jkt(t-1)}$$

Ω_{jt} is the set of destinations to which firm j is selling (product g) to in year t. Summing equation (A5) within each firm-year combination across destination k generates the following moment condition:

$$E[y_{jt} - \beta_k k_{jt} - \beta_l l_{jt} - \rho(\Phi_{jt-1} - \beta_k k_{jt-1} - \beta_l l_{jt-1}) \mid I_{jt-1}] = 0 \qquad (A6)$$

Following ACF (2015), we specify $I_{jt-1} = \{1, k_{jt}, l_{jt}, \Phi_{jt-1}, k_{jt-1}, l_{jt-1}\}$. Therefore, we use non-linear least squares to estimate equation (A7) to complete the second-stage estimation.

$$y_{jt} = \beta_k k_{jt} + \beta_l l_{jt} + \rho(\Phi_{jt-1} - \beta_k k_{jt-1} - \beta_l l_{jt-1}) + \xi_{jt} \qquad (A7)$$

$\xi_{jt} = \delta_{jt} \sum_k 1(k \in \Omega_{jt}) + \sum_{k \in \Omega_{jt}} \varepsilon_{jkt}$. $1(k \in \Omega_{jt})$ is a dummy variable indicating whether destination k is among one of the destinations where firm j sells product g in year t. This procedure jointly estimates β_k and β_l. So $\theta = \beta_k + \beta_l$ and $\alpha = \beta_k/\theta$. We can proceed to calculate the estimated value for $\ln \varphi_{jt}$, as in equation (A8):

$$\ln \varphi_{jt} = \frac{y_{jt} - \hat{\beta}_k k_{jt} - \hat{\beta}_l l_{jt}}{\theta \sum_k 1(k \in \Omega_{jt})} \qquad (A8)$$

We implement this control function approach for each IIS 4-digit product to obtain θ_g, α_g, and $\ln \varphi_{jgt}$.

9   Exporting and organizational change

*Lorenzo Caliendo, Ferdinando Monte and
Esteban Rossi-Hansberg*

1.   Introduction

Exporting affects the organization of production. In order to produce at the scale
needed to access export markets, firms need to hire teams of workers with a different set of skills, pay them different wages and give them different roles within
the organization. In this chapter we explore how a firm's organization reacts to
new or improved export opportunities. Guided by the theory of knowledge-
based hierarchies,[1] we understand organization as the characteristics and roles
played by the workers within a firm. Hence, we explore how the number of management layers, as well as the number of workers and wages in each of these
layers, change when the firm starts exporting or expands its presence in
foreign markets. Our goal is to document these relationships and attempt to rationalize them using available theories. Given that these reorganizations have important implications for the size, hiring practices and productivity of exporting firms,
the findings are relevant to understand the overall effects of trade liberalizations,
as demonstrated by Caliendo and Rossi-Hansberg (2012, from now on CRH).

   We follow the work in Caliendo, Monte and Rossi-Hansberg (2015, from now
on CMRH) that uses matched employer-employee data to document empirically
how firms change their organization when they grow. The paper identifies four hierarchical layers of the firm using a French classification of occupations (PCS) based
on an occupation's hierarchical position in the firm. That paper shows that firms
actively manage their organizational structure. When they grow substantially,
they reorganize by adding a layer of management,[2] lowering average wages in
all preexisting layers of the firm (including the layer of workers), and hiring
more employees in all of these layers. In contrast, when they grow little, they
tend not to reorganize, and so they grow by adding workers in preexisting layers
and increasing average wages. This behavior can be rationalized using the
theory of knowledge-based hierarchies. Firms that grow substantially want to economize on costly knowledge by concentrating it into a few managers and lowering
the knowledge of workers that do more routine tasks. Hence they add a management layer and lower skill, and consequently average wages, in preexisting
layers. Firms that grow little do not find this change profitable since it requires a
more costly management structure, so they prefer to grow by hiring more and

better workers and managers in preexisting layers that require less managerial help. In follow up work, using Portuguese data, Caliendo, Mion, Opromolla and Rossi-Hansberg (2015) confirm these findings for an additional country, but more importantly, show that they are associated with changes in quantity-based measures of productivity of the firm. So, reorganizations that add layers also increase the ability of the firm to transform inputs into physical units of output.

None of our work so far, however, has studied empirically the relationship between organization and exporting. This is our aim in this chapter using the same French dataset that we used in CMRH. This data set covers the vast majority of French manufacturing firms during the period 2002–2007.[3] We start by exploring the organization of exporters relative to non-exporters. Exporters are larger, employ more hours of labor, pay higher wages, and have more layers. Firms with more layers are much more likely to be exporters. For example, among firms with three layers of management (the highest number of layers given that they also have a layer of workers), 90.2 per cent of the value added is generated by firms that also export. All of these facts are consistent with the standard finding in the literature that exporters are larger and are also consistent with CRH where larger firms have weakly more layers. Hence, it is perhaps more interesting to turn our attention to new exporters.

We find that new exporters are more likely to add layers than non-exporters (and symmetrically firms that exit exporting are more likely to drop layers). In addition, new exporters that add layers decrease average wages in existing layers while exporters that do not add layers increase them. The well-known finding (Bernard and Jensen 1995, 1997, and Verhoogen 2008) that firms that become exporters pay higher wages is the result of a composition effect. In fact, the firms that expand significantly as a result of exporting, namely, the ones that add layers, reduce average wages. Furthermore, they do so at all pre-existing layers. In contrast, new exporters that do not change layers barely expand but do increase wages. Since there are more new exporters that do not change layers than there are exporters that do change layers, the average effect on wages is positive but small. The result is relevant for the conceptualization of new exporters. The notion that new exporters expand and increase the wages of their employees either because they upgrade their technology (and so the marginal product of labor is higher) or because profits are higher and they share them with workers (via a wage sharing or bargaining mechanism) is at odds with our data.[4] The data are consistent with a view in which new exporters that expand significantly change their organizational design and economize on knowledge by employing less knowledgeable employees who are paid less.

The findings above do not document the causal effect of exporting on organization, but rather the fact that exporting and organizational change are related in the data. To try to measure the causal effect of exporting on organization, we exploit pre-sample variation in the destination composition of a firm's exports, in conjunction with real exchange rate variation across countries, to build an instrument for exports. Similar instruments were used by Bertrand (2004), Brambilla, Lederman, and Porto (2012), Revenga (1992) and Verhoogen, (2008). We then use this instrument to evaluate if the probability of adding layers is causally related to increases in exports. We find that the first stage is somewhat noisy and weak across the subsamples of firms with different numbers of layers, but the second stage shows that for firms with one, two or three layers exporting does increase the probability of adding layers significantly. The result is not significant for firms with four layers, perhaps due to the fact that our identification of layers in the data allows for a maximum of only four layers so those firms can only reduce the number of layers. Perhaps more interesting is that, using this instrument, the causal effect of increases in the number of layers due to better access to foreign markets is to reduce wages in preexisting layers and to increase the number of employees in all of them. This holds for all layers in firms with any number of layers. More work is needed to establish this causality definitively, and we discuss several other papers that have tried to do so with other samples of firms and countries in Section 5, but this evidence is, we believe, encouraging.

The rest of the chapter is organized as follows. Section 2 reproduces some of the theory in CRH to clarify the logic behind the relationships that we look for in the data. Section 3 presents the empirical description of the relationship between organization and exporting. Section 4 presents our causal results and Section 5 reviews the related literature using occupations to understand the organization of the firm and its relationship to foreign markets in a variety of countries. Section 6 concludes.

2. Exports and reorganization: theoretical implications

In this section we discuss briefly the framework in CRH. Given that the purpose of the current chapter is to describe and understand the data, we present the theory in its simplest form and do not discuss all the details fully. The interested reader is directed to CRH for the more technical discussions and all proofs of the results.

We consider an economy with N identical agents. Agents acquire knowledge in order to solve the problems they encounter during production. Agents that acquire more knowledge command higher wages according to a function $w(z)$ with $\partial w(z)/\partial z > 0$.[5]

Firms are started and organized by a CEO. She pays a fixed entry cost f^E in units of labor to design her product. After doing so, she obtains a demand draw α from a known distribution $G(\alpha)$. The draw α determines the level of demand of the firm. If the entrepreneur decides to produce, she pays a fixed cost f in units of labor. Production requires labor and knowledge. Agents employed in a firm act as production workers (layer $\ell = 0$) or managers (layers $\ell \geq 1$). We denote by n_L^ℓ, z_L^ℓ, and w_L^ℓ, the number, knowledge, and total wage of employees at layer $\ell = 0, 1, 2\ldots$ of an organization with L layers of management (or $L + 1$ layers of employees, given that we call the layer of workers layer zero). Workers use their unit of time to generate a production possibility that can yield one unit of output. For output to be realized, the worker needs to solve a problem drawn from a distribution $F(z)$ with $F''(z) < 0$. Workers learn how to solve the most frequent problems, the ones in the interval $\left[0, z_L^0\right]$. If the problem they face falls in $[0, z_L^0]$, production is realized; otherwise, they can ask a manager one layer above how to solve the problem. Managers spend h units of their time on each problem that gets to them. A manager at layer $\ell = 1$ tries to solve the problems workers could not solve. Hence, they learn how to solve problems in $[z_L^0, z_L^0 + z_L^1]$. In general, the firm needs $n_L^\ell = hn_L^0(1 - F(Z_L^{\ell-1}))$ managers of layer ℓ, where $Z_L^\ell = \sum_{l=0}^\ell z_L^l$.[6]

Let $C(q; w)$ denote the minimum variable cost of producing q units, and $C_L(q; w)$ the same cost if we restrict the organization to producing with L layers of management, in an economy with an equilibrium wage function $w(\cdot)$. Then, the organizational problem of the firm is given by,

$$C(q; w) = \min_{L \geq 0} \{C_L(q; w)\} = \min_{L \geq 0, \, \{n_L^\ell, z_L^\ell\}_{l=0}^L \geq 0} \sum_{\ell=0}^L n_L^\ell w_L^\ell \tag{1}$$

subject to

$$q \leq F(Z_L^L)n_L^0, \tag{2}$$

$$w_L^\ell = w(z_L^\ell) \text{ for all } \ell \leq L, \tag{3}$$

$$n_L^\ell = hn_L^0[1 - F(Z_L^{\ell-1})] \text{ for } L \geq \ell > 0, \tag{4}$$

$$n_L^L = 1. \tag{5}$$

So one entrepreneur, $n_L^L = 1$, chooses the number of layers, L, employees at each layer, n_L^ℓ, and the interval of knowledge that they acquire, z_L^ℓ, subject to the output constraint (2), the prevailing wage function (3) and the time constraints of employees at each layer (4).

The problem above has several implications for the internal organization of firms as they grow. Consider first the choices z_L^ℓ and n_L^ℓ as functions of q, but conditional on L. That is, consider a firm that decides to produce more without changing the number of layers, that is, without reorganizing. To expand production, the firm needs to increase either total knowledge, Z_L^L, or the number of workers, n_L^0. Since knowledge and the number of workers are linked through the time constraint (4), the firm does a bit of both. The only way to have more workers is to make them more knowledgeable so they ask less often and the CEO can have a larger span of control. Since the knowledge of agents at different layers is complementary, the firm does so at all layers. Hence, the number of workers in all layers increases, as does the knowledge and, consequently, wages of all workers. Note also that since every worker has to learn more in order to expand the firm, the marginal cost of production is increasing in quantity conditional on the number of layers ($\partial^2 C_L(q;w)/\partial q^2 = \partial MC_L(q;w)/\partial q > 0$). It is increasingly costly to expand production in an organization with a fixed organizational structure as reflected by the number of layers.

In contrast, as proven in CRH, as firms increase the number of layers by one in order to produce more, the number of agents in each layer increases and the knowledge in all pre-existing layers, and therefore the wage, decreases. The logic is straightforward. Firms add layers to economize on the knowledge of their workers. So when they add a new top layer, they make the new manager deal with the rare problems and make lower level employees know less, and consequently they pay them less. The lower knowledge in all pre-existing layers reduces, by equation (4), the span of control of each manager in the organization. However, the number of employees in all layers still goes up since the span of control of the new top manager is larger than one. The marginal cost also declines discontinuously at the quantity produced where the firm adds a layer. The organization is building capacity by adding an extra layer, and that reduces the marginal cost discontinuously.

So far we have not said anything about how the quantity produced is determined. To do so we need to turn to the profit maximization and entry decision of the firm. CRH embed the cost function discussed above into a standard Melitz (2003) type framework with heterogeneity in demand. The model in CRH also allows us to study the effect of a new opportunity to export on the organization of firms. We sketch some of those arguments here.

We now embed our economy, that we denote by i, in a world with J foreign countries, with typical index j. Let $x_{ij}(\alpha)$ be the quantity demanded of an agent in country j for good α produced in country i, and let $p_{ij}(\alpha)$ denote its price. The name of the good α is also a demand shifter that implies that agents like varieties with higher α better. So that with constant elasticity of substitution (CES) preferences with elasticity of substitution $\sigma > 1$,

$$x_{ij}(\alpha) = \alpha \left(\frac{p_{ij}(\alpha)}{P_j} \right)^{-\sigma} \frac{R_j/N_j}{P_j} \tag{6}$$

where P_j, R_j and N_j denote the price index, total revenue and population in country j.

CEOs in the domestic country pay a fixed cost f_{ii} to produce. If they want to supply the foreign market, they also need to pay a fixed cost f_{ij}. Trading goods is costly. Let $\tau_{ij} > 1$ be the "iceberg" trade cost incurred by firms exporting to market j. Consider the problem of a firm with demand draw α in country i. It solves,

$$\pi_i(\alpha) \equiv \max_{(x_{ii}, \{x_{ij}\}_J) \geq 0} \left\{ p_{ii}(\alpha) N_i x_{ii}(\alpha) + \sum_J p_{ij}(\alpha) N_j x_{ij}(\alpha) - C(q_i(\alpha); w_i) - f_{ii} - \sum_J f_{ij} \right\}$$

subject to (6), where

$$q_i(\alpha) = N_i x_{ii}(\alpha) + \sum_J \tau_{ij} N_j x_{ij}(\alpha).$$

The cost function $C(\cdot; w_i)$ solves the cost minimization problem described above. The first-order conditions of this problem implicitly define the quantities sold in each market,

$$N_i x_{ii}(\alpha) = \alpha R_i P_i^{\sigma-1} \left(\frac{\sigma}{\sigma-1} MC(q_i(\alpha); w_i) \right)^{-\sigma},$$

and

$$N_j x_{ij}(\alpha) = \alpha R_j P_j^{\sigma-1} \left(\frac{\sigma}{\sigma-1} \tau_{ij} MC(q_i(\alpha); w_i) \right)^{-\sigma}. \tag{7}$$

In contrast with the standard model, $x_{ii}(\alpha)$ and $x_{ij}(\alpha)$ enter the marginal cost function through $q_i(\alpha)$ as well. That is, a firm's level of total production affects its marginal cost and therefore how much it sells in each market. Importantly, the decision to export affects the cost of production of the goods sold in the local market.[7] Hence, as usual, the price in each market is given by a constant markup over marginal cost, namely,

$$p_{ij}(\alpha) = \frac{\sigma}{\sigma-1} \tau_{ij} MC(q_i(\alpha); w_i) = p_{ii}(\alpha) \tau_{ij}.$$

Note that, as we argued above, since $\partial MC_L(q; w)/\partial q > 0$ the price of firms that expands increases conditional on the number of layers and declines discontinuously with a reorganization. Furthermore, a firm that starts to export to a new market, as a result of a marginal increase in α or an idiosyncratic reduction in τ_{ij} or f_{ij}, increases $q_i(\alpha)$, which results in higher marginal cost, higher wages and more employees in all layers, if the firm does not reorganize. However, if exporting to the new market makes the firm add a layer, it will reduce its marginal cost discontinuously which will decrease its price and expand its quantity more than in the previous case. The reorganization is accompanied by reductions in knowledge and wages in all preexisting layers, and increases in the number of workers in all layers, as discussed above.

When looking at the data, one must acknowledge that the way in which firms reach the new optimal organization depends on the particular institutional features and frictions of the labor market in which they operate. As we document in CMRH, French firms adjust mostly on the extensive margin: for example, to reduce the average knowledge in the layer, they hire new hours of work that are paid less than the average of the pre-existing hours. The development of a fully dynamic theory with adjustment costs is needed to account for these features.

To sum up, the model has the following implications.

1   Exporters are larger and have more layers than non-exporters.
2   A firm that becomes an exporter, or enters a new export market, as a result of a marginally higher α or marginally lower τ_{ij} or f_{ij} for some j,

   (a)   increases L weakly;
   (b)   if L does not change, it *increases* w_L^{ℓ} and n_L^{ℓ} at all ℓ;
   (c)   if L increases it *decreases* w_L^{ℓ} and *increases* n_L^{ℓ} at all ℓ.

Armed with these implications, we now turn to our empirical analysis.

3. Exporting and firm organization: evidence from France

We use confidential data collected by the French National Statistical Institute (INSEE) for the period 2002 to 2007. It combines the BRN dataset with manufacturing firm balance-sheet information with the DADS which includes worker characteristics. The details of the data construction can all be found in CMRH. Our sample includes 553,125 firm-year observations in the manufacturing sector and all monetary values are expressed in 2005 euros.

We use the PCS-ESE classification codes for workers in the manufacturing sector to identify the hierarchical layer in the firm. For manufacturing, it includes five occupational categories given by:

2   Firm owners receiving a wage (which includes the CEO or firm directors).
3   Senior staff or top management positions (which includes chief financial officers, heads of human resources, and logistics and purchasing managers).
4   Employees at the supervisor level (which includes quality control technicians, technical, accounting and sales supervisors).
5   Qualified and non-qualified clerical employees (secretaries, human resources or accounting employees, telephone operators and sales employees).
6   Blue collar qualified and non-qualified workers (welders, assemblers, machine operators and maintenance workers).

As in CMRH we merge classes 5 and 6, since the distribution of wages of workers in these two classes is extremely similar. Hence a firm can have a maximum of four layers, three of management and one of workers. We refer to the number of layers in the firm by the number of management layers. So a firm that has a layer of workers and one layer of managers is referred to as a firm with one layer.

3.1. Cross-sectional comparisons between exporters and non-exporters

It is well known by now that exporters are larger in terms of value added and employment (see Bernard and Jensen, 1999, and Bernard, Jensen, Redding and Schott 2007, among others). This is clearly the case in our data as well.[8] They also pay slightly higher wages. As Table 9.1 shows, they have more layers of management as well. The average number of layers of management among non-exporters is 1.25, meaning that the average exporter has a layer of workers, a layer of management and a fraction of a second layer of management. If we look at exporters, they have 2.11 layers of management on average. Hence, as we would expect from the fact that they are larger, exporters have more layers.

Table 9.1 Description of exporters

	Average				Firm-year obs.
	VA	Hours	Wage	# of layers	
Non-exporters	667.97	24,112.07	23.06	1.25	288,680
Exporters	6,754.35	164,534.30	23.71	2.11	162,795

Note: The difference in wages is significant at 1%.

In Figure 9.1 we present the distribution of value added by layer and by export status. For firms with a given number of layers, each of the panels compares the distribution of exporters and non-exporters. As can be seen from comparing the dark lines across panels, firms with more layers have a distribution of value added with a higher mean. We document this carefully in CMRH. Our emphasis in this chapter is the comparison between exporters and non-exporters. Clearly, for all layers exporters tend to be larger in terms of value added. The size advantage of exporters is present even conditional on the number of layers. Nevertheless, the size advantage of exporters is clearly larger across firms with more management layers. These figures look very similar after we control for time and industry fixed effects. The distributions of hours employed also exhibits similar shifts to the right for exporters with the difference growing larger for firms with more layers.

The comparison is not as clear when we compare the distribution of wages across exporters and non-exporters with a given number of layers in Figure 9.2. Exporters do tend to have a distribution of average hourly wage slightly shifted to the right, but the differences are small, and if anything, more pronounced for firms with less layers. Clearly, the fact that the average hourly wage combines employees with different skills and different roles in the organization that earn very different hourly wages, makes this comparison not particularly informative. As it is, the analysis combines the average wage of the CEO and the janitor. The theory of the organization of the firm outlined above can help us unpack these average effects. In fact, this theory tells us that exporters should pay more to the top layers, but less to the bottom ones. These two implications cancel each other out, at least partially, when we look at average wages.

About 44 per cent of the firms in our data export, and they account for slightly more than 83 per cent of value added, with some variation across years. More relevant for our purposes is that the firms that export tend to have more layers. As Table 9.2 shows, of the firms with three layers of management, 66.7 per cent of them export, while for firms with only workers, only 9.5 per cent of them export.

Table 9.3 presents the composition of firms by number of layers. Out of all exporters, only 15.5 per cent have only a layer of management, while 44.3 per cent have two layers of management, and 35.5 per cent have three. So there is substantial heterogeneity in the number of layers of exporters and

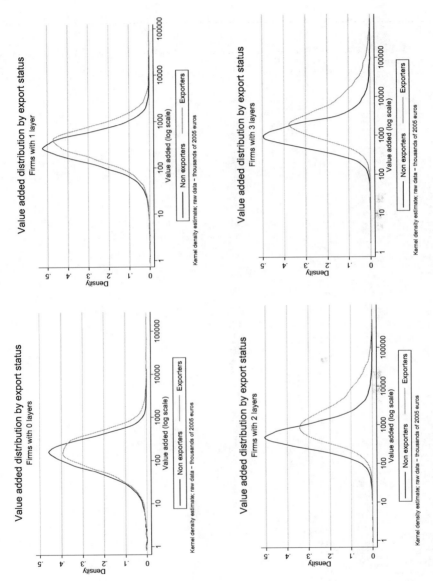

Figure 9.1 Value added distribution by number of layers and export status

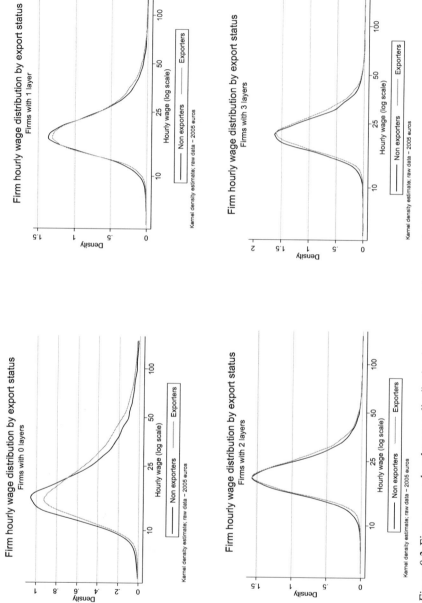

Figure 9.2 Firm average hourly wage distribution by number of layers and export status

Table 9.2 Share of exporters by number of layers

# of layers	Unweighted	Weighted by VA
0	9.5%	15.9%
1	20.3%	28.3%
2	45.0%	81.7%
3	66.7%	92.2%

Table 9.3 Composition of firms by number of layers

# of layers	Non-exporters	Exporters
0	25.2%	4.7%
1	34.3%	15.5%
2	30.5%	44.3%
3	10%	35.5%
Total	100%	100%

Table 9.4 Layer transitions for new exporters relative to non-exporters

		# of layers at t + 1			
		0	*1*	*2*	*3*
# of layers at *t*	0	−10.84	7.84	2.50	0.50
	1	−4.15	−2.91	6.40	0.67
	2	−0.91	−5.75	4.34	2.32
	3	−0.20	−2.85	−4.81	7.87

Note: All significant at 1%.

non-exporters. Furthermore, most exporters have many layers, while most non-exporters have only one or two.

Taken together, the results in this section corroborate Implication 1 of the theory. We now turn to the behavior of firms over time.

3.2. New exporters

We now focus on firms that become exporters during the period in our sample: new exporters. New exporters are more likely to add layers than non-exporters. Table 9.4 shows that the probability of adding one or more layers for new exporters is significantly higher than for non-exporters, regardless of the initial count of layers. The probability of keeping the same number of layers goes down if the firm has zero or one layer of management, while the probability of keeping the same number of layers increases for firms with two or three layers. Given that firms with three layers cannot add layers, this is natural. We conclude from this evidence that new exporters tend to add layers, consistent with the fact that they grow as a result. Of course, there are some that also drop layers, but there are fewer of those firms than those that do not start to export. Table 9.5

Table 9.5 Layer transitions for exporters exiting relative to exporters staying

		# of layers at t + 1			
		0	*1*	*2*	*3*
# of layers at *t*	0	4.51***	−1.84	−2.19***	−0.47***
	1	3.29***	0.30	−3.14***	−0.45**
	2	0.83***	6.50***	−3.73***	−3.60***
	3	0.14***	1.69***	5.46***	−7.30***

** significant at 5%
*** significant at 1%

Table 9.6 Behavior of firms that enter the export market

	All	*Increase* L	*No change in* L
d In total hours	0.031***	0.161***	0.019***
− detrended	0.046***	0.176***	0.034***
d In $\sum_{\ell=0}^{L} n_L^\ell$	0.012	1.233***	0.014**
− detrended	0.024**	1.244***	0.025***
d In *V A*	0.036***	0.117***	0.031***
− detrended	0.044***	0.125***	0.038***
d In avg wage	0.004*	−0.025***	0.010***
− detrended	−0.015***	−0.045***	−0.009***
− common layers	0.004	−0.143***	0.010***
− detrended	−0.016***	−0.163***	−0.010***
% firms	100	14.17	71.81
% *V A* change	100	46.59	49.49

* significant at 10%
** significant at 5%
*** significant at 1%

shows that firms that exit the export market are also more likely to drop layers than exporters that do not exit. So the effect is symmetric: firms that enter the export market are more likely to add layers and firms that exit are more likely to drop layers. These two tables corroborate our Implication 2a.

In fact, the new exporters that add layers expand on average much more than the ones that do not reorganize. Table 9.6 shows the changes in hours, normalized hours, value added and average wages for all new exporters, the ones that add layers, and the ones that do not change *L*. We present results when we detrend using trends for all firms in the economy (not only new exporters, of course). Firms that start exporting increase value added on average by 3.6 per cent. The ones that add layers increase value added by much more, 11.7 per cent, while the ones that do not change layers increase value added by only 3.1 per cent. We find similar numbers for hours and normalized hours. Namely, new exporters that add layers expand much more than firms that do not add layers.

Now let's look at wages. After detrending, new exporters pay wages similar to those paid before; so do firms that do not change layers. In contrast, firms that increase layers decrease wages by a significant 4.5 per cent. Perhaps more relevant is that this average change masks a composition effect between the new top manager and pre-existing layers. When we focus on wages of employees in pre-existing layers, we find that wages fall by 14.3 per cent in firms that add layers (16.3 per cent if we detrend), while they increase 1 per cent in firms that do not change layers (although the change is insignificant when we detrend).

The results paint a picture consistent with the one presented in the previous section. New exporters that reorganize reduce wages in pre-existing layers. Furthermore, these are the new exporters that actually expand significantly. The firms that add layers account for 14.17 per cent of new exporters and 46.59 per cent of the total increase in value added by new exporters. In sum, many firms expand little when they become exporters; these firms increase the salaries of all their employees. Some firms expand a lot when they start to export. They reorganize, add layers, and pay lower wages to employees in the pre-existing layers and higher than average wages to the new top manager.

We now proceed to verify that these results hold layer by layer. We look first at firms that do not add layers. We estimate the regression

$$d \ln \tilde{n}^{\ell}_{Lit} = \beta^{\ell}_{L} d \ln \widetilde{VA}_{it} + \varepsilon_{it} \tag{8}$$

where i denotes a firm, L denotes the total number of layers, t denotes time and d denotes a yearly time difference. $\tilde{n}^{\ell}_{Lit}$ represents normalized hours, and $\widetilde{VA}_{it}$ is the value added of a firm that stays at L layers for two consecutive years; we have removed from both variables the economy-wide trend. The only difference is that now we use only firms that either start to export or stop exporting in the year in which we measure the change in normalized hours. The results for β^{ℓ}_{L} are presented in Table 9.7. Many of these estimates are not significant. The ones that are, are positive as predicted by the theory. As we showed using Table 9.5, the firms that do not add layers expand very little, so it is hard to estimate β^{ℓ}_{L} precisely enough to have significant results.

Table 9.7 Elasticity of hours with $\widetilde{VA}_{it}$ for firms that change export status and do not change layers

# of layers	Layer	β^{ℓ}_{L}	s.e.	p-value	Obs
1	0	0.027	0.04	0.45	5,178
2	0	0.026	0.03	0.33	9,434
2	1	−0.010	0.03	0.73	9,434
3	0	0.117	0.04	0.01	4,789
3	1	0.103	0.05	0.03	4,789
3	2	0.066	0.05	0.17	4,789

Table 9.8 Elasticity of wages with $\widetilde{VA}_{it}$ for firms that change export status and do not change layers

# of layers	Layer	γ_L^ℓ	s.e.	p-value	Obs
0	0	0.065	0.02	0.00	2,064
1	0	0.072	0.02	0.00	5,178
1	1	0.087	0.02	0.00	5,178
2	0	0.122	0.02	0.00	9,434
2	1	0.143	0.02	0.00	9,434
2	2	0.152	0.02	0.00	9,434
3	0	0.194	0.03	0.00	4,789
3	1	0.202	0.03	0.00	4,789
3	2	0.204	0.03	0.00	4,789
3	3	0.260	0.04	0.00	4,789

We estimate a parallel equation for wages, for the sample of firms that change export status:

$$d \ln \tilde{w}_{Lit}^\ell = \gamma_L^\ell d \ln \widetilde{VA}_{it} + \varepsilon_{it} \tag{9}$$

where $\tilde{w}_{Lit}^\ell$ is the detrended change in layer-level wages. Results are presented in Table 9.8. Now the estimates are much more significant and robust. All the values of γ_L^ℓ are positive and significant and they tend to increase with ℓ given L. The ranking of the elasticities is not always significant, but it is in most cases, and when it is, it corresponds to the one predicted by the theory. Namely, the wage of the higher-level managers expands proportionally more than that of the lower-level ones. Hence, Implication 2b is also corroborated by the evidence.

The final prediction of the theory to contrast with our data is Implication 2c, which states that new exporters that add layers decrease w_L^ℓ and increase n_L^ℓ at all ℓ. We have already argued in the previous section that firms that add layers decrease wages and increase hours at all layers, and Table 9.4 shows that new exporters tend to add layers. So it is natural to expect that in fact the predictions of the theory will be corroborated by the data.

Table 9.9 presents the average log change in the number of hours for all transitions and all layers. The table uses the sample of firms that enter the export market and add layers and firms that exit the export market and drop layers. The results establish that, for all transitions and layers, firms that add layers increase the number of hours, while firms that drop layers decrease them.

The next step is to look at wages. Again, we study the change in average log wages for all transitions and layers for the sample of new exporters that add layers and firms that exit the export market and drop layers. The results are displayed in Table 9.10. The prediction in Implication 2c is broadly corroborated by the data (although the change in log wages for the case in which we do not have many observations is not significant). New exporters that add layers decrease wages and the firms that exit the export market and drop layers increase wages.[9] As

Table 9.9 Change in normalized hours for firms that transition and change export status

# of layers		Layer	Change	s.e.	p-value	Obs
Before	After					
0	1	0	1.476	0.10	0.00	347
0	2	0	1.786	0.24	0.00	62
0	3	0	2.815	0.31	0.00	9
1	0	0	−1.614	0.08	0.00	434
1	2	0	0.748	0.05	0.00	843
1	2	1	0.612	0.05	0.00	843
1	3	0	1.045	0.18	0.00	62
1	3	1	0.965	0.18	0.00	62
2	0	0	−1.952	0.22	0.00	85
2	1	0	−0.734	0.05	0.00	949
2	1	1	−0.558	0.05	0.00	949
2	3	0	1.073	0.06	0.00	676
2	3	1	1.008	0.06	0.00	676
2	3	2	0.822	0.07	0.00	676
3	0	0	−2.713	0.46	0.00	8
3	1	0	−1.125	0.15	0.00	94
3	1	1	−0.911	0.16	0.00	94
3	2	0	−1.248	0.05	0.00	860
3	2	1	−1.170	0.06	0.00	860
3	2	2	−1.042	0.06	0.00	860

Table 9.10 Change in wages for firms that transition and change export status

# of layers		Layer	Change	s.e.	p-value	Obs
Before	After					
0	1	0	−0.156	0.02	0.00	347
0	2	0	−0.697	0.14	0.00	62
0	3	0	−0.906	0.48	0.10	9
1	0	0	0.221	0.03	0.00	434
1	2	0	−0.082	0.01	0.00	843
1	2	1	−0.307	0.02	0.00	843
1	3	0	−0.215	0.09	0.01	62
1	3	1	−0.434	0.09	0.00	62
2	0	0	0.439	0.09	0.00	85
2	1	0	0.053	0.01	0.00	949
2	1	1	0.237	0.02	0.00	949
2	3	0	−0.039	0.01	0.67	676
2	3	1	−0.082	0.02	0.00	676
2	3	2	−0.217	0.02	0.00	676
3	0	0	1.053	0.60	0.12	8
3	1	0	0.175	0.07	0.01	94
3	1	1	0.430	0.07	0.00	94
3	2	0	0.043	0.01	0.00	860
3	2	1	0.061	0.01	0.00	860

Table 9.11 Decomposition of total log change in average wages

From/to	$\bar\omega_{L'it}^{\ell \leq L}/\bar\omega_{Lit}$			From/to	$\bar\omega_{L'it}^{L'}/\bar\omega_{Lit}$		
	1	*2*	*3*		*1*	*2*	*3*
0	0.935** (346)	0.734** (61)	0.706** (9)	0	1.454** (346)	1.331** (62)	1.666* (9)
1		0.912** (842)	0.838** (60)	1		1.902** (841)	2.015** (62)
2			0.975** (675)	2			7.336* (675)
From/to	*s*			From/to	$d \ln \bar\omega_{Lit}$		
	1	*2*	*3*		*1*	*2*	*3*
0	0.732** (346)	0.618** (62)	0.581** (9)	0	−0.014 (346)	−0.454** (61)	−0.184 (8)
1		0.856** (843)	0.775** (62)	1		−0.036** (843)	−0.070 (61)
2			0.946** (676)	2			−0.023 (675)

All results from trimmed sample at 0.05%.
* significant at 5%
** significant at 1%
Number of obs. in parenthesis.

we show in Table 9.4, new exporters tend to add more layers than non-exporters. Similarly, firms that exit the export market tend to drop more layers than exporters.

So, exporters tend to reduce wages as a result of adding layers. To consider an example, a new exporter that had one layer of management and added another as a result of its decision to start exporting *reduces* the wages of its workers in layer zero by 8.2 per cent, and the wage of managers in layer one *declines* by 30 per cent. In contrast, as Table 9.11 (discussed below) shows, the newly hired second layer manager earns 90.2 per cent more than the average wage in the firm before the change.

The result should change our view on the distribution of the gains from exporting. The view that new exporters pay higher wages is misleading. Most new exporters expand little and do not change their organization. They hire more hours and pay higher wages. The new exporters that expand substantially add layers of management. They hire substantially more workers but pay these workers less (since according to the theory they also know less). The new exporters that expand and add layers exhibit more dispersion in wages within the firm.

Table 9.11 separates the change in wages in the firm in the contribution to the average of the new top manager and the change in the wage of the pre-existing layers. The top left panel shows that the average wage of all existing layers decreases as firms add layers (and we know from Table 9.10 that it decreased for each layer individually). The top right panel shows the wage of the new top manager relative to the mean wage of the firm before the change. Clearly, wage dispersion in the firm increases substantially when it starts to export and adds layers.

We end this section with a graphical representation of the change in firms as they become exporters. Figures 9.3 to 9.5 show how the typical organization of firms change when they enter or exit the export market: in each figure, the first row in each graph represents the old and new organization when the firm adds layers and starts to export, while the second row represents a current exporter which leaves the export market.[10] Perhaps the most striking observation coming out of Figures 9.3 to 9.5 is how large the changes are as firms actively manage their organization. This is in stark contrast to the very small changes for those firms not reorganizing, as reported in Tables 9.7 and 9.8. Hopefully, these figures are convincing in showing that new exporters expand by adding layers, adding employment and reducing wages. The reduction in wages challenges, as far as we know, all theories of trade that do not add explicit organizational choices.

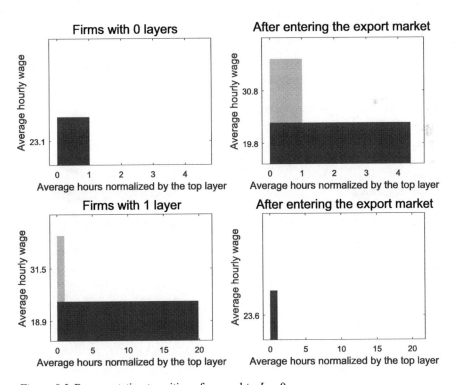

Figure 9.3 Representative transitions from and to $L = 0$

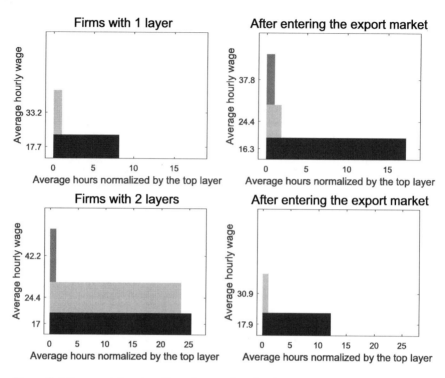

Figure 9.4 Representative transitions from and to $L = 1$

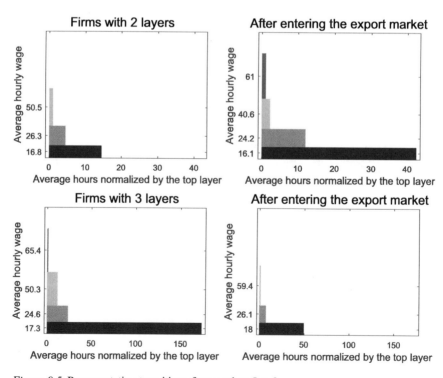

Figure 9.5 Representative transitions from and to $L = 2$

4. How do firms change the average wage in a layer?

Table 9.12 shows that for firms that change their export status (either entering or leaving the export market without adding layers), the only significant adjustments occur via changes in formal education, and especially at lower layers.

Table 9.13 shows that when a change in the export status is accompanied by a reorganization, firms tend to mostly act upon experience, while formal education

Table 9.12 Elasticity of knowledge with value added for firms that start or stop exporting and do not change *L*

# of layers	Layer	Experience	p-value	Education	p-value	Obs
0	0	0.003	0.745	0.006	0.023	2,062
1	0	−0.029	0.013	0.006	0.007	5,172
1	1	−0.006	0.628	0.007	0.002	5,172
2	0	−0.008	0.356	0.004	0.007	9,422
2	1	0.008	0.537	0.004	0.015	9,422
2	2	0.017	0.073	0.000	0.892	9,422
3	0	−0.008	0.437	0.003	0.170	4,783
3	1	0.008	0.602	0.000	0.884	4,783
3	2	0.002	0.871	−0.001	0.773	4,783
3	3	0.008	0.556	−0.002	0.678	4,783

Table 9.13 Elasticity of knowledge with value added for firms that start exporting and increase *L*, or stop exporting and decrease *L*

# of layers		Layer	Experience	p-value	Education	p-value	Obs
Before	After						
0	1	0	−0.161	0.000	0.004	0.413	346
0	2	0	−0.148	0.055	−0.014	0.174	62
0	3	0	−0.324	0.081	0.054	0.132	9
1	0	0	0.061	0.004	0.006	0.132	433
1	2	0	−0.030	0.017	0.000	0.817	841
1	2	1	−0.190	0.000	0.001	0.861	841
1	3	0	−0.049	0.250	0.006	0.652	62
1	3	1	−0.208	0.010	0.000	0.990	62
2	0	0	0.044	0.513	0.004	0.667	85
2	1	0	0.036	0.002	0.003	0.103	945
2	1	1	0.170	0.000	−0.007	0.039	945
2	3	0	−0.007	0.510	0.002	0.166	675
2	3	1	−0.036	0.020	0.001	0.739	675
2	3	2	−0.206	0.000	0.026	0.000	675
3	0	0	0.158	0.244	0.032	0.227	8
3	1	0	0.091	0.052	−0.004	0.591	94
3	1	1	0.189	0.007	−0.016	0.163	94
3	2	0	0.028	0.002	−0.001	0.391	860
3	2	1	0.013	0.284	0.002	0.356	860
3	2	2	0.111	0.000	−0.018	0.000	860

is almost never significant. These patterns are consistent (although somewhat more noisy) with our findings for the general population of firms.

5.   Exogenous export demand shocks and reorganization

In this section, we explore a more causal relation between reorganization and layer-level outcomes. In particular, we exploit variation in firm-level exports induced exogenously by country variations in real exchange rate as a "foreign demand shock". In the theory, firms close to the reorganization threshold should add a layer following a demand shock large enough; such reorganization will trigger changes in layer-level outcomes.

To compute plausibly exogenous firm-level demand shocks, we exploit pre-sample variation in the destination composition of exports, in conjunction with real exchange rate variation across countries. For each firm, we observe the shares of exports to all its destinations in 2002, s_{id}; we then build the following measures of exposure for firm i at time t:

$$W_{it}^{(k)} = \sum_d s_{id} w_{dt}^{(k)} \tag{10}$$

where $w_{it}^{(k)}$ is either the bilateral real exchange rate[11] between France and destination d in year t (denoted with $k = 1$), or the yearly change in the same bilateral real exchange rate between t and $t + 1$ (denoted with $k = 2$).

We start by estimating[12] the following model that relates export shocks to the probability of changing layers:

$$
\begin{cases}
d\log X_{Lit} = c_L^0 + \omega_L' W_{Lit} + v_L' V_{Lit} + \varepsilon_{Lit}^0 & (11.1) \\
\Pr\{dLayers_{Lit} = N\} = \{\alpha_{L,N-1} \le c_L^1 + \xi_L \cdot d\log X_{Lit} + \\
\qquad\qquad +\eta_L' V_{Lit} + \varepsilon_{Lit}^1 \le \alpha_{L,N}\} & (11.2)
\end{cases}
\tag{11}
$$

In this notation, i denotes a firm, t denotes time, and L denotes the number of layers firm i has at the beginning of time t.[13] c^j and ε_{Lit}^j for $j = 0, 1$ are constants and stochastic i.i.d. error terms, respectively.

The first equation is a linear regression; it describes the change over time in log exports as a function of exposure to real exchange rate variations $W_{Lit} = \{W_{Lit}^{(1)}, W_{Lit}^{(2)}\}$, and a vector V_{Lit} of controls: year dummies and log value added of firm i with L layers at the beginning of the year (to proxy for how close the firm is to the threshold).

The second equation is an ordered probit: it models the probability of any change in the number of layers as a function of the firm change in exports and the same set of controls (the parameters $\alpha_{L,N}$ are the standard thresholds for the latent variable).

We focus on the set of firms who export throughout the sample period. We estimate this model separately for all firms with initial number of layers L.

Table 9.14 Impact of change in export on $dLayers_{Lit}$

# of layers	ξ_L	s.e.	p-value	Obs	$Pr\left\{\begin{array}{l}dLayers_{Lit} = +1 \\ L, VA_{Lit} = p_{90}\,(L)\end{array}\right\}$
0	1.138	0.04	0.00	1,557	0.057
1	0.649	0.27	0.02	7,337	0.337
2	1.063	0.20	0.00	29,965	0.414
3	−0.193	0.36	0.59	28,816	–

Table 9.14 reports estimates for the coefficient ξ_L in equation (11.1).[14] Increases in exports induced by variations in the real exchange rate significantly affect the probability of reorganizing the firm. The last column in the table shows the probability of adding one layer for firms at the 90th percentile of value added implied by these coefficients, following a 10 per cent increase in export demand: for example, exporters with 1 layer at the 90th percentile of size within the group have a 33.7 per cent chance of reorganizing if they are hit by an exogenous 10 per cent increase in export demand.

To study how these demand shocks affect firm-level outcomes, we extend (11) and estimate the four-equations model:

$$
\left\{
\begin{aligned}
d\log X_{Lit} &= c_L^{\ell,0} + \omega_L^{\ell\prime} W_{Lit} + v_L^{\ell\prime} V_{Lit} + \varepsilon_{Lit}^{\ell,0} & (12.1) \\
\Pr\{dLayers_{Lit} = N\} &= \Pr\{\alpha_{L,N-1}^\ell \le c_L^{\ell,1} + \xi_L^\ell \cdot d\log X_{Lit} + \\
&\quad + \eta_L^{\ell\prime} V_{Lit} + \varepsilon_{Lit}^{\ell,1} \le \alpha_{L,N}^\ell\} & (12.2) \\
d\ln n_{Lit}^\ell &= c_L^{\ell,2} + \beta_{,L}^\ell \cdot dLayers_{Lit} + \varepsilon_{Lit}^{\ell,2} & (12.3) \\
d\ln w_{Lit}^\ell &= c_L^{\ell,3} + \gamma_L^\ell \cdot dLayers_{Lit} + \varepsilon_{Lit}^{\ell,3} & (12.4)
\end{aligned}
\right. \quad (12)
$$

As above, i denotes a firm, t denotes time, and L denotes the number of layers firm i has at the beginning of time t; in addition, ℓ denotes the layer-ℓ outcome. $c^{\ell,j}$ and $\varepsilon_{Lit}^{\ell,j}$ for $j = 0, \ldots, 3$ are constants and stochastic i.i.d. error terms, respectively.

Equations (12.1) and (12.2) are similar to (11.1) and (11.2) respectively, except that the coefficients are layer ℓ-specific. We estimate this model separately for each initial number of layers L and layer-level outcome ℓ: the estimation sample includes all firms that start with L layers and have at least ℓ layers the following period. For example, one model would only look at all firms with $L = 2$ layers initially, and study change in hours and wages at layer $\ell = 1$, using all the firms that have at least 1 layer the next period.

The third and fourth equations in model (12) are linear regressions that relate the change in normalized hours and wages, respectively, at a given layer ℓ for a firm with L layers initially, as a function of the change in layers.

Table 9.15 Impact of change in layers on layer-level outcomes

# of layers	Layer	β_L^ℓ	p-value	γ_L^ℓ	p-value	Obs
0	0	1.257	0.00	−0.362	0.00	1,557
1	0	1.037	0.00	−0.132	0.00	7,337
1	1	0.744	0.00	−0.312	0.00	6,854
2	0	1.851	0.00	−0.091	0.00	29,965
2	1	1.970	0.00	−0.179	0.00	29,965
2	2	1.929	0.00	−0.208	0.00	27,886
3	0	1.262	0.00	−0.066	0.00	28,816
3	1	1.299	0.00	−0.092	0.00	28,816
3	2	1.478	0.00	−0.144	0.00	28,816

Table 9.15 shows the estimates of the coefficients β_L^ℓ and γ_L^ℓ.[15] The coefficients can be read as the impact of adding 1 layer to the firm on the correspondent layer-ℓ outcome: for example, adding one layer in firms with $L = 1$ layers implies a decrease in average wages of $100(1 - \exp\{0.132\})\% = -14.1\%$ in wages, but an increase of $100\exp\{1.037\}\% = 282\%$ in the normalized number of hours in layer 0.

Overall, these results emphasize that firms react to shocks to their ability to trade by reorganizing in exactly the way we would expect from the logic in the theory. These reactions change their performance and in equilibrium have further repercussions both on trade and on other economic outcomes as emphasized by CRH. Other papers have also explored some of these responses empirically in other countries and context. In the next section we describe these contributions.

6. Organizational change and trade in other economic contexts

The starting point of this empirical agenda on organizations is that using changes in occupational categories to identify organizational structure and reorganizations is economically meaningful in that it is related to a variety of other firm characteristics like size, wages, employment, productivity, among others. CMRH presented the evidence for the case of France, and since then several studies document that mapping layers of management to occupations is meaningful across countries with very different labor market regulations and/or at very different stages of development. Moreover, some of these empirical studies find that reorganization not only has effects on firm level outcomes, but also aggregate implications for the economy.

A few studies have verified and reproduced the results in CMRH for different time periods and countries. For example, recent work by Bernini, Guillou and Treibich (2016) use French match-employer employee data as in CMRH. They validate all of CMRH's results for a more recent period, the years 2009 to 2013. Also for France, Spanos (2016b) also shows that higher ability workers are employed in the higher layers of firms, and presents evidence of positive assortative matching between workers in the different layers. Tåg (2013) uses the Swedish Standard Classification of Occupations 1996 (SSYK) which is a national version of the International Standard Classification of Occupations (ISCO-88 (COM)). He finds that the empirical patterns in Sweden match the theoretical predictions of CRH (2012). In particular, he finds that firms in Sweden are hierarchal, i.e. higher layers have less workers and a higher mean wage than lower layers. Reorganizing by adding layers is accompanied with an increase in firm size and decrease in firm wages at pre-existing layers, while the reverse holds for firms that reduce their layers.

In developing countries, Cruz, Bussolo and Iacovone (2016) study the Brazilian economy using the Classificao Brasileira de Ocupacao (CBO). Using this classification, they first document that firms are hierarchical in terms of hours and wages. Then, they find that in re-organized firms inequality of wages increases, as firms pay higher wages in added higher layers than in pre-existing ones. Also, and importantly for the main implications of the evidence in this chapter, they document how the change in firms' organization is positively correlated with export performance. So the results we find in France are very much consistent with their results for Brazil.

In order to try to be more detailed on the identification of the effect of exporting on organizational change, Friedrich (2016) uses confidential data collected by Statistics Denmark to study the internal organization of Danish firms. He finds evidence for how trade affects wage inequality, focusing on changes in firm hierarchies. Its main contribution is that the paper identifies a causal effect of trade shocks on firm hierarchies and wage inequality. Namely, Friedrich (2016) shows that trade shocks do generate changes in the way firms organize production and as a result the way in which wage inequality changes inside the firm. To do so, the paper uses two different identification strategies, one based on foreign demand and transportation costs, and the other using the Muslim boycott of Danish exports after the cartoon crisis. Both of these identification strategies result in robust effects of trade shocks on within-firm inequality through changes in the number of management layers. The evidence from the paper is consistent with models of knowledge-based hierarchies. He finds that adding a hierarchy layer significantly increases inequality within firms, ranging from 2 per cent for the 50–10 wage gap to 4.7 per cent for the 90–50 wage gap. These results reinforce our finding that reorganization can be an important channel by which trade affects wage inequality.

In this chapter our focus has been mostly in the reorganization associated with entry/exit behavior in foreign markets and the effects on layer-level changes in wages, span of control and knowledge composition. We have not explored the reverse channel by which organization affects trade, which is of course present in the general equilibrium theory of CRH. Spanos (2016c) complements our findings for France by looking at the effect of organization on export performance. He uses a similar dataset as our study and shows evidence that firms with more layers sell a larger number of products, and to more destinations, compared to the ones with fewer layers. He identifies these export margins as the ones more correlated to productivity and number of layers. In fact, these results complement nicely with the study on Portugal by Mion, Opromolla and Sforza (2016), who find that export experience acquired by managers in past organizations can result in more exports in their current firm. Put together, these results underscore that the channel from organization to export performance is also important and active in the data on top of the effect of exporting on organization that we have documented. Also using Portuguese data, Bastos, Monteiro and Straume (2018) find that foreign acquisitions lead to firm reorganization and an increase in within-firm wage inequality.

6.1. Other outcomes

The studies above look at the two-way link between organization and some firm level outcomes, including their participation in export markets. We have argued that this is important because the way firms organize determines their productivity and costs. Several papers have studied the link between organizational change and productivity. For example, Caliendo, Mion, Opromolla and Rossi-Hansberg (2015) show that the reorganization of firms is an important source of the aggregate productivity gains in the Portuguese economy. They first document that the empirical patterns in the Portuguese economy match the theoretical predictions of CRH. They then study empirically the prediction of the CRH model, that reorganization reduces the marginal cost of the firm, and therefore prices, while increasing the physical productivity of the firm by reducing average variable cost. As a result, revenue based productivity should fall, while quantity based productivity should increase, as firms add layers. The results are stark. The study does not find any case in which the evidence can falsify this prediction on how a reorganization affects both types of firm productivity. Moreover, the paper presents some evidence of a causal effect of changes in layers on productivity, using firm specific exchange rates based on a firm's import and export patterns. In sum, changes in organization affect significantly the physical productivity of the firm. For France, Spanos (2016a) finds that firms in larger markets have more layers and are more productive. Furthermore, Spanos (2016a) finds that between 8 per cent and 40 per cent of the productivity differences across locations within France can be explained by firms having a greater number of layers and more complex organizations. This provides a relevant rationale for why we care about the results on export opportunities and organization that we have documented in this chapter.

Finally, more recent research has also shown that using organizations can help to shed light on business creation. In particular, using a sample of 16 million observations of Swedish workers and occupational categories, Tåg, Åstebro and Thompson (2016) provide evidence that the hierarchical structure of a firm matters for the likelihood of business creation among its former employees. The results are striking; employees at the highest layers, namely CEOs, directors, and senior staff, are three to four times more likely than production workers to found a limited liability company. Unfortunately, given data limitations, the results cannot be interpreted as causal.

7. Conclusion

A firm's sales in foreign markets are correlated with a variety of firm level outcomes. Some of them are well known. For example, we know that trade makes firms more productive and larger in terms of total sales and employment. In this chapter we show that exporting is also associated with firm reorganizations. Firms that start to trade are more likely to add management layers. In fact, among all the firms that start to trade, the ones that grow significantly are the ones that reorganize. These firms also exhibit particular patterns for wages and employment in preexisting layers. In particular, the firms that reorganize when they start exporting pay workers in preexisting layers less, and workers in the top new layer much more. So, wage inequality within those firms increases. In contrast, firms that start to export but do not reorganize increase wages modestly at all layers.

Our first set of results only describes an equilibrium relationship between exporting and organization, not a causal effect. As such, these results are helpful to discriminate between theories, but not to understand the impact of, say, a trade liberalization on organization. So, we attempt to go further and estimate causal effects using a Bartik-style shock. The results are encouraging in that the causal effects are in general, significant and large. Still, more work needs to be done in identifying instruments that produce a more systematic first stage. Other studies have tried a variety of other instruments in other countries and yield results that are surprisingly consistent with ours.

All together, the evidence that we have presented, as well as the evidence in the existing literature, is starting to paint a consistent picture in which part of the effect of access to foreign markets is realized through the reorganization of production. Furthermore, as we argued in the last section, a variety of studies have linked these reorganizations to changes in productivity.

Firms are complex organizations that react to changes in their environment. Only if we understand how globalization affects the internal structure of firms are we ever going to understand its full and true impact. We hope this research is starting to illuminate some of the contents of one of the more resilient black boxes in economics.

Notes

Acknowledgement: We thank Francis Kramarz for helpful comments and suggestions. The computations in this chapter were done at a secure data center located at CREST, Paris.

1 As initially proposed by Rosen (1982) and Garicano (2000) and used in the context of heterogeneous firms in Caliendo and Rossi-Hansberg (2012).
2 Adding a layer is identified empirically as hiring an agent in an occupation classified in a layer where the firm did not hire before.
3 We refer the reader to CMRH for a detailed description of this data.
4 Felbermayr, Prat and Schmerer (2008), Egger and Kreickemeier (2009), Helpman, Itskhoki and Redding (2010) and Eaton, Kortum, Kramarz and Sampognaro (2011a) propose models where the exporter-wage premium is the outcome of a bargaining mechanism.

5 In CRH the wage is interpreted as the compensation for the time endomont of the workers, $\bar{w}$, plus the compensating differential for the cost of acquiring knowledge. Learning how to solve problems in an interval of knowledge of length z costs $\bar{w}cz$ (c teachers per unit of knowledge at cost $\bar{w}$ per teacher). Hence, the total wage of an employee with knowledge z is given by $w(z) = \bar{w}[cz + 1]$.

6 To derive some of the implications of the theory, CRH specify the distribution of problems as an exponential, so $F(z) = 1 - e^{-\lambda z}$.

7 This implies that even when $f_{ij} > f_{ii}$ all firms in the economy could enter the exporting market. Of course, if f_{ij} is large enough, then only the most productive firms will export. This is a key distinction with Melitz (2003) where, for the case of two symmetric countries, all firms will export if and only if $f_{ij} \leq f_{ii}$.

8 Part of our data is used in Eaton, Kortum and Kramarz (2011b) to study the exporting behavior of firms. As a result, some of these facts for France are known from their paper. However, they have no results on layers or firm reorganization conditional on changing or keeping constant the number of layers.

9 In CMRH, we show that the adjustment occurs mostly at the extensive margin: in an expanding firm, new hours hired in a layer receive a lower average wage than pre-existing hours active in the same layer; this action lowers the average wage in the layer.

10 To estimate the representative hierarchies before a transition, we compute the average number of normalized hours and wage only in the subset of firms with L layers that will enter the export market and have $L + 1$ layers the following period. To estimate the representative hierarchy after the transition, we use the estimated log changes for firms entering the export market from Tables 9.9 and 9.10. For transitions one layer up, the change in the hourly wage for the top layer after the transition is estimated as the average log change in the wage of the top layer ($\ln w_{L+1,t+1}^{L+1} - \ln w_{L,t}^{L}$).

11 We have defined the real exchange as $E_{eur}P_{for}/P_{france}$, where P_{for} is the CPI in the foreign country, P_{france} is the CPI in France, and E_{eur} is the price of a unit of foreign currency in terms of Euros. Hence, an increase in the real exchange rate corresponds to a depreciation, and should hence induce an increase in exports.

12 We use routines developed by Roodman (2011).

13 In the notation, the number of layers L is superfluous since it is uniquely identified by a firm and a time, i.e., $L = L(i, t)$. We keep L explicit however since we will be performing separate estimates according to L.

14 Table 9.A1 in the appendix reports the main coefficients in the second equation. While the contribution of individual regressors is noisily estimated, the joint model (11) is highly significant.

15 Note in this table that when estimating outcomes in the top layers, observations drop somewhat. This happens because outcomes in the top layer are not observed when the firm drops it. This is also why layer-3 outcomes in firms with 3 layers cannot be estimated: the sample only includes firms with which do not change layers ($dLayers_{Lit} = 0$), so that there is no variation on the RHS; morevoer, the left-hand side $d \ln \tilde{n}_{3it}^3$ also has no variation since normalized hours at the top are always 1.

Table 9.A2 in the appendix reports the main coefficients in the first two equations. As above, the contribution of individual regressors is noisily estimated, but the joint model (12) is highly significant.

References

Bastos, P., N. P. Monteiro, and O. R. Straume (2018), "Foreign Acquisitions and Internal Organization," *Journal of International Economics*, 114, 143–163.

Bernard, A. B. and J. B. Jensen (1995), "Exporters, Jobs, and Wages in U.S. Manufacturing: 1976–1987," Brookings Papers in Economic Activity: Microeconomics, 67–112.

Bernard, A. B. and J. B. Jensen (1997), "Exporters, Skill Upgrading and the Wage Gap," *Journal of International Economics*, 42, 3–31.

Bernard, A. B. and J. B. Jensen (1999), "Exceptional Exporter Performance: Cause, Effect, or Both?" *Journal of International Economics*, 47:1, 1–25.

Bernard, A. B., J. B. Jensen, S. Redding, and P. Schott (2007), "Firms in International Trade," *Journal of Economic Perspectives*, 21:3, 105–130.

Bernini, M., S. Guillou, and T. Treibich (2016), "Firm Export Diversification and Labor Organization," Working Paper.

Bertrand, M. (2004), "From the Invisible Handshake to the Invisible Hand? How Import Competition Changes the Employment Relationship," *Journal of Labor Economics*, 22:4, 723–765.

Brambilla, I., D. Lederman, and G. Porto (2012), "Exports, Export Destinations and Skills," *American Economic Review*, 102:7, 3406–3438.

Caliendo, L., G. Mion, L. Opromolla, and E. Rossi-Hansberg (2015), "Productivity and Organisation in Portuguese Firms," CEPR Discussion Papers 10993.

Caliendo, L., F. Monte, and E. Rossi-Hansberg (2015), "The Anatomy of French Production Hierarchies," *Journal of Political Economy*, 123:4, 809–852.

Caliendo, L. and E. Rossi-Hansberg (2012), "The Impact of Trade on Organization and Productivity," *Quarterly Journal of Economics*, 127:3, 1393–1467.

Cruz, M., M. Bussolo, and L. Iacovone (2016), "Organizing Knowledge to Compete: Impacts of Capacity Building Programs on Firm Organization," Policy Research Working Paper Series 7640, The World Bank.

Eaton, J., S. Kortum, F. Kramarz, and R. Sampognaro (2011a), "Dissecting the French Export Wage Premium," Working Paper.

Eaton, J., S. Kortum, and F. Kramarz (2011b), "An Anatomy of International Trade: Evidence From French Firms," *Econometrica*, 79:5, 1453–1498.

Egger, H., and U. Kreickemeier (2009), "Firm Heterogeneity and the Labor Market Effects of Trade Liberalisation," *International Economic Review*, 50, 187–216.

Felbermayr, G., J. Prat, and H. Schmerer (2008), "Globalization and Labor Market Outcomes: Bargaining, Search Frictions, and Firm Heterogeneity," IZA Discussion Paper No. 3363.

Friedrich, B. U. (2016), "Trade Shocks, Firm Hierarchies and Wage Inequality," Northwestern University, mimeo.

Garicano, L. (2000), "Hierarchies and the Organization of Knowledge in Production," *Journal of Political Economy*, 108:5, 874–904.

Helpman, E., O. Itskhoki, and S. Redding (2010), "Inequality and Unemployment in a Global Economy," *Econometrica*, 78, 1239–1283.

Melitz, M. J. (2003), "The Impact of Trade on Intra-Industry Reallocations and Aggregate Industry Productivity," *Econometrica*, 71:6, 1695–1725.

Mion, G., L. D. Opromolla, and A. Sforza (2016), "The Diffusion of Knowledge via Managers' Mobility," CESifo Working Paper 6256.

Revenga, A. L. (1992), "Exporting Jobs?: The Impact of Import Competition on Employment and Wages in US Manufacturing," *The Quarterly Journal of Economics*, 107:1, 255–284.

Roodman, D. (2011), "Estimating Fully Observed Recursive Mixed-process Models With cmp," *Stata Journal*, 11:2, 159–206.

Rosen, S. (1982), "Authority, Control, and the Distribution of Earnings," *The Bell Journal of Economics*, 13, 311–323.

Spanos, G. (2016a), "The Impact of Market Size on Firm Organization and Productivity," Working Paper.

Spanos, G. (2016b), "Sorting Within and Across French Production Hierarchies," Working Paper.

Spanos, G. (2016c), "Organization and Export Performance," *Economic Letters*, 146, 130–134.

Tåg, J. (2013), "Production Hierarchies in Sweden," *Economics Letters*, 121:2, 210–213.

Tåg, J., T. Åstebro, and P. Thompson (2016), "Hierarchies and Entrepreneurship," *European Economic Review*, 89, 129–147.

Verhoogen, E. A. (2008), "Trade, Quality Upgrading, and Wage Inequality in the Mexican Manufacturing Sector," *Quarterly Journal of Economics*, 123:2, 489–530.

Appendix

Supporting tables

Table 9.A1 shows the relevant coeffcients for equation (11.1) in model (11). Each row corresponds to a separate model estimate. $W_L^{(1)}$ and $W_L^{(2)}$ are measures of exogenous demand shocks as reported in the main text, and "p.v." are the associated p-values. Controls include year dummies and firm log value added at the beginning of the period. "model sig. p-value" reports the p-value for a test of the joint significance of model (11).

Table 9.A2 shows the relevant coefficients for equations (12.1), marked "Dep. var.:$d\log X_{Lit}$", and (12.2), marked "Dep. var.: $dLayers_{Lit}$", in model (12). As above, each row corresponds to a separate model estimate. $W_L^{(1)}$ and $W_L^{(2)}$ are

Table 9.A1 Export regression in model 11

# of layers	$W_L^{(1)}$	p.v.	$W_L^{(2)}$	p.v.	Controls	Model Sig. p-value	Obs
0	0.006	0.65	0.113	0.61	Yes	0.00	1,557
1	−0.099	0.01	−0.035	0.80	Yes	0.00	7,337
2	−0.033	0.20	0.021	0.68	Yes	0.00	29,965
3	−0.080	0.00	0.098	0.02	Yes	0.00	28,816

Table 9.A2 Export regression and ordered probit for model 12

# of layers	Layer	Dep. var.:d log X_{Lit}					Dep. var.: $dLayers_{Lit}$			Model sig. p-value	Obs
		$W_L^{(1)}$	p.v.	$W_L^{(2)}$	p.v.	Controls	ξ_L^ℓ	p.v.	Controls		
0	0	0.007	0.71	0.104	0.74	Yes	1.138	0.00	Yes	0.00	1,557
1	0	−0.099	0.01	−0.040	0.78	Yes	0.638	0.02	Yes	0.00	7,337
1	1	−0.100	0.01	−0.034	0.85	Yes	0.477	0.28	Yes	0.00	6,854
2	0	−0.032	0.21	−0.017	0.68	Yes	1.091	0.00	Yes	0.00	29,965
2	1	−0.033	0.21	0.014	0.73	Yes	1.082	0.00	Yes	0.00	29,965
2	2	−0.024	0.46	−0.011	0.63	Yes	1.144	0.00	Yes	0.00	27,886
3	0	−0.081	0.00	0.098	0.02	Yes	−0.058	0.87	Yes	0.00	28,816
3	1	−0.079	0.00	0.098	0.02	Yes	−0.034	0.93	Yes	0.00	28,816
3	2	−0.078	0.02	0.096	0.02	Yes	−0.084	0.83	Yes	0.00	28,816

measures of exogenous demand shocks as reported in the main text, and "p.v." are the associated p-values, in equation (12.1). ξ_L^ℓ is the coefficient multiplying the log change in export, and "p.v" the associated p-value, in equation (12.2) Controls include year dummies and firm log value added at the beginning of the period. "model sig. p-value" reports the p-value for a test of the joint significance of model (12).

10 Firm-to-firm connections in Colombian imports

Andrew Bernard, Esther Bøler and
Swati Dhingra

1. Introduction

Aggregate trade flows are composed of transactions between individual buying (importers) and selling (exporters) firms. The rise of the large literature on heterogeneous firms has recognized the importance of variation across exporters, and to a lesser extent across importers, in determining aggregate trade flows. However, even in that firm-focused research, the detailed trade transaction data are usually aggregated to the level of individual firms, summed across all buyers for exporters, or conversely, summed across all sellers for importers, before being used by researchers. Naturally, both empirical and theoretical work on international trade has also focused on firms on either side of the market, exporters in Melitz (2003) or importers in Antràs et al. (2017). In this chapter, we explore the individual matches between exporters and importers and examine the evolution of these microeconomic relationships.

During the decades since the end of WWII, the world has seen both immense progress on the reductions of tariffs and other barriers to international trade in goods as well as dramatic reductions in transport and communication costs. The rise of containerization, the successful multilateral rounds of the GATT and the WTO and the exponential increase in telecommunications capabilities have combined to allow the fragmentation of production across borders and have driven increases in the volume of global trade far faster than those for GDP (see Baldwin (2017)). However, in spite of these advances, estimates of trade costs between distant locations remained largely unchanged (Head and Mayer (2014)), suggesting that other forms of trade costs continue to be substantial impediments to global integration. This chapter explores the role of firm-to-firm connections in international trade both in the cross-section and over time as a first step towards a greater understanding of the firm-level costs of trade.

We have access to a rich data set for Colombian firms where the identities of both the exporter and the importer are known, and where each import transaction can be linked to a specific seller in a source country, and each Colombian firm's annual export transactions can be linked to specific buyers in every destination country. This allows us to develop a set of basic facts about sellers and buyers across markets at a point in time as well as the evolution of those buyer–seller relationships over time. We contribute to this nascent literature by confirming and extending previous findings on the importance of the extensive and intensive margins of trade.

The emergence of research examining firms on both sides of trade transactions has potentially important implications for policy and academic work on the origins of international trade. While substantial progress has been made on reducing tariffs on manufactured goods, especially for flows between higher income nations, empirical evidence suggests that substantial costs remain. Estimates of fixed and variable costs of trade are large, even as technology and policy have reduced costs of transport, communication and tariffs. To engender another round of global integration with its attendant increases in income, consumption and welfare, research must refocus attention on the nature of the trade costs between the firms that engage in trade.

This chapter contributes to that agenda by documenting the relationships between Colombian firms and their foreign suppliers. We find evidence that the extensive margin of importer–exporter connections is strongly correlated with aggregate country-level trade flows. In addition, there is substantial heterogeneity across both importers and exporters in terms of the numbers of partners and the levels of trade flows. Again, the extensive margin is crucial in explaining the variation in import levels across firms. Large importers do not import more from each partner but rather have many more partners than smaller importers.

International trade involves firms trading with each other, rather than directly with final consumers. Even domestic economies are comprised of a large network of buyers and sellers. The continuing revolution in international trade transaction data is opening up the black box of firm-to-firm connections across borders. One temptation is to think of this as just another extensive margin of trade. However, firm behavior is important on both sides of any international trade relationship and existing frameworks largely ignore the interaction between buyers and sellers each of whom may have market power (Bernard and Dhingra (2015)). Evidence in this chapter and elsewhere shows that the extensive margins of trade, including that of foreign partners, are important both in the aggregate and within firms. In addition variation in the extensive margins is one of the forces underlying the power of the gravity model in explaining aggregate trade volumes.

At a basic level we are still learning how firms structure their global supply and customer networks and know little about a range of important questions: do firms have multiple suppliers of the same product, how frequently do importers change their suppliers, do importers switch partners to replace one supplier of a product with another, what determines successful trade partnerships and what differences are there between the big, dominant global firms and the large number of smaller firms engaged in trade? This chapter will provide evidence on these questions for Colombian importers.

2.   Literature

Before turning to the Colombian trade data, we briefly review the literature on firms and trade. The role of heterogeneous firms in exporting has been the subject of a large literature, see surveys by Tybout (2003), Bernard et al. (2007), Redding (2011), Melitz and Redding (2014) and Bernard et al. (2012). However, it is important to note that in that large theoretical and empirical literature the role of partner importing firms is largely left unmentioned. The exporting firm is heterogeneous and "interesting" while the destination market is typically modeled as populated by a representative consumer. Similarly in the smaller and more recent literature on importing and global sourcing, the exporting firms are also largely "uninteresting". Our focus is on the role of firms on both ends of the trade transaction; we will first briefly review the emerging research on importing and then survey the smaller body of work looking at importer–exporter pairings.

2.1. Firms and importing

There has been substantial recent work examining the characteristics and choices of importing firms. Work on the characteristics of importers for the United States (Bernard et al. (2007) and Bernard et al. (2009)), Belgium (Muuls and Pisu (2009)) and Italy (Castellani et al. (2010)) shows that importers share many of the characteristics of exporting firms in terms of their larger size and higher productivity. In addition these papers find similar heterogeneity across importing firms with the largest importers sourcing many products from many countries. In fact, large importers and large exporters tend to be the same firms, (Bernard et al. (2007)), as well as the most likely to have foreign affiliates and be embedded in global production networks (Bernard et al. (2018b)). Our work extends this research by examining the connections between importers and exporters and exploring the link to firm size.

The causal nature of the relationship between importing and productivity has been examined by a number of authors. Amiti and Konings (2007) find large productivity gains from reductions in input tariffs on imported intermediate goods for Indonesian firms. Goldberg et al. (2010) also examine trade liberalization and imported inputs. They find substantial gains from trade through access to new imported inputs driven by increased firm access to new input varieties. Halpern et al. (2015) attribute one-quarter of Hungarian productivity growth during 1993–2002 to increases in imported inputs. Bøler et al. (2015) find that cheaper R&D stimulates imports of intermediates and that improved access to imported inputs promotes technological change. Our work contributes to this stream of research by examining the firm linkages underlying the import of intermediate inputs.

A different approach to importing firms examines the decision to source from abroad. Feenstra and Hanson (2005), Nunn and Trefler (2008), Bernard et al. (2010) consider contracting and contractability in the decision to offshore inside or outside the firm. Antràs et al. (2017) study the extensive and intensive margins of firms' global sourcing decisions, while Fort (2017) examines the interaction of technology and industry characteristics and shows substantial differences in the effects on domestic versus foreign outsourcing.

2.2. Firm-to-firm connections

One of the earliest authors to consider the role of networks and firm-to-firm connections in trade is Rauch (1999) who introduces the idea that information frictions might dampen trade and that the customer or supplier network might help reduce those frictions. Arkolakis (2010) provides an early model of the costly acquisition of consumers and while he does not model firm-to-firm connections, his framework is strongly linked to the emerging work on production and sales networks. Rauch and Watson (2004), Antràs and Costinot (2011), Petropoulou (2011) and Chaney (2014) model intermediaries as agents that facilitate matching between sellers/exporters and foreign buyers.

Work on firm-to firm connections is not limited to international trade. Additional theoretical and empirical contributions, often examining the role of production networks in the propagation of shocks, include Oberfeld (2013), Acemoglu et al. (2012), Carvalho et al. (2014), Magerman et al. (2016) and Bernard et al. (2017).

Recent work has started exploring the cross-section of trading relationships between exporters and importers. Blum et al. (2010; 2012) examine characteristics of trade transactions for the exporter–importer pairs of Chile-Colombia and Argentina-Chile while Eaton et al. (2014) consider exports of Colombian firms to specific importing firms in the United States. Using Norwegian data, Bernard et al. (2018a) find support for a model where exporters vary in their efficiency in producing differentiated intermediate goods and pay a relation-specific fixed cost to match with each buyer. Eaton et al. (2014) develop a model of search and learning to explain the dynamic pattern of entry and survival by Colombian exporters and to differentiate between the costs of finding new buyers and to maintaining relationships with existing ones. Monarch (2013) estimates switching costs using a panel of U.S. importers and Chinese exporters and Dragusanu (2014) explores how the matching process varies across the supply chain using U.S.-Indian data. Sugita et al. (2014) study matching patterns in U.S.-Mexico trade while Benguria (2014) estimates a trade model with search costs using matched French-Colombian data. Carballo et al. (forthcoming) focus on the role of importer heterogeneity across destinations, using data on exporters from Costa Rica, Ecuador and Uruguay.

Some stylized facts are emerging from this literature. The buyer margin accounts for a large fraction of the variation in aggregate trade, and is, in fact, as large or larger than the firm or product margins in accounting for cross-country trade flows. Bernard et al. (2018a) show this using Norwegian data. They also find that a firm's number of customers is significantly higher in larger markets and smaller in remote markets, i.e., importers per exporter vary systematically with GDP and distance. This response of the buyer margin to gravity variables is also shown by Carballo et al. (forthcoming).

The population of sellers and buyers are extremely concentrated. Bernard et al. (2018a) find that the top 10 per cent of exporters to an OECD country typically account for more than 90 per cent of aggregate exports to that destination. At the same time, the top 10 per cent of buyers from an OECD country are as dominant and also account for more than 90 per cent of aggregate purchases. This concentration of imports and exports in a small set of firms is similar to that found by Bernard et al. (2009) and Bernard et al. (2018b) for the United States and Mayer and Ottaviano (2008) for other European countries. Although a handful of exporters and importers account for a large share of aggregate trade, these large firms are matching with many partners; one-to-one matches are typically not important in the aggregate. Many-to-many matches, i.e., where both exporter and importer have multiple connections, make up almost two thirds of aggregate trade. Using trade data for Chile and Colombia as well as Argentine and Chile, Blum et al. (2012) similarly point to the dominance of large exporter–large importer matches among the total number of trading pairs.

The distributions of buyers per exporter and exporters per buyer are characterized by many firms with few connections and a few firms with many connections. Bernard et al. (2018a) plot the number of exporters per buyer in a particular market against the fraction of buyers in this market who buy from at least that many exporters. The distributions appear to be largely consistent with a Pareto distribution as the cdfs are close to linear except in the tails, consistent with the findings by Blum et al. (2010; 2012) and Carballo et al. (forthcoming). Within a market, exporters with more customers have higher total sales, but the distribution of exports across customers does not vary systematically with the number of customers. Firms with more buyers typically export more: in the Norwegian data, the average firm with 10 customers in a destination exports more than 10 times as much as a firm with only one customer.

In looking at the nature of the connections between firms, there is negative degree assortativity among sellers and buyers: the better connected a seller, the less well-connected is its average buyer. In recent work by Bernard et al. (2014), negative degree assortativity is found for buyer–seller links among Japanese firms. Their Japanese dataset covers close to the universe of domestic buyer-seller links and therefore contains information about the full set of buyer linkages (not only the linkages going back to the source market). Negative degree assortativity does not mean that well-connected exporters only sell to less-connected buyers; instead it suggests that well-connected exporters typically sell to *both* well-connected buyers and less-connected buyers, whereas less-connected exporters typically *only* sell to well-connected buyers. Degree assortativity is only a meaningful measure in economic environments with many-to-many matching. Moreover, negative degree assortativity can coexist with positive assortative matching on the intensive (export value) margin. Using the Colombian import data, we corroborate these main stylized facts and examine the nature of the evolution of trading partnerships over time.

3. Data

Our primary data source is the customs records of Colombia and includes a complete history of Colombian import and export transactions from 1995 to 2014.

This period includes dramatic changes in the Colombian economy, periods of external liberalization and domestic reforms as well as several economic crises.

The data include all the available information on the customs forms. We focus on a subset of the data. On the import side this includes the name of foreign firm i in country s selling quantity q of product p to Colombian firm j for x USD on date d. Products are defined at the HS 10-digit level using the Colombian classification matching the tariff line for Colombian imports. Colombian importers are identified by their national identification number, NIT, while foreign firms have alphanumeric names in the data. The foreign firm name data are very noisy. Using the information on the customs forms with no cleaning results in 1,847,822 foreign firms. We clean the foreign firms' names first by dropping or correcting typical prefixes and suffixes (e.g. "inc", "co.", "spa", etc), dropping non alpha numeric characters and then employing machine learning algorithms to group likely common spelling variants or misspellings. We vary the parameters on the machine learning algorithms to create sets of firms' names that are likely overmatched and under-matched. Throughout this chapter we use the overmatched set to avoid overemphasizing the extensive firm-to-firm margin.[1] After cleaning we are left with 432,156 unique foreign firms across the 20 years.

There are 3,023,055 million import transactions across 146,896 importer–exporter pairs in 2014. 27,927 Colombian firms imported while there were 82,762 foreign suppliers (see column 1 of Table 10.2).[2]

3.1.   *Colombian trade over time*

From 1995 to 2014, Colombia experienced a boom in international trade, both exports and imports. As shown in Figure 10.1, total imports into Colombia expressed in terms of US$ increased more than 450 per cent during the period. The data show clearly the effects of several crises in the Colombian and world economies. In 1999, following large devaluations and crises in Brazil and Russia, Colombia experienced its first recession in 60 years and was also forced to allow its exchange rate to float, resulting in a 30 per cent devaluation against the dollar. The reduction in imports from both the economic crisis and devaluation is apparent in the 27.5 per cent reduction in imports. The number of Colombian importers and foreign exporters fell far less during the same period, 10.7 and 8.6 per cent respectively. Import declines occurred again in 2001–2002 (0.9 per cent) and 2008–2009 (16.2 per cent) as a result of external economic shocks in Colombia's primary trading partners. Again the adjustments of the extensive margins of the number of trading firms was much lower, suggestive of the costs needed to create the relationships in the first place.

In Figure 10.2, we show the evolution of the mean number of exporters, products, and source countries per importer. The average number of foreign partners and source countries have been stable over time while the number of imported products rose steadily until the onset of the Great Recession and has been stable since.

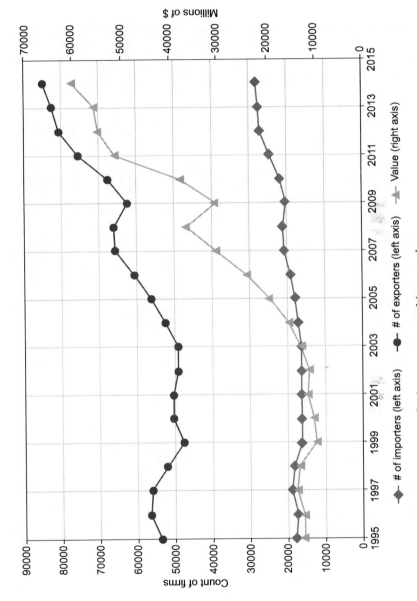

Figure 10.1 Colombian importers, foreign exporters, total import value

Source: Authors' calculations.

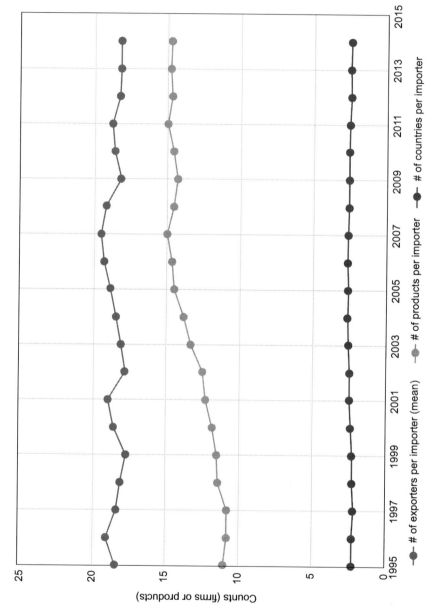

Figure 10.2 Foreign exporters per Colombian importer, imported products and source countries

Source: Authors' calculations.

4. Cross section

In this section, we examine the nature of firm-to-firm connections at a point in time. Whereas the emerging literature has documented facts from data on exports as described above, we document the firm-firm connections from the Colombian importing perspective.

4.1. Margins of trade

We start by decomposing aggregate country-level trade flows into their constituents parts, i.e the roles of exporting firms, importing firms, products and average value per exporter–importer-product per year. This already represents an aggregation from the raw transaction level data which includes the additional dimensions of the number of transactions per exporter–importer-product during the year. With this decomposition, total imports from country j into Colombia in any given year can be represented as

$$m_j = s_j p_j b_j d_j \bar{x}_j$$

with s_j , the number of sellers (exporters) in country j, p_j, the total number of products shipped by all sellers in country j, b_j, the number of Colombian firms that import from country j, $\bar{x}_j$, average value per buyer-seller-product, and d_j (or density), the fraction of actual *sbp* triples out of all possible exporter–importer-product combinations.

We regress each of the margins on total imports (in logs) using data from 2014 to assess the contribution of each of the three extensive margins (buyers, sellers, products) and the intensive margin (average imports per buyer-seller-product) in this decomposition. This set of regressions gives us a relatively simple way to examine the role of different microeconomic components of trade to aggregate trade flows. While previous research has examined the role of the number of exporters and the number of exported products, we are able to examine both the buyer and seller contribution to the variation of Colombian imports across source countries.[3]

Given that OLS is a linear estimator and its residuals have an expected value of zero, the coefficients for each set of regressions sum to unity, with each coefficient representing the share of overall variation in trade explained by the respective margin.[4]

The results in Table 10.1 confirm earlier work on extensive margin contributions to the cross-country variation in aggregate trade volumes. Both the number of importers and the number of products increase rapidly as total trade volumes rise. However, here we see that the role of the number of foreign partners, in this case exporters, is equally large. Large trade volumes between pairs of countries are associated with large numbers of firms on both sides of the border as well as large numbers of products. The intensive margin also covaries positively with total trade across countries but accounts for just under 40 per cent of the total variance.[5] Bigger trade volumes are associated with higher shipments per importer–exporter-product and particularly with increases in the extensive margins of more importers, more exporters and more products.

Table 10.1 Country-level regressions (2014)

Variables	(1) Buyers	(2) Sellers	(3) Products	(4) Intensive	(5) Density
Imports (log)	0.49[a]	0.48[a]	0.51[a]	0.39[a]	−0.87[a]
	(0.02)	(0.02)	(0.02)	(0.02)	(0.04)
Constant	−4.20[a]	−4.08[a]	−3.75[a]	4.85[a]	7.18[a]
	(0.31)	(0.33)	(0.33)	(0.37)	(0.55)
N	174	174	174	174	174
R^2	0.78	0.74	0.80	0.60	0.77

[a] indicates significance at the 1 per cent level.

Source: Authors' calculations.

Table 10.2 Summary stats 2014 – all and top 5 sources

Variables	All	U.S.	China	Mexico	Germany	Brazil
Total value in USD (millions)	55,199	19,229	3,728	3,254	1,820	1,691
# Colombian importers	27,927	13,680	9,278	2,851	2,831	2,829
# foreign exporters	82,762	24,557	16,076	2,431	3,501	2,641
Mean value per importer–exporter ($'000s)	375.77	405.71	138.93	687.27	295.76	308.71
Median value per importer–exporter ($'000s)	24.68	17.06	26.60	41.23	22.76	31.76
Mean exporters per importer	5.26	3.46	2.89	1.66	2.17	1.94
Median exporters per importer	2.00	1.00	1.00	1.00	1.00	1.00
Mean importers per exporter	1.78	1.93	1.67	1.95	1.76	2.07
Median importers per exporter	1.00	1.00	1.00	1.00	1.00	1.00
Log max/median import value		11.39	8.29	8.55	8.64	7.84

Source: Authors' calculations.

4.2.   Connections

In 2014, there are 146,896 trading relationships involving 27,927 Colombian importing firms and 82,762 foreign exporters. As shown in Table 10.2, the distribution of the value in these partnerships is highly skewed with the mean more than 15 times larger than the median. Similarly, the distributions of exporters per importer and importers per exporter reflect the presence of large trading firms. The mean importer has 5.26 foreign partners while the median has two. These distributions confirm that the findings of prior research on the importance of large firms in international trade flows also hold in Colombia, see Bernard et al. (2009), Mayer and Ottaviano (2008) and Bernard et al. (2018b).

Looking at individual source countries, the United States is by far the largest source for imports into Colombia, accounting for roughly one third of the trading partnerships and import value. Among Colombian importers, 49 per cent bought from at least one U.S. partner. The relative lower cost of trading with the United States is also reflected in the lower value imports for the median partnership, i.e., relatively smaller transactions with the U.S. are profitable. Across all the major source countries, the median Colombian importer has just one partner.

Figure 10.3 plots the distributions of exporters per Colombian importer and importers per foreign exporter across all relationships. The sub-figures are double log distributions with discrete steps, for example the upper panel has the number of suppliers per importer against the cumulative fraction of Colombian firms with at least x foreign suppliers. In both cases, the distribution is very close to a power law except in the extreme tails. There is a small number of firms, either Colombian importers or foreign exporters, with many partners and a large number of firms with a small number of partners.

The log linearity of the distributions appears at the country level as well for importers per exporter. This captures the stylized fact that a few firms, either exporters or importers, have large numbers of connections while large numbers of firms have just one or two foreign partners. For all five of the top source countries the distribution is indistinguishable from log-linearity (see Figure 10.4).[6]

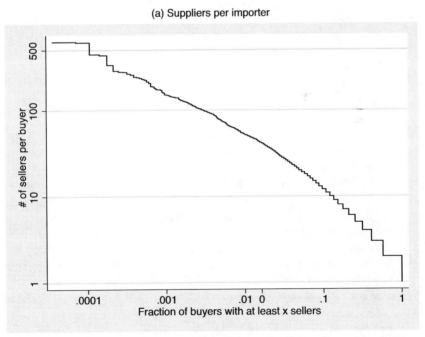

(a) Suppliers per importer

Figure 10.3 Suppliers per importer and importers per supplier – all countries, 2014

Source: Authors' calculations.

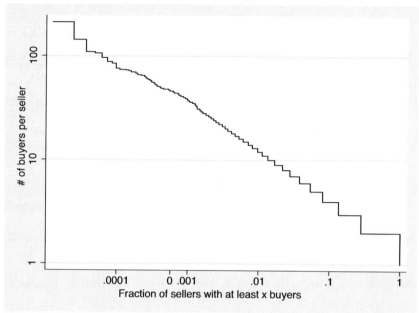

Figure 10.3   (Continued)

4.3.   Matching

The preceding results suggest that most Colombian importing firms have few partners while only a few are connected to many foreign exporters. However, we can group trading relationships and trade value by types of firms according to their number of partners. In Table 10.3 we place firms in two groups, one where the firm has only a single foreign partner and the other where the firm has multiple foreign partners.[7]

Table 10.3 confirms the important role for large, well-connected firms in international trade flows. Firms with more than one foreign partner appear in the vast majority, 88 per cent of partnerships in 2014. Those partnerships in turn account for the preponderance of Colombian import value, 91 per cent. In fact, more than half of Colombian imports by value are conducted between exporting and importing firms that each have multiple partners, i.e., there are large, well-connected firms on both sides of the transaction. These results are perhaps unsurprising given previous research that has emphasized the role of large, global firms in international trade.

The link between the number of foreign partners and total firm imports can be seen clearly in Figure 10.5. The vertical axis shows log imports, normalized such that log imports are relative to the average imports for one-supplier firms. On the horizontal axis is the number of suppliers. Log firm imports are strongly

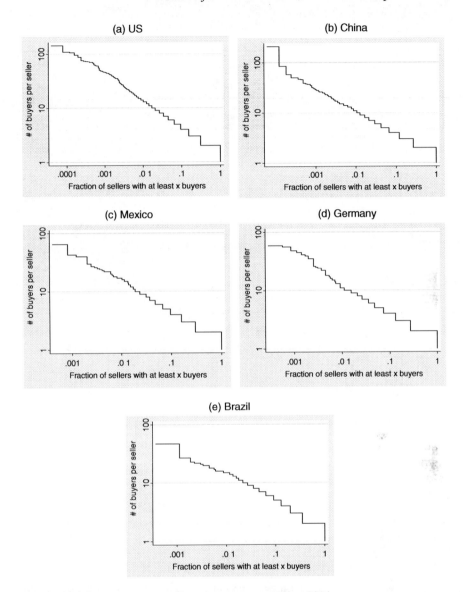

Figure 10.4 Importers per supplier – top source countries, 2014
Source: Authors' calculations.

positively and linearly related to the number of foreign partners of the Colombian importer. Big importers import from many firms.

However, while large importers import from many exporters, they do not import more from each partner. Figure 10.6 shows the log value of imports for suppliers at the 80th, 50th and 20th percentiles of the supplier distribution for

Table 10.3 Match types

Importer–exporter	1995		2004		2014	
	Count	*Value*	*Count*	*Value*	*Count*	*Value*
1-1	0.09	0.04	0.11	0.07	0.13	0.09
1-many	0.17	0.1	0.16	0.14	0.17	0.16
many-1	0.29	0.18	0.29	0.24	0.28	0.21
many-many	0.45	0.66	0.43	0.54	0.42	0.54

Source: Authors' calculations.

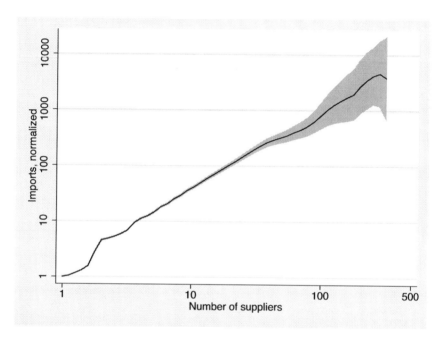

Figure 10.5 Log imports and the number of suppliers
Source: Authors' calculations.

importers with 5 or more suppliers.[8] The vertical axis is log imports in the partnership, normalized by source to be 1 for importers with a single foreign partner. The horizontal axis is the log number of foreign suppliers for the Colombian importer.

Sales from the median foreign supplier to the Colombian importer (the middle line) are invariant across firms, regardless of the number of foreign partners shipping to the Colombian firm. In addition, the value of shipments from the median exporter are the same as average purchases by Colombian firms with a single foreign partner. The same invariance holds for larger partners (80th percentile)

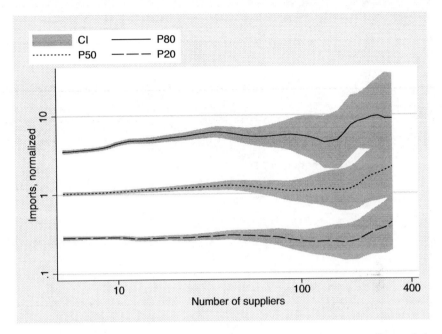

Figure 10.6 Log imports of 80th, 50th (median) and 20th percentile suppliers and the number of suppliers

Note: Log imports (vertical axis) are normalized so average log imports for single-supplier importers equal 1. The horizontal axis is the the number of suppliers for the firm.

Source: Authors' calculations.

and smaller partners (20th percentile). Large importers have more foreign suppliers but they do not purchase more from each of those suppliers.

This result is confirmed by work on Norwegian exports (Bernard et al. (2018a)) and on the domestic firm-to-firm production network in Belgium (Bernard et al. (2017)) and is of substantial significance for future research on firm size and aggregate export flows. Export volumes are large because of large numbers of partnerships, especially with a large firm on one or both sides of the relationship, and because large firms have many partners.

4.4. Assortativity

The literature on firm-to-firm connections in trade has many points of contact with the larger existing literatures on social and economic networks. One striking difference is in the assortativity of connections and the relationships between well-connected and poorly connected firms. Social networks display a common strong tendency for the best connected people (nodes) to be more likely to be connected to other well-connected people (nodes). This feature means that the

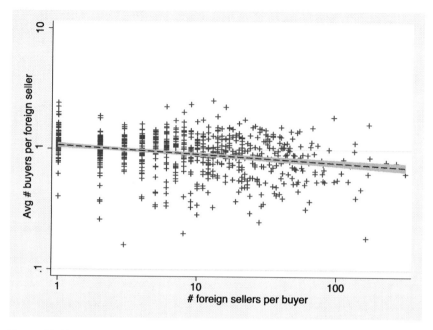

Figure 10.7 Degree assortativity
Source: Authors' calculations.

average connectedness of one's connections increases in your own number of connections, i.e., popular people are connected to other popular people.

Firm-to-firm connections systematically display negative assortativity. Figure 10.7 shows the number of suppliers per Colombian firm from a given source country j, a_j, on the x axis and the average number of Colombian connections among those suppliers, $s_j(a_j)$, on the y axis. The axes scales are in logs and both variables are demeaned at the source country level.

While there is a large amount of dispersion, as in many other studies of international trade and domestic connections, we find a significant negative relationship. Colombian firms that have large numbers of suppliers in a source country (to the right along the x axis) on average are connected with suppliers that have fewer Colombian partners. This finding suggests again that there is typically a large firm on one side of most Colombian import relationships. It does not mean that well-connected Colombian firms only connect with small (less well-connected) foreign firms. Rather, well-connected Colombian firms connect with large, medium and small foreign partners while small (less well-connected) Colombian firms are more likely to only match with a well-connected partner. Bernard et al. (2018a) document this finding in Norwegian export data and propose a model with match-specific fixed costs. In that framework small firms cannot profitably match with other small firms, while large firms can. In general this finding means that models designed to explain importer–exporter pairings cannot mirror the framework in the social network literature that often features preferential matching yielding positive assortativity.

4.5. Gravity and connections

The importance of distance and market size (gravity) in explaining international trade flows is the subject of a vast literature (see Head and Mayer (2014)). However, only recently have these forces been linked to the extensive margins of trade. In Table 10.4 we estimate a simple gravity regression for each of the margins discussed earlier including log distance and log GDP of the source country. As expected, distance and GDP are negatively and positively correlated with the margins respectively. The distance coefficient has similar magnitude for each of the extensive and intensive margins although it is not statistically significant in any single regression. The aggregate coefficient on distance is 0.74.[9] GDP is positive and significant for each margin and the magnitude of the relationship is stronger for the various extensive margins.

In Table 10.5 we look at the importance of distance and market size for import volume variation within importing firms. The table reports regressions for the number of foreign partners, the average value per partner and total firm

Table 10.4 Gravity and margins – Colombian imports (2014)

	(1) *Importers*	(2) *Exporters*	(3) *Products*	(4) *Intensive*	(35) *Density*
Distance	−0.37	−0.31	−0.38	−0.30	0.62
GDP	0.96[a]	0.91[a]	0.99[a]	0.67[a]	−1.7[a]
N	60,671	60,671	60,671	60,671	60,671
R^2	0.28	0.25	0.31	0.25	0.28

[a] indicates significance at the 1 per cent level.

Source: Authors' calculations.

Table 10.5 Within-firm gravity regression, 2014

	(1) *Foreign sellers*	(2) *Average imports*	(3) *Imports*
Distance (log)	−0.16[a]	−0.14[a]	−0.29[a]
GDP (log)	0.19[a]	0.04[a]	0.23[a]
Importer FE	Yes	Yes	Yes
N	65,866	65,746	65,746
R^2	0.47	0.55	0.54

[a] indicates significance at the 1 per cent level.

Source: Authors' calculations.

imports on source country log distance and log GDP. Distance is negatively related to the number of foreign partners in a source and the average value of purchases from the country with the magnitudes of the effects roughly equal. GDP, however, is much more strongly linked to the number of connections with the effect on the extensive margin almost five times larger than the effect on the average value of importer per partner. These results using the gravity framework in the aggregate and within firms point to the importance of understanding the barriers to making foreign connections.

5.   Connections over time

The existing work on firm-to-firm connections has emphasized the differences across trading firms in terms of the number and value of their partnerships. We now explore the evolution of these importer–exporter connections over time.

5.1.   *Margins of trade over time*

We start by examining the importance of the different margins, both extensive and intensive, in the growth of country-level shipments to Colombia. Similar to the decomposition for import levels done earlier, we regress the log differences of the margin of imports on the log difference in aggregate imports from each source country in Table 10.6. As before the coefficients sum to unity and the regressions allow us to assess the contribution of each margin to the variance in annual (and long-run) country growth rates. Panel A is an annual regression with no fixed effects; panel B includes country fixed effects in the annual growth rate regression, and Panel C runs a cross-section of long (19 year) differences.

The results are quite similar across the three specifications and are quite different from the cross-section decomposition of import levels reported above. The three extensive margins each contribute between 9 and 16 per cent to aggregate growth rate variation. Accordingly, the intensive margin is much more important in the growth rate decomposition than in the levels specifications. The variation in the growth of imports across source countries is strongly correlated with the variation in the growth in average imports per exporter–importer-product.

5.2.   *Adding and dropping suppliers*

While the recent round of research on firm-to-firm relationships in trade has documented a set of stylized facts that are robust across countries and years, there is less research on the evolution of importer–exporter connections over time. Table 10.7 divides importing firms into three mutually exclusively groups: those that increase the number of their suppliers, those that reduce the number, those that leave the number of their suppliers unchanged at annual and five-year horizons.[10] Less than a third of importers leave the number of suppliers unchanged from one year to the next, while over five-year intervals more than 95 per cent

Table 10.6 Import growth decompositions – country level regressions

Variables	(1) ΔBuyers	(2) ΔSellers	(3) ΔProducts	(4) ΔIntensive	(5) ΔDensity
(A) annual Δlog imports (without country fixed effect)					
ΔImports (log)	0.13[a]	0.12[a]	0.16[a]	0.82[a]	−0.23[a]
	(0.01)	(0.01)	(0.01)	(0.01)	(0.01)
Constant	0.03[a]	0.03[a]	0.04[a]	−0.05[a]	−0.05[a]
	(0.01)	(0.01)	(0.01)	(0.01)	(0.01)
N	2812	2812	2812	2812	2812
R^2	0.19	0.16	0.13	0.80	0.17
(B) annual Δlog imports (with country fixed effect)					
ΔImports (log)	0.13[a]	0.12[a]	0.16[a]	0.83[a]	−0.23[a]
	(0.01)	(0.01)	(0.01)	(0.01)	(0.01)
Constant	0.03[a]	0.03[a]	0.04[a]	−0.05[a]	−0.05[a]
	(0.01)	(0.01)	(0.01)	(0.01)	(0.02)
Country FE	Yes	Yes	Yes	Yes	Yes
N	2,812	2,812	2,812	2,812	2,812
R^2	0.19	0.16	0.13	0.80	0.17
(C) long difference Δlog imports					
ΔImports (log)	0.14[a]	0.15[a]	0.09[a]	0.88[a]	−0.25[a]
	(0.03)	(0.03)	(0.05)	(0.05)	(0.06)
Constant	−867.24	416.03	−2271.04	2147.14	575.10
	(2921.60)	(2849.81)	(4467.46)	(4299.15)	(5250.49)
N	93	93	93	93	93
R^2	0.18	0.21	0.04	0.80	0.18

[a] indicates significance at the 1 per cent level.

Source: Authors' calculations.

Table 10.7 Fraction of surviving firms that increase suppliers, reduce suppliers, unchanged

Year	Increase	Reduce	Unchanged
Annual	0.36	0.35	0.29
5-year	0.47	0.50	0.03

Source: Authors' calculations.

of firms adjust the count of suppliers up or down. Over short and longer intervals, most Colombian importing firms are changing their supplier mix.

Table 10.8 provides a different perspective on the changing buyer–supplier connections by reporting the fractions of Colombian importers that only add suppliers, only drop, both add and drop or leave their supplier mix unchanged. From year to year, only 13 per cent of importing firms maintain all their existing connections without adding or dropping. More than three quarters of firms add at

Table 10.8 Fraction that add at least one new supplier, drop at least one old supplier, do both, do neither

Year	Add	Drop	Both	Neither
Annual	0.77	0.76	0.66	0.13
5-year	0.94	0.97	0.92	0.01

Note: The annual numbers are the averages calculated across all pairs of years from 1995 to 1996 through 2013–2014 inclusive. The five-year numbers are the averages calculated across 1995–2000, 2002–2007 and 2009–2014.

Source: Authors' calculations.

Table 10.9 Supplier and import value shares at new, dropped and continuing suppliers

Year	New		Continuing	
	Value	Connections	Value	Connections
Annual	0.20	0.52	0.80	0.48
5-year	0.57	0.86	0.43	0.14

Year	Dropped		Continuing	
	Value	Connections	Value	Connections
Annual	0.17	0.52	0.83	0.49
5-year	0.46	0.75	0.54	0.25

Note: The annual numbers are the averages calculated across all pairs of years from 1995 to 1996 through 2013–2014 inclusive. The five-year numbers are the averages calculated across 1995–2000, 2002–2007 and 2009–2014.

Source: Authors' calculations.

least one supplier or drop at least one supplier while two-thirds of firms both add and drop on an annual basis. Over five-year intervals almost every firm is changing their supplier mix with more than 90 per cent of firms both adding and dropping.

Supplier churning is widespread among importing firms over short and especially longer horizons. Table 10.9 examines the importance of new and dropped partners in the overall number of connections and the share of import value for the firm. The four columns of the top panel report (i) the fraction of the value of firm imports accounted for by new foreign partners, (ii) the fraction of connections accounted by new foreign partners, (iii) the fraction of import value at continuing partnerships, and (iv) the fraction of connections at continuing partnerships. The rows give the fractions for one-year and five-year intervals.[11] While the majority of suppliers are new to the importer each year (52 per cent) those relationships are smaller on average accounting for 20 per cent of import value. Relationships begun before the previous year are, on average, more than four times larger than partnerships begun in the past year. Looking at five-year intervals, we see a similar pattern. The vast majority of connections are formed in a typical five-year interval but the older relationships are much larger.

The bottom panel considers a similar breakdown, reporting the fraction of this year's imports and connections that are accounted for by partnerships that will stop and those that will continue. Again more than half of today's suppliers will no longer be matched to the importer next year. Over a five-year horizon, three-quarters of the connections will disappear. The relationships that will continue one year into the future represent more than 80 per cent of today's import value, and those that will continue for five years represent half of today's import value.

These findings suggest that the typical importing firm is engaged in a substantial amount of churning of their supplier mix. Firms frequently add and drop partners which is at least suggestive of relatively low costs of matching. More research is needed to examine how this churning varies across importer and exporter industries.

Figure 10.8 shows the distribution of match length and match value for all importer–exporter pairs across all 20 years in the data. As reported by Eaton et al. (2008), more than half of all matches last only one year and are quite small in value. Aside from the big drop between matches of length one and two years, the distribution of match length suggests a relatively stable attrition rate of about 20 per cent annually. Match numbers fall off much more quickly than value, confirming that long-lived relationships are relatively more important in total import value and providing some additional evidence on the role of the intensive margin.

5.3. The 1997 cohort of new connections

In this and the next subsection, we focus on a single cohort of relationships starting in 1997.[12] First, we look at all new importer–exporter pairs in 1997 at new and continuing importers and then we consider only firms that were new to importing in the same year.

In 1997 across all importers, 64,432 importer–exporter connections were begun. This includes connections at new importers as well as new connections at firms that had previously imported from other partners. Of those new cross-border relationships 6,360 (2,916) were still active 5 (10) years later.[13] Considering all the importer–exporter connections that started in 1997, we find that they account for almost 30 per cent of total import value and more than 60 per cent of all importer–exporter connections in that first year (see Table 10.10). Over time the share of this cohort of new connections in total importer–exporter relationships falls both because specific matches end and because total Colombian imports, and thus the total number of connections, are growing. As we found earlier, the share of value falls less quickly than the share of connections and by their second year the surviving connections from the 1997 cohort are larger than average (value share is greater than the connection share).

Table 10.11 gives a similar path for that cohort of new partnerships in 1997 from the perspective of the importing firm. On average the new connections account for 74 per cent of connections and 58 per cent of import value for the

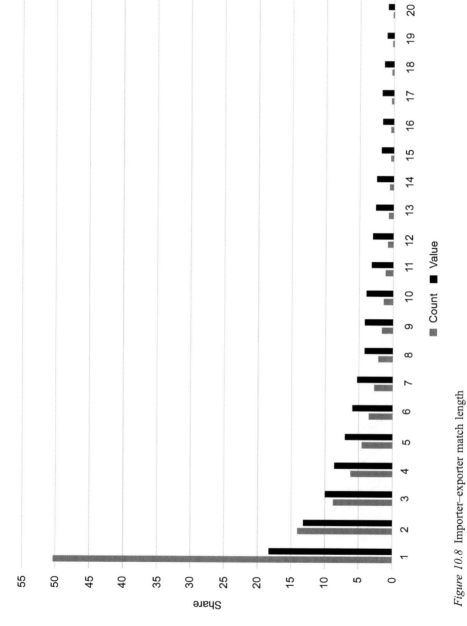

Figure 10.8 Importer–exporter match length

Source: Authors' calculations.

Table 10.10 New importer–exporter connections in 1997

Years	Connections	Value
1	0.63	0.29
2	0.17	0.19
3	0.10	0.12
4	0.06	0.09
5	0.04	0.08
6	0.03	0.06
7	0.02	0.05
8	0.02	0.04
9	0.01	0.03
10	0.01	0.03
11	0.01	0.03
12	0.01	0.03
13	0.01	0.02
14	0.00	0.02
15	0.00	0.02
16	0.00	0.02
17	0.00	0.02
18	0.00	0.02

Source: Authors' calculations.

Table 10.11 New importer–exporter connections in 1997 – importing firm

Years	Connections	Value
1	0.74	0.58
2	0.34	0.43
3	0.26	0.37
4	0.20	0.35
5	0.18	0.35
6	0.17	0.35
7	0.16	0.37
8	0.16	0.36
9	0.14	0.35
10	0.13	0.35
11	0.13	0.32
12	0.12	0.32
13	0.12	0.33
14	0.12	0.30
15	0.11	0.30
16	0.11	0.31
17	0.11	0.37
18	0.11	0.40

Source: Authors' calculations.

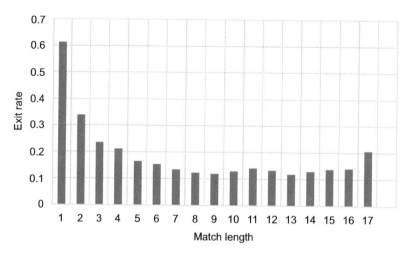

Figure 10.9 Importer–exporter (match) exit rates
Source: Authors' calculations.

importing firms that had at least one new connection. For those firms that con-tinue to import a decade later, that set of initial connections still accounts for more than a third of the firm imports although it represents just 13 per cent of their foreign supply relationships.

Figure 10.9 reports the exit rate for these new matches for the subsequent 17 years. As we saw earlier, match disintegration rates are highest in the early years of a match. For new importers the disintegration rate is higher, 61.3 per cent, than for new connections at all importing firms, 51.3 per cent, i.e. the age of the importer predicts the success of the match. Disintegration rates are high and declining for the first several years of the match and then stabilize between 10 and 15 per cent per year.

5.4.   *The 1997 cohort of new importers*

In 1997, 6,854 Colombian firms started importing, of which 929 (550) were still active 5 (10) years later and 309 survived as importers to 2014.[14] Importer failure rates also start quite high, two thirds of this entering cohort imported only once and an additional 17 per cent imported for only 2–3 years. After stabilizing the annual exit rate for Colombian importers is 7 per cent (see Figure 10.10).

Except for the start year, three-quarters of continuing importers start a new con-nection each year. Those new connections cover more than 1,400 products from more than 65 countries. First-year connections for continuing importers in this cohort average 1.22 suppliers per product. Total value of imports increases at an average rate of 9 per cent per year, while value per importer increases at 34 per cent per year as smaller importers exit and continuing importers increase

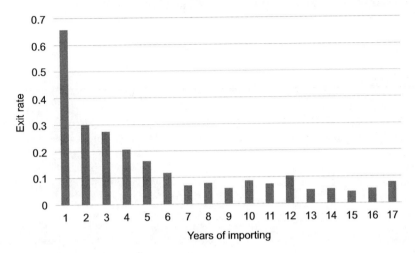

Figure 10.10 Importer exit rates – 1997 cohort
Source: Authors' calculations.

their transactions. For 1997 starting importers that continue for at least 10 years, 20 per cent have relationships that lasted the full period.

5.5. Match failure

In this section we look at factors that are correlated with the probability of failure of matches between importers and exporters. A match is defined between two firms and can potentially include multiple products. We consider characteristics of the importer and those of the exporter as well as match-specific variables. As before we are limited in the extent of firm characteristics to those available in the Colombian import data.

For Colombian importers we know the number of years the firm has been an importer since 1995 and the number of foreign partners from the particular source country. For the foreign exporter we know how long it has exported to Colombia, and the number of Colombian import partners. For the match itself, we include the current length of the match between the exporter and importer, the value in the current year and whether or not it is a multi-product relationship. Finally we consider the role of traditional gravity variables for the source country including GDP per capita, population and distance.

Table 10.12 reports results of linear probability models for the failure of the match in year t+1; the columns respectively include year fixed effects, importer and year fixed effects, importer-year fixed effects and match and year fixed effects. In column 1, including only year fixed effects, we find that the probability of match failure is lower the longer the Colombian firm has been importing and the greater the number of foreign partners in the source country. Similarly match

Table 10.12 Linear probability model of match failure

Variables	(1)	(2)	(3)	(4)
Importer age	−0.005[a]	−0.012[a]		
Log # of exporters per importer-source country	−0.001[a]	0.008[a]		−0.010[a]
Exporter age	−0.001[a]	0.000	0.0002[c]	
Log # of importers per exporter	−0.026[a]	−0.046[a]	−0.047[a]	−0.024[a]
Length of match	−0.023[a]	−0.016[a]	−0.018[a]	0.051[a]
Multi-product match dummy	−0.094[a]	−0.101[a]	−0.101[a]	−0.035[a]
Log match value	−0.048[a]	−0.049[a]	−0.049[a]	−0.037[a]
Log GDP per cap source country	0.001	0.004[a]	0.006[a]	0.141[a]
Log population source country	0.008[a]	0.004[a]	0.006[a]	0.419[a]
Log distance to source country	−0.042[a]	−0.021[a]	−0.023[a]	
Year FE	Yes	Yes	No	Yes
Importer FE	No	Yes	No	No
Importer-year FE	No	No	Yes	No
Match FE	No	No	No	Yes
N	2,183,257	2,183,257	2,183,257	2,183,257
R^2	0.19	0.26	0.29	0.42

[a] and [c] indicates significance at the 1 and 10 per cent level respectively.

Source: Authors' calculations.

failure is reduced if the foreign firm has been exporting for a longer time to Colombia and if it is connected to more Colombian importers. Unconditionally, and perhaps unsurprisingly, "better" firms, those that survive longer and have more partners, have lower rates of match failure. The "quality" of the match is also negatively correlated with match failure. The length of the match, the value of the match and multi-product matches all are associated with lower failure probabilities.

Gravity variables enter with perhaps unexpected coefficients. Unconditionally one would expect matches to be harder to sustain at greater distances or in smaller markets. However, we find that conditional on the value and characteristics of the partners, distance is negatively associated with match failure. While the number of connections and the value of connections is negatively related to distance, as shown earlier, the survival of individual matches increases with distance. This is suggestive of the possibility that the sunk costs of a match increase with distance and thus firms are less willing to break a match at longer distances. Market size, however, works in the opposite direction. Match failure rates are higher for markets with larger populations and higher GDP per capita.

Including importer, or importer-year, fixed effects does not substantially alter the findings of the match failure regressions. All the variables that potentially proxy for match quality are again negatively related to match failure. Years of importing for the Colombian firm are negatively correlated with match failure although the number of exporters in the source country now is positive and significant. Exporter age is positive but insignificant. The gravity-related source country variables are again negative for distance and positive for GDP per capita and population. Conditioning on match fixed effects, the results are largely unchanged, although we now find match length is positively related to failure.

6. Products

In this section we examine the relationship between importing firms and products. Table 10.13 reports summary statistics on products for all source countries, and for the top five sources of Colombian imports. As with other trade-related variables the number of products per importer is highly skewed. The mean number of products is 14.7 while the median is 4. A few firms are importing large numbers of products but most importers import multiple products. This contrasts with the evidence on the numbers of foreign partners and sourcing countries in Table 10.2, which showed that most importers sourced from a single partner in a single country. This supports evidence from numerous studies that document the prevalence of multi-product exporters in cross-border trade flows. On the other side of the transactions, the mean number of products exported by a foreign firm to Colombia is 6.3 and the median is 2 with relatively little variation across source countries. Within an importer–exporter pair, the mean number of products is 4.4 and the median is 1, again with modest variation across countries.

In their work modeling and documenting foreign sourcing by U.S. manufacturing firms, Antràs et al. (2017) report that the vast majority of firms source products from a single country. Looking at Colombian imports, we see that 38 per cent of importer-product combinations have more than one supplier. However, only 9 per cent of importer-product combinations source from multiple countries. When firms have multiple suppliers, three quarters of the time those suppliers are in the same source country. This provides some confirmatory evidence that there are substantial country-specific sourcing costs along with the sunk costs within an exporter–importer relationship suggested by the results in the previous section.

Table 10.13 Product summary statistics, 2014

	All	*U.S.*	*China*	*Mexico*	*Brazil*
Mean products per importer	14.73	11.31	8.18	5.85	6.32
Median products per importer	4.00	3.00	3.00	2.00	2.00
Mean products per exporter	6.30	7.17	5.16	5.68	5.89
Median products per exporter	2.00	2.00	2.00	2.00	2.00
Mean no. of products per importer–exporter	4.43	4.61	3.71	3.78	3.71
Median no. of products per importer–exporter	1.00	1.00	1.00	1.00	1.00
Share of importer-products > 1 supplier	0.38	0.13	0.11	0.05	0.07
Share of importer-products > 1 source country	0.09				

Source: Authors' calculations.

Looking at changes in sourcing partners over time, in Table 10.14, we calculate the fraction of product drops for single supplier relationships in year t that are replaced by a new supplier in year t+1. This excludes all importer-products with multiple suppliers in year t. Surprisingly very few product drops appear to be associated with churning of suppliers, on average fewer than 4 per cent of dropped products are imported in the following year from a different foreign firm. The second column shows that within the set of replaced suppliers, most changes remain within the same source country. More than two thirds of the new suppliers are from the same source country.

Over time, importers deepen their relationship with their suppliers. Within an importer over time, the number of products per supplier rises 3 per cent per year, see Table 10.15. We can see the growing importance of long-time suppliers in Table 10.16 which follows the product characteristics of matches started in 1997. As with other characteristics of the partnership such as import value, the distribution of the number of products supplied by foreign partners is highly skewed. In the first year of the match the mean products per supplier is close to 11 while the median is just 3. Over time the number of products traded within a match rises dramatically; the annual increase for the average surviving match is 20 per cent per year (24 per cent excluding the recession years), while the increase at the median surviving firm is 23 per cent per year (25 per cent excluding the recession years). The average partnership from this cohort involves more than 40 products after five years and more than 80 products after a decade.

Table 10.14 Product replacements

	Replacements	*Same country*
1995	0.03	0.69
1996	0.04	0.77
1997	0.03	0.77
1998	0.02	0.77
1999	0.03	0.77
2000	0.03	0.78
2001	0.02	0.78
2002	0.03	0.76
2003	0.03	0.74
2004	0.03	0.72
2005	0.02	0.67
2006	0.02	0.68
2007	0.03	0.67
2008	0.02	0.65
2009	0.03	0.67
2010	0.03	0.66
2011	0.03	0.65
2012	0.03	0.65
2013	0.03	0.61

Source: Authors' calculations.

Table 10.15 Relative evolution of imported products and foreign partners

Variables	(1) #products / #suppliers
Age of importer	0.03[a]
	(0.00)
Importer FE	Yes
Year FE	Yes
N	393,888
R^2	0.60

[a] indicates significance at the 1 per cent level.

Source: Authors' calculations.

Table 10.16 Products per connection and share of total imported products – 1997 match cohort

Years	# of products		Share of total	
	(mean)	(median)	(mean)	(median)
1	10.95	3.00	0.33	0.18
2	29.51	9.00	0.39	0.30
3	28.48	10.00	0.39	0.30
4	35.31	13.00	0.40	0.30
5	40.75	16.00	0.41	0.35
6	46.18	18.00	0.43	0.36
7	52.89	20.00	0.45	0.43
8	62.10	27.00	0.46	0.43
9	79.22	31.00	0.47	0.46
10	82.31	35.00	0.48	0.41
11	82.50	40.00	0.46	0.43
12	89.37	35.00	0.48	0.44
13	65.83	40.00	0.46	0.39
14	76.41	35.00	0.46	0.43
15	83.75	42.00	0.46	0.45
16	99.91	46.00	0.49	0.50
17	131.09	52.00	0.53	0.63
18	125.27	53.00	0.53	0.47

Source: Authors' calculations.

While surviving importers increase the number of suppliers, the last two columns of Table 10.16 show that the long-lived partnerships take on increasing significance for importers over time. Products from importer–exporter connections that started in 1997 and survived for five years account for 35–41 per cent of all imported products. After 10 years, these relationships supply 41–48 per cent of the foreign products bought by the Colombian firm.

7.   Conclusions

This chapter has explored a new comprehensive datasest of detailed firm-to-firm Colombian import transactions covering the period 1995–2014. The results shows that the extensive margin of foreign partner firms plays an important role in both aggregate and especially firm-level trade flows. Large importers are bigger precisely because they have many foreign partners and not because they trade more with each partner. Gravity relationships that do well in explaining aggregate trade flows are successful in part because they capture extensive margins effects.

Looking at importers and import partnerships over time, the findings are striking that most firms see substantial changing in their supplier mix over both annual and, especially, longer time horizons. Most importer–exporter pairs end within the first year or two, but those that survive grow rapidly. Also firms do not appear to be dropping foreign suppliers to replace them with new providers of the same product. The vast majority of changes are towards partners supplying different products than those dropped.

The results presented here suggest a path forward for future research. The ability of firms to create profitable and productive matches across borders is a key ingredient in aggregate trade flows and their growth. Large firms have more matches and thus larger trade volumes. However, the underlying sources of the frictions that prevent these matches, or cause them to be short-lived, are still unknown. Continued work using detailed firm-level trade transaction data with information on both the importer and exporter is needed to develop a deeper understanding of the barriers to trade in order to reduce them.

Notes

Disclaimer: Any opinions or conclusions expressed herein are those of the authors and do not necessarily reflect those of the NBER, CEPR, CEP or any other institution to which the authors are affiliated.

1 While there is also information on foreign addresses and telephone numbers, it is missing in many cases and subject to even more variation so we to date have not employed this in grouping transactions.
2 We retain all Colombian importers in our analysis including manufacturing and service firms. The latter group includes retailers, wholesalers and other service firms.
3 It is possible to examine the margins one at a time using the results from this analysis. For example, a decomposition into the number of importers and average imports per importer would correspond to column (1), importers, and the sum of columns (2)–(5), average importers per importer, in Table 10.1.
4 The coefficient on the density term is expected to be negative as the fraction of active importer–exporter-product triples from a country is decreasing as the total possible number of triples increases.
5 To see this consider the decomposition into the number of active importer–exporter-products which corresponds to the sum of columns (1)–(4) and the average shipments per importer–exporter-product, column (5).
6 Bernard et al. (2018a) develop a model with Pareto distributed productivity for importers and exporters that results in the log-log linear relationships shown in Figures 10.3 and 10.4.

7 For the foreign firms we can only see their Colombian exports, so the two groups are foreign exporting firms with one Colombian import partner and foreign firms with multiple Colombian importers.
8 For a Colombian firm with 10 suppliers, this represents the imports from foreign exporters with the 2nd, 5th and 8th largest sales to the Colombian importer.
9 Running the same regression on aggregate imports at the country level yields a significant coefficient.
10 In each case the actual suppliers may have changed.
11 The five-year intervals throughout the table represent averages for 1995–2000, 2002–2007 and 2009–2014.
12 Choosing 1997 gives us the longest continuous set of new importing relationships.
13 New connections in 1997 are defined as an import transaction in an importer–exporter pair in 1997 that did not transact in either 1995 or 1996.
14 New importers in 1997 are those who imported in 1997 but had not imported in either 1995 or 1996.

References

Acemoglu, Daron, Vasco M. Carvalho, Asuman Ozdaglar, and Alireza Tahbaz-Salehi, "The Network Origins of Aggregate Fluctuations," *Econometrica*, 2012, *80* (5), September, 1977–2016. 2.2.

Amiti, Mary and Jozef Konings, "Trade Liberalization, Intermediate Inputs and Productivity: Evidence From Indonesia," *American Economic Review*, 2007, *97* (5), 1611–1638. 2.1.

Antràs, Pol and Arnaud Costinot, "Intermediated Trade," *The Quarterly Journal of Economics*, 2011, *126* (3), 1319–1374. 2.2.

Antràs, Pol, Teresa C. Fort, and Felix Tintelnot, "The Margins of Global Sourcing: Theory and Evidence From U.S. Firms," *American Economic Review*, 2017, *107* (9), 2514–2564. 1, 2.1, 6.

Arkolakis, Costas, "Market Access Costs and the New Consumers Margin in International Trade," *Journal of Political Economy*, 2010, *118* (6), 1151–1199. 2.2.

Baldwin, Richard, *The Great Convergence: Information Technology and the New Globalization*, Belknap Press, 2017. 1.

Benguria, Felipe, "Production and Distribution of International Trade: Evidence From Matched Exporter-Importer Data," Technical Report 2014. 2.2.

Bernard, Andrew B., J. Bradford Jensen, and Peter K. Schott, "Importers, Exporters, and Multinationals: A Portrait of Firms in the U.S. that Trade Goods," in T. Dunne, J.B. Jensen, and M. Roberts, eds., *Producer Dynamics: New Evidence From Micro Data*, University of Chicago Press, 2009. 2.1, 2.2, 4.2.

Bernard, Andrew B., and Swati Dhingra, "Contracting and the Division of the Gains From Trade," Working Paper 21691, NBER October 2015. 1.

Bernard, Andrew B., Emmanuel Dhyne, Kalina Manova, Glenn Magerman, and Andreas Moxnes, "The Origins of Firm Heterogeneity: A Production Network Approach," Technical Report, Tuck School of Business 2017. 2.2, 4.3.

Bernard, Andrew B., Andreas Moxnes, and Karen H. Ulltveit-Moe, "Two-sided Heterogeneity and Trade," *Review of Economics and Statistics*, July 2018a, *100* (3), 424–439. 2.2, 6, 4.3, 4.4

Bernard, Andrew B., Stephen J. Redding, and Peter K. Schott, "Firms in International Trade," *Journal of Economic Perspectives*, Summer 2007, *21* (3), 105–130. 2, 2.1.

Bernard, Andrew B., Stephen J. Redding, and Peter K. Schott, "Intrafirm Trade and Product Contractibility," *American Economic Review*, May 2010, *100* (2), 444–448. 2.1.

Bernard, Andrew B., Stephen J. Redding, and Peter K. Schott, "The Empirics of Firm Heterogeneity and International Trade," *Annual Review of Economics*, 2012, *4*, 283–313. 2.

Bernard, Andrew B., Stephen J. Redding, and Peter K. Schott, "Global Firms," *Journal of Economic Literature*, 2018b, *56* (2), 565–619. 2.1, 2.2, 4.2.

Bernard, Andrew B., and Yukiko Saito, "Geography and Firm Performance in the Japanese Production Network," Discussion Paper 14-E-033, RIETI 2014. 2.2.

Blum, Bernardo S., Sebastian Claro, and Ignatius Horstmann, "Facts and Figures on Intermediated Trade," *American Economic Review*, 2010, *100* (2), 419–423. 2.2.

Blum, Bernardo S., Sebastian Claro, and Ignatius J. Horstmann, "Import Intermediaries and Trade Costs: Theory and Evidence," mimeo, University of Toronto 2012. 2.2.

Bøler, Esther Ann, Andreas Moxnes, and Karen Helene Ulltveit-Moe, "Technological Change, International Sourcing and the Joint Impact on Productivity," *American Economic Review*, December 2015, *105* (12), 3704–3739. 2.1.

Carballo, Jeronimo, Gianmarco I. P. Ottaviano, and Christian Volpe Martincus, "The Buyer Margins of Firms' Exports," *Journal of International Economics*, forthcoming. 2.2.

Carvalho, Vasco M., Makoto Nirei, and Yukiko U. Saito, "Supply Chain Disruptions: Evidence From Great East Japan Earthquake," Discussion Paper, Research Institute of Economy, Trade and Industry (RIETI) 2014.2.2.

Castellani, Davide, Francesco Serti, and Chiara Tomasi, "Firms in International Trade: Importers' and Exporters' Heterogeneity in Italian Manufacturing Industry," *The World Economy*, March 2010, *33* (3), 424–457. 2.1.

Chaney, Thomas, "The Network Structure of International Trade," *American Economic Review*, 2014, *104* (11), 3600–3634. 2.2.

Dragusanu, Raluca, "Firm-to-Firm Matching Along the Global Supply Chain," Working Paper 2014. 2.2.

Eaton, Jonathan, Marcela Eslava, David Jinkins, C. J. Krizan, and James Tybout, "A Search and Learning Model of Export Dynamics," Working Paper 2014. 2.2.

Eaton, Jonathan, Marcela Eslava, Maurice Kugler, and James Tybout, "Export Dynamics in Combia: Firm-Level Evidence," in E. Helpman, D. Marin, and T. Verdier, eds., *The Organization of Firms in a Global Economy*, Chicago: University of Chicago Press, 2008. 5.2.

Feenstra, Robert C. and Gordon H. Hanson, "Ownership and Control in Outsourcing to China: Estimating the Property-rights Theory of the Firm," *The Quarterly Journal of Economics*, 2005, *120* (2), 729–761. 2.1.

Fort, Teresa C., "Technology and Production Fragmentation: Domestic versus Foreign Sourcing," *Review of Economic Studies*, 2017, *84* (2), 650–687. 2.1.

Goldberg, Pinelopi K., Amit K. Khandelwal, Nina Pavcnik, and Petia Topalova, "Imported Intermediate Inputs and Domestic Product Growth: Evidence From India," *The Quarterly Journal of Economics*, 2010, *125* (4), 1727–1767. 2.1.

Halpern, Lazlo, Miklos Koren, and Adam Szeidl, "Imported Inputs and Productivity," *American Economic Review*, December 2015, *12* (105), 3660–3703. 2.1.

Head, Keith and Thierry Mayer, "Gravity Equations: Workhorse, Toolkit, and Cookbook," in E. Helpman, G. Gopinath, and K. Rogoff, eds., *Handbook of International Economics Vol. 4*, Amsterdam: Elsevier, 2014, pp. 131–195. 1, 4.5.

Magerman, Glenn, Karolien De Bruyne, Emmanuel Dhyne, and Jan Van Hove, "Heterogeneous Firms and the Micro Origins of Aggregate Fluctuations," Technical Report, KU Leuven 2016. 2.2.

Mayer, Thierry and Gianmarco Ottaviano, "The Happy Few: The Internationalisation of European Firms," *Intereconomics: Review of European Economic Policy*, May 2008, *43* (3), 135–148. 2.2, 4.2.

Melitz, Marc J., "The Impact of Trade on Intra-Industry Reallocations and Aggregate Industry Productivity," *Econometrica*, 2003, *71* (6), 1695–1725. 1.

Melitz, M. J. and S. J. Redding, "Heterogeneous Firms and Trade," in E. Helpman, G. Gopinath, and K. Rogoff, eds., *Handbook of International Economics Vol. 4*, Amsterdam: Elsevier, 2014, pp. 1–54. 2.

Monarch, Ryan, "'It's Not You, It's Me': Breakups in U.S.-China Trade Relationships," Working Paper 2013. 2.2.

Muuls, Mirabelle and Mauro Pisu, "Imports and Exports at the Level of the Firm: Evidence From Belgium," *The World Economy*, May 2009, *32* (5), 692–734. 2.1.

Nunn, Nathan and Daniel Trefler, "The Boundaries of the Multinational Firm: An Empirical Analysis," in Elhanan Helpman, Dalia Marin, and Thierry Verdier, eds., *The Organization of Firms in a Global Economy*, Cambridge: Harvard University Press, 2008, chapter The Boundaries of the Multinational Firm: An Empirical Analysis, pp. 55–83. 2.1.

Oberfeld, Ezra, "Business Networks, Production Chains, and Productivity: A Theory of Input-Output Architecture," Working Paper 2013. 2.2 .

Petropoulou, Dimitra, "Information Costs, Networks and Intermediation in International Trade," Globalization and Monetary Policy Institute Working Paper 76, Federal Reserve Bank of Dallas 2011. 2.2.

Rauch, James E., "Networks versus Markets in International Trade," *Journal of International Economics*, June 1999, *48* (1), 7–35. 2.2.

Rauch, James E. and Joel Watson, "Network Intermediaries in International Trade," *Journal of Economics & Management Strategy*, 2004, *13* (1), 69–93. 2.2.

Redding, Stephen J., "Theories of Heterogeneous Firms and Trade," *Annual Review of Economics*, 2011, 3, 77–105. 2.

Sugita, Yoichi, Kensuke Teshima, and Enrique Siera, "Assortative Matching of Exporters and Importers," Working Paper 2014. 2.2.

Tybout, J. R., "Plant-and Firm-level Evidence on 'New' Trade Theories," *Handbook of International Trade*, 2003, 1, 388–415. 2.

11   Chinese import exposure and U.S. occupational employment

Marco Del Angel, Sanjana Goswami
and Antonio Rodriguez-Lopez

1.   Introduction

Occupations differ along several characteristics such as their pay, degree of routineness, and required level of education. These differences should lead to heterogeneous responses of occupational employment levels to technology or international trade shocks. For example, automation is more likely to replace highly routine occupations, and an international offshoring relationship with an unskilled-labor abundant country is more likely to replace low-skilled occupations in the source country. For the United States, the greatest trade shock in the last few decades comes from the rise of China as the world's largest trader. In influential papers, Autor, Dorn and Hanson (2013), Acemoglu, Autor, Dorn, Hanson and Price (2016), and Pierce and Schott (2016) find a large negative impact of Chinese import competition on U.S. employment.[1] Contributing to this literature, the goal of this chapter is to estimate the impact of the 'China shock' on U.S. occupational employment from 2002 to 2014 by distinguishing occupations according to their wage, non-routineness, and education characteristics.

After sorting about 750 occupations from low to high wage, from routine to non-routine, and from low to high education, we document the decline in the share of lower-indexed occupations in total U.S. employment from 2002 to 2014, and an increase in the share of higher-indexed occupations during the same period. At the industry level, we show that the composition of employment in the vast majority of our industries changes in favor of higher-indexed occupations. Our empirical analysis confirms that Chinese import exposure is an important driver of these results, mainly through its large negative employment impact on lower-indexed occupations.

Following Acemoglu, Autor, Dorn, Hanson and Price (2016), henceforth AADHP, we construct industry-level measures of direct, upstream, and downstream import exposure from China. An industry's direct import exposure is simply related to the change in the industry's real imports from China, while upstream and downstream import exposure take into account input-output linkages across industries. The upstream measure captures Chinese exposure effects flowing from affected buying industries to domestic selling industries, while the downstream measure captures Chinese exposure effects flowing from affected selling industries to their domestic buying industries. From those industry-level variables, we construct occupation-specific measures of Chinese import exposure using industry shares of occupational employment as weights.

Our first empirical specification, which ignores occupational sorting, obtains large and negative employment effects of Chinese import exposure on U.S. occupational employment. We estimate the employment effects of direct import exposure, and of two combined measures of import exposure – the first combined measure adds the direct and upstream exposures, while the second measure adds the direct, upstream, and downstream exposures. From 2002 to 2014, the predicted employment losses are 1.05 million jobs from direct exposure, 1.51 million when we consider upstream exposure, and 2.12 million when we consider downstream exposure. These numbers are well in line with the employment losses calculated by AADHP from 1999 to 2011 in their industry-level analysis.

Our second empirical specification considers occupational sorting under our three criteria (real wage, non-routineness and education). Occupations are arranged into tertiles (low, middle and high) under each criteria, and we estimate the impact of Chinese import exposure on each occupational tertile – a regression is individually estimated for each occupation-sorting criteria. Our estimation obtains a large negative effect of all types of Chinese exposure on lower-indexed (low wage, routine, low education) occupations, suggesting that a high content of these occupations is embodied in U.S. imports from China.

Additionally, we obtain a mildly significant positive employment effect of Chinese direct import exposure on high-education occupations. These gains are either the result of (i) strong productivity effects – as described by Grossman and Rossi-Hansberg (2008) – by which firms importing cheaper inputs from China increase their productivity and market shares, allowing an expansion in occupations that remain inside the firm, or (ii) market share reallocation effects as in Melitz (2003), by which contracting or dying firms are displaced by more productive firms that hire high-education workers more intensively, or (iii) a combination of both. The associated employment gains in high-education occupations are sufficiently large to make up for the employment losses in low-education occupations.

Our third and last empirical specification investigates the effects of Chinese import exposure on occupational employment across different sectors. After classifying industries into three sectors (Chinese-trade exposed, non-exposed tradable and non-exposed non-tradable), this chapter finds large and negative employment effects of Chinese exposure on lower-indexed occupations across all sectors, with the exposed sector accounting for 55 to 63 per cent of employment losses due to direct exposure. Although the losses in the exposed sector's lower-indexed occupations are expected, the losses in lower-indexed occupations in the non-exposed sector are a novel result. The most likely explanation of this result is the existence of local-labor-market effects as in Autor, Dorn and Hanson (2013) along with a heavy regional concentration of lower-indexed occupations. Importantly, we find no evidence of Chinese-induced job reallocation of lower-indexed occupations from the exposed sector to the non-exposed sector.

The rest of the chapter is organized as follows. Section 2 briefly describes the relevant literature. In Section 3 we discuss our data sources, and present a brief overview of the 2002–2014 changes in occupational employment and in our occupation-specific measures of Chinese import exposure. Section 4 presents our empirical analysis for the impact of Chinese import exposure on U.S. occupational employment. Lastly, Section 5 concludes.

2.   Literature review

As mentioned above, this chapter builds on the recent contributions of Autor, Dorn, and Hanson (2013), AADHP and Pierce and Schott (2016), who study the impact of the China shock on U.S. employment. The main difference with those papers is that we use occupational employment data, which allows us to exploit differences in occupational characteristics to estimate differential effects of Chinese exposure.[2]

Related to our focus on occupations, there are papers that link trade exposure to U.S. outcomes at the occupational level. Ebenstein, Harrison and McMillan (2015) estimate the impact of trade exposure on occupational wages using worker-level data from the Current Population Survey (CPS). Similar to our approach, they construct occupation-specific measures of import penetration. Also focusing on U.S. wages, Ebenstein, Harrison, McMillan and Phillips (2014) find that the negative effects of globalization affect routine occupations the most, and argue – while highlighting the importance of labor reallocation across sectors and into different occupations – that globalization affects wages by pushing workers out of the manufacturing sector to take lower-paying jobs elsewhere. Using also CPS data, Liu and Trefler (2011) examine the impact of trade in services with China and India on U.S. unemployment, occupational switching, and earnings. They also find that routine occupations are the most adversely affected by service imports. Along those lines, Oldenski (2012) shows that U.S. firms are more likely to offshore routine tasks, while less routine tasks are more likely to be performed in their U.S. headquarters. More generally, we find that Chinese import exposure negatively affects employment in lower-indexed occupations whether they are classified by wage, non-routineness, or education.

Keller and Utar (2016) link Chinese import competition and occupational employment. Using Danish employer-employee matched data from 1999 to 2009, they show that import competition from China explains a large part of the increase in job polarization. They document the decline in employment in mid-wage occupations as well as the rise in employment in both low-wage and high-wage occupations. They also report that in the process of Danish job polarization there is substantial worker reallocation from the manufacturing sector to services. In contrast, in this chapter we find that Chinese import exposure reduces employment in low-wage occupations in every sector, and there is not statistically significant evidence of Chinese-induced job creation in the highest-wage occupations. Hence, we do not find evidence of Chinese-induced job polarization based on the wage criterion. We find, however, evidence of strong job destruction in mid-routine occupations in all sectors, which indicates Chinese-induced polarization under the non-routineness criterion. The last result points out that the adversely affected mid-routine occupations are more related to low-wage (and low-education) occupations than to mid-wage occupations.

Under the education criterion, this chapter finds that Chinese direct import exposure yields net employment gains due to large job creation in high-education occupations, which dominates the job destruction in low-education occupations. Relatedly, Wright (2014) uses manufacturing data and finds that offshoring – which we interpret as imports of intermediate inputs from China – reduces low-skill employment but increases high-skill employment, with the net effect being positive. Similar to our interpretation, he attributes these results to strong productivity effects.

In terms of welfare, Artuç and McLaren (2015) estimate a dynamic structural model using CPS data and find that an offshoring shock harms low-education workers and benefits high-education workers. Using Danish data in the estimation of a dynamic model of occupational choice, Traiber-man (2017) obtains similar evidence for the effects of lower import prices on earnings of low- and high-education workers. In a similar vein, Lee (2017) uses a multi-country Roy model and finds that "China effects" – measured by decreases in trade costs with China and increases in China's productivity – increase between-educational-type inequality in most of the 32 countries in her sample.

3. Data and overview

Our analysis for the impact of Chinese import exposure on U.S. occupational employment relies on data from several sources. We obtain (i) occupational wage and employment data from the Occupational Employment Statistics (OES) database of the Bureau of Labor Statistics (BLS), (ii) data on occupation characteristics from the O*NET database, (iii) data on trade flows from the United Nations Comtrade database and (iv) U.S. national and industry data from the Bureau of Economic Analysis (BEA).

This section describes the construction of our occupational employment and Chinese import penetration variables, and provides an overview of their evolution during our period of study (2002–2014).

3.1. Occupational employment and occupation characteristics

The OES database provides yearly occupational employment and mean hourly wage at the four-digit NAICS level. Although the classification of occupations changes across years, the BLS provides concordance tables that allow us to obtain 810 occupations at the six-digit 2010 Standard Occupational Classification (SOC) for the period 2002–2014. We also aggregate the data to 60 industries according to a three-digit NAICS classification of the BEA (see Table 11.A1 in the appendix for the list of industries). In the end, our employment-wage data is an industry-occupation panel for years 2002 to 2014.

We construct time-invariant rankings of occupations along three dimensions: from low to high wage, from routine to non-routine, and from low to high education. For the wage ranking, we first obtain the average yearly wage of each occupation across all industries (weighted by employment), and then convert wages to real terms using the BEA's Personal Consumption Expenditure Price Index (PCEPI). Last, we obtain each occupation's median real wage throughout the 2002–2014 period, and then rank all occupations from the lowest to the highest median real wage.

The non-routineness and education rankings are based on O*NET data on occupation characteristics. Based on Costinot, Oldenski, and Rauch (2011), the non-routineness ranking is constructed from the O*NET's rating (on a 0 to 100 scale) of the importance of "making decisions and solving problems" for each occupation. On the other hand, the education ranking is created from the O*NET's "job zone" rating (on a 1 to 5 scale) of the level of preparation needed to perform each occupation.[3]

Out of 810, we are able to sort 757 occupations using the wage ranking, and 749 occupations using the non-routineness and education rankings. For illustration and comparison purposes, we convert the three occupation rankings to percentile ranks – in the $(0,1)$ interval – so that, for example, a percentile wage rank of 0.4 for an occupation indicates that 40 per cent of occupations have a lower median wage. Hence, for occupation i, we define w_i as its percentile wage rank, q_i as its percentile non-routineness rank, and e_i as its percentile education rank. As expected, the correlation between the three percentile ranks is high and positive: 0.65 between w and q, 0.75 between w and e, and 0.59 between q and e.

Using our three sorting criteria, we can now look at changes in the composition of U.S. occupational employment during our period of study. Let $\bar{w}_{jt} \in (0,1)$ denote the *average real-wage index* of industry j in year t, defined as

$$\bar{w}_{jt} = \sum_i \left(\frac{L_{ijt}}{L_{jt}} \right) w_i,$$

where L_{ijt} is the total employment in occupation i in industry j at year t, and $L_{jt} \equiv \sum_i L_{ijt}$ is total employment in industry j at year t (L_{ijt}/L_{jt} is the employment share of occupation i in industry j at year t). Note that an increase in $\bar{w}_{jt}$ indicates a higher employment share of high-wage occupations in that industry, while the opposite is true for a reduction in $\bar{w}_{jt}$. With analogous definitions for $\bar{q}_{jt}$ and $\bar{e}_{jt}$ – the *average non-routineness index* and the *average education index* of industry j in year t – Figure 11.1 plots the 2014 values of our three average indexes against their 2002 values for our 60 industries. Most 2014 values are above the 45 degree line for each sorting criteria, showing a generalized change in

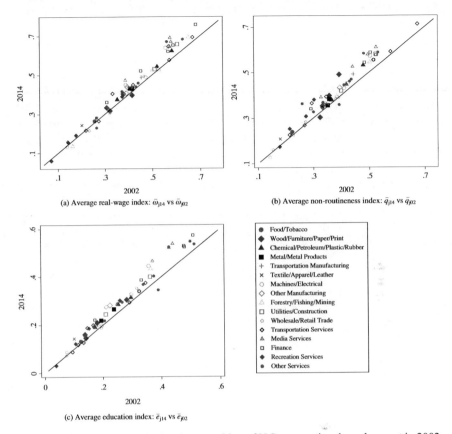

Figure 11.1 Average industry-level composition of U.S. occupational employment in 2002 and 2014

the composition of U.S. employment toward higher-indexed (higher wage, more non-routine, higher education) occupations. These findings are consistent with previous evidence by Berman, Bound, and Griliches (1994), who similarly reported a shift in employment towards skilled labor in manufacturing during the 1980s.

In addition, Figure 11.1 classifies our 60 industries into 16 categories. This allows us to identify which industries are more intensive in lower-indexed or higher-indexed occupations, and also to pinpoint similarities and differences across the three indexes. Along the three dimensions, the industries that are intensive in lower-indexed occupations are Recreation Services, Wholesale/Retail Trade, Textile/Apparel/Leather, and Food/Tobacco; the industries that are intensive in higher-indexed occupations are Finance and Media Services; and the industries that are in the middle of the pack are in general manufacturing industries such as Wood/Furniture/Paper/Print, Metal Products, Chemical/Petroleum/

Plastic/Rubber, and Machines/Electrical. On the other hand, Transportation Services is the most non-routine category, and while industries in this category have in general mid-to-high average real wages, they have low average education indexes.

Reinforcing the point of a generalized change in the composition of U.S. employment toward higher-indexed occupations, Figure 11.2 shows the kernel distributions of occupational employment in 2002 and 2014 under our three sorting criteria. Figure 11.2a shows that the decline in the employment share of lower-wage occupations occurs up to the 60th percentile, while Figure 11.2b shows that the decline in the employment share of routine occupations occurs up to the 40th percentile. An interesting fact from the distributions in Figures 11.2a and 11.2b is that they evolved from slightly bimodal in 2002 to

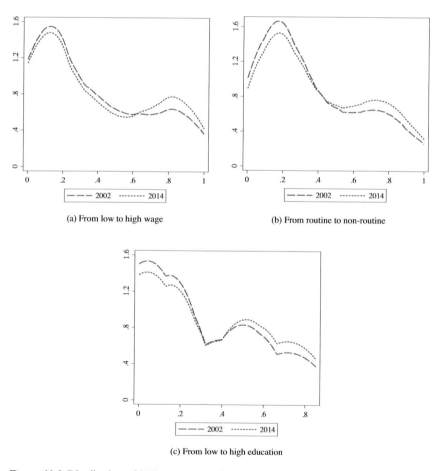

(a) From low to high wage

(b) From routine to non-routine

(c) From low to high education

Figure 11.2 Distribution of U.S. occupational employment in 2002 and 2014 (by sorting criterion)

distinctly bimodal in 2014. This shows that polarization in the U.S. labor market during the 2002–2014 period is mostly the result of an increase in relative employment in occupations on the right side of the distribution, rather than in occupations on the left side.

From Figure 11.2c we see that the kernel distribution of occupational employment based on the education ranking is not as smooth as the distributions based on the wage and non-routineness rankings. This is simply a consequence of the O*NET "job zone" rating, which clusters in integer values from 1 to 5 (corresponding to values 0, 0.05, 0.39, 0.66 and 0.85 in the percentile education rank, e). Nevertheless, the same story emerges: from 2002 to 2014 there has been a change in the composition of employment in favor of occupations that need a higher level of education.

3.2. Chinese import penetration

This section describes our measures of U.S. exposure to Chinese imports. First we discuss the construction of the industry-level measures, and then show how to construct from them the occupation-specific measures of Chinese import penetration.

3.2.1. Industry-level Chinese import penetration

We use the industry-level Chinese import penetration variables of AADHP. The differences are our industry classification, which is based on 60 BEA industries, and our period of study.

AADHP define Chinese import penetration in industry j in year t as the ratio of U.S. industry j's real imports from China in year t to industry j's real domestic absorption in a base year. Taking 2000 as our base year, the Chinese import penetration ratio in industry j in year t is given by

$$IP_{jt} = \frac{\mathbb{M}_{jt}^{C}}{\mathbb{Y}_{j00} + \mathbb{M}_{j00} - \mathbb{X}_{j00}}, \tag{1}$$

where $\mathbb{M}_{jt}^{C}$ are U.S. industry j's real imports from China in year t, $\mathbb{Y}_{j00}$ is industry j's real gross output in 2000, $\mathbb{M}_{j00}$ are industry j's real total imports in 2000, and $\mathbb{X}_{j00}$ are industry j's real total exports in 2000. Nominal U.S. imports from China come from the United Nations Comtrade Database, while U.S. industry-level gross output, total exports, and total imports come from the BEA's Industry and International Economic Accounts. All nominal values are converted to real terms using the BEA's PCE price index.[4]

AADHP are concerned about U.S. demand shocks possibly driving the increase in U.S. imports from China. To isolate the supply-driven component of the rise of China's exports to the U.S., AADHP follow Autor, Dorn and Hanson (2013) and instrument Chinese import penetration in the U.S. with

Chinese exports to other developed economies. Hence, and in line with AADHP, the instrument for our variable in equation (1) is

$$IP_{jt}^* = \frac{\mathrm{M}_{jt}^{C*}}{\mathrm{Y}_{j00} + \mathrm{M}_{j00} - \mathrm{X}_{j00}}, \tag{2}$$

where M_{jt}^{C*} is the sum of Chinese exports to Australia, Denmark, Finland, Germany, Japan, New Zealand, Spain and Switzerland in industry j at year t. The data on Chinese exports to these countries is obtained from Comtrade (in nominal U.S. dollars) and is deflated using the PCE price index.

Chinese import exposure may also affect an industry's employment indirectly through input-output linkages. Inspired by Acemoglu, Carvalho, Ozdaglar and Tahbaz-Salehi (2012), AADHP define *upstream* import penetration as the import effects flowing from directly impacted buying industries to their domestic supplying industries, and *downstream* import penetration as the effects flowing from directly impacted supplying industries to their domestic buying industries. While the impact of upstream import exposure on employment is expected to be negative (if buying industries shrink due to foreign competition, then their domestic providers will sell less and will shrink too), the impact of downstream import exposure on employment may be positive or negative (if domestic providers shrink due to foreign competition, then industries may contract due to less access to domestic inputs, but may also expand due to access to cheaper inputs from abroad). In this chapter we also take into account employment responses to Chinese import exposure due to first-order upstream and downstream linkages.[5]

The upstream and downstream import penetration variables are weighted averages of the direct import penetration variable in equation (1), with weights obtained from the BEA's 2000 Input-Output Table.[6] Let μ_{gj} denote the value of industry j's output purchased by industry g. Then, upstream weights are computed as $\omega_{gj}^U = \mu_{gj}/\sum_{g'} \mu_{g'j}$ for every g, where $\sum_{g'} \mu_{g'j}$ is industry j's total output value. Therefore, the upstream import penetration from China for industry j is given by

$$UIP_{jt} = \sum_g \omega_{gj}^U IP_{gt}. \tag{3}$$

Likewise, downstream weights for industry j are calculated as $\omega_{jg}^D = \mu_{jg}/\sum_{g'} \mu_{jg'}$ for every g, where $\sum_{g'} \mu_{jg'}$ is the value of industry j's total purchases; hence, downstream import penetration from China for industry j is

$$DIP_{jt} = \sum_g \omega_{jg}^D IP_{gt}. \tag{4}$$

Using (2), we construct the instruments for UIP_{jt} and DIP_{jt} as $UIP_{jt}^* = \sum_g \omega_{gj}^U IP_{gt}^*$ and $DIP_{jt}^* = \sum_g \omega_{jg}^D IP_{gt}^*$.

3.2.2.   Occupation-specific Chinese import penetration

Occupations vary in their degree of exposure to Chinese imports. For example, an occupation that is mainly employed in the computer and electronics industry is more exposed to Chinese imports than an occupation mainly employed in the real estate industry. To account for this, we construct occupation-specific measures of Chinese import exposure using the industry-level import penetration variables from the previous section.

Similar to Ebenstein, Harrison and McMillan (2015), the occupation-specific trade variables are weighted averages of the industry-level trade variables, with weights determined by each industry's share in the occupation's total employment. Using weights from 2002, which is the first year in our occupational employment data, we define the Chinese import penetration for occupation i as

$$IP_{it} = \sum_j \left(\frac{L_{ij02}}{L_{i02}}\right) IP_{jt}, \tag{5}$$

where L_{ij02} is the employment of occupation i in industry j in 2002, $L_{i02} \equiv \sum_j L_{ij02}$ is the total employment in occupation i in 2002, and IP_{jt} is the Chinese import penetration in industry j in year t as described in (1). As weights may respond endogenously to changes in Chinese import penetration – which may lead to selection bias in a measure with changing weights – the best approach in the construction of occupation-specific variables is to use the same weights throughout our period of study.[7] We follow the same formula (and weights) from (5) to construct occupation-specific upstream and downstream Chinese import penetration variables, UIP_{it} and DIP_{it}, as well as occupation-specific import penetration instruments, IP_{it}^*, UIP_{it}^*, and DIP_{it}^*.

We can now look at the evolution of occupation-specific variables during our period of study. For the 671 occupations that report employment in every year, Figure 11.3 shows the values in 2002 of the direct import penetration, IP_{it}, and the combined import penetration, $IP_{it} + UIP_{it} + DIP_{it}$, against their values in 2014. Two of our econometric specifications in Section 4 classify occupations into tertiles (low, middle, high) for each of our sorting criteria (wage, non-routineness, and education). In line with this, the graphics in the left side of Figure 11.3 show the same plot of direct import penetration, but differ in their sorting criteria, while the graphics on the right side do the same for the combined measure of import exposure. Occupations marked with a circle denote the lowest-tertile occupations (low wage, routine, low-education), those marked with a square denote the middle-tertile occupations (mid-wage, mid-routine, mid-education), and those marked with a triangle denote the highest-tertile occupations (high wage, non-routine, high-education).

First, note that the vast majority of occupations are well above the 45 degree line for both types of Chinese import penetration (direct and combined), indicating extensive occupational exposure to Chinese imports during the period. For the combined import penetration measure, for example, only six occupations

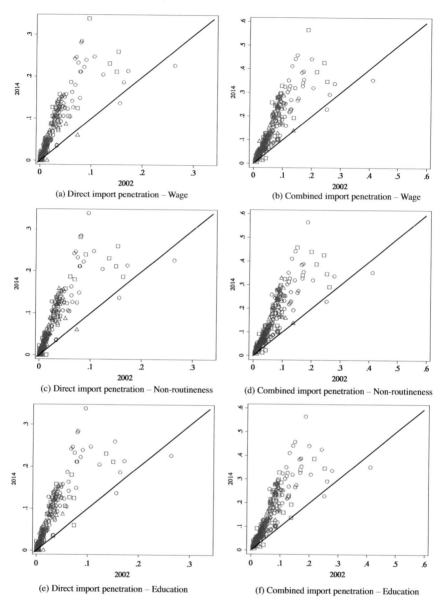

Figure 11.3 Occupation-specific import penetration measures in 2002 and 2014 under three sorting criteria (wage, non-routineness, education): ○ lowest tertile, □ middle tertile, △ highest tertile

(out of 671) had a decline in Chinese import exposure from 2002 to 2014. Second, note that across the three sorting criteria and for both measures of import penetration, lowest-indexed occupations are the most exposed to Chinese import competition, while the highest-indexed occupations are the least exposed. This highlights the strong heterogeneity in the exposure of different occupations to Chinese import competition.

3.3. *Occupation-specific capital exposure controls*

To control for automation forces, which may substitute workers of some occupations but may complement workers in other occupations, in our specifications below we include occupation-specific measures of capital exposure as regressors. Given that changes in capital stock throughout the period are likely to be endogenous, our time-invariant capital-exposure measures are based on 2002 data, which is the first year in our sample.

From the BEA's Fixed Assets accounts, we obtain the quantity index for net capital stock by asset type for each of our industries in 2002. Eden and Gaggl (2015) argue that information and communication technology (ICT) capital – which is related to software and computer equipment – is a closer to substitute to routine occupations than non-ICT capital (equipment, structures, and intellectual property) and suggest to distinguish between them. Following their classification, each asset is labeled as either ICT capital or non-ICT capital.[8] Then, an industry's ICT capital stock index is the weighted average of the industry's ICT-assets quantity indexes, with the weight of each asset determined by the ratio of the asset's current-cost value to the total current-cost of ICT assets in the industry. We follow an analogous procedure to calculate the non-ICT capital stock index.

Let K^I_{j02} denote the ICT capital stock index for industry j in 2002, and let K^N_{j02} denote the non-ICT capital stock index for industry j in 2002. Hence, similar to the construction of the occupation-specific import penetration variables in (5), the index of ICT capital exposure for occupation i is given by

$$K^I_i = \sum_j \left(\frac{L_{ij02}}{L_{i02}}\right) K^I_{j02}, \tag{6}$$

with a similar definition for K^N_i, which is occupation i's index of non-ICT capital exposure based on 2002 data.

4. Responses of U.S. occupational employment to Chinese import exposure

This section estimates the effects of Chinese import exposure on U.S. occupational employment. Given that the effects of import exposure may take some time before they are reflected in employment, we focus our analysis on a panel with three-year changes. Thus, we use periods 2002–2005, 2005–2008, 2008–2011, and 2011–2014. Following AADHP, we use the operator "Δ" to denote annualized changes times 100 so that for any variable X_{it}, we define ΔX_{it} as

$$\Delta X_{it} \equiv \frac{100}{3}[X_{it} - X_{it-3}].$$

We refer to ΔX_{it} as the "annualized change" in X between $t - 3$ and t.

4.1.   *Employment responses without occupational sorting*

We start by ignoring occupational sorting. Hence, our specification to estimate the average impact of Chinese import exposure on occupational employment is

$$\Delta \ln L_{it} = \alpha_t + \beta \Delta IP_{it} + \gamma Z_i + \varepsilon_{it}, \tag{7}$$

where for occupation i and between $t - 3$ and t, $\Delta \ln L_{it}$ is the annualized change in log employment, ΔIP_{it} is the annualized change in Chinese import exposure, α_t is a time fixed effect, and ε_{it} is an error term. For each occupation i, the term Z_i is a vector of time-invariant *production controls* that includes the 2002 values of the log average real wage, and the log of the ICT and non-ICT capital-stock indexes (K_i^I and K_i^N). Our coefficient of interest is β, which represents the semi-elasticity of occupational employment to Chinese import exposure.

Table 11.1 presents the results of the estimation of the specification in (7). All regressions in Table 11.1, as well as all the following regressions, are weighted by 2002 employment and show standard errors clustered at the occupation level. Columns 1–3 use as main regressor the annualized change in direct import penetration as defined in (5), while columns 4 and 5 use instead annualized changes of combined import penetration measures. The first combined measure adds the direct and upstream measures ($IP_{it} + UIP_{it}$), while the second combined measure adds the direct, upstream, and downstream measures ($IP_{it} + UIP_{it} + DIP_{it}$). Consequently, in the instrumental variables (IV) regressions, the instrument in columns 2–3 is ΔIP_{it}^*, the instrument in column 4 is $\Delta(IP_{it}^* + UIP_{it}^*)$, and the instrument in column 5 is $\Delta(IP_{it}^* + UIP_{it}^* + DIP_{it}^*)$.

All the estimates for β in the five columns of Table 11.1 are negative and statistically significant at least at the 5 per cent level, showing that – as found by Autor, Dorn, and Hanson (2013) at the commuting-zone level and by AADHP at the industry level – Chinese import exposure is associated with job losses in the United States. Column 1 presents the OLS estimation without production controls, and column 2 presents the analogous IV estimation. Note that the estimate for β in column 2 is almost twice as large as the coefficient in column 1, which highlights the importance of the IV approach to take care of a strong endogeneity bias. Columns 3–5 include production controls. Comparing columns 2 and 3, notice that the magnitude of the estimate for β declines by almost 40 per cent

Table 11.1 Estimation of U.S. occupational employment responses to Chinese import exposure

	OLS		IV estimation	
	(1)	(2)	(3)	(4)	(5)
Direct import exposure	−0.97***	−1.91***	−1.16***		
	(0.34)	(0.37)	(0.40)		
Combined import exposure I				−0.83**	
(direct + upstream)				(0.38)	
Combined import exposure II					−0.69**
(direct + upstream + downstream)					(0.30)
Production controls	No	No	Yes	Yes	Yes
Observations	2,672	2,672	2,444	2,444	2,444

Notes: All regressions include time-fixed affects (not reported) and are weighted by 2002 employment. Standard errors (in parentheses) are clustered at the occupation level. The coefficients are statistically significant at the *10%, **5%, or ***1% level.

(the coefficient changes from −1.91 to −1.16), which indicates that the exclusion of production controls leads to an overestimation of the negative impact of Chinese imports on U.S. employment.

From column 4, note that the coefficient on import exposure declines in magnitude if we use instead the combined measure of direct plus upstream import penetration (the coefficient changes from −1.16 to −0.83). This, however, does not imply that the negative effects of Chinese import exposure on U.S. occupational employment are smaller when we consider upstream input-output linkages. To know this, we need to separately calculate the 2002–2014 predicted employment losses from columns 3 and 4. Following Autor, Dorn, and Hanson (2013) and AADHP, the formula to calculate column 4's predicted employment changes from Chinese import exposure from 2002 to 2014 is

$$Predicted\ employment\ change = \sum_i \left[1 - e^{-\hat{\beta}\rho(IP_{i14} - IP_{i02})}\right]L_{i14}, \tag{8}$$

where $\rho = 0.78$ is the partial R-squared from the first-stage regression of ΔIP_{it} on ΔIP_{it}^* from the specification in column 2. We derive a similar expression to calculate column 4's predicted losses, with the value of ρ kept constant at 0.78.

Predicted employment losses from 2002 to 2014 are 1.05 million from direct exposure (column 3) and 1.51 million from the combined direct and upstream exposure (column 4). Therefore, upstream input-output links further reduce U.S. employment by about 0.46 million jobs. Column 5 adds downstream exposure to the combined measure and reports a smaller estimate for β (−0.69), but again, we need to calculate predicted employment losses because changes in the combined exposure measure are likely to be larger. Indeed, column 5's predicted employment losses from Chinese exposure are 2.12 million, so that about 0.61 million jobs (2.12 million minus 1.51 million) are lost due to downstream input-output linkages.[9]

4.2.   *Employment responses with occupational sorting*

The main contribution of this chapter is that we can analyze the effects of Chinese import exposure on different types of occupations classified by either wage level, degree of non-routineness, or required education. For each of these criteria, we sort occupations into tertiles (low, middle and high) using the percentile ranks described in Section 3.1. Thus, the econometric specification with occupational sorting is

$$\Delta \ln L_{it} = \sum_{k=1}^{3} \left[\alpha_{kt}^{\ell} + \beta_k^{\ell}\Delta IP_{it} + \gamma_k^{\ell}Z_i\right]\mathbb{1}_i\{T_k^{\ell}\} + \varepsilon_{it}, \tag{9}$$

where $\ell \in \{w, q, e\}$ denotes the sorting criteria (wage, non-routineness, or education), $k \in \{1, 2, 3\}$ indicates the tertile (from low to high), $\mathbb{1}_i\{T_k^{\ell}\}$ is a dummy variable taking the value of $\mathbb{1}$ if occupation i belongs to tertile k under criteria

ℓ, and α_{kt}^{ℓ} accounts for tertile-time fixed effects. This specification is estimated separately for each sorting criteria. Hence, for each $\ell \in \{w, q, e\}$, the coefficients of interest are β_1^{ℓ}, β_2^{ℓ} and β_3^{ℓ}, which indicate the employment semi-elasticity to Chinese import exposure for each occupational tertile.

Table 11.2 shows our IV estimation of (9) for the impact of direct import exposure. Production controls are included in even columns and excluded in odd columns. All six columns show strong and highly significant negative effects of direct Chinese import exposure on the lowest occupational tertiles (low-wage, routine, low-education occupations). Therefore, Chinese import exposure is related to job losses in all kinds of lower-indexed occupations, suggesting that a high content of these types of occupations is embodied in U.S. imports from China. As well, columns 3–4 show statistically significant evidence of Chinese-induced job losses in mid-routine occupations.

Under the education-sorting criterion with production controls, column 6 shows a positive and mildly significant coefficient for the impact of direct import exposure on high-education occupations. The predicted employment expansion in high-education occupations – while employment declines in occupations in the lowest tertiles – can be the result of (i) reallocation of workers from low- to high-education occupations, (ii) strong productivity effects in the presence of complementarities between low- and high-education occupations, or (iii) Melitz-type reallocation of markets shares from low-productivity firms to high-productivity firms.

The first scenario is, however, unlikely, as released low-educated workers would have to retool themselves with college degrees, or a large number of highly educated workers would have to be employed in low-education occupations in the first place. Regarding the second scenario, and as discussed by Grossman and Rossi-Hansberg (2008) and Groizard, Ranjan and Rodriguez-Lopez (2014), the offshoring of lower-indexed occupations allows firms to reduce marginal costs (so that productivity increases), which allows them to set lower prices and capture larger market shares; this translates to higher employment in occupations that remain inside the firm, with larger employment gains if there is complementarity across occupations.[10] Last, the third scenario requires that contracting or dying firms have a disproportionately large share of low-educated workers, while expanding high-productivity firms either upgrade their labor force or have a disproportionately large share of highly-educated workers.[11] The most plausible mechanism for the results in column 6 is a combination of the second and third scenarios.

Table 11.3 considers the occupational employment effects of combined import exposure. For both combined measures, the implications described from direct import exposure on lower-indexed occupations remain robust: there is Chinese-induced job destruction in low-wage, routine and mid-routine, and low-education occupations when we consider input-output linkages across industries. Similar to what we observed in Table 11.1, the import-exposure estimates decline in magnitude when we use the combined measures. However, this does not imply

Table 11.2 IV estimation of U.S. occupational employment responses to Chinese direct import exposure: by tertiles based on three occupation-sorting criteria

	Wage		Non-routineness		Education	
	(1)	*(2)*	*(3)*	*(4)*	*(5)*	*(6)*
Direct import exposure						
Lowest tertile	-2.42***	-1.81***	-2.07***	-1.46***	-2.19***	-1.63***
	(0.60)	(0.55)	(0.52)	(0.43)	(0.52)	(0.50)
Middle tertile	0.14	0.91	-2.73***	-2.25***	-0.78	-0.04
	(0.75)	(1.01)	(0.46)	(0.71)	(0.87)	(1.12)
Highest tertile	-0.21	2.35	0.63	3.42	3.40	7.08*
	(2.16)	(2.64)	(1.80)	(2.47)	(2.85)	(4.21)
Production controls	No	Yes	No	Yes	No	Yes
Observations	2,460	2,444	2,660	2,436	2,660	2,436

Notes: All regressions include tertile-time fixed affects (not reported). Standard errors (in parentheses) are clustered at the occupation level. The coefficients are statistically significant at the *10%, **5%, or ***1% level.

Table 11.3 IV estimation of U.S. occupational employment responses to Chinese combined import exposure: by tertiles based on three occupation-sorting criteria

	Wage		Non-routineness		Education	
	(1)	(2)	(3)	(4)	(5)	(6)
A. Combined import exposure I (direct + upstream)						
Lowest tertile	-2.00***	-1.47***	-1.69***	-1.16***	-1.72***	-1.19***
	(0.46)	(0.42)	(0.41)	(0.35)	(0.38)	(0.36)
Middle tertile	0.06	0.62	-1.86***	-1.55**	-0.24	-0.13
	(0.55)	(0.77)	(0.48)	(0.64)	(0.78)	(0.86)
Highest tertile	-0.37	1.76	0.60	3.08	1.64	4.83
	(1.62)	(2.12)	(1.45)	(2.08)	(2.03)	(3.25)
B. Combined import exposure II (direct + upstream + downstream)						
Lowest tertile	-1.55***	-1.12***	-1.30***	-0.87***	-1.40***	-0.99***
	(0.37)	(0.34)	(0.31)	(0.27)	(0.32)	(0.31)
Middle tertile	-0.13	0.17	-1.51**	-1.42***	0.29	-0.09
	(0.45)	(0.60)	(0.59)	(0.52)	(0.97)	(0.65)
Highest tertile	-0.36	1.08	0.44	2.17	1.52	3.78
	(1.41)	(1.70)	(1.35)	(1.82)	(1.83)	(2.69)
Production controls	No	Yes	No	Yes	No	Yes
Observations	2,460	2,444	2,660	2,436	2,660	2,436

Notes: All regressions include tertile-time fixed affects (not reported). Standard errors (in parentheses) are clustered at the occupation level. The coefficients are statistically significant at the *10%, **5%, or ***1% level.

smaller employment effects because changes in the combined import-exposure measures are likely to be larger. To shed light on this, we need to calculate predicted employment changes for each occupational tertile (under each sorting criteria) using formulas that are analogous to equation (8).

Table 11.4 presents the predicted employment changes from Chinese import exposure based on the regressions with production controls (in the even columns) of Tables 11.2 and 11.3, as well as for other specifications described below. For our three sorting criteria, the first three rows of Table 11.4 show that predicted employment losses for occupations in the lowest tertile are between 0.6 and 0.8 million due to direct exposure, are between 1.1 and 1.3 million when we consider upstream links, and further increase to between 1.43 and 1.75 million if we also consider downstream links. These losses are the main component of the average employment losses reported in the previous section. In addition, the statistically significant predicted job losses in mid-routine occupations range between 0.5 million from direct exposure to about 0.9 million when considering upstream and downstream linkages.

Column 6 in Table 11.2 shows a strong positive effect of direct import exposure on high-education occupations, with the first row of Table 11.4 showing that the 1.2 million predicted job gains in high-education occupations more than make up for the 0.8 million job losses in low-education occupations. However, column 6 of Table 11.3 shows that the high-education import exposure coefficient loses its statistical significance once we consider input-output linkages (for both combined measures). Hence, although the second and third row of Table 11.4 show predicted job gains in high-education occupations that continue to be larger than job losses in low-education occupations, these job gains are no longer statistically significant. Thus, the Chinese-induced positive productivity effects on U.S. firms occur through direct exposure, and not through input-output linkages.

The results of Tables 11.2, 11.3 and the first three rows of Table 11.4 suggest, not surprisingly, substantial overlap in the employment losses of low-wage, routine and low-education occupations. They also suggest an overlap between mid-routine occupations and low-wage, low-education occupations. Moreover, although there are always predicted job gains in the highest-tertile occupations along the three criteria, they are only significant for direct exposure in high-education occupations. This indicates either that (i) high-education occupations that benefit from Chinese exposure are not necessarily concentrated in non-routine, high-wage occupations, or that (ii) there is a large fraction of Chinese-impacted low-education occupations that are non-routine or high-wage, which average out employment gains in other higher wage and non-routine occupations, or (iii) a combination of both.

4.3. Employment responses by sector exposure

The last part of our empirical analysis expands the specification in equation (9) to account for different impacts of Chinese import exposure across occupational employment in different sectors. This exercise is motivated by AADHP, who

Table 11.4 Predicted employment changes (in thousands) from Chinese import exposure (2002–2014)

	Wage			Non-routineness			Education		
	Lowest tertile	Middle tertile	Highest tertile	Lowest tertile	Middle tertile	Highest tertile	Lowest tertile	Middle tertile	Highest tertile
Table 11.2									
Direct import exposure	**−731**	205	606	**−602**	**−497**	876	**−794**	−9	**1,227**
Table 11.3, panel A									
Direct + upstream	**−1,292**	266	813	**−1,101**	**−609**	1,352	**−1,216**	−56	1,580
Table 11.3, panel B									
Direct + upstream+downstream	**−1,751**	112	811	**−1,429**	**−907**	1,526	**−1,662**	−66	2,097
Table 11.5									
Direct import exposure									
Exposed	**−380**	122	2,187	**−243**	**−257**	1,954	**−401**	42	2,248
Non-exposed tradable	**−23**	**25**	5	**−22**	**−17**	**17**	**−32**	**16**	10
Non-exposed non-tradable	**−289**	117	−126	−119	−247	249	−216	−27	117
Table 11.6, panel A									
Direct + upstream									
Exposed	**−530**	199	3,083	**−293**	−290	2,464	**−508**	98	2,991
Non-exposed tradable	**−36**	**38**	13	**−32**	−18	**23**	**−46**	**20**	17
Non-exposed non-tradable	**−448**	81	−453	−448	−323	565	−148	−201	−122
Table 11.6, panel B									
Direct + upstream + downstream									
Exposed	**−720**	181	3,311	**−421**	**−381**	2,627	**−705**	67	3,277
Non-exposed tradable	**−40**	**45**	19	**−36**	−20	**29**	**−51**	**23**	19
Non-exposed non-tradable	209	−28	**−871**	−253	−801	1,070	94	−161	−282

Notes: Reported quantities represent the change in employment attributed to instrumented changes in import exposure in all specifications reported in Tables 11.2–11.5 with wage and capital controls. Negative values indicate that import exposure reduces employment. Equation (8) shows the general formula to calculate predicted employment changes. The numbers in bold denote predicted changes corresponding to statistically significant coefficients in Tables 11.2–11.5. The predicted employment changes changes from Table 11.1 are −1,051,651 for the direct effect, −1,512,415 for the direct and upstream combined effect and −2,122,630 for the direct, upstream and downstream combined effect of import exposure.

classify industries into three sectors – exposed, non-exposed tradable, and non-exposed non-tradable – according to industry-level measures of (direct and upstream) Chinese import exposure, to investigate different sectoral employment responses within a local-labor-market analysis, as well as to look for evidence of employment reallocation across sectors.[12]

As in AADHP, we begin by dividing our 60 industries into three sectors, $s \in \{1, 2, 3\}$, with '1' denoting the exposed sector, '2' denoting the non-exposed tradable sector and '3' denoting the non-exposed non-tradable sector.[13] The sectoral econometric specification can then be written as

$$\Delta \ln L_{ist} = \sum_{k=1}^{3} [\alpha_{kst}^{\ell} + \beta_{k1}^{\ell} \Delta IP_{it} \times \mathbb{1}_s\{1\} + \beta_{k2}^{\ell} \Delta IP_{it} \quad (10)$$

$$\times \mathbb{1}_s\{2\} + \beta_{k3}^{\ell} \Delta IP_{it} \times \mathbb{1}_s\{3\} + \gamma_{ks}^{\ell} Z_{is}] \mathbb{1}_i\{T_k^{\ell}\} + \varepsilon_{ist},$$

where, between $t - 3$ and t, $\Delta \ln L_{ist}$ is the annualized change in log employment of occupation i in sector s, ΔIP_{it} is the annualized change in Chinese import exposure of occupation i, and Z_{is} is a vector of time-invariant production controls of occupation i in sector s.[14] Also, $\mathbb{1}_s\{S\}$ is a dummy variable taking the value of 1 if $s \equiv S$, for $S \in \{1, 2, 3\}$, and $\mathbb{1}_i\{T_k^{\ell}\}$ is a dummy variable taking the value of 1 if occupation i belongs to tertile k under sorting criterion $\ell \in \{w, q, e\}$. The term α_{kst} denotes a tertile-sector-time fixed effect and ε_{ist} is the error term.

Table 11.5 shows the results from the estimation of equation (10) for the impact of Chinese direct import exposure on U.S. occupational-sectoral employment. Columns 1 and 2 use the occupation-sorting criterion based on wage, columns 3 and 4 use the non-routineness criterion, and columns 5 and 6 use the education criterion. Regressions in even columns include production controls, and regressions in odd columns do not include them. Note that each column reports estimates for nine β-coefficients: one coefficient for each tertile (low, middle, high) in each of the three sectors.

For the exposed sector, Table 11.5 shows that direct import exposure has negative and statistically significant effects in lower-indexed occupations under the three criteria, as well as on mid-routine occupations. Indeed, the job destruction effect on mid-routine occupations is larger in magnitude than the impact on the highly routine (lowest tertile) occupations, which suggests that an important fraction of mid-routine occupations are low wage and low education. In contrast, although there are large and positive coefficients for the higher-indexed occupations, none of them is statistically significant.

The non-exposed tradable sector also has statistically significant job destruction in lower-indexed (under the three criteria) and mid-routine occupations, but also shows mildly significant evidence of job creation in mid-wage, mid-education, and highly non-routine occupations. The implied job destruction in a non-exposed sector is likely a consequence of local labor market effects, as described by Autor, Dorn and Hanson (2013). The result that these job

Table 11.5 IV estimation of U.S. occupational employment responses to Chinese direct import exposure: by sector exposure under three occupation-sorting criteria

	Wage		Non-routineness		Education	
	(1)	(2)	(3)	(4)	(5)	(6)
Direct import exposure						
Exposed						
Lowest tertile	−2.33***	−1.47***	−1.77***	−1.07**	−2.21***	−1.21***
	(0.67)	(0.57)	(0.62)	(0.46)	(0.58)	(0.45)
Middle tertile	0.01	0.87	−2.66***	−1.54**	0.01	0.38
	(1.06)	(0.98)	(0.57)	(0.75)	(1.22)	(1.27)
Highest tertile	15.13	24.50	11.72	21.90	30.00	41.69
	(15.94)	(22.57)	(13.30)	(19.75)	(25.57)	(32.86)
Non-exposed tradable						
Lowest tertile	−1.42***	−1.00***	−1.28***	−0.88***	−1.41***	−1.00***
	(0.26)	(0.23)	(0.24)	(0.24)	(0.24)	(0.21)
Middle tertile	1.15	2.55*	−1.96***	−1.55***	2.31*	2.35*
	(1.08)	(1.35)	(0.63)	(0.58)	(1.34)	(1.30)
Highest tertile	0.94	0.60	2.17**	2.47*	2.60	2.40
	(1.31)	(1.52)	(1.09)	(1.31)	(2.51)	(2.38)
Non-exposed non-tradable						
Lowest tertile	−2.55*	−2.50*	−2.13**	−0.95	−2.42*	−1.81
	(1.33)	(1.31)	(1.04)	(0.99)	(1.26)	(1.16)
Middle tertile	2.08	1.67	−4.22***	−3.46***	−0.63	−0.31
	(1.51)	(1.39)	(1.29)	(1.14)	(1.40)	(1.30)
Highest tertile	−2.08	−0.98	1.73	2.18	−1.11	1.13
	(1.66)	(1.50)	(2.08)	(1.93)	(1.97)	(1.67)
Production controls	No	Yes	No	Yes	No	Yes
Observations	5,372	5,273	5,581	5,253	5,581	5,253

Notes: All regressions include tertile-sector-time fixed affects (not reported). Standard errors (in parentheses) are clustered at the occupation level. The coefficients are statistically significant at the *10%, **5%, or ***1% level.

destruction effects of direct exposure happen in the same types of occupations as in the exposed sector, indicates a heavy regional concentration of lower-indexed occupations.[15] On the other hand, the implied job creation in mid-wage, mid-education, highly non-routine occupations is evidence of job reallocation from negatively affected lower-indexed occupations; that is, some released workers are able to find better jobs in more sophisticated occupations.

The coefficients for the non-exposed non-tradable sector in Table 11.5 also show evidence of job destruction in lower-indexed and mid-routine occupations, which also points out toward the existence of local labor market effects under heavy regional concentration of lower-indexed occupations. Note, however, that the coefficients for the lower-indexed occupations under the non-routineness and education criteria lose their statistical significance once production controls are added to the regressions. Moreover, and in contrast to the findings for the non-exposed tradable sector, there is no evidence of job reallocation from occupations with shrinking employment to occupations in the non-exposed non-tradable sector.[16]

Table 11.6 considers the combined measures of Chinese import exposure. Panel A shows the estimation results that use the measure that adds upstream linkages and panel B shows the results that use the measure that adds upstream and downstream linkages. As before, the magnitudes of the coefficients are in general smaller when adding input-output linkages, but this is simply a consequence of the rescaling of the import exposure measure. The results from both panels are qualitatively similar to those discussed for direct import exposure from Table 11.5, though our previous findings for the non-exposed non-tradable sector become largely insignificant.

The only novelty for the non-exposed non-tradable sector comes from significant and negative import-exposure coefficients for high-wage occupations in both panels, which indicates Chinese-induced job destruction in high-wage occupations in this sector. This may be evidence of job reallocation of high-wage occupations from the non-exposed to the exposed sector, with the latter sector demanding more high-wage workers due to productivity effects. However, the evidence is not conclusive because in spite of very large and positive coefficients for high-wage occupations in the exposed sector (indicating a large expansion in these occupations' employment), they have large standard errors and are not statistically significant.

To gauge the importance of the effects obtained in our occupational-sectoral estimation, the last nine rows of Table 11.4 present the 2002–2014 implied employment changes from Tables 11.5 and 11.6 for the specifications including production controls. The predicted changes from direct import exposure show that the exposed sector accounts for the majority of the employment losses in occupations in the lowest tertile: the share of the exposed sector in lowest-tertile losses is 55 per cent under the wage criterion, 63 per cent under the non-routineness criterion and 62 per cent under the education criterion. Thus, between 38 and 45 per cent of predicted job losses in lower-indexed occupations are likely the consequence of local-labor-market effects à la Autor, Dorn and

Table 11.6 IV estimation of U.S. occupational employment responses to Chinese combined import exposure: by sector exposure under three occupation-sorting criteria

	Wage		Non-routineness		Education	
	(1)	(2)	(3)	(4)	(5)	(6)
A. Combined import exposure I (direct + upstream)						
Exposed						
Lowest tertile	-1.90***	-1.18***	-1.26***	-0.72*	-1.73***	-0.90****
	(0.51)	(0.44)	(0.46)	(0.38)	(0.43)	(0.34)
Middle tertile	0.18	0.85	-1.96***	-1.01	0.19	0.54
	(0.82)	(0.84)	(0.49)	(0.69)	(0.88)	(0.94)
Highest tertile	14.47	21.77	10.92	19.12	26.31	33.97
	(13.68)	(17.88)	(11.52)	(16.00)	(20.04)	(23.43)
Non-exposed tradable						
Lowest tertile	-1.21***	-0.86***	-1.09***	-0.75***	-1.16****	-0.82***
	(0.23)	(0.21)	(0.22)	(0.22)	(0.21)	(0.20)
Middle tertile	1.37*	2.32**	-1.26**	-0.90	1.86*	1.90*
	(0.82)	(0.95)	(0.56)	(0.55)	(1.08)	(1.06)
Highest tertile	1.12	0.89	1.93**	2.21**	2.76*	2.48
	(0.98)	(1.14)	(0.84)	(1.00)	(1.63)	(1.61)
Non-exposed non-tradable						
Lowest tertile	-1.44	-1.18	-2.22**	-1.22	-1.15	-0.38
	(1.39)	(1.37)	(1.03)	(0.98)	(1.32)	(1.28)
Middle tertile	0.64	0.49	-3.02*	-1.60	-1.30	-0.99
	(1.15)	(1.14)	(1.59)	(1.64)	(1.11)	(1.07)
Highest tertile	-2.81**	-1.78	1.65	2.52	-2.25	-0.58
	(1.35)	(1.21)	(2.02)	(2.03)	(1.69)	(1.47)

(Continued)

Table 11.6 (Continued)

	Wage		Non-routineness		Education	
	(1)	(2)	(3)	(4)	(5)	(6)
B. Combined import exposure II (direct + upstream + downstream)						
Exposed						
Lowest tertile	-1.70***	-1.18***	-1.14***	-0.74**	-1.54***	-0.92***
	(0.48)	(0.44)	(0.41)	(0.34)	(0.40)	(0.33)
Middle tertile	0.08	0.58	-1.70***	-0.99*	0.06	0.27
	(0.67)	(0.68)	(0.43)	(0.57)	(0.72)	(0.75)
Highest tertile	11.62	17.18	8.83	15.18	21.96	27.96
	(11.27)	(14.49)	(9.62)	(13.20)	(16.97)	(19.57)
Non-exposed tradable						
Lowest tertile	-0.93***	-0.68***	-0.82***	-0.59***	-0.89***	-0.64***
	(0.19)	(0.17)	(0.19)	(0.19)	(0.17)	(0.17)
Middle tertile	1.22*	1.93**	-0.99**	-0.72	1.56*	1.55*
	(0.71)	(0.81)	(0.44)	(0.44)	(0.86)	(0.85)
Highest tertile	1.20	1.02	1.85***	2.10***	2.25*	2.05
	(0.79)	(0.93)	(0.61)	(0.77)	(1.32)	(1.29)
Non-exposed non-tradable						
Lowest tertile	0.20	0.24	-0.82	-0.32	-0.31	0.12
	(1.39)	(1.41)	(0.72)	(0.78)	(1.25)	(1.26)
Middle tertile	-0.03	-0.09	-3.29*	-1.90	-0.55	-0.38
	(1.12)	(1.11)	(1.69)	(1.70)	(0.86)	(0.88)
Highest tertile	-2.53**	-1.80*	2.10	2.62	-1.85	-0.70
	(1.11)	(1.04)	(2.32)	(2.45)	(1.41)	(1.26)
Production controls	No	Yes	No	Yes	No	Yes
Observations	5,372	5,273	5,581	5,253	5,581	5,253

Notes: All regressions include tertile-sector-time fixed affects (not reported). Standard errors (in parentheses) are clustered at the occupation level. The coefficients are statistically significant at the *10%, **5%, or ***1% level.

Hanson (2013), which indicates – given the non-significant employment responses of higher-indexed occupations – that employment in lower-indexed occupations is heavily concentrated in particular regions.

Although the non-exposed tradable sector has statistically significant employment gains in mid-wage, mid-education, and highly non-routine occupations, these are relatively small – between 16,000 jobs in mid-education occupations and 25,000 jobs in mid-wage occupations – when compared to predicted changes in the exposed and non-exposed non-tradable sectors. This is the case because the non-exposed tradable sector is very small, accounting on average for only 2.3 per cent of total employment per year. Thus, although these gains are evidence of job reallocation toward better occupations, their overall impact is very small.

Across our three sorting criteria, upstream and downstream linkages in occupational exposure to Chinese imports increase the exposed sector's job losses in the lowest occupational tertile – considering both types of linkages, job losses increase 89 per cent under the wage criterion, 73 per cent under the non-routineness criterion and 76 per cent under the education criterion. Note that after adding downstream linkages, the significant job losses in high-wage occupations in the non-exposed non-tradable sector amount to 871,000 jobs (which is larger than the 720,000 job losses in low-wage occupations in the exposed sector). Although it is possible that this reflects job reallocation of high-wage occupations from the non-exposed to the exposed sector, the lack of significance of the large predicted gains in the latter sector does not allow us to reach a precise interpretation.[17]

5. Conclusion

Chinese import exposure has a differential impact in employment across occupations. After sorting occupations according to their real wages, degree of non-routineness, and education requirements, we find that employment losses from occupational-level Chinese import exposure are concentrated in low-wage, routine, low-education occupations. These losses occur in both Chinese-trade exposed and non-exposed sectors. Although the result of negative employment effects in the exposed sector's lower-indexed occupations is expected – these U.S. occupations would be the most adversely affected in the influential offshoring models of Feenstra and Hanson (1996) and Grossman and Rossi-Hansberg (2008) – our finding of employment reductions in lower-indexed occupations in the non-exposed sectors is novel and does not have a straightforward interpretation.

We argue that the latter result is a consequence of local labor market effects à la Autor, Dorn and Hanson (2013), in combination with a heavy concentration of lower-indexed occupations in particular regions. In support of this interpretation, exploratory analysis conducted by Van Dam and Ma (2016) using the Chinese import-exposure data of AADHP and Autor, Dorn and Hanson (2013) shows that the U.S. areas most affected by the China shock were "less educated, older and poorer than most of the rest of America."[18]

In a related paper, Asquith, Goswami, Neumark and Rodriguez-Lopez (2017) find that deaths of establishments account for most of the Chinese-induced job destruction in the United States. In conjuction with this chapter's findings, this implies that establishments that die due to the China shock have a larger proportion of workers in lower-indexed occupations than surviving establishments. Although this issue requires further investigation, previous work from Abowd, McKinney and Vilhuber (2009) shows evidence in that direction. Using Longitudinal Employer-Household Dynamics (LEHD) data, they find that firms that employ more workers from the lowest quartile of the human capital distribution are much more likely to die, while firms that employ workers from the highest quartile of the distribution are less likely to die.

We also find mild evidence that direct Chinese exposure drives an employment expansion in high-education occupations. This suggests the existence of productivity effects as in Grossman and Rossi-Hansberg (2008), by which the replacement of low-wage employment with imports from China allows U.S. firms to reduce marginal costs and expand their markets shares; consequently, this leads to higher employment in occupations that remain inside U.S. firms. Another possibility is the existence of effects à la Melitz (2003), by which low-productivity firms exposed to Chinese competition die, with market shares being reallocated toward more productive firms that use high-education occupations more intensively. Disentangling these effects is another relevant research topic spanning from our findings.

Notes

Acknowledgement: We thank Priya Ranjan and an anonymous reviewer for comments and suggestions. Rodriguez-Lopez thanks El Colegio de la Frontera Norte for its hospitality while working on part of this chapter.

1 For the 1999–2011 period, Acemoglu, Autor, Dorn, Hanson, and Price (2016) attribute to Chinese import exposure the loss of about 2.4 million jobs.
2 While Pierce and Schott (2016) use the U.S. policy change of granting Permanent Normal Trade Relations (PNTR) status to China as its measure of the China shock, our empirical analysis uses AADHP's measure of Chinese import exposure. However, we are not able to perform a local-labor-market analysis as in AADHP and Autor, Dorn, and Hanson (2013) because our occupational employment data does not have geographical information.
3 According to the O*NET's website (https://www.onetonline.org/help/online/zones), occupations in job zone 1 need little or no preparation (some may require high school), occupations in job zone 2 need some preparation (usually require high school), occupations in job zone 3 need medium preparation (usually require vocational school or an associate's degree), occupations in job zone 4 need considerable preparation (usually require a bachelor's degree) and occupations in job zone 5 need extensive preparation (usually require a graduate degree).
4 The Comtrade annual trade data from 2000 to 2014 is at the ten-digit Harmonized System (HS) product level. We then use the HS-NAICS crosswalk of Pierce and Schott (2012), available up to 2009, to convert the trade data to six-digit NAICS industries. For 2010 to 2014, we use the Foreign Trade Reference Codes from the U.S. Census Bureau (available since 2006): we aggregate up to the level of

six-digit HS codes and then use a unique mapping from six-digit HS codes to six-digit NAICS codes. Lastly, we aggregate to the BEA three-digit NAICS classification described in Table 11.A1.

5　AADHP also consider higher-order input-output linkages. We abstract from these higher-order effects in this chapter.

6　First we obtain the BEA's Use-of-Commodities-by-Industries Input-Output Table (in producer's prices) for 71 industries in the year 2000, and then we aggregate it to our 60 industries in Table 11.A1.

7　If we allow weights to change, IP_{it} may become irrelevant as a measure of occupation-specific import penetration due to selection bias. For example, suppose that 95 per cent of employment of an occupation is in the computer industry, and the remaining 5 per cent is in the food services industry. If Chinese import exposure depletes that occupation's employment in the computer industry but does not affect its employment in the food services industry, with weights changing to 10 per cent in the computer industry and 90 per cent in the other industry, the new import penetration measure for that occupation will likely decline, misleadingly indicating a reduction in that occupation's exposure.

8　The BEA report 96 types of fixed private assets. Following Eden and Gaggl (2015), 23 of them are classified as ICT capital, and 73 as non-ICT capital.

9　These predicted losses are well in line with the industry-level numbers reported by AADHP for the period from 1999 to 2011. They calculate direct losses of 0.56 million jobs, and combined direct and upstream losses of 1.58 million jobs. Considering higher-order upstream linkages – which we do not do – the losses increase to 1.98 million. AADHP do not report losses from downstream linkages because their downstream import exposure coefficients are not statistically significant. We only use combined measures of import exposure – instead of separately including them in the regressions as AADHP do – because the correlation between them is very high, which would highly reduce the precision of our estimation (the correlation is 0.63 between direct and upstream exposures, 0.61 between direct and downstream exposures, and 0.59 between upstream and downstream exposures).

10　Groizard, Ranjan and Rodriguez-Lopez (2014) show that the productivity effect is a source of job creation in offshoring firms even if tasks are substitutable (as long as the elasticity of substitution across tasks is smaller than the elasticity of substitution across goods), but the effect is stronger if tasks are complementary.

11　As mentioned below, Abowd, McKinney and Vilhuber (2009) show that U.S. firms are more likely to die if they hire a disproportionately large share of workers from the lowest quartile of the human capital distribution, and are less likely to die if they disproportionately hire workers from the highest quartile.

12　Within local labor markets, AADHP find that from 1991 to 2011, U.S. employment losses due to Chinese import exposure were concentrated in the exposed sector, and find no evidence of employment reallocation toward the other sectors.

13　Following AADHP, we classify industries into exposed and non-exposed sectors based on industry-level direct and upstream import penetration measures. First we calculate the change in each type of import penetration from 2002 to 2014, and then we classify as exposed those industries whose import penetration changes are equal or above the mean for at least one of the measures. Similar to AADHP, tradable industries are those in agriculture, forestry, fishing, mining, and manufacturing.

14　Note that production controls are at the occupation-sectoral level, so that we allow for an occupation i to be subject to different wages and capital exposures across sectors.

15　Unfortunately, we cannot directly verify this explanation because our occupational employment data does not contain geographical information.

16　Ebenstein, Harrison, and McMillan (2015) find evidence of job reallocation of high-wage workers in the manufacturing sector to lower-wage jobs in non-manufacturing.

In contrast, we do not find evidence of Chinese-induced job destruction in high-wage occupations (nor in non-routine or high-education occupations) in the exposed sector, which includes most manufacturing industries.

17 Note, however, that the statistically significant creation of 1.2 million jobs in high-education occupations reported in the first row of Table 11.4 (corresponding to the results from Table 11.2) present indirect evidence of an active job reallocation channel toward better occupations.

18 See http://graphics.wsj.com/china-exposure/ and http://chinashock.info/.

References

Abowd, J. M., K. L. McKinney, and L. Vilhuber (2009): "The Link Between Human Capital, Mass Layoffs, and Firm Deaths," in *Producer Dynamics: New Evidence From Micro Data*, pp. 447–472. University of Chicago Press, Chicago, IL.

Acemoglu, D., D. Autor, D. Dorn, G. H. Hanson, and B. Price (2016): "Import Competition and the Great US Employment Sag of the 2000s," *Journal of Labor Economics*, 34 (S1), S141–S198.

Acemoglu, D., V. M. Carvalho, A. Ozdaglar, and A. Tahbaz-Salehi (2012): "The Network Origins of Aggregate Fluctuations," *Econometrica*, 80(5), 1977–2016.

Artuç, E., and J. McLaren (2015): "Trade Policy and Wage Inequality: A Structural Analysis With Occupational and Sectoral Mobility," *Journal of International Economics*, 97 (2), 278–294.

Asquith, B. J., S. Goswami, D. Neumark, and A. Rodriguez-Lopez (2017): "U.S. Job Flows and the China Shock," Working Paper 24080, National Bureau of Economic Research.

Autor, D. H., D. Dorn, and G. H. Hanson (2013): "The China Syndrome: Local Labor Market Effects of Import Competition in the United States," *American Economic Review*, 103(6), 2121–2168.

Berman, E., J. Bound, and Z. Griliches (1994): "Changes in the Demand for Skilled Labor within U.S. Manufacturing: Evidence from the Annual Survey of Manufacturers," *Quarterly Journal of Economics*, 109(2), 367–397.

Costinot, A., L. Oldenski, and J. Rauch (2011): "Adaptation and the Boundary of Multinational Firms," *Review of Economics and Statistics*, 93(1), 298–308.

Ebenstein, A., A. Harrison, and M. McMillan (2015): "Why Are American Workers Getting Poorer? China, Trade and Offshoring," Working Paper 21027, National Bureau of Economic Research.

Ebenstein, A., A. Harrison, M. McMillan, and S. Phillips (2014): "Estimating the Impact of Trade and Offshoring on American Workers Using the Current Population Surveys," *Review of Economics and Statistics*, 96(4), 581–595.

Eden, M., and P. Gaggl (2015): "On the Welfare Implications of Automation," Policy Research Working Paper Series 7487, The World Bank.

Feenstra, R. C., and G. H. Hanson (1996): "Foreign Investment, Outsourcing, and Relative Wages," in *The Political Economy of Trade Policy: Papers in Honor of Jagdish Bhagwati*, ed. by R. C. Feenstra, G. M. Grossman, and D. A. Irwin. MIT Press, Cambridge, MA.

Groizard, J. L., P. Ranjan, and A. Rodriguez-Lopez (2014): "Offshoring and Jobs: The Myriad Channels of Influence," *European Economic Review*, 72, 221–239.

Grossman, G. M., and E. Rossi-Hansberg (2008): "Trading Tasks: A Simple Theory of Offshoring," *The American Economic Review*, 98(5), 1978–1997.

Keller, W., and H. Utar (2016): "International Trade and Job Polarization: Evidence at the Worker-Level," NBER Working Paper 22315, National Bureau of Economic Research.

Lee, E. (2017): "Trade, Inequality, and the Endogenous Sorting of Heterogeneous Workers," Discussion Paper, University of Maryland.

Liu, R., and D. Trefler (2011): "A Sorted Tale of Globalization: White Collar Jobs and the Rise of Service Offshoring," NBER Working Paper 17559, National Bureau of Economic Research.

Melitz, M. J. (2003): "The Impact of Trade on Intra-Industry Reallocations and Aggregate Industry Productivity," *Econometrica*, 71(6), 1695–1725.

Oldenski, L. (2012): "The Task Composition of Offshoring by US Multinationals," *International Economics*, 131, 5–21.

Pierce, J. R., and P. K. Schott (2012): "A Concordance Between Ten-Digit US Harmonized System Codes and SIC/NAICS Product Classes and Industries," *Journal of Economic and Social Measurement*, 37(1, 2), 61–96.

———— (2016): "The Surprisingly Swift Decline of US Manufacturing Employment," *American Economic Review*, 106(7), 1632–1662.

Traiberman, S. (2017): "Occupations and Import Competition: Evidence From Denmark," Discussion Paper, New York University.

Van Dam, A., and J. Ma (2016): "The Parts of America Most Vulnerable to China," *The Wall Street Journal*, August 11.

Wright, G. C. (2014): "Revisiting the Employment Impact of Offshoring," *European Economic Review*, 66, 63–83.

Appendix

Table 11.A1 Industry classification

	Industry	Three-digit NAICS		Industry	Three-digit NAICS
1	Forestry and fishing	113, 114, 115	31	Rail transportation	482
2	Oil and gas extraction	211	32	Water transportation	483
3	Mining, except oil and gas	212	33	Truck transportation	484
4	Support activities for mining	213	34	Transit and ground passenger transportation	485
5	Utilities	221	35	Pipeline transportation	486
6	Construction	236, 237, 238	36	Other transportation and support activities	487, 488, 492
7	Food, beverage, and tobacco products	311, 312	37	Warehousing and storage	493
8	Textile mills and textile product mills	313, 314	38	Publishing industries (includes software)	511, 516
9	Apparel, leather, and allied products	315, 316	39	Motion picture and sound recording	512
10	Paper products	322	40	Broadcasting and telecommunications	515, 517
11	Printing and related support activities	323	41	Information and data processing services	518, 519
12	Petroleum and coal products	324	42	Federal Reserve banks, credit intermediation	521, 522
13	Chemical products	325	43	Securities, commodity contracts, and investments	523
14	Plastics and rubber products	326	44	Insurance carriers	524
15	Wood products	321	45	Funds, trusts, and other financial vehicles	525
16	Nonmetallic mineral products	327	46	Real estate	531
17	Primary metals	331	47	Rental and leasing services	532, 533
18	Fabricated metal products	332	48	Professional, scientific, and technical services	541
19	Machinery	333	49	Management of companies and enterprises	551

(Continued)

Table 11.A1 (Continued)

Industry	Three-digit NAICS	Industry	Three-digit NAICS
20 Computer and electronic products	334	50 Administrative and support services	561
21 Electrical equipment	335	51 Waste management and remediation services	562
22 Transportation equipment	336	52 Educational services	611
23 Furniture and related products	337	53 Ambulatory health care services	621
24 Miscellaneous manufacturing	339	54 Hospitals, nursing, and residential care	622, 623
25 Wholesale trade	423, 424, 425	55 Social assistance	624
26 Motor vehicle and part dealers	441	56 Performing arts, spectator sports, and museums	711, 712
27 Food and beverage stores	445	57 Amusements, gambling, and recreation	713
28 General merchandise stores	452	58 Accommodation	721
29 Other retail	442, 443, 444, 446, 447, 448, 451, 453, 454	59 Food services and drinking places	722
		60 Other services, except government	811, 812, 813, 814
30 Air transportation	481		

12 The 'China shock' in trade: consequences for ASEAN and East Asia

Robert Feenstra and Akira Sasahara

1. Introduction

Countries in East Asia have experienced significant economic integration since 1990s due to tariff cuts and a decline of non-tariff barriers, including a reduction in tariffs with China since 2005 under the ASEAN-China Free Trade Agreement. This integration has contributed to economic efficiency by exploiting the comparative advantage of countries in production (e.g., Ando and Kimura, 2005; Los et al., 2015a). However, the impact of this economic integration on employment has not received much attention. While a number of policy articles highlight the role of China as an engine of global economic growth (e.g., World Bank, 2017; IMF, 2017) the role of China in employment creation has not been assessed quantitatively. This chapter aims to quantify the employment creation effect of China for the Association of Southeast Asian Nations (ASEAN) countries and Japan, South Korea, and Taiwan (hereafter ASEAN + JKT).

We employ two different techniques in order to quantify the employment effect of China. First, we use the technique proposed by Los, Timmer, and de Vries (2015a), investigating the impact of China's exports on employment creation in China, which is called the demand-side analysis. This technique makes it possible to quantify the employment compensation coming from foreign demand using a Global Input-Output Table. Results from the analysis in this chapter suggests the employment creation effect of China measured by USD value is growing at annual growth rates of 11 per cent during the period 1990–2013 and is responsible for employment compensation of 234 billion USD in 2013, which is equivalent to 6.5 per cent of the total employment compensation and 1.7 per cent of the total GDP in the ASEAN + JKT area.

We also employ the hypothetical extraction technique proposed by Los, Timmer, and de Vries (2016). We find that the employment effect due to China's final demand from this approach accounts for 5 per cent of employment compensation. In the last exercise, we decompose the employment effect obtained from the demand-side analysis by running a regression that uses the actual tariff reductions from China on the ASEAN + JKT countries as well as the growth in Chinese demand not associated with the tariff cuts, and other controls.

This chapter contributes to the literature investigating the employment effect of international trade. Recent studies can be classified into two categories, depending upon methodologies they employ. One strand of recent literature conducts regression analyses to investigate the impact of trade. A group of studies in this literature quantifies the inverse effect of import penetration from China and other low-wage developing countries (e.g., Autor, Dorn and Hanson, 2013, 2015; Acemoglu, Autor, Dorn, Hanson and Price, 2016, Pierce and Schott, 2016, for the U.S. economy; and Dauth, Findeisen and Suedekum, 2014, for Germany). Another group of studies in this literature argues that China has been playing a central role in the world economic growth and remains a powerful engine for growth even today (e.g., IMF, 2017; World Bank, 2017; Vianna, 2016; Dauth et al., 2014). These studies estimate regressions to examine the impact of exports on employment in source countries. Vianna (2016) estimates the impact of exports to China on GDP growth in Latin American counties by employing a panel estimation technique. He finds that exports to China have a positive effect on GDP growth in Latin American countries during 1994–2013. Dauth et al. (2014) examine the impact of trade with Eastern Europe and China on local labor markets in Germany during 1988–2008 by exploiting regional variations in industrial structure in the same spirit as Autor, Dorn and Hanson (2013). While they find a negative import competition effect in import competing industries, they also show that export-oriented industries experienced even stronger employment gains and lower unemployment. Likewise, Feenstra, Ma and Xu (2017) analyze the impact of Chinese imports and global exports from the U.S. on its employment.

The second strand of literature employs Input-Output Tables, including National Input-Output Tables (Feenstra and Hong, 2010; and see Baldwin, 1994, for a survey of earlier studies)[1] and Global Input-Output Tables (Kiyota, 2016; Koopman et al., 2008, 2014; Los, Timmer, and de Vries, 2015a; Timmer, Los, Stehrer, and de Vries, 2013; Timmer, Erumban, Los, Stehrer and de Vries, 2014).[2] For example, Kiyota (2016) examines the impact of exports on employment in China, Indonesia, Japan and South Korea using the WIOD Input-Output Table. He finds that, between 1995 and 2009, the employment creation effect of exports is increasing in the four countries. While prior literature tends to employ the Input-Output Table from the WIOD database, we use the EORA database (Lenzen et al., 2012 and Lenzen et al., 2013) because many of the ASEAN countries are included as the "rest of the world" in WIOD and unable to obtain country-specific effects for those countries. In addition to China, Indonesia, Japan and South Korea included in the WIOD database, our sample covers Brunei, Cambodia, Malaysia, Myanmar, Singapore, Taiwan, Thailand and Vietnam. Our analysis here is complementary to Feenstra and Sasahara (2017), who focus on the impact of U.S. imports and global exports on U.S. employment using an input-output analysis.

The rest of the chapter is organized as follows. In Section 2 we follow the method of Los, Timmer and de Vries (2015a), who measure the positive impact of Chinese exports for job growth in that country, to infer the positive impact on employment in East Asia. In Section 3 we measure the employment effect of China's final demand *per se* by employing the technique by Los, Timmer and de Vries (2016). Section 4 investigates the determinants of China's employment effect obtained from Section 2 and decompose it into contributions from tariff cuts, China's final demand *per se*, and other factors. Section 5 includes concluding remarks. Further details of the dataset and techniques are in the appendixes.

2.   Demand-side analysis

2.1.   *Structure of the Global Input-Output Table*

In this section we employ the technique proposed by Los et al. (2015b) to quantify the employment effect of China on the ASEAN + JKT economies. Before describing the technique, we briefly discuss the structure of the IO table. Figure 12.1 depicts a global IO table for a three country case – country A, country B, and China (country C). The EORA IO table includes 26 sectors and six final demand categories (see Appendix B for details) and Figure 12.1 shows the case where the six final demand categories are collapsed into one by taking summation over the six final demand categories. The left half of the matrix, denoted as Matrix T, portrays flows of intermediate goods across countries including domestic transactions. For example, the top left cell of matrix T describes domestic intermediate good flows within country A and the top center cell shows international intermediate good flows from country A to country B. The right half of the matrix, denoted as matrix F, portrays final good flows and the same structure applies as matrix T.

A mathematical representation of the simplified IO table Figure 12.1 is as follows. Let $m_{A,B}(r,s)$ denote the value of intermediate goods produced in sector r of country A and used by sector s of country B. Final good flows are also described in a similar manner: $f_{A,B}(r)$ indicates the value of final good produced in sector r of country A and consumed in country B. The gross output of sector s of country A, $y_A(s)$, is computed as the horizontal sum of numbers in the corresponding row:

$$y_A(s) = \sum_j \sum_i m_{A,i}(r,j) + \sum_i f_{A,i}(r).$$

By dividing the intermediate good flows by the gross output in the destination sector of the destination country, we find Leontief coefficients (or input-output coefficients):

$$\mathbf{A} \equiv \begin{bmatrix} m_{A,A}(1,1)/y_A(1), & m_{A,A}(1,2)/y_A(2), & \dots, & m_{A,C}(1,2)/y_C(2) \\ m_{A,A}(2,1)/y_A(1), & m_{A,A}(2,2)/y_A(2), & \dots, & m_{A,C}(2,2)/y_C(2) \\ \vdots & \vdots & \ddots & \vdots \\ m_{C,A}(2,1)/y_A(1), & m_{C,A}(2,2)/y_A(2), & \dots, & m_{C,C}(2,2)/y_C(2) \end{bmatrix}$$

Source \ Destination	Country A Sectors 1, 2, …, 26	Country B Sectors 1, 2, …, 26	China Sectors 1, 2, …, 26	Country A 6 final demand categories	Country B 6 final demand categories	China 6 final demand categories
Country A — Sector 1, Sector 2, ⋮, Sector 26	Intermediate goods produced and used by Country A	Intermediate goods produced by Country A and used by Country B	Intermediate goods produced by Country A and used by China	Final goods produced and consumed by Country A	Final goods produced by Country A and consumed by Country B	Final goods produced by Country A and consumed by China
Country B — Sector 1, Sector 2, ⋮, Sector 26	Intermediate goods produced by Country B and used by Country A	Intermediate goods produced and used by Country B	Intermediate goods produced by Country B and used by China	Final goods produced by Country B and consumed by Country A	Final goods produced and consumed by Country B	Final goods produced by Country B and consumed by China
China — Sector 1, Sector 2, ⋮, Sector 26	Intermediate goods produced by China and used by Country A	Intermediate goods produced by China and used by Country B	Intermediate goods produced and used by China	Final goods produced by China and consumed by Country A	Final goods produced by China and consumed by Country B	Final goods produced and consumed by China

Matrix T

Matrix F

Figure 12.1 The structure of the Global Input-Output Table: a three country case

Notes: The Global Input-Output Table comes from the EORA database. The original EORA table includes 189 countries. However, we re-construct the table with 52 countries including the rest of the world as one country. This figure shows the case with four countries for simplicity. Also, see Appendix A for the list of the countries. There are 26 sectors and six final demand categories. A big sub-matrix in the left indicated by a red box (denoted as matrix T) is the matrix for intermediate good flows and. Another big sub-matrix in the right (denoted as matrix F) is the matrix for final good flows. Diagonal boxes in matrices T and F indicate domestic transactions within each country while the rest of the boxes are international transactions. See Lenzen et al. (2012) and Lenzen et al. (2013) for further details.

Following Leontief (1936)'s idea and using this matrix **A** and the final demand from a country, say country j, $\mathbf{f}_j$, gross production absorbed by country j is estimated as

$$\mathbf{y}_j = (\mathbf{I} - \mathbf{A})^{-1}\mathbf{f}_j, \tag{1}$$

where **I** denotes a unit matrix. As noted in Johnson and Noguera (2012), $(\mathbf{I} - \mathbf{A})^{-1}$ is the "Leontief inverse" of the input-output matrix and it can be expressed as a geometric series: $(\mathbf{I} - \mathbf{A})^{-1}\mathbf{f}_j = \sum_{k=0}^{\infty} \mathbf{A}^k\mathbf{f}_j$. The first term $\mathbf{f}_j$ is the direct output absorbed as final goods, and the second term $\mathbf{Af}_j$ is the intermediate goods used to produce that final goods, and the third term $\mathbf{A}^2\mathbf{f}_j$ includes the additional intermediate goods employed to produce the first round of intermediate goods $\mathbf{Af}_j$, and so on.

2.2. Method to obtain the employment effect

We describe the technique proposed by Los et al. (2015b) to quantify the effect of China's final demand on the country's employment compensation. For simplicity, we define the "employment effect of China" as the impact of exports to China on the exporting country's employment compensation.[3] Suppose now that there are a number N of countries and each country comprised of a number S of sectors. We also introduce year subscript t because IO tables are available at the annual frequency. China is indicated by superscript C.

The employment effect driven by the final demand from China in year t, denoted as $\mathbf{k}_t^C$, is estimated by a similar method as equation (1) in the previous subsection:

$$\mathbf{k}_t^C = \hat{\mathbf{p}}_t(\mathbf{I} - \mathbf{A}_t)^{-1}\mathbf{f}_t^C \tag{2}$$

The only difference with equation (1) is that we post-multiply it by $\hat{\mathbf{p}}_t$ to obtain the employment effect of China's final demand, $\hat{\mathbf{p}}_t$ is a $(N \times S) \times (N \times S)$ diagonal matrix containing the share of labor compensation to the total output in each sector of each country. To be more precise, let $y^{(i,s)}$ be the gross output in industry s of country i, and let $l^{(i,s)}$ the compensation for labor in this industry. Then we can define $p^{(i,s)}$ as the labor compensation required per dollar gross output in industry s in country i, $p^{(i,s)} = l^{(i,s)}/y^{(i,s)}$, and create the column vector **p** with dimension $(N \times S) \times 1$ with the diagonal matrix $\hat{\mathbf{p}}$ with the elements of that vector on the diagonal. We re-express equation (2) as follows:

$$
\begin{bmatrix} \mathbf{k}_t^{1,C} \\ \mathbf{k}_t^{2,C} \\ \vdots \\ \mathbf{k}_t^{N,C} \end{bmatrix}_{(N \times S) \times 1} = \underbrace{\hat{\mathbf{p}}_t(\mathbf{I} - \mathbf{A}_t)^{-1}}_{(N \times S) \times (N \times S)} \begin{bmatrix} \mathbf{f}_t^{1,C} \\ \mathbf{f}_t^{2,C} \\ \vdots \\ \mathbf{f}_t^{N,C} \end{bmatrix}_{(N \times S) \times 1} \tag{3}
$$

where $\mathbf{k}_t^{i,C}$ is a $S \times 1$ submatrix of $\mathbf{k}_t^C$ describing the employment effect (in USD value) driven by China's final demand on country i in year t; $\mathbf{f}_t^{i,C}$ is a $S \times 1$ submatrix of $\mathbf{f}_t^C$ indicating final good flows from country i to China at year t. The total employment effect of China (in USD value) on country i is calculated as the sum of the employment effect on all of the S sectors, $\mathbf{1}'\mathbf{k}_t^{i,C}$, where $\mathbf{1}$ is a $S \times 1$ vector of ones. It is important to note that the employment effect of final demand from China estimated using this technique includes effects through other foreign countries. For example, final demand from China to Thailand can have impacts on Indonesia because Thailand purchases intermediate goods from Indonesia to produce final goods exported to China. The employment effect comes from not only bilateral trade but also trade with third countries. This technique makes it possible to include such effects, which is one of the advantages of using an input-output analysis.

Data: The Global Input-Output Table provided by the WIOD database includes major countries in the world – 40 countries in the WIOD IO table we use and 43 countries in the WIOD 2016 release. As a result, it is missing many of East Asian countries that we are particularly interested. Therefore, we employ the Global Input-Output Table from the EORA database, which includes 189 countries. We re-construct a new EORA including 40 WIOD countries and 10 countries from East Asia for computational simplicity.[4]

2.3. Results from the demand-side analysis

Results from the demand-side analysis are reported in Table 12.1, which shows that the employment effect of China is growing strongly in all of the ASEAN + JKT economies. On average, the employment effect of China is growing at an annual growth rate of 11 per cent in the area during 1990–2013. With regard to the time series variation, the highest growth rates are from 1990–1995 and 2005–2010 when the employment effect of China grew at a 15 per cent annual growth rate. The growth rate is relatively low in 1995–2000 and 2010–2013 – 4 per cent and 8 per cent, respectively. The Asian financial crisis in 1997 and the 2008–2009 global financial crisis are likely to be responsible for the former and the latter, respectively. The growth rate is particularly high for Brunei, Cambodia, and Laos – annual average growth rates of 18 per cent, 22 per cent, and 19 per cent, respectively. The lowest growth rate is observed from Taiwan, at 3 per cent. In the ASEAN + JKT area overall, the employment creation effect of China was USD 19.3 billion in 1990 and it reached to USD 234.3 billion in 2013. These results show that China is playing an increasingly important role in creating employment in the area.

One may argue, however, that this growing trend in the employment effect is not unique to China as there is strong deepening in economic integration in the East Asia during the period (see, for example, Ando and Kimura, 2005). To investigate if it is the case, we find the share of China's employment effect to the employment effect driven by the total demand $\mathbf{1}'\mathbf{k}_t^{i,All}$, which is the employment effect due to demand from all countries in the world including country i itself.[5] By looking at the share, $\mathbf{1}'\mathbf{k}_t^{i,-i}/\mathbf{1}'\mathbf{k}_t^{i,All}$, we can see whether the relative

Table 12.1 Employment effect of China on ASEAN + JKT countries, from the demand-side analysis

| | The employment effect of China (in million USD), $\mathbf{1}'\mathbf{k}_t^{i,C}$ | | | | | | Growth rate of the employment effect of China (annual average) | | | | | |
| | | | | | | | 5-year horizon (3-year horizon for 2010–2013) | | | | | |
	1990	1995	2000	2005	2010	2013	1990–1995	1995–2000	2000–2005	2005–2010	2010–2013	1990–2013
Brunei	4.3	10.8	22.8	63.2	168.3	239.5	19%	15%	20%	20%	12%	18%
Cambodia	0.5	7.3	11.8	34.4	48.2	70.3	54%	10%	21%	7%	13%	22%
Indonesia	230.6	774.8	984.6	2,148.4	7,213.1	10,243.0	24%	5%	16%	24%	12%	16%
Japan	8,474.5	22,571.0	25,622.0	45,607.0	94,611.0	111,370.0	20%	3%	12%	15%	5%	11%
Laos	0.6	2.4	3.9	9.1	37.0	55.0	27%	10%	17%	28%	13%	19%
Malaysia	511.4	1,342.8	1,451.9	3,345.8	9,790.6	13,339.0	19%	2%	17%	21%	10%	14%
Myanmar	11.0	26.8	60.8	65.8	242.1	379.8	18%	16%	2%	26%	15%	15%
Philippines	107.9	266.6	364.2	810.8	2,619.1	3,726.2	18%	6%	16%	23%	12%	15%
South Korea	1,530.7	5,060.4	6,745.2	16,342.0	42,540.0	59,195.0	24%	6%	18%	19%	11%	16%
Singapore	311.9	976.1	1,215.1	2,511.8	6,970.4	9,744.8	23%	4%	15%	20%	11%	15%
Taiwan	7,699.4	8,739.1	11,485.0	11,635.0	14,939.0	15,375.0	3%	5%	0%	5%	1%	3%
Thailand	296.7	870.7	1,007.6	2,286.8	5,426.4	8,126.5	22%	3%	16%	17%	13%	14%
Vietnam	96.1	266.4	562.9	1,149.3	1,848.3	2,419.4	20%	15%	14%	10%	9%	14%
ASEAN + JKT (Sum)	19,275.6	40,915.2	49,537.7	86,009.4	186,453.6	234,283.5	15%	4%	11%	15%	8%	11%

Notes: The table shows $\mathbf{1}'\mathbf{k}_t^{i,C}$ for each country i (in million USD). The estimated employment effect is based on the data from the EORA Input-Output Table. The employment effect is estimated for 26 EORA sectors and we aggregate the sectoral employment effects to find the overall effect on each country. The growth rate is annualized (e.g., the annual average growth rate of the employment effect from 1990 to 1995 is $g_{1,1990-1995} = [\ln(\mathbf{1}'\mathbf{k}_{1995}^{i,C}) - \ln(\mathbf{1}'\mathbf{k}_{1990}^{i,C})]/5$).

importance of China in creating employment has increased or not. We also compute the employment effect of China relative to country's GDP, $\mathbf{1}'\mathbf{k}_t^{i,-i}/GDP_{i,t}$, in order to investigate the relative importance of China comparing to country i's market size.

Panel A of Figure 12.2 shows the employment effect of China relative to the employment effect driven by the total demand $\mathbf{1}'\mathbf{k}_t^{i,-i}/\mathbf{1}'\mathbf{k}_t^{i,All}$ for 1990 and 2013. The share of China's employment effect to the overall employment compensation increased substantially in South Korea, Japan, Myanmar, and Vietnam – the shares increased by 26.5, 19.4, 18.9 and 18.7 percentage points, respectively. Cambodia and Taiwan have the smallest increase in the share of China's employment effect to the total employment effect yet the numbers are positive – 5.9 and 7.6 percentage points increase for Cambodia and Taiwan, respectively. Panel B describes the employment effect of China relative to country's GDP. It shows that the relative share of the China effect to GDP is increasing for all economies except for Taiwan. The largest increase in the share of the China effect to GDP comes from South Korea, Singapore, and Japan – 3.2, 2.5, and 2.2 percentage points, respectively. We can compare our estimates to those in Los et al. (2015b), who investigate the impact of foreign demand on China's employment. One issue is that the unit of the employment effect is different between this chapter and Los et al. (2015b). While the employment effect is measured by the number of workers in Los et al. (2015b), it is measured by employment compensation (in USD value) in this chapter. The difference stems from the fact that we use the Global Input-Output Table from the EORA Database while Los et al. (2015b) use the one from the WIOD database.

In order to make our estimates compatible with Los et al. (2015b)'s estimates, we compute the change in employment effect relative to the overall employment effect at the end of a period. Table 12.2 shows the change of number of employees induced by final demand from China reported in Table 1 of Los et al. (2015b). Table 12.2 shows that, for example, between 1995 and 2009, foreign demand created jobs for 31.2 million workers. This number is not compatible with our estimates because it is given by the number of workers while our estimates are in USD. Therefore, we normalize the employment effect by dividing by the total employment at the end of the period, 2009. Because the total employment in China in 2009 was 781.0 million, the change of employment induced by foreign demand in China is 31.2/781.0 × 100 = 3.99% of the total employment in 2009.

We normalize our estimates of the employment effect by dividing by the employment compensation at the end of a period.[6] Table 12.3 presents our normalized employment effects. It shows that the employment effect of China on ASEAN + JKT economies takes values that are not very different from Los et al. (2015b)'s estimates on the impact of foreign demand on China's employment. For example, our result shows that, between 1995 and 2009, the overall demand led to a 480.72 billion USD increase of employment compensation in ASEAN + JKT economies. This is equivalent to 12.53 per cent of the total employment compensation in the area at the end of the period, 2009 (3.8 trillion USD). This number, 12.53 per cent, is very similar to the impact of the overall

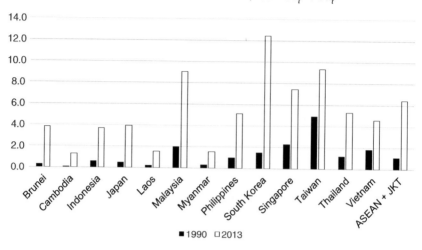

Panel A: Relative to the Overall Effect, $100 \times \mathbf{1}'\mathbf{k}_t^{i,C} / \mathbf{1}'\mathbf{k}_t^{i,All}$

■1990 □2013

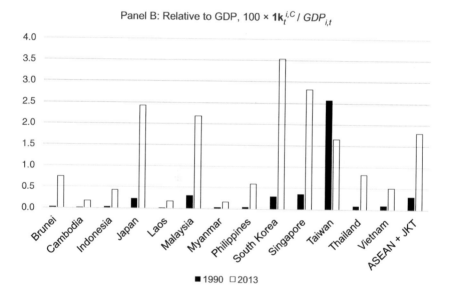

Panel B: Relative to GDP, $100 \times \mathbf{1k}_t^{i,C} / GDP_{i,t}$

■1990 □2013

Figure 12.2 Employment effect of China on ASEAN + JKT countries in 1990 and 2013, from the demand-side analysis

Notes: Panels A and B show $100 \times \mathbf{1}'\mathbf{k}_t^{i,C}/\mathbf{1}'\mathbf{k}_t^{i,All}$ and $100 \times \mathbf{1}'\mathbf{k}_t^{i,C}/GDP_{i,t}$, respectively, for each country i. The estimated employment effect is based on the data from the EORA Input-Output Table. The employment effect is estimated for 26 EORA sectors and sum of these are shown. The unit for the vertical axis is %. ASEAN + JKT is the weighted average of the China effect on the ASEAN + JKT economies.

Table 12.2 Change in number of workers induced by final demand (millions) in China

	Domestic final demand for		Foreign final demand	All demand	Total employment in the end of the period
	Merchandise	Non-merchandise			
Numbers without parentheses (million workers)	$\Delta\mathbf{k}^{DOM}_{(Merchandise)}$ $\dfrac{\Delta\mathbf{k}^{DOM}_{(Merchandise)}}{Emp}$	$\Delta\mathbf{k}^{DOM}_{(Non\text{-}merchandise)}$ $\dfrac{\Delta\mathbf{k}^{DOM}_{(Non\text{-}merchandise)}}{Emp}$	$\Delta\mathbf{k}^{FOR}$ $\dfrac{\Delta\mathbf{k}^{FOR}}{Emp}$	$\Delta\mathbf{k}$ $\dfrac{\Delta\mathbf{k}}{Emp}$	Emp
Numbers with parentheses (%)					
1995–2001	−14.7 (−2.02%)	68.9 (9.45%)	−4.6 (−0.63%)	49.6 (6.80%)	729.0
2001–2006	−65.6 (−8.58%)	28.7 (3.75%)	70.6 (9.23%)	33.8 (4.42%)	764.6
2006–2009	3.6 (0.46%)	47.2 (6.04%)	−34.8 (−4.46%)	16.0 (2.05%)	781.0
1995–2009	−76.7 (−9.82%)	144.8 (18.54%)	31.2 (3.99%)	99.3 (12.71%)	781.0

Source: Los et al. (2015b).

Table 12.3 Change in the employment effect induced by final demand (billion USD) in the ASEAN + JKT area

Panel A: The employment effect on ASEAN + JKT countries

	Foreign	China	All	Total
	Δk^{FOR}	Δk^{C}	Δk	EmpComp
Numbers without parentheses (billion USD) Numbers in parentheses (%)	$\frac{\Delta k^{FOR}}{EmpComp}$	$\frac{\Delta k^{C}}{EmpComp}$	$\frac{\Delta k}{EmpComp}$	
1990–1995	122.04 (**3.63%**)	21.64 (**0.64%**)	1414.99 (**42.17%**)	3,355.26
1996–2000	46.97 (**1.57%**)	8.62 (**0.29%**)	–356.31 (**–11.88%**)	2,999.14
2001–2005	155.30 (**4.78%**)	36.47 (**1.12%**)	246.12 (**7.58%**)	3,245.62
2005–2010	261.27 (**6.07%**)	100.44 (**2.33%**)	1060.99 (**24.64%**)	4,306.41
2010–2013	110.12 (**2.53%**)	47.83 (**1.10%**)	39.81 (**0.92%**)	4,346.13
1995–2009	302.72 (**7.89%**)	95.02 (**2.48%**)	480.72 (**12.53%**)	3,836.28
1990–2013	617.05 (**14.20%**)	200.40 (**4.61%**)	1316.85 (**30.30%**)	4,346.13

Panel B: The employment effect on China implied from Los et al. (2015b)

	Foreign	All
1995–2009	(**3.99%**)	(**12.71%**)

Notes: *EmpComp* denotes the employment compensation in billion USD. The data on employment compensation are directly obtained from the EORA database. Numbers without parentheses are the employment effect induced by each category of demand (in billion USD). Numbers in parentheses are the change in the employment effect relative to the overall employment at the end of the period.

demand on China's employment in the same period estimated by Los et al. (2015b). They find that the overall demand increased employment by 99.3 million workers, which is equivalent to 12.71 per cent of the total employment of 781.0 million workers at the end of the period, 2009.

Comparing Table 12.2 and Table 12.3 shows that the foreign demand is roughly twice as important for ASEAN + JKT economies than for China. Table 12.2 shows that, based on estimates by Los et al. (2015b), the foreign demand contributed to 3.99 per cent of the overall employment during 1995–2009 in China. Table 12.3 shows that that foreign demand contributed to 7.89 per cent of the overall employment compensation during the same period. Furthermore, the result suggests that the majority of the foreign demand comes from China – China contributed to 2.48 per cent of the overall employment compensation, which accounts for 31 per cent of the total foreign contribution.

3.   Hypothetical extraction exercise

3.1.   Method

This section estimates the employment effect stemming from a rise in China's final demand by exploiting the idea of "hypothetical extraction" in Los et al. (2016). The demand-side analysis conducted in the previous section quantifies the employment compensation generated by contemporaneous exports to China from each of ASEAN + JKT economies. The hypothetical extraction technique presented this section quantifies the employment effect of export opportunities to China relative to that from the base year, 1990. It is informative to know which economies experienced the greatest growth in employment benefits from China.

First, we find the employment effect due to the final demand from the world by keeping China's final demand at the 1990 level as:

$$\mathbf{k}_t^{All*} = \hat{\mathbf{p}}_t (\mathbf{I} - \mathbf{A}_t)^{-1} \mathbf{F}_t^{All*} \tag{5a}$$

where,

$$\mathbf{F}_t^{All*} = \begin{bmatrix} \mathbf{f}_{1990}^{1,C} + \sum_{k \neq C} \mathbf{f}_t^{1,k} \\ \mathbf{f}_{1990}^{2,C} + \sum_{k \neq C} \mathbf{f}_t^{2,k} \\ \vdots \\ \mathbf{f}_{1990}^{N,C} + \sum_{k \neq N} \mathbf{f}_t^{C,k} \end{bmatrix} \tag{5b}$$

The final demand vector $\mathbf{F}_t^{All*}$ makes it clear that China's final demand is fixed at the 1990 level. Each element is the sum of final good flows from each sector of each country to all countries where the final good flows to China are fixed at the 1990 level while those to other countries are allowed to change over time. $\mathbf{k}_t^{All*}$ is the employment effect due to the final demand from all countries in a hypothetical world where China's final demand did not grow at all since 1990.

Using (5) and the actual total employment effect from the previous section $1'\mathbf{k}_t^{i,All}$, the contribution of the final demand from China on employment in country i, expressed in dollar value, is calculated as:

$$\text{Emp Effect of China's Final Demand}_{i,t} = 1'\mathbf{k}_t^{i,All} - 1'\mathbf{k}_t^{i,All*}, \tag{6}$$

The difference between the two is the employment effect purely due to a change in China's final demand. Using (4) and (5), we can re-express $\mathbf{k}_t^{All*}$ as

$$\text{Emp Effect of China's Final Demand}_{i,t} = 1'\hat{\mathbf{p}}_t (\mathbf{I} - \mathbf{A}_t)^{-1} (\mathbf{F}_t^{All} - \mathbf{F}_t^{*All})$$

$$= 1'\hat{\mathbf{p}}_t (\mathbf{I} - \mathbf{A}_t)^{-1} \begin{bmatrix} \mathbf{f}_t^{1,C} - \mathbf{f}_{1990}^{1,C} \\ \mathbf{f}_t^{2,C} - \mathbf{f}_{1990}^{2,C} \\ \vdots \\ \mathbf{f}_t^{N,C} - \mathbf{f}_{1990}^{N,C} \end{bmatrix} \tag{7}$$

In other words, the results from the hypothetical extraction exercise will be similar to that from the demand-side analysis, except that the hypothetical extraction exercise subtracts off final demand in China in 1990. The hypothetical extraction exercise is therefore accounting for the *growth* in Chinese final demand since 1990 rather than its *level* each year.

By scaling the dollar value of the employment effect (6) by the actual total employment effect $\mathbf{k}_t^{All*}$, we find the ratio of the employment effect due to China's final demand to the actual total employment effect as:

$$\% \text{ Emp Effect of China's Final Demand}_{it} = 100 \times (1'\mathbf{k}_t^{All} - 1'\mathbf{k}_t^{All*})/1'\mathbf{k}_t^{All}. \tag{8}$$

3.2.   Results from the hypothetical extraction exercise

The calculated share of the employment effect with the base year 1990 based on equation (8) is presented in Figure 12.3 for three years, 1993, 2003, and 2013.[7] It shows that the employment effect of the growth in China's final demand since 1990 is increasing over time for all sample countries. The employment effect of China increased the most in South Korea, Malaysia, Taiwan, and Singapore – increased by 10.9, 7.6, 5.8, and 5.6 percentage points, respectively, from 1990 and 2013. In the ASEAN + JKT area overall, the employment effect increased from 0.4 per cent to 4.6 per cent during the period. As expected, the share of China's employment effect implied from the demand-side analysis $100 \times 1'\mathbf{k}_t^{i,C}/1'\mathbf{k}_t^{i,All}$ is slightly greater than that implied by the hypothetical extraction exercise $100 \times (1'\mathbf{k}_t^{i,All} - 1'\mathbf{k}_t^{i,All*})/1'\mathbf{k}_t^{i,All}$: the former is 6.4 per cent and the latter is 4.58 per cent for the ASEAN + JKT area overall in 2013. The difference

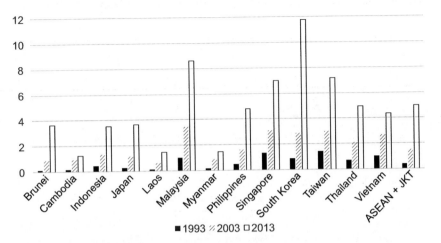

Figure 12.3 Employment effect of China on the ASEAN + JKT area in 2013, from the
hypothetical extraction exercise, in 1993, 2003 and 2013, $100 \times (1'k_t^{i,All} - 1'k_t^{i,All*})/1'k_t^{i,All}$

Notes: The figure shows the employment effect driven by China's final demand *per se* in percentage of
the actual employment effect of China, $100 \times (1'k_t^{i,All} - 1'k_t^{i,All*})/1'k_t^{i,All}$, from the hypothetical
extraction exercise for each country *i*. The estimated employment effect is based on the data from
the EORA Input-Output Table. The employment effect is estimated for 26 EORA sectors and we
aggregate the sectoral employment effects to find the employment effect on a country as a whole.
The unit for the vertical axis is %. ASEAN + JKT is the weighted average of the China effect on
the ASEAN + JKT economies.

comes from the fact that the demand-side analysis includes the employment effect
through changes in the labor share and input-output linkages while the hypothetical extraction does not include these. The next section decomposes the employment effect of China from the demand-side analysis into that due to China's final
demand *per se* and other factors.

4.   Demand-side analysis versus hypothetical extraction

4.1.   *Decomposing the employment effect from the demand-side analysis*

We next investigate the determinants of the employment effect of China from the
demand-side analysis. We are particularly interested in the impact of tariff cuts
and China's final demand *per se*. Import tariff rates imposed by China have
been continuously falling since the 1990s. Table 12.4 shows the average tariff
rates imposed by China on each of the ASEAN + JKT economies. The table
shows that there is a continuous decline of tariff rates since 1990s. That final
year marks the remaining tariff cuts under the ASEAN-China Free Trade Area
for the ASEAN 6 countries (Brunei, Indonesia, Malaysia, Philippines, Singapore

Table 12.4 The average tariff rates imposed by China to the ASEAN + JKT economies

	1991	*1996*	*2001*	*2006*	*2011*
Brunei	38.4	25.3	14.3	9.5	8.5
Cambodia	35.1	23.6	19.3	13.1	10.1
Indonesia	35.5	32.4	17.2	11.1	9.9
Japan	40.0	32.4	16.8	10.5	9.7
Laos	41.9	27.7	16.5	10.9	8.1
Malaysia	35.5	32.7	17.2	10.6	9.0
Myanmar	33.8	29.1	14.6	8.7	9.1
Philippines	41.0	37.7	17.6	11.0	9.2
South Korea	42.3	32.2	16.8	10.8	9.9
Singapore	38.9	31.5	16.8	10.1	9.9
Taiwan	38.1	32.7	16.7	10.8	9.8
Thailand	37.8	28.7	18.1	10.7	9.9
Vietnam	23.9	28.9	17.7	11.7	9.9

Notes: The table shows the simple average of tariff rates (in per cent) imposed by China on each of the ASEAN + JKT economies. The data on tariffs come from Caliendo et al. (2015). The original tariff data are provided by SITC 4-digit level, and we match the tariff data to the 11 merchandise sectors in EORA. See Appendix F for the crosswalk between SITC and EORA. The tariff rates shown in the table are the simple average of the tariff rates in 11 EORA sectors.

and Thailand), whereas the other ASEAN countries that are party to that agreement have had their tariffs eliminated by 2015. In order to investigate the impact of these tariff cuts and other factors on the employment effect of China, we estimate the following equation:

$$OLS : \ln k_t^{(i,s),C} = \beta_0 + \beta_1 \ln Tariff_t^{(i,s),C} + \mathbf{X}_t^{(i,s)}\boldsymbol{\beta}_2' + \mathbf{X}_t^i\boldsymbol{\beta}_3' + \varphi_{OLS}^{(i,s)} + \varepsilon_{OLS,t}^{(i,s)}, \quad (9)$$

where $k_t^{(i,s),C}$ is the employment effect of China on sector s of country i in year t from the demand-side analysis; $Tariff_t^{(i,s),C}$ is one plus the tariff rate imposed by China to sector s of country i in year t. We also include control variables that potentially have impact on the employment effect of China: $\mathbf{X}_t^{(i,s)}$ denotes a vector of control variables varying at the country-level and the sectoral-level. It includes log of total employment compensation, $\ln EmpComp_t^{i,s}$, capturing the labor market condition of sector s of country i at year t. It also includes log of sum of final good exports from the rest of the world to China, which we call the *multilateral demand from China*, capturing China's demand assumed to be orthogonal to country i's exports:

$$\ln MultiD_t^{(i,s),C} = \ln\left(\sum_{k \neq i} x_t^{(k,s),C}\right) \quad (10)$$

where $x_t^{(k,s),C}$ denotes the final good exports from sector s of country k to China in year t. We take summation over all available 189 EORA countries in addition to the ASEAN + JKT economies. This variable is expected to capture the impact of China's final demand *per se*. Therefore, estimated coefficient for (10) is interpreted as the impact of China's demand *per se* on the employment effect of China.

Because export flows to China can be increased by a decline in tariffs imposed by China, (10) can be affected by tariff cuts. In order to control for that, it is important to incorporate tariffs imposed by China on other countries by including the following variable:

$$
\ln MultiTariff_t^{(i,s),C} = \ln \left(\frac{\sum_{k \neq i} x_t^{(k,s),C}}{\sum_{k \neq i} \left(Tariff_t^{(k,s),C}\right)^{1-\sigma_s} x_t^{(k,s),C}} \right), \tag{11}
$$

which is the weighted average of the inverse tariffs where the weights are export flows $x_t^{(k,s),C}$. The elasticity of substitution σ_s acts as a scaling factor governing the weight on tariffs relative to export flows.[8] We set $\sigma_s = 6$ for all sectors. Because (11) is the weighted average of tariffs imposed by China to other countries, the coefficient for the variable is expected to be positive and it is included in the controls $\mathbf{X}_t^{(i,s)}$. Turning to the final variables in (9), $\mathbf{X}_t^i$ denotes a vector of country-level control variable including source country's GDP and source country k's nominal exchange rate against Chinese Yuan, $E_{k/Yuan,t}$, while $\phi_{OLS}^{(i,s)}$ indicates the country-sector fixed effects and $\varepsilon_{OLS,t}^{(i,s)}$ is the error term.

Empirical model: In order to isolate the impact of tariff cuts, we calculate predicted values using the estimated coefficients, the tariff level that are fixed at the early 1990s level, and current values of other control variables as follows:

$$
\hat{y}_{OLS,t}^{(i,s),C} = \hat{\beta}_0 + \hat{\beta}_1 \ln Tariff_{1990}^{(i,s),C} + \mathbf{X}_t^{(i,s)} \hat{\mathbf{\beta}}'_2 + \mathbf{X}_t^i \hat{\mathbf{\beta}}'_3 + \hat{\phi}_{OLS}^{(i,s)} + \hat{\varepsilon}_{OLS,t}^{(i,s)}, \tag{12}
$$

where a hat indicates that it is an estimated coefficient; $Tariff_{1990}^{(i,s),C}$ denotes the highest tariff level in the early 1990s, $Tariff_{1990}^{(i,s),C} = \max_t \{ Tariff_t^{(i,s),C} | t = 1990, 1991, \ldots, 1995 \}$, and $\hat{y}_{OLS,t}^{(i,s),C}$ denotes the predicted log employment effect of China. The reason why we use the highest tariff level in the early 1990s is that tariff levels were volatile in the early 1990s and we are interested in a hypothetical situation in which tariff levels are fixed at the highest level. In equation (12), even residuals are included in the prediction because we are particularly interested in isolating the impact of tariff cuts. Given the predictions (12), we compute the aggregate predicted employment effect of China on country i in a hypothetical world with tariff levels fixed at the early 1990s level:

$$
\mathbf{1}' k_{OLS,t}^{i,C} = \sum_{s=1}^{11} \exp(\hat{y}_{OLS,t}^{(i,s),C}). \tag{13}
$$

where we take sum over 11 merchandise sectors.

While the OLS estimates are employed as our benchmark, we also estimate the regression using another technique for robustness. In the derivation from equation

(8) to equation (13), we first transform $k_t^{(i,s),C}$ to a log form and estimate predictions, and then we transform them back to the USD value form. In this calculation procedure, we are concerned about loss of accuracy because Jensen's inequality implies that log of an average value is not equal to the average of log values. Following the estimation technique proposed by Santos Silva and Tenreyro (2006), we use the Poisson pseudo-maximum likelihood estimator (hereafter PPML). The hypothetical employment effect implied from PPML is denoted as $\mathbf{1}'\mathbf{k}_{PPML,t}^{i,C}$. See Appendix H for further details. By calculating the difference between the actual employment effect of China and the predictions from OLS and PPML, respectively, we find the impact of tariff cuts on the employment effect of China:

$$\text{Impact of Tariff Cuts}_{OLS,t}^{i,C} = \mathbf{1}'\mathbf{k}_{Actual,t}^{i,C} - \mathbf{1}'\mathbf{k}_{OLS,t}^{i,C}, \tag{14}$$

$$\text{Impact of Tariff Cuts}_{PPML,t}^{i,C} = \mathbf{1}'\mathbf{k}_{Actual,t}^{i,C} - \mathbf{1}'\mathbf{k}_{PPML,t}^{i,C}. \tag{15}$$

We are also interested in isolating the impact of China's final demand *per se*. Therefore, we conduct a similar exercise by calculating a hypothetical employment effect of China keeping the final demand from China at the early 1990s level:

$$\ln \textit{Multi } D_{1990}^{(i,s),C} = \min_t\{\ln \textit{Multi } D_{1990}^{(i,s),C}|t = 1990, 1991, ..., 1995\}.$$

Data: The data on the employment effect of China come from the demand-side analysis in this chapter. The country-sector level employment compensation data are directly taken from the EORA database. The data on tariffs come from Caliendo et al. (2015). The multilateral demand from China and the weighted average of tariffs imposed by China to other countries are constructed based on the final good flows from the EORA Global Input-Output Table and tariff data from Caliendo et al. (2015). The other country-level control variables, GDP and the nominal exchange rate are from the Penn World Table 9.0 (Feenstra et al., 2015). The sample in this regression includes 13 countries: Brunei, Cambodia, Indonesia, Japan, Laos, Malaysia, Myanmar, Philippines, Singapore, South Korea, Taiwan, Thailand, and Vietnam. The sample period is from 1990 to 2011. Also, only merchandise sectors, which are EORA sector 1 to EORA sector 11, are included because tariff data are not available for non-merchandise sectors.

Regression results: Estimation results are presented in Table 12.5. The first three columns report OLS estimation results while the last three columns describe results from PPML. Column (1) regresses the log of the employment effect of China on log of tariffs only. The estimated elasticity is −6.32 and highly significant. The absolute value of the coefficient becomes even greater with PPML and it is −8.77. Adding the total employment compensation in order to control for the labor market conditions of each country-sector pair reduces the size of the tariff coefficients substantially, to −2.33 and −5.29 for OLS and PPML, respectively (see columns (2) and (5)). Columns (3) and (6) add more controls. These columns show that the tariff coefficients are much smaller than the previous columns but still significantly less than zero, at −0.49 and −1.15 for OLS and

Table 12.5 Regression result, the impact of tariff cuts and the final demand from China on the employment effect of China

Dep. Var. = ln $(k_t^{(i,s),C})$ for OLS; $k_t^{(i,s),C}$ for PPML

	OLS			PPML		
	(1)	(2)	(3)	(4)	(5)	(6)
ln(tariff imposed by China$_{is}$)	-6.319***	-2.328***	-0.485**	-8.766***	-5.285***	-1.152*
	(0.324)	(0.235)	(0.199)	(0.850)	(0.899)	(0.620)
ln(total emp. compensation$_{is}$)		1.311***	0.906***		1.574***	1.350***
		(0.041)	(0.084)		(0.094)	(0.181)
ln(China's final demand$_{is}$)			0.480***			0.510***
			(0.052)			(0.053)
ln(weighted average of tariffs$_{is}$)			0.213			0.372
			(0.239)			(0.308)
ln(GDP$_i$)			-0.108			-0.771***
			(0.116)			(0.238)
ln(nominal exchange rate against Chinese Yuan$_i$)			0.138***			0.012
			(0.033)			(0.058)
Country-sector fixed effect	Yes	Yes	Yes	Yes	Yes	Yes
R-squared	0.949	0.986	0.990			
# of observations	2,712	2,712	2,712	2,719	2,719	2,719

# of countries = 13, # of sectors = 11, the sample period = 1990–2011

***, **, and * indicate the statistical significance at 1%, 5%, and 10% level, respectively. The employment effect of China on Laos is zero for some sectors, which makes it impossible to find the log(employment) effect. As a result, these observations are dropped from the OLS regression. However, these observations can be included in PPML. Therefore, the number of observation is different between these two models.

PPML, respectively. Total employment compensation and the multilateral demand from China, measured by equation (9) and denoted by *China's final demand*, also make significant contributions to the regression.

The coefficients for the weighted average of tariffs have the expected sign but these are insignificant. The log of GDP is insignificant in OLS and it is significantly negative in PPML. The negative sign from PPML is presumably because an increase in country's GDP works to increase the total employment compensation and leads to a decline of the employment effect of China relative to overall labor compensation. Also, the nominal exchange rate has a positive sign, meaning that a depreciation of a country's currency against Chinese Yuan works to increase the employment effect of China. This makes sense because a depreciation of a currency increases exports by reducing the relative price of exports.

Decomposition results: Figures 12.4 and 12.5 show the decomposition result for the ASEAN + JKT economies, where the actual China's employment effect is different from the one from the demand side analysis because only 11 merchandise sectors are included in this regression analysis. Figure 12.4 describes the employment effect of China, holding tariffs at the early 1990s level, and Figure 12.5 shows the one keeping China's final demand constant at the early 1990s level. In Figure 12.4, the thick line with markers indicates the actual employment effect of China on the ASEAN + JKT economies. The thinner dashed line indicates the hypothetical employment effect of China when tariff levels were fixed at the early 1990s level, based on OLS. The thicker solid line indicates the hypothetical employment effect of China when tariff levels were fixed at the early 1990s level, based on PPML. Average tariff rates applied by China are shown by the dashed line with markers. The figure suggests that declining tariffs imposed by China seem to be related with the increasing employment effect of China. It also shows that the gap between the actual employment effect of China and the one obtained by fixing the tariff levels at the early 1990s becomes greater over time, regardless the two methods of estimation, OLS and PPML.

Estimated impacts of tariff cuts on the employment effect of China are shown in Table 12.6, for each of the Asian countries as well as for the area as a whole. It shows that, in the ASEAN + JKT area overall in 2011, the OLS estimates imply that tariff cuts account for 11.5 billion USD of China's employment effect, which is equivalent to 10.2 per cent of China's employment effect. The PPML estimates imply even greater contribution of tariff cuts, accounting for 25.0 billion USD of China's employment effect, which is 22.1 per cent of the total employment effect. The decomposition results for each country are shown in Table 12.6. Tariff cuts contributed the most for Brunei: 44.4 per cent and 42.5 per cent based on OLS and PPML, respectively. The contribution of tariff cuts is almost the same for the rest of the ASEAN + JKT economies: roughly 10 per cent and 20–25 per cent based on OLS and PPML, respectively.

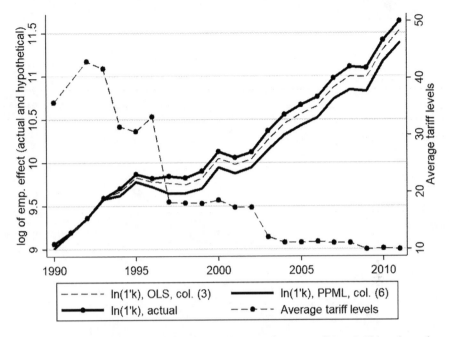

Figure 12.4 The impact of tariff cuts on the "employment effect of China from the demand-side analysis", in the ASEAN + JKT area

Notes: The thick line with markers indicates the actual employment effect of China on the ASEAN + JKT area, $1'k_{Actual,t}^{ASEAN+JKT,C}$. The dashed line indicates the hypothetical employment effect of China when tariff levels were fixed at the early 1990s level, based on OLS reported in column (3) of Table 12.5, $1'k_{OLS,t}^{ASEAN+JKT,C}$. The solid line without markers indicates the hypothetical employment effect of China when tariff levels were fixed at the early 1990s level, based on PPML reported in column (6) of Table 12.5, $1'k_{PPML,t}^{ASEAN+JKT,C}$. The difference between the actual employment effect $1'k_{Actual,t}^{ASEAN+JKT,C}$ and the hypothetical employment effects $1'k_{OLS,t}^{ASEAN+JKT,C}$ (and $1'k_{PPML,t}^{ASEAN+JKT,C}$) is the impact of tariff cuts on the employment effect of China. The simple average tariff rates imposed by China to the ASEAN + JKT area are also shown.

The contribution of China's final demand for the exports of the ASEAN + JKT economies is described in Figure 12.5. Unlike the previous case, the implied impact of China's final demand is almost the same for the OLS and PPML estimates. Table 12.7 shows that, in the ASEAN + JKT area overall in 2011, the OLS estimates imply that China's final demand *per se* accounts for 85.8 billion USD of China's employment effect, which is equivalent to 75.8 per cent of China's employment effect. The PPML estimates imply that China's final demand contributes to 87.0 billion USD employment creation, which is 76.9 per cent of China's total employment effect.

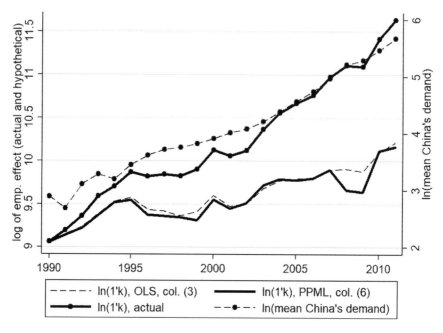

Figure 12.5 The impact of the final demand on the "employment effect of China from the demand-side analysis", in the ASEAN + JKT area

Notes: The thick line with markers indicate the actual employment effect of China on the ASEAN + JKT area, $1'k_{Actual,t}^{ASEAN+JKT,C}$. The dashed line indicates the hypothetical employment effect of China when China's final demand were fixed at the early 1990s level, based on OLS reported in column (3) of Table 12.5, $1'k_{OLS,t}^{ASEAN+JKT,C}$. The solid line without markers indicates the hypothetical employment effect of China when China's final demand were fixed at the early 1990s level, based on PPML reported in column (6) of Table 12.5, $1'k_{PPML,t}^{ASEAN+JKT,C}$. The difference between the actual employment effect $1'k_{Actual,t}^{ASEAN+JKT,C}$ and the hypothetical employment effects $1'k_{OLS,t}^{ASEAN+JKT,C}$ (and $1'k_{PPML,t}^{ASEAN+JKT,C}$) is the impact of China's final demand *per se* on the employment effect of China.

Table 12.6 Contribution of tariff cuts on the employment effect of China implied by the demand-side analysis

Panel A: Based on the OLS estimates

	The impact of tariff cuts on the employment effect of China (million USD)				% to the actual employment effect of China			
	1996	*2001*	*2006*	*2011*	*1996*	*2001*	*2006*	*2011*
Brunei	–	3.54	12.29	35.95	–	48.38	45.59	44.44
Cambodia	–	1.23	0.50	1.46	–	42.46	6.94	9.11
Indonesia	17.88	43.13	165.92	597.82	3.97	7.64	9.96	10.28
Japan	387.98	1,032.82	2,515.74	6,104.96	3.60	7.42	9.72	9.95
Laos	0.12	0.30	0.72	3.29	7.78	16.49	11.09	11.86
Malaysia	23.87	65.33	236.55	769.85	3.97	8.09	10.56	11.06
Myanmar	3.75	2.17	3.86	17.19	24.17	8.62	9.94	10.72
Philippines	6.35	16.94	63.69	221.72	4.33	8.19	10.47	10.87
South Korea	85.85	245.75	859.73	2,289.91	4.04	7.84	9.92	10.27
Singapore	16.49	44.03	138.26	402.86	4.02	7.92	10.19	10.33
Taiwan	114.74	240.56	408.16	551.87	3.62	7.51	9.68	10.01
Thailand	10.54	42.53	151.55	340.79	2.45	8.01	10.44	10.84
Vietnam	8.90	22.77	81.45	149.85	3.38	5.45	7.79	8.11
ASEAN + JKT	681.34	1,761.08	4,638.42	11,487.52	3.70	7.53	9.82	10.15

Panel B: Based on the PPML estimates

	1996	2001	2006	2011	1996	2001	2006	2011
Brunei	–	3.91	11.93	34.36	–	53.46	44.27	42.47
Cambodia	–	1.46	1.21	3.13	–	50.66	16.88	19.50
Indonesia	49.38	78.13	402.40	1,152.77	10.96	13.84	24.17	19.82
Japan	987.27	2,310.03	5,109.58	13,464.12	9.15	16.59	19.74	21.94
Laos	0.33	0.37	1.55	6.62	22.35	20.82	24.02	23.91
Malaysia	67.30	144.12	527.18	1,600.66	11.20	17.84	23.53	22 99
Myanmar	4.43	2.97	6.54	39.74	28.50	11.81	16.83	24.79
Philippines	11.04	32.05	154.11	485.82	7.51	15.49	25.33	23.82
South Korea	277.38	573.52	1,916.51	4,596.01	13.06	18.30	22.10	20.62
Singapore	38.91	89.41	298.40	906.44	9.49	16.09	21.99	23.24
Taiwan	210.47	529.69	993.23	1,619.70	6.64	16.53	23.55	29.38
Thailand	25.71	82.67	342.75	784.27	5.97	15.58	23.61	24.95
Vietnam	24.77	47.78	179.75	330.03	9.41	11.44	17.19	17.87
ASEAN + JKT	1,702.14	3,896.11	9,945.15	25,023.67	9.25	16.66	21.06	22.11

Notes: The table shows contributions of tariff cuts on the employment effect of China implied from the demand-side analysis. Panel A shows the contribution of tariff cuts based on the regression result reported in column (3) of Table 12.5, estimated by OLS. Panel B reports the one based on the result shown in column (6) of Table 12.5, estimated by PPML. Missing numbers for Brunei and Cambodia in 1996 are due to inadequate observations on tariffs.

Table 12.7 Contribution of the final demand from China on the employment effect of China implied by the demand-side analysis

Panel A: Based on the OLS estimates

	The impact of China's final demand on the employment effect of China (million USD)				% to the actual employment effect of China			
	1996	2001	2006	2011	1996	2001	2006	2011
Brunei	–	3.69	17.49	62.89	–	50.47	64.89	77.73
Cambodia	–	1.55	3.91	11.26	–	53.49	54.73	70.15
Indonesia	102.72	173.50	855.15	4,054.59	22.80	30.74	51.36	69.73
Japan	3,516.91	6,366.54	16,315.87	47,115.40	32.61	45.72	63.02	76.78
Laos	0.42	0.80	3.52	19.34	28.13	44.17	54.36	69.81
Malaysia	188.17	349.38	1,367.45	5,262.84	31.30	43.24	61.04	75.60
Myanmar	6.96	8.14	19.88	110.84	44.83	32.40	51.15	69.13
Philippines	47.86	94.31	382.90	1,570.70	32.59	45.60	62.94	77.02
South Korea	678.62	1,379.83	5,343.10	16,916.73	31.94	44.03	61.62	75.90
Singapore	133.16	249.37	843.37	2,979.50	32.48	44.87	62.16	76.39
Taiwan	1,008.03	1,406.24	2,617.45	4,207.36	31.81	43.88	62.06	76.31
Thailand	125.85	206.81	821.19	2,278.44	29.23	38.97	56.56	72.48
Vietnam	46.28	98.53	469.24	1,207.34	17.59	23.60	44.87	65.35
ASEAN + JKT	5,859.70	10,338.69	29,060.50	85,797.22	31.84	44.21	61.54	75.82

Panel B: *Based on the PPML estimates*

Brunei	—	4.21	15.97	55.05	—	57.56	59.28	68.05
Cambodia	—	1.36	3.35	13.15	—	47.01	46.98	81.95
Indonesia	118.64	148.58	982.49	3,656.00	26.34	26.32	59.00	62.87
Japan	4,037.36	6,600.07	15,477.36	48,182.28	37.44	47.40	59.79	78.52
Laos	0.64	0.65	3.79	19.19	43.09	36.31	58.51	69.27
Malaysia	236.89	361.43	1,441.68	5,125.29	39.41	44.73	64.36	73.62
Myanmar	9.05	4.65	15.84	126.04	58.25	18.50	40.77	78.60
Philippines	36.08	82.72	438.91	1,603.94	24.57	39.99	72.14	78.65
South Korea	1,007.58	1,521.72	5,558.01	15,738.74	47.42	48.56	64.10	70.61
Singapore	145.68	241.22	857.92	3,096.58	35 53	43.40	63.24	79.39
Taiwan	833.66	1,451.70	2,981.76	5,742.02	26.31	45.29	70.70	104.15
Thailand	118.20	189.38	878.67	2,453.60	27.45	35.68	60.52	78.05
Vietnam	51.46	95.61	479.62	1,238.79	19.55	22.90	45.86	67.06
ASEAN + JKT	6,600.32	10,703.30	29,135.36	87,050.67	35.87	45.77	61.70	76.93

Notes: The table shows contribution of China's final demand on the employment effect of China implied from the demand-side analysis. Panel A shows the contribution of the final demand from China based on the regression result reported in column (3) of Table 12.5, estimated by OLS. Panel B reports the one based on the result shown in column (6) of Table 12.5, estimated by PPML. Missing numbers for Brunei and Cambodia in 1996 are due to inadequate observations on tariffs. The number can be greater than 100% because the predicted employment effect of China can be greater than the actual employment effect of China.

5.   Conclusions

The empirical results presented in this chapter highlight positive employment creation effects of China on the ASEAN and other East Asian countries by providing export opportunities to these countries. We have quantified the employment effect of China on the ASEAN + JKT during 1990–2013 using the global IO table from the EORA database. We employ the two different techniques: the demand-side analysis from Los et al. (2015b) and the hypothetical extraction technique from Los et al. (2016). The two techniques yield large and strongly growing employment effects of China during the period. According to the results from the former technique, the employment creation effect of China on the ASEAN + JKT area overall is 19 billion and 234 billion USD in 1990 and 2013, respectively, meaning that the employment effect grew at an annual rate of 11 per cent. The China effect accounts for 6.5 per cent of the employment effect driven by the total demand in 2013, versus merely 1 per cent in 1990.

While this exercise is highly informative, it includes the employment effect through changes in tariffs such as the ASEAN-China Free Trade Agreement and through changes in China's final demand *per se* together. So we have also used a regression technique to decompose the portion of the employment creation that is due to each of these two sources, and we find that tariff cuts by China account for 10–25 per cent of the employment effect, with the remainder due to the expansion of Chinese demand *per se*. Through both its tariff liberalization and through its growth of final demand, therefore, China plays an important role in creating employment in the ASEAN and other East Asian countries.

Notes

Acknowledgement: The authors would like to thank Marcel P. Timmer, Robert C. Johnson, Ayumu Tanaka, Zadia M. Feliciano, Jung Hur, and participants at the Groningen Growth and Development Centre (GGDC) 25th Anniversary Conference and the Robert E. Lipsey Memorial Panel Sessions at the Western Economic Association International 2018 for their helpful suggestions.

1 Feenstra and Hong (2010) estimate the impact of export growth on China's employment using China's Input-Output Table. They find that export growth over 1997–2002 contributed to at most 2.5 million jobs per year where the total number of jobs increased by 7.5–8 million jobs per year.
2 Los, Timmer and de Vries (2015a) investigate the impact of China's exports on employment creation in China using the Global Input-Output Table from the WIOD database. They find that, between 2001 and 2006, Chinese exports added approximately 70 million jobs to the Chinese economy.
3 In an integrated global economy, it is also possible to consider third country effects. For example, increasing export opportunities to China from country A may have an impact on employment in country B through various linkages. However, this chapter focuses on the direct effect of export opportunities to China on the exporting country.
4 The advantages of employing the EORA database are as follows. First, and most important, it includes a number of ASEAN and East Asian countries that are not included in WIOD (see Appendix A). Second, the EORA database provides data on labor compensation rather than only the number of workers employed. Third, a

longer time-series, from 1990 to 2013, is available from the EORA database while the WIOD database covers 1995 to 2011.

5 See Appendix D for detailed derivation.

6 See Appendix D for details of our calculation.

7 Unlike the previous section, the share of China's employment effect in 1990 is not shown because it is zero by construction.

8 This multilateral tariff term can be derived more formally from a CES framework.

References

Acemoglu, Daron, David Autor, David Dorn, Gordon H. Hanson and Brendan Price, 2016, "Import Competition and the Great U.S. Employment Sag of the 2000s," *Journal of Labor Economics*, 34(S1), S141–S198.

Ando, Mitsuyo and Fukunari Kimura, 2005, "The Formation of International Production and Distribution Networks in East Asia," in: *International Trade (NBER-East Asia Seminar on Economics)*, Volume 14, edited by Takatoshi Ito and Andrew K. Rose, Chicago: The University of Chicago Press.

Autor, David H., David Dorn and Gordon H. Hanson, 2013, "The China Syndrome: Local Labor Market Effects of Import Competition in the United States," *American Economic Review*, 103(6), 2121–2168.

Autor, David H., David Dorn and Gordon H. Hanson, 2015, "Untangling Trade and Technology: Evidence From Local Labor Markets," *Economic Journal*, 125(584), May, 621–646.

Autor, David H., David Dorn, Gordon H. Hanson and Jae Song, 2014. "Trade Adjustment: Worker-Level Evidence," *Quarterly Journal of Economics*, 129(4), 1799–1860.

Baldwin, Robert E., 1994, "The Effects of Trade and Foreign Direct Investment on Employment and Relative Wages," *OECD Economic Studies*, 23, 7–54.

Caliendo, Lorenzo, Robert C. Feenstra, John Romalis and Alan M. Taylor, 2015, "Tariff Reductions, Entry, and Welfare: Theory and Evidence for the Last Two Decades," NBER Working Paper No. 21768.

Dauth, Wolfgang, Sebastian Findeisen and Jens Suedekum, 2014, "The Rise of the East and the Far East: German Labor Markets and Trade Integration," *Journal of European Economic Association*, 12(6), 1643–1675.

Feenstra, Robert C. and Chang Hong, 2010, "China's Exports and Employment," in: *China's Growing Role in World Trade*, edited by Robert C. Feenstra and Shang-Jin Wei, pp. 167–199. Chicago: The University of Chicago Press.

Feenstra, Robert C., Robert Inklaar and Marcel P. Timmer, 2015, "The Next Generation of the Penn World Table," *American Economic Review*, 105(10), 3150–3182.

Feenstra, Robert C., Hong Ma and Yuan Xu, 2017, "U.S. Exports and Employment," NBER Working Paper No. 24056.

Feenstra, Robert C. and Akira Sasahara, 2017, "The 'China Shock', Exports and U.S. Employment: A Global Input-Output Analysis," NBER Working Paper No. 24022.

International Monetary Fund, 2017, "World Economic Outlook Update: A Shifting Global Economic Landscape," January 2017, Washington, DC.

Johnson, Robert C. and Guillermo Noguera, 2012, "Accounting for Intermediates: Production Sharing and Trade in Value Added," *Journal of International Economics*, 86(2), 224–236.

Kiyota, Kozo, 2016, "Exports and Employment in China, Indonesia, Japan, and Korea," *Asian Economic Papers*, 15(1), 57–72.

Koopman, Robert B., Zhi Wang and Shang-Jin Wei, 2008, "How Much of Chinese Exports Is Really Made in China? Assessing Domestic Value-Added When Processing Trade is Pervasive," NBER Working Paper No. 14109.

Koopman, Robert B., Zhi Wang and Shang-Jin Wei, 2014, "Tracing Value-Added and Double Counting in Gross Exports," *American Economic Review*, 104(2), 459–494.

Lenzen, Manfred, Keiichiro Kanemoto, Daniel Moran and Arne Geschke, 2012, "Mapping the Structure of the World Economy," *Environmental Science & Technology* 46(15), 8374–8381. doi:10.1021/es300171x

Lenzen, Manfred, Daniel Moran, Keiichiro Kanemoto and Arne Geschke, 2013, "Building Eora: A Global Multi-regional Input-Output Database at High Country and Sector Resolution," *Economic Systems Research*, 25(1), 20–49. doi:10.1080/09535314.2013.769938

Leontief, Wassily W., 1936, "Quantitative Input-Output Relations in the Economic System of the United States," *Review of Economics and Statistics*, 18(3), 105–125.

Los, Bart, Mercel P. Timmer and Gaaitzen J. de Vries, 2015a, "How Global Are Global Value Chains? A New Approach to Measure International Fragmentation," *Journal of Regional Science*, 55(1), 66–92.

Los, Bart, Marcel P. Timmer and Gaaitzen J. de Vries, 2015b, "How Important Are Exports for Job Growth in China? A Demand-side Analysis," *Journal of Comparative Economics*, 43(1), 19–32.

Los, Bart, Marcel P. Timmer and Gaaitzen J. de Vries, 2016, "Tracing Value-Added and Double Counting in Gross Exports: Comment," *American Economic Review*, 106(7), 1958–1966.

Pierce, Justin R. and Peter K. Schott, 2016, "The Surprisingly Swift Decline of U.S. Manufacturing Employment," *American Economic Review*, 106(7), 1632–1662.

Santos Silva, João M.C. and Silvana Tenreyro, 2006, "The Log of Gravity," *Review of Economics and Statistics*, 88(4), 641–658.

Timmer, Marcel P., Abdul Azeez Erumban, Bart Los, Robert Stehrer and Gaaitzen J. de Vries, 2014, "Slicing Up Global Value Chains," *Journal of Economic Perspectives*, 28(2), 99–118.

Timmer, Marcel P., E. Dietzenbacher, Bart Los, Robert Stehrer and Gaaitzen J. de Vries, 2015, "An Illustrated User Guide to the World Input? Output Database: The Case of Global Automotive Production," *Review of International Economics*, 23, 575–605.

Timmer, Marcel P., Bart Los, Robert Stehrer and Gaaitzen J. de Vries, 2013, "Fragmentation, Incomes, and Jobs: An Analysis of European Competitiveness," *Economic Policy*, 28(76), 613–661.

Vianna, Andre C., 2016, "The Impact of Exports to China on Latin American Growth," *Journal of Asian Economics*, 47(1), 58–66.

World Bank, 2017, "Where We Work: China Overview", World Bank, Washington, DC, www.worldbank.org/en/country/china/overview.

Appendix A

List of countries

Our re-constructed EORA Input-Output Table includes 51 countries besides the rest of the world as one economy. The 51 countries include 40 WIOD countries and additional 11 economies from ASEAN and East Asia. The list of the countries is as follows. * indicates newly added non-WIOD countries and ISO Alpha 3 codes are in parentheses.

Australia (AUS), Austria (AUT), Belgium (BEL), Brazil (BRA), Brunei (BRN)*, Bulgaria (BGR), Cambodia (KHM)*, Canada (CAN), China (CHN), Cyprus (CYP), Czech Republic (CZE), Denmark (DNK), Estonia (EST), Finland (FIN), France (FRA), Germany (DEU), Greece (GRC), Hong Kong (HKG)*, Hungary (HUN), India (IND), Indonesia (IDN), Ireland (IRL), Italy (ITA), Japan (JPN), Laos (LAO)*, Latvia (LVA), Lithuania (LTU), Luxembourg (LUX), Macao SAR (MAC)*, Malaysia (MYS)*, Malta (MLT), Mexico (MEX), Myanmar (MMR)*, Netherlands (NLD), Philippines (PHL)*, Poland (POL), Portugal (PRT), South Korea (KOR), Romania (ROU), Russia (RUS), Singapore (SGP)*, Slovakia (SVK), Slovenia (SVN), Spain (ESP), Sweden (SWE), Taiwan (TWN), Thailand (THA)*, Turkey (TUR), the United Kingdom (GBR), the United States (USA), and Vietnam (VNM)*

Appendix B

List of sectors and final demand categories

Our Input-Output Table includes 26 sectors as in the one from the EORA Database. The list of the sectors is as follows.

1. Agriculture, 2. Fishing, 3. Mining and Quarrying, 4. Food and Beverages, 5. Textiles and Wearing Apparel, 6. Wood and Paper, 7. Petroleum, Chemical and Non-Metallic Mineral Products, 8. Metal Products, 9. Electrical Machinery, 10. Transport Equipment, 11. Other Manufacturing, 12. Recycling, 13. Electricity, Gas and Water, 14. Construction, 15. Maintenance and Repair, 16. Wholesale Trade, 17. Retail Trade, 18. Hotels and Restaurants, 19. Transport, 20. Post and Telecommunications, 21. Financial Intermediation and Business Activities, 22. Public Administration, 23. Private Households, 25. Others, 26. Re-export and Re-import

There six final demand categories. The list of the categories is as follows.

1. Household final consumption, 2. Non-profit institutions serving households, 3. Government final consumption, 4. Gross fixed capital formation, 5. Changes in inventories, and 6. Acquisitions less disposals of valuables

Appendix C

How to treat Hong Kong and Macau

Our Global Input-Output Table includes Hong Kong and Macau. These two economies are first treated as different from China. However, after computing the employment effects due to the final demand from Hong Kong and Macau, these two employment effects are aggregated into the employment effect of the mainland China. We clarify this by showing the equations below.

First, compute the employment effects due to the final demand from mainland China, Hong Kong, and Macau as follows:

$$\mathbf{k}_t^{Mailand\ China} = \hat{\mathbf{p}}_t(\mathbf{I} - \mathbf{A}_t)^{-1}\mathbf{f}_t^{Mailand\ China},$$

$$\mathbf{k}_t^{Hong\ Kong} = \hat{\mathbf{p}}_t(\mathbf{I} - \mathbf{A}_t)^{-1}\mathbf{f}_t^{Hong\ Kong},$$

$$\mathbf{k}_t^{Macau} = \hat{\mathbf{p}}_t(\mathbf{I} - \mathbf{A}_t)^{-1}\mathbf{f}_t^{Macau},$$

where $\mathbf{f}_t^{MainlandChina}$, $\mathbf{f}_t^{HongKong}$, and $\mathbf{f}_t^{Macau}$ are $(S \times C) \times 1$ matrices of the final demand from the mainland China, Hong Kong, and Macau, respectively. The same notations follow as the main text for the rest of the matrices. After finding the employment effects from the three economies, $\mathbf{k}_t^{MailandChina}$, $\mathbf{k}_t^{HongKong}$, and $\mathbf{k}_t^{Macau}$, we take sum of these to find the employment from China as follows:

$$\mathbf{k}_t^{China} = \mathbf{k}_t^{Mailand\ China} + \mathbf{k}_t^{Hong\ Kong} + \mathbf{k}_t^{Macau}.$$

Appendix D

Appendix to the demand-side analysis: the foreign effect and the total effect

This section presents mathematical details to estimate the employment effect due to total demand in the demand-side analysis. This employment effect is estimated as:

$$\mathbf{k}_t^{All} = \hat{\mathbf{p}}_t (\mathbf{I} - \mathbf{A}_t)^{-1} \mathbf{f}_t^{All}, \tag{A1}$$

where $\mathbf{k}_t^{All}$ is an $(N \times S) \times 1$ vector describing the employment effect driven by demand from overall demand. $\mathbf{f}_t^{All}$ denotes the final good flows to all countries, and can be written as follows:

$$\mathbf{f}_t^{All} = \begin{bmatrix} \sum_k \mathbf{f}_t^{1,k} \\ \sum_k \mathbf{f}_t^{2,k} \\ \vdots \\ \sum_k \mathbf{f}_t^{N,k} \end{bmatrix}.$$

For example, the first element of $\mathbf{f}_t^{All}$, $\sum_k \mathbf{f}_t^{1,k}$, is the value of final good flows from country 1 to all over the world including country 1 itself. The estimated employment effects based on equation (A1) can be expressed as:

$$\mathbf{k}_t^{All} = \begin{bmatrix} \mathbf{k}_t^{1,All} \\ \mathbf{k}_t^{2,All} \\ \vdots \\ \mathbf{k}_t^{N,All} \end{bmatrix}.$$

The employment effect of total demand on country is estimated as the sum of numbers in $\mathbf{k}_t^{i,All}$, which is written as $\mathbf{1}'\mathbf{k}_t^{i,All}$.

The employment effect on country i driven by final demand in China relative to the employment effect driven by final demand from all countries is computed as

$$\text{China Effect relative to Total Effect}_{i,t} = 100 \times \mathbf{1}'\mathbf{k}_t^{i,C}/\mathbf{1}'\mathbf{k}_t^{i,All}. \tag{A2}$$

Another way to normalize the employment effect of China is to compute the ratio to country's GDP:

$$\text{China Effect relative to GDP}_{i,t} = 100 \times \mathbf{1}\mathbf{k}_t^{i,C}/GDP_{i,t.}$$

Appendix E

Appendix to the demand-side analysis: the comparison with Los et al. (2015b)

This section gives more details regarding the calculation procedure for the numbers reported in Table 12.3. The employment effect induced by the foreign demand from year t to year $t+h$ $\sum_{i\in\{ASEAN+3\}}\mathbf{1}'\mathbf{k}_{t+h}^{i,-i} - \sum_{i\in\{ASEAN+JKT\}}\mathbf{1}'\mathbf{k}_t^{i,-i}$ is divided by the overall employment compensation at year $t+h$, $\sum_{i\in\{ASEAN+JKT\}}EmpComp_{i,t+h}$, which leads to:

$$\frac{\sum_{i\in\{ASEAN+JKT\}}\mathbf{1}'\mathbf{k}_{t+h}^{i,-i} - \sum_{i\in\{ASEAN+JKT\}}\mathbf{1}'\mathbf{k}_t^{i,-i}}{\sum_{i\in\{ASEAN+JKT\}}EmpComp_{i,t+h}},$$

where $\{ASEAN+JKT\}$ is a set of the ASEAN+JKT economies; h is a time horizon; $EmpComp_{i,t}$ denotes the total employment compensation in country i in year t. A similar calculation applies to the employment effects induced by China's demand and the total demand. These are calculated as follows:

$$\frac{\sum_{i\in\{ASEAN+JKT\}}\mathbf{1}\mathbf{k}_{t+h}^{i,C} - \sum_{i\in\{ASEAN+JKT\}}\mathbf{1}\mathbf{k}_t^{i,C}}{\sum_{i\in\{ASEAN+JKT\}}EmpComp_{i,t+h}},$$

$$\frac{\sum_{i\in\{ASEAN+JKT\}}\mathbf{1}\mathbf{k}_{t+h}^{i,All} - \sum_{i\in\{ASEAN+JKT\}}\mathbf{1}\mathbf{k}_t^{i,All}}{\sum_{i\in\{ASEAN+JKT\}}EmpComp_{i,t+h}},$$

respectively, where C indicates China and All indicates all countries including country i itself.

Appendix F

Sectoral crosswalk between EORA and SITC

The tariff data from Caliendo et al. (2015) are given in 4-digit SITC classification. We match the tariff data with the 11 merchandise sectors from EORA. The crosswalk between SITC and EORA sectors is shown in Table 12.A1.

Table 12.A1 Crosswalk between EORA sectors and SITC code

EORA no.	EORA sectors	SITC code
1	Agriculture	00–02, 12,21–23,29
2	Fishing	03
3	Mining and Quarrying	32–34
4	Food & Beverages	04–09, 11,41–43
5	Textiles and Wearing Apparel	26,27,61,62,65,66,85
6	Wood and Paper	24, 25, 63, 64
7	Petroleum, Chemical and Non-Metallic Mineral Products	51–59
8	Metal Products	28, 67–69, 96, 97
9	Electrical and Machinery	35,71–77
10	Transport Equipment	78,79
11	Other Manufacturing	81–84,87–89,91,93
12	Recycling	
13	Electricity, Gas and Water	
14	Construction	
15	Maintenance and Repair	
16	Wholesale Trade	
17	Retail Trade	
18	Hotels and Restaurants	
19	Transport	Not included in regression
20	Post and Telecommunications	
21	Finacial Intermediation and Business Activities	
22	Public Administration	

(Continued)

Table 12.A1 (Continued)

EORA no.	EORA sectors	SITC code
23	Education, Health and Other Services	
24	Private Households	
25	Others	
26	Re-export & Re-import	

Notes: The table shows the correspondence between 11 EORA merchandise sectors and SITC 2 digit classification code employed in order to match the tariff data from Caliendo et al. (2015) with the EORA sectors.

Appendix G

Summary statistics

Summary statistics for the variables employed in the regression analysis are presented in Table 12.A2.

Table 12.A2 Summary statistics for variables in regression analysis

	# of obs.	Mean	Std. dev.	Min	Max
ln(employment effect of China)	3,126	2.40	3.11	−4.61	10.45
ln(1+tariff/100)	2,719	0.17	0.11	0.00	0.82
ln(total emp. compensation)	3,146	6.02	2.52	−0.69	12.35
ln(multilateral final demand from China)	3,024	3.60	1.34	0.99	6.82
ln(weighted average of tariffs imposed by China)	3,024	0.21	0.24	0.01	1.48
ln(GDP)	3,024	12.23	1.77	8.64	15.32
ln(nominal exchange rate against Chinese Yuan)	3,146	2.94	3.07	−1.77	8.06

Notes: See the main text for data sources.

Appendix H

Decomposition exercise using estimates from PPML

In Section 4, we estimate a regression equation in order to investigate the determinants of the employment effect of China using OLS and the Poisson pseudo-maximum likelihood (PPML) estimator. This section provides mathematical details in order to calculate the prediction based on the PPML estimator. We first estimate the following equation:

$$
\text{PPML}: k_t^{(i,s),C} = \exp\{\gamma_0 + \gamma_1 \ln \text{Tariff}_t^{(i,s),C} \tag{A3}
$$
$$
+ \mathbf{X}_t^{(i,s)} \gamma_2' + \mathbf{X}_t^i \gamma_3' + \varphi_{PPML}^{(i,s)}\} + \varepsilon_{PPML,t}^{(i,s)}
$$

where $k_t^{(i,s),C}$ is the USD value of the employment effect of China on sector s of country i in year t; $\text{Tariff}_t^{(i,s),C}$ denotes the tariff rate imposed by China on sector s of country i; $\mathbf{X}_t^{(i,s)}$ is a vector of control variables varying at the country-level and the sector-level including total employment compensation, multilateral demand from China, and the weighted average of tariff rates imposed by China to other countries (see the main text for the definition of these variables). $\mathbf{X}_t^i$ is a vector of control variables varying at the country-level including GDP and the nominal exchange rate against China. $\varphi_{PPML}^{(i,s)}$ denotes country fixed effects and $\varepsilon_{PPML,t}^{(i,s)}$ indicates the error term. γ_0 and γ_1 are scalar parameters to be estimated and γ_2 and γ_3 are vectors of parameters to be estimated.

Predictions from equation (A3) are in USD value:

$$
\hat{y}_{PPML,t}^{(i,s),C} = \exp\{\hat{\gamma}_0 + \hat{\gamma}_1 \ln \text{Tariff}_{1990}^{(i,s),C} + \mathbf{X}_t^{(i,s)} \hat{\gamma}_2' + \mathbf{X}_t^i \hat{\gamma}_3' + \hat{\varphi}_{PPML}^{(i,s)}\} + \hat{\varepsilon}_{PPML,t}^{(i,s)}. \tag{A4}
$$

where a hat indicates estimated coefficients or prediction. Using the prediction from (A4), we compute the aggregate predicted employment effect on country i as follows:

$$
\mathbf{1}' \mathbf{k}_{PPML,t}^{i,C} = \sum_{s=1}^{11} \hat{y}_{PPML,t}^{(i,s),C}.
$$

13   Modern spatial economics: a primer

Treb Allen and Costas Arkolakis

1. Introduction

Space: Economic Science's final frontier. Over the past twenty years a revolution in the exploration of space in Economics led by a combined effort from geographers, trade, and urban economists has finally brought the required technology to analyze space in all its glory: An armada of tools from mathematics, physics, cartography, and computer science has gradually formed the necessary equipment to explore space and its consequence for growth and allocation of economic activity.

Spearheading this exploration is spatial theory's dreadnought: The gravity model. This mathematical design strikes a careful balance between two key ingredients behind any successful theory. It is intuitive and pedagogical while at the same time rich enough to provide an incredibly good fit to the empirical observations. In other words, it is beautiful and it works like a charm!

The key force that spatial models with mobility of goods and people need to harness is space itself. In an environment with N locations, mobility of goods and people implies that N^2 number of trade interactions and N^2 migration flows have to be modeled. These many complex interactions could potentially obscure the main forces that determine economic activity across space. The resolution that the gravity model provides cuts right through these complexities: It allows for as many (exogenous) frictions as relationships, but assumes that the elasticity of the flows to (endogenous) push and pull factors are governed by only a single parameter. This lets the theory capture the first-order impacts of the effects of geography on economic outcomes while ignoring the (potentially) less important impact of varying bilateral elasticities.

To understand the model and the impact of space on economic activity we present a generalized, yet simple, version of the gravity model that allows for mobility of goods and people across space limited by frictions specific to these flows.[1] In particular, we employ an extension of the Allen and Arkolakis (2014) framework with an exogenous population in each location and mobility frictions across locations. Variations of this extension have been more formally modeled by Tombe, Zhu et al. (2015), Bryan and Morten (2015), Caliendo, Dvorkin and Parro (2015), Desmet, Nagy and Rossi-Hansberg (2016), Faber and Gaubert (2016), Allen, Morten and Dobbin (2017) and Allen and

Donaldson (2017). Within this environment we can answer a number of important questions: What is the allocation of economic activity across space and how is it determined by location fundamentals or bilateral frictions of mobility. When does a solution of the model exists and when is it unique? Do different assumptions on the frictions of moving goods and people imply that policies have different implications?

Finally, we should note that the brief literature review of gravity models above is by no means complete and refer the interested reader to the excellent review articles by Baldwin and Taglioni (2006), Head and Mayer (2013), Costinot and Rodríguez-Clare (2013) and Redding and Rossi-Hansberg (2017), where the latter two focus especially on quantitative spatial models.

2.   Gravity: the evidence

We begin by explaining and documenting the "gravity" relationship. Empirically, the notion of gravity introduced by Tinbergen (1962) postulates that flows decline with distance. We illustrate that both the flow of goods (trade) and people (migration) exhibit gravity. Moreover, this gravity relationship is robust to different scales of distance: it is prevalent for the flow of people and goods both across countries and within countries. Finally, gravity has been present in the data for (at least) the past fifty years, and shows no signs of attenuating over time.

2.1.   *Gravity in the flow of goods*

We first examine the flow of goods (trade). We use two different data sets: the first, from Head, Mayer and Ries (2010), comprise the value of trade between between countries from 1948 to 2006; the second, from CFS (2007, 2012), are the Commodity Flow Surveys, comprise the value of trade between U.S. states for 2007 and 2012. To reduce concerns of selection bias, we constrain each sample to be balanced by only including origin-destination pairs that reported positive trade flows for each year in the sample; moreover, to avoid having to take a stand on what constitutes the "distance-to-self", in each sample we exclude own trade flows.

Let X_{ijt} be the value of trade flows from location i to location j in time t. The gravity relationship postulates that the (log) of the value of trade flows declines in the distance between locations, conditional on (endogenous) origin-specific push factors γ_{it}^T and destination-specific pull factors δ_{jt}^T:

$$\ln X_{ijt} = f(\ln dist_{ij}) + \gamma_{it}^T + \delta_{jt}^T, \tag{1}$$

where $\frac{\partial f}{\partial \ln dist_{ij}} < 0$. Figure 13.1 overlays a non-parametric function $f(\cdot)$ on top of a scatter plot of the relationship between log trade flows and log distance after partitioning out the origin-year and destination-year fixed effects for international trade in both 1950 and 2000; as is evident, there is a strong negative (and approximately log-linear) relationship in both years, with the negative effect being

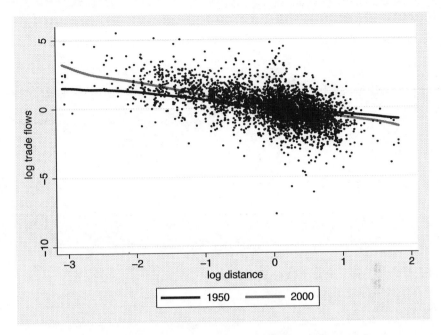

Figure 13.1 Across country gravity: trade flows between countries over time

Notes: Data are from Head, Mayer and Ries (2010). Only bilateral pairs with observed trade flows in both 1950 and 2000 are included. The thick lines are from a non parametric regression with Epanechnikov kernel and bandwidth of 0.5 after partitioning out the origin-year and destination-year fixed effects.

especially pronounced in the year 2000. In Figure 13.2, we impose a linear function $f(\ln dist_{ij}) = \gamma_t \ln dist_{ij}$ and estimate the coefficient γ_t separately for each year; we find a precisely estimated negative relationship that appears to be getting stronger over time, with a coefficient γ_t of between -0.5 and -1.5.

This strong gravity relationship in the flow of goods is also prevalent within countries. Figure 13.3 is the analog of Figure 13.1 for trade between U.S. states. In both 2007 and 2012 there is a strong negative (and approximately log-linear) relationship between log trade flows and log distance. As with the international trade flows, the trade coefficient is about -1, showing that the effect of distance is similar within and across countries.

We can also examine how the origin push factor γ_{it} and destination pull factor δ_{jt} are correlated with various observables. Figure 13.4 shows that both the push and pull factors in international trade are strongly positively correlated with GDP – even after partitioning out time-invariant country effects and country-invariant year effects. Put another way, changes in GDP within a country over time (relative to total world GDP) are strongly positively correlated with both a country's imports and exports. This strong positive correlation is also present within

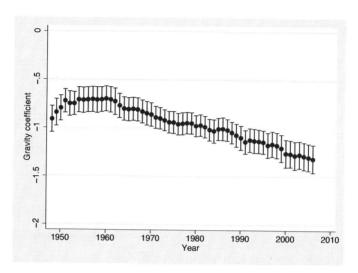

Figure 13.2 Across country trade gravity: the gravity coefficient over time

Notes: Data are from Head, Mayer and Ries (2010). This figure plots the estimated coefficient of distance in a trade gravity regression with origin-year and destination-year fixed effects over time. The bars indicate the 95 per cent confidence interval, where the standard errors are two-way clustered by country of origin and country of destination.

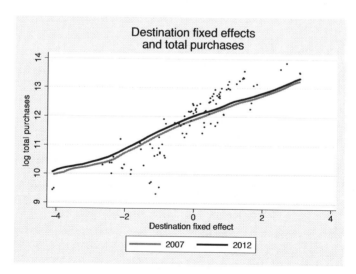

Figure 13.3 Within country gravity: trade flows between U.S. states

Notes: Data are from 2007 and 2012 Commodity flow surveys CFS (2007, 2012). The figure excludes trade flows within each state. The thick lines are from a non parametric regression with Epanechnikov kernel and bandwidth of 0.5 after partitioning out the origin-year and destination-year fixed effects.

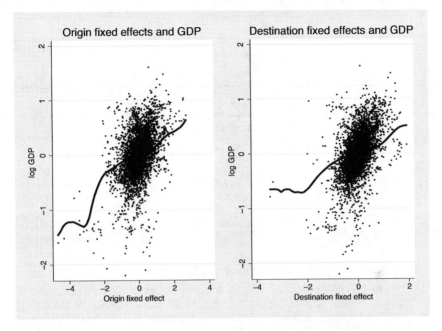

Figure 13.4 Location size and gravity fixed effects: trade flows between countries

Notes: Data are from Head, Mayer and Ries (2010). The country-year fixed effects are from a series gravity regression of trade flows on distance x year and origin-year and destination-year fixed effects. The thick lines are from a non parametric regression with Epanechnikov kernel and bandwidth of 0.5 after partitioning out both a country and year fixed effect.

country trade flows, as is evident in Figure 13.5. Moreover, Figures 13.6 and 13.7 show a strong positive correlation between the push and pull factors both across and within countries. As we will see below, this positive correlation will be predicted by a gravity spatial model with balanced trade and symmetric trade costs.

2.2. Gravity in the flow of people

The flow of labor (migration) exhibits similar – but not identical – patterns as the flow of goods. We analyze the flow of labor both across and within countries. For international migration, we turn to the WBG (2011) dataset, which provides bilateral flows of people across countries every ten years from 1960 to 2010. For intranational migration, we construct flows of people across U.S. states using their state of birth and current location for each decennial census from 1850 to 2000 from Ruggles, Fitch, Kelly Hall and Sobek (2000). As with the trade data, we consider a balanced sample of location pairs for which there is a positive flow of people in all years and exclude own-flows of people (i.e., those that do not migrate).

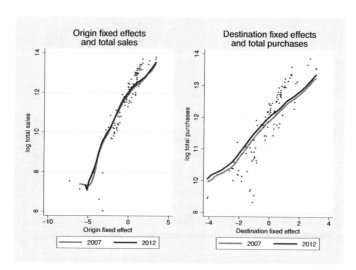

Figure 13.5 Location size and gravity fixed effects: trade flows between U.S. states

Notes: Data are from 2007 and 2012 Commodity flow surveys (CFS, 2007, 2012). Fixed effects are from a gravity regression of trade flows on distance and origin and destination fixed effects within year. Total sales (purchases) are caculated by summing trade flows across all destinations (origins). The thick lines are from a non parametric regression with Epanechnikov kernel and bandwidth of 0.5.

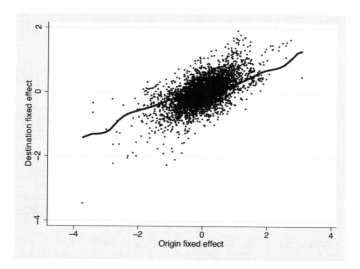

Figure 13.6 Origin and destination fixed effects: trade flows between countries

Notes: Data are from Head, Mayer, and Ries (2010). The country-year fixed effects are from a gravity regression of trade flows on distance x year and origin-year and destination-year fixed effects for each year. The thick lines are from a non parametric regression with Epanechnikov kernel and bandwidth of 0.5 after partitioning out both a country and year fixed effect.

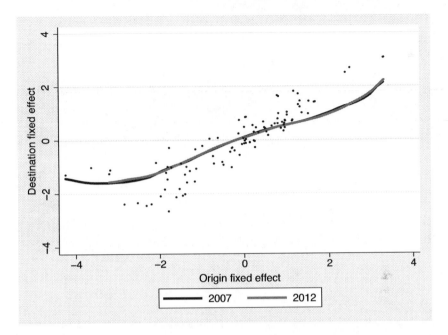

Figure 13.7 Origin and destination fixed effects: trade flows between U.S. states

Notes: Data are from 2007 and 2012 Commodity flow surveys (CFS, 2007, 2012). Fixed effects are from a gravity regression of trade flows on distance and origin and destination fixed effects within year. The thick lines are from a non parametric regression with Epanechnikov kernel and bandwidth of 0.5.

As with the flow of goods, we can construct a simple empirical gravity speci-fication for the flow of people from location i to location j at time t, L_{ijt}:

$$\ln L_{ijt} = g(\ln \ dist_{ij}) + \gamma_{it}^L + \delta_{jt}^L, \tag{2}$$

where gravity implies $\frac{\partial g}{\partial \ln \ dist_{ij}} < 0$. Figure 13.8 overlays a non-parametric function $g(\cdot)$ on top of a scatter plot of the relationship between log migration flows and log distance after partitioning out the origin-year and destination-year fixed effects for international migration in both 1960 and 2010; like with the flow of goods, there is a strong negative (and approximately log-linear) relationship in both years. In Figure 13.9, we impose a linear function $g(\ln \ dist_{ij}) = \gamma_t \ln \ dist_{ij}$ and estimate the coefficient γ_t separately for each year of data; again, as with the flow of goods, we find a precisely estimated negative relationship with a coef-ficient γ_t of between -1 and -2.

Figure 13.10 shows that the gravity relationship also exists for within country migration and is remarkably stable over the 150 years of data; indeed, as

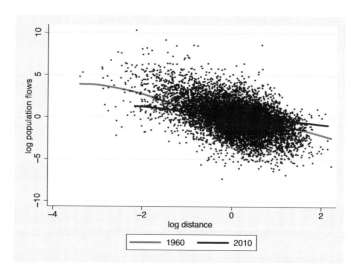

Figure 13.8 Across country gravity: migration flows between countries over time

Notes: Data are from Yeats (1998). Excludes own country population shares (i.e. nonmigrants). The thick lines are from a non parametric regression with Epanechnikov kernel and bandwidth of 0.5 after partitioning out the origin-year and destination-year fixed effects.

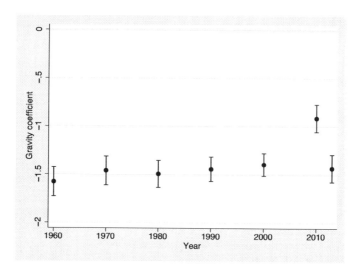

Figure 13.9 Across country gravity: the migration gravity coefficient over time

Notes: Data are from Yeats (1998). This figure plots the estimated coefficient of distance in a gravity migration regression with origin-year and destination-year fixed effects over time. The bars indicate the 95% confidence interval, where the standard errors are two-way clustered by country of origin and country of destination.

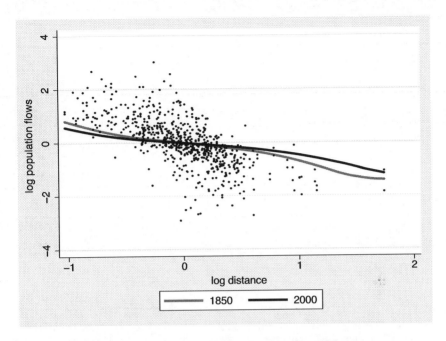

Figure 13.10 Within country gravity: migration flows between U.S. states

Notes: Data are from the 1850 and 2000 U.S. Censuses Ruggles, Fitch, Kelly Hall and Sobek (2000), where migration flows are comparing current state of residence of 25–34 year olds to their state of birth. The thick lines are from a non parametric regression with Epanechnikov kernel and bandwidth of 0.5 after partitioning out the origin-year and destination-year fixed effects.

Figure 13.11 illustrates, the effect of distance on the flow of people is nearly identical within the United States as it is across countries, with a coefficient hovering of about −1.5. (It is interesting to note that unlike for the flow of goods, the gravity coefficient of migration shows no evidence of getting more negative over time.)

While the gravity relationship with distance is quite similar for trade and migration, the "push" and "pull" factors (γ_{it}^L and δ_{jt}^L, respectively) are substantially different for migration. Figure 13.12 shows that there is no systematic relationship between population and either the push or pull factor across countries; within the United States, however, Figure 13.13 shows the lagged population is strongly correlated with the push factor and the contemporaneous population is strongly correlated with the pull factors. Unlike the flow of goods, there is no systematic correlation between the push and pull factors across countries (Figure 13.14), but there is a negative correlation between push and pull factors across U.S. states (Figure 13.15). As we will see below, this is consistent with a theoretical model of migration when the population is not in a steady state and/or migration costs are not symmetric.

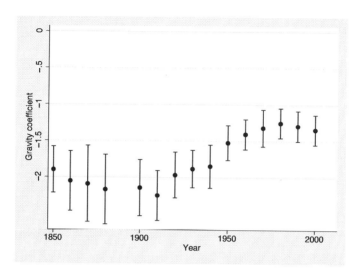

Figure 13.11 Within country gravity: the migration gravity coefficient over time

Notes: Data are from the U.S. Censuses from 1850 to 2000 Ruggles, Fitch, Kelly Hall and Sobek (2000), where migration flows are comparing current state of residence of 25–34 year olds to their state of birth. This figure plots the estimated coefficient of distance in a gravity migration regression with origin-year and destination-year fixed effects over time. The bars indicate the 95% confidence interval, where the standard errors are two-way clustered by state of origin and state of destination.

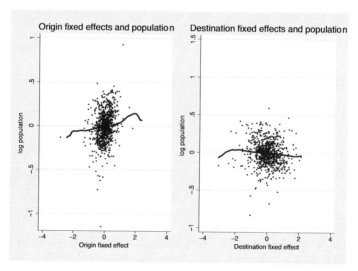

Figure 13.12 Location population and gravity fixed effects: migration flows between countries

Notes: Data are from Yeats (1998). The country-year fixed effects are from a gravity regression of migration flows on distance x year and origin-year and destination-year fixed effects. The thick lines are from a non parametric regression with Epanechnikov kernel and bandwidth of 0.5 after partitioning out both a country and year fixed effect.

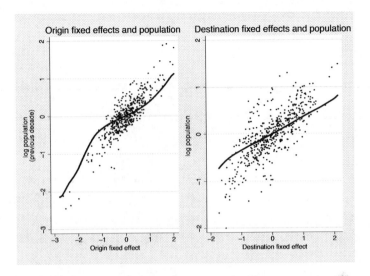

Figure 13.13 Location size and gravity fixed effects: migration flows between U.S. states

Notes: Data are from the U.S. Censuses from 1850 to 2000 Ruggles, Fitch, Kelly Hall and Sobek (2000), where migration flows are comparing current state of residence of 25–34 year olds to their state of birth. The state-year fixed effects are from a series gravity regression of migration flows on distance x year and origin-year and destination-year fixed effects. The thick lines are from a non parametric regression with Epanechnikov kernel and bandwidth of 0.5 after partitioning out both a state and year fixed effect.

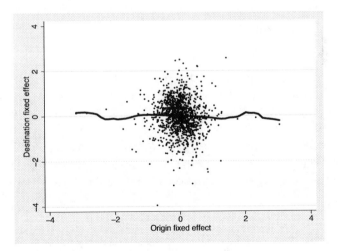

Figure 13.14 Origin and destination fixed effects: migration flows between countries

Notes: Data are from Yeats (1998). The country-year fixed effects are from a gravity regression of migration flows on distance x year and origin-year and destination-year fixed effects. The thick lines are from a non parametric regression with Epanechnikov kernel and bandwidth of 0.5 after partitioning out both a country and year fixed effect.

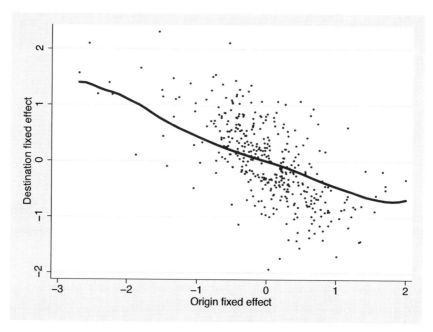

Figure 13.15 Origin and destination fixed effects: migration flows between U.S. states

Notes: Data are from the U.S. Censuses from 1850 to 2000 Ruggles, Fitch, Kelly Hall and Sobek (2000), where migration flows are comparing current state of residence of 25–34 year olds to their state of birth. Fixed effects are from a gravity regression of migration flows on distance x year and origin-year and destination-year fixed effects. The thick lines are from a non parametric regression with Epanechnikov kernel and bandwidth of 0.5 after partitioning out both a state and year fixed effect.

3. Gravity: a simple framework

We now introduce a simple model that can generate the prevalence of gravity in the data. Suppose there are N locations, where in what follows we define the set $S \equiv \{1, \ldots, N\}$, each producing a differentiated good. The only factor is labor, and we denote the allocation of labor in location $i \in S$ as L_i and assume the total world labor endowment is $\sum_{i \in S} L_i = \bar{L}$. Given the evidence from the previous section that gravity holds both within and across countries, locations can be interpreted as either regions within a country or countries themselves.

3.1. Demand for goods: gravity on trade flows

We assume that workers have identical Constant Elasticity of Substitution (CES) preferences over the differentiated varieties produced in each different location. The total welfare in location $i \in S$, W_i, can be written as:

$$W_i = \left(\sum_j q_{ji}^{\frac{\sigma-1}{\sigma}} \right)^{\frac{\sigma}{\sigma-1}} u_i, \tag{3}$$

where q_{si} is the per-capita quantity of the variety produced in location s and consumed in location i, $\sigma \in (1, \infty)$ is the elasticity of substitution between goods ω, and u_i is the local amenity, discussed below.[2]

Each worker in location i earns a wage w_i and thus the budget constraint is

$$\sum_j p_{ji} q_{ji} = w_i \tag{4}$$

where p_{ji} is the price of good from location j in i. Optimization of the worker utility, equation (3), subject to the budget constraint, equation (4), yields the total expenditure in location j on the differentiated variety from location i:

$$X_{ij} = (p_{ij})^{1-\sigma} P_j^{\sigma-1} w_j L_j \quad \text{for all } j \tag{5}$$

where L_j is the total number of workers residing in location j (determined endogenously below) and $P_j \equiv (\sum_i (p_{ij})^{1-\sigma})^{\frac{1}{1-\sigma}}$ is the Dixit-Stiglitz price index.

The production function of each variety is linear in labor and the productivity in location i is denoted by A_i. Thus, the cost of producing variety i is $p_i = w_i/A_i$. Shipping the good from i to final destination j incurs an "iceberg" trade friction, where $\tau_{ij} \geq 1$ units must be shipped in order for one unit to arrive. Thus, the price faced by location j for a factor from i can be written as:

$$p_{ij} = \frac{w_i}{A_i} \tau_{ij}, \tag{6}$$

where τ_{ij} are bilateral trade frictions. Substituting this solution to equation (5) and rearranging we obtain

$$X_{ij} = (\tau_{ij})^{1-\sigma} \left(\frac{w_i}{A_i}\right)^{1-\sigma} P_j^{\sigma-1} w_j L_j. \tag{7}$$

This equation is the modern version of a gravity equation initially derived by Anderson (1979) and is ubiquitous in modern work in international trade. It is characterized by a bilateral term that is a combination of model parameters, trade costs and the trade elasticity, and origin and destination specific terms which are combinations of endogenous variables and parameters.

More recent work provides a wealth of microfoundations for this structural equation based on comparative advantage, increasing returns, or firm heterogeneity (see, for example, Eaton and Kortum (2002); Chaney (2008); Eaton, Kortum and Kramarz (2011); Arkolakis (2010); Arkolakis, Costinot and Rodríguez-Clare (2012); Allen and Arkolakis (2014); Redding (2016) among others). Taking log of this equation generates the empirical gravity trade equation (1) presented in Section 13.2.

To incorporate agglomeration forces in production – which Allen and Arkolakis (2014) show creates an isomorphism with the monopolistic competition models with free entry as in Krugman (1980) – we assume that the productivity of a location is subject to spillovers: $A_i = \bar{A}_i L_i^\alpha$ where $\bar{A}_i$ is the exogenous productivity.[3] We focus on the empirically relevant cases of $\alpha \geq 0$, capturing among others agglomeration externalities due to endogenous entry and scale effects.

3.2. Demand for labor: gravity on worker flows

We next determine the allocation of labor across location. We assume that there is an initial (exogenous) distribution of workers across all locations i denoted by L_i^0, from which all workers choose where to live subject to migration frictions. In particular, the indirect utility function of an owner of one unit of aggregate factor originating from location i and moving to location j is equal to the product of the utility realized in the destination and a bilateral migration disutility v_{ij}:

$$W_{ij} = \frac{w_j}{P_j} u_j \times v_{ij},$$

where $v_{ij} = \frac{(L_{ij}/L_i^0)^{-\beta}}{\mu_{ij}}$ depends both on an (exogenous) iceberg migration friction $\mu_{ij} \geq 1$ and on the (endogenous) number of migrating workers L_{ij}. The parameter $\beta \geq 0$ governs the extent to which migration flows create congestion externalities.

In equilibrium, labor mobility implies that the utility of all agents originating from i is equalized:

$$W_i = \frac{w_j \, \bar{u}_j}{P_j \, \mu_{ij}} (L_{ij}/L_i^0)^{-\beta}. \tag{8}$$

Inverting this expression, we obtain the number of workers that migrate from i to j:

$$L_{ij} = \frac{\left(\frac{w_j \, \bar{u}_j}{P_j \, \mu_{ij}}\right)^{\frac{1}{\beta}}}{W_i^{\frac{1}{\beta}}} L_i^0. \tag{9}$$

Equation (9) is a gravity equation on worker flows as it determines the share of workers in location i as a function of the real wage in location i. By taking logs, it provides a theoretical justification of the empirical gravity specification for the flow of people in equation (2) in Section 2.

We should at this point note that when modeling bilateral migration flows many authors choose alternative, possibly more intuitive, formulations. These formulations yield the same functional form as (8) but capture a variety of microfoundations such as competition for an immobile factor (e.g., land or housing markets) or heterogeneous location preferences across workers. In this latter approach, an agent's utility in location j is the product of the local real wage times a heterogeneous component. This heterogeneity results to different decisions for otherwise identical agents. Assuming a Frechet distribution for this heterogeneity following Eaton and Kortum (2002); Ahlfeldt, Redding, Sturm and Wolf (2015); Redding (2016) leads to a similar formulation to equation (9), as discussed in Allen and Arkolakis (2014).

3.3. Closing the model

To close the model we need to satisfy four equilibrium conditions. The first two are associated with the flow of goods. First, the total amount of labor used for the production of goods for all countries equals the labor available in each country i. Written in terms of labor payments, this implies that the total payments accrued to labor in location i must equal to the sales of this location to all the locations in the world, including i,

$$w_i L_i = \sum_j X_{ij}. \tag{10}$$

The second equilibrium condition is that total expenditure equals total labor payments and in turn this equals total payments for goods produced for location j,

$$E_j = w_j L_j = \sum_i X_{ij}. \tag{11}$$

Using equation (7) this expression can be written,

$$w_j L_j = \sum_i (\tau_{ij})^{1-\sigma} \left(\frac{w_i}{A_i}\right)^{1-\sigma} P_i^{\sigma-1} w_j L_j \Rightarrow P_i^{1-\sigma} = \sum_i (\tau_{ij})^{1-\sigma} \left(\frac{w_i}{A_i}\right)^{1-\sigma}, \tag{12}$$

which is the expression for the Dixit-Stiglitz price index defined above.

The third and fourth equilibrium conditions are associated with the flow of labor. The third condition is that the initial population in location i is equal to the total flows of persons from location i, i.e.:

$$L_i^0 = \sum_j L_{ij}. \tag{13}$$

Combined with the migration gravity equation (9) above allows us to write equilibrium welfare of migrants from location i W_i as the CES aggregate of their bilateral utility:

$$L_i^0 = \sum_j \frac{\left(\frac{w_j \bar{u}_j}{P_j \mu_{ij}}\right)^{\frac{1}{\beta}}}{W_i^{\frac{1}{\beta}}} L_i^0 \Leftrightarrow W_i = \left(\sum_j \left(\frac{w_j \bar{u}_j}{P_j \mu_{ij}}\right)^{\frac{1}{\beta}}\right)^{\beta}. \tag{14}$$

Substituting this expression for welfare back into the migration gravity equation then allows us to write migration shares of people analogously to expenditure shares on goods:

$$L_{ij}/L_i^0 = \frac{\left(\frac{w_j \bar{u}_j}{P_j \mu_{ij}}\right)^{\frac{1}{\beta}}}{\sum_j \left(\frac{w_j \bar{u}_j}{P_j \mu_{ij}}\right)^{\frac{1}{\beta}}}. \tag{15}$$

Finally, the fourth equilibrium condition requires that the in-flow of migrants to location i is equal to its total population:

$$L_j = \sum_{i \in S} L_{ij}. \tag{16}$$

Define the *geography* of the economy as the set of trade costs $\{\tau_{ij}\}$, migration frictions $\{\mu_{ij}\}$ productivities $\{\bar{A}_i\}$, amenities $\{\bar{u}_i\}$, and initial population $\{L_i^0\}$. For any set of elasticities $\{\sigma, \alpha, \beta\}$ and any geography, an equilibrium is defined as a set of wages, labor allocations, price index, and welfare, that satisfy the following four equations:

$$w_i L_i = \sum_j (\tau_{ij})^{1-\sigma} \left(\frac{w_i}{\bar{A}_i L_i^\alpha}\right)^{1-\sigma} P_i^{\sigma-1} w_j L_j \tag{17}$$

$$P_i = \left(\sum_j \left(\frac{\tau_{ji} w_j}{\bar{A}_j L_j^\alpha}\right)^{1-\sigma}\right)^{\frac{1}{1-\sigma}} \tag{18}$$

$$L_i = \sum_{j \in S} (\mu_{ji})^{-\frac{1}{\beta}} \left(\frac{w_i}{P_i} \bar{u}_i\right)^{\frac{1}{\beta}} (W_j)^{-\frac{1}{\beta}} L_j^0 \tag{19}$$

$$W_i = \left(\sum_j \left(\frac{w_j \bar{u}_j}{P_j \mu_{ij}}\right)^{\frac{1}{\beta}}\right)^\beta \tag{20}$$

This yields a system of $4 \times N$ equations and $4 \times N$ unknowns (with one equation being redundant from Walras' Law and one price being pinned down by a normalization). Note the symmetry of the labor and goods market clearing conditions: each consists of one market clearing condition and one composite "price index": P_i for goods and W_i for labor.

Precise restrictions that guarantee existence and uniqueness are provided by Allen and Donaldson (2017). Product differentiation implies that there are gains to moving to locations with low population in order to provide labor for the global demand of the local good. In addition agglomeration and dispersion forces act upon this basic mechanism. Intuitively, the agglomeration forces, governed by parameter α, imply increased concentration of economic activity. Dispersion forces, governed by parameter β, imply dispersion of economic activities away from locations with large populations. When agglomeration forces are stronger than dispersion forces the possibility of multiple equilibria arises. In these cases agglomeration may act as a self-sustaining force and equilibria where different locations are the ones with the largest population can arise, similar to the spatial models of Krugman (1991); Helpman (1998); Fujita, Krugman and Venables (1999). In fact, in the version of the model where migration costs are infinite, this happens exactly at $\alpha > \beta$, as discussed in Allen and Arkolakis (2014). Existence of equilibria with positive population is always guaranteed. However, when the agglomeration forces are very strong black hole equilibria with all the activity concentrated in one point may be the only ones that satisfy some refined notion of equilibrium related to stability.[4]

Finally, it may be apparent from the above discussion that particular microfoundations of the two key gravity equations do not play a key role in determining many of the properties of the model. A long tradition on modeling gravity in international trade flows is summarized in Arkolakis, Costinot and Rodríguez-Clare (2012) (see discussion in Proposition 2) by a class of models governed by a single parameter, the elasticity of trade, hereby captured by $1 - \sigma$. In addition, more recently, microfoundations for the migration gravity equation have been provided as well. It can be shown that, as far as it concerns the positive properties and the counterfactuals of this expanded class of models, with respect to wages and labor, two composite parameters (in this case functions of the three parameters α, β and σ) determine all its predictions. This class of models that includes geography models with labor mobility, intermediate inputs, non-traded goods and other economic forces is discussed in Allen, Arkolakis and Takahashi (2014).

4.   Model characterization

We proceed next to characterize this setup by imposing assumptions on the geography of trade costs, τ_{ij}, and the geography of fundamentals, i.e. productivities and amenities, $\bar{A}_i$, $\bar{u}_i$.

4.1.   Geography and the distribution of economic activity

We first provide intuition about how geography shapes the spatial distribution of economic activity; these results build upon Allen and Arkolakis (2014), Allen, Arkolakis and Takahashi (2014) and Allen and Donaldson (2017).

Suppose that trade costs are bilaterally symmetric, i.e. $\tau_{ij} = \tau_{ji}$ for all i and j. Then the goods gravity equation (7), and two equilibrium conditions, equations

(10) and (11), together imply that the origin and destination fixed effects of the *trade* gravity equation are equal up to scale, i.e.:

$$\left(\frac{w_i}{\bar{A}_i L_i^\alpha}\right)^{1-\sigma} \propto P_i^{\sigma-1} w_i L_i \; \forall i \in S \tag{21}$$

This accords well with the finding in Section 2.1 that the origin and destination fixed effects of the trade gravity equation are strongly correlated.

What about on the migration side? Suppose that migration costs are bilaterally symmetric, i.e., $\mu_{ij} = \mu_{ji}$ for all i and j. One might wonder if this symmetry, along with the labor gravity equation (9), and the two labor adding up conditions, equations (14) and (16) correspondingly imply that the origin and destination specific terms of the *labor* gravity equation are equal up to scale. It turns out that the answer in general is no, unless the population distribution is in a steady state where $L_i^0 = L_j$. In that case (and only in that case) we have:

$$\left(\frac{w_i}{P_i}\bar{u}_i\right)^{\frac{1}{\beta}} \propto W_i^{-\frac{1}{\beta}} L_i \; \forall i \in S \tag{22}$$

Recall from Section 2.2 that we empirically find virtually no correlation in the origin and destination fixed effects in the migration gravity equation both across countries and across states within the U.S., suggesting that we are either far from a steady state or migration costs are asymmetric (or both). Combining equations (21) and (22), we can express the equilibrium steady-state population and wage of each location solely as a function of that location's productivity, amenity, and geographic location (with the effect of trade costs being summarized by P_i and the effect of migration costs being summarized by W_i):

$$\gamma \ln L_i = \frac{1}{\beta}(\sigma-1)\ln \bar{A}_i + \frac{\sigma}{\beta}\ln \bar{u}_i + \frac{\sigma}{\beta}\ln W_i - \frac{2\sigma-1}{\beta}\ln P_i + C_1 \tag{23}$$

$$\sigma\gamma \ln w_i = \sigma(\sigma-1)\ln \bar{A}_i + (\alpha(\sigma-1)-1)\frac{\sigma}{\beta}\ln \bar{u}_i + (\alpha(\sigma-1)-1) \tag{24}$$
$$\frac{\sigma}{\beta}\ln W_i - \sigma\left((\sigma-1)\left(1-\frac{\alpha}{\beta}\right)-\frac{1}{\beta}\right)\ln P_i + C_2$$

where $\gamma \equiv \left(\sigma + \frac{1}{\beta}(1-\alpha(\sigma-1))\right)$, C_1 is a constant determined by the size of the aggregate labor market and C_2 is a constant determined by the choice of numeraire. Focusing on the equilibrium distribution of population and assuming $\alpha < \frac{1}{\sigma-1}$, we can see that more productive places (higher $\bar{A}_i$), higher amenity places (higher $\bar{u}_i$), places with lower migration costs (higher W_i), and places with lower trade costs (lower P_i) all have higher populations, with the responsiveness of the population to the geography governed by the strength of spillovers through the composite term γ.[5]

4.2.   Special cases

We now illustrate a number of interesting special cases of this general framework. First, consider the case where workers cannot move from their original location, i.e. where $\mu_{ij} = \infty$ for all $i \neq j$. This is an assumption maintained in gravity trade models such as Anderson (1979); Eaton and Kortum (2002); Chaney (2008); Arkolakis (2010); Arkolakis, Costinot and Rodríguez-Clare (2012); Costinot and Rodríguez-Clare (2013); Allen, Arkolakis and Takahashi (2014). Since labor is fixed, we can determine the wage and the price index, w_i and P_i by using equations (17) and (18), equation (19) implies $L_i = L_i^0$, and equation (20) simplifies to $W_i = \frac{w_i}{P_i} \bar{u}_i$.

Second, consider the case where there are no migration frictions, i.e. $\mu_{ij} = \infty$ for all $i \neq j$. This is an assumption maintained in economic geography models such as Krugman (1991); Helpman (1998); Redding and Sturm (2008) and in the gravity new economic geography models of Allen and Arkolakis (2014); Redding (2016). In this case, equation (20) implies welfare is equalized across locations,

$$W = W_i = w_i / P_i,$$

Moreover, equation (19) implies that the population residing in location i is

$$\frac{L_i}{\bar{L}} = \frac{\left(\frac{w_i}{P_i} \bar{u}_i\right)^{1/\beta}}{\sum_{i'} \left(\frac{w_{i'}}{P_{i'}} \bar{u}_i\right)^{1/\beta}}. \tag{25}$$

A third special case is where there is both free trade and free migration, i.e. μ_{ij}, $\tau_{ij} = 1$ for all $i \neq j$. This setup is the celebrated Rosen-Roback (1982) model put to use in a number of urban applications (see Glaeser and Gottlieb (2008) and Moretti (2011) for review of applications of this model). With free labor mobility, equation (20) again implies that $W_i = W$ while with free goods mobility, equation (18) implies that the price index equalizes across locations $P_i = P$.[6] Notice that in this special case equations (23) and (24) give an explicit solution of wages and labor in terms of geography of each location. These solutions are intuitive (e.g., under reasonable restrictions labor is increasing in productivities and amenities) and have been heavily exploited by the urban literature.

4.3.   Analytical solutions

In this section, we provide analytical solutions for the equilibrium above for two simple geographies. (Note that the characterization of the equilibrium from equations (23) and (24) provide only partial characterization in the case with positive trade or migration frictions as they are functions of two equilibrium objects, namely the price index and the expected welfare of a location.)

4.3.1. Two countries

In the special case of two countries we assume that the population is fully mobile across locations so that utility equalization holds. Here we do not impose any restriction on the geography of trade costs but we do impose the assumption of symmetry in the geography of productivities and amenities so that $\bar{A}_i = \bar{u}_i = 1$ for all i. Using equation (10) and the gravity equation for trade flow simplies

$$w_i L_i = w_i^{2-\sigma} P_i^{\sigma-1} L_i + \tau_{ij}^{1-\sigma} w_i^{1-\sigma} w_j L_j P_j^{\sigma-1} \Leftrightarrow \tag{26}$$
$$L_i = w_i^{1-\sigma} P_i^{\sigma-1} L_i + \tau_{ij}^{1-\sigma} w_i^{-\sigma} w_j L_j P_j^{\sigma-1}$$

We next impose utility equalization resulting from the zero migration costs: $\frac{w_i}{P_i} = \frac{w_j}{P_j} = \bar{W}$. This implies that:

$$\frac{P_j^{\sigma-1}}{P_i^{\sigma-1}} = \frac{w_j^{\sigma-1}}{w_i^{\sigma-1}}.$$

Using the definition of the price index we have that

$$\frac{w_i^{1-\sigma}\tau_{ij}^{1-\sigma} + w_j^{1-\sigma}}{w_j^{1-\sigma}\tau_{ji}^{1-\sigma} + w_i^{1-\sigma}} = \frac{w_j^{\sigma-1}}{w_i^{\sigma-1}} \Rightarrow \left(\frac{w_i}{w_j}\right) = \left(\frac{\tau_{ji}}{\tau_{ij}}\right)^{\frac{1}{2}}. \tag{27}$$

Combining the two results yields:

$$L_i = \bar{W}^{1-\sigma}\left(L_i + \tau_{ij}^{1-\sigma}\left(\frac{w_j}{w_i}\right)^{\sigma}L_j\right).$$

Now take the ratio of the two region's populations:

$$\frac{L_i}{L_j} = \frac{L_i + \tau_{ij}^{1-\sigma}\left(\frac{\tau_{ij}}{\tau_{ji}}\right)^{\frac{\sigma}{2}}L_j}{\tau_{ji}^{1-\sigma}\left(\frac{\tau_{ji}}{\tau_{ij}}\right)^{\frac{\sigma}{2}}L_i + L_j} = \frac{\left(\frac{L_i}{L_j}\right) + \tau_{ij}^{1-\sigma}\left(\frac{\tau_{ij}}{\tau_{ji}}\right)^{\frac{\sigma}{2}}}{\tau_{ji}^{1-\sigma}\left(\frac{\tau_{ji}}{\tau_{ij}}\right)^{\frac{\sigma}{2}}\frac{L_i}{L_j} + 1} \Rightarrow \frac{L_i}{L_j} = \left(\frac{\tau_{ij}}{\tau_{ji}}\right)^{\frac{1}{2}} \tag{28}$$

In other words, if country j is more open than country i, $\tau_{ij} < \tau_{ji}$, then the population in country i is smaller but wages are higher.

4.3.2. The line

We now assume that the topography of the world is described by a line, largely drawing from the analysis of Allen and Arkolakis (2014). Let space S be the $[-\pi, \pi]$ interval and suppose that $\alpha = \beta = 0$ and $\bar{A}_i = \bar{u}_i = 1$, i.e. there are no spillovers and all locations have homogeneous exogenous productivities and amenities. Suppose that trade costs are instantaneous and apart from a border b in the middle of the line at location 0; that is, trade costs between locations on the same side of the line are $\tau_{is} = e^{\tilde{\tau}|i-s|}$ and those on different sides are $\tau_{is} = e^{b+\tilde{\tau}|i-s|}$.[7]

Taking logs of equation (23) and differentiating yields the following differential equation:

$$\frac{\partial \ln L_i}{\partial i} = (1 - 2\sigma)\frac{\partial \ln P_i}{\partial i}. \tag{29}$$

It is easy to show that $\frac{\partial \ln P_{-\pi}}{\partial i} = -\tilde{\tau}$ and $\frac{\partial \ln P_{\pi}}{\partial i} = \tilde{\tau}$ in the two edges of the line and $\frac{\partial \ln P_0}{\partial i} = \tilde{\tau}(1 - e^{(1-\sigma)b})/(1 + e^{(1-\sigma)b})$ in the location of the border which gives us boundary conditions for the value of the differential equation at locations $i = -\pi, 0, \pi$. Intuitively, moving rightward while on the far left of the line reduces the distance to all other locations by τ, thereby reducing the (log) price index by τ. To obtain a closed form solution to equation (29), we differentiate equation (23) twice to show that the equilibrium satisfies the following second order differential equation:

$$\frac{\partial^2}{\partial i^2}L_i^{\tilde{\sigma}} = k_1 L_i^{\tilde{\sigma}} \text{ for } i \in (-\pi, 0) \cup (0, \pi), \tag{30}$$

where $\tilde{\sigma} \equiv (\sigma - 1)/(2\sigma - 1\sigma)$ and $k_1 \equiv (1 - \sigma)^2\tau^2 + 2(1 - \sigma)\tau W^{1-\sigma}$ can be shown to be negative. Given the boundary conditions above, the equilibrium distribution of labor in both intervals is characterized by the weighted sum of the cosine and sine functions (see example 2.1.2.1 in Polyanin and Zaitsev (2002)):

$$L_i^{\tilde{\sigma}} = k_2\cos(i\sqrt{-k_1}) + k_3|\sin(i\sqrt{-k_1})|.$$

The values of k_1 and the ratio of k_2 to k_3 can be determined using the boundary conditions. Given this ratio, the aggregate labor clearing condition determines their levels.[8] Notice that in the case of no border or an infinite border, the solution is the simple cosine function or two cosine functions one in each side of the border, respectively, and $k_3 = 0$, so that the aggregate labor clearing condition directly solves for k_2.[9]

Figure 13.16 depicts the equilibrium labor allocation in this simple case for different values of the instantaneous trade cost but no border. As the instantaneous trade cost increases, the population concentrates in the middle of the interval where the locations are less economically remote. The lower the trade costs, the less concentrated the population; in the extreme where $\tau = 0$, labor is equally allocated across space. With symmetric exogenous productivities and amenities, wages are lower in the middle of the line to compensate for the lower price index. Figure 13.17 shows how a border affects the equilibrium population distribution with a positive instantaneous trade cost. As is evident, the larger the border, the more economic activity moves toward the middle of each side in the line; in the limit where crossing the border is infinitely costly, it is as if the two line segments existed in isolation.

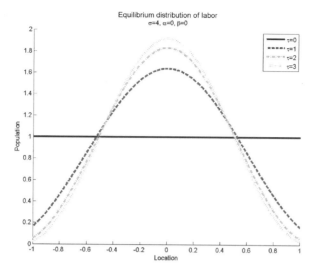

Figure 13.16 Economic activity on a line: trade costs

Notes: This figure shows how the equilibrium distribution of population along a line is affected by changes in the trade cost. When trade is costless, the population is equal along the entire line. As trade becomes more costly, the population becomes increasingly concentrated in the center of the line where the consumption bundle is cheapest.

Source: Allen and Arkolakis (2014).

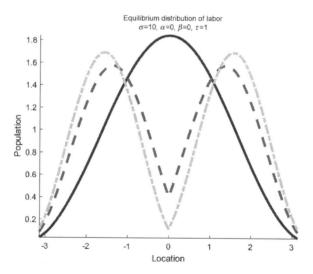

Figure 13.17 Economic activity on a line: border costs

Notes: This figure shows how the equilibrium distribution of population along a line is affected by the presence of a border in the center of the line. As crossing the border becomes increasingly costly, the equilibrium distribution of population moves toward the center of each half of the line.

Source: Allen and Arkolakis (2014).

Differences in exogenous productivities, amenities and the spillovers also play a key role in determining the equilibrium allocation of labor and wages. The numerical solutions for these cases can be found in Allen and Arkolakis (2014).

5. Taking the model to the data

In this section, we discuss how one can estimate the parameters of the structural model from the previous section and use the model to perform counterfactuals. We conclude the section by illustrating how different assumptions regarding the mobility of goods and labor affects such counterfactual results.

5.1. Estimation

We first discuss how to estimate all the model parameters using readily available data. One particular highlight of the methodology that follows is that it does not require observing all bilateral flows of goods and labor. This is helpful, as often-times (especially in sub-national data) such bilateral data is unavailable.

5.1.1. Estimating bilateral frictions

Assume that the log of the trade and migration bilateral frictions (to the power of their 1 respective elasticities, i.e., $\tau_{ij}^{1-\sigma}$ and $\mu_{ij}^{\frac{1}{\beta}}$) are functions of observables (e.g. distance), i.e. $(1-\sigma)\ln\tau_{ij} = f(X_{ij}^{T};\gamma^{T})$ and $\frac{1}{\beta}\ln\mu_{ij} = g(X_{ij}^{L};\gamma^{L})$, where $f(\cdot)$ and $g(\cdot)$ are functions known up to a vector of parameters γ^{T} and γ^{L}, respectively. Then taking logs of the goods and labor gravity equations (7) and (9) yield:

$$\ln X_{ij} = f(X_{ij}^{T};\gamma^{T}) + \gamma_{i}^{T} + \delta_{j}^{T} + \varepsilon_{ij}^{T} \tag{31}$$

$$\ln L_{ij} = g(X_{ij}^{L};\gamma^{L}) + \gamma_{i}^{L} + \delta_{j}^{L} + \varepsilon_{ij}^{L}, \tag{32}$$

where γ_{i}^{T} and γ_{i}^{L} are the origin fixed effects of the trade and labor gravity equations, δ_{j}^{T} and δ_{j}^{L} are the respective destination fixed effects, and we interpret ε_{ij}^{T} and ε_{ij}^{L} as measurement error in the observed bilateral flows. Note that equations (31) and (32) are virtually identical to the empirical gravity equations (1) and (2) presented in Section 2; the key difference is we have now provided a theoretical justification for them.

By far the most common assumption in the literature is that bilateral frictions are increasing in bilateral distance $dist_{ij}$, i.e. $f(\cdot) = \gamma^{T}\ln dist_{ij}$ and $g(\cdot) = \gamma^{L}\ln dist_{ij}$. However, several recent innovations have allowed researchers to go beyond simply using straight-line distances between locations. Donaldson and Hornbeck (2012); Donaldson (forthcoming) uses Dijkstra's algorithm to calculate the least cost route between locations on a graph of the transportation network. Allen and Arkolakis (2014) apply the Fast Marching Method to calculate the least cost route between locations over a continuous geography. Both these methods rely on algorithms originally developed in computer science, leaving $f(\cdot)$ and $g(\cdot)$ implicit functions of the underlying geography. More recently Allen and Arkolakis (2017) derive a closed form solution for $f(\cdot)$ and $g(\cdot)$ as a function of the underlying transportation network assuming that many heterogeneous traders each choose the least cost route over the network.

Regardless of the choice of $f(\cdot)$ and $g(\cdot)$, the fixed effects regression only recovers estimates of the combination of the bilateral frictions and their respective elasticities, i.e. $\tau_{ij}^{1-\sigma}$ and $\mu_{ij}^{-\frac{1}{\beta}}$. However, as we will see, this is all that is needed to recover the remainder of the parameters and conduct counterfactuals. To make this clear, define $T_{ij} \equiv \tau_{ij}^{1-\sigma}$ and $M_{ij} \equiv \mu_{ij}^{-\frac{1}{\beta}}$ for what follows. Moreover, note that estimation can be accomplished even if bilateral flow data is only available for a subset of location pairs, as long as the observables are available for all bilateral pairs. This is helpful, for example, if trade flow data is only available for a subset of countries, but one wishes to construct a model for the entire world.

5.1.2.   Recovering location fundamentals and estimating model elasticities

Given estimates of $T_{ij} \equiv \tau_{ij}^{1-\sigma}$ and $M_{ij} \equiv \mu_{ij}^{-\frac{1}{\beta}}$, we can use the equilibrium structure of the model to recover information about endogenous outcomes in each location, namely the productivities A_i, the amenities u_i, the price index P_i, and the welfare W_i.

To see this, we re-write the equilibrium equations (17)–(20) as follows:

$$p_i^{\sigma-1} = \sum_j T_{ij} \left(\frac{Y_j}{Y_i}\right) P_i^{\sigma-1} \tag{33}$$

$$\left(P_i^{\sigma-1}\right)^{-1} = \sum_j T_{ji} \left(p_j^{\sigma-1}\right)^{-1} \tag{34}$$

$$\left(\omega_i^{\frac{1}{\beta}}\right)^{-1} = \sum_j M_{ji} \left(\frac{L_j^0}{L_i}\right) \left(W_j^{\frac{1}{\beta}}\right)^{-1} \tag{35}$$

$$W_i^{\frac{1}{\beta}} = \sum_j M_{ij} \omega_j^{\frac{1}{\beta}} \tag{36}$$

where $p_i \equiv \frac{w_i}{A_i L_i^\alpha}$ is the price of a good produced in location i and $\omega_i \equiv \frac{w_i}{P_i} u_i$ is the welfare of residents residing in location i. Since $\{T_{ij}\}$ and $\{M_{ij}\}$ were estimated in the previous step and assuming the income Y_i, initial population $L_i^0 = L_i$ and current population L_i are all observed in the data, it can be shown (see Allen and Donaldson (2017)) that there exists a unique (to-scale) set of $\left\{p_i^{\sigma-1}, P_i^{\sigma-1}, \omega_i^{\frac{1}{\beta}}, W_i^{\frac{1}{\beta}}\right\}$ that are consistent with equations (33)–(36). That is, the equilibrium structure of the model allows one to uniquely invert the model to recover these parameters for each location.

There are three important things to note about this inversion procedure. First, the inversion itself does *not* require knowledge of the any model elasticities, i.e. conditional on the bilateral frictions $\{T_{ij}\}$ and $\{M_{ij}\}$, the choice of σ, β, or α does not affect the equilibrium $\left\{ p_i^{\sigma-1}, P_i^{\sigma-1}, \omega_i^{\frac{1}{\beta}}, W_i^{\frac{1}{\beta}} \right\}$ Second, if one does know the values of σ, β, and α one can identify the exogenous productivity and amenity of each location, since:

$$\ln p_i^{\sigma-1} = (\sigma - 1) \ln w_i - \alpha(\sigma - 1) \ln L_i - (\sigma - 1) \ln \bar{A}_i \tag{37}$$

$$\ln \omega_i^{\frac{1}{\beta}} = \frac{1}{\beta} \ln \frac{w_i}{P_i} + \frac{1}{\beta} \ln \bar{u}_i, \tag{38}$$

where the left hand side of both equations ($\ln p_i^{\sigma-1}$ and $\ln \omega_i^{\frac{1}{\beta}}$) are values recovered from the inversion and the right hand side are either observed in the data (the $\ln w_i$ and $\ln L_i$), are recovered from the inversion (the $\ln P_i^{\sigma-1}$) or are the exogenous productivities and amenities (the $\ln \bar{A}_i$ and $\ln \bar{u}_i$).

Third, and perhaps most importantly, note that equations (37) and (38) are estimating equations that allow one to recover the model elasticities σ, α, and β. Specifically, one can regress the $\ln p_i^{\sigma-1}$ recovered from the model inversion on the observed wages $\ln w_i$ and population $\ln L_i$ to recover estimates of σ and α. Given the estimate of σ, one can construct P_i from the model inversion of $P_i^{\sigma-1}$ and then regress $\ln \omega_i^{\frac{1}{\beta}}$ on the observed real wage to recover β. Crucially, because the exogenous productivity and amenity of each location are the residuals of these two equations – and the model tells us that the wage and population will be correlated with the exogenous productivities and amenities (see equations (23) and (24)), ordinary least squares estimation will yield biased estimates. Instead, estimation of the structural parameters requires valid instruments for the wage (both real and nominal) and population that are both correlated with the observed wage and population but uncorrelated with the fundamental productivity and amenity of a location. Two plausible sets of instruments are as follows. First, Allen, Arkolakis and Takahashi (2014) suggest that the model structure could be used to generate instruments. In particular, the authors calculate the equilibrium wages, price indices, and populations of a hypothetical world where bilateral frictions are a solely a function of observed bilateral distance and local characteristics (e.g., productivity and amenities) are solely a function of known geographic variables (e.g., distance to coast, ruggedness, soil quality, etc.). One could then use these equilibrium variables as instruments for the actual wages, price indices, and populations. This procedure is valid as long as the geographic variables used are also controlled for directly in the regression; indeed, Adao, Arkolakis and Esposito (2017) show that a two-stage procedure using such a model implied instrument is optimal in the sense that it minimizes the variance of the estimates. An alternative approach would be to use a shock to either trade or migration costs; for example Allen, Morten and Dobbin (2017) use the construction of wall segments along the border between the U.S. and Mexico as a shock to migration costs. This can be implemented either in a reduced form way (e.g., instrumenting for wages, populations, and the price indices using distance to the border wall, as in Ahlfeldt, Redding, Sturm and Wolf (2015)) or by using the structure of the model to predict how the trade cost shock changes each of the endogenous variables and using these model-predicted changes in wages, populations, and price indices to estimate the elasticities using the first-differenced versions of equations (37) and (38).

5.2.   Conducting counterfactuals

Given estimates of $T_{ij} \equiv \tau_{ij}^{1-\sigma}$ and $M_{ij} \equiv \mu_{ij}^{-\frac{1}{\beta}}$ and the structural elasticities σ, α and β from the previous section, it is straightforward to use the equilibrium structure of the model to conduct counterfactuals. Consider any counterfactual change in the bilateral frictions that change $\{T_{ij}, M_{ij}\}$ to $\{T'_{ij}, M'_{ij}\}$. Following Dekle, Eaton, and Kortum (2008), we can express the equilibrium system using the "exact hat algebra" approach where the notation $\hat{x} \equiv \frac{x'}{x}$ is the ratio of the counterfactual value of a variable its current value. We start by writing equilibrium equations (17)–(20) for the future period and using the the identity $x' = \hat{x} \times x$ as follows:

$$\hat{Y}_i = \sum_j \pi_{ij} \hat{T}_{ij} \hat{p}_i^{1-\sigma} \hat{P}_i^{\sigma-1} \tag{39}$$

$$\hat{P}_i^{1-\sigma} = \sum_j \chi_{ji} \hat{T}_{ji} \hat{p}_j^{1-\sigma} \tag{40}$$

$$\hat{L}_i = \sum_{j \in S} \rho_{ji} \hat{M}_{ji} \hat{\omega}_i^{\frac{1}{\beta}} \hat{W}_j^{-\frac{1}{\beta}} \tag{41}$$

$$\hat{W}_i^{\frac{1}{\beta}} = \sum_j \upsilon_{ij} \hat{M}_{ij} \hat{\omega}_j^{\frac{1}{\beta}}, \tag{42}$$

where $\pi_{ij} \equiv \frac{T_{ij} p_i^{1-\sigma} P_j^{\sigma-1} Y_j}{Y_i} = \frac{X_{ij}}{Y_i}$ is the trade export share, $\chi_{ji} \equiv \frac{T_{ji} p_j^{1-\sigma} P_i^{\sigma-1} Y_i}{Y_i} = \frac{X_{ji}}{Y_i}$ is the trade import share, $\rho_{ji} \equiv \frac{M_{ji} W_j^{-\frac{1}{\beta}} L_j^0 \omega_i^{\frac{1}{\beta}}}{L_i} = \frac{L_{ji}}{L_i}$ is the in-migration share, and $\upsilon_{ij} \equiv \frac{M_{ij} W_i^{-\frac{1}{\beta}} L_i^0 \omega_j^{\frac{1}{\beta}}}{L_i^0} = \frac{L_{ij}}{L_i^0}$ is the out migration share. There are several important things to note about the system of equations (39)–(42). First, the kernel of each equation

– i.e., π_{ij}, χ_{ji}, ρ_{ji}, and υ_{ij} – are solely a function of observed variables (income Y_i, initial and final populations L_i and L_i^0), estimated variables (the bilateral frictions T_{ij} and M_{ij}) and variables that are re-covered from the model inversion (i.e., $\left\{ p_i^{\sigma-1}, P_i^{\sigma-1}, \omega_i^{\frac{1}{\beta}}, W_i^{\frac{1}{\beta}} \right\}$). Moreover, no element of the kernel requires any knowledge of the model elasticities to recover. Hence, even if the bilateral shares are not directly observed, all necessary components of the shares are observed so that the kernels of each equation can be treated as observable. This shows that the "exact hat algebra" approach of Dekle, Eaton, and Kortum (2008) does not require observing bilateral trade or migration flows to implement. Second, the change in bilateral frictions $\hat{M}_{ij}$ and $\hat{T}_{ij}$ depend on the counterfactual of interest, so they are known as well. Hence, equations (39)–(42) comprise $4N$ equations for $6N$ unknowns, namely $\left\{ \hat{Y}_i, \hat{L}_i, \hat{p}_i^{1-\sigma}, \hat{P}_i^{\sigma-1}, \hat{\omega}_i^{\frac{1}{\beta}}, \hat{W}_j^{-\frac{1}{\beta}} \right\}$.

Since the $4N$ equations in the system (39)–(42) do not depend on any of the model elasticities $\{\sigma, \alpha, \beta\}$, one might reasonably ask how these elasticities affect the counterfactuals. The answer is that the choice of model elasticities affects how one can express the changes in incomes $\hat{Y}_i$ and populations $\hat{L}_i$ as a function of the changes in the other endogenous variables $\left\{ \hat{p}_i^{1-\sigma}, \hat{P}_i^{\sigma-1}, \hat{\omega}_i^{\frac{1}{\beta}}, \hat{W}_j^{-\frac{1}{\beta}} \right\}$. Taking first differences of equations (37) and (38) – using the fact that $\hat{\bar{A}}_i = \hat{\bar{u}}_i = 1$ and $\ln \hat{Y}_i = \ln \hat{L}_i + \ln \hat{w}_i$ – and inverting yields:

$$\ln \hat{Y}_i = \frac{\beta(1+\alpha)}{\alpha} \ln \hat{\omega}_i^{\frac{1}{\beta}} - \frac{1+\alpha}{\alpha(\sigma-1)} \ln \hat{P}_i^{\sigma-1} - \frac{1}{\alpha(\sigma-1)} \ln \hat{p}_i^{1-\sigma}$$

$$\ln \hat{L}_i = \frac{\beta}{\alpha} \ln \hat{\omega}_i^{\frac{1}{\beta}} - \frac{1}{\alpha(\sigma-1)} \ln \hat{P}_i^{\sigma-1} - \frac{1-\alpha}{\alpha(1+\alpha)(\sigma-1)} \ln \hat{p}_i^{1-\sigma},$$

which allows us to re-write equations the $4N$ equations in the system (39)–(42) as a function of only $4N$ unknowns:

$$\left(\hat{\omega}_i^{\frac{1}{\beta}} \right)^{\frac{\beta(1+\alpha)}{\alpha}} \left(\hat{P}_i^{\sigma-1} \right)^{-\frac{1+\alpha}{\alpha(\sigma-1)}} \left(\hat{p}_i^{1-\sigma} \right)^{-\frac{1}{\alpha(\sigma-1)}} = \sum_j \pi_{ij} \hat{T}_{ij} \hat{p}_i^{1-\sigma} \hat{P}_i^{\sigma-1} \tag{43}$$

$$\left(\hat{P}_i^{\sigma-1} \right)^{-1} = \sum_j \chi_{ji} \hat{T}_{ij} \hat{p}_j^{1-\sigma} \tag{44}$$

$$\left(\hat{\omega}_i^{\frac{1}{\beta}} \right)^{\frac{\beta}{\alpha}} \left(\hat{P}_i^{\sigma-1} \right)^{-\frac{1}{\alpha(\sigma-1)}} \left(\hat{p}_i^{1-\sigma} \right)^{-\frac{1}{\alpha(1+\alpha)(\sigma-1)}} = \sum_{j \in S} \rho_{ji} \hat{M}_{ji} \hat{\omega}_i^{\frac{1}{\beta}} \hat{W}_j^{-\frac{1}{\beta}} \tag{45}$$

$$\left(\hat{W}_j^{-\frac{1}{\beta}} \right)^{-1} = \sum_j \upsilon_{ij} \hat{M}_{ij} \hat{\omega}_j^{\frac{1}{\beta}}, \tag{46}$$

and a normalization on prices. These four equations can then be solved to determine the effect of the counterfactual on all endogenous variables.

5.3.   An example: the Interstate Highway System

Finally, we illustrate the procedure above with a counterfactual based on Allen and Arkolakis (2014): the effect of the construction of the Interstate Highway System (IHS). In particular, we consider five different versions of that counterfactual with different assumptions regarding the mobility of goods and labor: First, we consider a "trade" model where labor is fixed in each location and the movement of goods is costly; second, we consider the reverse where each location is in autarky (trade costs are infinite) but migration is possible (but costly); third, we consider an "economic geography" model where trade is costly but the movement of labor is costless; fourth, we consider a "labor" model where trade is costless but the movement of labor is costly; and finally we consider the full model where both labor and trade are mobile but subject to bilateral frictions.

For each version of the model, we use data on the wage and population from the 2000 Census as in Allen and Arkolakis (2014) and invert the model using the methodology discussed in Section 5.1 to recover the unique set of variables for each location so that the model exactly matches the data given assumptions on labor and goods mobility.[10] (For models with labor mobility, we assume that the population in the 2000 Census is the steady state population.) We use the estimates of the removal of the IHS from Allen and Arkolakis (2014) to construct $\hat{T}_{ij}$ and $\hat{M}_{ij}$ (assuming migration costs and trade costs are affected equally) and apply the counterfactual procedure from Section 5.2 to calculate the change in populations $\hat{L}_i$ and real wages $\frac{\hat{w}_i}{\hat{P}_i}$ in each location. For all simulations, we set $\sigma = 4$, $\alpha = 0.1$, and $\beta = 0.25$, which are (roughly) in line with estimates from the existing literature, see e.g. Simonovska and Waugh (2014) and Rosenthal and Strange (2004).

Figures 13.18 through 13.22 present the results; each figure shows the spatial distribution in the change in population and real wage across all U.S. counties by decile, with white indicating the greatest decline and black indicating the greatest increase. The most important thing to see from the simulations is that the assumptions regarding the mobility of goods and people play a hugely important role in dictating the effects of the removal of the IHS. For example, in the first counterfactual, there is zero correlation between the change in population and the change in real wages – for the simple reason that the population is assumed to be immobile (see Figure 13.18). Contrast this with the second counterfactual, where there is a perfect correlation between the (log) change in population and the (log) change in real wages – for the simple reason that the change in real wages is determined solely by the change in the location population when each location is in autarky (see Figure 13.19). This is also true when trade is costly but migration is costless (as is assumed in Allen and Arkolakis (2014)), as welfare will be equalized across all locations (see Figure 13.20). However, when migration is costly (and trade is possible), the correlation between the change in population

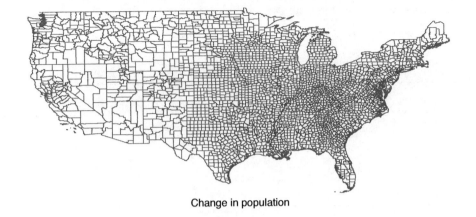

Change in population

Change in real wage

Figure 13.18 Effect of removing the Interstate Highway System: no migration, costly
          trade

Notes: These maps show the predicted change in population and real wage in every county from
removing the Interstate Highway System under the assumption that migration is infinitely costly
and trade is costly. The model is calibrated to match the observed population and income in each
county from the 2000 Census. The effect of the IHS on trade costs are taken from Allen and Arkolakis
(2014). The model parameters assumed are an elasticity of substitution (σ) of 5, a productivity spillover (α) of 0.1 and a disamenity spillover (β) of 0.25, yielding trade and migration elasticities of
4. The shading of a county indicates its decile, with white indicating the greatest decline and black
indicating the greatest increase.

and the change in real wages is far from perfect, as Figures 13.21 and 13.22
highlight.

Table 13.1 depicts the pair-wise correlations in predicted changes in real wages
and populations across the different model variants. It is somewhat surprising to
see how varied the predictions for population changes are: for example, the

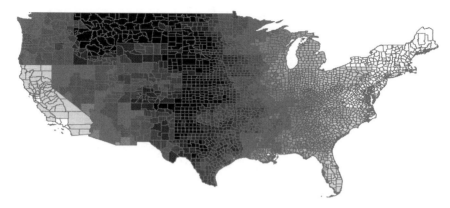

Change in population

Change in real wage

Figure 13.19 Effect of removing the Interstate Highway System: no trade, costly
migration

Notes: These maps show the predicted change in population and real wage in every county from
removing the Interstate Highway System under the assumption that migration is costly and trade is
infinitely costly. The model is calibrated to match the observed population and income in each
county from the 2000 Census. The effect of the IHS on migration costs are set equal to the change
in trade costs estimated in Allen and Arkolakis (2014). The model parameters assumed are an elasticity of substitution (σ) of 5, a productivity spillover (α) of 0.1 and a disamenity spillover (β) of 0.25,
yielding trade and migration elasticities of 4. The shading of a county indicates its decile, with white
indicating the greatest decline and black indicating the greatest increase.

predictions of model variant #2 (no trade, costly migration) is strongly negatively
correlated with the other model variants. Even across the other model variants
with labor mobility, the correlation in predicted labor changes is as low as 0.74
(comparing costly trade, free migration to costly trade, costly migration). In contrast, the model variants (with the exception of variant #2) largely agree on the
change in real wages, with all pair-wise correlations exceeding 0.95.

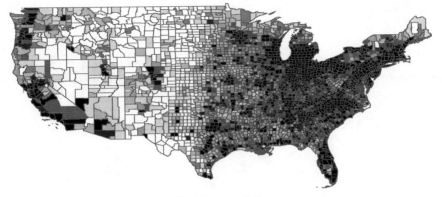

Change in population

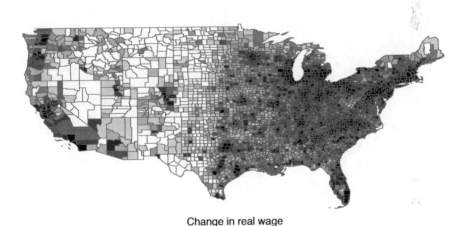

Change in real wage

Figure 13.20 Effect of removing the Interstate Highway System: costly trade, free migration

Notes: These maps show the predicted change in population and real wage in every county from removing the Interstate Highway System under the assumption that migration is costless and trade is costly. The model is calibrated to match the observed population and income in each county from the 2000 Census. The effect of the IHS on trade costs are equal to those estimated in Allen and Arkolakis (2014). The model parameters assumed are an elasticity of substitution (σ) of 5, a productivity spillover (α) of 0.1 and a disamenity spillover (β) of 0.25, yielding trade and migration elasticities of 4. The shading of a county indicates its decile, with white indicating the greatest decline and black indicating the greatest increase.

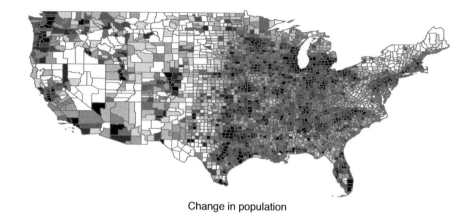

Change in population

Change in real wage

Figure 13.21 Effect of removing the Interstate Highway System: free trade, costly migration

Notes: These maps show the predicted change in population and real wage in every county from removing the Interstate Highway System under the assumption that migration is costly and trade is costless. The model is calibrated to match the observed population and income in each county from the 2000 Census. The effect of the IHS on migration costs are equal to those estimated for the change in trade costs in Allen and Arkolakis (2014). The model parameters assumed are an elasticity of substitution (σ) of 5, a productivity spillover (α) of 0.1 and a disamenity spillover (β) of 0.25, yielding trade and migration elasticities of 4. The shading of a county indicates its decile, with white indicating the greatest decline and black indicating the greatest increase.

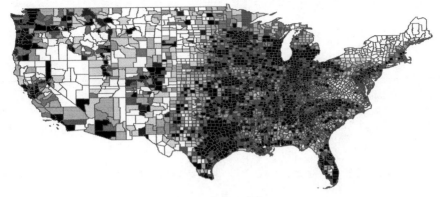

Change in population

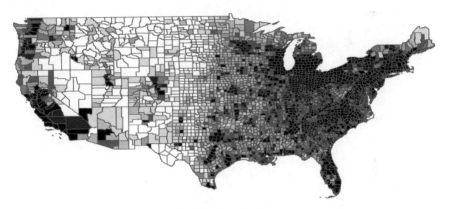

Change in real wage

Figure 13.22 Effect of removing the Interstate Highway System: costly trade, costly migration

Notes: These maps show the predicted change in population and real wage in every county from removing the Interstate Highway System under the assumption that both migration and trade are costly. The model is calibrated to match the observed population and income in each county from the 2000 Census. The effect of the IHS on both migration and trade costs are equal to those estimated for the change in trade costs in Allen and Arkolakis (2014). The model parameters assumed are an elasticity of substitution (σ) of 5, a productivity spillover (α) of 0.1 and a disamenity spillover (β) of 0.25, yielding trade and migration elasticities of 4. The shading of a county indicates its decile, with white indicating the greatest decline and black indicating the greatest increase.

Table 13.1 Correlation of counterfactual predictions across different model specifications

	Population				
	Costly trade, no migration	*No trade, costly migration*	*Costly trade, free migration*	*Free trade, costly migration*	*Costly trade and migration*
Costly trade, no migration	N/A				
No trade, costly migration	N/A	1			
Costly trade, free migration	N/A	−0.6104	1		
Free trade, costly migration	N/A	−0.0945	0.8216	1	
Costly trade and migration	N/A	0.0244	0.742	0.9852	1

	Real wage				
	Costly trade, no migration	*No trade, costly migration*	*Costly trade, free migration*	*Free trade, costly migration*	*Costly trade and migration*
Costly trade, no migration	1				
No trade, costly migration	−0.5083	1			
Costly trade, free migration	0.9949	−0.5886	1		
Free trade, costly migration	0.9555	−0.7301	0.9787	1	
Costly trade and migration	0.9841	−0.6506	0.996	0.99	1

Notes: This table shows the pair wise correlations in changes in real income (top) and population (bottom) across the five different model specifications. The shock considered is the removal of the Interstate Highway System (IHS). The models differ only in their assumptions regarding the mobility of goods and labor; when trade and/or migration is "costly", the change in the costs due to the destruction of the Interstate Highway System are those estimated for trade costs in Allen and Arkolakis (2014). Each model is calibrated to exactly match the county level population and income data from the 2000 Census given assumed bilateral trade and migration costs. The model parameters assumed are an elasticity of substitution (σ) of 5, a productivity spillover (α) of 0.1 and a disamenity spillover (β) of 0.25, yielding trade and migration elasticities of 4.

6. Conclusion

In this primer, we present a review of the simple gravity framework that nests many leading spatial economic models, succinctly incorporates a rich real world geography and matches a number of important empirical patterns in the flow of people and goods. Using a set of newly developed solution techniques and mathematical methods the model can be solved efficiently and be used to conduct relevant policy experiments. Within this environment, the analysis of the economic impact of the interstate highway network highlights the importance of the assumptions on the mobility of labor and goods for evaluating infrastructure policies. We expect that these new tools will further advance the way economists conduct the exploration of space – Economic Science's final frontier.

Notes

Acknowledgement: We thank Xiangliang Li and Jan Rouwendal for helpful comments. All errors are our own. The authors would like to thank Lili Yan Ing, Miaojie Yu and an anonymous reviewer for their insightful comments. They also acknowledge NSF support under grants SES-1658875 and 1658838.

1 Examples of gravity trade models included in our framework are perfect competition models such as Anderson (1979), Anderson and Van Wincoop (2003), Eaton and Kortum (2002) and Caliendo and Parro (2015); for monopolistic competition models such as Krugman (1980), Melitz (2003) as specified by Chaney (2008), Arkolakis, Demidova, Klenow and Rodríguez-Clare (2008), Di Giovanni and Levchenko (2008) and Dekle, Eaton and Kortum (2008); and the Bertrand competition model of Bernard, Eaton, Jensen, and Kortum (2003). Economic geography models incorporated in our framework include Allen and Arkolakis (2014) and Redding (2016) and the geography-trade framework of Allen, Arkolakis and Takahashi (2014).

2 While the model attains a non-trivial solution even for $\sigma \in (0,1)$, we focus on the case where $\sigma > 1$ so that the elasticity of trade flows to trade costs is negative.

3 See Allen and Arkolakis (2014) for a precise discussion of the various isomorphisms to this formulation.

4 The system of equations has the form of the multi-equation multi-location gravity system analyzed by Allen, Arkolakis and Li (2014). Using their approach equilibrium existence and uniqueness can be characterized in generalized gravity systems. In addition, their approach provides algorithms to compute the equilibrium of these multi-equation systems efficiently. Refined notions of stability are discussed in Allen and Arkolakis (2014).

5 When $\alpha \geq \frac{1}{\sigma-1}$, the only type of stable equilibria possible is a black-hole equilibrium where all the population is concentrated in a single location; see Allen and Arkolakis (2014) for an in-depth discussion and formal definition of "stability" in this context.

6 In fact, the baseline Rosen-Roback (1982) framework also imposes that elasticity of substitution is infinite across goods, i.e., the goods are perfect substitutes. The assumption is not essential for what is obtained below.

7 This border cost is reminiscent of the one considered in Rossi-Hansberg (2005). As in that model, our model predicts that increases in the border cost will increase trade between locations that are not separated by border and decrease trade between locations separated by the border. Unlike Rossi-Hansberg (2005), however, in our model the border does not affect what good is produced (since each location produces a distinct differentiated variety) nor is there an amplification effect through spillovers (since spillovers are assumed to be local).

8   More general formulations of the exogenous productivity or amenity functions result to more general specifications of the second order differential equation illustrated above (see Polyanin and Zaitsev (2002) section 2.1.2 for a number of tractable examples).

9   Mossay and Picard (2011) obtain a characterization of the population based on the cosine function in a model where there is no trade but agglomeration of population arises due to social interactions that decline linearly with distance. In their case, population density may be zero in some locations while in our case the CES Armington assumption generates a strong dispersion force that guarantees that the equilibrium is regular when agglomeration forces are not too strong, as discussed in Theorem 2.

10   To ease computation, we approximate the model variants with "infinitely" costly trade or migration with very large (but finite) trade or migration costs, respectively. Similarly, we approximate model variants with "costless" trade or migration with very small (but positive) trade or migration costs, respectively.

References

Adao, R., C. Arkolakis, and F. Esposito (2017): "Trade, Agglomeration, and Labor Markets: Theory and Evidence," Manuscript.

Ahlfeldt, G. M., S. J. Redding, D. M. Sturm, and N. Wolf (2015): "The Economics of Density: Evidence From the Berlin Wall," *Econometrica*, 83(6), 2127–2189.

Allen, T., and C. Arkolakis (2014): "Trade and the Topography of the Spatial Economy," *The Quarterly Journal of Economics*, 29(3), 1085–1140.

——— (2017): "The Welfare Effects of Transportation Infrastructure Improvements," Manuscript.

Allen, T., C. Arkolakis, and X. Li (2014): "On the Existence and Uniqueness of Trade Equilibria," mimeo, Northwestern and Yale Universities.

Allen, T., C. Arkolakis, and Y. Takahashi (2014): "Universal Gravity," NBER Working Paper 20787.

Allen, T., and D. Donaldson (2017): "The Geography of Path Dependence," Manuscript.

Allen, T., M. Morten, and C. d. C. Dobbin (2017): "The Welfare of Walls: Migration and the U.S.-Mexican Border," Manuscript.

Anderson, J. E. (1979): "A Theoretical Foundation for the Gravity Equation," *American Economic Review*, 69(1), 106–116.

Anderson, J. E., and E. Van Wincoop (2003): "Gravity with Gravitas: A Solution to the Border Puzzle," *American Economic Review*, 93(1), 170–192.

Arkolakis, C. (2010): "Market Penetration Costs and the New Consumers Margin in International Trade," *Journal of Political Economy*, 118(6), 1151–1199.

Arkolakis, C., A. Costinot, and A. Rodríguez-Clare (2012): "New Trade Models, Same Old Gains?" *American Economic Review*, 102(1), 94–130.

Arkolakis, C., S. Demidova, P. J. Klenow, and A. Rodríguez-Clare (2008): "Endogenous Variety and the Gains From Trade," *American Economic Review, Papers and Proceedings*, 98(4), 444–450.

Baldwin, R., and D. Taglioni (2006): "Gravity for Dummies and Dummies for Gravity Equations," Discussion Paper, National Bureau of Economic Research.

Bernard, A. B., J. Eaton, J. B. Jensen, and S. Kortum (2003): "Plants and Productivity in International Trade," *American Economic Review*, 93(4), 1268–1290.

Bryan, G., and M. Morten (2015): "Economic Development and the Spatial Allocation of Labor: Evidence From Indonesia," Manuscript, London School of Economics and Stanford University.

Caliendo, L., M. Dvorkin, and F. Parro (2015): "The Impact of Trade on Labor Market Dynamics," Discussion Paper, National Bureau of Economic Research.

Caliendo, L., and F. Parro (2015): "Estimates of the Trade and Welfare Effects of NAFTA," *The Review of Economic Studies*, 82(1), 1–44.

CFS (2007): "2007 Commodity Flow Survey," Bureau of Transportation Statistics.

―――― (2012): "2012 Commodity Flow Survey," Bureau of Transportation Statistics.

Chaney, T. (2008): "Distorted Gravity: The Intensive and Extensive Margins of International Trade," *American Economic Review*, 98(4), 1707–1721.

Costinot, A., and A. Rodríguez-Clare (2013): "Trade Theory With Numbers: Quantifying the Consequences of Globalization," Discussion Paper, National Bureau of Economic Research.

Dekle, R., J. Eaton, and S. Kortum (2008): "Global Rebalancing With Gravity: Measuring the Burden of Adjustment," *IMF Sta Papers*, 55(3), 511–540.

Desmet, K., D. K. Nagy, and E. Rossi-Hansberg (2016): "The Geography of Development," mimeo, Princeton University.

Di Giovanni, J., and A. A. Levchenko (2008): "Putting the Parts Together: Trade, Vertical Linkages, and Business Cycle Comovement," *American Economic Journal: Macroeconomics*, 2(2), 95–124.

Donaldson, D. (forthcoming): "Railroads of the Raj," *American Economic Review*.

Donaldson, D., and R. Hornbeck (2012): "Railroads and American Economic Growth: New Data and Theory," Discussion Paper.

Eaton, J., and S. Kortum (2002): "Technology, Geography and Trade," *Econometrica*, 70(5), 1741–1779.

Eaton, J., S. Kortum, and F. Kramarz (2011): "An Anatomy of International Trade: Evidence From French Firms," *Econometrica*, 79(5), 1453–1498.

Faber, B., and C. Gaubert (2016): "Tourism and Economic Development: Evidence From Mexico's Coastline," Discussion Paper, National Bureau of Economic Research.

Fujita, M., P. Krugman, and A. J. Venables (1999): *The Spatial Economy: Cities, Regions, and International Trade*. MIT Press, Boston, MA.

Glaeser, E. L., and J. D. Gottlieb (2008): "The Economics of Place-making Policies," Discussion Paper.

Head, K., and T. Mayer (2013): "Gravity Equations: Workhorse, Toolkit, and Cookbook." Centre for Economic Policy Research.

Head, K., T. Mayer, and J. Ries (2010): "The Erosion of Colonial Trade Linkages After Independence," *Journal of International Economics*, 81(1), 1–14.

Helpman, E. (1998): "The Size of Regions," *Topics in Public Economics. Theoretical and Applied Analysis*, 33–54.

Krugman, P. (1980): "Scale Economies, Product Differentiation, and the Pattern of Trade," *American Economic Review*, 70(5), 950–959.

―――― (1991): "Increasing Returns and Economic Geography," *Journal of Political Economy*, 99(3), 483–499.

Melitz, M. J. (2003): "The Impact of Trade on Intra-Industry Reallocations and Aggregate Industry Productivity," *Econometrica*, 71(6), 1695–1725.

Moretti, E. (2011): "Local Labor Markets," *Handbook of Labor Economics*, 4, 1237–1313.

Mossay, P., and P. M. Picard (2011): "On Spatial Equilibria in a Social Interaction Model," *Journal of Economic Theory*, 146(6), 2455–2477.

Polyanin, A., and V. Zaitsev (2002): *Handbook of Exact Solutions for Ordinary Differential Equations*. Boca Raton: Chapman & Hall/CRC.

Redding, S. J. (2016): "Goods Trade, Factor Mobility and Welfare," *Journal of International Economics*, 101, 148–167.

Redding, S. J., and E. A. Rossi-Hansberg (2017): "Quantitative Spatial Economics," *Annual Review of Economics*, 9(1).

Redding, S. J., and D. Sturm (2008): "The Costs of Remoteness: Evidence From German Division and Reunification," *American Economic Review*, 98(5), 1766–1797.

Roback, J. (1982): "Wages, Rents, and the Quality of Life," *The Journal of Political Economy*, 1257–1278.

Rosenthal, S. S., and W. C. Strange (2004): "Evidence on the Nature and Sources of Agglomeration Economies," *Handbook of Regional and Urban Economics*, 4, 2119–2171.

Rossi-Hansberg, E. (2005): "A Spatial Theory of Trade," *American Economic Review*, 95 (5), 1464–1491.

Ruggles, S., C. A. Fitch, P. Kelly Hall, and M. Sobek (2000): "IPUMS-USA: Integrated Public Use Microdata Series for the United States," *Handbook of International Historical Microdata for Population Research*. Minneapolis: Minnesota Population Center, pp. 259–284.

Simonovska, I., and M. E. Waugh (2014): "The Elasticity of Trade: Estimates and Evidence," *Journal of International Economics*, 92(1), 34–50.

Tinbergen, J. (1962): "Shaping the World Economy; Suggestions for an International Economic Policy," *The International Executive*, 5(1), 27–30.

Tombe, T., X. Zhu, et al. (2015): "Trade, Migration and Productivity: A Quantitative Analysis of China," Manuscript, University of Toronto.

WBG (2011): "2011 World Bank Bilateral Migration Database," World Bank Group.

Yeats, A. J. (1998): "Just How Big Is Global Production Sharing?," Policy Research Working Paper 1871, The World Bank.

Index

Note: Page numbers in *italics* indicate figures and in page numbers in **bold** indicate tables on the corresponding pages.